Pattern Languages
of Program Design 5

The Software Patterns Series

Series Editor: John M. Vlissides

The Software Patterns Series (SPS) comprises pattern literature of lasting significance to software developers. Software patterns document general solutions to recurring problems in all software-related spheres, from the technology itself, to the organizations that develop and distribute it, to the people who use it. Books in the series distill experience from one or more of these areas into a form that software professionals can apply immediately.

Relevance and *impact* are the tenets of the SPS. Relevance means each book presents patterns that solve real problems. Patterns worthy of the name are intrinsically relevant; they are borne of practitioners' experiences, not theory or speculation. Patterns have impact when they change how people work for the better. A book becomes a part of the series not just because it embraces these tenets, but because it has demonstrated it fulfills them for its audience.

Titles in the series:

Data Access Patterns: Database Interactions in Object-Oriented Applications; Clifton Nock

Design Patterns Explained, Second Edition: A New Perspective on Object-Oriented Design; Alan Shalloway and James Trott

Design Patterns in C#; Steven John Metsker

Design Patterns in Java™; Steven John Metsker and William C. Wake

Design Patterns Java™ Workbook; Steven John Metsker

.NET Patterns: Architecture, Design, and Process; Christian Thilmany

Pattern Hatching: Design Patterns Applied; John M. Vlissides

Pattern Languages of Program Design; James O. Coplien and Douglas C. Schmidt

Pattern Languages of Program Design 2; John M. Vlissides, James O. Coplien, and Norman L. Kerth

Pattern Languages of Program Design 3; Robert C. Martin, Dirk Riehle, and Frank Buschmann

Pattern Languages of Program Design 5; Dragos Manolescu, Markus Voelter, and James Noble

Patterns for Parallel Programming; Timothy G. Mattson, Beverly A. Sanders, and Berna L. Massingill

Software Configuration Management Patterns: Effective Teamwork, Practical Integration; Stephen P. Berczuk and Brad Appleton

The Design Patterns Smalltalk Companion; Sherman Alpert, Kyle Brown, and Bobby Woolf

Use Cases: Patterns and Blueprints; Gunnar Övergaard and Karin Palmkvist

Pattern Languages of Program Design 5

Edited by

Dragos Manolescu
Markus Voelter
James Noble

♦♦Addison-Wesley

Upper Saddle River, NJ • Boston • Indianapolis • San Francisco
New York • Toronto • Montreal • London • Munich • Paris • Madrid
Capetown • Sydney • Tokyo • Singapore • Mexico City

Many of the designations used by manufacturers and sellers to distinguish their products are claimed as trademarks. Where those designations appear in this book, and the publisher was aware of a trademark claim, the designations have been printed with initial capital letters or in all capitals.

The authors and publisher have taken care in the preparation of this book, but make no expressed or implied warranty of any kind and assume no responsibility for errors or omissions. No liability is assumed for incidental or consequential damages in connection with or arising out of the use of the information or programs contained herein.

The publisher offers excellent discounts on this book when ordered in quantity for bulk purchases or special sales, which may include electronic versions and/or custom covers and content particular to your business, training goals, marketing focus, and branding interests. For more information, please contact:

U.S. Corporate and Government Sales
(800) 382-3419
corpsales@pearsontechgroup.com

For sales outside the U.S., please contact:

International Sales
international@pearsoned.com

Visit us on the Web: www.awprofessional.com

Library of Congress Cataloging-in-Publication Data

Pattern Languages of Program Design 5 / Dragos Manolescu, Markus Voelter, James Noble.
    p.   cm.
Includes bibliographical references and index.
ISBN 0-321-32194-4 (pbk. : alk. paper)
    1. Computer software—Development.   2. Object-oriented programming (Computer science)
3. Software patterns.   I. Manolescu, Dragos.   II. Voelter, Markus.   III. Noble, James, 1967–

QA76.76.D47P3754 2006
005.1—dc22   2006000154

ISBN 0-321-32194-4
Text printed in the United States on recycled paper at R.R. Donnelly in Crawfordsville, Indiana.
First printing, April 2006

To the memory of our friend and colleague John Vlissides,
who called on us to assemble this volume
and passed away during its production.

Contents

Acknowledgments . . . . *ix*

Preface . . . . *xi*

Introduction . . . . *xvii*

PART I   *Design Patterns*   *1*

    1 Dynamic Object Model   *Dirk Riehle, Michel Tilman,*
       and Ralph Johnson   3
    2 Domain Object Manager   *John Liebenau*   25
    3 Encapsulated Context   *Allan Kelly*   45

PART II   *Concurrent, Network, and Real-Time Patterns*   *67*

    4 A Pattern Language for Efficient, Predictable, and Scalable
       Dispatching Components   *Irfan Pyarali, Carlos O'Ryan,*
       and Douglas C. Schmidt   69
    5 "Triple-T"—A System of Patterns for Reliable Communication
       in Hard Real-Time Systems   *Wolfgang Herzner,*
       Wilfried Kubinger, and Manfred Gruber   89
    6 Real Time and Resource Overload Language
       Robert S. Hanmer   127

PART III   *Distributed Systems*   *153*

    7 Decentralized Locking   *Dietmar Schütz*   155
    8 The Comparand Pattern: Cheap Identity Testing
       Using Dedicated Values   *Pascal Costanza and Arno Haase*   169
    9 Pattern Language for Service Discovery   *Juha Pärssinen,*
       Teemu Koponen, and Pasi Eronen   189

PART IV *Domain-Specific Patterns*   **211**

    10 MoRaR: A Pattern Language for Mobility and Radio
       Resource Management   *Rossana Maria de Castro Andrade*
       and Luigi Logrippo   213
    11 Content Conversion and Generation on the Web:
       A Pattern Language   *Oliver Vogel and Uwe Zdun*   257

PART V *Architecture Patterns*   **299**

    12 Patterns for Plug-ins   *Klaus Marquardt*   301
    13 The Grid Architectural Pattern: Leveraging Distributed
       Processing Capabilities   *Raphael Y. de Camargo,*
       Andrei Goldchleger, Márcio Carneiro, and Fabio Kon   337
    14 Patterns of Component and Language Integration   *Uwe Zdun*   357
    15 Patterns for Successful Framework Development
       Andreas Rüping   401

PART VI *Meta-Patterns*   **431**

    16 Advanced Pattern Writing   *Neil B. Harrison*   433
    17 A Language Designer's Pattern Language
       Tiffany Winn and Paul Calder   453
    18 The Language of Shepherding   *Neil B. Harrison*   507
    19 Patterns of the Prairie Houses   *Paul R. Taylor*   531

About the Authors 555

Index. 565

Acknowledgments

We would like to acknowledge the following pattern experts who volunteered their time to help us assemble this volume:

Alejandra Garrido, University of Illinois at Urbana-Champaign
Andy Longshaw, Blue Skyline Ltd.
Arno Haase, Arno Haase Consulting
Arno Schmidmeier, AspectSoft
Brian Foote, The Refactory, Inc.
Brian Marick, Exampler
Charles Weir, Penrillian
David Trowbridge, Microsoft
Diethelm Bienhaus, University of Cooperative Education North Hesse
Dirk Riehle, Bayave Software GmbH
Doug Lea, State University of New York at Oswego
Douglas C. Schmidt, Vanderbilt University
Dwight Deugo, Carleton University
Erich Gamma, IBM
Eugene Wallingford, University of Northern Iowa
Fabio Kon, University of São Paulo
Gregor Hohpe, Google
Jens Coldewey, Coldewey Consulting
Jim Coplien, University of Manchester, and DAFCA, Inc.
Joe Yoder, The Refactory, Inc.
Joel Jones, University of Alabama
John Vlissides, IBM
Kevlin Henney, Curbralan Ltd.
Klaus Marquardt, Dräger Medical

Kyle Brown, IBM
Neil B. Harrison, Utah Valley State College
Patricia M. Carlin, ThoughtWorks
Peter Sommerlad, HSR Hochschule für Technik Rapperswil
Ralph Johnson, University of Illinois at Urbana-Champaign
Richard P. Gabriel, Sun Microsystems
Robert S. Hanmer, Lucent Technologies
Uwe Zdun, Vienna University of Economics and BA

In addition, Dragos Manolescu is indebted to: John Vlissides for entrusting him with the job of editing this volume, and Markus Voelter and James Noble for joining their forces in getting it done; Neil Harrison and Brian Foote for sharing insight from their editing the PLoPD4 volume; Chris McMahon for commenting on the chapter summaries; and Mara, Nora, Traian, and Beth for putting up with bringing a PowerBook on several trips to the Rockies to work on this manuscript. James Noble would like to thank Katherine and Amy, for letting him get away with it, *again*.

Dragos Manolescu, Lawrence, Kansas, USA
Markus Voelter, Heidenheim, Germany
James Noble, Wellington, New Zealand

Preface

On the first day of EuroPLoP, my workshop said to me,
"Delete everything on page three."

It is strange for us to realize that the design patterns movement in software design is at least ten years old. Erich Gamma, Richard Helm, Ralph Johnson and John Vlissides' *Design Patterns*—the urtext of patterns in software design—was unleashed into an unsuspecting world (or at least, the OOPSLA conference) in late 1994—although, following in the grand tradition of book publishers, its copyright date is 1995. Jim Coplien's *Software Patterns*, and the first volume (by Frank Buschmann, Regine Meunier, Hans Rohnert, Peter Sommerlad, and Michael Stal) in the enduring *Patterns of Software Architecture* followed in 1996, setting the template or the blueprint—well, the pattern for what would follow. Inspired by these large-scale efforts, many other authors have also taken up the cause of writing patterns, centered around the Pattern Languages of Programming conference series—the first, PLoP in Monticello, Illinois, beginning in 1994 followed by EuroPLoP beginning at Kloster Irsee in 1995, and then expanding to a series of conferences held worldwide. We are all older: many of us have much less hair than we did back then.

Design Patterns—and all the work that was contemporaneous, that followed, that was inspired, or that reacted against it—really has two key values. First, to understand and to catalogue successful, proven software designs. Second, to explain and name those designs so that they can be understood, communicated, and adopted by others. To that end, software designs are described as "patterns": small, independent, interdependent pieces of a design that can be combined in many ways with many other patterns and programming techniques to generate many designs for whole programs, just as words in a language may be combined in many ways to generate an infinity of sentences, paragraphs, novels, or book prefaces. This book, and the Pattern Languages of Program Design series of which this is the latest volume, are a testament to the flexibility, diversity, and openness of patterns and the community that has grown up around them.

On the second day of Europlop, my workshop said to me,
"Too many patterns."

This volume represents the fifth installment in a series that collects first-rate patterns from Pattern Languages of Programs conferences. These conferences are unique in that they consist of working sessions. Instead of presenting their work in front of a passive and sometimes dormant audience, pattern authors receive feedback from their peers. During writer's workshops, a group of pattern authors discusses a draft and provides constructive criticism to the author.

All the papers in this book were workshopped at PLoP conferences from 1998 through 2004. We invited top submissions from PLoP and ChiliPLoP (USA), EuroPLoP and VikingPLoP (Europe), KoalaPLoP (Australia), SugarLoaf PLoP (Brazil), and MensorePLoP (Japan) conferences. To maintain the tradition of previous PLoPD volumes while adding unique color to this collection, the editing team was comprised of three editors with different backgrounds (and also from different continents), who are themselves pattern authors and long-time members of the patterns community.

Current and past pattern authors welcomed the PLoPD5 call for contributions with enthusiasm. Consequently, we received over 70 papers to be considered for this volume. The submissions covered architecture, analysis, and design patterns on a wide range of topics, including aspects, Web-based applications, security, middleware, distributed workflow, finite state machines, patterns about patterns (i.e., meta-patterns), and others. To tackle this repertoire, we enlisted seasoned members of the pattern community to help us with the selection process. Each submission was reviewed for quality as well as fit by at least three reviewers and ultimately the decision of which patterns to include was made by the editors—or, as two of us (or the other two, depending on the frame of reference) would say after finishing this project, "It's all Dragos' fault."

On the third day of Europlop, my workshop said to me,
"Three known uses."

How can you trust the patterns you find in this book? Why should you trust them? Part of the answer to this question is in the review process described above: The patterns in this book are not simply the crazed imaginings of a programmer who has been up too many nights and has drunk too much coffee;

they are the crazed imaginings of a programmer who as been up too many nights and has drunk too much coffee—*and* they have been rigorously reviewed and edited by pattern experts.

Really, though, the patterns in this book stand on their own much more than on their heritage of shepherding, workshops, conferences, and reviewers. We hope that in reading them you will be able to identify the three known uses of each pattern: descriptions of at least three documented instantiations that were not designed or implemented by the author of the patterns in this book, but yet that clearly contain instances of these patterns as part of their design.

Famously, the three known uses for almost all the patterns in the original *Design Patterns* book were Smalltalk, ET++, and Interviews. It is a testament to the adoption of object-oriented design throughout the software industry—catalyzed, no doubt, due to the success of *Design Patterns*—that the three known uses of the patterns in this book are much more varied. Smalltalk and C++ graphical user interface frameworks are no doubt still lurking just under the surface, but the patterns here are much broader: object-oriented systems, middleware, management, telephony, weapons systems, jet fighters, meta-patterns, the list goes on and on. But the principle remains: these patterns are trustworthy not because the authors or us editors postulate it, but because each has been proven in at least three known practical, successful systems.

On the fourth day of Europlop, my workshop said to me,
"Four forces."

A design pattern is more than just a description of a software design—that's what UML diagrams are for. Christopher Alexander, who developed patterns to describe architectural designs, defined a pattern as a "three part rule describing a solution to a problem in a context." A software pattern, however, has to be more than just a well-delineated problem and a description of a solution (with three known uses of solving that problem).

A good pattern should convince its reader first that the problem it describes is real, is hard, and is worth the time and effort of being solved properly (and thus the time and effort to write the pattern in the first place). Then, it needs to surprise the reader with its solution—what Ward Cunningham calls an "Aha! moment." Finally, a good pattern needs to make a solid argument about why the solution actually solves the problem, and how.

Alexander called the important considerations in applying a pattern the "forces." A pattern may resolve forces, rendering them unimportant after its application, or expose them where using a particular pattern requires programmers to think about things they didn't need to think about beforehand. A good pattern will discuss not only what is good about it (its benefits, the forces it resolves) but also what is bad (its liabilities, the forces it exposes). A pattern doesn't just provide advocacy, but also argument, analysis, and rationale, convincing programmers why the solution it proposes is reliable, repeatable, and trustworthy.

On the fifth day of Europlop, my workshop said to me,
"Five good things, four forces, three known uses, too many patterns,
and delete everything on page three."

One hundred years ago, Albert Einstein had a "miraculous year." He published several papers that have forever changed relativity, quantum theory, and molecular theory. His paper, "On the Electrodynamics of Moving Bodies," introduced the theory of special relativity and a new way of understanding the relation between space and time. Today, most people agree that Einstein's replacing Isaac Newton's absolute space and time and regarding them as relative is a manifestation of his genius. However, genius alone would not have been enough to articulate his ideas and solve the puzzle. The formulation of special and general relativity relied on ideas developed by Einstein's predecessors and contemporaries, including Galileo Galilei, Ernst Mach, Carl Friedrich Gauss, Georg Friedrich Bernhard Riemann, Gregorio Ricci-Curbastro, Tullio Levi-Civita, Hermann Minkowski, and Hendrik Antoon Lorenz.

Although very different from theoretical physics, software development also tackles complexity. We have come a long way since the days of the first programmable machines. Today the people involved in software development must deal with complex problems on many different fronts. They build Web-based, distributed applications. They write software that powers portable devices. They build systems that receive and process events in real time. They craft applications that others extend in ways never imagined. They build software for entire product lines. They design systems that must deal with widely heterogeneous environments. Just like with special and general relativity, it would be hard or even impossible to solve all of these problems from scratch without leveraging ideas and techniques developed by others. Patterns of software, such as those presented in this volume, and the other volumes in the series, represent the best attempt we have to catalogue and explain these ideas and techniques for software design. We hope you find them useful.

To cover the breadth of the papers selected for this volume, we structured the book in six parts. Part I focuses on design and contains patterns aimed at people designing object systems. As the Internet and embedded systems continue to expand their reach, they bring with them concurrency and resource management problems; Part II contains patterns on these topics. Part III continues the shift from one to many applications and contains patterns for distributed systems. The domain-specific patterns from Part IV focus on mobile telephony and Web-based applications. Part V shifts gears to architecture and comprises patterns that tackle composition, extensibility, and reuse. Finally, Part VI offers a smorgasbord of meta-patterns for improving the quality of pattern papers and helping their authors.

Introduction

Amazingly, it has been more than a decade since we held the first patterns conference known as PLoP and published the first volume of collected works on programming patterns, nicknamed PLoPD. In a world where most bright and shiny new ideas in software become tarnished and forgotten in a few years, it is significant that the development of software patterns continues to flourish. And paradoxically, no one got rich from the technology.

Even lacking an economic incentive to spread the word, the message spread. Void of a well-funded marketing effort, the idea thrived at the hands of many very talented professionals volunteering their time and talent, famously so. Patterns-related conferences have been held in eleven different locations in nine countries on five continents.

Confronted with a decade of success, so rare in our field, we should pause and examine our journey to see what wisdom might be found. Maybe there are patterns waiting to be distilled on how to launch other initiatives, or help the patterns community sustain its mission and momentum. Our field has begun to embrace the ritual of a retrospective as a way to reflect and learn from our experiences, and I think it is the perfect vehicle to organize the next few pages.

A retrospective is founded on a review of history, so let's draw upon the introductory material from each of the previous PLoPD volumes to understand a bit of this decade-long journey. Starting with the first volume, published in 1995, we learned: "PLoP was founded to create a new literature. The founders ... had come to realize that the advance of their discipline was limited by... the traditions of scientific publication that favored the new, the recent invention or discovery over the ordinary, no matter how useful."

Consequently, the Patterns Community was established to write about what works well based on practitioners' experience. It was a well-received idea and in short order, we had worldwide interest in discovering, writing, and publishing the best wisdom from our field.

Scores of authors began presenting their best work, in a variety of pattern formats and approaches. With this growing collection of pattern papers, researchers began to understand the effects of expressing solutions in a pattern form. Volume 2 of PLoPD came out in 1996, and in it is where we learned how much this new research had grown.

The emphasis shifted from "What are patterns all about?" to "What makes a pattern good, and a good pattern better?" This profound shift was a sign of rapid maturing in people's thinking about patterns. It was a shift away from introspection toward a healthy activism. Many now appreciate that a pattern's value is in neither its discovery nor its definition, but in its relevance, its quality, and its impact. Patterns in software are as much about great literature as they are about technology.

In 1998, as the popularity of patterns continued and pattern names became an integral part of a software developer's vocabulary, the third volume appeared. It was common to find patterns from the best-selling *Design Patterns* book cited in the general software literature, while many other patterns and pattern languages were quietly being put to work. The authors of this third preface rejoiced in the success of improving our field, but warned us of a new problem: "Robert Martin spoke at a conference in Chicago to a rather large audience regarding design patterns. He asked who had purchased the *Design Patterns* book. About 80 percent raised their hands. Then he asked everyone who had not actually read the book to put their hands down. About half the hands went down. Then he asked who could explain the Visitor pattern. Nearly all the hands went down."

The message was clear—patterns had reached that certain level of notoriety in our field where many programmers were aware of the new technology but few had mastered the literature well enough to make good use of patterns. Why? Because the common over-worked software professional working hard to meet unrealistic schedules, bought a patterns book with the best intentions to grow in his/her profession but found only a few brief moments to dedicate to learning. Our profession needs to mature to the point where continuing education is expected and even required by employers and managers. But this line of thought is well addressed in a sub-family of patterns literature, so I will return to our quick history of the patterns movement.

In 2000, the introductory material for PLoPD4 showed a maturing in our understanding about patterns, our experiences applying patterns, and the importance of writing about the ordinary patterns that are our field's best practices. At this point in history, the glitz of a concentrated media focus has moved away from patterns, and in spite of that, the association of patterns authors continues to thrive, with participation from even more corners of the world.

As a worn-out patterns pioneer, I was puzzled why this community continued to grow. However, as new leaders of the movement emerged and as new patterns authors joined the effort, they explained, "It is hard to describe, but there is something about this culture."

From the beginning, our patterns community had embraced norms that fostered respect and dignity for all. Our way turned out to be universal across cultures, as it was recreated in each of the PLoP conferences held around world. Our tenets and practices help an individual develop his skills, both in the technical aspects and in the writing aspects, from within a safe and nurturing environment. So PLoPD 4 told us a bit about this culture.

"...PLoP is a very different kind of conference because we focus on the humans in the human activity of software development. The conferences make an enormous effort to generate a comfortable and welcoming environment. They are the only conferences with a nap-time scheduled. EuroPLoP limits the number of attendees, not to be exclusive but to ensure the intimacy and cohesion that comes with a small group. And all PLoP Conferences provide a number of social activities and services that help attendees build a community."

After five years of collegiality, we had come to realize that the patterns community had a special way of interacting. We knew it worked, but we couldn't say what "it" was. Another four years would pass before Jim Coplien explained this mystery in his scholarly paper, *The Culture of Patterns*.

This ends my all too quick review of our history, but a retrospective is not just a story of past events; it is a search for lessons learned or wisdom mined from our experiences. One way to go about a retrospective is by seeking answers to a few well-chosen questions, such as the ones below.

Question 1: What did we do well, that we must not forget?

Our goal was to create a new body of literature, based on the experiences of what works in the software field. Not since Donald Knuth's classic volumes has so much ordinary wisdom been published. Not only are the PLoPD volumes a good source of patterns, but many patterns-influenced books have been published on such diverse relevant topics as:

- small memory systems
- real-time embedded systems
- distributed systems
- server systems
- large-scale systems

- concurrent systems
- requirements
- software architecture
- software reuse
- refactoring
- integration
- testing
- configuration management
- building product lines
- team organization
- installing change in an organization
- enterprise architecture
- language specific wisdom: C++, Smalltalk, Java, etc.

Thus, we must not forget that our mandate is to harvest, distill, write about, learn about, and use those ideas that serve our profession well.

Question 2: What did we learn?

There were two simple practices the founders of the patterns movement embraced, with only a little discussion, that I think made this community so vibrant and long lived: 1) Shepherds were assigned to help authors refine their papers into a fine works of literature, and 2) Patterns papers were discussed at conferences in Writer's Workshops, rather than presented in front of a passive audience.

Shepherds helped authors in a way quite different from the way traditional reviewers judged papers, sometimes painfully so. Writer's Workshops honored the written work by giving the author a rare opportunity to listen as a circle of readers discussed the paper.

Out of these two simple ideas came community norms that fostered respect for a variety of ideas, even those counter to one's own. And from novice to expert, every reader's opinion on a written work held equal value. We built a community where it was safe to say what you were thinking, and even to state what you do not understand.

Question 3: What would we do differently next time?

In the early days of the patterns movement, finding wisdom and writing a single pattern of exceptional quality was hard. As a profession, we had few skills to draw on as we consciously reflected upon our work while studying colleagues' work, hoping to uncover the common wisdom.

Thus the early successes in patterns literature were those of single patterns and of collections of single patterns. Admittedly, these works had a profound impact on our profession, but they also set a direction for other researchers to follow. It was like a gold rush of miners looking for single nugget patterns—and ignoring the potentially more valuable interrelated systems of patterns, referred to by Christopher Alexander as "pattern languages."

While a single pattern might dramatically improve a critical piece of a system, or have an important effect on the micro aspects of a software architecture, only a pattern language can comprehensively address how we might approach wicked problems and complicated systems. It is through pattern languages that the masters of our field can share their lifelong wisdom with the rest of us. Our profession's great software architects build amazing systems over and over—and for the most part, we don't even know who they are, so how can we expect to learn from them?

I think what I would do differently next time is speak up more strongly for the search for pattern languages, while still appreciating the great single patterns that are uncovered. I will try to make amends here.

While many colleagues worked on single patterns, I quietly experimented with pattern languages and found the discipline of thinking about systems of patterns most valuable. To distill wisdom from my years of experience leading retrospectives, I set out to develop a retrospective facilitator's pattern language. As a work in progress, my pattern language made holes in my thinking apparent, and often as I struggled to fix a single bulky pattern, I was led to the discovery of deeper wisdom and multiple new patterns. It was a methodology by which I could uncover and refine a complex system of interrelated concepts without becoming overwhelmed.

When my retrospectives pattern language was finished, I was most satisfied with the process, but worried that the pattern language form would be foreign to most readers. Accordingly, I translated my pattern language into an "easy to read" book format more commonly found on bookstore shelves, *Project Retrospectives*. Reverse engineering the pattern language from my book is easy for the reader familiar with pattern languages, but what was lost on our community was the awareness that constructing a pattern language is a powerful method to uncover and organize intricate wisdom.

I was not alone in this quiet exploration of patterns languages—eXtreme Programming grew out of Ward Cunningham's development of his EPISODES Pattern Language [PLoPD2]. And I suspect that other recent books have been built upon on the foundation of pattern language reasoning.

While pattern languages can be found in the other PLoPD volumes, it is this fifth volume that finally features a good collection of pattern languages. Finally, we are on a path to discover the true utility of Christopher Alexander's life work.

Question 4: What still puzzles me?

What puzzles me the most is "how to find the right pattern for the situation with which I'm currently confronted." While my bias is towards pattern languages, I recognize that my colleagues have produced a vast quantity of single patterns and confederations of patterns of significant value. In the early days, I was able to carry most of the approximately 100 published patterns in my head. Knowing about and deploying them was easy.

As our collected works of published patterns grew into the thousands, I found I had little chance of finding the perfect pattern at the moment I needed it.

For a brief moment in time in the year 2000, Linda Rising solved this puzzle with her book, *The Pattern Almanac*. Linda had undertaken the difficult task of categorizing and referencing all known published patterns, and she did it well. I regularly turned to her book for reference. Alas, for many reasons, not related to the almanac itself, the book went out of print.

Nevertheless, Linda's effort demonstrates that the discipline of library science can be applied to patterns; and it must be, or else our ever-growing pile of patterns will lie underutilized. This, I believe, is our next challenge—to bring order and widespread critical review to our literature.

Question 5: What was my greatest joy?

Over these past ten years, the community of patterns investigators has built a true fellowship—rare for our field. I believe this association has helped many strong but unknown practitioners develop their careers to international acclaim, and in the same way, many university students have become industry leaders. One might argue that the search for patterns attracts people destined to become leaders, but I prefer to think that the habit of looking at our work for great wisdom makes us into wise and respected leaders.

A Retrospective Challenge

And this brings us back to the ritual of retrospectives, which by the way is a good source to uncover patterns. I defined the retrospective ritual as "a community coming together, to collectively tell the story of past events in order to find wisdom greater than what any one person might have noticed." Thus my words here, while they have the flavor of a retrospective, are only one voice. May this be a beginning of a discussion by our community on how we came to this point in time and where we might head next.

Conclusion

Patterns authors do important work. We are distilling and documenting our best wisdom for the purpose of developing our field to a new level of professionalism. While it is work we take on as individuals, we receive help and support from our colleagues who act as shepherds and workshop attendees.

Our work is more than important; it continues to have a profound impact on the software field. In 2005, three of the four books considered as "finalists" for the 15th Annual Jolt book award were about patterns. The prestigious award went to *Head First Design Patterns*, with close competition from the books *Refactoring to Patterns* and *Software Factories: Assembling Applications with Patterns, Models, Frameworks and Tools*. For contrast, look back ten years at the other emerging ideas of the time—formal methodologies, use cases and UML; capability maturity models, ISO standards and continuous process improvement; software life-cycle refinement and rapid application development; reuse and re-engineering; process metrics and function points—how many of these competing ideas still affect our work?[1]

Good reader, you hold in your hands some of the finished products from the patterns community. This volume adds to the best wisdom our community has to offer. These works of literature have been worked, reworked, revised, and refined over the past months and years. You see not just the hard work of the author(s), but the hand of the shepherd, the refinements from workshop participants' discussions, and the awesome responsibility the editors of this volume to select just the best of the many papers.

But all this work is for naught unless you find some wisdom in this volume that you can incorporate into your professional practice. I hope what you find will profoundly improve the way you go about your work.

Norman L. Kerth
Portland, Oregon
July 2005

---

1. These topics were prominent in the issues of IEEE Software 1995, IEEE Computer 1995, and Software Development 1996.

References

J. O. Coplien. "The Culture of Patterns." *ComSIS Consortium*, Volume 01, Issue 02 (November 2004).

W. Cunningham. *EPISODES: A Pattern Language of Competitive Development (PLoPD2)*, pp. 371–390. Reading, MA: Addison-Wesley, 1999,

Eliz. Freeman, E. Freeman, B. Bates, and K. Sierra. *Head First Design Patterns*. O'Reilly, 2004.

E. Gamma, R. Helm, R. Johnson, and J. Vlissides. *Design Patterns*. Reading, MA:, Addison-Wesley, 1995.

J. Greenfield, K. Short, S. Cook, S. Kent, and J. Crupi. *Software Factories: Assembling Applications with Patterns, Models, Frameworks and Tools*. Wiley, 2004.

J. Kerievsky. *Refactoring to Patterns*. Boston: Addison-Wesley Professional, 2004.

L. Rising. *The Pattern Almanac 2000*. Boston: Addison-Wesley, 2000.

PART I

Design Patterns

Chapter 1: Dynamic Object Model

Many applications must accommodate elaborate flexibility requirements. Examples include applications that deal with a wide variety of products, such as insurance or financial products systems. In popular languages such as Java or C#, the classification relationship between classes and instances is too rigid for these requirements. The Dynamic Object Model pattern combines ideas from class-based and prototype-based languages to address this problem. Dirk Riehle, Michel Tilman, and Ralph Johnson explain how object-oriented developers using popular object-oriented languages could dynamically introduce new types in their applications without programming new classes.

Chapter 2: Domain Object Manager

The widespread adoption of application servers and other types of containers has shifted many systems from stand-alone applications to managed applications. In these applications, a dedicated container component manages the domain objects' life cycle, implementing operations such as insert, modify, remove, and find. The Domain Object Manager allows application code to handle transient and persistent domain objects while supporting multiple data stores or application servers. John Liebenau's compound design pattern provides object-oriented developers with a design for keeping their domain objects independent of the persistence or middleware APIs.

Chapter 3: Encapsulated Context

As designs go through changes and accommodate new requirements, the data exchange between collaborating objects also changes. Allan Kelly shows how to manage an increasing number of call parameters without introducing global variables. Although written for C++ developers, Encapsulated Context provides value to developers who are seeking ways to lower the ripple effects of code changes regardless of programming language.

CHAPTER 1

DYNAMIC OBJECT MODEL

Dirk Riehle, Michel Tilman, and Ralph Johnson

Intent

Allow a system to have new and changing object types without having to reprogram the system. Representing the object types as objects means that they can be changed at configuration time or at runtime, which makes it easy to change and adapt the system to new requirements.

Also Known As

OBJECT SYSTEM, RUNTIME DOMAIN MODEL, ACTIVE OBJECT MODEL, ADAPTIVE OBJECT MODEL

Motivation

Consider a banking system for handling customer accounts like checking or savings accounts. One option is to design a hierarchy of account classes, starting with the Account root class. However, banks provide many different types of accounts. It is not uncommon for a large bank to have more than 500 types of accounts. Many of these account types vary only by a few attributes, but these differences are important to the bank and need to be represented.

Rather than implementing 500 account classes, you decide to use the TYPE OBJECT[1] pattern [Johnson+1998] to represent each class as an object. You introduce the AccountType class whose instances represent a specific type of account, and the Account class whose instances represent a specific account of a customer, as shown in Figure 1–1. Instances of AccountType serve as type objects for instances of Account. All properties that are the same for a specific type of account go into the AccountType class (name of this type of account, interest rate for this type of account, etc.). All properties that may vary within instances of the same AccountType go into the Account class (account number, current balance, etc.).

After a while, you recognize that the Account and AccountType classes get bloated with a large number of fields and methods, most of which remain unused most of the time. After all, the two classes represent the union of some 500 account types! To slim down the Account class, you decide to use the PROPERTY LIST[2] and VALUE HOLDER[3] patterns [Riehle1997a][Foote+1998].

The Account class now holds a collection of instances of the new Property class. An instance of the Property class represents the value of an attribute that was formerly an attribute of the Account class, see Figure 1–2. The Property instances stores these values as generic Object instances, and it is up to a client of an account to properly interpret this value.

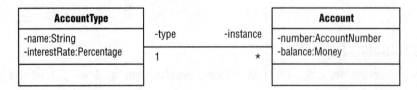

Figure 1–1 *Account and AccountType classes*

---

1. The TYPE OBJECT pattern centralizes common information about a set of instance objects in a TYPE OBJECT that is shared by all instances. TYPE OBJECTs provide application domain specific information, such as behavior shared by their instances or a description of the list of properties of their instances, rather than implementation information.

2. Objects implementing the PROPERTY LIST pattern contain a generic and extensible set of properties. Clients may access the list of properties, and use a naming scheme to set and get properties. Properties may even be added or removed at runtime. An example implementation is the Java HashMap.

3. The VALUE HOLDER pattern abstracts the concept of a variable in programming languages. It is often used in combination with the OBSERVER pattern. This allows interested parties to be notified when the value of the 'variable' changes.

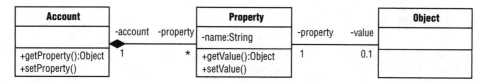

Figure 1–2 *Account with Property and Value objects*

Properties of Account like "name of owner" or "balance" now become instances of a generic Property class. The name of a property is stored in the name attribute of the Property class, and the Account class uses it to select a Property instance. A Property instance can hold any object that represents the value of the property.

However, something still worries you: The properties are not being type-checked. Therefore, a client might mistakenly set a string as the value of the balance of an account. So you need to check whether a value provided for a property is of the correct type, is in a proper range of values, and so on. Also, you need to define whether a certain type of Property is acceptable for an Account in the first place.

For example, a Swiss numbered account may not have an owner name. It does not have a property "owner name" and must not be given one. Thus, you use PROPERTY LIST again and define a collection of PropertyType objects for AccountType so that an Account instance can check with its AccountType object whether a specific Property is acceptable or not.

For this, we use the TYPE OBJECT pattern again, and use the type objects to check access to a property. Any given AccountType can now have a collection of PropertyType objects that represent the types and their allowed values for a given account type. Any Account object property can be checked for validity through the account's type object, which provides the property type objects.

What can be said about the design, as shown in Figure 1–3? First, we distinguish a type level from an instance level. On the left of each figure, we see the type objects, and on the right, we see the instance objects. Fowler also calls the type level the "knowledge level" and the instance level the "operational level" [Fowler1996]. Effectively, the type level is a model (on the left of the diagrams) of what makes up valid instances of the model (on the right of the diagrams).

This design lets you introduce new types of accounts at runtime without programming new classes. You simply create a new instance of AccountType and configure it with its PropertyType objects. You could now sit together with some bankers and explore new ideas for accounts and their behavior in real time (probably in a computational sandbox, though).

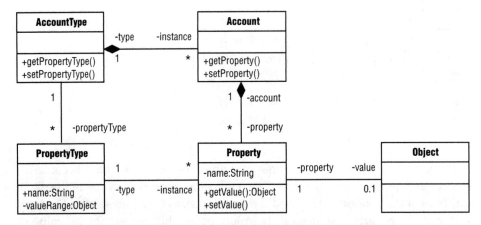

Figure 1–3 *The Account and AccountType classes with their type definitions and instance properties*

The AccountType class in Figure 1–3 no longer mentions the "name" and "interest rate" attributes, so where did they go? We want to identify each type of account, so we retain the name attribute for all account types. Not all type of accounts have interest rates though, but savings accounts do. Hence we introduce the class SavingsAccountType that subclasses AccountType with an extra "interest rate" attribute. Now the SavingsAccountType class has an interest rate attribute representing a value shared by all instances of the SavingsAccount-Type. At the instance level, we perform the same analysis. Some attributes (not their values), like balance, are shared by all instances; other attributes may be shared only by specific instances of Account. In both cases we have to decide whether to represent these attributes as dynamic property types or as regular member fields of Account or of a subclass thereof (see the Sample Code section for a more detailed description).

Problem

The DYNAMIC OBJECT MODEL pattern solves several different problems. Some systems only have one of these problems while others have several:

- A system is difficult to understand, change, and evolve, because it is complex. The system seems complex because there are so many types of objects, but they differ only in a few fields.

- A system requires frequent changes and rapid evolution. New types of objects must be created at runtime. For example, end users may need to specify these new types of objects, and they need to interact immediately with the objects without having to rebuild the system.

- A system needs a domain-specific modeling language, perhaps because it should be used by end users, perhaps because it needs custom type validation, or perhaps because it needs to generate complex behaviors from that model.

Usually a DYNAMIC OBJECT MODEL starts out as a way of making a system simpler and easier to change. Later it becomes apparent that it is possible for users to specify the changes without involving programmers, and then it becomes apparent that the system now has a domain-specific modeling language. But some DYNAMIC OBJECT MODELs do not allow end users to define new types, and sometimes a DYNAMIC OBJECT MODEL starts with the need for a domain-specific modeling language.

Languages like Smalltalk support class modification at runtime, even when classes have instances. They also allow developers to adapt—within limits—the meta-model describing what classes look like and how they behave. Java-like languages, on the other hand, are much more limited in this regard, even without considering class incompatibility problems resulting from serialization in a multiversion environment. So why not use one of these more dynamic programming languages? For a start, many customers have already standardized on one of the more widely used (but often more static) languages, and introducing yet another language is usually not an option. But the problem goes deeper than this, because it involves more than the mere technical issue of choosing the right implementation language. Usually one of the main underlying motivations of DYNAMIC OBJECT MODELs is to bring "configuration" of the solution closer to the end user. In several of the Known Uses examples, for instance, domain experts participate heavily in the process of developing end-user applications. Imposing general-purpose programming languages and traditional IDEs on these users then misses the stated goals. As a result, systems driven by DYNAMIC OBJECT MODELs are often accompanied by a set of domain-specific high-level development tools.

Solution Structure

The core of the DYNAMIC OBJECT MODEL pattern consists of the following classes and their respective clients: Component and ComponentType; Property and PropertyType. It is a composite (compound) pattern consisting of several other patterns. Figure 1–4 shows that it is composed of the TYPE OBJECT, PROPERTY LIST, and VALUE HOLDER patterns. Figure 1–4 uses UML collaboration specification

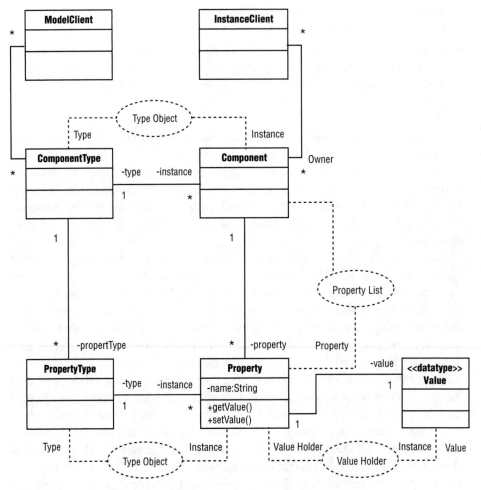

Figure 1–4 *Structure diagram of the DYNAMIC OBJECT MODEL pattern*

diagrams to show the participating patterns. Each collaboration specification is displayed as a dashed ellipsis.

Figure 1–4 shows how the TYPE OBJECT pattern separates the type level from the instance level. In the TYPE OBJECT pattern, an Instance object delegates type-specific behavior to its Type object [Johnson+1998]. Client objects may work both with the Instance and the Type object. The Type object serves as a specification of what is acceptable to its Instance objects. New instances of the Type class and hence new types of objects can be introduced at runtime.

In the PROPERTY LIST pattern, an Owner object maintains a set of Property objects that Client objects may request to learn more about the Owner object

[Riehle1997a]. Property objects are got and set dynamically, typically using strings as property names. The PROPERTY LIST pattern allows for runtime extension of the Owner's properties.

In the VALUE HOLDER pattern, a Client object retrieves a Value object from a VALUE HOLDER object [Foote+1998]. The VALUE HOLDER serves as an adapter for the Value that it makes available to the Client object using a homogeneous interface. Value objects can be any kind of value, primitive or non-primitive [Cunningham1995] [Bäumer+1998].

Thus, a Component class (Account in the Motivation section) is the *Owner* of a set of property objects, the *Client* of a property object acting as a value holder, and the *Instance* of the ComponentType object.

The Property class (Attribute in the Motivation section) is the *Property* of an account object, the *Instance* of a PropertyType object, and the *VALUE HOLDER* of value objects.

The Value class is the *Value* of a Property.

The ComponentType class (AccountType in the Motivation section) is the *Type* of a Component instance and the *Client* of its PropertyType objects.

The PropertyType class (AttributeType in the Motivation section) is the *Type* of its Property instances.

Tradeoffs

The DYNAMIC OBJECT MODEL has both advantages and disadvantages.

Simplicity

The DYNAMIC OBJECT MODEL pattern reduces the number of "real" classes. This is a design issue, much in the same way a developer might factor out common orthogonal variations on a theme by means of plug-in components. As such, this approach is essentially independent of the underlying programming language. This reduction is sometimes several orders of magnitude. However, a system based on the DYNAMIC OBJECT MODEL has its own kind of complexity. It is a composite pattern, which means that it uses several patterns that are tightly woven together. Many programmers do not know these patterns and find the system hard to understand. The TYPE OBJECT pattern is particularly hard for programmers of traditional object-oriented languages because it represents as instances what are normally represented as classes. A DYNAMIC OBJECT MODEL represents one logical class as a set of instances: one instance of ComponentType and several instances of PropertyType. For a programmer, this design is more complex and harder to understand than a traditional class inheritance hierarchy. When programmers understand the design, it seems simple and easy to change. However, it can take a long time for a programmer to understand it. This is even true for, say, Smalltalk programmers, who are fairly accustomed to classes being first-class citizens.

The DYNAMIC OBJECT MODEL pattern provides a complete, explicit model that can be consulted at runtime to automate many functions. When developing a generic store-retrieve relational database application, for instance, you can generate forms as well as query screens and SQL statements on the fly. Adding a new feature often means extending the DYNAMIC OBJECT MODEL in a single place rather than changing every type of domain object. For this to work, your model must be able to describe things like properties, relationships, and totality constraints, and you must be able to describe how object structures and data types are mapped onto the database. Up to a certain level we can also do this in statically typed languages like Java. But, as the DYNAMIC OBJECT MODEL pattern leaves all this up to the system designer, these model elements can all be domain-specific, which makes them both easier to implement (because they don't have to be fully general) and easier to understand. Nevertheless, as the model grows more detailed, it becomes harder to understand.

Flexibility

Type definitions can be created at runtime and can be changed at runtime. This makes applications easy to extend and easy to change. Part of the type definition can be constraints between types, and these can be changed at runtime as well. Of course, the more that can be changed at runtime, the harder it is to implement the system. For example, perhaps existing objects must be updated. Can objects change their type? All things are possible, but not all things are expedient. As a system gets more flexible, it gets slower. A system based on the DYNAMIC OBJECT MODEL has the potential to be very slow. Most systems are limited by something other than the DYNAMIC OBJECT MODEL, such as a database, a network, or the user, but there is always a performance penalty in both time and space. The designer has to decide how flexible to make the system. Most systems that use a DYNAMIC OBJECT MODEL find that lack of understandability is a bigger problem than lower performance, but this might be because designers are more afraid of performance problems than of understandability problems.

Languages like Smalltalk offer many of these benefits while still offering sufficient performance for most types of business applications. But without discipline, this flexibility may lead to chaos. Systems using DYNAMIC OBJECT MODELS may encapsulate these features in components performing, for instance, some sort of consistency checks. Most of the systems described in the Known Uses section use dynamic facilities of the implementation language, but they typically use them sparingly and in a tightly controlled way.

End-User Configuration

The DYNAMIC OBJECT MODEL pattern lets end users define key concepts from their application domain at runtime, without lengthy development cycles in between. The DYNAMIC OBJECT MODEL pattern acts like a (possibly domain-specific) language for users to describe their domain problems. End users need their own specialized development environment, because classic development environments are designed for software developers. Although end-user configuration means that programmers have less work to do, when a new feature cannot be added by the user, then it is harder for the programmer to know how to add it. Should the DYNAMIC OBJECT MODEL be extended? Should the entire feature be added to the DYNAMIC OBJECT MODEL, or only part? Perhaps the end users could have implemented the feature themselves, but just didn't know how?

End users usually don't understand the importance of testing, documentation, and configuration management. If they understand the importance, they don't know how to do it. The end-user environment must help them with these activities. End users will make mistakes, so sometimes they will report a bug when the mistake is really their own. End-user configuration is more likely to be successful when there is close communication between the end users and the programmers developing the core of the system.

Programming Environment

Programmers can no longer rely on their familiar development tools, such as browsers, to edit, view, and version TYPE OBJECTS. Other traditional tools break down because they are not effective anymore. Debuggers and inspectors, for instance, still work, but they are harder to use: type objects appear as any other field in an inspector, and to retrieve the value of a property, you must navigate through the implementation structures. You need to provide new tools that replace or enhance the existing tools. This need has been captured by many, for example, as the Visual Builder pattern of Roberts and Johnson [Roberts+1998]. An important concern is where to store the models and how to version and maintain the models in a multiuser environment. You can store, for instance, models in a database or as XML files in a source control system.

The inverse problem exists if we want to directly use a general-purpose programming language and make it available to domain-experts, because in general, we can not afford to present end users with the same tools as regular developers.

Dynamic Behavior

The core of the DYNAMIC OBJECT MODEL pattern provides only a structure to which dynamic behavior needs to be hooked up. However, there is no standardized way to do so (like a programming language for a traditional system). Hence you have to add a whole bunch of further patterns (like Strategy, Chain of Responsibility, Interpreter, or Observer) to do so [Johnson+1998]. The DYNAMIC OBJECT MODEL is easiest to use when there is little type-specific behavior.

Runtime Typing

The DYNAMIC OBJECT MODEL pattern introduces full-fledged typing information at runtime, including property types. This may be helpful in dynamically typed languages like Smalltalk, for instance, if we want to map objects onto a relational database.

Portability

The "language" described by the DYNAMIC OBJECT MODEL pattern is essentially independent of the implementation language. Putting more information in configuration files or repositories and less in classes in the implementation language means that the system can be ported by rewriting the implementation and reusing the configuration. In a sense this is no different from write-once-run-anywhere programs written in Java or VisualWorks Smalltalk running on top of a virtual object machine (except that these virtual machines are readily available for the major platforms).

Extensions

You can extend the DYNAMIC OBJECT MODEL pattern by adding structural features and by adding behavioral features. On the structural side, you enhance the core pattern by adding relationships like inheritance, aggregation, associations, and role-playing.

The two most common structural relationships are inheritance and aggregation.

- *Inheritance.* Give every TYPE OBJECT a link to its supertype, thereby building up a single inheritance tree. This gives you the power of type reuse. With it come the problems of preserving inheritance semantics. Can inherited properties be overwritten? Is an instance of a derived type just one instance or several? We can learn from traditional programming languages, but they also provide a variety of answers to these problems, and no general solution.

- *Aggregation.* Give every TYPE OBJECT a list of aggregate member types for its instances. An instance object must conform to this structure set up on the type level. A DYNAMIC OBJECT MODEL diagram enhanced with the aggregation relationship is not truly commutative: On the instance level, an object owns its aggregated subobjects, while on the type level, a TYPE OBJECT references, but does not own, the aggregated TYPE OBJECTs.

- *Constraints.* Some domain models have a lot of constraints between their various Instance objects. These constraints make it difficult to use the DYNAMIC OBJECT MODEL pattern, if they need to be addressed. To overcome this problem, you can introduce Constraint objects that describe how attribute values of Instance objects and links between Instance objects can and cannot relate. Effectively, you are adding a constraint-solving system to the domain model.

If you want to provide more than one relationship type between TYPE OBJECTs, consider introducing explicit *relationship type objects* that describe how a type relates to another type. Such a relationship type object can provide adornments like names, multiplicity, and visibility.

You can also apply the DYNAMIC OBJECT MODEL pattern recursively:

- *Recursive application.* Make ComponentType a subclass of Component to reuse its features. This lets you introduce further type levels. In Figure 1–3, there is only one instance and one type level. By making the Component/ComponentType relationship recursive, you can introduce new types of TYPE OBJECTs, which lets you handle not just one domain-specific language, but several.

To deal with behavioral aspects, you can include several patterns, including:

- *Strategy,* to hook up individual aspects of behavior to instance objects
- *Chain of Responsibility,* to connect objects with each other to delegate functionality
- *Interpreter,* to make a whole instance object hierarchy compute some algorithm
- *Observer,* to implement "rules" that check or implement consistency or that automate computations whenever particular events (such as state changes) occur at the instance *or* at the type level

Johnson and Oakes discuss this topic in more detail [Johnson+1998].

Implementation

A simple implementation of the DYNAMIC OBJECT MODEL pattern is straightforward, as is shown in the Sample Code section. However, such an implementation may be too inefficient. Let us therefore examine some possible performance bottlenecks.

The core DYNAMIC OBJECT MODEL pattern provides property access. Anything else is left to the designer, such as how to invoke behavior or how to map the classes of the DYNAMIC OBJECT MODEL pattern to a (typically) relational database. However, even these problems can be handled by observing a key guideline: *Use the type information of the system wherever possible to make ever stronger assumptions about runtime execution.*

Let us examine how we can use type information to speed up property access. The following two crucial issues are poorly handled by a naive implementation but can be handled nicely by using type information:

- *Type-checking property access.* In a straightforward implementation, properties are accessed using strings as their name. To check the name for validity, the string is used in at least one dynamic hashtable lookup, which typically leads to a PropertyType object. Because it occurs with every property access, this lookup is costly.

  We can overcome this problem by requiring clients to use unambiguous keys to identify a property. Such a key should be immutable (a value object) and handed out by the component itself. This way, the component can make sure that the key will always be a valid key, so that type checking property access can be omitted.

  One option for such a key is the PropertyType object of a property itself. Client code that is written in terms of PropertyType objects received from a component (rather than strings) is guaranteed to ask the Component only type-safe questions. In general, however, it is better to introduce dedicated key objects.

- *Accessing the property.* Given a valid name or key for a property, a straightforward implementation requires another dynamic lookup: from the key to the actual property, typically stored in a hashtable. Here, the costly part is the calculation of the hash code and the lookup in the table.

  However, because component types don't change frequently, we can separate two different phases in the lifetime of a component type and its instances. Most of the time, the type definition is stable, and nothing changes. This regular operating phase is occasionally interrupted by short phases in which we change the type.

  Most property accesses take place during regular operation with a stable ComponentType definition. During this time, we assign each PropertyType (and hence each key) a unique index into an array. We then replace the properties hashtable with an array and store component properties in that array exactly at those indices provided by their keys. This reduces the dynamic hashtable lookup to a simple indexed array lookup.

The second performance improvement highlights one drawback of our ever-smarter implementations: the need to perform more bookkeeping. It is interesting (and not surprising) to note that the techniques described here are similar to what happens in a virtual machine that allows for runtime modification of classes with existing instances, see [Riehle+2001]. In fact, we can borrow several ideas from interpreter and VM implementations as well as from other domains. Which techniques work best for you ultimately depends on your application requirements.

Sample Code

We describe how we use the pattern to model accounts as illustrated in the Motivation section by means of the following Java code snippets. We do not present the "final" solution at once. Instead, we retrace some of the steps in the Motivation section. We do not show all member fields, methods, or classes.

Let us begin with the class SavingsAccount that captures what makes up a savings account.

```java
public class SavingsAccount {
  protected Money balance;
  protected Percentage interestRate;

  public Money getBalance() {
    return balance;
  }

  public Percentage getInterestRate() {
    return interestRate;
  }

  public synchronized void deposit(Money deposit) {
    balance = balance.add(deposit);
  }

  public synchronized void withdraw(Money amount) {
    Money newBalance = balance.subtract(amount);
    if (newBalance.getAmount() >= 0) {
      balance = newBalance;
    }
  }

  public void accrueDailyInterest() {
    deposit(InterestCalculator.calcDailyInterest(getBalance (),
            getInterestRate()));
  }
}
```

Each instance of the SavingsAccount class contains a field called "interest-Rate" that stores the interest rate for the account. The SavingsAccount class provides a number of fields that are value objects, like Money and Percentage.[4] For simplicity's sake, let's assume that each day the method "accrueDailyInterest" is called and the interest is added to the account's balance.

Obviously, it is not very efficient to make every Account object store the interest rate. We could make it a static field of the SavingsAccount class, but this makes changing the interest rate rather difficult, in particular if it involves database persistence. It is better to provide a SavingsAccount type object class that provides the field "interestRate" for all the different variations of SavingsAccount that our anonymous bank provides to its customers.

```
public class SavingsAccountType {
  protected Percentage interestRate;

  public Percentage getInterestRate() {
    return interestRate;
  }

  public synchronized void setInterestRate(Percentage ir) {
    interestRate = ir;
  }
}
```

The SavingsAccount class can now retrieve the interest rate from its type object and use it to calculate the daily interest payments.

```
public class SavingsAccount {
  protected Money balance;
  protected SavingsAccountType type;

  public Money getBalance() {
    return balance;
  }

  public SavingsAccountType getType() {
    return type;
  }

  public void accrueDailyInterest() {
    Percentage interestRate= getType().getInterestRate();
    deposit(InterestCalculator.calcDailyInterest(getBalance (),
        getInterestRate()));
  }
}
```

---

4. For an efficient implementation of such value objects, see www.jvalue.org.

We can now change the interest rate for all accounts of a specific SavingsAccount type by changing the field in the SavingsAccountType object.

Next to our SavingsAccount class, we are also designing and implementing a CheckingAccount class. Because SavingsAccount and CheckingAccount have so many fields in common, we introduce a superclass Account that captures fields like owner id, balance, and most importantly, the reference to the type object. For the type object, we introduce a class AccountType, which provides fields shared by all types of accounts.

```java
public class Account {
   protected PartyId ownerId;
   protected Money balance;
   protected AccountType type;

   public AccountType getType () {
      return type;
   }
}

public class AccountType {
   protected String name;

   public String getName() {
      return name;
   }
}
```

However, not all fields are common to all classes. For example, a savings account typically has no overdraw limit, but a checking account does. We could now use inheritance to add the different fields for different subclasses of Account and AccountType. However, as initially noted, the class hierarchy can quickly become so deep that handling and changing it becomes unwieldy. Our bank, successful in its business, not only has individual retail customers, but also wealthy individual (private banking) customers, corporate clients, pension funds, and others, all of which come with special requirements that need to be catered to.

Quickly losing the oversight of the resulting class hierarchy, we decide to use a PROPERTY LIST to hold the fields of an account. We drop the SavingsAccount class and extend the generic Account class with a PROPERTY LIST (actually a hashtable of generic property objects). The PROPERTY LIST maintains all fields for savings accounts or for checking accounts, and others that are not stored in a dedicated member field.

In the following code we provide a uniform way to access properties, regardless of their representation as regular fields or as entries in the PROPERTY LIST.

```
class Account {
   protected PartyId ownerId;
   protected Money balance;
   protected Map properties;
   protected AccountType type;

   public AccountType getType () {
      return type;
   }

   public Money getBalance() {
      return balance;
   }

   public Object getProperty(String name) {
      if (isFieldPropertyName(name)) {
         return getFieldProperty(name);
      }
      else {
         return getDynamicProperty(name);
      }
   }

   protected Object getFieldProperty(String name) {
      if (name.equals("balance")) {
         return getBalance();
      }
      else {
         return null;
      }
   }

   protected Object getDynamicProperty (String name) {
      return properties.get(name);
   }

   public synchronized void setProperty(String name, Object value) {
      if (isFieldPropertyName(name)) {
         setFieldProperty (name, value);
      }
      else {
         setDynamicProperty(name, value);
      }
   }
```

```
   protected void setFieldProperty(String name, Object value) {
      // no code for balance, but maybe for additional member fields.
   }

   protected void setDynamicProperty(String name, Object value) {
      properties.put(name, value);
   }
}
```

There may be valid reasons to retain some fields considered common to all types of accounts as individual fields rather than dynamic property types. This usually allows, for example, for more efficient database querying (assuming that the PROPERTY LIST will be stored as a non-queryable BLOB). Also, for some types of fields, it may not be acceptable to directly set them, so that access needs to be controlled. (For example, the balance is either added to or subtracted from, but it is never directly set a value.)

As we can see from the implementation of Account, it is possible to set arbitrary properties to an instance of it. This is certainly not desirable, because some accounts may not even know properties that are falsely set to them! Hence we extend our AccountType implementation and provide means to describe what properties are valid for a specific type of account.

First, we must capture the types of properties that an Account instance may receive. Hence we conceive a PropertyType class that describes one particular type of property available for instances of a given type of account.

```
class PropertyType {
   protected String name;
   protected Class type;
   protected boolean isMandatory;

   public String getName() {
      return name;
   }

   public boolean isSupertypeOf(Class type) {
      return type.isAssignableFrom(type);
   }

   public boolean isValidValue(Object value) {
      // add correct test, possibly delegate to a strategy
      return true;
   }
}
```

Now we make the AccountType class provide a set of PropertyType objects, each of which represents a property that its instances may or must have. Again, using a hashtable to store the property type objects is a reasonable choice.

```
class AccountType {
  protected String name;
  protected Map propertyTypes;

  public boolean hasPropertyType(String name) {
    return propertyTypes.containsKey(name);
  }

  public PropertyType getPropertyType(String name) {
    return (PropertyType) propertyTypes.get(name);
  }

  public boolean isValidProperty(String name, Class type, Object
      value) {
    PropertyType propertyType = getPropertyType(name);
    if (propertyType == null) {
      return false;
    }
    return propertyType.isSupertypeOf(type) &&
      propertyType.isValidValue(value);
  }
}
```

We now have shown how to model and implement the motivating example using the DYNAMIC OBJECT MODEL pattern.

Known Uses

Most object-oriented programming languages work according to this model. However, the relationships we describe are subdued to efficient implementations and hence are non-obvious. An important question is whether the programming language supports modification at runtime. Another key feature is the ability to adapt the meta-model toward a specific business domain. Clearly, languages like Java with their limited introspective reflective facilities currently fall short, which means we must turn toward languages like Smalltalk or CLOS. Even the current aspect-oriented extensions of Java lack various benefits of the DYNAMIC OBJECT MODEL pattern. Another useful perspective is to extend our comparison to prototype-based languages, because the DYNAMIC

OBJECT MODEL pattern contains traces of both class-based and prototype-based concepts.

Fortunately, there are also many systems that make the model explicit. And as the Sample Code section demonstrates, we can fairly easily implement such systems in most modern languages.

At Argo we developed a framework to support Argo's administration when the organization itself was in a great state of flux. The framework provides generic components and tools (such as query screens, overview lists, and an authorization rulebase) driven at runtime by the business model. We used the DYNAMIC OBJECT MODEL pattern with several extensions (see the Extensions section) to implement the business model (this includes organizational model, data, documents, relationships, and business rules) [Tilman+1999]. A lot of effort went into making sure we got good performance while retaining the flexibility of DYNAMIC OBJECT MODELS [Tilman1999].

A second application of DYNAMIC OBJECT MODELS consists in a business rules engine to allow the Belgian's Social Security to adapt the business rules to legislative changes [Tilman2005].

At UBS, we developed Dynamo 1 and Dynamo 2. Dynamo 1 was a research prototype used to sell the idea to bankers [Riehle+1998]. It featured a full-fledged type level with all relevant relationship types. After successfully getting contracts, we implemented Dynamo 2 in the corporate client business [Wegener1999]. Dynamo 2 uses a slimmed down version of the Dynamo 1 model that is similar to the core of the pattern described here. It was used to capture the plethora of types of loans available to corporate clients of UBS.

At SKYVA, we developed a UML virtual machine that loads UML models and runs them [Riehle+2001]. The virtual machine was part of a larger development effort that comprised an integrated development environment (IDE) for UML, several domain-specific language extensions of UML, and runtime support for dynamic object models on both the type and instance level in the form of libraries. UML and its extensions are cast as dynamic object models, and the virtual machine is their implementation. The implementation made use of many well-known interpreter and virtual machine techniques like those discussed earlier, for example, using keys rather than strings, perfect hashtables, and so on. Of particular interest is the focus on domain-specific languages and tooling to support working in these domains.

The Hartford has a framework for representing insurance policies that is a DYNAMIC OBJECT MODEL [Johnson+1998].

The thesis by Witthawaskul describes a simple DYNAMIC OBJECT MODEL [Witthawaskul2001] for editing databases.

Related Patterns

As a composite pattern, the DYNAMIC OBJECT MODEL pattern imposes constraints on its composed patterns:

- Compared to the TYPE OBJECT pattern, types now explicitly describe the structure of their instances.
- Compared to the PROPERTY LIST pattern, properties are now constrained by their types.
- When extending the pattern with Composite, the components of an aggregate are constrained by their type.

The OBJECT SYSTEM pattern [Noble2000] provides components with properties but does not introduce a type level distinct from the instance level. Effectively, it is a type-less generic object model.

Martin Fowler's book, *Analysis Patterns*, introduces the concepts of knowledge level and operational level (for accountability) [Fowler1997]. Essentially, knowledge level means the same as type level, and operational level means the same as instance level. Fowler describes various aspects of the knowledge level for accountability, which can be viewed as a domain-specific use of the DYNAMIC OBJECT MODEL pattern.

Robert Haugen's Dependent Demand pattern refers to Fowler's knowledge level [Haugen1997]. The knowledge level underlies all operations of the demand networks (order networks) that he describes for supply chain management. Through this indirection, Dependent Demand relies on the DYNAMIC OBJECT MODEL pattern, and most instances of the Dependent Demand pattern are likely to use the DYNAMIC OBJECT MODEL pattern.

Acknowledgments

This chapter was initially shepherded for and workshopped at PLoP 2000. We would like to thank Joshua Kerievsky, our shepherd, and Robert Haugen for helping us improve the description of the DYNAMIC OBJECT MODEL pattern. We would further like to thank the workshop participants and the anonymous reviewers of the PLoPD 5 submission for helping us improve the pattern description as well.

References

[Bäumer+1998] D. Bäumer, D. Riehle, W. Siberski, C. Lilienthal, D. Megert, K. H. Sylla, and H. Züllighoven. "Values in Object Systems." *Ubilab Technical Report 98.10.1*. Zurich, Switzerland: UBS AG, 1998. Available: *http://www.riehle.org/computer-science/research*.

[Cunningham1995] W. Cunningham. "The Checks Pattern Language of Information Integrity." In J. O. Coplien and D. C. Schmidt (eds.), *Pattern Languages of Program Design*, pp. 147–162. Reading, MA: Addison-Wesley, 1995.

[Foote+1998] B. Foote and J. Yoder. "Metadata." *Technical Report #WUCS-98-25* (PLoP '98). Dept. of Computer Science, Washington University, 1998.

[Fowler1997] M. Fowler. *Analysis Patterns*. Reading, MA: Addison-Wesley, 1997.

[Haugen1997] R. Haugen. "Dependent Demand." *Technical Report #WUCS-97-34* (PLoP '97). Dept. of Computer Science, Washington University, 1997.

[Haugen+2000] R. Haugen and W. E. McCarthy. "REA, a Semantic Model for Internet Supply Chain Collaboration." Available: *http://www.supplychain-links.com/Rea4scm.htm*.

[Johnson+1998] R. Johnson and B. Woolf. "Type Object." In R. C. Martin, D. Riehle, and F. Buschmann (eds.), *Pattern Languages of Program Design 3*, pp. 47–66. Reading, MA: Addison-Wesley, 1998.

[Johnson+1998] R. Johnson and J. Oakes. "The User-Defined Product Framework." Unpublished manuscript. Available: *http://st-www.cs.uiuc.edu/users/johnson/papers/udp*.

[Noble2000] J. Noble. "Prototype-Based Object System." In *Pattern Languages of Program Design 4*. Boston: Addison-Wesley, 2000.

[Riehle1997b] D. Riehle. "Composite Design Patterns." In *Proceedings of the 1997 Conference on Object-Oriented Programming Systems, Languages and Applications* (OOPSLA '97), pp. 218–228. ACM Press, 1997.

[Riehle1997a] D. Riehle. "A Role-Based Design Pattern Catalog of Atomic and Composite Patterns Structured by Pattern Purpose." *Ubilab Technical Report 97-1-1*. Zürich, Switzerland: Union Bank of Switzerland, 1997. Available: *http://www.riehle.org/computer-science/research*.

[Riehle+1998] D. Riehle and E. Dubach. "Why a Bank Needs Dynamic Object Models." *Position Paper for OOPSLA '98 Workshop 15 on Metadata and Active Object Models*. UBS AG, 1998. Available: *http://www.riehle.org/computer-science/research*.

[Riehle+2001] D. Riehle, S. Fraleigh, D. Bucka-Lassen, and N. Omorogbe. "The Architecture of a UML Virtual Machine." In *Proceedings of the 2001 Conference on Object-Oriented Programming Systems, Languages, and Applications* (OOPSLA '01), pp. 327–341. ACM Press, 2001.

[Roberts+1998] D. Roberts and R. Johnson. "Patterns for Evolving Frameworks." In R. C. Martin, D. Riehle, and F. Buschmann (eds.), *Pattern Languages of Program Design 3*, pp. 471–486. Reading, MA: Addison-Wesley, 1998.

[Tilman+1999] M. Tilman and M. Devos. "A Reflective and Repository-Based Framework." In M. E. Fayad, D. C. Schmidt, and R. E. Johnson (eds.), *Implementing Application Frameworks*, pp. 29–64. Wiley Computer Publishing, 1999.

[Tilman1999] M. Tilman. "Active Object-Models and Object Representations," Position Paper for the OOPSLA '99 MetaData and Active Object-Model Pattern Mining Workshop. Available: *http://users.pandora.be/michel.tilman/ Publications*.

[Tilman2005] M. Tilman, Ph.D. (in progress). Available: *http://users.pandora.be/ michel.tilman/Publications*.

[Vlissides1998] J. Vlissides. "Composite Design Patterns—They Aren't What You Think." *C++ Report* (June 1998).

[Wegener1999] H. Wegener. "Dynamo 2 System Documentation." UBS AG, 1999.

[Witthawaskul2001] W. Witthawaskul. "A Customizable Database Editor based on an Adaptive Object Model." Master's thesis, University of Illinois at Urbana-Champaign. Available: *http://weerasak.com/witthawaskul_ms_thesis.pdf*.

CHAPTER 2

Domain Object Manager

John Liebenau

Intent

Separate an object's domain interface from its repository interface to encapsulate domain object insertion, update, removal, and query. Let concrete subclasses adapt specific repository APIs to conform to the standard repository interface. DOMAIN OBJECT MANAGER enables domain object clients to be independent of specific persistence repositories or application servers.

Also Known As

Repository

Motivation

Suppose you are building a framework that implements a key part of your enterprise's business logic. The central components of this framework are domain objects that represent important entities in your business. These domain objects will be part of multiple applications that run on different operating systems, use a variety of middleware, and depend on several types of persistence mechanisms. Because it is central to your enterprise, the framework is also expected to adapt to future technologies as they become available.

How will you keep the domain object code simple and focused on business logic while also supporting multiple persistence mechanisms (some of which may not yet exist)? You might be tempted to solve this problem with inheritance. You could define a hierarchy for each domain type with the business logic in the base class and specific persistence or middleware functionality in derived classes, but there are drawbacks to this approach. Business code and persistence code can mix too easily using inheritance. For example, clients of your framework may commonly need to extend domain types to fit their particular application. They would have to find the derived class that implements their kind of persistence and extend it with a subclass that contains the additional business logic. This would result in a class hierarchy that has persistence code sandwiched between two levels of business code. A better solution is to completely separate business logic from persistence. The DOMAIN OBJECT MANAGER design pattern does this by keeping the business logic in a domain object class and encapsulating the persistence and middleware functionality behind a common manager interface that can be implemented with adapters for each specific API.

Consider an order-processing framework that provides key functionality to a brokerage firm. At the core of this framework is the Order class that represents buy and sell orders, tracks reports on successful trades, and records order modification requests. Orders are created from client data, updated with trade reports and additional client instructions, retrieved with various kinds of search criteria, and sometimes destroyed. The order-processing framework is used in multiple applications such as trading management systems, order routing servers, and electronic crossing networks. Each application imposes its own constraints on the environment in which the framework will operate, including operating systems, databases, file systems, middleware, and application servers. We can keep the framework simple and reusable by defining: an Order class that encapsulates the business logic for order processing, an OrderFinder interface for specifying and executing the query process for Orders, and an OrderManager interface for inserting, updating, and removing Orders from a repository. The OrderManager interface is also used as the access point for obtaining OrderFinders for retrieving Order objects. The Order subsystem of our framework will have the interface structure shown in Figure 2–1.

Application code will only depend on the interfaces provided by OrderManager, OrderFinder, and Order. For each persistence repository or middleware API, the framework provides concrete subclasses of OrderManager and OrderFinder that adapt the specific life-cycle code to the common API.

For example, the application could use a relational database as its persistence repository and a homegrown object-to-relational mapping to bring objects in and out of the database. RdbOrderManager implements the OrderManager interface by providing insert, update, and remove methods that internally generate SQL and operate on a relational database (see Figure 2–2).

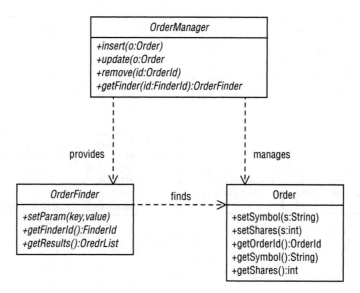

Figure 2–1 *Order subsystem interfaces*

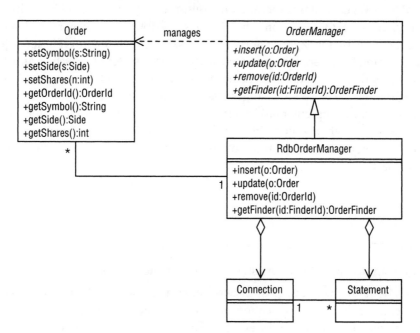

Figure 2–2 *OrderManager implemented with relational database*

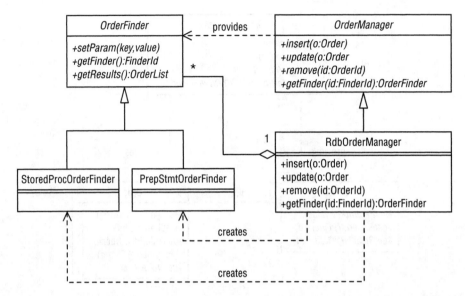

Figure 2–3 *OrderFinder relational database implementations and reference management*

OrderManager declares methods for returning OrderFinder objects that are used to retrieve Orders from the database. RdbOrderManager implements those methods by managing references to a set of concrete OrderFinder objects and returning the reference associated with a finder's identifier (see Figure 2–3). This allows the set of finders to be open to extension while keeping the Order-Manager interface closed to changes [Meyer1988][Martin1996].

New concrete implementations of OrderManager and OrderFinder can be provided to use other technologies, such as object oriented databases or component Frameworks like EJB without disturbing the application's use of Order domain objects.

Applicability

Use the DOMAIN OBJECT MANAGER pattern when:

- You want to implement persistent or componentized domain objects.

- Each domain object can exist in two states: a transient state in which the object exists only in the application's primary memory, and a persistent state in which the object has been inserted or transformed so that it exists in the persistence repository or application server.

- Your framework code must be independent of the operating environments on which it is deployed.

- Your framework must have the capability of choosing a specific persistence repository or application server from multiple choices, usually at deployment time but possibly at runtime or linktime as well.

- You want to insulate your framework against changes in the underlying persistence repository or application server.

Structure

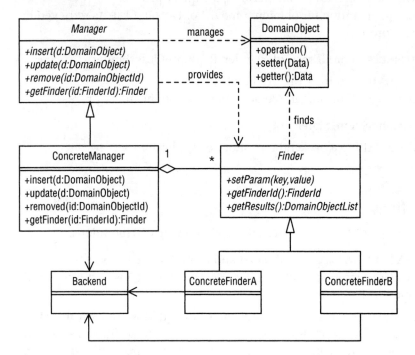

Figure 2–4 *Structure diagram for DOMAIN OBJECT MANAGER pattern*

Participants

- MANAGER (OrderManager...)
  - Declares operations for inserting, updating, and removing DOMAINOBJECTS
  - Declares an operation for choosing FINDERS in order to retrieve DOMAIN-OBJECTS

- CONCRETEMANAGER (RdbOrderManager...)
  - Adapter for inserting, updating, and removing DOMAINOBJECTS from the BACKEND repository
  - Maintains the set of CONCRETEFINDERS used to retrieve DOMAINOBJECTS

- DOMAINOBJECT (Order...)
  - Declares an interface for some business logic

- FINDER (OrderFinder...)
  - Declares an operation for identification
  - Declares operations for parameterizing the query process
  - Declares an operation for obtaining the list of DOMAINOBJECTS retrieved by the query process

- CONCRETEFINDER (StoredProcOrderFinder, PrepStmtOrderFinder...)
  - Implements the interface declared by FINDER
  - Provides a specific search implementation used in the query process

- BACKEND (Connection, Statement)
  - Provides an API to a backend repository or application server

Collaborations

The DOMAIN OBJECT MANAGER pattern has the following collaborations:

- *Insertion*–A DOMAINOBJECT is validated and passed to the CONCRETEMANAGER via the MANAGER interface that uses the DOMAINOBJECT to insert the appropriate data into the BACKEND.

- *Query*–Client code gets a FINDER from the CONCRETEMANAGER via the MANAGER interface. The FINDER is optionally configured with additional search information provided by the client. The DOMAINOBJECTS are retrieved through the Finder's getResults() method.

- *Update*–A DOMAINOBJECT's state has changed. The DOMAINOBJECT is passed to the CONCRETEMANAGER via the MANAGER interface. The CONCRETEMANAGER updates the BACKEND with the new DOMAINOBJECT data.

- *Removal*–Client code passes a DOMAINOBJECT to the CONCRETEMANAGER via the MANAGER interface. The CONCRETEMANAGER removes the DOMAINOBJECT from the BACKEND.

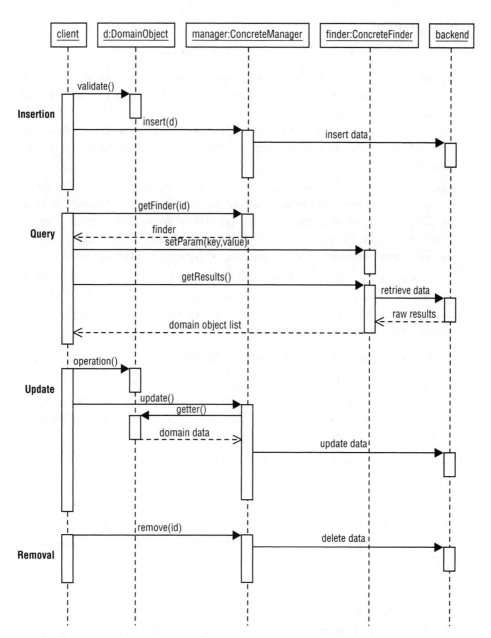

Figure 2–5 *Collaboration diagram for DOMAIN OBJECT MANAGER pattern*

Consequences

The DOMAIN OBJECT MANAGER pattern has the following benefits:

- *Separates life cycle from business logic.* DOMAIN OBJECT MANAGER allows you to evolve life-cycle mechanisms independently of business domain mechanisms. This separation reduces risks associated with relying on a single application server or persistence technology. It also increases the application's flexibility to change as new component and persistence technologies become available.

- *Enables multiple kinds of persistence repositories or application servers.* A single application may need to run in a variety of operating environments, each necessitating a different persistence repository or application server. DOMAIN OBJECT MANAGER enables applications to choose between multiple kinds of operating environments to suit a particular deployment requirement.

- *Provides extensible query mechanism.* DOMAIN OBJECT MANAGER provides an open-ended query mechanism that can be extended to handle practically any kind of query and retrieval required by an application. It accomplishes this with a simple and compact interface.

DOMAIN OBJECT MANAGER has the following liability:

- *Introduces additional layers of indirection that could slow performance.* By encapsulating the life-cycle mechanisms behind generic interfaces, performance can be slowed due to the additional indirection and the mapping between the generic interfaces and the concrete repository mechanisms.

DOMAIN OBJECT MANAGER has the following tradeoff:

- *Complex implementations versus easy usage.* Each ConcreteManager/ConcreteFinder implementation becomes internally more complex due to mapping the native life-cycle API to conform to the common repository interfaces. However, the internal complexity of the repository interfaces enables the rest of the application to become simpler.

Implementation

The following implementation issues should be considered when using the DOMAIN OBJECT MANAGER pattern:

- *Identifying DomainObjects.* DOMAINOBJECTS may need to provide multiple schemes for identifying themselves. A common approach is to generate object ids (OIDs) for each new DOMAINOBJECT instance. The OID acts as a

DOMAINOBJECT's unique address and can be used to represent relationships between DOMAINOBJECTS or as a search key for use in FINDERS. However, an additional identification scheme may be provided to identify DOMAINOBJECTS based on an attribute such as a name or time stamp.

- *DomainObject persistence states.* From a persistence point of view, DOMAINOBJECTS can be in one of the following states:
  - Transient–An in-memory object that has not yet been persisted
  - Persistent–An object that has been persisted and both its in-memory representation and its persistent data are equivalent
  - Modified–An object that has been previously persisted but its in-memory representation has been modified and not yet re-persisted

  Managers should provide a method for determining the persistence state of DOMAINOBJECTS.

- *Validating DomainObjects.* Domain objects need to be validated prior to being inserted into the repository. This can be accomplished by adding a validate() method to the DOMAINOBJECT or by implementing a separate DomainObjectValidator class if the validation process is complex.

- *Parameterizing Finders.* Many concrete search mechanisms, such as stored procedures or prepared statements, require data to be passed to them in order to configure their queries to retrieve the desired objects. The FINDER interface can accommodate these mechanisms by declaring various setInput(...) methods that the concrete implementations can override if necessary:

```
interface Finder ...
    void setInput(int input);
    void setInput(double input);
    void setInput(String input);
    // ...


class ConcreteFinderThatTakesOneStringParam implements Finder
{
    private String queryInput;
    // ...
    public  void    setInput(int input) {}
    public  void    setInput(double input) {}
    public  void    setInput(String input) { queryInput = input }
    // ...
}
```

The FINDER's setInput(...) methods should be general enough to be applicable for all CONCRETEFINDER implementations allowing the Finder to be open for extension but closed to change [Meyer1988][Martin1996]. The FINDER interface can also provide versions of the `setInput(...)` method that can accommodate queries that require multiple inputs by specifying the inputs' names, by specifying the inputs' positions, or by passing in a Parameter Object [Fowler1999] that contains all of the inputs:

```
interface Finder ...
    void setInput(String name,double input);
    void setInput(int position,String input);
    void setInput(Parameter input);
    // ...
```

- *Returning Finders that have state.* The MANAGER declares methods for getting FINDERS and returning them for use in client code. If the FINDERS maintain state in the form of input data, there may be conflicts as each caller of the FINDER sets its input data overwriting the previous caller's input data. The Prototype design pattern [Gamma+1995] can eliminate this problem by having the CONCRETEMANAGER's getFinder() method return a clone of the requested FINDER. FINDERS that do not have state can implement a clone() method that returns a reference to themselves. The CONCRETEMANAGER then becomes a Prototype-based factory [Gamma+1995][Vlissides1998a].

- *Configuring the ConcreteManager with Finders.* There are two approaches to configuring the CONCRETEMANAGER with its FINDERS. The first approach is to have the CONCRETEMANAGER explicitly create and store instances of the ConcreteFinders needed by the client. The second approach is to have the MANAGER provide an interface for registering FINDERS. The first approach has the advantage of freeing the clients from the responsibility of configuring the finders, but it has the disadvantage of requiring the CONCRETEMANAGER to be recompiled and relinked if additional CONCRETEFINDERS are added to the system. The second approach has the advantage of flexibility in that additional CONCRETEFINDERS can be added without affecting the CONCRETEMANAGER, but it clutters up client code with configuration details. By combining both approaches, we can reach a balanced medium in which the default CONCRETEFINDERS are configured by the CONCRETEMANAGER and custom CONCRETEFINDERS can be added by clients.

- *Specification-based queries versus Finders.* Some DOMAINOBJECTS and BACKENDS may lend themselves to specification-based queries. A specification is a set of criteria that is applied to DOMAINOBJECT attributes. DOMAINOBJECTS matching the specification are returned as results. This approach can further simplify the query process by eliminating the need for separate FINDER objects. The MANAGER interface would provide a matching(Specification) method in place of the getFinder(id) method:

```
interface Manager ...
    List matching(Specification spec);
    // ...
```

Specification-based queries are generally useful when the DOMAINOBJECT structure can be described by relatively simple specifications and the BACKEND has features that allow the specifications to be incorporated into the BACKEND query mechanism. Evans and Fowler call this variation the Repository pattern [Evans2004][Fowler2003]. Given the right kind of DOMAINOBJECT, specification-based queries can make retrieving DOMAINOBJECTS from the Manager as simple as a single method call. However, the Finder approach has some advantages of its own. Finders provide a very close abstraction over stored procedures and prepared statements. In essence, Finders are implemented as rather simple adapters on top of stored procedures and prepared statements, which makes them very efficient. One disadvantage to specification-based queries is that they may limit optimization by preventing you from exploiting some features provided by the BACKEND, such as highly optimized stored procedures.

Sample Code

The sample Java code is taken from the example given in the Motivation section. It illustrates some of the key features required for using DOMAIN OBJECT MANAGER to integrate a persistence infrastructure into an application.

The OrderManager interface declares methods for inserting, updating, removing, and finding Orders.

```
interface OrderManager
{
    void          insertOrder(Order o);
    void          updateOrder(Order o);
    void          removeOrder(Order o);
    OrderFinder   getOrderFinder(String id);
}
```

The RdbOrderManager class implements the OrderManager as an object-to-relational mapper that stores and retrieves objects to and from a relational database.

```
class RdbOrderManager implements OrderManager
{
    private Connection    connection;
    private Map           finders;
    // ...

    public RdbOrderManager(Connection conn)
    {
        connection = conn;
        finders = new TreeMap();

        finders.put(
            "ORDERS_FOR_CLIENT",
            new StoredProdOrderFinder(connection,"orders_for_client")
);
        finders.put(
            "BUY_ORDERS",
            new StoredProdOrderFinder(connection,"get_buy_orders") );
        finders.put(
            "SELL_ORDERS",
            new StoredProdOrderFinder(connection,"get_sell_orders") );
        // ...
    }

    public void insertOrder(Order p)
    {
        Statement inserter = connection.createStatement();
        inserter.executeUpdate(
            "INSERT INTO Order VALUES(" +
            p.getOrderId() + "," + p.getSymbol() + "," +
            p.getSide() + "," + p.getShares() + ")" );
    }
    // ...
}
```

The Order class is the domain type managed by the OrderManager. It provides basic operations for manipulating Orders in a stock trading application.

```
class Order ...
    void    setSymbol(String symbol);
    void    setSide(Side side);
    void    setShares(int shares);
```

```
OrderId getOrderId();
String  getSymbol();
Side    getSide();
int     getShares();
// ...
```

The OrderFinder interface declares the methods for: identifying each Order-
Finder instance, retrieving a List of Orders, and setting parameters to configure
concrete queries with addition information.

```
interface OrderFinder
{
    void    setInput(int pos,int value);
    void    setInput(int pos,double value);
    void    setInput(int pos,String value);

    String  getFinderId();
    List    getResults();
}
```

The StoredProcOrderFinder class implements the OrderFinder interface by executing a stored procedure to retrieve Orders matching the given inputs (if any).
The stored procedure returns a JDBC ResultSet that is processed and transformed into a list of Orders.

```
class StoredProcOrderFinder implements OrderFinder
{
    private Connection        connection;
    private CallableStatement procedure;
    //  ...

    public StoredProcOrderFinder(Connection conn,String name)
    {
        super();
        connection = conn;
        procedure  = connection.prepareCall( "{call " + name + "}" );
    }
    public void    setInput(int pos,int value)
                        { procedure.setInt(pos,value); }
    public void    setInput(int pos,double value)
                        { procedure.setDouble(pos,value); }
    public void    setInput(int pos,String value)
                        { procedure.setString(pos,value); }
    public String  getFinderId() { return( "ORDERS_FOR_CLIENT" ); }
```

```
    public List getResults()
    {
        ResultSet results = procedure.executeQuery();
        List      output = new ArrayList();
        Order     order;

        while ( results.next() )
        {
            int    orderId = results.getInt( "ORDER_ID" );
            String symbol  = results.getString( "SYMBOL" );
            String side    = results.getString( "SIDE" );
            int    shares  = results.getInt( "SHARES" );

            output.add( new Order( orderId,symbol,side,shares ) );
        }
        return( output );
    }
}
```

The following is an excerpt of code that makes use of the various participants of the DOMAIN OBJECT MANAGER pattern. A list of Orders is loaded into the application. They are validated and then inserted into the persistence repository. Finally, a list of Orders belonging to a single client is retrieved through the finder.

```
OrderManager manager = new RdbOrderManager();
List         orders  = getOrdersToInsert();
OrderFinder  finder  = manager.getOrderFinder( "ORDERS_FOR_CLIENT" );
String       clientName = "Order Management Inc.";
List         clientOrders = null;

try
{
    for (Iterator terator i = orders.getIterator();i.hasNext();)
    {
        Order order = (Order)i.next();
        try { order.validate(); }
        catch (ValidationException e) { e.printStackTrace(); }
        manager.insertOrder( order );
    }
}

finder.setInput( 1,clientName );
clientOrders = finder.getResults();
```

Known Uses

Object-to-Relational Mapping frameworks such as JDO [Jordan+2003] *and Hibernate* [Bauer+2005] are instantiations of the DOMAIN OBJECT MANAGER pattern that provide a higher level of abstraction on top of relational database persistence. JDO specifies a PersistenceManager interface that plays the MANAGER role and a Query interface that plays the FINDER role. Concrete implementations of these interfaces are provided for each kind of persistence backend. Relational databases connected via JDBC are the most common backend. Hibernate is similar to JDO and provides equivalent interfaces and functionality.

Enterprise Java Beans [Matena+1999][Monson-Haefel2000] use the DOMAIN OBJECT MANAGER pattern to achieve portability across EJB component container implementations such as IBM's WebSphere and BEA's WebLogic application servers. An enterprise bean provides client code with a Home interface that acts as the MANAGER by providing life-cycle methods for creating, destroying, and finding DOMAINOBJECTS. DOMAINOBJECTS implement a Remote interface that provides business methods. The Home interface is implemented by an automatically generated component container class that manages creation, search, and destruction of Remote objects in the same way as a CONCRETEMANAGER does. EJBs are portable between vendor implementations, because applications only depend on the Home and Remote interfaces. When an application changes EJB component container implementations, the component container-related classes (CONCRETEMANAGER and MANAGED) are regenerated for the new component container.

CORBA Object Factories [Henning+1999] use the DOMAIN OBJECT MANAGER pattern, in much the same way as Enterprise Java Beans, to achieve portability across implementations. Object factories in CORBA provide life-cycle methods for creating, destroying, and finding CORBA objects. An object factory is represented by an IDL interface (Manager) on the client side and a class implementation on the server side. Object factories return references to user-defined CORBA domain objects (DOMAINOBJECT). The IDL compiler provided by a CORBA implementation will automatically generate proxy classes that implement the Object factory and user-defined CORBA domain object interfaces.

Many domain-specific frameworks use the DOMAIN OBJECT MANAGER pattern to encapsulate object persistence and open it to extension. The Order example from the Motivation section is based on several proprietary trading systems.

Related Patterns

DOMAIN OBJECT MANAGER is a compound design pattern [Riehle1997] [Vlissides1998b] combining the Manager [Sommerlad1998], Adapter, Façade [Gamma+1995], and Query Object [Fowler2003] design patterns. The Manager design pattern serves as the center for drawing the other patterns together to form a cohesive whole. The Manager design pattern acts as a Façade that encapsulates the components associated with the concrete repository. Table 2–1 shows how the DOMAIN OBJECT MANAGER participants map onto the participants of its component patterns.

Table 2–1 *Mapping between Domain Object Manager and Component Patterns*

DOMAIN OBJECT MANAGER Participants		Component Patterns Participants
Manager	→	$\text{Manager}_{\text{Manager}}$, $\text{Target}_{\text{Adapter}}$, $\text{Façade}_{\text{Façade}}$
ConcreteManager	→	$\text{Manager}_{\text{Manager}}$, $\text{Adapter}_{\text{Adapter}}$
Backend	→	$\text{Adaptee}_{\text{Adapter}}$
DomainObject	→	$\text{Subject}_{\text{Manager}}$, $\text{Subject}_{\text{Query Object}}$
Finder	→	$\text{Query}_{\text{Query Object}}$
ConcreteFinder	→	$\text{ConcreteQuery}_{\text{Query Object}}$

DOMAIN OBJECT MANAGER is also known as the Repository pattern, which is described in different forms in [Evans2004] and [Fowler2003]. The main difference between DOMAIN OBJECT MANAGER and Repository is that DOMAIN OBJECT MANAGER describes separate Finder objects for implementing the query process while Repository generally describes specification-based queries.

DOMAIN OBJECT MANAGER is also closely related to many of the patterns described in "Connecting Business Object to Relational Databases" [Yoder+1998]. DOMAIN OBJECT MANAGER is one way of implementing the CRUD pattern described in [Yoder+1998]. DOMAIN OBJECT MANAGER is more general than the CRUD patterns because DOMAIN OBJECT MANAGER can encapsulate component containers such as EJB in addition to persistence repositories such as relational databases.

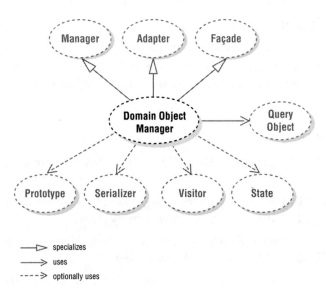

```
            ┌───────⊳      ┌──────⊳       ┌──────⊳     specializes
            ──────⊳   uses
            ----⊳   optionally uses
```

Figure 2–6 *Pattern relationships diagram for DOMAIN OBJECT MANAGER pattern*

DOMAIN OBJECT MANAGER can optionally use the following patterns in its implementation:

- The Prototype design pattern [Gamma+1995] can be used to return clones of FINDERS in order to avoid problems with overwriting FINDER state.

- The Serializer design pattern [Riehle+1997] can be used internally by the CONCRETEMANAGER participant to implement DOMAINOBJECT persistence.

- The Visitor design pattern [Gamma+1995] can be used to validate a composite DOMAINOBJECT by applying validation logic to each element of the DOMAINOBJECT.

- The State design pattern [Gamma+1995] can be used to represent the DOMAINOBJECT persistence state and control state-specific behavior.

The following diagram illustrates the relationships between DOMAIN OBJECT MANAGER and other patterns (see Figure 2–6). The notation is based on Noble's pattern relationship notation [Noble1998][Noble+2001].

Acknowledgments

Thanks go to my PLoP-01 shepherd, Wolfgang Keller, for providing many iterations of helpful feedback. I would also like to thank the anonymous PLoP05 review board for providing valuable suggestions during the editing process.

References

[Bauer+2005] C. Bauer and G. King. *Hibernate in Action*. Manning Publications Co., 2005.

[Evans2004] E. Evans. *Domain-driven Design: Tackling Complexity in the Heart of Software*, pp. 147–161. Boston: Addison-Wesley, 2004.

[Fowler1999] M. Fowler. *Refactoring: Improving the Design of Existing Code*, pp. 295–299. Reading, MA: Addison-Wesley, 1999.

[Fowler2003] M. Fowler. *Patterns of Enterprise Application Architecture*, pp. 316–327. Boston: Addison-Wesley, 2003.

[Gamma+1995] E. Gamma, R. Helm, R. Johnson, and J. Vlissides. *Design Patterns: Elements of Reusable Object-Oriented Software*. Reading, MA: Addison-Wesley, 1995.

[Henning+1999] M. Henning and S. Vinoski. *Advanced CORBA Programming in C++*. Reading, MA: Addison-Wesley, 1999.

[Jordan+2003] D. Jordan and C. Russell. *Java Data Objects*. O'Reilly, Inc., 2003.

[Martin1996] R. Martin. "Open Closed Principle." *C++ Report* (January 1996). Available: *http://www.objectmentor.com/publications/ocp.pdf*.

[Matena+1999] V. Matena and M. Harper. *Enterprise Java Beans Specification v1.1*, pp. 41–47, 88–94, 114–115. Sun Microsystems, Inc., 1999.

[Meyer1988] B. Meyer. *Object-Oriented Software Construction*, 1st Edition, pp. 23–25. Prentice Hall International Ltd., 1988.

[Monson-Haefel2000] R. Monson-Haefel. *Enterprise Java Beans*, 2nd Edition, pp. 23–29, 135–147, 161–165. O'Reilly, Inc., 2000.

[Noble1998] J. Noble. "Classifying Relationships between Object-Oriented Design Patterns." In *Proceedings of the Australian Software Engineering Conference (ASWEC)*, Adelaide, Australia: IEEE Computer Society Press, 1998.

[Noble+2001] J. Noble and Charles Weir. *Small Memory Software: Patterns for Systems with Limited Memory*, pp. 16–17. Boston: Addison-Wesley, 2001.

[Riehle1997] D. Riehle. "Composite Design Patterns." In *Proceedings of the 1997 Conference on Object-Oriented Programming Systems, Languages and Applications*

(OOPSLA '97), pp. 218–228. ACM Press, 1997. Available: *http://www.riehle.org/ papers/1997/oopsla-1997.html.*

[Sommerlad1998] P. Sommerlad. "Manager." In R. C. Martin, D. Riehle, and F. Buschmann (eds.), *Pattern Languages of Program Design 3.* Reading, MA: Addison-Wesley, 1998.

[Vlissides1998a] J. Vlissides. "Pluggable Factory Parts I & II." C++ Report, November 1998, February 1999. Available: *http://www.research.ibm.com/designpatterns/pubs/ph-nov-dec98.pdf* and *http://www.research.ibm.com/designpatterns/ pubs/ph-feb99.pdf.*

[Vlissides1998b] J. Vlissides. "Composite Design Patterns (They Aren't What You Think)." *C++ Report June 1998.* Available: *http://www.research.ibm.com/ designpatterns/pubs/ph-jun98.pdf.*

[Yoder+1998] J. Yoder, R. Johnson, and Q. Wilson. "Connecting Business Objects to Relational Databases." In *Pattern Languages of Programming Conference Proceedings, 1998.* Available: *http://jerry.cs.uiuc.edu/~plop/plop98/final_submissions/ P51.pdf.*

CHAPTER 3

Encapsulated Context

Allan Kelly

Audience

ENCAPSULATED CONTEXT was principally written for software developers who design and write programs. The pattern was originally written for C++ developers, but examples have been reported from other languages such as Java and Smalltalk. It is believed that users of many languages will find the pattern useful, although C++ developers may find the pattern of particular interest.

This chapter explores the pattern in depth and offers a rigorous explanation of where the pattern occurs, the forces of the pattern, and the consequences of using the pattern. For reference purposes, a summary section has been included at the end of the chapter. Experienced developers may prefer to read the summary before reading the entire chapter.

Example

In traditional structured programming, global data is minimized by use of function call parameters. This tradition has continued with some modifications in object-oriented programming. For example:

```
void ProcessMarketTrade( MarketMessage& msg,
                         MarketDataStore& store) {
    if (msg.Trade() == Sell)
        store.Sell(msg.Commodity(), msg.Price(), msg.Quantity());
    else
        store.Buy(msg.Commodity(), msg.Price(),msg.Quantity());
} // ProcessMarketTrade
```

We now decide that any trade that results in a negative quantity should result in an error message. Hence the function Sell must have access to the log manager, and a handle must be passed down. The code becomes:

```
void ProcessMarketTrade( MarketMessage& msg,
                         MarketDataStore& store,
                         LogManager* log) {
  if (msg.Trade() == Sell)
      store.Sell( msg.Commodity(), msg.Price(),msg.Quantity(), log);
  ... as before ...
```

Such changes have a habit of recurring, so when we add a transaction history, the code changes again:

```
void ProcessMarketTrade( MarketMessage& msg,
                         MarketDataStore& store,
                         LogManager* log,
                         TransactionHistory& history) {
  if (msg.Trade() == Sell)
        store.Sell(msg.Commodity(), msg.Price(), msg.Quantity(),
              log, history);
  ... and so on ...
```

Several problems are clearly apparent. First, the parameter list is growing, with a negative effect on comprehensibility; even though the additional code is trivial, it increases the bulk. Second, we are breaking encapsulation. Sell was initially an encapsulated function, but adding more and more parameters exposes its inner workings.

More ominously, we have a ripple effect running through interface and implementation code. The function that calls ProcessMarketTrade must itself have access to LogManager and TransactionHistory, and in turn, the function that calls that function, and so on. Even though these functions only act as pass-throughs for the handles, they need modification.

Less obvious is the capacity for redundant code to enter the system. If at some future date we dispense with the transaction history, then removal impacts at least three different functions. To be sure, the temptation would be to disable the code while leaving it in place. Hence we simply use an anonymous parameter in Sell:

```
void MarketStore::Sell( Commodity& c, Price& p,
                        Quantity& q, LogManager* log,
                        TransactionHistory&) {
   ....
```

In choosing not to delete the history in full, we are storing up complications for future refactorings, and we are also halfway to implementing the Poltergeist anti-pattern [Brown+1998].

These problems are exacerbated if the design is refactored; we may decide to recast our market message processing as a Command pattern [Gamma+1995]:

```
class MarketMessageCommand {
public:
    virtual void Action(MarketDataStore&, LogManager*) = 0;
    ....
};

class Buy : public MarketMessageCommand {
public:
    virtual void Action(MarketDataStore&, LogManager*);
    ....
};

class Sell : public MarketMessageCommand {
public:
    virtual void Action(MarketDataStore&, LogManager*);
     ....
};
```

To ensure substitutability, each `MarketMessageCommand` must implement `Action` with the same signature as the abstract base class. Consequently, commands such as `Buy` are complicated with parameters that are unused. What's worse is the magnified potential for ripple effects across all objects in the hierarchy. Let's say the market introduces a programmatic way of signaling a transition point in the trading day by an enumeration such as:

```
enum TradingDay {
    Closed, PreOpen, Open, Settlement, Suspended
};
```

A new market message is thus needed to handle this, but so too is a state variable:

```
class TradingDayChange : public MarketMessageCommand {
public:
    virtual void Action(MarketDataStore&, LogManager*,
                        TradingDay& activity);
    ....
};
```

Since our new message can change the state activity, a new parameter is needed, and to maintain a common signature, this new parameter must be added to `MarketMessageCommand` and all derived classes. Again, we are increasing the length of the parameter list, introducing a ripple effect, and adding complexity. Our main loop may look like:

```
int main() {
    MarketDataStore marketData;
    LogManager *log(LogFactory());
    TradingDay exchangeStatus(Closed):
    MessageSource source;
    while (true) {
        auto_ptr<MarketMessageCommand> w(source.NextMessage());
        w->Action(marketData, log, exchangeStatus);
    }
    delete log;
    return 0;
}
```

Faced with the problem of adding yet more parameters, we may be tempted to consider global variables. After all, a market is open or closed, and there is surely only one instance of such a flag. It's a tempting solution, because the market status is a simple variable, initialization is not a significant problem, and because it's stack-based, a memory leak is a non-issue.

However, a global variable for `LogManager` is decidedly less tempting. The example just presented strictly controls the use of `log` through scope and parameter passing; were the same variable global, it could potentially be accessed before creation. For example, the `MarketDataStore` constructor may choose to log a message.

We would then be forced into the position of trying to enforce creation before use. This is known to be problematic, and the best-known solution (access through a function) suffers from known issues in multithreaded systems. The same problems also occur in reverse when cleanly ending the program.

While we may be able to survive one or two such global variables, we quickly find the number increasing: the market status, log manager, loaded DLLs. As we add more global variables, it becomes harder to reason about the initialization sequence for each, and this is particularly important when one variable makes use of another. It is also more difficult to reason about the internal state of the program because it is dispersed and has no central point of reference.

Judicious use of namespaces and careful coding may offset the issues with globals, but the issues do not go away; they are merely repositioned or hidden for a while. Each additional parameter or global variable increases coupling, which makes classes more specific to the environment and less of a commodity.

At first sight, the ever-expanding parameter list may appear simply unsightly, but as we can see, the need to pass more and more parameters is a real problem.

Problem

Access to common data is important to many systems. Many systems contain data that must be generally available to divergent parts of the system: configuration data, runtime handles, and in-memory application data.

However, we wish to avoid using global data—such data is normally regarded as poor engineering practice. The problem is traditionally addressed by passing such data as function call parameters, but parameter lists become longer over time. Long parameter lists themselves have an adverse effect on maintainability and on object substitutability.

While access to such data is a common requirement, neither of the two common techniques are without problems. Access to the data is not as trivial as it first appears, and as any system grows, the drawbacks of each solution become greater.

Forces

There are several forces that any widely applicable solution to this problem must accommodate.

Substitutability

Software designs based on common interfaces with object substitutability—either runtime polymorphic or compile-time polymorphic—are restricted in the parameters that can be easily passed to an object. This is because all objects must conform to a common interface with common function signatures to ensure commonality of access, that is, they must conform to the Liskov Substitution Principle (LSP) [Liskov+1988][Martin+1996b].

However, where all data is supplied to objects and function via call parameters, if any object requires additional data it must be passed via a call parameter, and to conform to LSP, all similar objects must also accept this parameter even if they have no functional requirement for it.

For an object, changing any function-method call signature, whether by addition, revision, or removal, breaks LSP. The object in question can no longer be substituted for other similar objects. The compiler should refuse to compile the resulting program. Typically, we must either change every class in the same hierarchy to match the new signature, change every call to the function-method, or both.

Having broken LSP, we are forced to restore LSP by changing other parts of the system. This creates ripple effects through the code base. A good solution to the overall problem would ensure that LSP is not broken and that ripple effects within the code base are thus minimized.

Encapsulation

Good software practice values encapsulation, but traditional solutions threaten encapsulation in the following ways:

- Overlong parameter lists to function calls reduce encapsulation because the parameters suggest the internal workings to developers.
- Global variables break encapsulation by definition. They are considered a poor programming practice that lead to side-effects and increased coupling.
- Within C++ systems there are additional problems associated with instantiation and destruction—particularly in multithreaded developments. Although C++ namespaces allow better management of globals, they do not resolve instantiation and coupling problems.

A good solution would preserve encapsulation, thereby minimizing side-effects and coupling.

Coupling to the Environment

The parameters passed to a function or method define the state of the system external to the object in question. An object receiving a method call knows its own state (even if this is stateless). What it does not know is the state of the rest of the system, that is, the context in which it is called. If global data is used, it becomes harder to reason about the state of the system at the point of call.

Likewise, a simple function maintains little or no state between calls. The external state is everything; the result of the function call depends on the context in which it is called.

The more tightly coupled an object is to its environment, the more difficult it is to use the object in a different setting. Opportunities for using the object in a different environment, for example, within a test harness, or for reuse in a different system, are much reduced. At the same time, developers must pay more attention to the object's environment, thereby reducing readability, understandability, and maintainability.

A solution that minimized coupling would do much to improve understandability and maintainability, and it would improve the opportunities for alternative uses.

Avoid Data Copying

One solution to the global or parameter conflict would be to retain a copy of such data in individual objects. Unfortunately, this is not always practical, especially when the system has a large number of small objects and/or objects exist in difference execution threads.

Reasons for not copying pieces of data may include, but are not limited to, the following:

- Data such as equity market prices may change rapidly and needs to be available in several different locations in the program.

- Data and operations on the data may overwhelm the class. For example, a simple command class used in a Command pattern may only have one significant method; to additionally store data, handles, and accessors would rob the class of its simplicity.

- Overhead of a copy operation is high, both in terms of time and memory used, and this is particularly so if the data is seldom accessed (e.g., command line options).

- Data may be singleton in nature, or may encounter problems when copied. For example, a handle to a log file may be easily copied, but we may not wish to store multiple copies of the handle—to do so increases the chances of introducing a dangling pointer (or reference) when the file is closed. However, use of the Singleton [Gamma+1995] pattern may not be appropriate.

Since these potential solutions are unavailable, they represent forces in their own right. Furthermore, because modern systems frequently end up with a large number of small objects, these problems are increasing.

Solution

Provide a Context container that collects data together and encapsulates common data used throughout the system (see Figure 3–1).

For example:

```
class Context {
    LogManager*          log_;
    CommandLineOptions   cmdOpts_;
    ApplicationData*     store_;
    ...
};
```

Rather than supply multiple parameters, we supply a Context object. The object acts as a container for program state data, a central repository for widely used data within the system. The Context object provides few, if any, functions itself. The object is passed, or more likely a reference is passed, to functions when they are called—utilizing the "parameterize from above" paradigm.

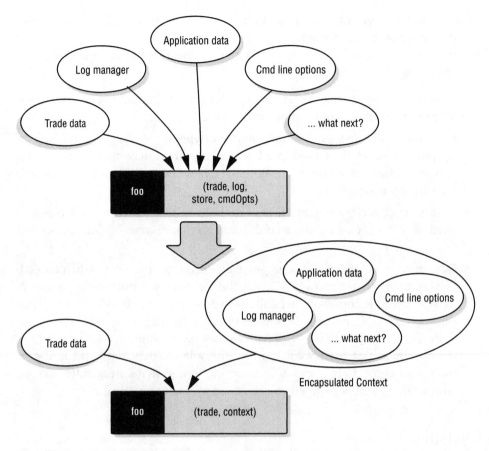

Figure 3–1 *Solution places context data in a single container.*

Three types of data are typically found in a Context class:

• Configuration data such as command line options.
• Application data such as market data.
• Transient runtime data such as handle to log manager.

Implementation

The example given here uses one Context class for simplicity. While the simplicity of a single Context has a lot to recommend it, without careful attention, the class may become a kitchen sink—that is, it may be overwhelmed with any and all data in a system. When this happens, we start to see the emergence of a Blob anti-pattern [Brown+1998].

To counter the drift toward Blob, we can split the class into two or more discrete classes: one for system data and handles, and the second for application data.

Specifically, we can distinguish three types of split:

- *Temporal*: Separating data on the basis of its lifespan. Data that is short-lived is kept separate from data that exists for long periods of time. It is better not to mix transient data with persistent data in order to ensure that expired data does not remain in the container.

- *Horizontal*: Separating reference data from value data, usually needed when one application becomes large itself and inflates the size of the Context class. (Value data items have their own intrinsic value; reference data is a pointer to an item that exists elsewhere. Copying value data results in a second item with the same value, and copying reference data results in another pointer to the same underlying item.)

- *Vertical*: Separating the Context class into a small hierarchy, usually needed when the same Context is needed in a family of programs. This allows for specialization through inheritance in order to provide each family member with a specialized Context object and common code to be shared across the family.

Such splits will mitigate the Blob tendencies, but they also detract from the pattern simplicity. Splitting the Context class should also help improve compile times, since we can assume that although some functions will need to be passed all the fragments of the original Context, many will require fewer fragments, thus reducing dependencies.

However, while it may be desirable to split the Context class for a variety of reasons, this can be taken too far. The use of many fine-grained Context objects may return us overlong parameter lists.

Thus, any implementation of the ENCAPSULATED CONTEXT pattern should consider the following issues:

- Is a single Context class the best answer? The initial simplicity of a single Context may lead to difficulties later.

- What is the life expectancy of the data? Bundling short-lived or rapidly changing data together with constant data may lead to confusion or inaccuracies.

- Is there a family of programs under development? Is there benefit from creating vertical hierarchy of Context classes? This may facilitate code transfers between programs

- Are we creating problems by mixing reference and value data in the same Context? Could this data be split horizontally between several Context classes?

- Are we in danger of creating too many, fine-grained, Context classes?

These issues must be addressed together, because the answers to each question influence the answers to the others.

Resolution

Applying this solution to the example given at the start of this chapter, we get:

```
// MarketContext.hpp
class LogManager;
class CommandLineOptions;
class MarketDataStore;

class MarketContext {
    LogManager*          log_;
    CommandLineOptions   opts_;
    MarketDataStore*     marketData_;
public:
    MarketContext( LogManager*, CommandLineOptions&,
                   MarketDataStore*);
    LogManager* Log();
    MarketDataStore* MarketData();
    CommandLineOptions& CmdOptions() const;
};
```

With this Context class, the presence or absence of a `TransactionLog` is abstracted to a detail about `MarketContext`.

The class should take a minimal role in the lifetime of enclosed classes; it is better to present these as ready-constructed to the class. This removes life-cycle issues from the domain of the Context class. And because enclosed classes are often just references or pointers, the .hpp interface file should only need forward declarations, thereby reducing potential ripple effect.

(The decision on whether to use pointers or references to objects is outside the scope of this chapter.)

Continuing this example, the body of the program is refactored:

```
class MarketMessageCommand {
public:
    virtual void Action(MarketContext&) = 0;
    ....
};
```

```
int main() {
    LogManager* log(LogFactory());
    CmdLineOptions options(argc, argv);
    MarketDataStore marketData;
    MarketContext context(log, options, &marketData);
    MessageSource source;
    while (true) {
        auto_ptr<MarketMessageCommand> w(source.NextMessage());
        w->Action(context);
    }
    return 0;
}
```

The Context provides access to data such as the `LogManager` that otherwise may be made Singleton, global, or both.

In this example, the Context object is passed to the `Action` method; an alternative would be to pass the Context to the `MarketMessageCommand` constructor and store a reference. This would allow `Action` to be parameterless at the cost of adding state to the class. Furthermore, by renaming `Action` to `operator()`, the class acquires the characteristics of a *function object* [Stroustrup+1997] or *functor*. For example:

```
class MarketMessageCommand {
    MarketContext& context_;
public:
    MarketMessageCommand(MarketContext& mc) : context_(mc) {}
    virtual void operator()();
    ....
};
```

While this potentially increases the design's flexibility, more attention must be given to lifetime management of the Context object in this case.

Variations

- Provide parent's `this` pointer.

  The passing of `this` pointers to *worker objects* can be seen as a variation on this theme; in effect, the calling object is itself acting as a Context object for the worker objects. (One consequence of using Context classes is that the need to pass `this` is usually reduced.)

  While this solution may be economical in terms of lines of code, it does introduce a more complex structure. The parent object is attempting to fulfill two objectives: to provide its own *raison d'etre* and to provide Context to the worker. When applied widely, code becomes harder to follow. Frequently, although not always, this pointers are passed to *worker object* so that the state of the *this object can be queried. It is possible to view this arrangement as a variation on ENCAPSULATED CONTEXT in which the calling object acts as a Context object itself.

In such a situation, the parent state may be refactored as a Context object and accessed by both of the original objects. The new class is only responsible for state, and the original classes are simplified.

- Provide forwarding functions to encapsulated data.

   Rather than expose an entire member class, the MarketContext class could implement forwarding methods. For example, the CmdOptions member could be replaced with:

```
class MarketContext {
    ...
    bool IsVerbose() const { return opts_.IsVerbose(); };
    ... and other forwarding functions ...
};
```

However, it is best to keep the class as lightweight as possible; to this end, the class exposes the key objects encapsulated rather than implementing pass-through calls onto the underlying data. It is the underlying class that decides what to expose rather than the Context class. Furthermore, although such forwarding functions may be convenient, they contribute to the tendency for the Context class to become a Blob [Brown+1998] and so are best avoided.

Consequences

As a result of the pattern, several of the forces detailed earlier are resolved or balanced.

Substitutability

Parameters passed to a function call can be restricted to Context objects containing system state data and parameters that specifically refer to the function call task at hand, such as market trades. Function signatures are free of the clutter that can make them fragile—there is no longer a need for every class method in the hierarchy to accept every parameter ever needed.

Encapsulation

The Context object effectively compacts the parameter list on a function call signature, thereby abstracting state variables and promoting encapsulation of the function. In addition, there is a reduction in the ripple effect as function signatures become more stable.

Having relieved the problems of passing parameter to a function, the attractions of global data are reduced. Indeed, the Context object provides a natural home for data with characteristics of global variables.

Coupling to the Environment

The Context class is encapsulated through its own well-known common interface. This allows the solution to be applied to compile-time and runtime polymorphic designs, using either template metaprogramming or v-table dispatch techniques.

By providing several Context classes, data is encapsulated along temporal, horizontal, or vertical lines, which further reduces coupling. It is difficult to eliminate all coupling, because some classes will always need other classes; choosing the granularity of the coupling is a design issue.

Additionally, by separating the classes that implement algorithms from the plumbing that supplies the data, the classes themselves are less coupled and more like commodities, which makes transfer to other developments easier.

Avoid Data Copying

Since the Context class contains common data with little overhead, there is no need to copy the data in local objects.

There may be multiple references to the Context object in the system, particularly if multiple threads are being used. Hence some care must be taken to avoid dangling references to Context objects.

In addition, there are other beneficial consequences:

Reasoning

State data that needs to be shared or retained is factored, and objects are left with either transient data or as completely stateless. By centralizing the core data within a system, we have made it easier to reason about the system. Instead of having to look in multiple places, we can halt the program and look in one place to see what state the program is in.

Instantiation

Instantiation issues are simplified because objects must be created before being placed in the Context object and are subsequently only accessed through the Context. Destruction issues are similarly handled, because all access is via the Context. The life-span of the Context object can be clearly defined at a high level.

Uncluttered Code

Pass-through code and long parameter lists have been minimized, and the potential for future redundant code has been reduced—it is easier to add and remove elements from the Context class. (This may entail a recompile of the whole system when the interface to the Context class is changed, but recompilation should be a well-defined procedure.)

Synchronization Point

The Context class can provide a useful place to add mutexes for multithreaded systems. In multithreaded environments, the Context object can hold all shared data, acting as a gatekeeper with mutex control. This is reminiscent of the Monitor Object pattern [Schmidt+2000] and has the same potential for bottlenecks if lock access is not carefully considered.

Bottlenecks may be avoided if the data is either immutable (e.g., command line options that do not change) or if data elements manage their own locking (e.g., a log manager that implements its own synchronization) and application data is absent.

Testing

Artificially configured Context objects can be used for testing. A test harness may create a Context object and populate it with data to simulate a scenario to be tested. Such test classes could validate inputs or dump "state" to a file for further examination.

However, there are several less desirable consequences:

Blob Tendencies

As already mentioned, care must be taken as systems develop that a Context class does not become a Blob. In the example given, we already see the mixing of value data and reference data. Without vigilance, Context classes may grow to encompass far more data and functionality than is strictly necessary.

Invariably, the Context class ends up touching most aspects of the system. It is therefore best placed low in the dependency hierarchy of classes—although this can lead to its own dependency inversion [Martin+1996a] problems and small changes necessitate a major recompile of the system. Once this happens, we are in danger of implementing the Blob anti-pattern.

Fortunately, changes to the Context class tends to be additive in nature and thus seldom breaks other parts of the system. However, the friction of change is still increased. One way to minimize this is to ensure that no operations are placed inside the Context class. A second technique is to use multiple Context classes, as described earlier, but introducing too many Context classes will introduce some of the original problems we sought to resolve.

Hidden Globals

Blind use of Context classes can give rise to an abuse known as "Hide Forbidden Globals." [Green+2001]. This abuse is characterized by a kitchen-sink approach to the Context class in which every second variable is listed. We typically see Context members that are referenced in only a few points within the system, and such data would usually be better embedded in specific classes rather than placed in the Context.

Dominant Sibling

Program families may share a common root Context class, which they embellish through inheritance. In this model, the Context underpins the common code of the family. If one family member becomes dominant, there will be pressure to enhance the common root in order to facilitate the dominant member. This has a negative effect on the other family members that start to see the common root as a Blob that forces upon them additional dependencies and complications they do not need.

In the program family, we find elements of functional overlap such as a market trading system and a market simulation system. Both may use the `Market-MessageCommmand` and hence rely on the `MarketContext` class described earlier. As one program, say, the simulation, becomes more important and bigger objects start to appear in the command hierarchy that are specific to the one application, one of these objects will eventually require some data that is not available in the Context class. For immediate simplicity, we are tempted to add this data into the Context. Unfortunately, the trading system now has this data even though it is never used. If continued, the trading system will be inhibited over time by a Context class that is obscured by unused functions.

Even more confusing are the results that occur if the trading system now develops its own specialist message commands and makes demands on the Context class for specific fields.

This is normally an indication that the Context class should be split vertically. We may choose to create a hierarchy of three classes: a common base class, a derived class with simulator enhancements, and a second derived class with the trading system enhancements.

At this point we may compile different versions that accept either a `SimulatorContext` or a `TradingContext`, or we may choose to down-cast the provided Context—assuming that the simulator message classes will only be passed a `SimulatorContext` by way of a `MarketContext` handle.

Known Uses

Chutney Technologies Apptimizer (C++)

Apptimizer uses a single Context object to store handles to important system objects such as `Configuration`, `CachedData`, and `ConnectionServer`. These system objects are accessed by polymorphic command objects that receive the Context as a parameter to their `execute()` method.

Reuters Liffe Connect Data Router (C++)

This system uses two Context objects split horizontally. The first encapsulates system data, log manager handles, a configuration cache, and COM parameters, while the second holds application data exclusively.

Jiffy (Parthenon Computing) XML Database Server (C++)

The Jiffy server has three Context objects split along temporal lines. One Context object exists for the length of the program run. This encapsulates process-wide context items such as log manager handle, command line options, and the database store index. A second Context class is used to represent data associated with connections. Each TCP connection is assigned a session Context to hold items such as the user id for the connection. Finally, the underlying database from Sleepycat uses its own database-Context object to maintain state between database calls.

In this case, the database-Context objects are short-lived; each one is limited to function call scope (although it will be passed to several underlying functions in turn). A session Context lives for the duration of the TCP connection, while the process Context is created shortly after the application starts running and is destroyed at the end of the program run.

Enterprise Java Beans

Enterprise Java makes use of Session Beans and Context Beans that encapsulate program state information. Although the objective of Java Beans is to implement component-based transaction programming, most of the underlying forces are the same, namely, substitutability of different beans, encapsulation of context from server to client, and clearly defined coupling.

However, the fourth force, *avoid data copying*, is absent. In the distributed environment for which Java Beans is designed, data copying is essential.

Interpreter Pattern Example

The C++ example given in *Design Patterns* [Gamma+1995] for the Interpreter pattern passes a Context object to the polymorphic Evaluate function.

Related Patterns

- *Command*, *Chain of Responsibility*, and *Methods for States*: Although the Command pattern is cited here, the same principles apply to any design based on the dependency inversion principle [Martin+1996a] using class hierarchies, for example, Chain of Responsibility [Gamma+1995] and Methods for States [Henney+2002]. In each of these, the hierarchy provides the algorithm while the Context object(s) provide the data.

- *Singleton*: ENCAPSULATED CONTEXT may be a useful alternative to Singleton [Gamma+1995] in many program designs.

- *Observer*: ENCAPSULATED CONTEXT may be contrasted with Observer [Gamma+1995]. Like the Subject in Observer, the Context class is a central repository of data. Like Observer, there is a many-to-one relationship. However, the critical difference lies in the updating mechanics.

  The subject in Observer knows its observers; when it is updated, it will update all its observers. This satisfies the motivation for the pattern that seeks to keep two or more objects consistent. Thus, when one Observer changes, and hence changes the Subject, the other Observers must be informed. In effect, Subject is an active participant in the execution of the program.

  In ENCAPSULATED CONTEXT there is no requirement on the Context class to inform its clients that something has changed. Indeed, it doesn't know who its clients are, so it cannot inform them. ENCAPSULATED CONTEXT keeps the various objects consistent by centralizing the data. It is essentially passive during execution.

While there is an obvious transformation for turning a Context object into a Subject, and hence ENCAPSULATED CONTEXT into an Observer pattern, and vice versa, there are fundamentally different motivations and forces underlying the two patterns.

- *Monitor Object*: As noted in the Consequences section, in multithreaded systems, mutex control can be added to ENCAPSULATED CONTEXT to assist with synchronization issues. In this, the pattern is acting like Schmidt's Monitor Object [Schmidt+2000]. While this can provide a simple way to synchronize access to resources, it is not without a cost.

  First, using the Context class as a monitor introduces pressure to perform more processing within the Monitor class. This contributes to the Blob tendencies already described.

  Second, the consequences encountered by Monitor Object are introduced into the design. Specifically, the liabilities associated with Monitor Object such as limited scalability, complicated extensibility semantics, inheritance anomaly, and nested monitor lockout need to be recognized.

  Readers are strongly advised to read Schmidt before using ENCAPSULATED CONTEXT as a synchronization point.

- *Arguments Object*: This pattern shares much in common with Noble's Arguments Object pattern [Noble+2000]. The key difference is that Noble suggests the pattern as a code level pattern for reducing the number of parameters passed to a function, while ENCAPSULATED CONTEXT advocates using the same paradigm as a high-level design pattern to encapsulate the state of the system.

- *Introduce Parameter Object*: Both the ENCAPSULATED CONTEXT and Arguments Object patterns resemble Fowler's Introduce Parameter Object refactoring pattern [Fowler+2000]. However, Fowler introduces this as only a refactoring pattern without discussion of the issues involved in grouping data or alternative solutions. It is possible to view Fowler's pattern as an application of either ENCAPSULATED CONTEXT or Arguments Object when refactoring code.

- *Parameter Block*: Some of the motivations of ENCAPSULATED CONTEXT are shared with Parameter Block [Patow+2003]. Both aim to provide a consistent interface through which diverse parts of a system may access parameters. The focus of Parameter Block is internal mechanisms of the Context object and how that object may support a dynamic set of parameters at runtime. In contrast, ENCAPSULATED CONTEXT focuses on parameter passing at compile-time. Parameter Block considers a parameter block that stores various param-

eters; this has clear parallels with the Context class in ENCAPSULATED CON-
TEXT. The two patterns do not exclude one another, and under the right
circumstances, they may be complementary.

- *New patterns*: Kevlin Henney presented several patterns that follow from EN-
CAPSULATED CONTEXT; these are ENCAPSULATED CONTEXT Object, Decoupled
Context Interface, Role-Partitioned Context, and Role-Specific Context Object. These patterns were presented at EuroPLoP 2005 and will appear in the
conference proceedings. This work places ENCAPSULATED CONTEXT within a
wider pattern sequence.

More Examples

The examples presented are given in C++, although it is expected that the pattern is generally applicable to all languages. The author looks forward especially to hearing of implementations in Java and C#.

Summary

In any nontrivial system, there will be a number of data elements that are widely
used throughout the program, for example, log manager and the application
data model. These will typically be classes in their own right and accessed
through handles (references or pointers). Since global data is regarded as a poor
practice, it is likely that these handles will be passed by way of function call parameters. However, this technique can soon lead to long parameter lists that are
not only difficult to understand, but tend to make the program more fragile.

Therefore, we create a Context class that encapsulates these data elements
and pass a handle to this object to the diverse functions.

While similar techniques have been suggested by others [Fowler+2000, No-
ble+2000], this pattern discusses the forces and consequences when applied
system-wide. This can bring considerable benefits to a design, but if used reck-
lessly, it can result in a number of known bad patterns.

Rather than use a single Context class, it may be appropriate to design a system with several of them. These are divided along temporal, horizontal, or vertical lines to ensure that each is consistent and promotes good design.

Acknowledgments

This pattern was the result of a conversation on the ACCU-General mailing list
entitled, "Overload 49 and State." Significant contributions were made by Kevlin

Henney and Josh Walker in June 2002. I am grateful to Kevlin for acting as initial pattern shepherd and to Josh for reviewing the results and providing an additional example. The chapter was further shepherded by Frank Buschmann in April 2003 for submission to EuroPLoP. Again, I am most grateful to Frank for his time and interest.

In addition, I am grateful to all in *Workshop D* at the EuroPLoP 2003 conference for their many varied and useful comments concerning the pattern, for their support, and for their suggestions for improvement.

References

[Brown+1998] J. B. Brown, R. C. Malveau, H. W. McCormick, and T. J. Mowbray. *Anti-Patterns*. New York: John Wiley & Sons, 1998.

[Fowler+2000] M. Fowler. *Refactoring: Improving the Design of Existing Code*. Object Technology Series. Boston: Addison-Wesley, 2000.

[Gamma+1995] E. Gamma, R. Helm, R. Johnson, and J. Vlissides. *Design Patterns: Elements of Reusable Object-Oriented Software*. Reading, MA: Addison-Wesley, 1995.

[Green+2001] R. Green. "How to Write Unmaintainable Code." Available at *http://mindprod.com/jgloss/unmaincamouflage.html*, accessed 26 June 2005.

[Henney+2002] K. Henney. "Methods for States." In *Proceedings of First Nordic Conference on Pattern Languages of Programs* (VikingPLoP), pp. 91–104. Højstrupgård, Denmark, 2003. Available at *http://www.two-sdg.demon.co.uk/curbralan/papers/vikingplop/MethodsForStates.pdf*.

[Liskov+1988] B. Liskov. "Data Abstraction and Hierarchy." *SIGPLAN Notices*, 5(23):17–34, May 1998.

[Martin+1996a] R. C. Martin. "The Dependency Inversion Principle." *C++ Report* (June 1996).

[Martin+1996b] R. C. Martin. "The Liskov Substitution Principle." *C++ Report* (March 1996).

[Noble+2000] J. Noble. "Arguments and Results." *The Computer Journal*, 6(43):439–450.

[Patow+2003] G. Patow and F. Lyardet. "Parameter Block." In *Proceedings of 8th European Conferences on Pattern Languages of Programs* (EuroPLoP), pp. 571–580. Irsee, Germany, June 2003.

[Schmidt+2000] D. Schmidt, M. Stal, H. Rohnert, and F. Buschmann. "Monitor Object." In (ed.), *Pattern-Oriented Software Architecture*, vol. 2. New York: Wiley, 2000.

[Stroustrup+1997] B. Stroustrup. *The C++ Programming Language*. Reading, MA: Addison-Wesley, 1997.

PART II

Concurrent, Network, and Real-Time Patterns

Chapter 4: A Pattern Language for Efficient, Predictable, and Scalable Dispatching Components

Distributed application development has graduated from a niche market to common practice. Currently, systems ranging from search engines to avionics control rely on middleware to handle requests between their components. Irfan Pyarali, Carlos O'Ryan, and Douglas Schmidt present a pattern language that addresses the challenges associated with developing dispatching components. These patterns provide one of the building blocks of a handbook for distributed real-time and embedded middleware.

Chapter 5: "Triple-T"—A System of Patterns for Reliable Communication in Hard Real-Time Systems

Software powers the majority of systems we're using today, from digital cameras, PDAs, and phones to digital TVs and personal video recorders (PVRs) to automotive and avionics controllers. Some of these systems have real-time or near real-time requirements. However, writing software for real-time processing is hard and poses unique challenges. In Triple-T, Wolfgang Herzner, Wilfried Kubinger, and Manfred Gruber present five patterns harvested from time-triggered bus architectures for safety-critical real-time systems such as the ones employed by Airbus airplanes or BMW and DaimlerChrysler automobiles.

Chapter 6: Real Time and Resource Overload Language

Many real-time systems receive and process external stimuli. As these systems' workload increases, they could eventually violate scheduling or other quality constraints, lowering the quality of service. Robert Hanmer presents a pattern language for designing reactive systems that gracefully accommodate load bursts. These patterns have been mined from carrier-grade systems (such as those used in the worldwide telephone network), a class of applications renowned for the way it deals with load variability. These patterns' applicability extends to any systems that process incoming requests, such as Web servers, middleware, OLTP, and so on.

CHAPTER 4

A Pattern Language for Efficient, Predictable, and Scalable Dispatching Components

Irfan Pyarali, Carlos O'Ryan, and Douglas C. Schmidt

Introduction

Dispatching components are a core feature of many systems, such as distributed object computing (DOC) middleware. For instance, the dispatching components in a CORBA Object Request Broker (ORB) are responsible for delivering incoming client events or requests to other ORB components and the application-level objects that implement application-defined behavior. In general, dispatching components must handle a variety of tasks, such as dispatching multiple requests simultaneously, handling recursive dispatches from within application-provided upcalls, dispatching the same upcall to multiple objects efficiently, and adding and removing objects in dispatching tables while upcalls are in progress.

This chapter presents a pattern language used to develop efficient, predictable, and scalable dispatching components in a variety of application domains, an example of which is shown in Figure 4–1. These domains include the TAO Real-Time CORBA [OMG2002a], ORB [Schmidt+1998], real-time avionics mission computing with strict periodic deadline requirements [Schmidt+2002a] [Sharp+2003] [Roll+2003], and distributed interactive simulations with high scalability requirements [O'Ryan+1999] [Noseworthy+2002]. In addition, various dispatching-oriented framework components, such as Reactors and Proactors [Schmidt+2000], Observers [Gamma+1995], and Model-View-Controllers [Buschmann+1996], are implemented using these patterns.

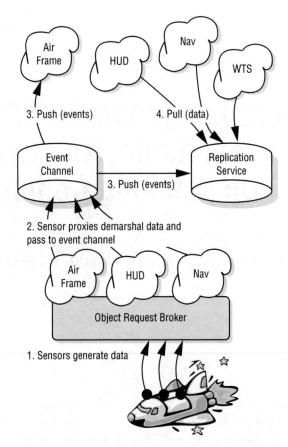

Figure 4–1 *Multiple dispatching components in DOC middleware*

This chapter is organized as follows: An Overview of Dispatching Components and Pattern Languages describes the context in which dispatching components are used and identifies common requirements for several typical use cases; A Pattern Language for Dispatching Components presents the pattern language used to implement efficient, predictable, scalable, and flexible dispatching components for both single and multiple targets; and Concluding Remarks presents some final thoughts.

An Overview of Dispatching Components and Pattern Languages

This section summarizes the functionality and requirements of two common use cases that illustrate the challenges associated with developing dispatching components. The first example is the Object Adapter [Pyarali+1998] component in a standard CORBA [OMG2002b] ORB. The second example is a event channel in a standard CORBA Event Service [OMG2001] or Notification Service [OMG2002c].

Object Adapter Dispatching Components

The core responsibilities of a CORBA Object Adapter include (1) generating identifiers for objects that are exported to clients, and (2) mapping subsequent client requests to the appropriate object implementations, which CORBA calls "servants." Figure 4–2 illustrates the general structure and interactions of a CORBA Object Adapter.

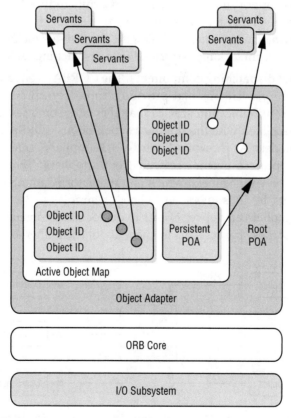

Figure 4–2 *Object adapter structure and interactions*

In addition to its core responsibilities, a CORBA Object Adapter must handle the following situations correctly, robustly, and efficiently:

- **Non-existent objects.** Clients may invoke requests on "stale" identifiers, that is, on objects that have been deactivated from the Object Adapter. In this case, the Object Adapter should not use the stale object, because it may have been deleted by the application. Instead, it must propagate an appropriate exception back to the client.

- **Unusual object activation/deactivation use cases.** Object Adapters are responsible for activating and deactivating objects on demand. Moreover, server application objects can activate or deactivate other objects in response to client requests. An object can even deactivate itself while in its own upcall, for example, if the request is a "shut yourself down" message.

- **Multithreading hazards.** Implementing an Object Adapter that works correctly and efficiently in a multithreaded environment is hard. For instance, there are many opportunities for deadlock, unduly reduced concurrency, and priority inversions that may arise from recursive calls to an Object Adapter while it is dispatching requests. Likewise, excessive synchronization overhead may arise from locking performed on a dispatching table.

- **Event channel dispatching components.** The CORBA Event and Notification Services define participants that provide a more asynchronous and decoupled type of communication service that alleviates some restrictions [Harrison+1997] associated with the standard synchronous CORBA ORB operation invocation models. As shown in Figure 4–3, "suppliers" generate events and "consumers" process events received from suppliers. That figure also illustrates the "event channel," which is a mediator [Gamma+1995] that dispatches events to consumers on behalf of suppliers. By using an event channel, a supplier can deliver events to one or more consumers without requiring any of these participants to know about each other explicitly.

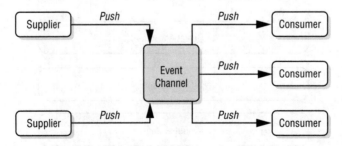

Figure 4–3 *Participants in the COS Event and Notification Service Architecture*

To perform its core responsibilities, a CORBA event channel must address the following aspects:

- **Dynamic consumer subscriptions.** A robust implementation of an event channel must support the addition of new consumers while dispatching is in progress. Likewise, it must support the removal of existing consumers before all active dispatching operations complete. In multithreaded environments, it is possible for multiple threads (potentially running at different priorities) to iterate over the dispatching table concurrently. Some consumers may trigger further updates, which also must be handled properly and efficiently.

  Naive implementations, such as copying the complete set of consumers before starting the iteration, may fail if one consumer is destroyed as a side-effect of the upcall on another consumer. In multithreaded implementations, this problem is exacerbated because separate threads may remove and destroy consumers in the table concurrently.

- **Variable dispatching times.** Dispatching events requires an event channel to iterate over its set of consumers. However, iterators make it even harder to provide predictable implementations because the number of consumers may vary. Some type of synchronization is therefore required during the dispatching process.

  Implementations of the Observer pattern [Gamma+1995] must also contend with problems similar to those faced in the CORBA Event Service. The Observer pattern propagates updates emanating from one or more suppliers to multiple consumers, that is, observers. An implementation of this pattern must iterate over the set of consumers and disseminate the update to each one of them. As with the event channel, subscriptions may change dynamically while updates are being dispatched.

Historically, a variety of ad hoc strategies have emerged to address the dispatching challenges outlined earlier. No one strategy is optimal for all application domains or use cases, however. For instance, real-time implementations may impose too much overhead for high-performance, "best-effort" systems. Likewise, implementations tailored for multithreading may impose excessive locking overhead for single-threaded reactive systems. In addition, strategies that support recursive access can incur excessive overhead if all upcalls are dispatched to separate threads or remote servers. Thus, what is required are strategies and methodologies that systematically capture the range of possible solutions that arise in the design space of dispatching components. One family of these strategies is described in the next section.

A Pattern Language for Dispatching Components

Certain patterns, such as STRATEGIZED LOCKING [Schmidt+2000] or STRATEGY [Gamma+1995], address some of the challenges associated with developing efficient, predictable, scalable, and flexible dispatching components. In other cases, however, the relationships and collaborations between dispatching components require more specialized solutions. Moreover, as noted in the Overview section, no single pattern or strategy alone resolves all the forces faced by developers of complex dispatching components. Therefore, this section presents "patterns" that address the challenges for dispatching components outlined in the Overview.

A pattern is a recurring solution to a standard problem within a particular context [Gamma+1995]. When related patterns are woven together, they form a "language" [Alexander+1977] that provides a process for the orderly resolution of software development problems. Pattern languages are not formal languages or programming languages, but rather a collection of interrelated patterns that provide a vocabulary for solving particular problems [Buschmann+1996]. Both patterns and pattern languages help developers communicate architectural knowledge, help developers learn a new design paradigm or architectural style, and help new developers avoid traps and pitfalls that have traditionally been learned only by costly experience.

Each pattern in our dispatching mechanism pattern language resolves a particular set of forces, with varying consequences on performance, functionality, and flexibility. In general, simpler solutions result in better performance but do not resolve all the forces that more complex dispatching components can handle. Application developers should not disregard simpler patterns, however. Instead, they should apply the patterns that are most appropriate for the problem at hand, balancing the need to support advanced features with the performance and flexibility requirements of their applications.

Dispatching to a Single Object

This subsection focuses on patterns for components where events or requests are dispatched to a single target object. The section Dispatching to Multiple Objects then describes patterns that are suitable for dispatching to multiple objects. The initial patterns are relatively straightforward and are intended for less complex systems. The latter patterns are more intricate and address more complex requirements for efficiency, predictability, scalability, and flexibility.

Serialized Dispatching

Context. Dispatching components are vital in DOC middleware and applications. They typically contain a collection of target objects that reside in one or more dispatching tables. These tables are used to select appropriate objects based upon identifiers contained in incoming requests. For example, as outlined in the Overview, the CORBA architecture [OMG2002b] defines an Object Adapter [Pyarali+1998] that maps client requests to objects supplied by server applications and helps dispatch operations on server objects.

Problem. Multithreaded applications must serialize access to their dispatching table to prevent data corruption.

Forces. Serialization mechanisms such as mutexes or semaphores should be used carefully to avoid excessive locking, priority inversions, and non-determinism. Distributed real-time and embedded systems can maximize parallelism by minimizing serialization. However, application correctness cannot be sacrificed to improve performance. For example, a multithreaded application should be able to add and remove objects registered with the dispatching table efficiently during runtime without corrupting the dispatching table.

Solution. Serialize dispatching of requests by using the MONITOR OBJECT pattern [Schmidt+2000] where a single monitor lock serializes access to the entire dispatching table, as shown in Figure 4–4. The monitor lock is held both while searching the table to locate the object and while dispatching the appropriate operation call on the application-provided code. In addition, the same monitor lock is used when inserting and removing entries from the table.

Consequences. A regular monitor lock is sufficient to achieve the level of serialization necessary for this dispatching component. Serialization overhead is minimal since only one set of acquire/release calls are made on the lock during an upcall. Thus, this design is appropriate when there is little or no contention for the dispatching table or when upcalls to application code are short-lived.

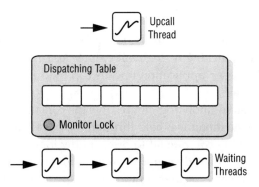

Figure 4–4 *Serialized dispatching with a Monitor Lock*

A simple protocol can control the life cycle of objects registered with the dispatching component. For instance, an object cannot be destroyed while it is still registered in the dispatching table. Since the table's monitor lock is used both for dispatching and modifying the table, other threads cannot delete an object that is in the midst of being dispatched.

Note, however, that this pattern may be inadequate for systems with stringent real-time requirements. In particular, the monitor lock is held during the execution of application code, which makes it hard for the dispatching component to predict how long it will take to release the monitor lock. Likewise, this pattern does not work well when there is significant contention for the dispatching table. For instance, if two requests arrive simultaneously for different target objects in the same dispatching table, only one of them can be dispatched at a time.

Serialized Dispatching with a Recursive Mutex

Context. Assume the dispatching component outlined in the section Serialized Dispatching is being implemented in multithreaded applications.

Problem. Monitor locks are not recursive on many OS platforms. When using non-recursive locks, attempts to query or modify the dispatch table while holding the lock will cause deadlock. Thus, application code cannot query or modify the dispatch table, since it is called while the lock is held.

Forces. A monitor lock cannot be released before dispatching the application upcall because another thread could remove and destroy the object while it is still being dispatched.

Solution. Serialize dispatching of requests by using a "recursive" monitor lock [McKinney+1996]. A recursive lock allows the calling thread to re-acquire the lock if that thread already owns it. The structure of this solution is identical to the one shown in Figure 4–4 except that a recursive monitor lock is used in lieu of a non-recursive lock.

Consequences. As before, the monitor lock serializes concurrent access to avoid corruption of the dispatching table. Unlike the SERIALIZED DISPATCHING pattern outlined earlier, however, application upcalls can modify the dispatching table or dispatch new upcalls.

Unfortunately, this solution does not resolve the concurrency and predictability problems, since the monitor is held through the upcall. In particular, it is still hard for the dispatching component to predict how long the monitor lock must be held and the component does not allow multiple requests to be dispatched simultaneously. Moreover, recursive monitor locks are usually more expensive than their non-recursive counterparts [Schmidt+2002b].

Dispatching with a Readers/Writer Lock

Context. In complex DOC middleware and applications, events and requests often occur simultaneously. Unless application upcalls are sharing resources that must be serialized, these operations should be dispatched and executed concurrently. Even if hardware support is not available for parallel execution, it may be possible to execute events and requests concurrently by overlapping CPU-intensive operations with I/O-intensive operations.

Problem. Serialized Dispatching patterns are inefficient for implementing concurrent dispatching upcalls since they do not distinguish between read and write operations and thus serialize all operations on the dispatching table.

Forces. Although dispatching table modifications typically require exclusive access, dispatching operations do not modify the table. However, the dispatching component must ensure that the table is not modified while a thread is performing a lookup operation on it.

Solution. Use a readers/writer lock to serialize access to the dispatching table. The critical path, that is, looking up the target object and invoking an operation on it, does not modify the table. Therefore, a `read` lock will suffice for this path. Operations that modify the dispatching table, such as adding or removing objects from it, require exclusive access, however. Therefore, a `write` lock is required for these operations. Figure 4–5 illustrates the structure of this solution, where multiple reader threads can dispatch operations concurrently, whereas writer threads are serialized.

Consequences. Readers/writer locks allow multiple readers to access a shared resource simultaneously, while only allowing one writer to access the shared

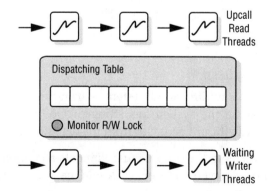

Figure 4–5 *Dispatching with a Readers/Writer Lock*

resource at a time. Thus, the solution described earlier allows multiple concurrent dispatch calls.

Some DOC middleware executes the upcall in a separate thread in the same process or on a remote object. Other middleware executes the upcall in the same thread after releasing the read lock. Thus, this readers/writer locking pattern [McKinney+1996] can be applied to such systems without any risk of deadlocks. However, this solution is not applicable to systems that execute an upcall while holding the read lock. In that case, changing the table from within an upcall would require upgrading the readers/writer lock from a read lock to a write lock. Unfortunately, standard readers/writer lock implementations, such as Solaris/UI threads, do not support upgradable locks. Even when this support exists, lock upgrades will not succeed if multiple threads require simultaneous upgrades.

Note that applications using readers/writer locks become responsible for providing appropriate serialization of their data structures since they cannot rely on the dispatching component itself to serialize upcalls. As with recursive locks, the serialization overhead of readers/writer locks may be higher compared to regular locks [Schmidt+2002b] when little or no contention occurs on the dispatching table.

Implementors of this pattern must analyze their dispatching component carefully to identify operations that require only a read lock versus those that require a write lock. For example, the CORBA Object Adapter supports activation of objects within upcalls. Thus, when a dispatch lookup is initiated, the Object Adapter cannot be certain whether the upcall will modify the dispatching table. Note that acquiring a write lock a priori is self-defeating since it may impede concurrent access to the table unnecessarily.

Finally, this solution does not resolve the predictability problem. In particular, unbounded priority inversions may occur when high-priority writer threads are suspended waiting for low-priority reader threads to complete dispatching upcalls.

Reference Counting During Dispatch

Context. As before, a multithreaded system is using the dispatching component. However, assume the system has stringent QoS requirements that demand predictable and efficient behavior from the dispatching component.

Problem. To be predictable, the system must eliminate all unbounded priority inversions. In addition, system efficency should be maximized by reducing bounded priority inversions.

Forces. During an upcall, an application can invoke operations that modify the dispatching table. In addition, the dispatching component must be efficient and scalable, maximizing concurrency whenever possible.

Solution. Reference count the entries of the dispatching table during dispatch by using a single lock to serialize changes to the referenced count and modifications to the table. As shown in Figure 4–6, the lock is acquired during the upcall, the appropriate entry is located, its reference count increased, and the lock is released before performing the application upcall. Once the upcall completes, the lock is reacquired, the reference count on the entry is decremented, and the lock is released

As long as the reference count on the entry remains greater than zero, the entry is not removed and the corresponding object is not destroyed. Concurrency hazards are avoided, therefore, because the reference count is always greater than zero while a thread is processing an upcall for that entry. If an object is "logically" removed from the dispatching table, its entry is not "physically" removed immediately since outstanding upcalls may still be pending. Instead, the thread that brings the reference count to zero is responsible for deleting this "partially" removed entry from the table.

In programming languages such as C and C++ that lack built-in garbage collection, the dispatching table must collaborate with the application to control the objects' life cycle. In this case, objects are usually reference counted.[1] For example, the reference count is usually incremented when the object is registered with the dispatching table and decremented when the object is removed from the dispatching table.

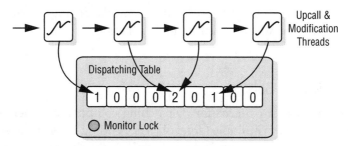

Figure 4–6 *Dispatching with Reference Counted Table Entries*

---

1. Note that this reference count is different from the per-entry reference count described earlier.

Consequences. This pattern supports multiple simultaneous upcalls since the lock is not held during the upcall. For the same reason, this model also supports recursive calls. An important benefit of this pattern is that the level of priority inversions does not depend on the duration of the upcall. In fact, priority inversions can be calculated as a function of the time needed to search the dispatching table. Our previous research [Pyarali+1999] has shown that very low and bounded search times can be achieved using techniques like active demultiplexing and perfect hashing. Implementations that use these techniques in conjunction with the serialization pattern described here can achieve predictable dispatching with bounded priority inversions.

A disadvantage of this pattern, however, is that it acquires and releases the lock *twice* per upcall. In practice, this usually does not exceed the cost of a single recursive monitor lock or a single readers/writer monitor lock [Schmidt+2002b]. This solution does, however, warrant extra care in the following special circumstances:

- **Accessing "logically deleted" objects**. A new request arrives for an object that has been logically, but not physically, removed from the dispatching table. Additional state can be used to record that this object has been removed and should therefore receive no new requests.

- **Activating "partially removed" objects.** An implementation must handle the case where an object has been partially removed (as described earlier) and a client application requests a new object to be inserted for the same identifier as the partially removed object. Typically, the new insertion must block until upcalls on the old object complete and the old object is physically removed from the dispatching table.

Table 4–1 summarizes the different patterns for dispatching to a single object and compares their relative strengths and weaknesses.

Dispatching to Multiple Objects

This section focuses on patterns for dispatching components where events or requests are delivered to multiple target objects. Sending the same event to multiple target objects adds another level of complexity to dispatching component implementations. For instance, an implementation may need to iterate over the collection of potential targets and invoke upcalls on a subset of the objects in the dispatching table.

In many use cases, modifications to the collection invalidate any iterators for that collection [Kofler+1993], even for single-threaded configurations. In gen-

Table 4–1 *Summary of Dispatching to Single Object*

Pattern	Times lock acquired	Nested upcalls	Priority inversion	Appropriate when
Serialized dispatching	1	No	Unbounded	Little or no contention Short-lived upcalls
Recursive mutex	1	Yes	Unbounded	Same as above
Readers/Writers lock	1	Limited	Unbounded	Concurrent upcalls
Reference counting	2	Yes	Bounded	Predictable behavior

eral, an implementation must ensure that no modifications are performed while a thread is iterating over the dispatching table. For distributed real-time and embedded systems, moreover, simple serialization components such as conventional mutexes can result in unbounded priority inversions if higher priority threads wait for lower priority threads to finish iterating.

Interestingly, the most sophisticated pattern for dispatching to a single target object (which was presented in the section Reference Counting During Dispatch) is not suitable for dispatching to multiple targets. In particular, its lock would have to be acquired for the entire iteration and upcall cycle, thereby worsening priority inversion problems. If the lock were released, it could lead to an inconsistent view of the dispatching table. We now present a series of patterns that addresses these problems.

Copy-then-Dispatch

Context. An event or request must be dispatched to multiple objects concurrently.

Problem. The challenge is how to optimize throughput while minimizing contention and serialization overhead.

Forces. Modifications to the dispatching table are common during the dispatch loop. The dispatching table does not provide robust iterators [Kofler+1993], or the iterators are not thread-safe. There are no stringent real-time requirements.

Solution. Make a copy of the entire dispatching table before initiating the iteration, as shown in Figure 4–7. Although some serialization mechanism must be used during the copy, its cost is relatively low since it is outside the critical path. As an optimization, the dispatching component can acquire the lock, copy only the target objects that are interested in the event, and then release the lock. At this point, the dispatching component iterates over the smaller set of interested target objects and dispatches upcalls.

To apply this pattern, applications must collaborate with the dispatching component to control object life cycle. For example, an object cannot be destroyed simply because it was removed successfully from the dispatching table. Other threads may still be dispatching events on an older copy of the dispatching table and thus still have a reference to the object. Therefore, objects in the dispatching table copy must be marked "in use" until all dispatching loops using it complete.

Consequences. This pattern allows multiple events or requests to be dispatched concurrently. In addition, it permits recursive operations from within application upcalls that can modify the dispatching table, either by inserting or removing objects.

However, making copies of the dispatching table does not scale well when the table is large, when memory allocation is expensive, or when object life-cycle management is costly. In this case, other patterns, such as THREAD-SPECIFIC STORAGE [Schmidt+2000], which eliminates locking overhead, can be used to minimize these costs, thereby making the COPY-THEN-DISPATCH pattern applicable for systems that have small dispatching tables.

Copy-On-Demand

Context. As in the section Copy-then-Dispatch, an event or request must be dispatched to multiple objects concurrently.

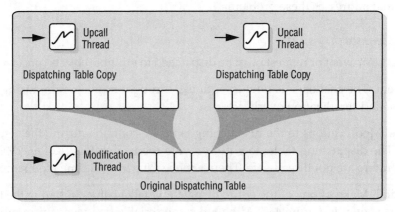

Figure 4–7 *Copy-then-Dispatch*

Problem. Making copies of the dispatching table is expensive and non-scalable.

Forces. Changes to the dispatching table are infrequent. The dispatching table does not provide robust iterators [Kofler+1993], or the iterators are not thread-safe. In addition, there are no stringent real-time requirements.

Solution. Copy the table on demand, as shown in Figure 4–8. When starting an iteration, a counter flag is incremented to indicate that a thread is using the table. If a thread wishes to modify the table, it must *automatically* make a copy of the dispatching table, make the modication on the copy, and replace the reference to the old table with a reference to the new one. When the last thread using the original dispatching table finishes its iteration, the table must be deallocated. In programming languages that lack garbage collection, a simple reference count can be used to accomplish this memory allocation strategy.

Consequences. Since the solution does not copy the dispatching table when initiating the dispatch loop, the COPY-ON-DEMAND pattern improves the dispatch latency when compared to COPY-THEN-DISPATCH pattern described in Section 3.2.1. Note that locks are not held while executing the upcalls. Thus, an application upcall can invoke recursive operations without risking deadlock.

One downside of this pattern is that it acquires the lock at least twice. The first acquisition occurs when the table state is updated to indicate the start of an iteration. The second acquisition indicates the end of the same iteration. Thus, when there is little or no contention, this solution is slightly more expensive than simply holding a lock over the entire dispatch loop.

Moreover, when threads contend to initiate a dispatch iteration, some priority inversions may occur. Since the lock is held for a short and fixed period of

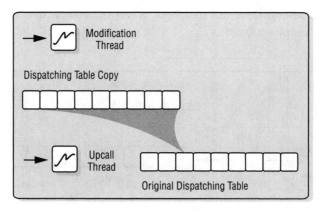

Figure 4–8 *Copy-On-Demand*

time, however, the priority inversion is bounded. In contrast, when a thread makes changes to the dispatching table, the amount of time for which it holds the lock depends on the size of the table, which may result in longer priority inversions. Thus, this pattern may be unsuitable for distributed real-time and embedded systems with stringent timing requirements.

Asynchronous-Change Commands

Context. An application with stringent real-time requirements where events or requests must be dispatched to multiple objects concurrently.

Problem. Modifications to the dispatching table must be serialized. However, the amount of time locks are held must be bounded to minimize priority inversions.

Forces. Upcalls are executed in the same thread that dispatches the event. The application can add and remove objects from the dispatching table dynamically.

Solution. Postpone changes to the dispatching table while threads are dispatching upcalls. Before iterating over the dispatching table, the dispatching thread atomically increments a counter that indicates the number of threads iterating over the dispatching table currently. When an iteration completes, it decrements the counter atomically. If a change is requested while the dispatching table is "busy," the request is converted into a Command Object [Gamma+1995], as shown in Figure 4–9, and queued to be executed when the dispatching table becomes "idle," that is, when no more dispatching threads are iterating over the table.

Consequences. Queueing a change to the dispatching table requires a bounded amount of time, thus preventing unbounded priority inversions. For similar reasons, this solution does not deadlock when upcalls request modifications, since they are simply queued.

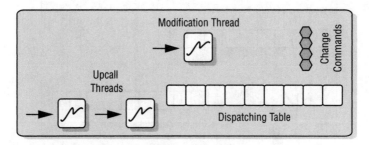

Figure 4–9 *Asynchronous-Change commands*

Table 4–2 *Summary of Dispatching to Single Object*

Pattern	Times lock acquired	Nested upcalls	Priority inversion	Appropriate when
Copy-then-Dispatch	2	Yes	Unbounded	Small dispatch table
Copy-on-Demand	2	Yes	Unbounded	Rare table modifications
Asynchronous-Changes	2	Yes	Unbounded	Predictable behavior

There is, however, a more subtle priority inversion in this Asynchronous-Change Command pattern implementation. A high-priority thread can request a modification, but the modification will not occur until the potentially lower priority threads have finished dispatching events. In many systems this is an acceptable tradeoff since priority inversions must be avoided in the critical path, that is, the dispatching path.

In addition, it is hard to ascertain when requested modifications actually occur, because they execute asynchronously. Likewise, it is hard to report errors when executing change requests, because the thread requesting the change does not wait for operations to complete.

Table 4–2 summaries the different patterns for dispatching to multiple objects and compares their relative strengths and weaknesses.

Concluding Remarks

This chapter described a pattern language for developing and selecting appropriate solutions to common problems encountered when developing efficient, scalable, predictable, and flexible dispatching components. This pattern language is part of ongoing efforts [Buschmann+1996][Schmidt+2000][Kircher+2004] [Gill+2005] to develop a handbook of patterns for developing DOC middleware for distributed real-time and embedded (DRE) systems. Patterns help middleware researchers and developers reuse successful strategies and practices. Moreover, they help developers communicate and reason more effectively about what they do and why they use particular designs and implementations. In addition, patterns are a step toward an engineering handbook for DOC middleware.

The pattern language presented in this chapter has been applied to the TAO real-time ORB [Schmidt+1998] on a range of DRE systems, including the Boeing

Bold Stroke avionics mission computing system [Harrison+1997][Gill+1999] [Doerr+1999][Sharp+2003][Roll+2003] and the SAIC Run Time Infrastructure (RTI) implementation [O'Ryan+1999][Noseworthy+2002] for the Defense Modeling and Simulation Organization's (DMSO) High Level Architecture (HLA) [Kuhl+1999]. The source code and documentation for the TAO ORB and its Event and Notication Services are freely available at www.dre.vanderbilt.edu/TAO.

References

[Alexander+1977] C. Alexander, S. Ishikawa, M. Silverstein, M. Jacobson, I. Fiksdahl-King, and S. Angel. *A Pattern Language*. New York: Oxford University Press, 1977.

[Buschmann+1996] F. Buschmann, R. Meunier, H. Rohnert, P. Sommerlad, and M. Stal. *Pattern-Oriented Software Architecture—A System of Patterns*. New York: John Wiley & Sons, 1996.

[Doerr+1999] B. S. Doerr, T. Venturella, R. Jha, C. D. Gill, and D. C. Schmidt. "Adaptive Scheduling for Real-time, Embedded Information Systems." In *Proceedings of the 18th IEEE/AIAA Digital Avionics Systems Conference (DASC)*, 1999.

[Gamma+1995] E. Gamma, R. Helm, R. Johnson, and J. Vlissides. *Design Patterns: Elements of Reusable Object-Oriented Software*. Reading, MA: Addison-Wesley, 1995.

[Gill+1999] C. D. Gill, F. Kuhns, D. L. Levine, and D. C. Schmidt. "Applying Adaptive Real-time Middleware to Address Grand Challenges of COTS-based Mission-Critical Real-Time Systems." In *Proceedings of the 1st IEEE International Workshop on Real-Time Mission-Critical Systems: Grand Challenge Problems*, Nov. 1999.

[Gill+2005] C. Gill and L. DiPippo. *Design Patterns for Distributed Real-Time Systems*. Norwell, MA: Kluwer Academic Publishers, 2005.

[Harrison+1997] T. H. Harrison, D. L. Levine, and D. C. Schmidt. "The Design and Performance of a Real-time CORBA Event Service." In *Proceedings of the 1997 Conference on Object-Oriented Programming Systems, Languages, and Applications (OOPSLA '97)*, pp. 184–199. ACM Press, 1997.

[Kircher+2004] M. Kircher and P. Jain. *Pattern-Oriented Software Architecture, vol. 3: Patterns for Resource Management*. New York: John Wiley & Sons, 2004.

[Kofler+1993] T. Koer. "Robust Iterators for ET++." *Structured Programming*, vol. 14, no. 2, pp. 62–85, 1993.

[Kuhl+1999] F. Kuhl, R. Weatherly, and J. Dahmann. *Creating Computer Simulation Systems*. Upper Saddle River, NJ: Prentice Hall, 1999.

[McKinney+1996] P. E. McKinney. "Selecting Locking Designs for Parallel Programs." In J. O. Coplien, J. Vlissides, and N. Kerth (eds.), *Pattern Languages of Program Design 2*. Reading, MA: Addison-Wesley, 1996.

[Noseworthy+2002] R. Noseworthy. "IKE 2–Implementing the Stateful Distributed Object Paradigm." In *5th IEEE International Symposium on Object-Oriented Real-Time Distributed Computing (ISORC 2002)*, Washington, DC: IEEE, 2002.

[OMG2001] Object Management Group. *Event Service Specication Version 1.1*, OMG Document formal/01-03-01 ed., Mar. 2001.

[OMG2002a] Object Management Group. "Real-time CORBA Specication." OMG Document formal/02-08-02 ed., Aug. 2002.

[OMG2002b] Object Management Group. *The Common Object Request Broker: Architecture and Specification*, 3.0.2 ed., Dec. 2002.

[OMG2002c] Object Management Group. *Notification Service Specification*. Object Management Group, OMG Document formal/2002-08-04 ed., 2002.

[O'Ryan+1999] C. O'Ryan, D. C. Schmidt, D. Levine, and R. Noseworthy. "Applying a Scalable CORBA Events Service to Large-scale Distributed Interactive Simulations." In *Proceedings of the 5th Workshop on Object-oriented Real-time Dependable Systems*. Monterey, CA: IEEE, 1999.

[Pyarali+1998] I. Pyarali and D. C. Schmidt. "An Overview of the CORBA Portable Object Adapter." *ACM StandardView*, vol. 6, Mar. 1998.

[Pyarali+1999] I. Pyarali, C. O'Ryan, D. C. Schmidt, N. Wang, V. Kachroo, and A. Gokhale. "Applying Optimization Patterns to the Design of Real-time ORBs." In *Proceedings of the 5th Conference on Object-Oriented Technologies and Systems*, pp. 184–199. San Diego, CA: USENIX, 1999.

[Roll+2003] W. Roll. "Towards Model-Based and CCM-Based Applications for Real-Time Systems." In *Proceedings of the International Symposium on Object-Oriented Real-time Distributed Computing* (ISORC). Hakodate, Hokkaido, Japan: IEEE/IFIP, 2003.

[Schmidt+1998] D. C. Schmidt, D. L. Levine, and S. Mungee. "The Design and Performance of Real-Time Object Request Brokers." *Computer Communications*, vol. 21, pp. 294–324, Apr. 1998.

[Schmidt+2000] D. C. Schmidt, M. Stal, H. Rohnert, and F. Buschmann. *Pattern-Oriented Software Architecture: Patterns for Concurrent and Networked Objects*, vol. 2. New York: John Wiley & Sons, 2000.

[Schmidt+2002a] D. C. Schmidt and C. O'Ryan. "Patterns and Performance of Real-time Publisher/Subscriber Architectures." *Journal of Systems and Software, Special Issue on Software Architecture-Engineering Quality Attributes,* 2002.

[Schmidt+2002b] D. C. Schmidt and S. Huston. *C++ Network Programming: Mastering Complexity Using ACE and Patterns.* Boston: Addison-Wesley, 2002.

[Sharp+2003] D. C. Sharp and W. C. Roll. "Model-Based Integration of Reusable Component-Based Avionics System." In *Proceedings of the Workshop on Model-Driven Embedded Systems in RTAS 2003,* May 2003.

"Triple-T"—A System of Patterns for Reliable Communication in Hard Real-Time Systems

Wolfgang Herzner, Wilfried Kubinger, and Manfred Gruber

Introduction

A system is considered to be "real-time," if response (to events, etc.) has to occur within given time spans, making timely response an essential feature [Pont2001]. Think of a PC, equipped with a framegrabber being able to convert an incoming video signal into a digitized format like MPEG at a rate of 25 frames per second. If it cannot encode a frame within 40 milliseconds, it will be too slow and eventually lose frames. In contrast, a word-processing application on the same PC: Of course, users want it to work as fast as possible, but besides raising their frustration level, it will have no effect if the application runs slower than promised or assumed.

As long as a real-time system may miss a deadline without causing significant risk to humans or environment, as can be assumed with the framegrabber example, it is called "soft real-time." If there is risk, however, it is called "hard real-time." For instance, electronic brake controls in cars are considered to be "hard real-time" because untimely reactions may easily lead to accidents.

In general, hard real-time systems become increasingly widespread in safety-critical application areas like automotive, avionics, robotics, and so forth. Although hard real-time and dependability are not automatically connected, they are closely related by implication, because only those real-time systems that may cause severe damage when failing are considered "hard," and those systems are also safety-critical.

Since the failure of a hardware component of a safety-critical system may compromise the operability of the whole system, it must be tolerant against hardware failures. This can usually be achieved by means of redundancy, that is, with duplicated hardware components, where a breakdown of some component is compensated for by its duplicate. Redundancy requires communication among the system's components and realization in a distributed form, at least for allowing negotiation between the duplicates and the rest of the system.

Since we are dealing with hard real-time, it becomes essential that communication among system components also adhere to strict transmission durations, which leads to the topic of this chapter: reliable communication with guaranteed transmission durations for hard real-time systems.

Such systems are often "embedded," in the sense of being part of larger structures like cars or airplanes. However, the patterns described in this chapter do not necessarily require "embeddedness" of the systems where they are applied.

It should be noted that many solutions for distributed hard real-time systems try to avoid the concept of a (communication) master. Although redundancy could solve the problem of having such a master as a critical part of the whole system, the implied architectural asymmetry makes it less feasible than symmetrical approaches, where each node may act as a temporary master in certain situations, if necessary.

We consider the presented patterns as a basic set for reliable hard-real-time systems. This set of patterns will be extended in the future. It should also be noted that task scheduling for hard real-time applications is not a topic of Triple-T, which concentrates merely on communication. We use a running example in order to illustrate how the described patterns are used.

A terminology glossary and an outline of the bus architectures where the described patterns have been found, and which are referenced in the Known Uses sections of the patterns, are given in the appendix at the end of the chapter.

Running Example: Brake-by-Wire

To illustrate application of the patterns, we use the so-called "Electro Mechanical Brake" (EMB). The EMB is considered the brake of the future for cars (pure brake-by-wire technology) because it entirely eliminates brake fluid and hydraulic lines. Furthermore, it can include all brake, safety, and stability functions in one system. The basic layout of an EMB is given in Figure 5–1. On each wheel, braking force is generated by an independent brake node. Wheel speed is measured and sent to the pedal node, which acts as the main control node of

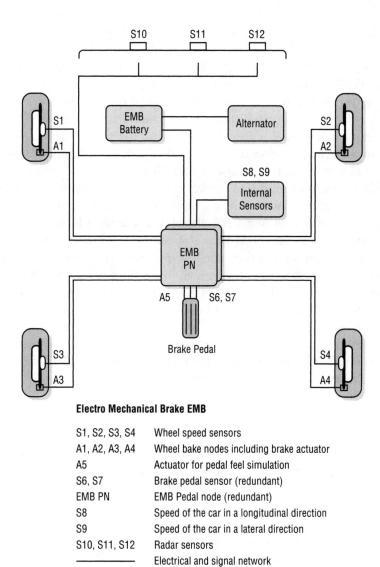

Electro Mechanical Brake EMB

S1, S2, S3, S4	Wheel speed sensors
A1, A2, A3, A4	Wheel bake nodes including brake actuator
A5	Actuator for pedal feel simulation
S6, S7	Brake pedal sensor (redundant)
EMB PN	EMB Pedal node (redundant)
S8	Speed of the car in a longitudinal direction
S9	Speed of the car in a lateral direction
S10, S11, S12	Radar sensors
————————	Electrical and signal network

Figure 5–1 *Electro Mechanical Brake*

the system. It measures the position of the brake pedal via two sensors, calculates the brake force for each wheel, transmits its new value to each wheel node, and simulates the real pedal feeling for the driver. Both pedal nodes and pedal sensors are replicated.

We added sensors S8 to S12 to show a further safety function, namely, automatic emergency braking. For its realization, the pedal node needs both information about the car's speed and the distance to the next obstacle in the driving direction. While S8 and S9 serve to measure the car's speed in the longitudinal and lateral directions, respectively, S10 to S12 are distance-measuring sensors (e.g., radar) for obtaining the distance to objects in front of the car. If the emergency braking algorithm calculates that a crash is likely to occur (e.g., if the distance to an obstacle falls below the "safe" braking distance), it initiates emergency braking to minimize the harm caused by a collision.

The need for reliable and time-critical communication in this example (and hence its justification as a running example in this chapter) can be justified by the following scenario. Assume the electrical connection to one of the brake nodes is interrupted. Since this now isolated node cannot receive the brake force messages anymore, it immediately stops braking (as long as it is not in the emergency braking state), and the needed brake force is redistributed over the remaining three nodes. This again requires that all remaining nodes, and the pedal nodes in particular, learn about the lost node as fast as possible and with maximum trust.

In contrast to this scenario, the force feedback to the real pedals is not of the same time-criticality (though it still has to occur reliably). It will therefore not be considered as important in the rest of this chapter.

Patterns Outline

Triple-T is a system of five patterns that together establish a base for the development of distributed safety-critical (hard) real-time systems. While fault-tolerance patterns have already been described (for example, in [Adams+1996] and its update [Hanmer+1999] for user interfaces in real-time control systems; in [Saridakis2002] for fault-tolerance against system failures; or in [Saridakis 2003] for fault containment, and patterns for time-triggered embedded systems on dedicated hardware platforms in books like [Pont2001]), Triple-T concentrates on reliable communication among nodes in a distributed system with high safety and hard real-time requirements.

As shown in Figure 5–2, PRESCHEDULED PERIODIC TRANSMISSION is the entry point into Triple-T. It describes how guaranteed transmission times can be achieved to meet hard deadlines. TIME-TRIGGERED CLOCK SYNCHRONIZATION provides a solution for keeping the local clocks synchronized without a central master. SYNC FRAME addresses how the whole communication can be initiated, as well as how nodes can enter an already running communication. The BUS GUARDIAN is necessary for keeping faulty nodes from disturbing the communi-

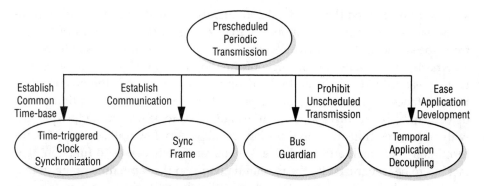

Figure 5–2 *Relationship among Triple-T patterns.*

cation among healthy nodes. Finally, TEMPORAL APPLICATION DECOUPLING describes how application tasks can be decoupled from the communication process to ease both their development and their scheduling.

These patterns are described in the following sections.

Prescheduled Periodic Transmission

Also known as: Time-Triggered Communication, Time-Division Multiple Access (TDMA)

Context

Distributed (embedded) hard real-time systems where communication among the components shows the following characteristics:

- Most, if not all, of the messages to be exchanged between components are small (e.g., single-sensor measures) but have to be frequently transmitted.
- Transmission times must be guaranteed (a consequence of being hard real-time).
- Breakdown of a node must be detected by the remaining nodes within a given time (a consequence of being fault-tolerant).

Example

Consider the brake-by-wire system in a car as discussed in the introduction. Here, typical components are sensors for brake-pedal position, wheel angle speeds, vehicle speed (longitudinal and lateral), and distance measures to frontal obstacles. Computing components analyze the situation in front of the car from speed and distance measures, they evaluate the resulting brake forces for all wheels, and actuators turn force information into physical brake forces. Actuators also provide feedback to the driver by adjusting both the position and the resistance strength of the brake pedal. Perhaps with the exception of the driver feedback, all corresponding information has to be transmitted frequently, with an ensured transmission duration, usually every few milliseconds. The information is of small and fixed size. Whenever a node ceases to function, that fact has to be recognized by the remaining nodes in the same time range so that the system's behavior can be adapted immediately to the new situation (e.g., by redistributing the needed brake force over the remaining three brake nodes).

Problem

How can requested transmission times of many, mostly small, messages be guaranteed, and how can a node failure be recognized as soon as possible?

As we will now see, conventional communication techniques will not solve this problem.

Why Ethernet-Like Communication Won't Work

When using conventional event-driven communication, where each node sends a message as soon as it has one to transmit, we are faced with several problems. First, it is almost impossible to guarantee requested transmission times, due to the risk of collisions on the bus. If, for instance, two nodes start to send almost simultaneously, so that they have not yet recognized each other, both messages are corrupted and have to be retransmitted, which then raises the danger of another collision. A well-known consequence of this effect is that (non-switched) Ethernet loads of more than about 30% of the maximum capacity significantly raise transmission times. Figure 5–3 illustrates this effect.

As shown in Figure 5–3, Nodes A and B send almost simultaneously, so their transmissions collide and are disturbed. Then each waits a node-specific time before it retransmits. In the meantime, the same happens to nodes C and D. Due to their individual retransmission times, C collides with A at its next try, while D succeeds. Happy about its successful transmission, it starts to transmit a new message, which collides with the third try of A, while C succeeds at its fourth try. So, in the interval shown, there have been 12 transmission tries with only 2 of them successful.

Another concern is that nodes may malfunction in various ways. If they are able to send corresponding information to the other nodes before shutting

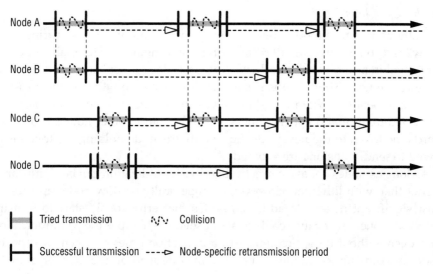

Figure 5–3 *Example of collisions on Ethernet*

down, the remaining system can adjust to the new situation. If, however, a node ceases without warning, the other nodes may recognize this only by detecting that they are no longer receiving messages from that node. (This presumes that any node sends at least one message regularly, even pure actuator nodes.) Although such behavior of regularly sending "alive" messages is possible, it both consumes bandwidth and may cause additional transmission delays due to collisions, as previously discussed, which may cause unacceptable delays or jitter.

Finally, a rather minor issue is that we need headers for each message. The headers must contain the sender identification, the type/meaning of the transmitted information, sending/creation time, and possibly the intended recipient(s) if we do not broadcast. The headers tend to need significantly more bits than the actual data. If, for instance, only one data byte is to be transmitted, for example, brake pedal position (such as percent of "fully pressed"), a major part (two-thirds or more) of the available bandwidth is consumed by framing information, not relevant data. If we take the first problem of message collision into consideration as well, then we have to conclude that in the given context the net utilization of the available bandwidth must stay clearly below 10% to be able to ensure a requested transmission time with a probability of about 99% or more—which is still below the 10^{-9} failures/hour required for hard real-time systems.

Why Not Using Token Ring?

An alternative to Ethernet-like transmission could be a token ring (e.g., www2.rad.com/networks/1996/toknring/toknring.htm). Here, all nodes are connected in a ring-like network, where a so-called "token" is passed from one node to the next. The token is some sort of message to which other messages may be appended. When a node receives the token, it removes all messages dedicated to itself and appends messages to be sent to other nodes. It then forwards the token to the next node. Since only the node holding the token is allowed to send, collisions are avoided.

As long as nodes behave correctly, bandwidth utilization can be significantly higher than with Ethernet. However, a single faulty or slow node can cause at least significant delays. In addition, nodes that erroneously start to transmit without a token may cause collisions and severely hamper the communication. And even without these problems, communication times between two specific nodes are difficult to guarantee, because they depend on the number of nodes between them.

As a consequence, token ring does not represent a reasonable solution to the given problem.

Solution

Use a periodic transmission schedule with a period short enough to fulfill the longest needed transmission duration within the system, assign each message at least one time slot, and define the precise phase of the period during which each message must be sent.

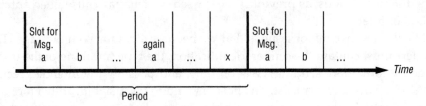

Figure 5–4 *Example of periodic transmission schedule*

As soon as time passes the slot of a certain message, the respective sender node (or the corresponding tasks, respectively) sends the data exactly as prescribed by the schedule, whether the data changed since the previous period or not. Since the meaning of data sent is completely described by its phase within the period, it is not necessary to send a header with it. Only the pure information needs to be contained in a message (besides error correction codes for handling transmission errors, which have to be used anyway). Data that have to be transmitted more frequently than with the largest period may have more than one time slot assigned within a period, as indicated with message *a*.

(Use BUS GUARDIAN for prohibiting nodes from transmitting outside of their slots.)

Basically, this pattern implies broadcast communication rather than multicast or even point-to-point communication. Of course, each node listening on the bus can ignore data not relevant for it or the tasks running on it.

This communication is called "time-triggered" (the opposite of "event-triggered"), because the progression of time is the only reason for a transmission.

Sometimes the set of all transmitted information within a period is considered as the "public state" of the system, which gets continuously updated, so that after each round, each node within the system has conceptual knowledge of the most recent state values.

Implementation

The first implementation step is the specification of the schedule, which must be done during the design of the overall system. Several constraints must be considered when preparing the schedule.

Constraints for the Schedule

- *Highest transmission frequency needed.* This will define the shortest period. It essentially depends on the highest possible and desired refresh rate for any information to be transmitted.

- *Lowest refresh rate needed.* Some data may be generated with frequencies significantly lower than the shortest transmission time needed. If, for instance, some measure value cannot be read more than four times a second, but requires a greater amount of bytes (which, for example, could apply to visual sensor data), it can make sense to consider this in the schedule.

- *Validity time spans.* Messages have to be scheduled so that their data are not outdated before they can be processed by the receiving node(s), that is, the sum of time data stay in sending node and receiving node(s) must not exceed that time span.

- *A-periodic messages.* It may be necessary to allow transmissions of a-periodic or even sporadic messages, for example, diagnostic information.

- *Future extensions.* If available bandwidth is not already exhausted, it is wise to anticipate the need for new messages within existing slots and for new slots for future additions by adding free "space" to both time slots and transmission period. The reason for this is that as long as future extensions do fit into the free time slots, no re-design is needed for the existing communication, because it is safely not affected by these extensions.

- *Available bandwidth.* Of course, available bandwidth affects the free space left over for a-periodic transmissions and future extensions.

Preparing the Schedule

The highest needed transmission frequency determines the shortest period within the schedule. To leave room for positioning messages within the schedule with respect to their validity time spans, it is sensible to take even a shorter period than implied by the highest needed transmission frequency.

If there are transmission frequencies significantly lower than the highest one, as indicated by the lowest refresh rate needed, it may make sense to use more than one period, resulting in hierarchical periods, where the number of shorter periods is an integer multiple of the longer one. For instance, the shortest period is 10 ms, while the longest is 250 ms, resulting in 25 short periods within one long period. Of course, that hierarchy may consist of more than two levels.

Message slots are now placed within the periods in a way that validity time spans are not violated. In particular, so-called "processing pipes" have to be considered: if task A (e.g., a sensor task) on node 1 sends message X to task B (a computing task) on node 2, which processes it and sends message Y to task C (an actuator task) on node 3, then X and Y have to be scheduled so that both B can process X before its validity time span expires and produce Y just in time to be processed by C before Y's validity time span is exceeded.

If time slots for a-periodic messages are needed, they are scheduled in unused spaces of the schedule prepared so far. Since these slots will serve for transmission of data from various nodes, a special protocol is needed to control communication within such time slots.

Finally, free transmission time is computed by subtracting all defined time slots from the available transmission bandwidth.

See "Running Example Resolved" for a diagram showing a possible schedule.

Using the Schedule

The schedule will finally be installed at each node of the system in a way that the transmission control unit of each node knows the whole system schedule at runtime, or at least those parts relevant to it.

Running Example Resolved

First, we list the assumed frequencies with which individual data are or can be provided (see Table 5–1).

If "front distance credibility" is 1, the "minimum front distance" will indicate the smallest measured distance to an obstacle, or the latter value is not valid. The 9 milliseconds for data provided by the EMB processing nodes are assumed to result from strong WCET (worst case execution time) estimations. Actuators are not considered, because they only receive data (their malfuction is detected by the wheel speed sensors), but let's assume that the wheel brake nodes cannot process brake force commands more often than every 10 ms.

Table 5–1 *EMB-Example, Characteristics of Transmitted Data*

Data	Unit	Source	Size (Bytes)	Min. Time (ms)[a]
Brake pedal position	mm.	S6, S7	1 (unsigned int.)	44
Wheel speed (front left … rear right)	°/sec	S1 … S4	2 (signed int.)	2
Car speed longitudinal	cm/sec	S8	2 (signed int.)	5
Car speed lateral	mm/sec	S9	2 (signed int.)	18
Minimum front distance	cm	S10 … S12	2 (unsigned int.)	95
Front distance credibility	0→no, 1→ok	S10 … S12	1 bit	95
Wheel brake force (per wheel)	milliNewton	PN1, PN2	2 (unsigned int.)	9
Brake pedal feed back position	mm	PN1, PN2	1 (unsigned int.)	9
Brake pedal feed back force	milliNewton	PN1, PN2	1 (unsigned int.)	9

a. Minimal sampling time for sensors; WCET for control algorithms

Obviously, the maximum of the PN's 9 ms and the actuator nodes' 10 ms define a basic transmission frequency. However, it is not the best way to force the whole data exchange into one 10 ms period, because some data like brake pedal position cannot be provided with the same frequency. But the longer intervals can appropriately be fit into multiples of this period, making a hierarchical schedule plausible, as shown in Figure 5–5. There, messages are denoted by their source sensor, or "a"..."c" for the processor nodes' (PN1/2) output as given in the order of Table 5–1.

The period consists of 10 sub-periods of 10 ms each, resulting in a period of 100 ms. Each message has its own defined slot. Every message with a delivery period up to 10 ms is transmitted in each sub-period, and lateral car speed is transmitted every second sub-period. Other less frequently provided messages are distributed so that the lengths of the sub-periods are nicely balanced, resulting in a net bandwidth of less than 20 bytes per sub-period, or some 20 Kbit. Even with modest bus capacities, there is enough spare space per sub-period for future extensions, which is indicated by the blank areas at the end of each sub-period.

	ms0														ms10
Subperiod 1	S1	S2	S3	S4	S8	a1	b1	c1	a2	b2	c2	S12			
Subperiod 2	S1	S2	S3	S4	S8	a1	b1	c1	a2	b2	c2	S9			
Subperiod 3	S1	S2	S3	S4	S8	a1	b1	c1	a2	b2	c2				
Subperiod 4	S1	S2	S3	S4	S8	a1	b1	c1	a2	b2	c2	S9			
Subperiod 5	S1	S2	S3	S4	S8	a1	b1	c1	a2	b2	c2	S6	S7		
Subperiod 6	S1	S2	S3	S4	S8	a1	b1	c1	a2	b2	c2	S9			
Subperiod 7	S1	S2	S3	S4	S8	a1	b1	c1	a2	b2	c2	S10			
Subperiod 8	S1	S2	S3	S4	S8	a1	b1	c1	a2	b2	c2	S9			
Subperiod 9	S1	S2	S3	S4	S8	a1	b1	c1	a2	b2	c2	S11			
Subperiod 10	S1	S2	S3	S4	S8	a1	b1	c1	a2	b2	c2	S9	S6	S7	

Figure 5–5 *EMB example schedule*

Consequences

Benefits

- *Guaranteed transmission time.* Transmission time of a message within a time-triggered slot can be guaranteed to the frequency it is scheduled, because due to the schedule each node sends only when it is planned and therefore no transmission collisions occur. (See Bus Guardian for assuring that this remains true even in the presence of faulty nodes.)

- *Fast detection of erroneous nodes.* That a node misses its slot is conceptually detected immediately by the other nodes. Hence, fail-silent nodes can inform the remaining nodes in the system simply by not sending anymore. This is a significant advantage of time-triggered communication over event-triggered communication, which needs various additional mechanisms for detecting erroneous nodes like I Am Alive or You Are Alive [Saridakis2002].

- *Minor message header needed.* Since message content is completely defined by its position within the schedule, no information about sender, content type, creation time, and so forth needs to be attached to the message. However, some framing information may be needed to let both receiving communication controllers detect the transmission and to safely distinguish data messages (data frames) from synchronization frames (see Time-Triggered Clock Synchronization). However, for small messages like sensor values or control values for actuators, which are often represented by single or small sets of bytes, this may be a significant reduction of transmission overhead.

- *High bandwidth utilization.* Since within the time-triggered parts of the schedule no collisions occur, bandwidth can be utilized up to almost 100%.

- *Composability.* If new messages can be placed into free slots (unused parts of the transmission period), the communication can be extended without any risk of affecting existing transmissions, which cannot be guaranteed with event-triggered transmission. With only the latter available, communication has to be redesigned (retested, recertified) as a whole every time messages are added.

  Of course, this argument applies only to transmission, while all affected tasks (that send the new message and read it) have to be retested/certified. But if a new subsystem is added that uses its own messages, only this subsystem as a whole has to be tested and certified.

Liabilities

- *Synchronization needed.* Time-triggered communication relies on synchronization of all participating nodes, which has to be kept much stronger than in event-driven communication. Time-Triggered Clock Synchronization provides a solution for that, based on Prescheduled Periodic Transmission, while Sync Frame helps to establish communication.

- *Risk of transmission disturbance.* Fault nodes can easily disturb communication by transmitting out of phase. Bus Guardian helps to avoid this.

- *More complex application development.* Application tasks must adhere to the transmission schedule with respect to sending and receiving data. Temporal Application Decoupling explains how this complexity can be significantly reduced.

- *Inflexibility.* Time-triggered transmission is highly inflexible at runtime. For instance, communications that need more than half of the bandwidth to be occupied by one sender at some time, and to be occupied by another node at some other time, cannot be realized with a transmission schedule defined at design time. Of course, it is possible to switch between different schedules, but this is hard to implement with respect to maintain dependability during schedule switching.

- *High design effort.* Developing correct schedules is an NP-hard problem. No methods currently exist that can evaluate the optimal schedule for any given set of constraints. Instead, so-called heuristic schedulers are used that may fail to find a solution even if one exists.

- *Transmission overhead through unnecessary transmission.* It can be argued that the avoidance of message headers is traded against superfluous transmission. This will be the case if development tools used do not allow various transmission periods or the use of a-periodic (event-triggered) messages in dedicated time slots.

- *Power consumption.* Highly periodic transmission may consume more power than event-driven transmission. In power-aware environments, this could become a critical issue.

Known Uses

All bus architectures outlined in the appendix at the end of this chapter support time-triggered transmission, mainly as described. FlexRay and TTCAN also support event-triggered transmission. In TTP (Time-Triggered Protocol), the periodic transmission schedule is named MEDL (Message Description List). TTP provides two levels of schedule hierarchy: A so-called "bus cycle" can consist of a power of two "TDMA rounds," where all rounds are of equal length and layout with respect to node-specific time slots, but within each round, each node may send different messages (or none at all).

FlexRay differs slightly from the others in the way that each node gets only those parts of the schedule loaded that concern messages it is interested in. This has the advantage of a somewhat higher flexibility, because when adding a new node to an existing system without affecting the existing schedule, existing nodes need not be updated, at the cost of a higher start-up complexity (see the Known Uses section of Sync Frame). Likewise, a TTCAN controller only gets the information it needs for time-triggered sending and receiving of messages as well as for sending of spontaneous messages.

Related Patterns

For executing both application tasks and system tasks serving for transmission, the Cyclic Executive pattern or—in special cases—the ROUND ROBIN pattern can be applied [Douglass2003]. CO-OPERATIVE SCHEDULER [Pont2001] can be used on the operating system level to execute tasks in alignment with the transmission schedule.

Time-Triggered Clock Synchronization
Context

Distributed (embedded) hard real-time systems, where PRESCHEDULED PERIODIC TRANSMISSION is applied to guarantee that requested transmission times are not violated, and where a central clock is not available.

Problem

How can the clocks of all nodes be kept synchronized with sufficient precision for the requested transmission rates in the absence of a central clock?

Each node has a local clock oscillator. Even optimally calibrated clocks on different nodes will diverge due to different physical and environmental parameters. But keeping the clocks of all nodes synchronized is crucial for a successful time-triggered communication.

Example

Consider our brake-by-wire application. It consists of five nodes, each of which uses its own quartz oscillator, which will gradually drift apart due to temperature differences (even if they start with exactly the same frequency).

Solution

Precisely compare the actual arrival times of messages received from other nodes with the scheduled arrival times, and then use an error compensating function of these differences to correct the node's clock.

The solution is based on the transmission schedule. As soon as a node has successfully joined the communication on a time-triggered bus, it can simply compare the arrival times of the messages within time slots of the other nodes with the corresponding times given in the schedule. If, for instance, on a node K, message a from node 1 arrives two ticks later than scheduled, message b from node 2 five ticks later, and message c from node 3 one tick earlier, then K can deduce that it is a bit too early (that is, $(2+5-1)/2 = 3\ ticks$) and should therefore delay its own clock for that value.

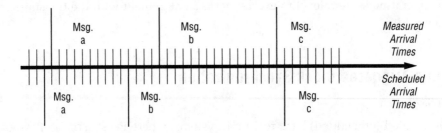

Figure 5–6 *Comparison of scheduled with measured message arrival times*

Implementation

Since TIME-TRIGGERED CLOCK SYNCHRONIZATION is vulnerable to "wild clock readings,"[1] it is desirable to exclude these from the clock correction calculation. This could be done by limiting the allowed difference between scheduled and measured arrival time to a maximum value. Nodes whose messages arrive too early or too late (that is, the corresponding arrival time differences exceed this limit) not only are excluded from clock correction, but could also be regarded as being faulty. This limit can even be used to judge a node's own clock: Having all (or most) readings from other nodes too early or too late indicates that a node's own clock has gone wild rather than that of the others.

---

1. This term denotes effects caused by an erroneous node clock, which runs significantly faster or slower than those of other nodes in a system, or even irregularly.

A variant is the Welch-Lynch algorithm, also known as "t-fault-tolerant midpoint" [Welch+1988]. If up to t faulty nodes are to be tolerated by $n+1$ nodes in the system, then the differences are increasingly or decreasingly ordered, and the average of the $(t+1)^{st}$ and $(n-t)^{th}$ value computed. Of course, this requires $n > 3t$.

Once a necessary clock correction has been identified, several methods exist to apply it. If a node's own clock counter (that is, the mapping of quartz periods to clock ticks) can be adjusted, then it is feasible to apply the correction by appropriately adjusting this mapping; this has the advantage of a maximally smooth clock correction. If, however, such an adjustment is not supported, excess ticks must be skipped and missing ticks must be added. This could be done at the beginning of the next transmission period. However, since such a correction is a "hard" or "jumping" clock correction and affects the whole node, including the operating system and application tasks, jumps of several ticks may be dangerous. It therefore appears preferable to distribute the insertion or omission of clock ticks over a longer period of time.

This leads to the question of the frequency with which these measurements and corrections should be executed. The highest frequency would be that of the transmission schedule; that means that after each transmission round, the arrival time deviations are measured and the resulting clock correction computed. Since the necessary calculations are rather simple, and the resulting corrections can be expected to be very small, this appears to be a reasonable solution.

Consequences

Benefits

- *No further mechanism needed.* Since this pattern relies on the periodic transmission schedule, it can be implemented without the need for further communication such as distributing specific clock-sync messages.

- *Fault-tolerance included.* Arrival time deviations that are too large automatically indicate faulty nodes. Likewise, methods like Welch-Lynch automatically avoid poor clock sync due to wild clock readings.

Liabilities

- *No sync with external time.* All clocks will synchronize to the average of all participating clocks. If this average deviates significantly from standard time, the whole system will drift away from standard time.

- *Minimum number of nodes needed.* If the clock synchronization is to be tolerant against t simultaneously faulty nodes, then at least $2t+2$ nodes are needed ($2t$ for ignoring t extreme measures on both ends, 1 for the good reading, and 1 recipient).

Known Uses

TTP uses Welch-Lynch. However, there is a distinction between nodes with ordinary clocks and those with accurate clocks (expensive), and only the latter are considered.

FlexRay also uses the standard Welch-Lynch, and adjusts the clock counter.

Related Patterns

An alternative is to use a "central clock," as described in the Shared-Clock (S-C) Scheduler [Pont2001], where a master sends tick messages at regular intervals within the framework of the transmission schedule, and all slave nodes adapt their time to these master ticks. As already discussed, this is vulnerable to faulty masters, as long as no smart fault-tolerance mechanisms like duplicating failsafe masters are applied, and needs special clock messages. However, a benefit of this pattern is that it can be coupled with an external clock, thus permitting alignment of a whole cluster with standard time.

Sync Frame

Context

Distributed (embedded) hard real-time systems without a master node, which use Prescheduled Periodic Transmission to guarantee that requested transmission times are not violated.

Problem

How can time-triggered periodic transmission be commenced, and how can a node join a running communication?

Once a node is started (or restarted after a failure) and ready to join the communication, how does it synchronize with the other nodes? That is, how does it recognize the current transmission phase? Since transmitted information contains essentially application-specific data and presumably error correcting code like CRC for transmission error detection, it is difficult for a node that wants to join to interpret the received bit sequences correctly.

Example

Consider our brake-by-wire application. When the ignition key is turned, all nodes boot, and after initialization and self-test, they are ready to communicate.

However, since no node is sending so far, how can the synchronized communication, which is necessary for running the predefined transmission schedule, become established? Note that without an established communication, no local node clocks are synchronized at this point.

Solution

Let special messages be transmitted that unambiguously identify the phase of the transmission schedule within which they are sent. These messages are called "synchronization frames," or "sync frame" for short.

In detail, the solution consists of several steps.

First, define a sync frame containing a unique bit pattern that can safely be distinguished from application data. It should also contain additional information, such as the actual phase in the schedule within which it is sent.

Second, for each node—or at least a number of nodes (see Implementation section), reserve a special part of its time slot for transmitting the sync frame, usually at the beginning of the slot. If a hierarchical schedule is used, then this reservation may be needed only on the highest level.

An "out-of-sync" node that wants to join a running communication listens until it recognizes the bit pattern of a sync frame. From the additional information, it learns the current phase within a transmission period, and this information allows it to settle its own transmission control.

If it does not receive a sync frame for a certain period of time, for example, somewhat longer than the longest period within the predefined schedule, then it starts sending such a frame itself. If other nodes also in the start-up phase receive this sync frame, they can synchronize and start to transmit. This, again, is detected by the sender of the sync frame, which can now start to transmit in its time slots, and the communication is established. If no node is responding, either because no other node is ready, or due to a collision on the bus, the sending of sync frames is usually repeated.

If two starting nodes send sync frames simultaneously, these will be corrupted and not successfully received by any node of the system. To avoid the same collision occurring again, each node must wait a different time so that in the worst case, after any possible combination of collisions among nodes, one will finally succeed. See the next section, Implementation, for how these different waiting times are determined.

In Figure 5–7, "Synchronized" means that the node knows the current phase within the transmission schedule and can therefore start to send and/or receive messages. "Send sync-frame" includes initiating local processing of the transmission schedule; hence, a sync frame is sent at precisely that phase for which it

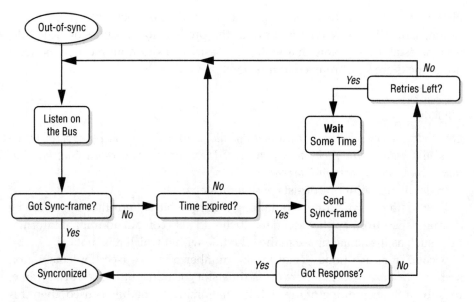

Figure 5–7 *Control diagram of Sync Frame*

is scheduled in the given node. Consequently, "Got response?" = "yes" means that the sync frame sending node receives valid messages from other nodes, which indicates that other nodes have successfully received its sync frame and established their transmission schedules in synchronization with its own.

Implementation

How the identification bit pattern of a sync frame looks depends on the general encoding of application data and other information on the bus. Since some form of redundancy will be needed to detect transmission errors, for example, CRC or some other error correcting encoding, application data are usually embedded into small control frames or encoded. Embedding data allows for reserving specific patterns for the sync frame. In most cases, quite a few bytes are needed for it.

It is not necessary for each node to send sync frames during the normal transmission period. Instead, each node has only to be guaranteed that even in the worst case at least one healthy node remains that sends sync frames. If m nodes are allowed to fail simultaneously, then obviously at least $m+1$ nodes must transmit sync frames. With the common "single fault hypothesis," this means at least two nodes. Therefore, Figure 5–7 shows how nodes that have sync frames scheduled behave at start-up (we will call those nodes "sync nodes"); those that have no sync frames scheduled simply listen.

An important prerequisite for efficient application of Sync Frame is that the waiting periods between two consecutive sync frame transmissions are sufficiently different for all nodes. In particular, no waiting period must be an integral multiple of some other within a system. Since these periods are defined prior to runtime (e.g., at installation or even at system design time), it is straightforward to fulfill this request. For instance, consecutive odd numbers where the product of the smallest with the number of sync nodes is larger than the largest number could be used. Then a sync-node will safely transmit a sync frame successfully without collision after at most one collision with each of the other sync-nodes in the system. Of course, the number of retries (see Figure 5–7) has to be larger than the number of sync-nodes. As a consequence, the individual waiting periods should be determined during scheduling.

This constraint has to be considered whenever a system is reconfigured, such as during maintenance in a car when an old node is replaced by a new one, or even new nodes added.

A risk of this pattern is that a faulty node may be incapable of detecting sync frames or even any communication, even though it is already going on. In this case, it will start to send sync frames without need. To avoid this, further mechanisms are necessary, like Bus Guardian.

A further risk is the appearance of so-called "Byzantine" situations at start-up. This includes all situations where either a node switches irregularly between faulty and non-faulty behavior (e.g., due to a loose contact), or the healthiness of a node is judged differently by different nodes. Many possible faults can be detected by healthy nodes (by sophisticated extensions of the algorithm sketched in Figure 5–7 or by methods not addressed by Triple-T) and corrected by the whole system as long as the underlying fault hypothesis is not violated. However, if not all components are fail-silent, it is impossible to safely exclude undetectable and hence unsolvable Byzantine situations. For a more thorough discussion of this topic, see, for example [Driscoll+2003].

A possible effect could be that several nodes that are successfully emitting sync frames establish communication among a subset of the whole cluster, thus creating so-called "cliques."

Running Example Resolved

In our running example, we assume that it is sufficient to transmit sync frames once per period, and by two nodes. We choose the processor nodes (PN1, PN2) for that. Since currently in sub-period 3 the fewest messages are scheduled (see

Figure 5–5), we add the sync frames there at the beginning of the time slots of PN1 and PN2, namely before a1 and a2, respectively, as indicated by boxes "1" and "2" in Figure 5–8.

For the content of these sync frames, we choose a unique bit pattern, followed by one bit indicating the number of the processing node it is sending, that is, '0' for PN1, and '1' for PN2. And we choose 111 and 117 ms as their waiting periods between sync frame transmissions.

Subperiod 3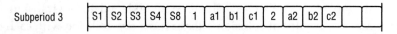

Figure 5–8 *Sub-period 3 with sync frames*

Consequences

Benefits

- *Decentralized start-up.* There is no need for a master to initialize communication.

- *Speed.* A new (or restarted) node may join within two periods. And as long as no series of increasingly unlikely sync frame collisions occur, start-up of a whole system will occur within a few periods.

- *Self-stabilization.* As long as no faulty or malicious node disturbs working transmissions of good nodes, this pattern finally integrates all good nodes into a communicating system.

Liabilities

- *Limited fault-tolerance.* In the presence of faulty nodes, communication may not settle or could be significantly hampered as long as no further mechanisms are used to suppress erroneous sync frame emission of such nodes. Bus Guardians allow for coping with deterministically detectable faulty nodes.

- *Increased complexity.* Sync frames have to be considered during evaluation of the transmission schedule, and different waiting times for all nodes must be computed.

- *Reduced bandwidth.* Sync frames don't carry application-relevant information and therefore reduce the bandwidth available for that. However, since sync frames are rather short and need not be sent too frequently, the bandwidth loss is usually about 1% or less.

Known Uses

In ARINC 659, two flavors of sync frames are actually used. "Long Resync" frames are transmitted during a running communication. Hence, an out-of-sync node first listens for such a "Long Sync." If it fails to recognize any for a certain length of time, it sends an "Initial Resync," indicating to the other nodes that it wants to restart the whole communication.

On TTP, sync frames are called "I-frames." If they are transmitted in a time slot together with application data, the whole frame is called an "x-frame." In addition, clever algorithms are implemented to minimize the danger of Byzantine errors during start-up.

Since FlexRay nodes get only their own part of the transmission schedule loaded, they have to learn the full configuration by observing message traffic during start-up, which again makes communication initialization more complicated and vulnerable to misbehaving nodes. This risk is reduced by restricting the creation of sync frames to dedicated nodes, which then can be built more expensively, but also more reliably, than the majority of the remaining nodes. Of course, this approach weakens the symmetry property intrinsic to SYNC FRAME.

Related Patterns

PRESCHEDULED PERIODIC TRANSMISSION is a precondition for applying SYNC FRAME. BUS GUARDIAN helps to avoid sending invalid sync frames by faulty nodes during rejoin.

Bus Guardian

Context

Distributed (embedded) hard real-time systems, where PRESCHEDULED PERIODIC TRANSMISSION is applied to guarantee that requested transmission times are not violated.

Problem

How can it be guaranteed that a node actually sends data only in its time slots?

In particular, how can it be ensured that an erroneous node or its communication handler, respectively, does not disturb the communication among correct nodes by "babbling" into their time slots? (In general, a "babbling idiot" failure occurs, if an erroneous node does not adhere to the rules of the communication protocol and sends messages at arbitrary points in time.)

Examples

Consider, for instance, a node basically following the transmission schedule of the whole system of which it is a member. However, due to an electrical fault (perhaps induced by a transient electromagnetic field disturbance), it sporadically produces noise on the bus outside its own time slots.

Another typical problem are so-called "slightly out of specification" (SOS) errors, caused when digital devices work close to the voltage border between the representation of "0" and "1." For example, in TTL "0" is represented by 0 Volt and "1" is represented by 5 Volt, and the border is 2 Volt. A device that loses power will represent "1" increasingly closer to this border. This may result not only in transmission errors, which should be detected by recipients, but also in complete misbehavior of that device, which again can turn it into a "babbling idiot."

Solution

For each node, provide a separate device—the "bus guardian"—which restricts transmission to the nodes' own time slots.

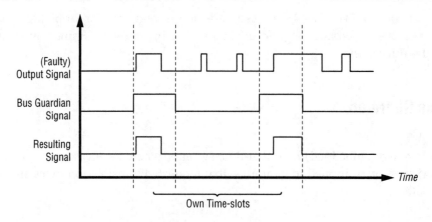

Figure 5–9 *Bus guardian effect on faulty output signal*

Essentially, the bus guardian's signal is ANDed with the output signal of the communication handler. Of course, partially truncated signals, when transmission overlaps their own time slots, will not be received correctly by healthy nodes; therefore, these will recognize that incorrectly sending node as being faulty.

Implementation

There are several implementations of Bus Guardian possible. One solution is to realize it as some sort of filter; another is to AND its output with that of the communication handler through a simple AND-gate, as indicated in Figure 5–10.

A variant of alternative b) would be that the guardian itself controls a gate in the output line of the node communication handler.

An important aspect is the independence of the bus guardian from the element it has to guard. If, for instance, it shares physically the schedule presentation, internal clock, and power supply with the communication handler, and is even located on the same board close to it, then common mode failures are more likely to occur, diminishing the effectiveness of the Bus Guardian pattern. Geographic separation, its own power supply, duplicated schedule presentation, and a separate clock source raise the implementation costs, though.

When a bus guardian fails, it may not allow any transmission of its guarded node at all, which results in a fail-silent FCU containing the bus guardian and the node guarded by it. Or it may allow transmission at the wrong period phases. As long as the guarded node transmits correctly, its transmission will be corrupted, resulting in being considered as faulty by the remaining nodes. As a consequence, a faulty bus guardian will be recognized in the same way as a faulty node.

Alternative: Central Bus Guardian

A possible alternative to individual bus guardians is to use a star configuration of the bus and place the bus guardian into the center of the star, where it opens

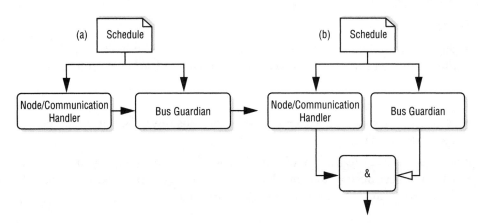

Figure 5–10 *Possible implementations of Bus Guardian*

the line for each node corresponding to the schedule. Then, only one bus guardian is needed for the whole network, which, however, turns it into a single point of failure. This can be neutralized by duplicating the whole network (which is necessary for fault-tolerance in any case). And since only two bus guardian units are needed, they can be more expensive.

Bus guardians essentially consist of two functional components: the one that—according to the schedule—decides when to open and close the output channel of its guarded output unit, and the one that actually controls that channel. While the first component is usually realized in software, the latter is in general realized in hardware, because it is much simpler and its correctness can easier be proved.

BUS GUARDIAN adds an important aspect of fault-tolerance to PRESCHEDULED PERIODIC TRANSMISSION and is easier realized when TEMPORAL APPLICATION DE-COUPLING has been applied. BUS GUARDIANS often apply TIME-TRIGGERED CLOCK SYNCHRONIZATION by themselves, to avoid common mode failure with their guarded node.

Running Example Resolved

In our EMB application, we will use the solution shown in Figure 5–10 b). All bus guardians share the schedule description with their guarded nodes and are placed on the same board as the communication controller (to reduce development costs), but possess their own power-supply and apply TIME-TRIGGERED CLOCK SYNCHRONIZATION independently from their guarded nodes.

Consequences

Benefits

- *Suppression of out-of-sync transmissions.* Actually, without BUS GUARDIAN, a time-triggered communication cannot be considered as being fault-tolerant.

Liabilities

- *Increased system costs.* The usage of bus guardians raises the hardware costs of the whole system.

- *Increased complexity.* Bus guardians add complexity to the system architecture, which affects design and development as well as maintenance. A possible countermeasure is the use of centralized guardians.

Known Uses

ARINC 659 uses a pair of communication handlers called BIUs (Bus Interface Units); each operates as bus guardian of the other. The new TTP version uses the central solution, while previous versions used the individual bus guardian, which was located on the same chip as the guarded communication controller, even sharing the MEDL with it but having its own power supply and clock. Recently, the FlexRay consortium decided not to use BUS GUARDIAN explicitly in the first generation of available hardware and to defer its use to later releases. In SPIDER, bus guardians are separated from nodes and placed in a central hub or star coupler.

Related Patterns

BUS GUARDIANS often apply TIME-TRIGGERED CLOCK SYNCHRONIZATION by themselves to avoid common mode failure with their guarded host. BUS GUARDIAN can be regarded as a temporal variant of OUTPUT GUARD [Saridakis2003].

Temporal Application Decoupling

Also known as: Application/Communication Buffer

Context

Distributed (embedded) hard real-time systems, where Prescheduled Periodic Transmission is applied to guarantee that requested transmission times are not violated.

Problem

How can application tasks adhere to the strict transmission schedule?

While such a periodic transmission provides a group of significant benefits for communication in dependable hard real-time systems, it lays a severe burden on the application tasks executed on the nodes of the distributed system: They have both to send and receive at precise points in time. Being a bit too early or too late (typically counted in microseconds or even nanoseconds) for the corresponding I/O-operation, a task will definitely miss its time slot.

One could think of performing each I/O-dependent task in its own thread, which is suspended at the corresponding position and reactivated when the appropriate operation has to be performed. This approach, however, requires a potentially large number of threads, which may be difficult, if not impossible, to realize in the main application area of the Triple-T patterns, namely, embedded systems. It may also lead to poor CPU utilization and therefore increased risk of deadline violation. Furthermore, it may introduce some level of indeterminism, which is undesirable in hard real-time applications.

Example

Consider our brake-by-wire application, with a couple of sensors and actuators. Each of them must be read (sensors) or written (actuators) at a specific point in time. Coordinating these timing constraints with those of the transmission schedule would be very challenging for the application developer.

Solution

Decouple the production and processing of data to be transmitted from the actual transmission by providing a buffer into which application tasks put the data to be transmitted as soon as they are available, and in which received data are stored for consumption by the application tasks. Further, a system task (with highest priority), which is activated according to the transmission schedule, sends data when the corresponding time slots are encountered and puts received data relevant for the application tasks on its node into the buffer.

Therefore, this pattern has the following participants (see Figure 5–11):

- The "application task" is responsible for producing and putting data into the buffer to be transmitted *before* the corresponding time slot within the current period arrives. Likewise, it is responsible to read data from the buffer *after* they have been received.

- The "communication handler" adheres strictly to the periodic transmission schedule. According to the schedule, it puts data to be sent from the buffer to the bus as it takes data received from the bus into it.

Note that for data transmitted in time-triggered mode, no queuing is necessary, because according to the system state semantics of such data, every new value written to the buffer overwrites the previous value of the same (state) variable. This, however, is not necessarily true for information transmitted in time slots reserved for event-triggered data. Here, application tasks have to read received information before it is overwritten in the next period.

Figure 5–12 shows an example of buffer access during a schedule period.

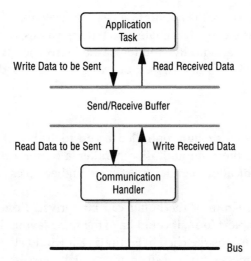

Figure 5–11   *Temporal Application Decoupling structure*

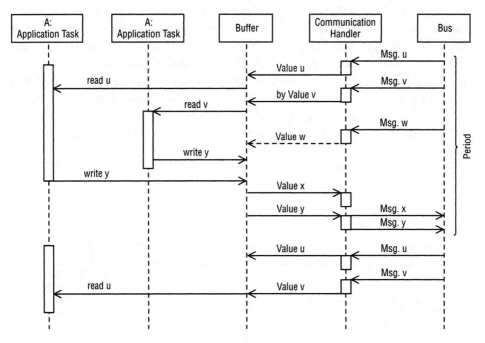

Figure 5–12   *Example sequence diagram for Temporal Application Decoupling*

The activation boxes of the application tasks indicate that these do not necessarily start with reading and terminate with writing values, and are not necessarily executed strictly periodically. And the dashed arrow for "value w" indicates that data not needed on local host may, but need not, be placed in the buffer.

Implementation

To allow simultaneous, though controlled, access to the buffer from both the application tasks and the communication handler, a dual-ported RAM could be used. The communication handler must have higher access priority than any application task.

The size and structure of the buffer can be derived from the transmission schedule. In its simplest form, it could have the same layout. For example, with respect to the schedule as sketched in Figure 5–4, it would start with an entry for message a, one for message b, and so on, thus making no distinction between entries for sending and receiving, respectively. Of course, no space is needed for messages received from other nodes, which are not relevant for application tasks on the local node. For them, no space needs to be reserved in the buffer.

Depending on the specific application, it may be necessary to ensure that application tasks update their output fields in the buffer every time these fields have been sent, as they read and process their input fields every time these have been received. Typically, tasks have to write data to the buffer (and read data from it) within the same period they are transmitted. This can be checked by setting a flag for each buffer entry when it is written and resetting it when it is read. Detecting a flag in the wrong state by the communication handler when accessing the corresponding buffer entry indicates a late application task, which can be interpreted as a deadline violation and which may trigger appropriate fault handling.

If executing the communication handler on the same CPU as the application tasks is too risky, it may be installed on another CPU.

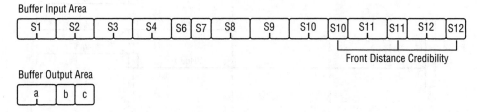

Figure 5–13 *Layout of Temporal Application Decoupling buffer of EMB PNs*

In Figure 5–13, the same message identifiers are used as in Figure 5–5, with the exception that PN output values are simply named "a"…"c", because processing nodes do not care about the output of their replicas. For simplification, single bit values are represented by one byte in the buffer.

Consequences

Benefits

- *Simplification of application task scheduling.* Equation constraints (i.e., "*operation x of task A has to be performed at time t*"), where "x" denotes sending or receiving data, are replaced by range constraints ("*operation y of task A has to be performed between t0 and t1*"), where "y" denotes writing data to the buffer or reading data from it, respectively.

- *Better CPU utilization.* Since there is more freedom for placing tasks along the time line, a more compact scheduling is usually possible.

- *Simple task monitoring.* The read/write flags as mentioned in the Implementation section can be used to easily detect deadline violations of application tasks.

Liabilities

- *Synchronized access on buffer needed.* Race conditions have to be avoided where some buffer value is changed from one side while the other is reading it. If the hardware of the buffer memory does not directly support synchronized access, appropriate software mechanisms are not trivial.

- *Memory waste.* The decoupling is done by memory cells (e.g., DPRAM). If memory is expensive, as is usually the case for embedded systems, it must be kept as small as possible. FlexRay and TTCAN address this problem by storing only messages that are processed at this node.

Known Uses

In ARINC 659, a so-called "bus interface unit" (BIU) is used to decouple applications from the bus; in FlexRay, "controller host interfaces" (CHI) is used for the same purpose; and TTP calls the communication handler "communication controller" and the buffer "communication network interface" (CNI). In TTCAN, a "Module Interface" is used for accessing Message RAM and Trigger Memory.

Related Patterns

The HALF-SYNC/HALF-ASYNC architectural pattern [Schmidt+2000] resembles TEMPORAL APPLICATION DECOUPLING in that it separates synchronous from asynchronous processing layers. In contrast to HALF-SYNC/HALF-ASYNC, however, in TEMPORAL APPLICATION DECOUPLING the layering appears to be reverted. The lower layer (that is, the communication system) is synchronous. In addition, TEMPORAL APPLICATION DECOUPLING does not use a queuing mechanism; instead, missing deadlines by the tasks within the upper, asynchronous layer is considered as failure.

If tasks and communication handler are realized as threads within the same computing environment, the "synchronization patterns" (e.g., THREAD-SAFE INTERFACE) as described in [Schmidt+2000] can be used for controlling buffer access.

Acknowledgments

We offer our gratitude to our EuroPLoP'04 shepherd, Michael J. Pont. He helped us to add details that transformed this chapter from being understandable mainly by people already familiar with the topic into its current shape, which we hope is helpful to all who are interested in reliable communication in hard real-time systems.

We'd also like to express our gratitude to Arno Haase, Kevlin Henney, Kaspar von Gunten, Frank Buschmann, Juha Pärssinen, Andreas Rüping, Aimilia Tsanavari, Paris Avgeriou, and Asa MacWilliams, who workshopped this chapter at the EuroPLoP'04 conference in a very constructive and encouraging way.

Appendix

Terminology

- *Component*: A component is an encapsulated building block that is of use when building a large system. Components are characterized by their interfaces with respect to composability and are described by their data properties and their temporal properties [Kopetz1997].

- *Fail silent*: If a system either produces correct results or no results at all, that is, it is quiet when it cannot deliver correct service, it is fail-silent [Kopetz1997].

- *Fault/error/failure*: A failure is an event that denotes a deviation between the actual service and the specified service, caused by an error. An error is an unintended incorrect internal state of a computer system. The cause of an error and therefore the indirect cause of a failure, is a fault [Kopetz1997].

- *Fault hypothesis*. Fundamental assumption about the fault-tolerant behavior of a system. One that is commonly used is the "single fault hypothesis," which holds that a system must continue to operate correctly as long as no more than one of its components fail.

- *FCU*: An FCU (fault containment unit) can fail in an arbitrary failure mode without affecting the proper operation of the components not affected by the fault [Kopetz 2003].

- *FTU*: An FTU (fault-tolerant unit) is an abstraction that is introduced for implementing fault tolerance by active replication. An FTU consists of a set of replicated units that produce replica determinate result messages, that is, the same results at the sufficiently same points in time [Kopetz1997].

- *Hard real-time*: A real-time system must react to stimuli from the controlled object within time intervals dictated by its environment. If a catastrophe could result if the deadline is missed, the deadline is called hard [Kopetz1997].

- *Jitter*: A measure for variability of processing or communication actions, for example, the difference between maximum and minimum durations of a certain kind of action, or the variance of arrival times. Jitter has to be distinguished from delay: a transmission system with high but constant delay has no jitter.

- *Node*: A node is a self-contained computer with its own hardware and software, which performs a set of well-defined functions within the distributed system [Kopetz1997].

- *NP-hard/NP-complete*: The complexity class of decision problems that are intrinsically harder than those that can be solved by a nondeterministic Turing machine in polynomial time. When a decision version of a combinatorial optimization problem is proven to belong to the class of NP-complete problems, which includes well-known problems such as satisfiability, travelling salesman, the bin packing problem, and so forth, then the optimization version is NP-hard (e.g., www.nist.gov/dads/HTML/nphard.html).

- *Periodic/sporadic/a-periodic/ (task)*: A periodic task has many iterations, and there is a fixed period between two consecutive releases of the same task. The request time of a sporadic task is not known a priori, and there is a minimum separation between any two requests of a sporadic task. If there is no constraint on the request times of task activations, the task is called a-periodic [Cheng2002][Kopetz1997].

- *Task*: A task is the execution of a sequential program. It starts with the reading of the input data and the internal state, and terminates with the production of the results and updating the internal state [Kopetz1997].

- *TDMA*: Time Division Multiple Access is a distributed static medium access strategy where the right to transmit a frame is controlled by the progression of real time. To every node that has to transmit data, at least one sending slot is assigned, where it transmits one data frame. If there are no data to send, an empty frame is transmitted [Kopetz1997].

- *Validity (time) span*: The information content, valid at time of updating the internal state, stays valid for the amount of time defined by the validity span [Poledna+2001].

- *Worst Case Execution Time (WCET)*: The maximum time some task or processing step may need to execute to completion [Kopetz1997].

Known Uses

The patterns described in this chapter have been found in a number of bus architectures for safety-critical real-time systems, which are briefly outlined in this section. See [Rushby2001] for more details.

ARINC 659 (SAFEbus)

The standard ARINC 659 [ARINC1993] was developed by Honeywell under the name SAFEbus for the Boeing 777, where it serves as Airplane Information Management System (AIMS). It is presumably the most expensive (and mature) time-triggered bus architecture, because not only are all bus interfaces duplicated per node, but the bus itself is quad-redundant, and the whole AIMS is duplicated.

TTP

TTP (Time-Triggered Protocol) realizes the time-triggered architecture (TTA), which has been developed for about 20 years by Kopetz and colleagues at the Technical University of Vienna [Kopetz1994], [Poledna+2001]. Although only the interconnect bus is duplicated, it offers a degree of dependability not much lower than that of ARINC 659, due to a number of clever algorithms—where fundamental ones like the clock synchronization have been formally verified—and the possibility to use node and task replicas in a well supported manner. Applications can be found in avionics, the automotive industry, and special vehicles. At present, it supports transmission rates up to 25 Mbit/s.

FlexRay

FlexRay has been developed by a consortium that includes BMW, Daimler-Chrysler, Motorola, and Philips. It can be regarded as a combination of TTP and

Byteflight (www.byteflight.com), which provides up to 10 Mbit/s transmission rates, message priorities that ensure deterministic behavior for high-priority messages, and the possibility of mixing synchronous and asynchronous transmission.

In FlexRay, the synchronous data transmission enables time triggered communication to meet the requirement of dependable systems, while asynchronous transmission allows each node to use the full bandwidth for event-driven communications. With the first versions of FlexRay controllers, the FlexRay consortium intends to provide somewhat less safety and fault-tolerance than TTP to achieve lower costs and higher flexibility. It primarily targets the automotive domain; first hardware components are already available.

TTCAN

The TTCAN (time-triggered communication on CAN) protocol is based on CAN. It provides a mechanism to schedule CAN messages as time-triggered and as event-triggered. TTCAN is based on the CAN data link layer protocol and does not infringe it at all [Zeltwanger2004]. The main focus of TTCAN is on substituting a CAN bus on segments in a car, where time-triggered communication is needed and CAN has already been deployed for years (e.g., power-train). TTCAN provides transmission rates up to 1Mbit/s [Führer+2000].

Spider

Spider is a "scalable processor-independent design for electromagnetic resilience" (SPIDER) that has been developed by Miner and colleagues at the NASA Langley Research Center [Miner2000]. Serving primarily as research platform for recovery strategies for faults caused by radiation-induced high-intensity radiated fields and electromagnetic interference (HIRM/EMI), Spider supports several bus configurations like bus, star, or central ring. It uses a time-triggered protocol only.

Cost Comparison

Although this chapter does not primarily focus on cost issues, it may be of interest to get a rough impression of what has to be paid for a certain level of dependability. Since, however, it is almost impossible to get real cost figures from providers or implementers, only a relative estimation of the deployment costs of known systems can be given: CAN (<)< TTCAN < FlexRay < TTP < SAFEbus. Since Spider is primarily a research platform, is has not been considered in that relation. This means that any of the techniques introduced is (considerably) more expensive than the commonly used CAN-bus [Bosch1991], which also shows the lowest level of dependability.

References

[Adams+1996] M. Adams, J. O. Coplien, R. Gamoke, R. Hanmer, F. Keeve, and K. Nicodemus. "Fault-Tolerant Telecommunication System Patterns." In J. Vlissides, J. O. Coplien, and N. L. Kerth (eds.), *Pattern Languages of Program Design 2*, pp. 549–562, Reading, MA: Addison-Wesley, 1996.

[ARINC1993] Aeronautical Radio, Inc. "ARINC Specification 659: Backplane Data Bus." Annapolis, MD: Airlines Electronic Engineering Committee, 1993.

[Bosch1991] Robert Bosch Gmbh. *CAN Specification, Version 2.0.* Stuttgart, Germany, 1991.

[Cheng2002] A. M. K. Cheng. "Real-Time Systems–Scheduling, Analysis, and Verification." Hoboken, NJ: Wiley & Sons, 2002.

[Driscoll+2003] K. Driscoll, B. Hall, H. Sivenkrona, and P. Zumsteg. "Byzantine Fault Tolerance, from Theory to Reality." In *Proceedings of SAFECOMP 2003.* Edinburgh, UK: 2003. *Lecture Notes in Computer Science*, vol. 2788, pp. 235–248. Berlin: Springer-Verlag, 2003.

[Douglass2003] B. P. Douglass. *Real-Time Design Patterns: Robust Scalable Architecture for Real-Time Systems.* Boston: Addison-Wesley, 2003.

[Hanmer+1999] R. Hanmer and G. Stymfal. "An Input and Output Pattern Language: Lessons From Telecommunications." In N. B. Harrison, B. Foote, and H. Rohnert (eds.), *Pattern Languages of Program Design 4*, pp. 503–538, Reading, MA: Addison-Wesley, 1999.

[Führer+2000] Th. Führer, B. Müller, W. Dieterle, F. Hartwich, R. Hugel, and M. Walther. "Time Triggered Communication on CAN (Time Triggered CAN–TTCAN)." In *Proceedings of 7th International CAN Conference 2000*, Amsterdam, Oct. 2000.

[Kopetz+1994] H. Kopetz and G. Grünsteidl. "TTP–A Protocol For Fault-Tolerant Real-Time Systems." *IEEE Computer*, 27(1), pp. 14–23, Jan. 1994.

[Kopetz1997] H. Kopetz. *Real-Time Systems–Design Principles for Distributed Embedded Applications.* Norwell, MA: Kluwer Academic Publishers, 1997.

[Kopetz2003] H. Kopetz. "Time Triggered Architecture." *ERCIM News*, 52, pp. 24–25, Jan. 2003.

[Miner2000] P. S. Miner. "Analysis of the Spider Fault-Tolerance Protocols." In C. M. Holloway (ed.), *Proceedings of LFM 2000: 5th NASA Langley Formal Methods Workshop*, Hampton, VA, June 2000.

[Poledna+2001] S. Poledna, W. Ettlmayr, and M. Novak. "Communication Bus for Automotive Applications." In *Proceedings of the 27th European Solid-State Circuits Conference*, Villach, Austria, Sep. 2001.

[Pont2001] M. J. Pont. *Patterns for Time-Triggered Embedded Systems–Building Reliable Applications with the 8051 Family of Microcontrollers.* Boston: Addison-Wesley, 2001.

[Rushby2001] J. Rushby. "A Comparison of Bus Architectures for Safety-Critical Embedded Systems." *CSL Technical Report*, SRI International, Sept. 2001.

[Saridakis2002] T. Saridakis. "A System of Patterns for Fault Tolerance." In A. O'Callaghan, J. Eckstein, and Ch. Schwanninger (eds.), *Proceedings of the 7th EuroPLoP*, pp. 535–582. Irsee, Germany: 2002; Konstanz, Germany: UVK, 2003.

[Saridakis2003] T. Saridakis. "Design Patterns for Fault Containment." In K. Hennley and D. Schütz (eds.), *Proceedings of the 8th EuroPLoP*, pp. 493–516. Irsee, Germany, June 2003; Konstanz, Germany: UVK, 2004.

[Schmidt+2000] D. C. Schmidt, M. Stal, H. Rohnert, and F. Buschmann. *Pattern-Oriented Software Architecture, vol. 2: Patterns for Concurrent and Networked Objects (POSA2).* Chichester, UK: Wiley & Sons, 2000.

[Welch+1988] J. L. Welch and N. Lynch. "A new fault-tolerant algorithm for clock synchronization." *Information and Computation*, 77(1), pp. 1–36, April 1988.

[Zeltwanger2004] H. Zeltwanger. "Time-Triggered Communication on CAN." In *Proceedings of Embedded World 2004 Conference*, pp. 229–233. Nürnberg, Germany, Feb. 2004.

CHAPTER 6

Real Time and Resource Overload Language

Robert S. Hanmer

Introduction

Many real-world computing systems are "reactive." They react to stimuli as it arrives. Examples of real-world reactive systems include: time-sharing computing systems, telephone switches, servers in client-server architectures, Web servers, online transaction systems, avionics systems, and so on. In fact, many people believe "that most real-time systems are reactive in nature" [Jagadeesan+1995].

When the load on a reactive computing system is light, most systems will have no difficulty processing all the stimuli they receive. This stimuli represents work that must be performed by the system. As the quantity of stimuli received increases, the workload increases. If the quantity of stimuli continues to increase, it will eventually reach the amount where even well-designed systems will start failing to handle the work adequately (see Figure 6–1). They will begin to miss Quality of Service requirements, scheduling constraints, or user expectations. In these cases, only the systems that were designed to be able to handle this excessive amount of stimulation/workload will be able to succeed.

The patterns in this chapter provide proven techniques that can move a well-designed system into the realm of exceptional capabilities. These Real Time and Resource Overload patterns describe solutions to typical problems in the creation of a system that can robustly handle overload situations that result from either a shortage of real time for processing or a shortage in some essential resource. They work with patterns published previously, both by this author and others to form a pattern language to address this topic.

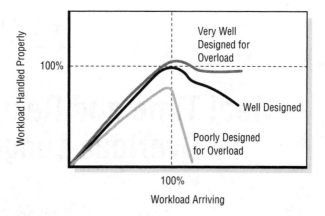

Figure 6–1 *Quality of design influences performance*

The public switched telephone network (PSTN) provides a ready source of examples to illustrate the behavior that these patterns engender in their systems. An example of a period with low stimuli (low "traffic") is the middle of the night, when most people are asleep and hence not making telephone calls. The middle of a typical workday provides an example of a period in the telephone network where there is a higher amount of traffic but one that should be manageable by most systems. Consider these two examples of periods of high traffic when the workload taxes even the well-designed systems: a natural disaster occurs and everyone telephones the affected region to determine if their friends and family are okay; tickets for the most sought-after event (soccer game, rock concert, etc.) go on sale only via the telephone. Because these examples are easy for most readers to understand, and since these patterns were most directly mined from telecommunications systems, telecom examples will be used throughout this chapter.

The problem arises during system design. For what workload should the reactive system be designed? For the idle periods when only a small level of stimuli is arriving, for example, no one is telephoning? For the extremely busy times when the concert tickets are on sale? Or for a normal workday? Designing for the idle periods will be the most inexpensive—until the costs of failing to handle the busier periods is considered. Designing for the periods of highest workload (even if they can be predicted effectively) is wasteful, because the system will be over-engineered for the average case of the business day. The most effective way has proven to be designing for the average business day with provisions to handle the excess traffic encountered in the case of abnormal events. When the excess stimulation is being received, a poorly designed system might crash. A well-designed system, that makes use of these patterns, will continue to process the workload that it is given (or a major part of it), and after the workload returns to normal the system will also return to normal operation automatically.

The patterns of Real Time and Resource Overload describe how to design for these periods of excessive workload caused by abnormal levels of stimuli. They are presented as a small language of patterns that work together to solve the problem of handing levels of stimulation in excess of the normal design levels.

A "pattern language" is a collection of patterns that work together to solve a problem that is larger than any of the patterns can solve individually [Hammer+2004]. The pattern map, Figure 6–2, shows the relationships among the patterns graphically. Looking at this chart you can see particular patterns that are of the most interest to the design problem that you are addressing, and what patterns are most closely related to the resolution of that problem. Following the language map is a description, in words, of the relationships among the patterns.

Not all of the patterns in this pattern language are presented in this chapter. In addition to helping to design better reactive systems, a purpose of this language is to show the effectiveness of merging published collections of patterns into one language.

In Chapter 35 in *Pattern Language of Program Design 2*, Gerard Meszaros wrote: "This language refers to a number of patterns that are known to exist but have not yet (to my knowledge) been documented. I invite others to "flesh out" these patterns based on their own experience, and perhaps submit the expanded forms for discussion at future PLoP conferences." [Meszaros1996] That is exactly what this chapter does.

Because the reader might not have the other patterns immediately at their fingertips, thumbnail sketches of the patterns are presented at the end of this chapter. In these thumbnails, you will see a brief synopsis of the pattern as well as a reference to where you can find the complete pattern text.

Language Map

Figure 6–2 shows patterns that enhance the solutions of other patterns, resolve previously unresolved forces in a pattern, or take advantage of an earlier pattern to provide some new system capability. For example, FINISH WORK IN PROGRESS (13)[1] refines the pattern OVERLOAD EMPIRES (1), helping to solve unresolved forces or new problems that OVERLOAD EMPIRES (1) introduced.

---

1. Either an internal reference number contained within parenthesis, or a reference to a published paper, will follow all the patterns. Internal reference numbers one through eight refer to patterns contained within this chapter. Internal references greater than eight refer to patterns that are part of this language but are not presented in their entirety here. They are thumbnailed at the end.

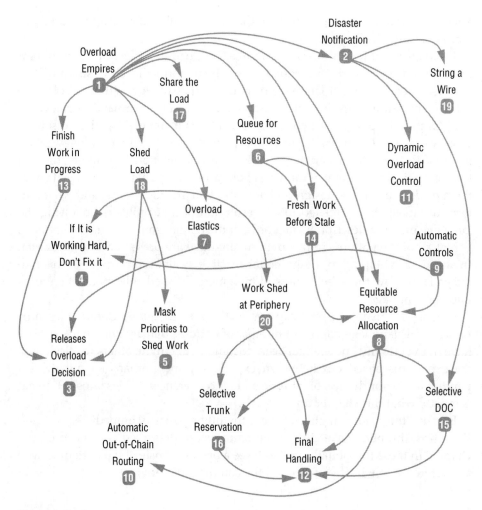

Figure 6–2 *Language map*

Language Context

The patterns within this language are intended to gracefully handle excess stimuli that results in a workload that exceeds the amount of available resources. The resource might be processor CPU time, or it might be a tangible resource such as memory or a special piece of hardware. By gracefully handling whatever traffic arrives at the system, the Quality of Service standards can best be achieved.

When a system is intended to handle errors autonomously, it must first decide if a given system state is due to the manifestation of a fault[2], or an excess of stimuli. This requires the System Integrity Control (SICO FIRST AND ALWAYS) [Adams+1996] to evaluate and determine global system status. If the Integrity Controller decides that it is indeed a fault situation, fault-handling patterns, such as those in [Adams+1996], are to be applied. If an overload is present, responses can be grouped into two broad categories: processor and resource. There will be times when both a real-time and a resource overload will occur simultaneously. Many techniques apply to only one of these categories, so a mechanism is needed to resolve the question of which OVERLOAD EMPIRE (1) is overloaded.

To handle a real-time overload situation, the system should attempt to FINISH WORK IN PROGRESS (13) to prevent the time spent switching between tasks from exceeding the amount of time spent processing tasks. When events arrive that require tangible resources, they can be QUEUED FOR THE RESOURCE (6). Recent requests for service should take precedence over those that have been in the queue longer, that is, complete FRESH WORK BEFORE STALE (14). This is especially important when dealing with human behavior.

If the system has idle resources reserved for fault handling, such as spare processors, or if the system has adjunct processors that can help with certain tasks, a real-time overload can be handled by SHARING THE LOAD (18) among processors. System architecture sometimes precludes this, however. In these cases, the system must be designed to SHED LOAD (17) that cannot be handled.

In fault-tolerant systems, the system generally has many maintenance tasks executing simultaneously. If the system is performing well, and is still overloaded, these tasks can be deferred. In other words, IF IT IS WORKING HARD, DON'T FIX IT (4). Resources must be ALLOCATED EQUITABLY (8). One way of doing this is to use predetermined allowable PRIORITY MASKS (5) to select which runable task should be executed.

Work should be shed as close to the edges of the system as possible (WORK SHED AT THE PERIPHERY (20)). The work to bring events into the processors' core is wasted if the work is to be canceled. When requests for service are canceled, a record should be kept for troubleshooting and already allocated resources should be freed by FINAL HANDLING (12) the request.

Existing metrics, such as OVERLOAD ELASTICS (7), can be used to decide the extent of a processor CPU time overload. The system architects must decide what

---

2. A "fault" is a deviation from correctness. When a fault is encountered in program execution, an "error" occurs, which is incorrect result. The effect on the system's user is a "failure."

the system should do when attempts to shed work are unsuccessful. One approach to deal with this is found in the pattern OVERLOAD OUT-OF-CONTROL (3): If all other attempts to reduce the level of stimuli are unsuccessful, cease processing all new stimuli until the situation improves and real time becomes available. This might be difficult for some system architects to implement.

Requests for tangible resources should be handled in an EQUITABLE MANNER (8). Requests for these resources are controlled through either protective or expansive AUTOMATIC CONTROLS (9). Expansive controls allow the use of resources that are not normally available for use, such as AUTOMATIC OUT-OF-CHAIN ROUTING (10). Protective controls restrict access in order to protect the system. Examples of these are SELECTIVE TRUNK RESERVATION (16), DYNAMIC OVERLOAD CONTROL (11), and SELECTIVE DYNAMIC OVERLOAD CONTROL (15). Whenever the system cancels and ignores a stimulus, FINAL HANDLING (12) should be performed on the stimuli to report status and to aid in diagnosing problems.

1. OVERLOAD EMPIRES

… The situation within the system has been analyzed and the decision has been made that it is not an error caused by faulty hardware or software. Overload situations occur when the system loses the resources necessary to handle its workload efficiently. This might be due to internal problems such as memory leaks or excessive maintenance work requests that are really faults within the system and should be handled through the fault recovery system (SICO FIRST AND ALWAYS [Adams+1996]). When external systems send too many requests for service too quickly, the system must handle as many as possible and then degrade as smoothly and as little as possible.

How should situations of overload be handled?

Too many requests for service can be taxing on a system in a number of ways:

- Memory: More memory than the system has available might be required to store the requests.
- Peripheral equipment: The requests might require the use of tangible peripheral resources that are already in use.
- Processor CPU time: Processing the requests might take more time than the system has.

There are a variety of techniques designed to address these resource overloads. Some, such as queuing for memory resources, work for some types of requests but not others. Some techniques will work for all three. Trying to manage one type of overload with a mechanism designed for another type of overload might have devastating results.

Therefore:

Administer multiple OVERLOAD EMPIRES, one for managed resources like peripheral equipment (such as telephone trunks and lines), another for memory, and yet another for processor CPU time. Avoid grouping all of the possibilities together, because they will only rarely work well for overloads in other empires (see Figure 6–3).

An effective technique to deal with overloads of the tangible variety is to QUEUE FOR RESOURCES (6). EQUITABLE RESOURCE ALLOCATION (8) discusses a way to divide up the tangible resources such as memory and peripheral equipment.

A technique similar to QUEUING FOR RESOURCES (8) that works for the intangible of CPU cycles is FRESH WORK BEFORE STALE (14). ENABLING THE SYSTEM TO SHARE LOAD (17) or to SHED LOAD (18) also helps with CPU time.

Resource Overload   Processor Overload   Memory Overload
Tools   Tools   Tools

Figure 6–3 *Overload Empires*

In order to know whether we are in processor or resource overload, there has to be some way of measuring the overload. OVERLOAD ELASTICS (7) discusses metrics that should be used to evaluate overloads.

Consumer/user behavior must be considered in deciding how to deal with an excess amount of work. FRESH WORK BEFORE STALE (14) and FINISH WORK IN PROGRESS (13) both discuss a way of dealing with too much work while considering the user's behavior.

In a network of peers, strategies can be designed to allow one peer to Notify (2) its neighbors that it is in overload and seek assistance in handling the traffic or in reducing the load from its peers. ...

2. DISASTER NOTIFICATION

... The system is in trouble. The trouble might be the result of an excess of requests for service from external sources, or it might be caused by the handling of errors. In either case, the system is dealing with an excessive demand for some kind of resources: CPU time, tangible resources, or memory.

Overloads happen when too many requests for service arrive too fast. What can a single system do to slow down the influx of requests?

Within a network of systems, what happens in one system will influence what happens in the others. "Regenerative switching delays, if left uncontrolled, can quickly spread throughout the network, causing the type of decline in carried load shown in [Figure 6–4]." [Green+1977]

You can resolve much of the internal inefficiency through rigorous testing and good design practices and algorithms. These are things done before the system is placed into service.

External stimuli causes system overloads during execution. By definition, nothing internal can be done when the system's peers are sending too much traffic to an overloaded system, since the stimuli are "external." But the peers can help if they are informed that they are sending too much information.

Therefore:

Call for help! Institute a method of communication between systems to help throttle the workload at systems in overload (see Figure 6–5). If a system receives such a signal, it should assist by reducing the amount of work being sent to the troubled system.

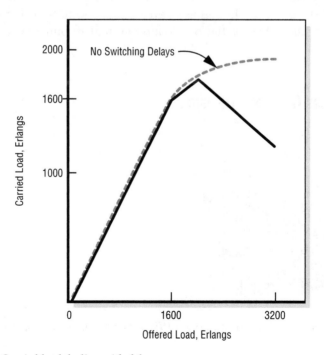

Figure 6–4 *Carried load decline with delays*

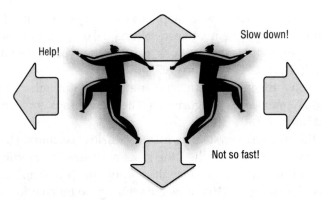

Help!

Slow down!

Not so fast!

Figure 6–5 *Calling for help*

DYNAMIC OVERLOAD CONTROL (11) and SELECTIVE DYNAMIC OVERLOAD CONTROL (15) are examples of such mechanisms for different types of overload responses.

STRING A WIRE (19) from the Telecommunications Input Output Language [Hanmer+2000] describes how these signals can be sent. By using a fixed permanent connection, few of the overloaded system resources will be used to send the signal. …

3. REASSESS OVERLOAD DECISION[3]

… The system is attempting to FINISH WORK IN PROGRESS (13) as well as to SHED LOAD (18).

---

3. Strategy alluded to in [Green+1977, p. 1177]

What should the system do when the usual load reduction techniques are not working to diminish the workload?

What happens if load keeps increasing in spite of all attempts to slow the system down (see Figure 6–6)?

The system is well engineered so that work shedding keeps the system from crashing. The mechanisms instituted to SHED LOAD (18) are working, yet the influx of new requests or the compounding of internal inefficiencies are not producing the desired reduction in workload. These mechanisms create a negative feedback loop that should keep load from getting out of hand.

Something's wrong if we haven't had any new requests for service in a long time. The system is designed to perform some work, such as processing telephone calls. If that is skipped for too long a period of time, it doesn't make any money for its owner.

A major goal of the overload handling mechanisms is to preserve system sanity[4] so that when the overload period is ended, the system can handle the routine level of traffic.

If feedback isn't enough to bring the system out of saturation, then the overload may be coming from a source other than traffic.

For example, when there's congestion (such as communications bandwidth), the overload handler will make a note that this facility type is congested, and

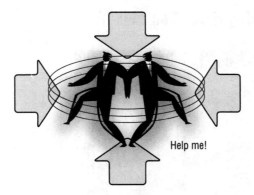

Help me!

Figure 6–6 *Work that keeps coming*

---

4. Sanity as it is used here refers to the system executing as designed with a clear task or set of tasks in control of the Program Counter in some manner intended by the system's developers.

Desired Effects?

Figure 6–7 *Reexamining prior decisions*

the handler doesn't do anything. It checks again some time later; if the congestion is still there, it applies an overload control or might trigger fault handling.

Therefore:

Provide the ability for the system to reexamine its decision that this is an overload instead of an error (see Figure 6–7). This might mean that the system decides that it is not an overload but really an error.

Unless reexamination is possible, the system can get further and further into trouble by following the wrong path. The same Integrity Controller introduced by SICO FIRST AND ALWAYS [Adams+1996] can make the decisions needed to prevent following this wrong path.

4. If it is Working Hard, Don't Fix it[5]

---

5. Strategy alluded to in [Green+1977, p. 1177]

... More work is arriving than the system can handle. The system is SHEDDING LOAD (18) and thus passing up revenue opportunities because it must be able to actually complete some work in order to realize the revenue. The system is always performing some overhead work to keep the system well maintained and fault-tolerant.

What work should be shed?

There aren't enough CPU resources both to handle the capacity and to continue the overhead work. This overhead includes the auditing and maintenance functions that keep the system fault-tolerant. It might be skipping some of its main application work already due to congestion. The choice is to reduce even more the revenue-producing work or to restrict some of the activities that guarantee the system's fault tolerance.

The system has very stringent availability requirements, which is why a system of audits, defensive checks, and integrity monitors must be kept in place. These parts of the system ensure that the system is working at its peak efficiency and detect errors in order to contain and correct them.

But if we're in traffic-induced overload, the peripheral hardware must be working and the software must be working, since we're doing work—so let's defer the tasks that come into play when we're *not* working properly. These deferrable items do work that isn't critical to the primary application. If it works, don't check if it works—release the time so that we can concentrate on the primary money-making aspects of operation.

Therefore:

Defer maintenance work. Use the system's task scheduler to implement this strategy. If the system is tending toward overload, chances are that the periphery and software are working—if it were otherwise, where would all that work be coming from (see Figure 6–8)?

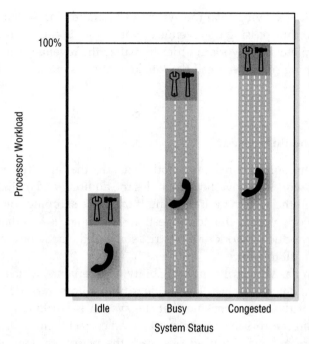

Figure 6–8 *Congestion squeezes maintenance*

There's an outside chance that the system just *seems* like it's in overload, that instead it may actually be reacting to errors. In that case, employ REASSESS OVERLOAD DECISION (3). REASSESS OVERLOAD DECISION (3) also addresses when this strategy is not working sufficiently and the system isn't recovering from the overload. MASK PRIORITIES TO SHED WORK (5) discusses one way that this pattern can be implemented.

Everything that the system does is important to someone. But not everything is directly related to the primary purpose of the system. Tasks should not be deferred forever. MASK PRIORITIES TO SHED WORK (5) provides an equitable way to do this. ...

5. MASK PRIORITIES TO SHED WORK

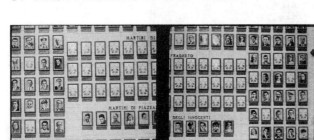

… You want to SHED LOAD (18), and in particular, you are implementing IF IT IS WORKING HARD DON'T FIX IT (4).

How do you spread out the workload under overload without skewing priorities?

There are many ways to select certain tasks to defer temporarily. Some involve development time decisions of what is more important. Some involve execution time decisions, as in IF IT IS WORKING HARD DON'T FIX IT (4). The best way is something that is fair.

All the work that the system performs is important; nothing should be totally eliminated during overload. Requirements upon execution frequency may be stretched, but eventually all tasks need to be scheduled.

If we were to alternate tasks that normally are all executed, and execute one-half this time and the other half on the next, every task would be executed eventually. The time period between successive task executions would be increased, but during periods of overload, everything is running more slowly, so this is acceptable. The time between subsequent iterations with this alternation might be less than if nothing was done.

One way of implementing this is through the use of bit masks. Every task should have its allowable bit set in at least one of the masks (see Figure 6–9).

Figure 6–9 *Ready task bitmaps*

Tasks that are runable and allowable will be executed. Some tasks that are "more" important might have bits set in several masks so that they get entered more frequently.

Sometimes there are interactions between multiple tasks that will dictate that certain of them must be executed together (or without certain others intervening).

Therefore:

Use bit masks to overlay the runable task words. Every scheduling loop, overload toggles between several of these "allowable" masks. By alternating allowable masks (see Figure 6–10), and making sure that every task appears in the masks, every task will eventually get scheduled.

When several tasks interact strongly and the mask mechanism might not guarantee correctness, the general scheduler and its mask might not be the appropriate scheduling technique.

Good engineering judgment is required to determine how tasks should be sorted onto the different masks.

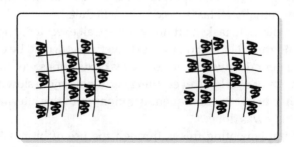

Figure 6–10 *Alternating masks*

6. QUEUE FOR RESOURCES[6]

... The system is overloaded, and not in the midst of failure processing. Too many requests for tangible services such as memory or peripheral equipment are being received. (OVERLOAD EMPIRES (1)).

What should be done with requests for tangible resources that cannot be handled at the moment?

The system is receiving too many stimuli for the moment, but in general can handle the excess requests for service.

You could throw up your hands and reject all requests that can't be handled as they appear. This supports the pattern FRESH WORK BEFORE STALE (14). But it results in work that, if deferred for only a short period, might be handled.

If you can store the work in a queue for later processing, then the work might complete eventually. The risks of doing this are that the queue might get longer than can be effectively managed. There is also the risk that the work won't need to be done when the task is finally ready.

Therefore:

Store requests for service that cannot be handled immediately in a queue. Give the queue a finite length to improve the likelihood that the request is still necessary when it reaches the head of the line (see Figure 6–11).

---

6. Reference: [Wake+1996]

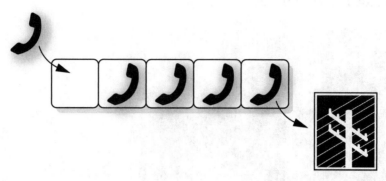

Figure 6–11 *Queue requests*

❖ ❖ ❖

The queue should use a LIFO strategy (as in FRESH WORK BEFORE STALE (4)) to govern insertion and removal from the queue. This will help people think that they are receiving good service. Allocation of resources under the guidance of EQUITABLE ALLOCATION (8) should recognize both the requests that have been queued and those that are fresh and have never been queued. ...

7. OVERLOAD ELASTICS[7]

... The problem appears to be one of processor CPU time overload (OVERLOAD EMPIRES (1)). This is an overload of an intangible resource.

---

7. Strategy alluded to in [Cieslek+1977, p. 1116]

How should we judge the severity of too many requests for resources?

Artificial indicators can be created to measure the severity of the overload. This introduces additional overhead work that will be most needed just when the system has the least resources available.

Or already existing indicators can be used. Some indicator such as per cent CPU idle time can be used. This does not increase overhead, since the computation is already routinely done.

The CPU idle time is a metric that system designers include as a measure of workload and its variability.

In some scheduling regimes, such as round robin, there is no idle time by definition. Round robin is used in many real-time systems. Generally, in these cases some sort of existing measurement, similar to idle time, is used to allow the system owners to gauge its performance. In these systems the length of time spent traversing the loop appears quite elastic.

Therefore:

Use an indicator already tied to the resource as an indicator of the system's sanity and overload condition.

Figure 6–12 shows CPU utilization and idle percentages which can be used as a workload indicator.

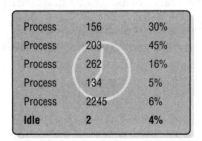

Process	156	30%
Process	203	45%
Process	262	16%
Process	134	5%
Process	2245	6%
Idle	2	4%

Figure 6–12 *Process CPU percentage as indicator*

It is important to periodically REASSESS THE OVERLOAD DECISION (3) by checking the overload indicators. ...

8. Equitable Resource Allocation

… You are trying to handle Fresh Work Before Stale (14) and yet you have many requests Queued For Resources (6). There are distinct types of resources that need to be allocated to requests. The system is capable of instituting Automatic Controls (9).

How should requests for scarce resources be handled?

You could strictly follow Fresh Work Before Stale (14) and only give the newest requests service, even if they are from predominantly one type/class/area. Customers might be paying for a premium service, however, and will not appreciate being lumped into the resource allocation pool with the bargain-rate customers.

There might be a specific resource that is especially overloaded. If requests are allocated based only upon their newness, that is, their position in the queue, then they might end up blocking on this resource anyway.

Another strategy would be to look at all the requests for service, both fresh and queued, and allocate resources equitably to all of them. While this requires additional bookkeeping, work can be directed around extremely specific resource overloads. This helps ensure the greatest common good by providing service to as many requests as possible.

Therefore:

Pool all similar requests and allocate resources to the pools based upon their availability and priority (see Figure 6–13). This allows all types of work to be accomplished even if concentrated overloads from a certain category of type/class/area exist.

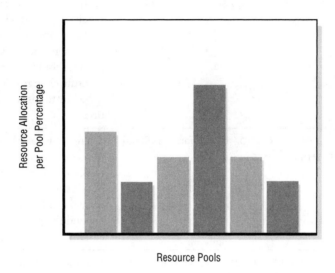

Figure 6–13 *Balance resource allocation*

FINAL HANDLING (12) is required for those requests for service that are abnormally terminated.

SELECTIVE TRUNK RESERVATION (16) can be helpful when the resources needed by the bulk of the overloading requests can be isolated. SELECTIVE DYNAMIC OVERLOAD CONTROL (SELECTIVE DOC) (15) reduces congestion due to traffic flow by providing DISASTER NOTIFICATION (2) to the sources of the traffic. If the flow of traffic is extremely mismatched, then the expansive control of AUTOMATIC OUT-OF-CHAIN ROUTING (10) can help. …

Previously Published Patterns

Internal Reference Number	Pattern	Source	Intent
9	AUTOMATIC CONTROLS	[Hanmer+2000]	Human operators are slow when compared with the speed of the computing system. When conditions dictate, the switch should automatically institute changes to normal behavior to respond to conditions.
10	AUTOMATIC OUT-OF-CHAIN ROUTING	[Hanmer+2000]	There are rules of communications that apply during periods of normal workload. During overloaded periods, automatically use different rules to expand the possibility of successful communication.
11	DYNAMIC OVERLOAD CONTROL	[Hanmer+1999]	Provide mechanism to tell peers to slow down the rate at which they send stimuli.
12	FINAL HANDLING	[Hanmer+2000]	Gracefully remove allocated resource and create records of termination for work that is abnormally terminated. This prevents memory leaks and provides a diagnostic tool.
13	FINISH WORK IN PROGRESS	[Meszaros1996]	Categorize arriving work as either new work or related to something that is already in progress. Give priority to work that continues already in progress work.

Internal Reference Number	Pattern	Source	Intent
14	FRESH WORK BEFORE STALE	[Meszaros1996]	Giving better service to recent requests enables at least some of the requests to get good service. If all requests wait in a QUEUE FOR RESOURCES then none receives good service.
15	SELECTIVE DYNAMIC OVERLOAD CONTROL	[Hanmer+2000]	Tell peers that parts of our system are overloaded, and request that they reduce the rate at which they send stimuli intended for those parts.
16	SELECTIVE TRUNK RESERVATION	[Hanmer+2000]	Give preference to stimuli that is intended for parts of the system that are not currently overloaded. This provides a rule that the WORK SHED AT THE PERIPHERY mechanism can use to select work to allow through.
17	SHARE THE LOAD	[Meszaros1996]	Move some processing to another processor. When deciding what to move, look for things that are clearly partitioned, because this will reduce the amount of synchronization that is required.
18	SHED LOAD	[Meszaros1996]	Throw away some requests for service to offer better service to other requests. Recognize that the system will not be able to process all requests and preemptively shed some, to ensure that the rest can be handled correctly.

(continued)

Internal Reference Number	Pattern	Source	Intent
19	STRING A WIRE	[Hanmer+2000]	Sometimes system state, such as overload, keeps the normal methods of communicating from being sufficient. For these times, provide a system-to-system emergency information channel.
20	WORK SHED AT THE PERIPHERY	[Meszaros1996]	As work proceeds further into the system, more effort is expended on it. To minimize the wasted effort on work that will be shed, discard it where it first enters the system.

Acknowledgments

Mike Adams was a co-author on previous versions of DYNAMIC OVERLOAD CONTROL, EQUITABLE ALLOCATION, OVERLOAD EMPIRES, IF IT'S WORKING HARD, DON'T FIX IT and DISASTER NOTIFICATION.

Karen Hanmer researched the photos that accompany these patterns and scanned several images.

Ward Cunningham was PLoP 2000 shepherd for this language.

Thanks to my PloP2K Writers' Workshop group for their valuable comments. Bill Opdyke, Carlos O'Ryan, Brian Foote, Rossana Andrade, Todd Coram, Brian Marick, Juha Pärssinen, and Terunobu Fujino were members of the group "Network of Learning."

Thanks also to the PLOPD5 editors and reviewers for helping me improve the version of the patterns that you see here.

Image Credits

Images introducing patterns:

OVERLOAD EMPIRES photo by James H. Pickerell, IF IT IS WORKING HARD, DON'T FIX IT photos by Flip Schulke, and QUEUE FOR RESOURCES are all used courtesy of the U.S. National Archives and Records Administration.

EQUITABLE RESOURCE ALLOCATION, photo by Jack Delano; and DISASTER NOTIFI-
CATION by Theodor Horydczak both used courtesy of The Library of Congress.

REASSESS OVERLOAD DECISION and OVERLOAD ELASTICS photographs by Karen
Hanmer.

MASK PRIORITIES TO SHED WORK *"Italian Diptych 5"* copyright © 1997 Steve
Harp.

Other images

Figure 6–4, in DISASTER NOTIFICATION, is taken from [Green+1977] and is re-
printed with permission of Lucent Technologies Inc./Bell Labs.

References

[Adams+1996] M. J. Adams, J. O. Coplien, R. J. Gamoke, R. S. Hanmer, F. H.
Keeve, and K. L. Nicodemus. "Fault-Tolerant Telecommunication System
Patterns." In R. C. Martin, D. Riehle, and F. Buschmann (eds.), *Pattern Lan-
guages of Program Design 3*. Reading, MA: Addison-Wesley, 1998.

[Cieslak+1977] T. Cieslak, L. Croxall, J. Roberts, M. Saad, and J. Scanlon. "No 4
ESS: Software Organization and Basic Call Handling." *Bell System Technical
Journal*, 56(7):1113–1138, 1977.

[Green+1977] T. V. Green, D. G. Haenschke, B. H. Hornbach, and C. E. Johnson.
"No 4 ESS: Network Management and Traffic Administration." *Bell System
Technical Journal*, 56(7):1169–1202, 1977.

[Hanmer+1999] R. Hanmer and M. Wu. "Traffic Congestion Patterns." In *Proceedings of 1999 Pattern Languages of Programming Conference*. Monticello, IL, USA:
1999. Available: *http://hillside.net/plop/plop99/proceedings/hanmer/hanmer629.pdf.*

[Hanmer+2000] R. S. Hanmer and G. Stymfal. "An Input and Output Pattern
Language: Lessons from Telecommunications." In N. Harrison, B. Foote, and
H. Rohnert (eds.), *Pattern Languages of Program Design 4*. Boston: Addison-
Wesley, 2000.

[Hanmer+2004] R. S. Hanmer and K. F. Kocan. "Documenting Architectures
with Patterns." *Bell Labs Technical Journal*, 9(1): 143–163, 2004.

[Jagadeesan+1995] L. J. Jagadeesan, C. Puchol, and J. E. Von Olnhausen. "A Formal Approach to Reactive Systems Software: A Telecommunications Application in ESTEREL." In *Proceedings of Workshop on Industrial-Strength Formal
Specification Techniques*, pp. 132–145. Boca Raton, FL, USA, April 1995.

[Meszaros1996] G. Meszaros. "A Pattern Language for Improving the Capacity of Reactive Systems." In J. M. Vlissides, J. O. Coplien, and N. L. Kerth (eds.), *Pattern Languages of Program Design 2*. Reading, MA: Addison-Wesley, 1996.

[Wake+1996] W. Wake, B. Wake, and E. Fox. "Improving Responsiveness in Interactive Applications Using Queues." In J. M. Vlissides, J. O. Coplien, and N. L. Kerth (eds.), *Pattern Languages of Program Design 2*. Reading, MA: Addison-Wesley, 1996.

_____

PART III

Distributed Systems

Chapter 7: Decentralized Locking

A little over a decade ago, few people built software for distributed systems. The ubiquity of networked systems in the enterprise and also in the embedded world changed that, and today many developers are in fact working on distributed systems. Locking is one of the key techniques in their toolbox. Drawing upon examples from several systems that deal with distribution, Dietmar Schütz distilled a pattern for managing locks. Infrastructure developers and builders of distributed systems alike will find Decentralized Locking useful.

Chapter 8: The Comparand Pattern: Cheap Identity Testing Using Dedicated Values

Identity represents one of the key characteristics of objects. However, while straightforward on the surface, dealing with identity is quite complex when working with objects from different hosts or processes within a distributed system. How does one tackle object identity and equality then? Pascal Costanza and Arno Haase answer this question in the Comparand Pattern.

Chapter 9: Pattern Language for Service Discovery

Since marketers started to abuse service-oriented architecture (SOA) it is hard to find a book that doesn't use the word "service" one way or another. Juha Pärssinen, Teemu Koponen, and Pasi Eronen helped us add the "s" word to this book. However, they don't talk about three-letter acronyms that people don't seem to agree about. Instead, the Pattern Language for Service Discovery tackles a common problem in practical ways, distilling solutions from well-established examples such as SLP, JXTA, UPnP, LDAP, DNS, and the now-ubiquitous IEEE 802.11.

CHAPTER 7

Decentralized Locking

Dietmar Schütz

Introduction

The DECENTRALIZED LOCKING design pattern provides fast acquisition and release of locks without network communication even in distributed systems built around a central lock server. Instead of plain locks, the server manages "permits to lock," and passes them to those clients that probably need the lock next. If a client hosts a permit, the associated lock can be acquired immediately without server interaction.

Also Known As

Lock-Permit, Distributed Locking

Example

A network management system provides access to a large amount of telecommunication hardware. The switches, routers, and transmission units are supervised and controlled by human operators as well as automated network administration tools. Since the hardware components are highly distributed, a model of the complex network resides on a central server. The set of hardware components is, depending on the workload, temporally organized into subsections, each with an operator assigned to it (see Figure 7–1). Therefore, there is almost no potential for collisions when accessing the components. But since they

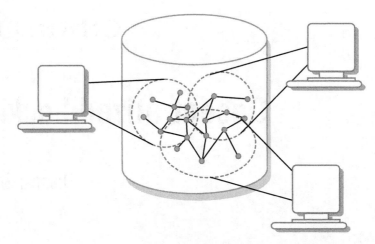

Figure 7–1 *Non-disjoint assignment of hardware components to subsection operators*

are still possible, it is necessary to serialize access to the hardware in order to prevent interference between different operators or tools. This is done by means of locking capabilities, also provided by the central server. Although seldom a real benefit, the pessimistic lock acquisition and release causes most of the network traffic, thereby wasting a lot of communication bandwidth for "administrative" sugar, just in case...

Context

A distributed application or system containing shared resources accessed concurrently by multiple clients in a somewhat regular pattern. Examples of regular patterns are a "soft" assignment of resources to clients or a standard sequence of steps when accessing different resources or "passing" resources to other clients.

Problem

In a distributed system with many clients accessing a base of common resources concurrently, it is necessary to avoid access collision or data corruption due to race conditions. How can such locks be provided in an efficient and consistent way?

The following forces influence the solution:

- *Simple deployment structure.* Since locking is a pessimistic approach, it provides a service that in most cases isn't necessary. Therefore, the organizational and development effort should be minimal, as shown in the example by use of a single centralized server for managing the locks.

- *Response times.* Clients should not be hindered and slowed down unnecessarily, such as when waiting for a response from an overloaded server.

- *Locking Overhead.* Especially in usage scenarios with very short interactions, acquiring and releasing locks can cause significant overhead for clients.

- *Availability.* In the event of partial failure (such as the server being down or not responding, or the network not being available), remaining clients should be able to continue operation.

Solution

Introduce a *permit to lock* that allows the client to immediately obtain a lock without communicating to the lock server. Instead of hosting locks, let the lock server keep track of the permits. If a client releases a lock, don't notify the lock server, but keep the permit at the client site. Revoke permits from clients if another client requests the corresponding locks.

Within the server, the semantics when handling permits are the same as with usual locks. If the server, for example, supports multiple read access, it can grant a write permit only if all read permits have been revoked successfully.

Structure

The DECENTRALIZED LOCKING design pattern defines six participating components.

A *Resource* provides a common service that is shared by multiple clients. In order to prevent race conditions and invalid states, access to the resource needs to be serialized.

Each resource is associated with a *Lock*. Only the temporal owner of this lock is allowed to access the resource.

Every lock is associated with a corresponding *Permit*, which is understood as an "option to lock": when a permit is owned, the corresponding lock can be obtained immediately upon request.

A *Client* makes use of resources, carefully complying with the locking conventions. Hence, before accessing the resource, the client tries to acquire the corresponding lock. Access to the resource is delayed until the lock is available and obtained successfully. After accessing the resource, the lock is released.

The *LockManager* is a central service that maintains the locks and permits. From the LockManager's point of view, locks and permits are semantically equal and therefore are treated as a unity. The LockManager provides a common interface to clients who want to acquire or release a lock/permit. Since a lock/permit can only be granted to one client at a time, an acquisition request is answered immediately only if the lock/permit is free. If the lock/permit is in use, the request is queued. Meanwhile, the lock/permit is revoked from its actual owner. As soon as it is passed back, the initial request is answered.

The *LockManager Proxy* shields the clients from network addresses and interprocess communication protocols when addressing the remote LockManager (see PROXY pattern [Gamma+1995]); every communication of clients with the LockManager is performed via the LockManager Proxy. The LockManager Proxy resides within the client's address space and provides an interface for acquiring and releasing that is semantically equal to the LockManager's interface. In addition, the LockManager Proxy mediates between permits and locks: the communication with the LockManager handles only permits, whereas the client interface works with the corresponding locks. Hence, the LockManager Proxy also shields the client from the permit semantics, providing a usual locking interface. The LockManager Proxy also manages the subset of permits granted to it.

The following class diagram (see Figure 7–2) shows the participants of the DECENTRALIZED LOCKING pattern and their relationships.

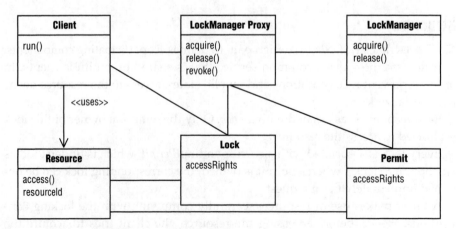

Figure 7–2 *Participants and their relationships*

Dynamics

Typical runtime scenarios cover the acquisition and release of locks. The acquisition scenarios further distinguish where the lock and the respective permit reside.

For simplicity, the following diagrams and descriptions are based on the assumptions that every client has its own LockManager Proxy and that all calls are performed in a synchronous blocking manner.

The initial scenario, **Server Lock Acquisition** (see Figure 7–3), takes place when the lock is acquired for the first time after system startup. In this state, the permit is stored on the lock server, and so the call sequence is very familiar.

The client initiates the acquisition of a specific lock with the LockManager Proxy. The LockManager Proxy determines whether the client is hosting the corresponding permit. Since this is not true, the call is forwarded to the Lock-Manager, which grants the permit to the LockManager Proxy. Now the lock acquisition can be completed successfully and the client is ready to access the resource.

The next interesting thing to happen is the **Lock Release** scenario (see Figure 7–4). After using the resource, the client addresses the LockManager Proxy in order to release the lock. The LockManager Proxy simply indicates the permit (which has been obtained during a former acquisition) to be "available" and returns the call immediately. The permit remains within the LockManager Proxy; no communication with the remote LockManager is established.

Starting from the state left behind by a previous lock release, the **Local Lock Acquisition** scenario (see Figure 7–5) is very compact. After the client invokes the acquisition routine, the LockManager Proxy determines if the corresponding

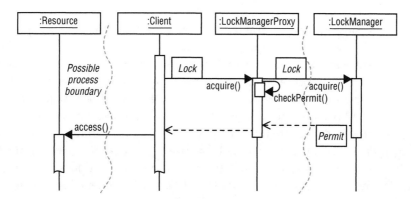

Figure 7–3 *Acquire a lock from the server*

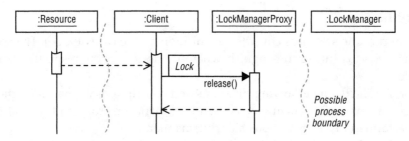

Figure 7–4 *Lock release*

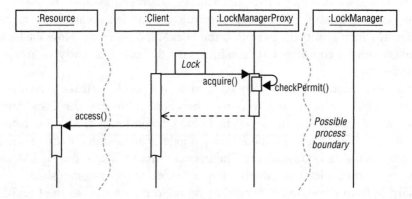

Figure 7–5 *Local lock acquisition using permit*

permit is already (has been) granted to him. That being the case, the permit is marked as "in use" and the acquisition is successful.

The **Permit Revoke** scenario (see Figure 7–6) shows the acquisition of lock via a permit that is hosted neither by the (acquiring) client nor the central server. The first steps are identical to those of the Server Lock Acquisition. But as soon as the LockManager discovers that it has granted the permit to somebody else previously, it initiates a revoke for that permit from the other Lock-Manager Proxy. If the permit is not "in use" (no lock is derived from that permit), it is given away immediately. If the corresponding lock is active, the permit is sent back as soon as the lock is released by the other client. During that time, the client waiting for the permit is blocked.

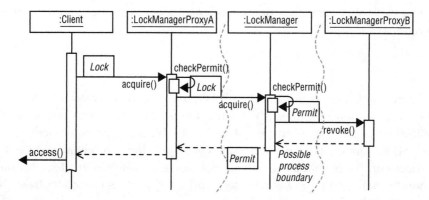

Figure 7–6 *Revoking a permit from a client*

Implementation

To implement this pattern, carry out the following steps:

Step 1

Determine how revocation requests are dealt with. Although this issue seems to be simple within the pattern, it may have a major impact on the system architecture. The first idea is to let the LockManager Proxy provide an interface that allows the LockManager to revoke a permit. Such an interface forces the Proxy to be reactive itself (a server in terms of CORBA), which causes a lot of additional infrastructure: an extended (or second) message queue, at least two threads of control for outgoing and incoming requests, precise locking on the container for permits to prevent deadlocks if the Proxy is blocked when waiting for a permit, detection of lost connections or dead targets, and so on. Thus, this approach is elegant, but it is expensive to implement. Therefore, if the revocation interface is the *only* reason to make the proxy reactive, a reactive Proxy may not be the best choice.

Another way to get permits back to the LockManager on demand is to poll the LockManager for revocation requests. This approach is much easier to implement, but causes additional network traffic due to the polling calls. If this traffic can be kept at a reasonably low level, for example, by using a low polling rate and longer revocation delays, a polling approach is a viable option. In addition, the polling method can also serve as an "alive" signal that allows the server to give away permits of "dead" clients to others.

Since this policy is much easier to implement, it is used throughout the example code.

Step 2

Define the interface of the LockManager. This interface contains methods for acquisition and release of permits. The acquisition function can, with respect to the availability of the requested permit, either be blocking or non-blocking. For blocking semantics, the LockManager has to provide a mechanism to detect deadlocks of clients with mutual dependencies. If an acquisition attempt should be non-blocking, no permit is returned, and the client has to recover from that failure by itself.

Although there is no explicit release of a permit in the scenarios just described, this method is needed in response to revoking a permit. The interface may also (see Step 1) provide a method to poll for revocation requests.

The structure of a permit carries the Id of the corresponding resource as well as the granted access rights. The granularity of the access rights allows concurrent read-only access to one resource by multiple clients.

The resulting CORBA interface is defined as shown here, based on non-blocking acquisition semantics.

```
module DBAccess
{
 enum Permission {u,r,w,rw};
  // u  unspecified: no permission
  // r  read permission
  // w  write permission
  // rw read & write permission
 struct Permit
  { long    resource_id;
   Permission access_rights;
  };
 interface LockManager
 { Permit acquire(in long resource_id,
        in Permission access_type);
     // return a u-Permit if not available
  void release(in Permit release_lock);
  boolean check_revoke(out long resource_id);
 };
};
```

Step 3

Implement the LockManager functions. The central part of the LockManager is a map, indexed by the Id's of the managed resources. For each resource, this map stores which access rights have been granted to which clients (loan list). For a blocking acquisition, it also offers a semaphore to queue additional acquisition requests. Access to the map is protected by a mutex.

If a permit is acquired, the map is inspected in order to determine if this permit is available with respect to the requested access rights. If yes, the client is added to the loan list, and the permit is returned. Otherwise, a revocation is initiated. The active revoke approach calls the corresponding method on the Lock-Manager Proxy that hosts the permit. The polling approach adds the resource Id to a pool of active revocations that is inspected by the polling calls. The acquisition thread may sleep a while to wait for a release in the meantime. If the resource Id is not known yet, it can be added to the map in order to implement a "lazy loading" of resource Id's into the LockManager or to cope with environments where resource Id's are not known in advance.

If a permit is released, the client is removed from the loan list, and its list of active revocations is shortened by the corresponding resource Id. The check_revoke method returns the first entry from a client's revocation list.

Less clear, but more effective, is an additional out parameter for the acquire and release methods, which is used to indicate a revocation request aside from the polling procedure.

Step 4

Build the LockManager Proxy. This task incorporates three parts.

Implement a Remote Proxy for the LockManager. Identify all responsibilities that deal with accessing the remote LockManager and encapsulate them into a Proxy class. See [Buschmann+1996] for details.

Make the Proxy smart. Extend the Proxy implementation with a map of resource Id's similar to that of the LockManager. This map keeps the permits that have been granted by the LockManager. If the acquire method is called, first look up the resource Id in the map. Only if it is not present, forward the call to the remote "original." If the release method is called, do *not* forward this call.

Implement the revocation mechanism. For an active revocation, a thread of the LockManager Proxy is responsible for handling the revocation requests. The permit map within the Proxy is checked to determine if the permit asked for is in use. If it is not, the permit is removed from the map and the call returns successfully. If a lock is derived from that permit, the revocation fails, but the permit is marked in order to be sent back as soon as it is released.

In accordance with the polling approach, a second thread needs to be started as soon as the Proxy is instantiated: periodically invoking check_revoke on the LockManager. If the call returns a revocation request, remove the resource Id from the local map and call the release method with that resource Id.

```
while(1){
 sleep(2);
 if ( resource_hash_map_.current_size() > 0 ){
  try {
   revoke_flag =
    lock_manager_var_->check_revoke(resource_id);
   catch (...) { /*...*/ };
  }
  if (revoke_flag) {
   try {
    revoke_flag =
     lock_manager_var_->release(resource_id);
    catch (...) { /*...*/ };
   }
  }
 }
}
```

Step 5

Integrate the Proxy into the client. The Proxy is integrated into the client as described by the PROXY pattern [Buschmann+1996]. From the client's view, there is no difference between the usual proxy and its smart implementation.

Example Resolved

Because a set of hardware components is assigned to each human operator, after normal operation for a period of time, most of the corresponding permits are granted to that person's workstation. Therefore, almost all operator actions are performed after the local lock acquisition scenario. Message traffic is reduced significantly across the whole network: most of the "administrative" remote lock requests have been eliminated successfully, and the remaining ones contribute very little to the communication workload.

During a responsibility shift, if some of the components are assigned to other operators, a transition phase takes place. In that time period, the first access to newly assigned components initiates revocation of corresponding permits, slightly increasing the network traffic. Soon, however, most of the permits have "moved" to their new locations, and the communication workload goes down to its previous low level.

Variants

The **Release Strategy** variant adds flexibility to what happens to the permit after a lock is released in order to prevent foreseeable revocations. Besides granting a permit, the LockManager selects or parameterizes a release strategy to be followed by the client or its LockManager Proxy. A simple strategy regarding the management of permits is, for example, the distinction between "keep it" and "return immediately" behavior, built upon preferences in the assignment of resources to clients. Other more complex strategies incorporate timing models or even solutions based on application state, which work well in environments with short-term collaboration patterns or highly dynamic relationships. Time-based handling of permits can be implemented using the LEASING pattern [Jain+2000]. Implementations of permit management based on state may benefit from using the STATE pattern [Gamma+1995] or its refinement [Dyson+1997].

A further extension of a state-based release strategy enables the LockManager to push a permit to a specific client that is indicated by the current state of the permit. This variant may be useful in reducing load peaks on the server.

The **Lock Relay** variant supports forwarding permits from one client to another. This feature applies, for example, to applications that implement a well-defined workflow among several clients. In accordance with succeeding operations by other clients, the permit is pushed ahead, simultaneously notifying the LockManager about the location change of the permit. With this technique, the client-server interaction is reduced to a minimum as long as operations follow the standard workflow. If the resources and the central LockManager are not colocated, even the location change notification can be omitted for the cost of a more expensive revoke.

Known Uses

The **ObjectStore** object-oriented database management system (www.objectdesign.com/htm/object_prod.htm or www.exceloncorp.com) uses permits within its cache-forward architecture for faster acquisition of read and write locks on database pages. The LockManager Proxy is implemented by the cache manager located on the client host; the LockManager is integrated into the central database server. The permits are always retained after releasing a lock, since the database libraries are generic and cannot make use of knowledge about the surrounding application. At any rate, this strategy works well in an environment with short transactions, which are typical in the context of object-oriented databases.

In accordance with the lock philosophy of a database, which allows either multiple read locks or a single write lock for each object at a time, the server may grant more than one concurrent read permit at a time, but it will revoke all of them if a write lock is acquired.

Objectivity, an object-oriented database system, uses this pattern for implementing the configurable "commit and hold" policy. If enabled, after writing back data to the server due to a commit, the client cache is *not* cleared, and the lock is held. This behavior reduces the load on the server in most interaction scenarios.

The **Oracle** relational database management system uses this pattern to improve client and server performance.

A known use from the "real world" can be found in large **service centers**, where customers and their contracts are assigned to specific employees. In most cases, a request is directly routed to the standard employee, but the files (that present the data and a lock) can be retrieved by anybody else, if necessary.

Consequences

The DECENTRALIZED LOCKING pattern offers a set of **benefits**:

- *Simple server structure.* The permits are managed by a single centralized server that needs no extraordinary availability features.

- *Performance.* In an environment with an almost constant relationship between clients and resources, the use of permits significantly increases the performance and reduces network traffic, since communication across the network is almost totally devoted to accessing the resource. This benefit can turn into a liability if the pattern is applied in the context of frequently changing associations between clients and resources; that is, if a resource is accessed by the same client less than two times in succession, the revocation overhead causes more network traffic than the usual lock acquisition and release without permits.

- *Fallback operation.* Even if the lock server is down, clients can continue their operation as long as they don't need any new locks.

- *No effects to usual client implementation.* The interaction schemes specific to this pattern only involve the LockManager and its proxies. Therefore, it can be implemented without modifying the client's interface to the LockManager Proxy, enabling an easy transition from a standard locking approach to permit-based locking.

The DECENTRALIZED LOCKING pattern has the following **liabilities**:

- *More sensitivity for abnormal network conditions.* Sometimes the server needs to revoke locks from clients that would be unaffected in a normal implementation. Hence, this solution needs more remote connections and is therefore more susceptible to nearly overloaded network conditions.

- *Revocation of multiple read permits.* In applications that make intensive use of multiple read locks, the average costs of revoking permits are much higher. In order to grant a write permit, the LockManager has to recall *all* corresponding read permits from variant LockManager Proxies. To draw a performance benefit from permits, the overall number of reuses of multiple read permits must be higher than the maximum number of clients hosting them before the permits are revoked.

Aside from these runtime benefits and liabilities, the design and implementation of DECENTRALIZED LOCKING may be quite complex if the LockManager Proxy has to provide an active interface for revoking permits. This problem is typical for all concurrent and distributed applications where components act (in CORBA terms) as server *and* client at the same time, and where the solutions clearly exceed the scope of this pattern.

Related Patterns

The Remote Proxy variant of the PROXY pattern [Buschmann+1996] provides a solution to shield clients from network addresses and inter-process communication protocols when dealing with locks. The STATE pattern [Gamma+1995] and its refinement, STATE PATTERNS [Dyson+1997], may be useful patterns for implementing state-dependent permit release strategies. STRATEGY [Gamma+1995] is applicable for more complex approaches or active assignment of permits to clients. SCOPED LOCKING and STRATEGIZED LOCKING [Schmidt+1999] refine locking mechanisms and semantics. From the collection of resource management patterns [Jain+2000], CACHING helps in designing the client side caches, and LEASING provides approaches regarding the time based on permit release semantics.

Acknowledgments

Thanks to my shepherd, Prashant Jain, who exercised plenty of patience going through the first versions of this paper. The complete example code has been contributed by my colleague and friend Martin Botzler. He also helped me with discussions on variant implementation issues. I would like to thank the participants of the workshop at EuroPLoP 2001 for their encouraging comments and suggestions. Thanks go also to my wife, Sigrid Becker, who endured all the time I took from our family when working on this pattern.

References

[Buschmann+1996] F. Buschmann, R. Meunier, H. Rohnert, M. Stal, and P. Sommerlad. *Pattern-Oriented Software Architecture: A System of Patterns*. London: John Wiley & Sons Ltd., 1996.

[Dyson+1997] P. Dyson and B. Anderson. "State Patterns." In R. C. Martin, D. Riehle, and F. Buschmann (eds.), *Pattern Languages of Program Design 3*. Reading, MA: Addison-Wesley, 1998.

[Gamma+1995] E. Gamma, R. Helm, R. Johnson, and J. Vlissides. *Design Patterns: Elements of Reusable Object-Oriented Software*. Reading, MA: Addison-Wesley, 1995.

[Jain+2000] P. Jain and M. Kircher. *Pattern Oriented Software Architecture: Patterns for Resource Management*. London: John Wiley & Sons Ltd, 2000.

[Schmidt+2000] D. Schmidt, M. Stal, H. Rohnert, and F. Buschmann. *Pattern-Oriented Software Architecture: Patterns for Networked and Concurrent Systems*. London: John Wiley & Sons Ltd., 2000.

CHAPTER 8

The Comparand Pattern: Cheap Identity Testing Using Dedicated Values

Pascal Costanza and Arno Haase

Thumbnail

The COMPARAND pattern provides a means for interpreting different objects as being the same for certain contexts. It does so by introducing an instance variable in each class of interest—the comparand—and using it for comparison. Establishing the sameness of different objects is needed when more than one reference refers to conceptually the same object. In distributed systems, the COMPARAND pattern provides for efficient comparison of (possibly) remote objects.

Example

Suppose you want to implement the Java Platform Debugger Architecture (JPDA), a specification of a debugging framework for the Java Virtual Machine (JVM).

The JPDA consists of three levels: the Java Virtual Machine Debug Interface (JVMDI), an API that is to be implemented in native code, at the level of the JVM; the Java Debug Wire Protocol (JDWP), which allows debuggers to remotely employ the capabilities offered by the JVMDI; and finally, the Java Debug Interface (JDI), a high-level Java API that abstracts from the details of the other levels and thus allows for the implementation of a concrete debugger in a pure object-oriented fashion (see Figure 8–1).

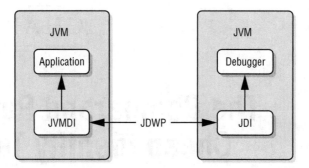

Figure 8–1 *The Java Platform Debugger Architecture*

This architecture expects a debugger to be executed on an instance of the JVM that is different from that of the target application. Therefore, the target application's objects cannot be directly referred to in the debugger by references as offered by the Java Programming Language. They have to be represented instead as objects that act as remote references.

If a debugger needs to compare variables holding such remote references in order to determine if they refer to the same remote object, care has to be taken to do so correctly. Different remote references might refer to the same remote object, since they can be created independently, for example, by consecutive retrieval operations. Therefore, if comparison of remote references yields `false`, it is not guaranteed that they actually represent different remote objects.

The straightforward solution is to execute an operation on the remote system that determines the correct answer. However, beyond the performance penalty that this solution incurs, it also interferes with the goal of the Java Platform Debugging Architecture, which is to isolate the debugger from the target application as far as possible in order to avoid potential side effects.

The COMPARAND pattern solves this problem by adding an attribute to the remote references, the so-called "comparand." The comparand of a particular reference is assigned a value that uniquely identifies its remote object.

Consequently, only a comparison of comparands is needed in order to determine sameness or difference of the respective remote objects. Comparands can therefore be used to carry out the comparison operation efficiently. Interferences with the execution of the target application are reduced to the actual creation of comparands inside the JVM of the target application.

Context

Comparison of objects with reference semantics without comparing their references.

Problem

Object comparison is usually taken to mean either comparison for sameness (object identity) or comparison of state. The first of these approaches corresponds to so-called *reference semantics,* usually based on comparison of references or pointers; the second approach corresponds to *value semantics,* using all or a subset of the attributes.[1]

On the lowest level, reference semantics is traditionally implemented via pointers—machine addresses—and the sameness of two pointers/references is determined simply by detecting whether they point to the same memory location. This is very useful, because it allows otherwise separate program parts to communicate via shared sections of memory. This is actually one of the origins of object-oriented programming: Objects can be understood as shared containers of state.

However, neither plain reference semantics nor value semantics are sufficient when reference semantics is to be maintained but reference comparison does not ensure sameness. This is the case when there are different references that can refer to conceptually the same object. In the introductory example, remote references are represented as objects on their own; for this reason, the target object together with its remote references form a conceptual entity that should be indistinguishable from the outside. So the issue is not how to change reference semantics to value semantics but how to have reference semantics with a comparison operation that does not simply compare the references. As another example, particularly in distributed systems, several proxies [Gamma+1995] in the same address space refer to either the same or to different remote objects (see Figure 8–2). In this case, the fact that a lack of a direct reference mechanism for remote objects has to be overcome results in potentially ambiguous references.

Another example is an implementation of the DECORATOR pattern [Gamma+ 1995], where not only different decorators may be applied to the same core object, but they can even decorate each other since decorators and decorated objects have the same interfaces in general. (See [Gamma+1995] for examples.) Here, comparison of references might not reveal that they actually refer to the same core object, but there is a need to establish sameness for decorator objects that are strictly different.[2]

---

1. Other semantics for object comparison include more complex equality operations that, for example, take structural equivalence into account. See [Baker1993] and [Grogono+2000] for discussions on the range of possible equality semantics.
2. The latter is also known as an example of a split object [Bardou+1996].

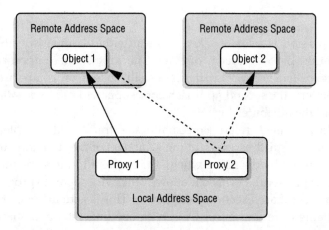

Figure 8–2 *Do the two proxies refer to the same remote object or not?*

In such circumstances, the following forces have to be balanced:

- A comparison of object state does not yield the intended result since reference semantics is desired.

- A comparison of references cannot be relied upon since one wants to consider different objects to be the same. These objects might even be instances of different types.

- The sameness of objects in general depends on the context. Objects that are considered the same in one context can be different in another. For example, no matter which objects are required to be regarded the same at the application level, the runtime libraries—garbage collector, middleware services, and so on—need a view of sameness that is closer to the machine level. Likewise, there can be different "sameness requirements" in different parts of the same application.

- If an object is copied,[3] care must be taken in defining the comparison between original and copy. There are cases where comparison between the two should yield true—leaning more towards value semantics—but others where they must be distinguished.

---

3. For the purposes of this paper, the clone method is just one means of allowing an object to be copied. Therefore the two are used interchangeably except where implementation details are discussed.

- Sometimes comparison of objects of different types must yield `true`, for example, different decorators of the same object, especially decorators of decorators.

- A system may want detailed control of the possible results of object comparisons. For example, when the cost of object creation is to be lowered by introducing a recycling mechanism, the expected result of comparison even changes over time.

- Comparison must be a cheap operation in terms of runtime overhead if it is performed frequently. This requires particular attention in distributed systems.

- In a distributed system, it is usually nontrivial to determine sameness of object references locally, and executing a remote call for comparison introduces a significant performance overhead.

- The additional memory overhead associated with achieving the desired comparison behavior often needs to be small, especially if many objects are involved.

Several programming languages provide ways to override equality operators in order to achieve different comparison semantics. For example, in Java the `equals` method can be overridden and subsequently invoked in client code. However, the COMPARAND pattern is not primarily concerned with the technical details of how to invoke new comparison semantics, but rather with the semantic details of a specific kind of comparison semantics that balances these forces.

Solution

Introduce an instance variable in each class of interest—the comparand—that does not belong to the conceptual state of their respective objects, and compare objects by comparing their comparand values.[4]

```java
public class MyClass {
    protected static long comparandCounter = 0;

    protected long comparand = comparandCounter++;
```

---

4. We have chosen the artificial name COMPARAND for this pattern to stress that this instance variable is a passive entity that is not used for referencing, but within comparison operations only. Elsewhere, names like "key" and "identifier," or acronyms like "OID" and "id" are used for this concept, but these names are used ambiguously and with overloaded meanings throughout the literature. Many brainstorming sessions have not revealed a better name, so we have opted for COMPARAND.

```
    public boolean equals(Object obj) {
        if (obj instanceof MyClass) {
            MyClass that = (MyClass)obj;
            return this.comparand == that.comparand;
        }
        return false;
    }

    // rest of class body
    ...
}
```

The comparands stored in the objects under consideration can be either values of a primitive type or instances of a compound type. Primitive values of 64 bits are large enough to allow 10 billion unique comparands per second to be created for half a century, which is good enough for almost all applications.[5] In this case, unique comparands can always be created efficiently by just increasing a global counter. Therefore, in a local context that allows the management of comparands to be centralized, there is no reason to use compound comparands with the associated performance and memory overhead.[6]

Implementation

There are some subtle issues when applying the COMPARAND pattern, which are discussed in the following sections. We do not provide "obviously correct" solutions for all issues mentioned here, because some of them depend too strongly on the needs of a concrete application and the concrete language and environment it is implemented in. Nevertheless, it is important to be aware of these issues, and they should be taken into account when designing a concrete system.

The "Right" Comparison Semantics

It is important to thoroughly understand what exactly object comparison is supposed to mean in the context at hand. The COMPARAND pattern is applicable

---

5. On the other hand, 32-bit values are usually not big enough to ensure uniqueness for long-running applications. At a rate of 1000 comparands per second, they wrap around after roughly 1.5 months. In the rare cases when even 64 bits are insufficient, two or more long integers can easily be combined in a customized value type with a larger range of numbers.
6. This need only arises in the case of distributed applications. See Comparands in Distributed Environments in the Implementation section for further details.

only if the intended behavior is that of reference semantics and not that of value semantics or even of some intermediate semantics.[7]

Sometimes different contexts require different comparison semantics. For example, after application of the DECORATOR pattern, the core object and its decorators represent the same conceptual entity. However, certain clients expect the comparison of decorator objects to determine whether their respective core objects are the same, whereas other clients need to differentiate between the decorators. The introduction of more than one comparison operation (for example, `equals` and `equalsDecorator`) is advisable under these circumstances.

Comparison of Clones

If an object can be copied or cloned, typically afterwards both objects have exactly the same state, but they are not identical. The COMPARAND pattern offers the flexibility to define any desired degree of sameness. There is a free choice to assign the copy the original comparand or a new one which can even be based on dynamic properties of the environment. However, then one must consider the question what the correct behavior should be in a given context. In the general case, a new comparand should be assigned by default, as illustrated in the following example, since clones can usually be regarded as independent instances.

```
public class MyClass implements Cloneable {
   // comparand and equals() as above
   ...

   public Object clone() {
      try {
         MyClass myClone = (MyClass)super.clone();
         myClone.comparand = comparandCounter++;
         return myClone;
      } catch (CloneNotSupportedException e) {
         // since MyClass implements Cloneable
         // this exception cannot occur
         throw new InternalError();
      }
   }
}
```

---

7. Sometimes, comparison of objects needs to take sophisticated aspects into account, for example, structural equivalence of complex object types. A thorough treatment of these issues is given in [Grogono+2000].

However, an example of a system that may need to treat objects and their clones as equal is one that offers transactional services. It creates copies of objects to operate on them instead of the original ones, so that a rollback operation is easily implemented by just discarding these copies. From a system programmer's point of view, the disambiguation of copies from original objects is clearly needed, but from an application programmer's point of view it is not desirable to distinguish between them. Again, the introduction of more than one dedicated comparison operation (with different access rights, if applicable) may solve this problem.

Which Classes Are Comparable to Each Other?

Another important issue is the determination of the classes that are supposed to be comparable. If it is required to potentially establish identity for any two objects of arbitrary type, further effort is needed. For example, in Java an interface can be introduced that otherwise unrelated classes can implement, allowing their objects to be compared as follows.

```
public interface Comparable {
    public long getComparand();
}
```

Since in this case the creation of comparands does not naturally belong to one of the comparable classes anymore, it should be factored out into a class of its own.[8]

```
public class ComparandFactory {

    private static long comparandCounter = 0;

    public long getNewComparand() {
        return comparandCounter++;
    }
}

public MyClass implements Comparable {
```

---

8. Note that the getNewComparand() method must be synchronized in the presence of multithreading.

```
protected long comparand = ComparandFactory.getNewComparand();

public long getComparand() {
   return this.comparand;
}

public boolean equals(Object obj) {
   if (obj instanceof Comparable) {
      Comparable that = (Comparable)obj;
      return this.comparand == that.getComparand();
   }
   return false;
}

// rest of class body
...

}
```

Provided that each `Comparable` class implements `equals` in this way, any two `Comparable` objects can be made the same by assigning their comparands the same value.

Boundary Conditions of a Given System

A good understanding of the properties and the "feel" of the environment at hand is important. Are there standard ways to establish and determine sameness? For example, in C++ sameness is usually determined via the `operator==`, so it is advisable to redefine it accordingly, whereas in Java the `==` operator cannot be redefined, but instead the `equals` method has to be overridden and used.

What kinds of comparison and guarantees of uniqueness are provided or required by the programming language and the libraries and frameworks to be used?

For example, libraries for collections usually expect comparison operations to behave well, as in the case of Java's Collection Framework that requires the standard `hashCode` method to return the same result for two objects that are equal in terms of the standard `equals` method. In fact, the comparand should be used as a hash code value for this reason, as shown in the code fragment on the next page.[9]

---

9. See the JDK documentation on `hashCode()` in `java.lang.Object` for further details [Sun2004].

```
public class MyClass {
   // comparand and equals() as above
   ...

   public int hashCode() {
      return (int)this.comparand;
   }
}
```

Reuse of an Existing Attribute

There are cases where there is no need to define and create comparands specifically. For example, in frameworks that map objects to table entries in relational database systems, primary keys are good candidates for comparands, especially when they are created by some kind of sequence number generator inside the database system. However, care must be taken to ensure that the preexisting attribute exactly reflects the intended comparison semantics. There are deceptive cases where an attribute "accidentally" reflects the intended semantics without being conceptually bound to it, in which case it is better to introduce a dedicated attribute.

Execution of Comparison Operations

There are two options in this dimension of variance. On the one hand, the objects that hold the comparands can offer methods to carry out the comparison, hiding the fact that the COMPARAND pattern is used for this purpose (*internal comparison*). This allows one to change the implementation later on and base it on a technique other than the COMPARAND pattern as required. The implementation can be scaled down to even a comparison of plain references as offered by the programming language when the reasons for an advanced solution have vanished.[10]

On the other hand, objects can allow one to access the comparands and perform the comparison directly (*external comparison*). This variant may be opted for when comparands offer additional functionality and there is therefore already a need to access them. For example, comparands can also serve as keys for later retrievals of the same object. In this case, comparison of two objects

---

10. Other details of the specific implementation are also encapsulated and therefore easily exchanged, like the issues of primitive types vs. compound types, and so on. See Comparands in Distributed Environments for further details on compound comparands.

looks like follows. (Note that casts to the `Comparable` interface are not always necessary.)

```
if ((obj1 instanceof Comparable) &&
    (obj2 instanceof Comparable)) {
  Comparable comp1 = (Comparable)obj1;
  Comparable comp2 = (Comparable)obj2;
  if (comp1.getComparand() == comp2.getComparand()) {
    ....
  }
}
```

The two options are not mutually exclusive: an object can offer both internal and external comparison. However, in this case, the specific advantage that internal comparison hides the implementation details of the COMPARAND pattern vanishes, and therefore, pure internal comparison is a better alternative in the general case.

Comparands in Distributed Environments

Especially in the case of distributed systems, the COMPARAND pattern can significantly reduce the runtime overhead of comparison operations. When the comparand of a remote object is cached within each of its remote references,[11] comparisons do not require any remote execution at all (see Figure 8–3). Instead of allowing various remote references for the same remote object to coexist, a system can choose to unify remote references as soon as they enter an address space. Since this guarantees the uniqueness of remote references they can directly be compared as such.

However, in order to check if an old reference must be reused or a new one must be created, the system has to keep a table that maps comparands, which are determined via the underlying communication mechanism, to the actual remote references.[12]

In distributed systems, the goal of unique comparands can be achieved only at great expense. Uniqueness can be complicated even further when a heterogeneous application has to be built which consists of independently developed subsystems. The following variants of the COMPARAND pattern offer different solutions for this problem.

---

11. Thus, it is a simple instance of the CACHE PROXY pattern [Rohnert1996].

12. Note that comparands should always be implemented with value semantics rather than reference semantics, since only values can be copied across machine boundaries.

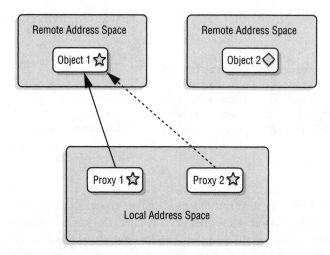

Figure 8–3 *The sameness of a remote object can be determined locally by comparing the comparands.*

Ambiguous Comparands

Instead of trying to achieve the goal of globally unique comparands, the requirements can be relaxed by letting all participating subsystems independently create potentially overlapping sets of comparands.

In this case, two objects might have equal comparands by accident. Therefore, one needs to know whether these comparands stem from the same subsystem in order to definitely determine sameness. As a last resort, the comparison operation has to be executed remotely. However, two objects that have different comparands are guaranteed to be different. The aim of avoiding remote invocations is not fully achieved, but the looser coupling of the systems involved outweighs this loss of performance, depending on the frequency of comparison operations.

Compound Comparands

Instead of sacrificing uniqueness of comparands, compound comparands can store identifiers for the process in which the respective objects live. Comparand creation is then a process that involves several steps, such as the creation of a unique number within a server and incorporating a server identifier into comparands within clients.

The basic implementation scheme for compound comparands is as follows.

```
public class Comparand {

    protected java.net.URL remoteSystem;
    protected int processNo; // identifies an address space
    protected long remoteComparand;

    public Comparand(java.net.URL remoteSystem,
                     int processNo,
                     long comparand) {
        this.remoteSystem = remoteSystem;
        this.processNo = processNo;
        this.remoteComparand = comparand;
    }

    public boolean equals(Object obj) {
        if (obj instanceof Comparand) {
            Comparand that = (Comparand)obj;
            return this.remoteSystem.equals(that.remoteSystem) &&
                   (this.processNo == that.processNo) &&
                   (this.remoteComparand == that.remoteComparand);
        }
        return false;
    }

    public int hashCode() {
        return (int)remoteComparand;
    }

    // note: no redefinition of clone()!

}
```

A class for remote references that uses compound comparands looks as follows.

```
public class MyRemoteReference {

    protected Comparand comparand;

    public MyRemoteReference(java.net.URL host,
                             int processNo,
                             long comparand) {
        this.comparand = new Comparand(host, processNo, comparand);
    }
```

```
public boolean equals(Object obj) {
   if (obj instanceof MyRemoteReference) {
      MyRemoteReference that = (MyRemoteReference)obj;
      return this.comparand.equals(that.comparand);
   }
   return false;
}

public int hashCode() {
   return this.comparand.hashCode();
}

// note: no redefinition of clone()!

}
```

Note that there are some fundamental differences between this implementation and the example that is given for non-distributed applications earlier in this paper. Firstly, remote references do not request the creation of a totally new comparand but let a comparand be initialized with given values that identify an existing remote object. This information must be determined via the underlying communication mechanism (for example, IP). Secondly, the clone() method is not redefined since a clone of a remote reference refers to the same remote object by definition.

Computed Comparands

Comparands may be computed by an algorithm that takes considerable effort to ensure global uniqueness. For example, GUIDs in the Microsoft Component Object Model (COM) can be used as 128 bit comparands. Again, counters that are global for the current machine are taken into account, together with the local machine's network address and the current time in order to ensure (world-wide) global uniqueness [Box1998]. Since GUIDs store all this information in a standardized way, they may still be regarded as a special case of compound comparands. However, since GUID creation imposes a significant runtime overhead, in the general case ambiguous comparands and compound comparands are preferable.

Coordinated Comparands

Another viable alternative for ensuring unique comparands is the assignment of non-overlapping sets of comparands to each node of a distributed application. Then each node is responsible for providing objects with unique comparands from the range of permitted comparands. This implies the need for a central comparand server that coordinates the creation of these non-overlapping sets and their assignment to the respective nodes. A possible disadvantage of this approach is the dependency on the availability of the comparand server. On the other hand, the access rate can be scaled by the number of comparands that are granted on each request.[13]

Consequences

Using COMPARANDs to compare objects yields the following benefits:

- *Flexibility.* The use of comparands makes it easy to define sameness of objects in an arbitrary way. It is even possible to change sameness at run time without affecting the objects' state. In addition, it is possible to make objects of different types equal, for example, different decorators wrapping the same object.

- *Comparison is cheap.* Comparison using primitive comparands is about as cheap as possible in terms of performance overhead.

- *Comparison of remote objects.* Proxies of remote objects can cache comparands locally, allowing remote references to be compared without the need for network traffic. This provides an efficient way to implement unification of remote references.

There are, however, the following liabilities:

- *Complexity.* As is often the case, flexibility comes at the cost of increased complexity. The use of comparands makes it more difficult to understand which objects are the same by looking at their implementation. This is partially due to the fact that the COMPARAND pattern introduces at least two different views on objects, one in which each object is strictly different from all others, and one in which different objects can represent the same conceptual entity. The program needs to deal with those different views and must use the "right" one depending on the context of use. Furthermore, the code that determines equality of objects can be part of objects other than those being compared, scattering the definition of sameness across several classes.

- *Collections.* If the default comparison mechanism of the language (`equals` in Java, `operator==` in C++) is implemented with comparands, care must be

---

13. There is no completely satisfactory solution to this problem because of the inherent unreliability of distributed applications. For example, see [Deutsch1992].

taken when container classes are used. Many container implementations rely on comparison of the contained objects, and if several objects have the same comparands, unexpected behavior can result.

- *Memory overhead.* The COMPARAND pattern relies on the introduction of an additional attribute, incurring some memory overhead. This can be an issue if the number of objects is large or compound comparands are used.

Known Uses

Java Platform Debugger Architecture

The JPDA [JPDA] does not only include a set of specifications, as introduced earlier, but also a standard implementation of all key components. The implementation of the Java Debug Interface uses comparands extensively to compare general ("user-defined") objects, strings, arrays, class loaders, and threads as well as reified types, fields, and methods.

The comparands are implemented as `long integer` values (field `ref` in class `com.sun.tools.jdi.ObjectReferenceImpl`). In principle, the implementation allows a debugger to connect to more than one virtual machine at the same time. For this reason, objects that have the same comparands are not necessarily the same. Therefore, a representation of the originating virtual machine is also taken into account during comparison. Consequently, the comparands can be created independently by their respective hosts.

Although the Java Debug Interface offers methods to retrieve the comparands of remote references, these comparands cannot be used to carry out comparison operations because of their ambiguity. Therefore, dedicated comparison methods are offered in addition.

See [J2SE] for the source code of JDK 1.3, which also includes the sources of the standard implementation of the Java Platform Debugger Architecture.

Remote Method Invocation

In Java RMI [JRMI], remote objects are represented by objects that implement the `java.rmi.server.RemoteRef` interface. In the standard implementation of RMI (as of JDK 1.3), this interface is implemented by the `sun.rmi.server.UnicastRef` class. This class uses the COMPARAND pattern to compare remote objects by comparing the field ref of type `sun.rmi.transport.LiveRef` that is defined for this class. This field consists of a representation of a server ("Endpoint"), a unique address space within that server ("UID") and a unique `long integer` value corresponding to an object within that address space.

This representation of remote objects allows each server to create its own set of values representing actual objects. Since remote references always record the execution context of their remote objects, they are the same if and only if they have the same comparands.

The `java.rmi.server.RemoteRef` interface does not allow the retrieval of the comparands of remote references, but it completely hides the fact that comparands are used in the standard implementation. Instead, a `remoteEquals` method is offered to carry out the comparison operation.

Again, see [J2SE] for the source code of JDK 1.3, which also includes the sources of the standard implementation of RMI.

CORBA Relationship Service

In principle, CORBA does not provide any means to compare components. However, the Relationship Service Specification [OMG2000] defines the CosObjectIdentity module, which includes an `IdentifiableObject` interface. It defines a `long` integer attribute as a comparand ("ObjectIdentifier").

Since this value is not guaranteed to be unique, two objects that have the same comparands are not necessarily the same. In order to definitively determine if two component references refer to the same component, an `is_identical` operation is also defined that has to be carried out remotely.

The "ObjectIdentifier" comparands are explicitly meant to be used as keys in hash tables. Therefore, they can be accessed directly as read-only attributes.

Enterprise Java Beans

In Enterprise Java Beans [Sun2000], the so-called entity beans offer primary keys that can be obtained by `getPrimaryKey` methods. For example, they can be used to retrieve or remove the components they represent and they can also be used as comparands.

Again, comparison of such primary keys does not completely determine whether two references refer to the same component. If they are equal, it must be determined whether they are obtained from the same execution context (the so-called "home") or otherwise an `isIdentical` method has to be invoked remotely.

Whereas primary keys are technically realized as instances of possibly user-defined primary key classes, these classes are restricted to being legal Value Types in RMI-IIOP [OMG2003]. These Value Types are constrained in a way that essentially leads to classes with value semantics rather than reference semantics. For example, they are required to redefine Java's standard `equals` method accordingly.

Ginko

Ginko [Objectpark] is an e-mail client for the Apple Macintosh (including Mac OS X), and is implemented in Objective-C. One of its features is the unified handling of different copies of the same e-mail. E-mails are represented as objects and can be stored into more than one folder while keeping the same set of attributes, such as status information and priority markers. The repeated receipt of the same e-mail is also detected by Ginko.

Different instances of the same e-mail are identified by comparison of the standard MESSAGE-ID, as specified by the Internet Request For Comments document number 822 [Crocker1982]. As RFC 822 states, the "uniqueness of the message identifier is guaranteed by the host which generates it." Therefore in Ginko, these MESSAGE-IDs are used as comparands and they are equal if and only if the corresponding e-mails are the same.

Related Patterns

Several of the standard patterns from [Gamma+1995] employ some kind of delegation to let methods of one object operate on behalf of another. If a multitude of objects delegate to a single object, implementations of these patterns can apply the COMPARAND pattern instead of delegating requests for comparison to the respective target objects. The patterns that can take advantage of the COMPARAND pattern in this way are ADAPTER, BRIDGE, DECORATOR, and PROXY.[14]

The OID pattern from [Brown+1996], which can be regarded as a special case of the COMPARAND pattern, is restricted to the context of integrating objects and relational database systems. It discusses only primitive types (integers or strings) as candidates for comparands, and it favors the use of sequence number generators, which are built into some relational database systems, as sources for comparand creation.

Conclusion

There are several techniques for implementing object comparison, depending on the desired semantics and the context of its use, with reference comparison being built into almost all programming languages and therefore being most

---

14. Other patterns from [Gamma+1995] that also use delegation are STATE and STRATEGY. However, they are not candidates for the application of the COMPARAND pattern, since in these cases, the respective target objects do not play an "identifying" role, so it makes no sense to compare them at all.

widely employed. An interesting distinction between the COMPARAND pattern and reference comparison is the following asymmetry. With the COMPARAND pattern, two objects are guaranteed to be the same if their comparands are equal; with reference comparison, two objects are guaranteed to be equal if their references are the same. The latter case is often utilized to optimize otherwise complex comparison operations.

We believe that these considerations could be extended into a useful pattern language covering the realm of object comparison. A few sources, among others, that should be taken into account are [Baker1993] and [Grogono+2000], which discuss various aspects of object comparison, and the EXTRINSIC PROPERTIES of [Fowler1997], which can also be used as a means to determine object equality.

Acknowledgments

The authors thank James Noble for shepherding this paper. They also thank the other members of this paper's Writers' Workshop at EuroPLoP 2001—Fernando Lyardet, Juha Pärssinen, Gustavo Rossi, Dietmar Schütz, and Sherif Yacoub as well as Tom Arbuckle, Michael Austermann, Peter Grogono, Axel Katerbau, Günter Kniesel, Thomas Kühne, Markus Lauer, Oliver Stiemerling, Clemens Szyperski, Dirk Theisen, and Kris De Volder—for their participation in the many fruitful discussions on earlier drafts and related publications that led to substantial improvements.

Pascal Costanza's contribution to this work has been carried out for the TAILOR project at the Institute of Computer Science III of the University of Bonn. The TAILOR project was directed by Armin B. Cremers and supported by Deutsche Forschungsgemeinschaft (DFG) under grant CR 65/13.

References

[Baker1993] H. G. Baker. "Equal Rights for Functional Objects or, The More Things Change, The More They Are the Same." ACM OOPS Messenger 4(4):2–27, 1993.

[Bardou+1996] D. Bardou and C. Dony. "Split Objects: A Disciplined Use of Delegation within Objects." OOPSLA 1996: 122–137.

[Box1998] D. Box. *Essential COM*. Reading, MA: Addison-Wesley, 1998.

[Brown+1996] K. Brown and B. Whitenack. "Crossing Chasms: A Pattern-Language for Object-RDBMS Integration." In J. Vlissides, J. Coplien, and N. Kerth (eds.), *Pattern Languages of Program Design 2*. Reading, MA: Addison-Wesley, 1996.

[Crocker1982] D. H. Crocker. "Standard for the Format of ARPA Internet Text Messages." Internet Request For Comments (RFC) 822, 1982. Available: *http:// www.ietf.org/rfc/rfc0822.txt*.

[Deutsch1992] P. Deutsch. "The Eight Fallacies of Distributed Computing." 1992. Available: *http://today.java.net/jag/Fallacies.html*.

[Fowler1997] M. Fowler. "Dealing with Properties." 1997. Available: *http:// www.martinfowler.com/apsupp/properties.pdf*.

[Gamma+1995] E. Gamma, R. Helm, R. Johnson, and J. Vlissides. *Design Patterns: Elements of Reusable Object-Oriented Software*. Reading, MA: Addison-Wesley, 1995.

[Grogono+2000] P. Grogono and M. Sakkinen. "Copying and Comparing: Problems and Solutions." ECOOP 2000, Object-Oriented Programming: 226–250.

[J2SE] Java 2 Platform, Standard Edition (J2SE). Sun Community Source Licensing. Available: *http://www.sun.com/software/communitysource*.

[JPDA] Java Platform Debugger Architecture. Available: *http://java.sun.com/ products/jpda*.

[JRMI] Java Remote Method Invocation. Available: *http://java.sun.com/products/ jdk/rmi*.

[OMG2003] Object Management Group, Inc. "Java Language Mapping to OMG IDL." 2003. Available: *http://www.omg.org/technology/documents/formal/ java_language_mapping_to_omg_idl.htm*.

[OMG2000] Object Management Group, Inc. "Relationship Service Specification, Version 1.0." Available: *http://www.omg.org/technology/documents/formal/ relationship_service.htm*.

[Objectpark] Objectpark Group. Available: *http://www.objectpark.org*.

[Rohnert1996] H. Rohnert. "The Proxy Design Pattern Revisited." In J. Vlissides, J. Coplien, and N. Kerth (eds.), *Pattern Languages of Program Design* 2. Reading, MA: Addison-Wesley, 1996.

[Sun2000] Sun Microsystems, Inc. "Enterprise JavaBeans Specification, Version 2.0." 2000. Available: *http://java.sun.com/products/ejb/docs.html*.

[Sun2004] Sun Microsystems, Inc. "JDK 5.0 Documentation." 2004. Available: *http://java.sun.com/j2se/1.5.0/docs/index.html*.

CHAPTER 9

Pattern Language
for Service Discovery

Juha Pärssinen, Teemu Koponen, and Pasi Eronen

In this chapter, a pattern language for service discovery is introduced. These patterns were mined from several existing service discovery protocols and from protocols generally used for service discovery that have not been discussed under the theme of service discovery in the research community. This language gives the reader an overview of different aspects of service discovery and enables easier comparison of different existing approaches to this problem domain.

Service discovery is about discovering services in a dynamic network environment. Everything in this chapter preceding the actual service usage is considered as service discovery, regardless of the actual used mechanism. We consider basically everything that can be accessed over the network as services. A service may be a low-level infrastructure service offering critical functionality such as IP connectivity or DNS name resolution. Other services are associated with physical devices such as printers, while Web sites and Web services are more independent of a particular computer implementing them. Certain services operate in more or less ad hoc networks characterized by wireless connections, mobility, lack of fixed infrastructure, decentralized control, and little planning, configuration, or administration, while others are implemented in professionally operated fixed networks with centralized control.

In this chapter, **client** means the party that initiates service discovery, and **service** means the party being discovered. As the result of the service discovery, the client obtains information necessary to choose the right service and communicate with it, such as its capabilities and addresses. However, this does not directly imply in-service discovery; one always has distinct roles for a client and a server. For instance, in voice-over-IP the caller may need to discover the current location (address) of the called party, but both peer-to-peer and client-server architectures are possible.

While some of the presented patterns assume the client is a device operated by a person, such as a Personal Digital Assistant (PDA) or a laptop, the kinds of clients are not limited to such devices. For example, an enterprise application component could implement service discovery to find the current location of a component offering a certain CORBA interface.

A road map of the pattern language is shown in Figure 9–1. In it, the node *How to discover?* is the starting point of this language. An example of the usage of some of the patterns in the Service Location Protocol (SLP) [Guttman+1999] appears at the end of this chapter.

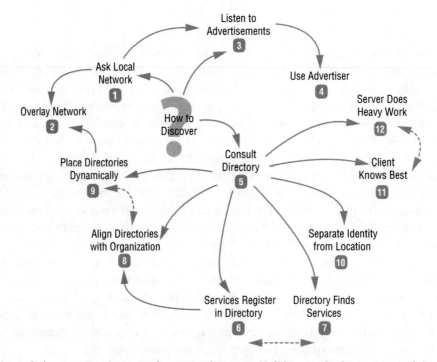

Figure 9–1 *A pattern language for service discovery. (Solid arrows lead to patterns solving a problem in the resulting context; a dashed line indicates an alternative solution or trade-off.)*

The Patterns

1. ASK LOCAL NETWORK

Context

There is a dynamic network of parties; that is, any node in the network can join or leave, usually without involving any centralized administration. Some nodes are offering services to others, mostly to others within broadcast/multicast scope. Service in this context can be almost anything, and the roles of the nodes are not necessarily fixed: the client is the party who wishes to find a service, and service is the party being discovered.

Problem

The client has an idea of what kind of service it needs, but it does not have enough information to contact the service yet.

Forces

- Deploying new services should be easy, and involve as little manual administration as possible.
- Services themselves often know best where they are, and what kind of services they provide.
- Introducing new network elements, such as dedicated directory servers, may not be feasible.

Solution

The client sends a query to nodes that are near it (in terms of network topology) that indicates what kind of services it is looking for. The query is typically sent using some kind of multicast or broadcast message. All services listen to these messages, but only the nodes that have information relevant to the query will actually answer. An illustrated example of this pattern appears at the end of this chapter.

Resulting Context

Clients can discover services that are in the broadcast/multicast scope without requiring fixed infrastructure (such as a directory server) or manual administration. The network topology often approximates physical location and other relevant context, so the services the client is interested in are likely to be near the client in network topology.

However, the client may also be interested in services that are not near it in network topology. One option is to extend the multicast scope, either using normal IP multicast routing or an OVERLAY NETWORK. However, if the number of nodes in the network is large, using multicast messages may become inefficient. This is typically solved by introducing dedicated directory servers, discussed in CONSULT DIRECTORY pattern.

If the client is interested in detecting when new services appear on the network, periodic polling is required. To avoid polling, this pattern is often combined with LISTEN TO ADVERTISEMENTS pattern.

Choosing the right one from the large amount of possible services is considered in patterns CLIENT KNOWS BEST and SERVER DOES HEAVY WORK.

Known Uses

Service discovery protocols supporting operation without a centralized directory, such as Rendezvous [Apple+2004], SLP [Guttman+1999], and UPnP [UPnP+2003], allow clients simply to broadcast their queries to everybody. Services considering the query to match their properties answer and thus inform clients about their presence.

2. OVERLAY NETWORK

Context

Clients ASK LOCAL NETWORK to find services.

Problem

The client's local broadcast/multicast scope does not contain the services the client is looking for. Moreover, only a limited set of nodes in the network containing the services is relevant for answering the query; thus, flooding the queries to everyone is inefficient. How to communicate with a possibly large amount of other nodes while still keeping the benefits of ASK LOCAL NETWORK?

Forces

- The network may not provide an efficient way to implement multicast, for example, normal IP multicast routing may not be available.
- There may be no centralized directories to ask.

Solution

Clients and services build an "overlay network" that allows "application layer multicast" queries to be sent regardless of the underlying network topology. The deployed overlay network enables more intelligent techniques than simple multicasting in order to more efficiently distribute queries. For example, the overlay network nodes could implement caches to store query results. Thus, centralized directories can be avoided.

Resulting Context

Application layer multicast facilitates multicast in environments in which it is not otherwise possible. However, the price is increased client/service complexity and increased usage of resources.

While an overlay network may not require any centralized directory servers that store information about other services, some nodes become more important than others. They are responsible for duplicating multicast messages for leaf nodes in the overlay network. Thus, PLACE DIRECTORIES DYNAMICALLY and ALIGN DIRECTORIES WITH ORGANIZATION patterns may be useful in selecting these more vital nodes. In other words, this pattern blurs the line between multicasting and (dynamically placed) directory servers.

Known Uses

Peer-to-peer file sharing networks, and peer-to-peer applications in general, commonly use a variety of application layer multicast approaches; see, for instance, JXTA Search [Waterhouse+2001].

3. LISTEN TO ADVERTISEMENTS

Context

There is a dynamic network of parties; that is, any node in the network can join or leave, usually without involving any centralized administration. Some nodes are offering services to others, and usually many of the nodes within broadcast/multicast scope are interested in the services.

Problem

Clients want to find out what services are available, when new services appear on the network, and when old services leave.

Forces

- Deploying new services should be easy, and involve as little manual administration as possible.
- Introducing new network elements, such as dedicated directory servers, may not be feasible.
- The network has a large number of clients compared to the number of services.

Solution

Services periodically send advertisement messages, normally using some kind of multicast or broadcast messages. Using advertisements is especially suitable if most clients are likely to be interested in the same services. An illustrated example of this pattern appears at the end of this chapter.

Resulting Context

There is a trade-off between reactiveness and bandwidth usage: if the services send advertisements more often, clients can discover the current situation faster, but more bandwidth and other resources are required. For this reason, periodic advertisements are sometimes used together with ASK LOCAL NETWORK pattern. If the number of services grows larger, other alternatives such as CONSULT DIRECTORY pattern can be considered.

If a service is not able to advertise itself, it can USE ADVERTISER.

Known Uses

Many service discovery protocols, such as SLP [Guttman+1999] and UPnP [UPnP+2003], use periodical multicast advertisements. Other examples include IEEE 802.11 wireless LAN Beacon messages [IEEE+1999] and ICMPv6 Router Advertisements [Thomson+1998].

4. USE ADVERTISER

Context

Clients LISTEN TO ADVERTISEMENTS to find services.

Problem

A service may not be able or willing to advertise itself.

Forces

- The service may not support the service discovery protocol that is used in the current environment.

- Advertising consumes the limited resources of the service.

Solution

A service delegates advertising to an advertiser that can, and is able to, advertise on behalf of the service. In order to advertise, the advertiser requires the service information. This transfer of information may be either manual or automatic.

While the first requires support from service administrators, the latter requires the advertiser to have a transfer interface available for services.

Resulting Context

Services that are not able to advertise themselves, or are too busy serving clients, can now use LISTEN TO ADVERTISEMENTS pattern. If the service does not know an advertiser by using automatic delegation, it can LISTEN TO ADVERTISEMENTS, ASK LOCAL NETWORK, or CONSULT DIRECTORY to discover one.

Known Uses

Service discovery protocol implementations often support manual registration of legacy services (without support for modern service discovery protocols). For example, OpenSLP's SLP daemon supports manual service registrations [Peterson+2004].

5. CONSULT DIRECTORY

Context

There is a dynamic network of parties; that is, any node in the network can join or leave at any time. There is possibly a large number of nodes offering services to others. The service in this context can be almost anything from low-level infrastructure services such as DNS name resolution to Web sites such as Amazon.com.

Problem

The client has an idea of what kind of service it needs, but it does not have enough information to contact the service yet.

Forces

- The services are not necessarily near the clients in the network topology.
- Using broadcast/multicast queries and advertisements may not scale to a large number of services.
- Centralized administration is often involved in setting up a new service.

Solution

Let the client consult a directory server that manages a database containing contact information for available services. An illustrated example of this pattern appears at the end of this chapter.

Resulting Context

The network requires the presence of a directory or directories. The administrator or service discovery protocol developer must decide whether being a directory is a permanent role assumed by one or more nodes in the network. One can ALIGN DIRECTORIES WITH ORGANIZATION, or the network can PLACE DIRECTORIES DYNAMICALLY by itself.

In order to give meaningful answers, a directory must be provisioned with the information to be shared with clients. Either SERVICES REGISTER IN DIRECTORY or DIRECTORY FINDS SERVICES is normally used. Moreover, to contact the directory, the client needs to know its contact information. This "bootstrap provisioning" could be done manually (by configuring the network address), or the client can LISTEN TO ADVERTISEMENTS or ASK LOCAL NETWORK to find the directory.

Clients are also occasionally interested in the appearance of new services on the network. To avoid needless polling, the PUBLISHER-SUBSCRIBER [Buschmann+ 2000] pattern, a variant of the OBSERVER [Gamma+1995] pattern, could be used to allow the directory to notify interested clients of new services.

Known Uses

Several service discovery protocols have a directory entity. For example, SLP has Directory Agent (DA) [Guttman+1999], and Jini has a lookup service [Sun+2001a]. Service discovery protocols also often support subscription to notifications about service appearances (e.g., [Kempf+2001] and [Sun+2001a]). Moreover, the network may have a LDAP directory [Hodges+2002] or authoritative DNS server [Mockapetris+1987].

General Web search engines (e.g., [Brin+1998]) and directories such as Google Directory, Yahoo!, and telephone directory services, are also examples of the pattern.

Related Patterns

Directories can be avoided in small networks by using ASK LOCAL NETWORK and LISTEN TO ADVERTISEMENTS patterns.

The LOOKUP pattern [Kircher+2004] describes a directory service, but combines querying, registering, bootstrapping, and aspects of directory placement into a single pattern. We consider these aspects in separate patterns in this chapter.

6. SERVICES REGISTER IN DIRECTORY

Context

Clients CONSULT DIRECTORY to find information about services. Each service is typically listed in only one directory or perhaps in a few.

Problem

The directory needs to get the information about services to share with the clients.

Forces

- Manually storing the information in the directory may be feasible, but is tedious.
- Service administrators may want to control what information is stored in the directory.
- Services themselves know best where they are, what kind of services they provide, and when this information changes.
- It's acceptable for services to become service discovery-aware.

Solution

Let services register themselves in directories. The directories must provide a special service registration interface so services can provision their information. An illustrated example of this pattern appears at the end of this chapter.

Resulting Context

The directory has the information it needs to answer service discovery queries from clients. In addition, services can update their own information so that any changes propagate in a timely fashion. However, information about services that no longer exist can still remain in directories: the LEASING [Kircher+2004] pattern provides a solution to this.

As a result, services have to be aware of service discovery and know how to register themselves, which is likely to complicate their implementation and operation. If this is not desired, DIRECTORY FINDS SERVICES can be used instead.

Moreover, if there is more than one independent directory to register in, services may have to first find the directories (e.g., using LISTEN TO ADVERTISEMENTS or ASK LOCAL NETWORK) and register with each of them. Therefore, DIRECTORY FINDS SERVICES may enable the services to reach a larger audience of clients in environments with several directories.

The problem that remains unanswered is how to ensure overall validity of the service information stored in the directories. For example, can anyone register a service or are there access control mechanisms in place?

Known Uses

Many service discovery protocols have a protocol and messages for registering purposes: SLP has service registration messages [Guttman+1999], Jini has "join protocol" [Sun+2001b], DNS has dynamic update messages [Vixie+1997], and UDDI provides a Publishing API [OASIS+2002].

7. DIRECTORY FINDS SERVICES

Context

Clients CONSULT DIRECTORY to find information about services. However, services do not require explicit control in publishing their information. In certain operational environments, there can also be a need to have multiple directories that contain the same services in order to facilitate an even wider audience for services.

Problem

The directory or directories must obtain the information about services to share with the clients. Requiring services to register themselves in a directory places the burden on the services. Moreover, services might not possess the information for all directories, or the number of directories may simply be overwhelming from a service's point of view. Unfortunately, services that don't want to, or can't, register themselves won't be listed in the directories.

Forces

- Manually storing the information in the directory may be feasible, but is tedious.
- Making services unaware of service discovery can simplify their implementation and deployment.
- Directories can be more comprehensive if they do not require active cooperation from the services.

Solution

Let the directories find the services by implementing a mechanism to examine networks to the directories. The mechanism should be executed periodically. It can be manual (e.g., Google Directory or Yahoo) or automatic (e.g., Google). A more comprehensive examination will yield a more comprehensive directory of services. The services can now provide information about themselves in a way that is independent of the way the directories work.

Resulting Context

This pattern decouples services from directories: services don't have to know where they are listed. It is easier to have multiple directories covering the same services—service information can be more easily distributed to a larger audience. Multiple directories and even competition between them could be useful in some situations (e.g., Web search engines).

Since services do not know where they are listed, timeliness of information may become problematic, because services cannot notify the directory when something has changed. To improve the validity of the service contact information, directories should execute the basic measure by using SEPARATE IDENTITY FROM LOCATION.

The directory has to find the services somehow, and a Web search engine, for example, will not find pages that are not linked anywhere. Also, finding services by following links is especially suitable for hypertext, but may not be applicable to other types of services.

Known Uses

Web search engines typically use this pattern (e.g., [Brin+1998]). Even in a closed environment such as a corporate intranet, it would be difficult to register every Web page in a search engine. Instead, the search engine crawler is given a couple of starting points and finds other pages by following hyperlinks.

In certain manually maintained directories, the directory maintainers are responsible for finding the services and sorting them into relevant categories; examples include Google Directory, Yahoo!, and Web-based restaurant guides. It is also possible to combine this pattern in a case where services ask to be listed in the directory using SERVICES REGISTER IN DIRECTORY.

8. ALIGN DIRECTORIES WITH ORGANIZATION

Context

Clients CONSULT DIRECTORY to find information about services on the network. Each service is usually associated with an organization or organizational unit responsible for it.

Problem

Where should directory servers be placed, and who should operate them?

Forces

- Availability of directory servers is critical.
- An organizational unit's information is accessed most often inside the unit.

- Organizations may want to control the contents of directories and who can access the data.

- Organizational units want to influence the division of responsibilities and allocation of costs.

Solution

Let organizational units, such as departments or divisions, establish their separate directories and then connect the directories to reflect the organization's hierarchy or other relevant static structure.

Resulting Context

Organizational units gain more control of the directory contents. Local directories allow local authorization and implementation decisions, such as who is allowed to modify information and how modifications are done.

The overall system becomes more scalable and fault tolerant. Moreover, because the network topology is often also aligned with organizational structures, local directories improve the overall performance of the directory system.

If static alignment of directories is impractical due to the dynamics of the organization, or if support for dedicated directories is uncertain in the organization, it's better to PLACE DIRECTORIES DYNAMICALLY.

Known Uses

Hierarchical directories such as DNS [Mockapetris+1987], LDAP [Hodges+2002], and Microsoft Active Directory [Microsoft+2004a] support deployment aligned with the organization.

9. PLACE DIRECTORIES DYNAMICALLY

Context

Clients CONSULT DIRECTORY to find information about services on the network. No static structures exist in the service discovery environment that support the further categorization of nodes to directories and regular nodes.

Problem

Where should directory servers be placed, and who should operate them?

Forces

- Technical differences among network nodes are insignificant in terms of providing directory functionality.

- No external restrictions or preferences are set for the directory servers—all network nodes are equally valid.

- The technical and non-technical support that dedicated directories can get is uncertain or must be kept minimal due to the environment.

Solution

Let all (or at least many) nodes implement directory functionality and then dynamically select node(s) that will assume the directory role. Depending on the context, several directory node-selection algorithms may be available. The selection can be based on the abilities of the nodes to operate as a directory (e.g., most processing power or best network connectivity) or if no such information is available, the choice can even be random.

Resulting Context

Dynamically selected directories provide fewer possibilities for controlling the directories and their contents. Moreover, the stability properties of the directories' services may be unknown. In certain environments, however, the overall availability may in fact improve, because other nodes can more easily take over in case of a failure.

If the directory functionality is dynamically placed, clients have to find the directory. This is usually accomplished by means of either LISTEN TO ADVERTISEMENTS or ASK LOCAL NETWORK pattern.

Known Uses

In NetBIOS networks, the nodes "elect" a domain master browser among themselves [Microsoft+2004b].

10. SEPARATE IDENTITY FROM LOCATION

Context

Clients and directories store information about gathered services in a dynamic environment. Directories do this as part of their normal operations—after all, they need to be able to answer service queries from clients—but clients can also store the service contact information in order to contact the same service later.

Problem

What should clients and directories store as service contact information in order to maintain the usability of the information later in such a dynamic environment?

Once again, the whole purpose of storing service contact information is to reuse it later.

Forces

- A service may be moved from a server to another server.

- A service may be running on a mobile terminal whose network attachment point constantly changes.

- The network address (location) of a server can be dynamically assigned.

Solution

Let clients and directories use an identifier, which remains valid for a long time, to identify services. In other words, clients and directories refer to services using identifiers, instead of network addresses, in their service information storages. One must also provide an additional mapping service to map these persistent identifiers, as needed, to more transient network addresses—information that will be needed to locate and contact the actual services. Mapping service implementation determines the allocation method of the identifiers. An illustrated example of this pattern appears at the end of this chapter.

Resulting Context

Clients and directories can store information for a longer time, but they also need a service to map the identifiers to network addresses (e.g., IP addresses). The mapping service may be distributed—that is, clients ASK LOCAL NETWORK— or centralized if clients CONSULT DIRECTORY (e.g., DNS, SIP). If the identifier resolution is based on a directory, there has to be a way to update the information; usually the SERVICES REGISTER IN DIRECTORY pattern is used.

There can be several layers of identifiers and service discovery. For example, a query for printers can result in a URL that is mapped to an IP address using DNS (an example of CONSULT DIRECTORY) and to an Ethernet MAC address using ARP (an example of ASK LOCAL NETWORK).

Known Uses

Domain names [Mockapetris+1987], Jini service identifiers [Sun+2001b], HIP host identities [Nikander+2003], SIP URIs [Rosenberg+2002], UPnP unique device names [UPnP+2003], and URLs [Berners-Lee+1994] are all examples of identifiers that can be stored for a long time and mapped to the service's current location (IP address, port number, etc.) when needed in order to obtain valid service contact information.

Related Patterns

The CLIENT-DISPATCHER-SERVER pattern [Buschmann+2000] describes a dispatcher service that knows the current location of services. Moreover, the dispatcher enables a communication channel between clients and services; clients merely identify the needed service with a service identifier while performing a service call. In this chapter, however, we consider service discovery not to include service access and thus SEPARATE IDENTITY FROM LOCATION contains the relevant aspects of the pattern: location and identity separation.

The IDENTIFICATION patterns [Zdun+2004] separate identifiers and locators in the context of distributed object middleware solutions. In the identification, patterns' interpretation of an object identifier is local to a server and thus identifiers do not translate to locators as such. In a way, SEPARATE IDENTITY >FROM LOCATION is an addition to these patterns; it makes a clearer functional distinction between locators and identifiers than the IDENTIFICATION patterns do.

11. CLIENT KNOWS BEST

Context

A client can discover services with or without consulting directories, but it is subject to receiving information about multiple services as an answer to a service query.

Problem

How can a service or a directory answering a query decide which services are the most relevant for the specific client and especially for its user?

Forces

- The relevance of services depends on the context of a client and its user's preferences.
- Usually only a limited amount of context information can be sent with the query.
- Increasing the expressive power of queries increases the complexity of both clients and directories.
- Services and directories do not know how to process the context and preference information.
- The user may not know how to formulate a specific query, but can pick the right service when shown the alternatives.

Solution

Use a simple query language, even if that means returning several matches to the client. Let the client, or even its user, decide which of the matches is the desired one. This moves the responsibility of handling context information and user preferences to the client software.

Resulting Context

The client obtains the information necessary to access a service fulfilling the current need. However, there is a risk that a service or directory has too much information to transmit to the client or the client has too much information to show to the user. It then becomes essential that the SERVER DOES HEAVY WORK.

Known Uses

The service discovery query language of UPnP has minimal expression power, namely, keywords; UPnP services accept their unawareness of clients' contexts and require more participation from their clients [UPnP+2003].

In many service discovery protocols, the user is presented with a list of best-matching services, and the final decision about which to use is made by the user. A typical example of this would be a Web search engine.

Related Patterns

PROFILE-BASED SERVICE BROWSING pattern [Gitsels+2000] recommends that the client software filters the list based on user's preferences and terminal capabilities when shown what services are available. This pattern was also inspired by PEOPLE KNOW BEST pattern in [Adams+1995].

12. SERVER DOES HEAVY WORK

Context

Clients CONSULT DIRECTORY to discover services; the directory contains information about a large number of services.

Problem

How do we optimize the processing and communication requirements of the clients? It is often impractical, or even impossible, to transfer a large set of service information to the client due to limited bandwidth, limited storage, and processing requirements.

Forces

- Clients can often better use context information and user preferences to select the right service among several alternatives: CLIENT KNOWS BEST.

- It is impractical to move the complete decision-making process into clients due to constraints.

- Answering the query may require complex algorithms and the processing of large amounts of data.

- Directory servers have better processing resources.

Solution

Let the directory server perform complex search operations. This reduces the amount of information that needs to be sent to the client. However, as with CLIENT KNOWS BEST, the directories must not be too aggressive—a careful equilibrium between minimization of communication requirements and maximizing of the client's abilities to leverage its context awareness and preferences must be obtained.

Resulting Context

The client obtains the information necessary to access a service fulfilling the current need. However, the directory servers become more complex and their resource requirements increase. It then might make sense to distribute the directory further, for example, by using ALIGN DIRECTORIES WITH ORGANIZATION.

Known Uses

Service discovery protocols (e.g., [Apple+2004], [Guttman+1999], [Sun+2001a], and [UPnP+2003]), Web search engines (e.g., [Brin+1998]), and directories in general (e.g., LDAP [Hodges+2002] and UDDI [OASIS+2002]) allow clients to define search criteria, possibly even with complex query languages. Implementing complex algorithms for ranking the results (such as Google's PageRank) is also possible.

Combining the Patterns: SLP as an Example

Actual service discovery protocols usually use several of the patterns presented here. In this section, we present an example in which a client discovers a printer using Service Location Protocol (SLP) [Guttman+1999]. Please note that this example shows only one possible scenario and thus does not cover all features of SLP.

1. The directory agent sends a multicast advertisement when it is started, and periodically after that. Services that are interested in directory agents, such as the printer in this example, LISTEN TO ADVERTISEMENTS.

2–3. When a new directory agent has been found, SERVICES REGISTER IN DIRECTORY. The registration contains information about the service being offered and where the service can be reached.

4–5. When Client 1 appears on the network, it decides to send a multicast message—or in other words, ASK LOCAL NETWORK—to find a directory agent. The directory agent answers with its IP address.

6–7. When Client 1 wants to print a document, it has to CONSULT DIRECTORY to find what printers are available.

8–9. The answer returned by the directory agent can contain a domain name instead of an IP address. In this case, Client 1 has to contact the DNS server, which is an example of SEPARATE IDENTITY FROM LOCATION.

10. Finally, Client 1 can connect to the printer (see Figure 9–2).

Acknowledgments

We would like to thank our EuroPLoP 2004 shepherd, Michael Kircher, and the participants of the workshop for their encouraging comments and suggestions. Mari Korkea-aho and Sanna Liimatainen also provided valuable comments on work that lead to these patterns.

References

[Adams+1995] M. Adams, J. Coplien, R. Gamoke, R. Hanmer, F. Keeve, and K. Nicodemus. "Fault-Tolerant Telecommunication System Patterns." In *Proceedings of the Second Annual Conference on the Pattern Languages of Programs.* Monticello, Ill., September 1995.

[Apple+2004] Apple Computer. Rendezvous. Apple Developer Connection, 2004. Available: *http://developer.apple.com/macosx/rendezvous/*.

[Berners-Lee+1994] T. Berners-Lee, L. Masinter, and M. McCahill. Uniform Resource Locators (URL). RFC 1738, IETF, December 1994.

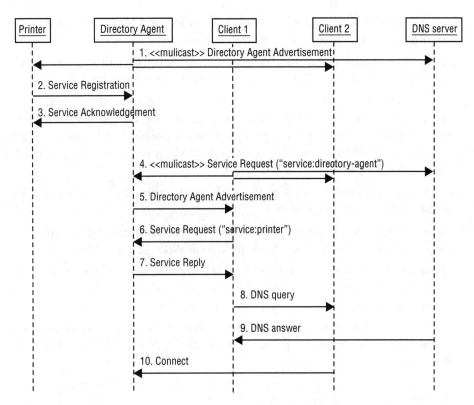

Figure 9–2 *Printer discovery using SLP as an example of using the service discovery patterns*

[Brin+1998] S. Brin and L. Page. "The Anatomy of a Large-Scale Hypertextual Web Search Engine." *Computer Networks and ISDN Systems*, 30(1–7):107–117, 1998.

[Buschmann+2000] F. Buschmann, R. Meunier, H. Rohnert, P. Sommerlad, and M. Stal. *Pattern-Oriented Software Architecture: A System of Patterns*. New York: John Wiley & Sons, 1996.

[Gamma+1995] E. Gamma, R. Helm, R. Johnson, and J. Vlissides. *Design Patterns: Elements of Reusable Object-Oriented Software*. Reading, MA: Addison-Wesley, 1995.

[Gitsels+2000] M. Gitsels and J. Sauter. "Profile-Based Service Browsing—A Pattern for Intelligent Service Discovery in Large Networks." The Jini Pattern Language Workshop at OOPSLA 2000, Minneapolis, Minn., October 2000.

[Guttman+1999] E. Guttman, C. Perkins, J. Veizades, and M. Day. Service Location Protocol, Version 2. RFC 2608, IETF, June 1999.

[Hodges+2002] J. Hodges and R. Morgan, Lightweight Directory Access Protocol (v3): Technical Specification, RFC 3377, IETF, September 2002.

[IEEE+1999] Institute of Electrical and Electronics Engineers. Information Technology—Telecommunications and Information Exchange between Systems—Local and Metropolitan Area Network—Specific Requirements—Part 11: Wireless LAN Medium Access Control (MAC) and Physical Layer (PHY) Specifications, IEEE Standard 802.11, 1999.

[Kempf+2001] J. Kempf and J. Goldschmidt. Notification and Subscription for SLP. RFC 3082, IETF, March 2001.

[Kircher+2004] M. Kircher and P. Jain. *Pattern-Oriented Software Architecture: Patterns for Resource Management.* New York: John Wiley & Sons, 2004.

[Microsoft+2004a] Microsoft. Active Directory Architecture. Microsoft TechNet, 2004. Available: *http://www.microsoft.com/technet/prodtechnol/windows2000serv/technologies/activedirectory/deploy/projplan/adarch.mspx.*

[Microsoft+2004b] Microsoft. Description of the Microsoft Computer Browser Service. Microsoft Knowledge Base Article 188001, 2004. Available: *http://support.microsoft.com/?kbid=188001.*

[Mockapetris+1987] P. Mockapetris. Domain names—concepts and facilities. RFC 1034, IETF, November 1987.

[Nikander+2003] P. Nikander, J. Ylitalo, and J. Wall. "Integrating security, mobility, and multi-homing in a HIP way." In *Proceedings of the 10th Annual Network and Distributed Systems Security Symposium* (NDSS), San Diego, CA, February 2003.

[OASIS+2002] Organization for the Advancement of Structured Information Standards (OASIS). UDDI API Specification, Version 2.04, 2002. Available: *http://uddi.org/pubs/ProgrammersAPI-V2.04-Published-20020719.htm.*

[Peterson+2004] M. Peterson, et al. OpenSLP home page, 2004. Available: *http://www.openslp.org.*

[Rosenberg+2002] J. Rosenberg, H. Schulzrinne, G. Camarillo, A. Johnston, J. Peterson, R. Sparks, M. Handley, and E. Schooler. SIP: Session Initiation Protocol. RFC 3261, IETF, June 2002.

[Sun+2001a] Sun Microsystems. Jini Architecture Specification, Version 1.2. December 2001. Available: *http://wwws.sun.com/software/jini/specs/jini1.2html/jini-title.html.*

[Sun+2001b] Sun Microsystems. Jini Technology Core Platform Specification, Version 1.2. December 2001. Available: *http://wwws.sun.com/software/jini/specs/ jini1.2html/core-title.html*

[Thomson+1998] S. Thomson and T. Narten. IPv6 Stateless Address Autoconfiguration, RFC 2462, IETF, December 1998.

[UPnP+2003] UPnP Forum. UPnP Device Architecture, Version 1.0.1. December 2003. Available: *http://www.upnp.org/resources/documents.asp.*

[Vixie+1997] P. Vixie, S. Thomson, Y. Rekhter, and J. Bound. Dynamic Updates in the Domain Name System (DNS UPDATE), RFC 2136, IETF, April 1997.

[Waterhouse+2001] S. Waterhouse. JXTA Search: Distributed Search for Distributed Networks, May 2001. Available: *http://search.jxta.org/JXTAsearch.pdf.*

[Zdun+2004] U. Zdun, M. Kircher, and M. Völter. "Remoting Patterns." *Internet Computing*, 8(6):60–68, 2004.

PART IV

Domain-Specific Patterns

Chapter 10: MoRaR: A Pattern Language for Mobility and Radio Resource Management

For years, the telecom field has been fertile ground for new ideas and techniques. Seasoned software architects often look at and adopt solutions from this space. Several telecom patterns and pattern languages already exist, and new patterns are emerging in the area of mobile telecommunications. Based on insights from 2, 2.5, and 3G mobile wireless systems, Rossana Andrade and Luigi Logrippo are the first to write a pattern language focused on mobility and radio resource management. People who design mobile telecommunications systems, people who need to know how these systems work, and even people who deal with similar problems may find these patterns useful.

Chapter 11: Content Conversion and Generation on the Web: A Pattern Language

When eBay, Amazon, and Yahoo! opened up ten years ago, skeptics questioned the viability of using the Web as a medium for building highly dynamic applications. Nowadays, Web-based applications are ubiquitous. We use them when we shop online, browse movie schedules, locate restaurants, print boarding passes, make rental car reservations, pay bills, trade stocks, and so on. All these applications generate content on demand. In Content Conversion and Generation on the Web, Oliver Vogel and Uwe Zdun present a pattern language aimed at people building applications that deal with dynamic HTML generation.

CHAPTER 10

MoRaR: A Pattern Language for Mobility and Radio Resource Management

Rossana Maria de Castro Andrade and Luigi Logrippo

Introduction

Mobile users are able to roam with a large variety of mobile wireless communication systems. For instance, the Global System for Mobile communications 900 (GSM-900) is a European-based technology that is the foundation for the digital cellular system 1800 (GSM-1800) [Mouly+1992] [Redl+1995] and the Personal Communication System 1900 (PCS-1900) [Grinberg1996]. General Packet Radio Services (GPRS) [Ghribi+2000] and Universal Mobile Telecommunications System (UMTS) [Kriaras+1997] are evolutions of GSM. Furthermore, the Digital Advanced Mobile Phone System (D-AMPS) (also known as Interim Standard 54-B) [Black1999], which is a North American technology, defines a hybrid air interface that allows mobile stations to operate in a dual-mode fashion (analog and digital). These cellular systems provide basic and supplementary telecommunications services [Grinberg1996]. The D-AMPS air interface is supported by the American National Standards Institute-41 (ANSI-41) [ANSI/TIA/EIA1997] [Gallagher+1997]. ANSI-41 provides registration, roaming, call features, and other mobile application protocol features on the network side.

These systems have substantial differences related to their architecture, protocols, and services [Grinberg1996]. Interfaces among components, cryptography algorithms, and types of handoff are proprietary solutions. However, these systems adopt common solutions for dealing with recurring mobility, communication, and radio resource management problems, as already discussed in [Andrade+2000a], [Andrade2001a], and [Andrade+2001b].

Third-generation standards such as the International Mobile Telecommunications 2000 (IMT-2000) Systems [ITU1999a][ITU1999b][ITU2000] have been developed to overcome the incompatibilities among the second-generation systems mentioned earlier and to integrate standardization activities. Meanwhile, other solutions such as signaling protocols for Wireless mobile Asynchronous Transfer Mode (WmATM) systems have been proposed to provide mobility and radio resource management functions for high-speed Local Area Networks (LANs) and Wide-Area Networks (WANs) [Bora1997][Cheng+1997] [Wesel998]. IMT-2000 systems and WmATM networks present commonalities with second-generation systems with regard to the architectural elements and the functional behaviors involved in mobility and radio resource management.

This chapter investigates the commonalities among mobile wireless communication systems as presented in [Andrade2001a] in order to identify, to capture, and to document patterns. We identify and capture commonalities related to mobility and radio resource management functions among the following second- and third-generation mobile systems: GSM and GPRS, ANSI-41, Wireless Intelligent Network (WIN) [Amyot+1999], UMTS, IMT-2000, and WmATM.

These patterns are grouped into a pattern language for mobility and radio resource management (MoRaR) that shows possible relationships among them. Several alternative scenarios can be derived from these relationships. Furthermore, this set of patterns allows designers to recognize similarities among legacy systems at the early stages of the system development process and evolution, and to reuse good solutions independent of implementation. However, MoRaR is useful not only to design a mobile system but also to know how one works.

This chapter is organized as follows. The next section gives an overview of mobile wireless systems, which are the pattern language context. The MoRaR Pattern Language section introduces the MoRaR pattern language and shows the relationship between the patterns related to mobility management introduced in [Andrade+2000a] and the radio resource management patterns presented in [Andrade+2001b]. These patterns are detailed in the Patterns Related to Mobility Management Functions section and the Patterns for Radio Resource Management section, respectively. Finally, the Conclusion of this chapter addresses the main contributions of the pattern language and potential patterns to be documented. A table with a summary and an index of all patterns presented in this chapter (by chapter section and pattern name) is provided in the Appendix.

Mobile Wireless Systems: Architectural Concepts

The geographical area covered by a mobile system is divided into **cells** that are grouped into location areas [FCC2006]. Typically, a **location area** is a group of cells that constitute the domain of an operator, although an operator can have several location areas. A mobile station needs to **register** when it enters a new location area, and it remains registered as long as it remains in that location area. A mobile station has a **home location area** where it is initially registered (this area typically includes the principal address of the user); it is said to be **roaming** when it goes to other location areas (**visited area**). Roaming must occur without interruption of service. Mobility management operations are responsible for keeping a record of the mobile user's location (**location registration** function) and for finding the correct location of a mobile station in a group of cells (**paging** function). A mobile user's privileges are also checked during mobility management (**authentication** and **ciphering** functions) in order to minimize the possibility of fraud.

Every time a powered-on mobile station crosses certain boundaries or detects a better channel in another location area, it requests a location update to the network. The network is in charge of the databases that keep information about the user. If a call is coming to the mobile user, the network requests a paging operation to locate the mobile station and establish the connection.

Authentication is applied to validate the user's identity and ciphering is used to protect the information exchanged between the mobile station and the network. Authentication and ciphering operations give the mobile user privacy and security. At a high level of abstraction, these solutions are the same for GSM/GPRS/UMTS, ANSI-41/WIN, IMT-2000, and WmATM systems. Implementations, however, differ: The ciphering and authentication algorithms and the sequences of exchanged messages or parameters between network entities during this process may be different.

Figure 10–1 shows the typical components of a mobile wireless communication system (PLMN—Public Land Mobile Network), which is an example of the systems under consideration in this chapter. The mobile system functions mentioned earlier involve mobile stations (MSs), home database (commonly called "home location register" or "HLR"), visitor database (also called "visitor location register" or "VLR"), security database (called "authentication center"), and mobile switching centers (MSCs). This scenario shows a mobile station (represented by a car) that is roaming from its home location area to a visited area. The mobile station movement is represented by the colors gray (previous locations) and black (current location).

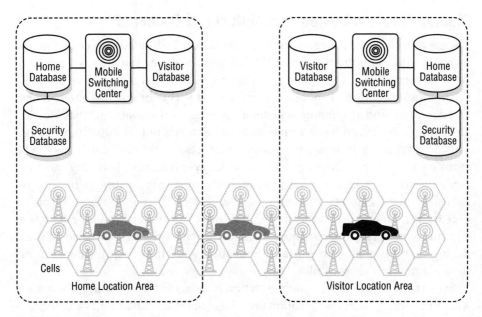

Figure 10–1 *Typical components of a mobile wireless communication system*

The MS is the equipment used to terminate the radio path at the user side. At the network side, base station controllers (BSCs) and mobile switching centers (MSCs) are also involved.

The mobile switching center is the interface between the base station controller (BSC), which is not shown in the figure, and the home database as well as the visitor database. Each mobile switching center is responsible for one or more location areas and for the exchange of messages between the network side and the mobile stations through common or dedicated radio channels. The MSC also constitutes the interface for user traffic between the cellular network and other public switched networks (or other MSCs in the same or other cellular networks). There is typically an MSC and one location area for each operator. However, standards leave considerable freedom for different implementations. Operators responsible for large geographical entities can have several MSCs and location areas. Initially, the MS of a mobile user is registered with the MSC that is responsible for the user's home location area.

The home database permanently keeps information about the mobile user profile while the visitor database temporarily keeps part of the mobile user profile, the part that is needed to perform the current call. The security database is responsible for the sensitive data related to authentication and ciphering functions. In short, these databases are responsible for keeping information about a mobile user's location, services, and equipment.

As shown in Figure 10–2, a cell is the region covered by the radio signal of a base station transceiver (BST). A BSC is responsible for monitoring a certain number of cells grouped in a location area. The set of BST and BSC is often called a base station (BS).

Radio resource management functions handle the connection, which is done through radio access ports (known as "air interface"), between a BST and MS. The handoff procedure (also known as "handover" in Europe) guarantees the quality of the connection (i.e., the dedicated radio channel between the MS and the network), which allows each mobile user to roam. In this chapter, we capture and document patterns related to handoffs, which constitute the main issues for radio resource management, on the basis of the architectural elements involved and their functional behavior.

Handoff is a critical functionality for mobile systems because all communication services should be maintained while the user is roaming. Without handoffs, calls would be dropped as soon as the user moves from the home location area. As shown in Figure 10–2, handoffs can occur in three different ways depending on the network equipment involved [Grinberg1996] [ITU1999a] [Mouly+1992].

Interbase station transceiver handoff involves modifications only in the radio channel between BSTs and the MS (position 1 in the figure). Interbase station

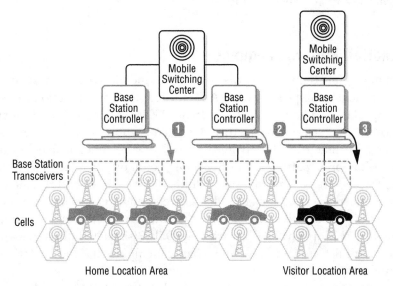

Figure 10–2 *Types of handoffs*

controller (or intra-MSC) handoff also includes changes in the BST (position 2). These types of handoffs are also known as "intrasystem handoff." Finally, the inter-mobile switching center handoff (also known as "intersystem handoff") involves different MSCs (position 3).

As Figure 10–2 shows, BSTs and BSCs are important components of the handoff process; however, this chapter considers only the so-called "intersystem handoffs," which involve different MSCs. At the upper layers, intersystem handoffs are managed by MSs and MSCs. BSTs and BSCs act as complex transmission systems and can be ignored. This handoff requires specialized signaling protocols between the current and the candidate MSCs that are involved in the process.

It is worth mentioning that architectural models of mobile wireless systems distinguish among functional entities, network entities, and physical entities. The highest level of abstraction is described in terms of functional entities, and these are incorporated into network entities at a lower level of abstraction. Network entities are then mapped to real physical entities at the implementation level. In this chapter, we use the term **architectural** (or **structural**) **element** as a synonym for a functional or network entity. As mentioned earlier, common architectural (or structural) elements are identified among these systems [Andrade2001a] [Black1999] [Grinberg1996]. Thus, the sections that follow take into consideration the following common architectural elements: MS, MSC, BST, BSC, and databases such as the Home Location Register (HLR) and the Visitor Location Register (VLR).

The MoRaR Pattern Language

The common functional behaviors among the mobile wireless systems mentioned previously are presented in [Andrade2001a] using a notation called Use Case Maps (UCMs) [Amyot+1999] [Andrade+2000b] [Andrade2000c] [Buhr1998]. These commonalities are analyzed, and when it is appropriate, a pattern is captured and documented. The patterns based on the functional behavior are called **behavioral patterns**. Furthermore, common architectural elements among the chosen systems are also identified in [Andrade2001a], where each system architecture is described with UCM components and the common elements are extracted. Accordingly, when the pattern concept can be applied [Alexander+1977] [Coplien1996] [Meszaros+1997] [Rising1999], these network or functional entities are translated to the pattern template and they constitute the structural patterns.

After identifying behavioral and structural patterns from the commonalities presented in [Andrade2001a], the motivation for designing a pattern language arises from the need to show the interactions among them. The pattern language for mobility and radio resource management (MoRaR) shown in Figure 10–3 offers designers the possibility of generating different scenarios related to mobile systems. Designers are then able to find the patterns that are relevant for what they intend to do at the requirements and analysis stages. It should be mentioned that the pattern language shows alternative ways to combine patterns.

Figure 10–3 shows the pattern language with the behavioral (ovals) and architectural (plain rectangles) patterns classified into two categories (dashed rectangles): mobility management and radio resource management. In short, these two categories describe the functional layers discussed in [Andrade2001a] that are often used in the literature when discussing protocols for mobile communication systems. The dashed and plain black arrows illustrate the relationship among the patterns. The gray arrows with outgoing call, incoming call,

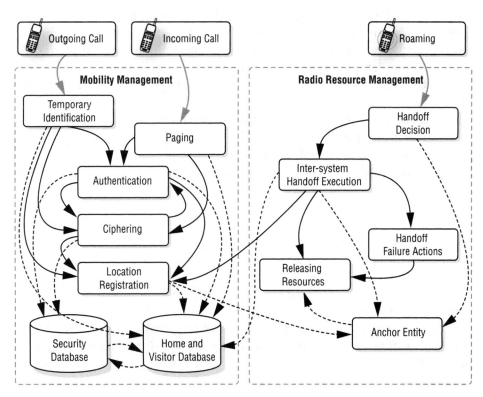

Figure 10–3 *Relationships of the patterns within the MoRaR pattern language*

and roaming labels depict three possible start points for scenarios derived from the pattern language. Each pattern name also identifies the subsection in which it is discussed.

Dashed arrows represent the exchange of the following information requests between the behavioral and the structural patterns: a request for data items, a request for operations on data items, or a request for control or release of resources. For instance, *location registration* requests the *home and visitor databases* to store, update, and delete data items related to the mobile users' location. On the other hand, *paging, temporary identification* assignment, *authentication*, and *intersystem handoff execution* request data items that are stored in the databases. In addition, the *home database* requests data items that are stored in the *security database* and vice versa. A request from the *handoff decision* or from the *location registration* triggers the *anchor* mobile switching center *entity*, which controls the resources (e.g., *releasing resources*) for the *intersystem handoff execution*.

Plain arrows represent the order in which the patterns occur. A designer chooses either a set of patterns or an individual pattern that best suits the system needs. In other words, the first pattern in a sequence or a single pattern is chosen according to the specific scenario that the designer wants to generate (e.g., outgoing call, incoming call, or roaming). The context of each pattern in a specific sequence is related to the resulting context of the previous pattern. As mentioned earlier, the following systems have been using these patterns: GSM/GPRS/UMTS, ANSI-41/WIN, and IMT-2000-based systems as well as WmATM networks.

For instance, a scenario with the sequence of patterns that describe what happens when a user powers on the mobile station and tries to make a call starts with an outgoing call request, as shown in Figure 10–3. First, the network queries the mobile station for its *temporary identification*; then, *authentication* and *ciphering* provide a secure environment for the communication. The *security database* separates the user's authentication information from the user's profile and accesses it during the previous two steps. After this, a new *temporary identification* is assigned to the mobile station and the *location registration* updates the *home and visitor databases* that keep track of the mobile user's current location information whenever the user roams.

When an incoming call (see gray arrow in Figure 10–3) arrives to a mobile station that is powered on, *paging* is performed to reach the mobile station before the *authentication* and *ciphering* that guarantee security and privacy for the establishment of the connection between the users. A *temporary identification* is assigned to the mobile user to avoid sending the real user's identity through the air interface.

Table 10–1   *Reusable Units of the MoRaR Pattern Language*

Reusable Software	Development Stage
Behavioral Patterns	Requirements
Structural Patterns	Analysis

Meanwhile, a handoff decision monitors the quality of the link between the mobile station and the network whenever a user moves from one location to another (see the roaming gray arrow in Figure 10–3). The *intersystem handoff execution* guarantees the communication when the roaming occurs. However, unsuccessful handoff outcomes also occur in this case and handoff failure actions handle them. The ability to release resources (i.e., *releasing resources*) after a handoff is also supported by the network. As presented earlier, an anchor mobile switching center entity maintains the control of the resources (e.g., transmission links) during the call processing.

The patterns gathered in the MoRaR pattern language are general and abstract enough to allow freedom with respect to future implementation decisions and to be reused at the early stages of the system development process and evolution of mobile systems. Table 10–1 presents an overview of the MoRaR pattern language in terms of its reusable software units and their correlation to the software development stages. These units can be reused at the requirements and analysis stages of a mobile system development process; see [Andrade2000c] for an approach that adds rigor to the pattern reuse and validation. It validates requirements, analysis, and design models against validation test cases that are derived from the pattern solutions.

The next sections introduce the mobility and radio resource patterns, which are used in different second- and third-generation systems, as stated earlier. Pattern names appear as subsection headings. When we reference patterns that are included in the MoRaR pattern language, we identify them within the context or the resulting context subsections. However, a separate subsection describes other patterns related to *ciphering*, *authentication*, and *location registration*.

Patterns Related to Mobility Management Functions

Mobility management functions solve problems related to the user's security and location. For instance, mobile communication systems use wireless technologies, such as the Time Division Multiple Access (TDMA) technique, that are by nature more prone to eavesdropping and fraud on the radio interfaces than are fixed networks. Furthermore, in such systems, other facilities are required to manage location aspects related to users who roam from cell to cell and to reach a user who is being called. This contrasts with the situation in fixed systems, where the location of the user (or the user's terminal) is always known because it is associated to the subscriber's number.

The following sections present patterns that solve mobility management problems such as: guaranteeing security and privacy (*temporary identification, security database, ciphering,* and *authentication*); reaching a mobile user who receives an incoming call (*paging*); keeping a record of the subscriber's location information that enables the establishment of calls efficiently (*home and visitor databases*); and keeping the location information of the mobile station (*location registration*) up to date.

Temporary Identification

Context

A user has just powered on the mobile station, traveled to a new location area, or an incoming call has just arrived to a mobile user. In all these cases, common control channels are used for network management messages before the establishment of a dedicated control channel between the mobile station and the network [Redl+1995]. At this time, privacy and security operations are the main concerns of the network in order to protect the communication over the air interface against illegal scanning of these control channels [Gallagher+1997].

Problem

How does one ensure privacy of the subscriber's identity when sending it on the radio path?

Forces

- When telecommunications services are enabled to a mobile station, identities are assigned by the network to identify the mobile station user anywhere.

- All the information exchanges in clear text on the radio path are vulnerable to a third party listening to the control channels. As a result, the subscriber's identity can be easily captured on the air interface. Then, a fraudulent mobile station can be programmed with this valid identification and make calls at the original mobile station's expense (known as "mobile cloning fraud").

- Although encryption is very efficient for confidentiality, it is not possible to protect every single information exchange on the radio path, for example:
  - When common channels are used simultaneously by all mobile stations in the cell and in the neighboring cells, *ciphering* (see Ciphering) is not applied because a key known to all mobile stations has a low level of security.
  - When a mobile user moves to a dedicated channel, there is a period during which the subscriber's real identity is unknown to the network and ciphering methods are not applied.

Solution

Assign a temporary identification to the mobile station in order to avoid exchanging the subscriber's real identity and the electronic serial number of the mobile station over a non-*ciphering* (see Ciphering) radio path.

Each mobile station has a unique temporary identification that is composed of a location area identity and a digit string. The temporary identification, which is dynamically allocated by the network when the mobile user registers in the location area, is stored in the mobile station and in the *visitor database* (see Home and Visitor Databases). When a mobile user powers off the mobile station or changes to another location area, this identification is released in the old *visitor database*. The network reduces signaling messages and resources by storing the temporary identification in the *visitor database*.

Figure 10–4 shows two scenarios that represent, respectively, a *temporary identification* inquiry and a *temporary identification* assignment. The former is used by GSM, ANSI-41-C, and IMT-2000-based systems when a mobile station powers on or tries to make a call. Two messages are exchanged in this message sequence chart [ITU1996], as follows: temporary identification request, which represents a request from MSC to MS for the temporary identification, and temporary identification indication, which contains the MS temporary identification. The latter can be performed by these systems when a mobile station receives a call or changes location area. Four messages are exchanged in this scenario as follows: temporary identification assignment request, which represents a request from the visitor database (i.e., VLR) to MSC for the temporary identification assignment; temporary identification assignment indication, which contains the new temporary identification from MSC to MS; the temporary identification assignment response and confirmation, which represent a positive or negative assignment acknowledgment; and then, when the mobile station changes location, in addition to the temporary identification assignment, the old temporary identification is released from the old *visitor database*.

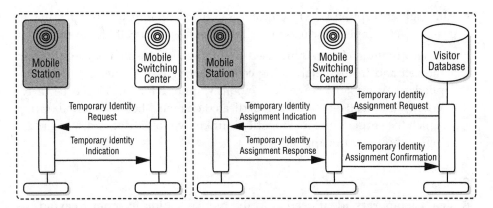

Figure 10–4 *(a) Temporary identification Inquiry and (b) Temporary identification Assignment*

Rationale

Temporary identification adds an extra level of protection in a mobile wireless environment. It is used instead of the real subscriber's identity when the user powers on a mobile station or when the user tries to make a call and has been previously assigned an identity by the network. The advantage of the use of this identity is observed when ciphering (see Ciphering) is not applied to the traffic. In that case, even if someone is listening to the radio path, the identity does not have any meaning outside the serving network (e.g., an illegal mobile station cannot be programmed with this number).

Resulting Context

The *temporary identification* protects the mobile user and the network from third parties that could otherwise get information about the subscriber's real identity by listening on the radio path. Once the temporary identification has been assigned to the mobile station, the user identity can be validated through *authentication* (see Authentication) and the exchanged information over the dedicated channel can be secured through *ciphering* (see Ciphering).

Known Uses

Temporary identification is called Temporary Mobile Subscriber Identity (TMSI) in GSM/GPRS and ANSI-41 Specifications, and Temporary Mobile User Identity (TMUI) in IMT-2000 Systems and UMTS.

Security Database

Context

Security and privacy management functions handle information such as authentication keys and security-related parameters. They also check the validity of received authenticated data and perform confidentiality controls.

On the other hand, location management functions manage mobile users' location information as well as their identification and profiles, which are relevant to the provision of telecommunications services. This information is stored in the *home and visitor databases* (see Home and Visitor Databases).

Problem

How does one handle the mobile user's sensitive information while assuring its protection on the network side?

Forces

- All the security mechanisms, including keys and algorithms, should be a concern for operators and manufacturers of mobile systems. For example, *ciphering* (see Ciphering) and *authentication* (see Authentication) not only rely on the secrecy of the information that are provided by them, but they also rely on the secrecy of their keys and algorithms.

- Even though security management functions involve the same protocols and architectural elements as location management functions, the location information and user profile are often accessed by the network while performing *paging* (see Authentication) and *location registration* (see Home and Visitor Databases). The information in the *home and visitor databases* is thus vulnerable to attacks and failures due to this frequent access.

- It is also not possible to store the security-related information only in the *visitor database*, because this database is in charge of temporarily storing information related to subscribers who are currently in its location area.

Solution

Create a repository of the user's sensitive information that is only accessed by functions involved in the security management process. This database does not transmit any sensitive information (e.g., secret keys and algorithms); it performs the *ciphering* and the *authentication* computations itself.

The authentication center is the security database for ANSI-41 and GSM-based systems. The same secret keys and algorithms are permanently stored in the internal memory of the mobile station when its activation occurs. In GSM, the Subscriber Interface Module (SIM) stores this information.

The *home and visitor databases* (see Home and Visitor Databases) have small roles during the security management process. For example, they store complementary information that is required when performing the authentication and ciphering computations.

Rationale

The amount of security information in a wireless environment, such as keys and algorithms that are used to perform ciphering and authentication calculations, justifies their separation from the user profile information stored permanently in the home database. Any problem that home databases face will not affect the *authentication* or *ciphering* procedures. This decision gives an extra level of security to any mobile system.

Resulting Context

Sensitive data has been stored in the *security database*, which provides an additional layer of protection around this information. Consequently, the *ciphering* (see Ciphering) and the *authentication* (see Authentication) functions use this information in order to guarantee privacy and security to the mobile user.

Known Uses

Security Database is called Authentication Center (AC) in ANSI-41 Specifications, IMT-2000 Systems, and GSM/GPRS/UMTS.

Ciphering

Context

In the idle mode, common control channels are used for all mobile stations that are in a particular cell as well as for the ones in the neighboring cells. Once a mobile station sends its *temporary identification* (see Temporary Identification) to the network, a dedicated control channel and a traffic channel, which is reserved for user information, are allocated. As a result, the mobile user changes from idle mode to dedicated mode.

After this, the type of information transmitted through the radio path belongs to different categories such as user information (voice or data), user-related signaling (messages carrying the user's identity numbers), and system-related signaling (messages carrying radio results measurement).

Problem

How does one protect the privacy of the communication over an insecure wireless communication channel?

Forces

- If the information is sent in clear text on the radio path, third parties are able to eavesdrop on the communication.

- A good protection against unauthorized listening is not easy with analog transmission, which is used by first-generation systems such as AMPS. For instance, analog mobile systems have to apply more than one mechanism to encrypt selected parameters in the signaling messages or to encrypt the user traffic. However, digital transmission, which is used by second-generation systems such as GSM, provides privacy and security to mobile subscribers by protecting all the transmitted information (e.g., voice, data, and signaling).

- Encryption of the same data must not generate the same encrypted sequence on the network each time in order to prevent replication fraud (e.g., playback of the encrypted sequence from a previously intercepted sequence).

Solution

Apply encryption mechanisms to the digital information that is transmitted through control and traffic channels when the mobile station is in dedicated mode. These mechanisms are independent of the exchanged information type.

Figure 10–5 shows two scenarios that involve the setup of the ciphering mode and the transmission of the ciphering information in IMT-2000 systems. In Figure 10–5a, the network instructs the mobile station that the *ciphering* mode should be employed during the transmission process. Figure 10–5b shows the mobile station sending an encrypted data stream on the radio interface.

Before setting up the encryption mechanisms as shown in Figure 10–5a, the mobile station and the network have already agreed on the inputs that allow the ciphering and deciphering methods, which are the following: a frame number, an encryption algorithm, and a ciphering key. The frame number, which is provided by the network for each ciphering sequence, prevents replication fraud. The encryption algorithm, which is specified for use in several countries, generates the ciphering sequence. The ciphering key is calculated for each communication according to a random number, a computation algorithm, and a secret key. The mobile station, the home and visitor databases (see Home and Visitor Databases), and the security database (see Security Database) are responsible for storing the inputs and calculating the encryption operations mentioned previously.

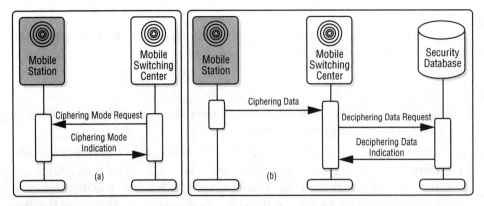

Figure 10–5 *(a) Ciphering mode setup and (b) Ciphering data exchange*

In order to ensure that the ciphered data from the mobile user's side can be deciphered on the network side, the encryption algorithm should be reversible. For instance, if the encryption algorithm is used to cipher a data stream, the same algorithm is used twice to decipher this data and get back to the original stream.

Rationale

The wireless environment does not protect against eavesdropping. There is thus the need to cipher the traffic in the air interface. Ciphering provides algorithms for encrypting signaling messages and data that are exchanged in the air interface.

Resulting Context

In dedicated mode, encryption mechanisms provide an enhanced degree of privacy over the radio channel by preventing unauthorized access to the information exchanges. For instance, when an incoming call has been requested through *paging* (see Paging), *ciphering* is applied to ensure the privacy of the information exchanges between the network and the user who is being called. In addition to ciphering, mobile user authentication (see Authentication) should be performed to prevent fraudulent access.

Known Uses

Ciphering is used in ANSI-41 Specifications, IMT-2000 Systems, GSM/GPRS/UMTS, and WmATM networks.

Related Patterns

Secure-channel communication, information secrecy, secrecy with sender authentication, and *secrecy with signature* are presented in [Braga+2000] within a pattern language for cryptographic software.

Information secrecy has the same purpose as *ciphering*. In other words, both patterns support encryption and decryption of data. However, *ciphering* documents the specific characteristics of mobile systems and concentrates on the requirements and analysis stages, while *information secrecy* focuses on the design stage of cryptographic software that is used in different domains. *Secrecy with sender authentication* and *secrecy with signature* are modifications of the *information secrecy* with the addition of *sender authentication* (see patterns related to Authentication) and *signature*, which guarantees the authorship of the message (non-repudiation requirement of the cryptographic process).

Authentication

Context

A *temporary identification* (see Temporary Identification) has been requested from a mobile user who has powered on the mobile station or entered a new location area. Once the network has provided a dedicated channel, *ciphering* (see Ciphering) prevents the eavesdropping on communications through the radio path. Nevertheless, transmissions could have been intercepted before using the temporary identification or before enabling the ciphering methods whenever a *location registration* (see Home and Visitor Databases) has occurred or when a mobile user has received an incoming call request through *paging* (see Paging). As a result, the stolen identification codes could have been used to obtain air time fraudulently.

Problem

How does one prevent unauthorized or fraudulent access to cellular networks by mobile stations illegally programmed with counterfeit identification and electronic serial numbers?

Forces

- If the subscriber's identity is transmitted without encryption over the air interface and special radio scanners capture this information, the valid user's identity (and the user's account) can be illegally used by someone else.
- If the identity of the mobile station cannot be verified, any fraudulent mobile station programmed with a valid subscriber's identification can make calls,

which leads to the possibility of incorrect billing to the legitimate user or the possibility of receiving calls with false identification (impersonation).

- Passwords can limit physical access to the mobile station but are of little value when sent over an open channel on the air interface.

- A robust method of validating the true identity of a subscriber in a wireless environment requires no subscriber intervention and no exchange of keys or algorithms through the air interface.

Solution

Perform an authentication operation on both the mobile station and the network sides based on an encryption algorithm and a secret key number. These values are stored in the legitimate mobile station and in the *security database* (see Security Database) at the initiation of the service (e.g., at the time of mobile station activation). Furthermore, they are neither displayable nor retrievable and never transmitted over the air or passed between systems.

The operation consists of applying the encryption algorithm with the following inputs: a random value dynamically provided by the network, the secret key number, an electronic serial number that identifies the mobile station, and the user's identification number. According to the comparison of both authentication results, the mobile station is either authorized or denied access to the network. The user's identification number is sent over a *ciphering* (see Ciphering) radio path and the electronic serial number has been previously stored in the *home database* (see Home and Visitor Databases).

Figure 10–6 shows a typical mobile wireless communication environment with a scenario that shows the authentication operations performed by a mobile station and its home network provider. The architectural elements shown in the figure are related to the following scenario: a mobile user powers on the mobile station inside the home location area and an *authentication* is requested.

First, the network sends a random value to the mobile station (random_value in the figure) from a pool of free numbers. The mobile station performs the authentication operation based on the encryption algorithm (AuthAlg in the figure) with this random value and the inputs previously assigned (i.e., the secret key number–Usr_key, the electronic serial number–MS_serial, and the user's identification number–Usr_ID). The operation result is sent to the network. The comparison between these results (respectively, UsrAuth and NetAuth) is made at the network side with the following network entities involved: mobile switching center, *home database* (see Home and Visitor Databases), and *security database* (see Security Database). The mobile user is successfully authenticated and able to access communication services when results are identical. Access is denied otherwise.

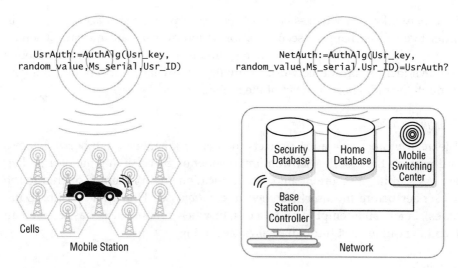

Figure 10–6 *Authentication operations*

The message sequence chart shown in Figure 10–7 shows the architectural elements of a system based on ANSI-41-C that are involved in the authentication of the mobile station shown in Figure 10–6.

Rationale

There is a need to verify the authenticity of every mobile station that tries to access a network in order to avoid problems such as mobile cloning. Unlike in

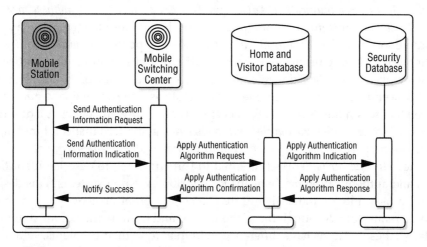

Figure 10–7 *Authentication: ANSI-41 message sequence diagram*

fixed networks, in a wireless environment extra protection is also necessary in order to avoid exchanging security information over the air interface when ciphering is not available. *Authentication* combines the verification of the mobile station's identity on the network side with the exchange of random numbers through the radio ports instead of the mobile user's identity.

Resulting Context

The *authentication* operation protects the network against unauthorized access and protects the mobile user from impersonation by certifying the user's identity. As a result, a secure mobile communication environment is offered to the subscriber before the user's *location registration* (see Home and Visitor Databases), before an attempt to make a call, or when a mobile user has received an incoming call request through *paging* (see Paging).

Known Uses

On the basis of the air interface protocol (e.g., IS-95 or IS-136), which is used to access mobile systems, or of a roaming agreement between the home and the serving systems, it is possible to determine whether the MS is authentication-capable or not. The ANSI-41-C mobile application part (MAP) contains operations and algorithms that are responsible for the authentication tasks [Gallagher+ 1997]. The authentication operations are done by a set of algorithms called Cellular Authentication and Voice Encryption (CAVE) and two secret keys, A-key and SSD.

Related Patterns

Secure-channel communication, sender authentication, and *secrecy with sender authentication* are presented in [Braga+2000] within a pattern language for cryptographic software. *Sender authentication* has the same purpose as *authentication*. In other words, both patterns guarantee that the sender is genuine and authentic. However, *authentication* documents specific characteristics of mobile systems and concentrates on the requirements and analysis stages, while *sender authentication* focuses on the design stage of cryptographic software, which is a different domain. *Secrecy with sender authentication* is a design pattern that combines *information secrecy (ciphering)* and *sender authentication (authentication)*.

The *authenticator pattern* is presented in [Brown+1999] to describe identification and authentication mechanisms for distributed object systems. This design pattern uses a login-and-authenticate protocol to grant or deny access to individual requestors. Although the authenticator and the authentication intents are related, these patterns have differences with regard to their problems, solutions, resulting context, and applicability.

Paging

Context

A network has received an incoming call request that is addressed to a mobile user whose current location area is kept by the *home and visitor databases* (see Home and Visitor Databases). This request contains the mobile user's identity (dialed number). The network refers to the user as the terminating or called party.

Problem

How does one reach the terminating mobile user and route the call to the actual location of the mobile station?

Forces

- The precise location of a terminating mobile station needs to be known in order to establish the communication.

- In a fixed telecommunication environment, the user's location is always known, because it is associated to the subscriber's number. In a mobile network, however, the dialed number has no information about the terminating user's current location, because it changes with the user's movements from one location to another.

- The mobile environment is split into cells, and each location area includes several cells managed by a single mobile switching center. When a user roams within a location area, this user eventually changes cells.

- When an incoming call request is sent to the network, *home and visitor databases* (see Home and Visitor Databases) are queried about the terminating user's current location area. However, each location area is composed of several cells, and the current cell location of the mobile station needs to be found by the network.

- The amount of information transmitted and processed by the network increases considerably if smaller cells are used. For instance, when a large number of mobile users are transmitting information about their locations through every cell, both base stations and the spectrum in use by them are overloaded.

Solution

Send a paging message to reach the terminating mobile user in a set of cells where the user is expected to be (for example, several dozen cells). The location area information is retrieved from the *home and visitor databases* (see Home and

Visitor Databases), which are kept updated by the *location registration* (see Location Registration). Based on the mobile station reply, the network precisely knows the cell where the terminating user is currently located.

Figure 10–8 shows a successful *paging* scenario after the network receives an incoming call request. MSC then sends a paging request message to reach the target MS, which responds with a paging response message if it is reachable.

Rationale

When there is an incoming call for a mobile user, it is not possible to locate the user on the basis of the dialed number. The location of the terminating user is not included in the number because it is not fixed. *Paging* solves the problem of locating the terminating user with the information provided in the user profile of the home database.

Resulting Context

Once the network has found the terminating mobile user and allocated a dedicated channel, the call establishment proceeds. The terminating user's *authentication* (see Authentication) and *ciphering* (see Ciphering), which is used to protect the information on the radio path, can also follow *paging*, depending on implementation decisions.

In large networks, this solution provides a balance between the amount of location information to be exchanged among architectural elements and the number of necessary *paging* messages to be sent on the radio path. Besides locating

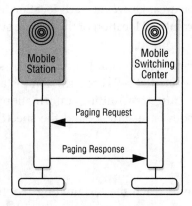

Figure 10–8 *Paging message sequence diagram*

the user, the paging procedure minimizes resource consumption—both the signaling load on the radio path and the processing load on the network.

Known Uses

Paging is used in ANSI-41 Specifications, IMT-2000 Systems, GSM/GPRS/UMTS, and WmATM networks.

Home and Visitor Databases

Context

In the mobile wireless network world, the fact that a user moves from one location area, which groups a set of cells, to another is called roaming. Roaming occurs when a user moves to a location area other than the home area. In practice, this usually means that a user is changing from one provider's domain to another provider's domain, although it is possible for a provider to have several domains.

Problem

How does one enable a user's mobility between location areas of the same provider or between location areas of different providers?

Forces

• Unlike fixed users' identification, a mobile user's identification includes no information about the subscriber's current location.

• Mobile communication providers are responsible for keeping information about the users permanently registered in their networks as well as about the ones currently visiting these networks. Not all visiting users have preregistered with a network upon which they appear.

• Information about mobile users' home, previous, and current locations are essential for enabling telecommunications services when one or several providers are involved in the roaming.

• Telecommunications services are only obtained from a current visiting location area if a mobile station is registered in that particular area. Such registration relies on the home and previous location areas providing the information about the mobile user.

Solution

Create two types of repositories to handle the mobile user's information. One is the home database, which is a primary repository for information (such as current location) about a set of users permanently registered in a location area. The other repository is the visitor database, which temporarily stores part of the information (e.g., home location) about the users who are currently visiting a particular location area. The visitor database reduces the signaling messages to the home database when the user is roaming.

Every time a mobile user registers in a new location area, the *location registration* (see Home and Visitor Databases) procedure updates the home, previous, and current location information.

Rationale

Databases are used in fixed networks to keep information about their subscribers, such as billing information and features. In mobile systems, these databases are still necessary, and they also have to keep other information, including a user's current location area, *temporary identification*, and security information. Some of this information is kept permanently in databases and some is kept only temporarily. The permanent information is stored in the user's home network, which can be far from the current user's location. The temporary information is often accessed by the network and should be close to the current user's location. *Home and visitor databases* are used for this purpose.

Known Uses

Mobile systems based on GSM, ANSI-41, and IMT-2000 maintain a home database that is called Home Location Register (HLR) and a visitor database that is called Visitor Location Register (VLR). The GSM-900 VLR is physically integrated with the Mobile Switching Center (MSC).

ANSI-41's specifications describe the *visitor database* as the VLR functional entity. The ANSI-41 serving system is described as a single entity composed of the MSC and VLR functional entities. Most of the ANSI-41 implementations currently in service also describe a single MSC/VLR; however, there is potential for their separation at the implementation level.

Resulting Context

Home and visitor databases keep track of users' information through *location registration* (see Home and Visitor Databases). As a result of having these databases, the roaming capability is guaranteed and the restriction of offering services only in a specific area within a particular network is removed. In addition, the *visitor database* stores the *temporary* identification (see Temporary Identification) as well as part of the user's profile information.

The mobile user's location information is needed for *authentication* (see Authentication) purposes and for *paging* (see Paging) the terminating mobile user. Furthermore, the *security database* (see Security Database) requests information from the *home and visitor databases* in order to perform the *authentication* and *ciphering* calculations, whose results are requested by the *home and visitor databases*.

Location Registration

Context

A user has changed location area in a mobile wireless environment that contains *home and visitor databases* (see Home and Visitor Databases). The user's location has changed as a consequence of a power-on event,[1] an outgoing call, or an incoming call. Optionally, an *authentication* operation (see Authentication) has been successfully performed.

Problem

How does one keep up-to-date information about a mobile user's location every time the user changes location area?

Forces

- A visitor database has limited storage capacity that is easily overloaded with a large number of mobile users roaming in its location area.
- The accuracy of the location information is necessary in order to offer telecommunications services such as information exchange between users.
- The location information in the previous *visitor database* is no longer up to date or useful when the mobile user moves to a new location area.

Solution

Perform a location registration procedure that consists of updating and inserting the mobile user's location, respectively, in the *home and* current *visitor databases* (see Home and Visitor Databases) every time the mobile user changes location area. This registration operation also includes a request message to the previous *visitor database* to delete the mobile user's temporary location record.

---

1. A mobile user changes location area before powering on the mobile station.

Figure 10–9 shows a location registration in ANSI-41-C networks. This scenario considers that the mobile user's home network is different from the previous location area (previous network). At the end of this scenario, the user is registered in a new network (current network).

A location registration failure occurs in two cases: the mobile user's previous location information is not reachable or the mobile station does not support the new area for technical reasons, such as network failure. As a result, the location information is not updated and the network notifies the mobile user.

Rationale

In order to handle the user's mobility, there is a need to update the home and visitor databases every time a user enters into a new location area. This must be done constantly in order to make it possible to complete calls or offer services to mobile users. Location registration not only takes care of this problem but also maintains the visitor database with temporary information about the users who are currently roaming its location area.

Resulting Context

When the current mobile switching center has successfully registered the mobile station in the new location area, the mobile station is allowed to operate in this area as well as to request services, to establish, and to receive calls. In addition, the temporary record containing out-of-date location information has been

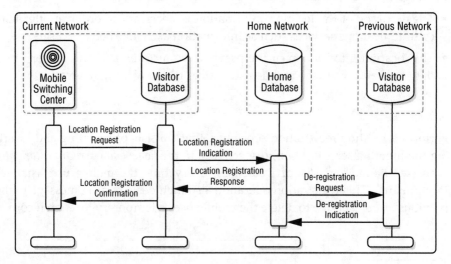

Figure 10–9 *Location registration message sequence diagram*

deleted from the previous *visitor database*. As a result, storage resources have been released.

However, information about user location does not change in the case of location registration failure.

Known Uses

The triggering events for location registrations are dependent on the protocol used for the air interface and on internal algorithms implemented in the serving systems [Gallagher+1997]. However, the air interfaces standards for AMPS, CDMA, and TDMA registrations support the following common registration events: mobile station power-on, timer-based (i.e., registration occurs at periodic intervals while the mobile station is powered on), transition to another system, and call origination. At a high level of abstraction, the actions involved in the location registration are common to systems based on ANSI-41, GSM, and WmATM networks.

Related Patterns

The *Parameter Database* [Utas1998] that is described within a *Pattern Language of Feature Interaction* solves the problem of two or more features accessing and modifying the same database parameter. This pattern language handles similar feature interactions occurring in telecommunications services (for fixed and mobile users).

Patterns for Radio Resource Management

After investigating the radio resource management concerns of the mobile systems that we have considered in our study, we identify the following patterns detailed in the next subsections: *handoff decision* (see Handoff Decision), *anchor entity* (see Anchor Entity), *intersystem handoff execution* (see Intersystem Handoff Execution), *handoff failure actions* (see Handoff Failure Actions), and *releasing resources* (see Releasing Resources).

A decision of doing handoff is taken every time it is appropriate to change a radio communication link. The execution of an intersystem handoff maintains the stability of the dedicated radio channel despite the user's move to a different location area. An anchor MSC handles the resources for information exchange during the intersystem handoff process. The network is also responsible for handling unsuccessful outcomes during the intersystem handoff execution. The use of radio resources is minimized by releasing circuits that are no longer necessary when a user roams.

Handoff Decision

Context

A dedicated radio communication channel has been assigned between a mobile station, which has changed from idle to dedicated mode, and a mobile switching center for transmitting signaling and data. The mobile user is moving from one place to another. This possibility of changing cells (and possibly location area) is called handoff and it is one of the major sources of complexity for mobile networks [Gallagher+1997] [Mouly+1992].

Problem

How do you monitor the quality of the radio communication link between the mobile station and the network to decide whether to trigger a handoff or not?

Forces

- Radio communication is interrupted as soon as the user leaves the radio coverage area of the current cell, whether a call is in progress or not.

- When a call is in progress, the radio communication cut-off has an important weight in the overall perception of voice quality from the user's point of view.

- When comparing the capabilities of two cells, the load of each base station transceiver and the overall interference level in each cell affect the radio link quality.

- Local geographic peaks can occur in events such as sport competitions, concerts, and festivals. It is possible in these situations that a cell is congested in the peak area while its neighbor cells are not.

Solution

The decision of whether a handoff should be triggered or not is based on the signal measurements of the transmission quality for ongoing dedicated radio connections. These measurements are best taken by the current base station or by both the current base station and the mobile station, with parameters such as transmission error rate, propagation path loss, propagation delay, traffic considerations, and the cell capacity and load.

Mobile stations provide measurements of the received base station signal strength to the current mobile switching center. Although the signal measurements normally concern the allocated radio resources of the current cell, when it is necessary, adjacent base stations (in the neighbor cells) also provide measurements to the current mobile switching center while the mobile station moves towards their coverage areas.

The handoff decision can be taken by the mobile station (mobile station-controlled handoff), the serving mobile switching center (network-controlled handoff), or both (mobile station-assisted handoff, called MAHO), depending on implementation issues. When the handoff involves two radio channels that are controlled by the same mobile switching center (intrasystem handoff), the base station controller can also take the handoff decision.

Figure 10–10 shows a handoff decision involving two or more mobile switching centers (intersystem handoff).

The current mobile switching center queries adjacent mobile switching centers to determine whether the mobile station should be assigned to another mobile switching center. The adjacent mobile switching centers send the collected handoff measurements, which contain the radio signal strength that is being received on the specific channel. The current mobile switching center examines each measurement to determine whether a handoff is appropriate or not. In Figure 10–10, the handoff is successfully done with the allocation of a dedicated channel to the mobile station.

Figure 10–11 shows a possible scenario for applying an intersystem handoff decision. The diagram starts when the mobile station moves near the border of a location area. In this scenario, a mobile switching center receives the measurements from the mobile station and decides whether the handoff is necessary or not. These measurements can also be taken by the base station or both the mobile station and base station.

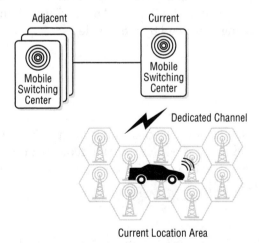

Figure 10–10 *Handoff decision with different MSCs*

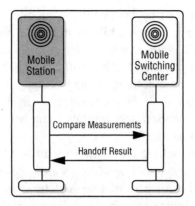

Figure 10–11 *A scenario for handoff decision*

Known Uses

The handoff decisions taken by the signaling alternatives for WmATM presented in [Bora1997], the ANSI-41 Handoff Measurement Request scenario presented in [Gallagher+1997], and GSM-based systems such as GSM-900 and GSM-1800 [Black1999] [Mouly+1992] follow this pattern.

Resulting Context

After the decision about the need for a handoff, an intrasystem or an *intersystem handoff* (see Intersystem Handoff Execution) can occur. There is otherwise no need for handing off. An *anchor entity* (see Anchor Entity) handles the network resources without being perceived by the mobile user.

Anchor Entity

Context

A *handoff decision* (see Handoff Decision) has been taken and an intersystem handoff, which involves the modification of a dedicated transmission path between a mobile station and a mobile switching center, must be performed [Black1999] [Mouly+1992].

Problem

How do you manage the network resources involved in information exchanges during an intersystem handoff?

Forces

- The physical transmission path, which includes the dedicated radio channel between the mobile station and the network, and the fixed transmission path within the network, is constantly modified by handoffs.

- If the transmission path is released as soon as an intersystem handoff decision is taken, all call information that should be transmitted to the new mobile switching center is lost. This can happen regardless of whether a new channel is allocated successfully or not.

- Charging is complicated because more than one mobile switching center is responsible for a call.

Solution

The mobile switching center that has first established the dedicated channel with the mobile station will be in charge of the call. This mobile switching center, called the anchor, keeps control of the call processing information, including the billing record, during the intersystem handoff. Figure 10–12 shows an example of an anchor MSC.

When an intersystem handoff occurs, the network configuration changes and other mobile switching centers become involved. The anchor remains the same, and the other MSCs become just relays. As an example of anchor entity use when the anchor mobile switching center is different from the previous mobile switching center, consider the case where the quality of the new channel is

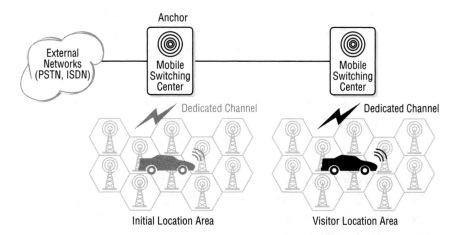

Figure 10–12 *ANSI-41 Successful handoff-forward with Anchor entity [Andrade+2001b]*

worse than the quality of the previous one. The anchor requests the previous base station controller to redirect the transmission to the previous mobile switching center.

Figure 10–13 shows a scenario that contains an *anchor entity mobile switching center* as a component. This scenario describes *intersystem handoff execution*. Furthermore, *anchor entity* also participates in the *handoff failure actions* and *releasing resources*.

Resulting Context

The *anchor entity* is responsible for controlling the resources that guarantee the signaling and data information exchanges during intersystem handoffs. The handoff process includes *intersystem handoff execution* (see Intersystem Handoff Execution) and eventually *handoff failure actions* (see Handoff Failure Actions).

When a *location registration* (see [Andrade+2000a]) occurs as a consequence of a handoff, the *anchor entity* mobile switching center is also in charge of the resources for the information exchanges.

Known Uses

Anchor Entity Mobile Switching Center is used in ANSI-41 Specifications (see Figure 10–12), IMT-2000 Systems (called MSC), and GSM/GPRS/UMTS (called anchor MSC).

Intersystem Handoff Execution

Context

A *handoff decision* (see Handoff Decision) has been taken and it is necessary to perform a handoff that involves different mobile switching centers. The *anchor entity* (see Anchor Entity) controls the resources for the information exchanges.

Problem

How do you guarantee continuous communication service for mobile users, even if they change location area?

Forces

• The current service can be cut off as a result of one of the following:

  – The candidate mobile switching center (MSC) does not support the requested radio channel characteristics. For example, a TDMA digital channel is required but not available.

   – The signal quality of the candidate MSC is below an acceptable threshold.
   – The current traffic conditions on the candidate MSC do not allow handoff traffic.

- Users' expectations are not met by the candidate MSC concerning the reliability and consistency of the signaling and data transmission.

- A similar situation could hold for security requirements.

Solution

Identify the candidate MSC that is being considered for handoff purposes and evaluate its characteristics before executing the handoff. If the evaluation is successful, the candidate mobile switching center is selected to handle the communication. After this, the mobile switching center detects and accepts the mobile station in its location area, and the mobile station tunes to the new channel.

Figure 10–13 shows a possible scenario for performing an intersystem handoff. The scenario starts with a request-triggering event, which represents the positive handoff decision (see Figure 10–11). After this, a new channel is allocated. The mobile station tunes to the new channel, and according to the communication status (whether a communication between the two users is occurring or not), the call is also rerouted. The new channel is verified in order to guarantee that the new link has a better quality of transmission than the previous one. Successful or unsuccessful subpaths can be generated as a result of this action.

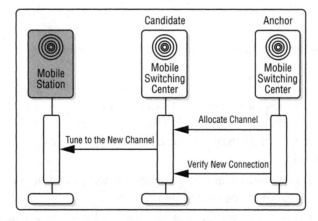

Figure 10–13   *A scenario for the Intersystem Handoff Execution*

Resulting Context

If successful, the *intersystem handoff execution* is completed and the mobile station characteristics become stable. The *anchor entity* (see Anchor Entity) is then able to release the resources that are no longer needed (see Releasing Resources). Meanwhile, *home and visitor databases* (see [Andrade+2000a]) update the mobile user's location information. This successful outcome is transparent to the user.

However, when a handoff failure occurs during this process, the network takes *handoff failure actions* (see Handoff Failure Actions) and notifies the user.

Known Uses

Intersystem Handoff Execution is used in ANSI-41 Specifications, IMT-2000 Systems, GSM/GPRS/UMTS, and WmATM networks. For instance, the handoff is performed through previous or candidate ports in the case of WmATM. ANSI-41 documents also present different scenarios for handoff backward and forward.

Handoff Failure Actions

Context

A failure has occurred during the *intersystem handoff execution* (see Intersystem Handoff Execution) due to the lack of radio or terrestrial resources or due to propagation loss (for example, obstacles such as bridges or tunnels). As mentioned earlier, an *anchor entity* (see Anchor Entity) controls the allocated resources during intersystem handoffs when the mobile station is in dedicated mode.

Problem

How does the network handle an intersystem handoff failure?

Forces

- The *handoff decision* (see Handoff Decision) and the *intersystem handoff execution* reduce the chances of handoff failure. However, the possibility of failure is not eliminated completely and the communication with the current cell can be effectively lost.

- The current communication service is cut off with possible loss of information. This failure can be perceived by the user.

- Before the failure occurred, several communication resources were allocated including the transmission path.

Solution

Choose one of the following alternatives: a new handoff attempt towards the same cell, a new handoff attempt toward another cell, or tuning to the previous channel (see Figure 10–1). Then request the release of all the previously allocated resources (*releasing resources* in Section Releasing Resources) along the path in which the failure has occurred. One alternative that should be avoided is losing the communication between the users or the ability to access network services. The *anchor entity* (see Anchor Entity) chooses one of the previous alternatives. When the alternative is to tune to the previous channel, it also includes the proper actions to deallocate the candidate channel, which is performed by *Releasing resources.*

Resulting Context

Either a handoff has been reinitiated (first and second alternatives described in the pattern solution) or the mobile station has tuned to the previous channel (the last alternative). Furthermore, all the resources in use during the failed handoff have been deallocated (see *releasing resources*).

Known Uses

Handoff Failure Actions is used in ANSI-41 Specifications, GSM/GPRS, and WmATM networks. Third-generation systems such as IMT-2000 Systems and UMTS also use this solution.

Releasing Resources

Context

An *intersystem handoff execution* (see Intersystem Handoff Execution) has successfully occurred or *handoff failure actions* (see Handoff Failure Actions) have been performed. Meanwhile, the *anchor entity* (see Anchor Entity) is controlling the allocated resources despite handoffs.

Problem

How does the network minimize the use of resources that are no longer needed, such as the circuits between the mobile switching centers?

Forces

- The circuits between mobile switching centers are limited, and resources may also be required by other users for handoff execution or for location registration.

- If the user is out of coverage, or has powered off the mobile station in the middle of a call, the network infrastructure has to detect that the resources are no longer needed and make sure that the mobile station is back to idle mode.

- Before a mobile station is back to idle mode (after finishing a call or due to a network failure), a frame loss can occur because the mobile station can still transmit on its dedicated channel while the network is allocating the same channel to another mobile station.

Solution

Release the unnecessary inter-mobile switching center circuits using a request from the *anchor entity* (see Anchor Entity) to mobile switching centers previously involved in the handoff. In order to avoid conflict on the allocation of channels, the mobile station goes back to idle mode (in case of *handoff failure actions*) or stand-by mode (in case of *intersystem handoff execution*) and stops using the channels before the network releases the resources.

Resulting Context

Once the inter-mobile switching center circuits have been released, they are available for allocation to other purposes.

Known Uses

Resources are released by the signaling alternatives for WmATM networks. This pattern can be found also in the ANSI-41 Handoff scenarios and in the GSM Handoff scenarios. *Releasing Resources* is also used in IMT-2000 Systems and UMTS.

Conclusion

This chapter presents the MoRaR pattern language to describe mobility and radio resource management functions at a high level abstraction. In practice, the pattern problems and their respective solutions are recognized by investigating different mobile systems and by capturing their commonalities. MoRaR captures common functional behaviors and architectural elements used in various mobile systems while looking for similarities and the solution of specific design problems associated with the commonalities. GSM/GPRS/UMTS [Gast2002] [Mouly+1992] [Kriaras+1997], ANSI-41/WIN [Amyot+1999] [ANSI/TIA/EIA1997] (D-AMPS [Black1999] is a system based on ANSI-41), IMT-2000

[ITU1999a] [ITU1999b] [ITU2000], and WmATM [Bora1997] [Wese1998] are the systems investigated in this work. In [Andrade+2000a], we have published the patterns related to mobility management functions and in [Andrade+2001b] those related to radio resource management. The MoRaR pattern language presents the patterns in their context.

After commonalities among existing systems are recognized, it is easier to iron out differences and enable them to inter-work. Furthermore, these solutions become more accessible and better understood to novices and experts when documented as patterns. Whether designers are maintaining existing systems or building new ones, they can identify similarities and differences with respect to actual or future systems using MoRaR. The MoRaR patterns are general and abstract enough to allow freedom with respect to implementation decisions and can be reused at the early stages of system development and in the evolution of systems.

This chapter did not intend to cover all common functional behaviors and architectural elements among mobile systems. We believe that common functionalities for communication management can be further investigated and other patterns can be extracted from these commonalities. These patterns can be included in the MoRaR pattern language within new categories (e.g., communication management) if they are not directly related to mobility or radio resource management.

A case study of pattern language reuse and validation in a WmATM environment is presented in [Andrade2000c]. Furthermore, the MoRaR pattern language is applied in [Albano+2004] to design a hybrid network [IEEE1999] that aims to integrate cellular and IP networks. Other wireless systems, such as IEEE 802.11 [Gast2002] and Bluetooth [Gratton2003], can also reuse MoRaR. As future case studies, the mobility and radio resource management functions used by the IS-95 systems (i.e., CDMA systems) [Gallagher+1997] can be investigated in order to find out which of the radio resource management patterns are suitable for them.

A framework that graphically describes the MoRaR pattern language with UCMs is presented in [Andrade+2000b]. This framework includes not only mobility and radio resource management functions (i.e., commonalities) but also variabilities such as communication management functions and the network reference model presented in [Amyot+1999].

It is worth mentioning that even though the MoRaR patterns are not presented in the object-oriented paradigm, designers should be able to apply object-oriented approaches [Jacobson+1992] [Fowler+2000] to implement them.

In addition, we believe that a more complete identification of the intersection between the software patterns presented in the literature [Gamma+1995]

[Rising2000] and the requirements and analysis patterns documented in this chapter should be done to point out more *related patterns*. This was attempted in some of the behavioral patterns presented earlier in this chapter. This identification can help to migrate from requirements and analysis models to object-oriented design and implementation.

Acknowledgments

We would like to thank our PLoP 2000 shepherd, Todd Coram, and the participants of the workshop for their insightful and valuable comments. We also thank our PloP 2001 shepherd, Dennis DeBruler, and the participants of the MensorePLoP 2001 workshop for their encouraging suggestions. John Visser motivated us to investigate this area and gave us much valuable information. We are also grateful to Jim Coplien for encouraging us to be involved in the PloP conferences. Many thanks go also to Paula Cibele Cavalcante Fernandes and João Gustavo Gomes Prudêncio for their help formatting the final version of this chapter. Finally, we acknowledge CAPES, CITO, Mitel, and Nortel Networks for their financial support during our research.

References

[Albano+2004] W. Albano, W. Sales, R. Andrade, R. Cavalcanti, and J. N. Souza. *SiGMA: Uma entidade para localização e autenticação de dispositivos móveis entre áreas de micromobilidade.* 22nd Brazilian Symposium on Computer Networks (SBRC 2004), Gramado (RS), Brazil, May 2004. (in Portuguese)

[Alexander+1977] C. Alexander, S. Ishikawa, and M. A. Silverstein. *Pattern Language: Town, Buildings, Constructions,* Volume 2. New York: Oxford University Press, 1977.

[Amyot+1999] D. Amyot and R. Andrade. *Description of Wireless Intelligent Networks with Use Case Maps,* Proc. 18th Brazilian Symposium on Computer Networks (SBRC 99). Salvador (BA), Brazil, May 1999: 418–433.

[Andrade+2000a] R. Andrade, M. Bottomley, L. Logrippo, and T. Coram. *A Pattern Language for Mobility Management.* In *Proceedings of the 7th Conference on the Pattern Languages of Programs* (PLoP 2000), Monticello, Illinois, August 2000.

[Andrade+2000b] R. Andrade and L. Logrippo. *Reusability at the Early Development Stages of the Mobile Wireless Communication Systems.* In *Proceedings of the 4th World Multiconference on Systemics, Cybernetics, and Informatics* (SCI 2000), Orlando, Florida, July 2000.

[Andrade2000c] R. Andrade. *Applying Use Case Maps and Formal Methods to the Development of Wireless Mobile ATM Networks.* In *Proceedings of the Fifth NASA Langley Formal Methods Workshop,* Williamsburg, Virginia, June 2000.

[Andrade2001a] R. M. C. Andrade. *Capture, Reuse, and Validation of Requirements and Analysis Patterns for Mobile Systems.* 2001. 226 f. Thesis (Doctor of Philosophy in Computer Science); School of Information Technology and Engineering (SITE), University of Ottawa—Carleton Institute of Computer Science, Ottawa, Ontario, Canada, 2001.

[Andrade+2001b] R. Andrade and L. Logrippo. *A Pattern Language for Radio Resource Management.* Submitted and discussed in the Shepherding Process of the 8th Conference on the Pattern Languages of Programs (PLoP 2001). Workshopped in the 1st Japan Conference on the Pattern Languages of Programs (MensorePLoP 2001), Okinawa, Japan, November 2001.

[ANSI/TIA/EIA1997] ANSI/TIA/EIA. ANSI-41-D. *Cellular Radiotelecommunications Intersystem Operations,* 1997.

[Black1999] U. Black. *Second Generation Mobile & Wireless Networks.* Prentice Hall Series in Advanced Communication Technologies, Prentice Hall, 1999.

[Bora1997] A. Bora. "Signaling Alternatives in a Wireless ATM Network." *IEEE Journal on Selected Areas in Communications,* Vol. 15, No. 1, January 1997.

[Braga+2000] A. M. Braga, C. M. F. Rubira, and R. Tropyc Dahab. "A Pattern Language for Cryptographic Software." In *Pattern Languages of Program Design 4,* N. D. Harrison, B. Foote, H. Rohnert (eds.). Boston: Addison-Wesley, 2000.

[Brown+1999] F. L. Brown, Jr., J. DiVietri, G. D. Villegas, and E. D. Fernandez. *The Authenticator Pattern.* In *Proceedings of Pattern Language of Programs (PloP'99),* August 15–18, 1999.

[Buhr1998] R. J. A. Buhr. *Use Case Maps as Architectural Entities for Complex Systems.* In *IEEE Transactions on Software Engineering,* Special Issue on Scenario Management, Vol. 24, No. 12, December 1998.

[Cheng+1997] F. C. Cheng and J. M. Holtzman. "Wireless Intelligent ATM Network and Protocol Design for Future Personal Communication Systems." *IEEE Journal on Selected Areas in Communications,* Vol. 15, No. 7, September 1997.

[Coplien1996] J. O. Coplien. *Software Patterns.* SIGS books and Multimedia, June 1996.

[FCC2006] Federal Communications Commission Web site. Available at *http://www.fcc.gov/cgb/consumerfacts/cellcoverage.html,* last access on February 20th, 2006.

[Fowler+2000] M. Fowler and K. Scott. *UML Distilled: A Brief Guide to the Standard Object Modeling Language, Second Edition.* Boston: Addison-Wesley, 2000.

[Gallagher+1997] M. D. Gallagher and R. A. Snyder. *Mobile Telecommunications Networking with IS-41.* McGraw-Hill, 1997.

[Gamma+1995] E. Gamma, R. Helm, R. Johnson, and J. Vlissides. *Design Patterns: Elements of Reusable Object-Oriented Software.* Reading, MA: Addison-Wesley, 1995.

[Gast2002] M. S. Gast. 802.11 *Wireless Network: The Definitive Guide.* O'Reilly & Associates, Inc., 2002.

[Gratton2003] Dean A. Gratton. *Bluetooth Profiles: The Definitive Guide.* Upper Saddle River, NJ: Prentice Hall, 2003.

[Ghribi+2000] B. Ghribi and L. Logrippo. *Understanding GPRS: The GSM Packet Radio Service.* Computer Networks, 2000.

[Grinberg1996] A. Grinberg. *Seamless Networks: Interoperating Wireless and Wireline Networks.* Reading, MA: Addison-Wesley, 1996.

[ITU1996] International Telecommunications Union. Recommendation Z. 120: *Message Sequence Chart (MSC).* Geneva, 1996.

[ITU1999a] International Telecommunications Union. Recommendation Q.1701: *Framework for IMT-2000 Systems.* Geneva 1999.

[ITU1999b] International Telecommunications Union. Recommendation Q.1711: *Network Functional Model for IMT-2000.* Geneva 1999.

[ITU2000] International Telecommunications Union. Recommendation Q.1721: *Information Flows for IMT-2000* (in preparation).

[Jacobson+1992] I. Jacobson, M. Christerson, P. Jonsson, and G. Overgaard. *Object-Oriented Software Engineering: A Use Case Driven Approach.* Reading, MA: Addison-Wesley, 1992.

[Meszaros+1997] G. Meszaros and J. Doble. "A Pattern Language for Pattern Writing." *Pattern Language of Program Design 3,* R. C. Martin, D. Riehle, and F. Buschmann, (eds.). Reading, MA: Addison-Wesley, 1997.

[Mouly+1992] M. Mouly and M. B. Pautet. *The GSM System for Mobile Communications,* 1992.

[Kriaras+1997] I. N. Kriaras, A. W. Jarvis, V. E. Phillips, and D. J. Richards. "Third-Generation Mobile Network Architectures for the Universal Mobile Telecommunications System (UMTS)." In *Bell Labs Technical Journal,* Summer 1997.

[IEEE1999] "Provision of Communication Services over Hybrid Networks." *IEEE Communications Magazine,* Vol. 37, No. 7, July 1999 (Special issue).

[Redl+1995] S. H. Redl, M. K. Weber, and W. Oliphant. *An Introduction to GSM.* Artech House, Inc., 1995.

[Rising1999] L. Rising. *Patterns: A Way to Reuse Expertise*. In *IEEE Communications Magazine*, Vol. 37, No. 4, April 1999.

[Rising2000] L. Rising. *The Pattern Almanac 2000*. Boston: Addison-Wesley, 2000.

[Utas1998] G. Utas. "A Pattern Language of Feature Interaction." In *Feature Interaction in Telecommunications and Software System V*. IOS Press, 1998.

[Wesel998] E. K. Wesel. *Wireless Multimedia Communications: Networking Video, Voice, and Data*. Reading, MA: Addison-Wesley, 1998.

Appendix

Table 10–2 summarizes the patterns for mobility and radio resource management presented in this chapter. For more information about each pattern solution, the reader should refer to the respective sections.

Table 10–2 *MoRaR Pattern Language Summary: Patterns Related to Mobility and Radio Resource Management*

Pattern/Section Name	Problem	Solution
Temporary Identification	How does one ensure privacy of the subscriber's identity when sending it on the radio path?	Assign a temporary identification to the mobile user in order to avoid exchanging the subscriber's real identity and the electronic serial number of the mobile station over a non-ciphering (see Ciphering) radio path.
Security Database	How does one handle the mobile user's sensitive information while ensuring its protection on the network side?	Create a repository of the user's sensitive information that is only accessed by functions involved in the security management process.
Ciphering	How does one protect the privacy of communication over an insecure wireless communication channel?	Apply digital cryptography mechanisms to the communication when the mobile subscriber uses a digital traffic channel in the dedicated mode.

(continued)

Table 10–2 *MoRaR Pattern Language Summary: Patterns Related to Mobility and Radio Resource Management (continued)*

Pattern/Section Name	Problem	Solution
Authentication	How does one prevent unauthorized or fraudulent access to cellular networks by mobile stations illegally programmed with counterfeit identification and electronic serial numbers?	Perform an authentication operation in both the mobile station and the network sides based on an encryption algorithm and a secret key number.
Paging	How does one reach the terminating mobile user and route the call to the user's actual location?	Send a paging message to reach the terminating mobile user to the cells within the user's current location area where the user is expected to be (for example, several dozen cells).
Home and Visitor Databases	How does one enable a user's mobility between location areas of the same provider or between location areas of different providers?	Create two types of repositories to handle the mobile user's information: one is the home database that is responsible for mobile users permanently registered in a location area, and the other is the visitor database that takes care of mobile users currently visiting a particular location area.
Location Registration	How does one keep up-to-date information about a mobile user's location every time the user changes location area?	Perform a location registration procedure that consists of updating and inserting the mobile user's location, respectively, in the home and current visitor databases (see Home and Visitor Databases) every time the mobile user changes location area.
Handoff Decision	How do you monitor the quality of the radio communication link between the mobile station and the network to decide whether to trigger a handoff or not?	The decision of whether a handoff should be triggered or not is based on the signal measurements of the transmission quality for ongoing dedicated radio connections. These measurements are best taken by the current base station or by both the current base station and the mobile station, with parameters such as transmission error rate, propagation path loss, propagation delay, traffic considerations, and the cell capacity and load.

Pattern/Section Name	Problem	Solution
Anchor Entity	How do you manage the network resources involved in information exchanges during an intersystem handoff?	The mobile switching center that has first established the dedicated channel with the mobile station is put in charge of the call. This anchor mobile switching center entity keeps control of the call processing information, including the billing record during the intersystem handoff.
Intersystem Handoff Execution	How do you guarantee continuous communication service for mobile users, even if they change location area?	Identify the candidate MSC that is being considered for handoff purposes and evaluate its reliability before executing the handoff. If the evaluation is successful, the candidate mobile switching center is selected to handle the communication. After this, the mobile switching center detects and accepts the mobile station in its location area, and the mobile station tunes to the new channel.
Handoff Failure Actions	How does the network handle an intersystem handoff failure?	Choose one of the following alternatives: a new handoff attempt toward the same cell, a new handoff attempt toward another cell, or tuning to the previous channel (see Figure 10–1). Then, request the release of all the previously allocated resources (see Releasing Resources) along the path in which the failure has occurred.
Releasing Resources	How does the network minimize the use of resources that are no longer needed, such as the circuits between the mobile switching centers?	Release the unnecessary inter-mobile switching center circuits by using a request from the anchor entity (see Anchor Entity) to mobile switching centers previously involved in the handoff.

CHAPTER 11

Content Conversion and Generation on the Web: A Pattern Language

Oliver Vogel and Uwe Zdun

Content conversion and generation is required by many interactive, Web-based applications. Simplistic implementations of content converters, creators, and templates often cannot satisfy typical requirements such as high performance, end-user customizability, personalization, dynamic system updates, and integration with multiple channels. In this chapter, we present a pattern language that resolves central forces in this context. A GENERIC CONTENT FORMAT can be used to integrate content from different supported content sources. PUBLISHER AND GATHERER are central instances to trigger back and forth conversion to the GENERIC CONTENT FORMAT, and to handle other central content management tasks such as cache lookup and storage. Conversions are performed by CONTENT CONVERTERS. The patterns CONTENT CREATOR, CONTENT FORMAT TEMPLATES, and FRAGMENTS generate content on request. A CONTENT CACHE is used to store and retrieve the content in a central repository, and FRAGMENTS are the basic elements stored in the cache.

Introduction

Interactive, Web-based applications generate formatted content on request. That is, the content is not available or only partially available in pre-built files.

In typical application scenarios, the generated content has to be formatted in different markup languages, such as HTML, WML, and XML. Other formats, such as graphical user interfaces or textual representations, need to be supported as well. The content might be provided to different channels with different protocols, such as HTTP, COM, CORBA, MMS, and WAP.

First, interactive, Web-based applications represent their services using HTML pages. An HTTP server transfers HTML pages with the HTTP protocol. A Web user agent, such as a browser, communicates with a Web server, and the Web server "understands" that certain requests are handled interactively.

Thus, it forwards the request and all its information to another module running in another thread or process. This handler may handle the request solely and generate an HTML page in response. Or it may translate and forward the HTTP request to a legacy system's API, and then the response has to be decorated with HTML markup.

At first glance, content creation on the Web seems to be a simple effort, especially when a given legacy system with a distinct API should be reengineered to the Web. In our experience, this naive view is fundamentally wrong, and it leads to severe problems when the resulting system has to be further evolved later on (see [Zdun2002b] for a detailed discussion). In many systems, HTML pages are simply generated by string concatenation:

```
StringBuffer htmlText = new StringBuffer();
String name = legacyObject.getName();
...
htmlText.append("<BR> <B> Name: </B>");
htmlText.append(name);
```

Such hard-coding of HTML markup in the program will inevitably lead to problems because central requirements of modern Web engineering are violated. Such central requirements for interactive, Web-based applications are:

- Content, representation style, and application behavior should be changeable ad hoc.

- Web-based applications typically have to represent business logic on the Web in a coherent way, say, in a common representation style.

- In many cases, the same content is presented to other channels, possibly with different representation formats than HTML, as well.

- Often rapid integration of new functionality is required, perhaps within a few hours, and it should be possible to evolve the system incrementally.

- In many cases, the running system cannot be stopped during changes.

- Many (large-scale) Web applications have very high performance and memory demands.

- Many applications require highly personalized presentations of content.

- Customization of content and behavior by non-programmers, such as content editors, domain experts, and end-users, might be required.

- Content, content structure, and content presentation should be separated.

These requirements are met by many different Web architectures. In this chapter we discuss a pattern language that documents "successful" solutions in the realm of converting and generating content on the Web. These patterns lead, in a mostly technology-neutral form, to flexible and generic software architectures for Web applications. The patterns' consequences and variants lead to decisions about which technological choices are appropriate. During the stepwise and sequential application of the patterns, different consequences and forces have to be compared with the technological options and the concrete application's requirements.

Intended Audience

This chapter is intended to help software and information architects faced with the development of highly dynamic, personalized, and content-centric Web applications. The patterns within this chapter can be used as a road map for building architectures capable of serving clients with dynamic Web pages in a consistent and efficient manner.

A Note on the Form

For convenience and clarity, each of our patterns has the same format. In this chapter we use a modification of a form called Alexandrian form that is inspired by the writings of Christopher Alexander, especially *A Pattern Language–Towns, Buildings, Construction* [Alexander+1977]. Each of our patterns begins with a name. This is followed by an introductory paragraph, which sets forth the context of the pattern and its basic relations to other patterns in the pattern language. Then, there are three diamonds to mark the beginning of the problem, and, in bold type, the problem is summarized in one or two sentences. The following body of the problem explains the problem in more detail and discusses the set of forces on which the pattern focuses. Then, again in bold type, the solution is given in the form of an instruction. In the following paragraphs, the solution is discussed in more detail, diagrams present the solution, dependencies to contained patterns are introduced, and consequences of applying the pattern are discussed. Another three diamonds show that the main body of the pattern is finished. And finally, there is a discussion of variants of the pattern and variations in the pattern's relationships to other patterns.

Pattern Language Overview

The pattern language consists of the patterns summarized in Table 11–1 as thumbnails. We give a thumbnail table here as an initial overview of the entire pattern language, because some of the pattern descriptions that follow refer to other patterns that are described in later sections.

Figure 11–1 illustrates the most important pattern dependencies in the pattern language. GENERIC CONTENT FORMAT is used to represent content from any supported content source. Usually, the pattern language is applied incrementally. Typically, at first, an initial GENERIC CONTENT FORMAT is defined to start off, and it is refined as the application evolves.

PUBLISHER AND GATHERER are central instances triggering conversion to and from the GENERIC CONTENT FORMAT. They also handle other central content management tasks. Therefore, it is quite usual to design and build PUBLISHER AND GATHERER very early in a project. There are some external patterns that are often integrated with the pattern language:

- The PUBLISHER AND GATHERER has to be integrated with the mapping of URLs (or other document/service IDs) to service implementations. This task is often handled by the MESSAGE REDIRECTOR pattern [Goedicke+2001].

- If multiple channels have to be served, often the PUBLISHER AND GATHERER is integrated with a SERVICE ABSTRACTION LAYER [Vogel2001] as well.

- Usually, PUBLISHER AND GATHERER trigger the content conversion, generation, and caching components, and they are FACADES [Gamma+1995] to this subsystem.

Conversions are performed by CONTENT CONVERTERS. Converters are triggered by PUBLISHER AND GATHERER. For each supported content format, one converter has to be written for conversion to and from the GENERIC CONTENT FORMAT. These may be hand-built or one can use one of the patterns for content generation.

Concerning the patterns CONTENT CREATORS, FRAGMENTS, and CONTENT FORMAT TEMPLATES, we want to introduce a major distinction of content generation models: template-based approaches (generating pages by substituting certain elements in template files) and constructive approaches (constructing a Web page on the fly). CONTENT CREATORS are implementing the constructive approach. They are highly flexible and programmable, but not the fastest alternative and

Table 11–1 *Pattern Thumbnails*

Pattern Name	Problem	Solution
GENERIC CONTENT FORMAT	How can we use content from different sources such as legacy systems, DBMS, or Web services in a system without having to know its concrete representation in advance?	Provide a generic representation that is used to represent content from any anticipated content source. Along with the generic representation, provide a class structure representing the elements of the generic representation. Convert the content from its concrete representation into the generic representation before you process it within your Web application.
PUBLISHER AND GATHERER	How can we convert to and from a GENERIC CONTENT FORMAT (semi-) automatically, provide access to all content required on the target platforms centrally, and integrate other content management tasks such as caching?	Provide central instance(s) for publishing and gathering of content. The content is given either in the GENERIC CONTENT FORMAT(S), or in other formats delivered to target platforms. The PUBLISHER AND GATHERER trigger conversions, lookup in the cache, and other central content management tasks.
CONTENT CONVERTER	How can we automatically convert content in one format to a different format, and/or update the content according to a set of change rules?	For each required conversion type, provide a converter that has callback methods to be called when a conversion should take place. Content conversion includes input processing of the input format, data conversion and manipulation, and output processing to the target format.
CONTENT CREATOR	How can we build up content in different content formats dynamically and reuse the same code for different content formats? How do we avoid hard-coding content format specifics in the business logic code?	Provide an abstract class that determines the common denominator of the used interfaces. Build special classes that implement that interface for each supported content format, as well as special methods (e.g., as callbacks) for required specialties.

(continued)

Table 11–1 *Pattern Thumbnails (continued)*

Pattern Name	Problem	Solution
CONTENT FORMAT TEMPLATE	How can we build up content in target content format and allow the content editor to add highly dynamic content parts in a simple way that yields high performance?	Provide a template written in the content format that contains special code in a template language to be substituted by a template engine.
FRAGMENTS	How can Web pages be designed in order to allow the generation of Web pages dynamically by assuring the consistency of its content? Moreover, how do you provide these dynamic Web pages in a highly efficient way?	Provide an information architecture that represents Web pages from smaller building blocks called FRAGMENTS. Connect these FRAGMENTS so that updates and changes can be propagated along a FRAGMENTS chain.
CONTENT CACHE	How can you increase the performance of Web page delivery and thereby increase efficiency of the underlying Web architecture?	Provide a central cache for caching already created dynamic content. Consider the lifetime of the content and cache content as long as it is still valid in the application's context.

not well-suited for end-user customization. FRAGMENTS and CONTENT FORMAT TEMPLATES are template-based approaches. Potentially, FRAGMENTS offer a very high performance but can only assemble pre-built parts. A compromise is CONTENT FORMAT TEMPLATES that integrate program elements in the content source. They are thus customizable with behavior and offer sufficient performance, but they are less flexible and less well-integrated with the programming model than CONTENT CREATORS. There are several systems supporting more than one of the approaches in different combinations.

FRAGMENTS, CONTENT CREATORS, and CONTENT FORMAT TEMPLATES can be seen as alternatives for implementing dynamic content generation. However, FRAGMENTS act at a different abstraction level than the other two patterns because they are used as elements of the content cache. Therefore, often the patterns are integrated. For instance, CONTENT CREATORS and CONTENT FORMAT TEMPLATES create FRAGMENTS

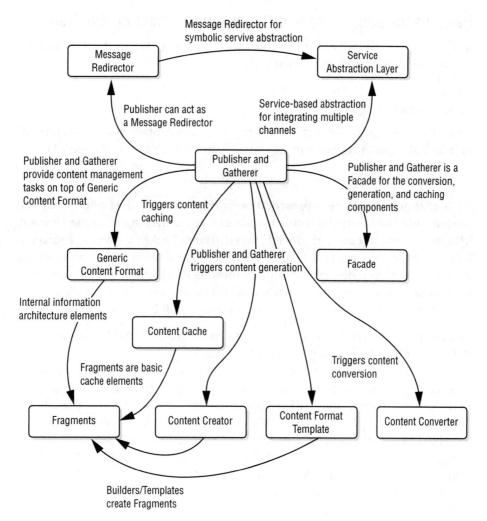

Figure 11–1 *Pattern interactions in the pattern language*

as results that are stored in the cache. The information architecture of the GENERIC CONTENT FORMAT pattern can be implemented with FRAGMENTS.

A CONTENT CACHE is used to store and retrieve the content in a central repository. Content caching is a central document management task. Therefore, the CONTENT CACHE is usually triggered by the PUBLISHER AND GATHERER. Besides complete documents, FRAGMENTS are the primary information elements stored in the cache.

Patterns for Converting and Generating Content on the Web

In this section, we present seven individual patterns that we have mined for content conversion and generation on the Web.

Generic Content Format

You are developing a Web application that provides content in different formats to different types of clients over different channels such as HTTP and WAP.

Each channel has its own presentation format that requires you to convert content into the channel-specific format before publishing it on the channel. Moreover, content can be retrieved from different backend systems characterized by their own content formats. This can lead to an N*M combination problem because potentially N source formats (backend formats) have to be converted into M target formats (channel formats). How can we integrate content from different sources such as legacy systems, DBMS, or Web services?

The code for conversion to and from different formats should be reusable, and the number of conversions should be minimal.

Often different programming languages and programs should be able to access the same information base. Suppose you are developing a Web application that retrieves content from a RDBMS and displays it using HTML. Usually the logic necessary to generate the HTML page operates directly on the content. It thus has to know the concrete format of the content (the database schema in this case). This approach works well if the number of input formats (N) and the number of output formats (M) are very small, because there is a N*M conversion between the different formats.

If there is a large number of different formats or if new formats will be supported in the future, changes in any content format might influence the channel-specific presentation logic directly. This prohibits the straightforward integration of new content sources, because a change in one of the N formats might require changes in all M output formats.

A simple and straightforward mapping of content formats and information architecture representation is necessary for efficient content conversion and generation.

Therefore:

Provide a generic representation that is used to represent content from any anticipated content source. This generic representation typically uses a (tex-

tual) markup format that represents at least the common denominator of all known input formats. Along with the generic representation, provide a class structure representing the elements of the generic representation closely (i.e., one class for each representation format element type). Convert the content from its concrete representation into the generic representation before you process it within your Web application.

When choosing a generic representation, often it is important that it is readable and changeable easily, so that, for instance, end users can manipulate it without programming experience. XML nowadays is often used to represent the GENERIC CONTENT FORMAT. Note that other (e.g., binary) formats may as well be chosen, for instance, if the overhead of processing XML is a problem.

The GENERIC CONTENT FORMAT should enable the representation of arbitrary content models, including primitive types like String, Integer, and Double as well as compound types like Address, Customer, or Account. Furthermore, binary data such as images and multimedia formats should be supported. By using a GENERIC CONTENT FORMAT, new content sources can be integrated without having to modify the presentation logic responsible for generating output formats such as HTML and WML. The number of potential conversions from the input to the output formats is thereby reduced to N+M.

The GENERIC CONTENT FORMAT represents the application-specific superset of content types. Thus, the ontological problem of integrating content from any source is not tackled by the pattern. Each content type is described by one class of the information architecture.

Figure 11–2 illustrates a possible generic structure of an information architecture following the GENERIC CONTENT FORMAT pattern concept. Here, we use dynamic typing with a string-based type property. Of course, static types can be used as well. Content is often represented using an XML vocabulary expressing the abstractions necessary to model a GENERIC CONTENT FORMAT. In Figure 11–2, we can see that there is a one-to-one correspondence of types in the XML vocabulary and the class hierarchy. Also in Figure 11–2, compound types in the XML vocabulary are modeled as COMPOSITE [Gamma+1995] classes.

A PrimitiveContent class is used to represent primitive data types like Integer, String, and Double as well as Images or arbitrary binary content. CompoundContent can contain other content like PrimitiveContent or other CompoundContent. An Address may consist of a PrimitiveContent Street of type String and a PrimitiveContent Number of type String.

The GENERIC CONTENT FORMAT pattern offers a set of benefits: GENERIC CONTENT FORMAT serves as "data glue" for integrating content from heterogeneous sources. It reduces the necessary number of converters to N input format converters plus

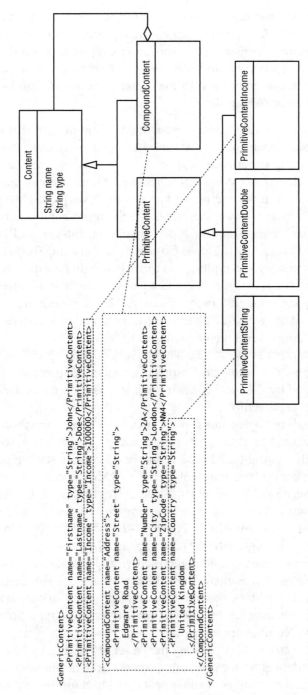

Figure 11–2 *Generic Content Format representation using the Composite pattern*

M target format converters. Automatic conversions with CONTENT CONVERTERS often rely on a GENERIC CONTENT FORMAT as a central conversion (and storage) format. A GENERIC CONTENT FORMAT helps us to implement an efficient content conversion and generation architecture, which is the primary intent of the pattern language.

The GENERIC CONTENT FORMAT pattern can also incur the following liabilities: A GENERIC CONTENT FORMAT has to be defined centrally; thus, as applications evolve, it may be hard to evolve the GENERIC CONTENT FORMAT non-centrally (in a distributed and collaborative working environment). Therefore, initial formats have to be well designed for the particular domain, and extension processes have to be defined. Most GENERIC CONTENT FORMATS are domain-dependent. Conversion can mean losing information if the expressive power of other supported formats and the GENERIC CONTENT FORMAT are significantly different. In unknown documents, it may be hard to guess automatically which parts of GENERIC CONTENT FORMAT conform to which part of the unknown document.

The COMPOSITE [Gamma+1995] pattern can be applied to model the information architecture required to support GENERIC CONTENT FORMAT in the software architecture of a Web application system. However, the GENERIC CONTENT FORMAT does not mandate the use of the COMPOSITE pattern. The COMPOSITE pattern is just a convenient and proven way to model tree structures.

The pattern also occurs in non-hierarchical structures. For instance, RDF [Lassila+1998] is a graph-based GENERIC CONTENT FORMAT that can be linearized to hierarchical XML structures.

Usually, if a FRAGMENTS architecture is supported, the FRAGMENTS architecture is also used as the information architecture of the GENERIC CONTENT FORMAT pattern.

We have discussed typed data for the GENERIC CONTENT FORMAT. In some variants, types are omitted, and a central data conversion type such as a string is used for all data. In such cases, each supported type must be convertible to and from Strings.

Publisher and Gatherer

In the context of a GENERIC CONTENT FORMAT, several issues with regard to central content management are important: delivering content to clients, receiving incoming content, content conversion and generation in different formats, content caching, ensuring content consistency, and other content management tasks.

In a content conversion and generation architecture, we have to handle
incoming and outgoing requests. How can we integrate central content management tasks with request handling?

Multiple different clients need to access content in a GENERIC CONTENT FORMAT.
Somehow these different kinds of requests have to be handled. Clients should
access different devices on which the content is stored, such as disk drives, network devices, databases, optical devices, via a unique interface so that they can
abstract from the storage devices used.

Sometimes, multiple GENERIC CONTENT FORMATS have to be created. For instance, in the Web context, often Web content is converted to XML, unsup-
ported image formats are converted to GIF or JPEG, and proprietary text
formats are converted to PDF. A Web application has to coordinate what should
be converted to what.

Some content is delivered statically; some other content is dynamically processed on the fly. Content change detection and content change propagation can
also induce dynamic changes in already processed static content. A Web application has to handle and integrate static and dynamic content (and possibly
handle caching of content).

Central access points to Web portals and services often have very high hit
rates; therefore, high scalability is required.

Therefore:

**Provide central instance(s) for publishing and gathering of content. For con-
tent gathering, the content is provided either in the GENERIC CONTENT FOR-
MAT(S), or in other formats delivered to target platforms. Then it is converted
to the GENERIC CONTENT FORMAT and (perhaps) cached. Published content can
be requested by clients in any supported content format. Upon a request, the
content is looked up in the cache, perhaps the content parts are dynamically
created, and content conversion to the requested channel is triggered. All
these central content management tasks are fulfilled by the PUBLISHER AND
GATHERER.**

PUBLISHER AND GATHERER are usually two entities, such as objects, threads, or
processes. Sometimes, such as in smaller systems, they are represented by the
same entity. Usually, there are distinct access points on these entities for each
specific type of content, for example, PUBLISHER AND GATHERER are two objects
with handler methods for each request type or they are realized as two daemons that fork handlers for each individual request. The content may be stored

in a cache and/or on different devices, for example, on the disk, in the memory, in a database, on optical devices, or on a network device. A CONTENT CACHE is used to abstract from these storage device specifics.

For each specific content type supported, the PUBLISHER AND GATHERER can access CONTENT CONVERTERS for back-and-forth conversion to the GENERIC CONTENT FORMAT. The CONTENT CONVERTERS may have to operate on the fly. Once the content is converted to GENERIC CONTENT FORMAT, it is stored in the PUBLISHER AND GATHERER'S CONTENT CACHE. FRAGMENTS of the CONTENT CACHE are the basic internal information entity used by the PUBLISHER AND GATHERER.

Content consistency issues are central content management tasks as well. For instance, content changes and updates may be induced by content change detection and content change propagation.

As central access points, the PUBLISHER AND GATHERER handle integration with channels other than the Web if required. Depending on the URL, different channels can be served. Usually the publisher is triggered by a MESSAGE REDIRECTOR [Goedicke+2001] used for redirecting URL calls to implementations. Each of these implementations is a service that should be published to the Web (and other channels). The URL usually denotes which document or service is requested, which format is required, and which protocol is used. One or more publishers can be integrated as services into this architecture (see Figure 11–3), or the MESSAGE REDIRECTOR can be part of the publisher if the publisher is the

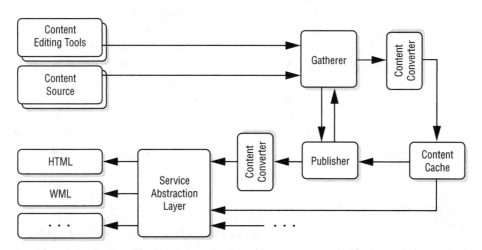

Figure 11–3 *Content Converters, Publisher and Gatherer, Content Cache, and Service Abstraction Layer*

only service supported. The presented structure is a SERVICE ABSTRACTION LAYER [Vogel2001]. It is quite common for PUBLISHERS AND GATHERERS to be combined with a SERVICE ABSTRACTION LAYER if multiple services are offered to a number of channels.

PUBLISHER AND GATHERER architecturally integrate the other patterns of the pattern language, and they also integrate other related services and channel abstractions.

The PUBLISHER AND GATHERER pattern offers a set of benefits: PUBLISHER AND GATHERER are central instances that enable service access from different platforms and with different protocols. Correct content conversion and generation is triggered automatically, and caching is handled. PUBLISHER AND GATHERER can be easily integrated with sophisticated service abstraction architectures.

The PUBLISHER AND GATHERER pattern can also incur the following liabilities: Using a central instance means that we have to care about scalability and performance issues. The converters are stateless, so they can be replicated. Only the caches must be shared. To enable automatic conversion means that all converters have to be written and maintained, whereas hand-built architectures can only rely on the relevant converters.

PUBLISHERS AND GATHERERS can be implemented in different variants. First, we can decide whether PUBLISHER AND GATHERER are implemented as two separate entities or as one entity of the programming language. In many more advanced server architectures, PUBLISHER AND GATHERER are separated. Often they can be forked or redirect to other servers to provide a higher scalability of the architecture. Often there is a central instance to receive requests and multiple workers to handle individual requests. Of course, this is only an issue if they run in different threads or processes. This architecture is actually quite typical for PUBLISHERS AND GATHERERS in systems with high hit rates.

In SERVICE ABSTRACTION LAYERS [Vogel2001] the publisher can either be used as a service or as a MESSAGE REDIRECTOR [Goedicke+2001] for resolving URLs.

Content Converter

Content has to be represented in multiple different formats. Typical target formats for the Web include XML, WML, and HTML. Sometimes formats such as PDF are required as well. Often pictures in formats, such as GIF, JPEG, and PNG, have to be generated.

How to automatically convert content in one format to a different format and/ or update the content according to a set of change rules?

Content in different formats has to be generated for an interactive Web application. Important considerations in this context are performance and scalability issues: For high-performance Web applications (typically with high hit rates), generating all content on the fly is usually costly in terms of memory and performance, and this imposes severe requirements on the scalability of the application.

In the context of migrating legacy applications to the Web (or other new media platforms), usually the original format has to be supported as well. Thus, we cannot change the legacy application to directly support Web-enabled output as its primary output format. It is necessary to convert either the legacy format or the Web format.

Converting one content format to another often means reducing the expressiveness of the application to the common denominator of all target (and input) formats involved. If we do not do this, we have to live with lossy conversions.

Usually, conversions should take place either on request or upon certain events.

Therefore:

For each required conversion type, provide a converter class that has callback methods to be lazily called when a conversion should take place. In general, content conversion includes input processing of the input format, data conversion and manipulation, and output processing to the target format.

A CONTENT CONVERTER is constructed from three elements that are ordered in a CHAIN OF RESPONSIBILITY [Gamma+1995]; each of them is optional:

1. Input processing creates a representation in memory from a given input format. As a result, an intermediate representation is created. Usually, this is a representation in memory. In exceptional cases, such as operating on very large data sets (that do not fit into memory), we may use different intermediate representations. If the conversion is very simple, we can also directly operate on the input format.

2. Data conversion and manipulation routines on the intermediate representation (i.e., most often in memory) apply a set of change rules. The result is manipulated data in the intermediate format. Of course, this step can be repeated multiple times.

3. Output processing is used to create and convert the intermediate format to the target format.

The CHAIN OF RESPONSIBILITY and the produced data formats of a CONTENT CONVERTER are depicted in Figure 11–4. All parts of the CHAIN OF RESPONSIBILITY are optional; however, most often all parts are present. For instance, if steps 2 and 3 are performed on the input format, input processing is not required. If there is only a one-to-one conversion from one format to another one without any manipulations (e.g., to adapt the differences of the two formats), then step 2 is obsolete. If the intermediate format is equal to the target format, then step 3 is not required.

There are different events that trigger CONTENT CONVERTERS. The CONTENT CONVERTER can be triggered on demand, such as when an HTTP request is coming in. The conversion can also be caused by events like content changes. Finally, the content can be pre-processed when the system is idle or has a low workload.

The converter may be able to operate back and forth. It unifies all different conversions to and from the target format. Therefore, usually the converter has two TEMPLATE METHODS [Gamma+1995] on an abstract converter class that call the three CHAIN OF RESPONSIBILITY methods for input processing, conversions, and output processing. One TEMPLATE METHOD handles conversion to the target format, and one handles conversion to the GENERIC CONTENT FORMAT, such as XML. Special converter classes implement the hook methods for the target format that they represent (such as HTML). Figure 11–5 illustrates this design.

Often static and dynamic content FRAGMENTS have to be combined to create one page. CONTENT FORMAT TEMPLATES and FRAGMENTS can be used for specifying in a static page where dynamic parts have to be inserted. CONTENT CREATOR can

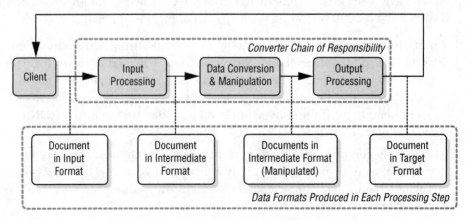

Figure 11–4 *Content Converters: Chain of Responsibility and Product Data Formats*

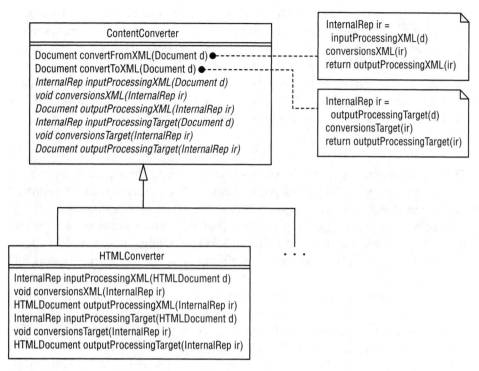

Figure 11–5 *Generic XML and special HTML content converter classes*

be used to build up content dynamically in a specific format using a generic interface. Thus, of course, it can be used to build up the target format processed by the CONTENT CONVERTER.

The CONTENT CONVERTER pattern offers a set of benefits: It unifies different APIs for data transformation and manipulation to one abstract converter interface. Thus, in a content management environment, different converters can be applied in an automated fashion. Automatic data conversion is required for automatically updating dynamic data in CONTENT CACHES and for dynamically applying conversion in PUBLISHER AND GATHERER. Moreover, the pattern allows for combining different content conversion approaches, such as the event-based, tree-based, and rule-based processing models. Content conversion is an efficient way to (re-)construct FRAGMENTS when new or changed input arrives.

The CONTENT CONVERTER pattern can also incur the following liabilities: Content conversion offers only a limited expressiveness compared to FRAGMENTS, templates, or creators. Therefore, higher-level manipulations of content should be implemented using these patterns. However, they can be triggered by a CONTENT CONVERTER. In many problem settings, there are certain exceptional conversions that should be handled differently. Here, the CONTENT CONVERTER offers only limited diversity of conversions because it does not make much sense to produce a new converter for each exception. Better solutions are to provide a MESSAGE INTERCEPTOR [Zdun2003][Goedicke+2002] or other callback mechanisms on the converter object for these cases.

There are different CONTENT CONVERTER variants. Since all three parts of a CONTENT CONVERTER are optional, all parts can be omitted. The internal creation of content can be hand-built, or it can use CONTENT CREATOR, TEMPLATES, or FRAGMENTS.

In some variants, the CONTENT CONVERTER object is also used to store the internal (generic) and the target format (instead of using an external CONTENT CACHE). This especially makes sense in automatic type conversion systems following the AUTOMATIC TYPE CONVERTER pattern [Zdun2004]. Here, the CONTENT CONVERTER object potentially "knows" the two representations in the two supported formats. However, at any time, one of them may be undefined if it is possible to create the content without losing information in both directions. The conversion is performed when the typed or untyped object is requested the next time. When the information changes in one of the representations, the other representation is automatically invalidated. This variant is especially useful for integrating FRAGMENTS objects and a GENERIC CONTENT FORMAT. At any time, only one of the representations has to be valid, and the other one can be lazily created on demand. Lazy resource acquisition is also the focus of the LAZY ACQUISITION pattern [Kircher2001].

Content Creator

In interactive Web applications, dynamically generated content in HTML format, and most often in multiple others formats, is required. Sometimes the same application supports the same format in different variants. For instance, HTML may be delivered pretty printed in a debugging version and compressed for optimizing file size in the released version. CONTENT CONVERTERS require a facility to build up a representation in a target format dynamically.

How can we build up content in different content formats dynamically and reuse the same code for different content formats? How do we avoid hardcoding content format specifics in the business logic code?

Different content formats have different characteristics and specialties; however, the requirement for supporting multiple formats exists in many systems. As an example of this diversity, consider classical widget sets and markup formats, such as HTML and XML. Moreover, format types are heterogeneous in different incarnations. For instance, some widget sets have highly static and monolithic programming interfaces (such as Swing, AWT, or MFC), whereas other interfaces are highly dynamic (such as TK). Some markup formats such as XML are well-formed and can be validated with a DTD or schema, whereas HTML, for instance, is only loosely defined.

Converting one content format to another often means reducing the expressiveness of the application to the common denominator of all target (and input) formats involved. If we do not do this, we have to live with lossy conversions.

Often, we have to create the same content in the same format in different ways. Consider, for instance, generation of HTML text. Ideally, we would like to have pretty-printed and indented HTML output that is easily readable. However, for larger pages this may become problematic: Pretty printing HTML text means to insert a lot of white space and carriage returns. Therefore, in such cases, we require a more compressed output. When different platforms have to be supported, often we want to leave out marked parts of the content, such as leaving out larger pictures in HTML text to better support mobile devices. Another common example is stripping out comments.

Therefore:

Provide an abstract CONTENT CREATOR class that provides operations to build up content incrementally in the memory. These operations support at least the common denominator of the used content formats. Build special classes that implement that interface for each supported content format, as well as special methods (e.g., callbacks) for required specialties of the respective content formats.

The classes' instances enable the application to incrementally build up pages in the user interface and to retrieve the result. Usually, for each user interface element we have methods for starting and ending the element, so that elements may be placed in between.

Sometimes, the CONTENT CREATOR builds up a string, such as for generating XML or HTML directly. The CONTENT CREATOR'S internal data representation can also be a COMPOSITE that is built up incrementally from the content format elements (which are then represented as objects). This variant has the advantage that the content representation in memory can be changed. That is, if the internal format of a CONTENT CREATOR and a CONTENT CONVERTER are identical (e.g., a DOM tree), we do not have to perform input processing in the CONTENT CONVERTER after generating content on the CONTENT CREATOR, but we can directly use the internal format generated. Those objects may also be of the internal FRAGMENTS structure.

CONTENT CREATORS let us abstract specialties and characteristics of different user interfaces. However, we have to "simulate" the more advanced formats in the less advanced ones, or reduce the output to the common denominator. Another variant is to live with lossy conversions.

Sometimes, living with lossy conversions is intended, such as if we want to provide a rich Web interface and reduced content for smaller mobile devices or set-top boxes. In such cases, we can either leave out certain parts of the content during the building process or use different CONTENT CREATOR objects as STRATEGIES [Gamma+1995]. Note that it is often easier and less memory and performance consuming to use CONTENT FORMAT TEMPLATES to create multiple different variants of the same content in the same format. Here, the content to be provided only on some platforms can be marked in the template definition.

In Figure 11–6, a typical design of a CONTENT CREATOR is shown. An abstract CONTENT CREATOR class determines the common interface for all derived creators. Here, four special Creator classes are derived: the GENERIC CONTENT FORMAT XML, HTML pages on the Web, MMS pages for mobiles, and DVB-J Java classes that represent pages on interactive digital television platforms such as the Multimedia Home Platform (MHP).

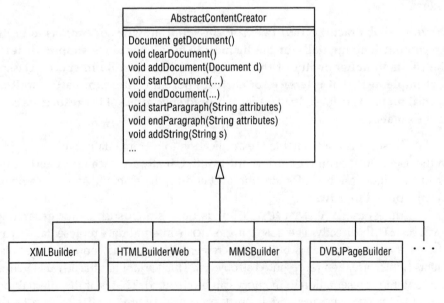

Figure 11–6 *Example of abstract and special Content Creators*

The CONTENT CREATOR pattern offers a set of benefits: The CONTENT CREATOR allows for abstracting multiple target formats. Compared to implementing each target format by hand, the CONTENT CREATOR results in shorter code that is easier to maintain, for example, in cases of changing Web standards and new features. CONTENT CREATORS avoid scattering format specifics throughout the business logic code. In comparison to template or fragment approaches, the constructive approach of the CONTENT CREATOR is more flexible. Syntax errors in the target format can be detected a priori, for example, the creator can raise an error if a content element is opened but not closed.

The CONTENT CREATOR pattern can also incur the following liabilities: In comparison to template or fragment approaches, the constructive approach of the CONTENT CREATOR is rather slow. Problems of lossy conversions and reducing all inputs to the common denominator of the target formats can only be avoided by programming specialties of target formats for all other formats by hand. CONTENT CREATORS require programming efforts to create and customize content; thus, they are hardly applicable at the end-user level without tool support.

CONTENT CREATORS let us generically program how to build up the content format; thus, they are a generic constructive approach. In contrast, CONTENT FORMAT TEMPLATES and FRAGMENTS are template-based approaches for the same problem (but both have a different set of forces in focus).

CONTENT CREATORS can be structured as class hierarchies with methods for each content element, as discussed earlier, or as alternative variants, other descriptive structures can be chosen. As a runtime structure, an object can be created for each content element. Sometimes simpler list structures are appropriate as well.

Content Format Template

In interactive Web applications, content in HTML format, and most often in multiple other formats, has to be dynamically generated. CONTENT CONVERTERS need a facility to build up a representation in a target format dynamically.

How can we build up content in a target content format and allow the content editor to add highly dynamic content parts in a simple way that yields high performance?

An important limitation of CONTENT CREATOR is that it requires programming to create and customize the content created. End-user-level customizability, however, is important for many Web applications since changes to the content presentation can be applied more quickly.

Compared to static HTML content, CONTENT CREATORS are rather slow. For high-performance systems, a performance closer to using static content is required. Most often only small parts of a page are dynamic, and others are given statically. In suitable cases, we should not build up the whole page dynamically but use static content where possible.

The same content in the same format may be presented in different ways. For example, when different platforms are supported, often we want to leave out marked parts of the content, such as leaving out larger pictures in HTML text for better support of mobile devices.

FRAGMENTS solve both of these issues to a certain extent. However, for highly dynamic content elements, we still have to create these Fragments, for example, using CONTENT CREATORS. Therefore, in such cases the problems appear again during construction of the FRAGMENTS.

Therefore:

Provide a template written in the content format that contains special code in a template language to be substituted by a template engine. This way, content editors can work directly using a (familiar) content format and add dynamic elements to it. As large parts of the content do not have to be processed dynamically, such a CONTENT FORMAT TEMPLATE provides potentially high performance.

A CONTENT FORMAT TEMPLATE enriches the content with meta-information. A template language is needed for specifying the substitutions to be performed by the template engine. In some variants, this is a whole scripting language.

A typical example structure is AOL Server's ADP templates that use Tcl. For instance, in the following example, a Web page is created dynamically in which the user's browser type and the time is displayed:

```
<%
  set header [ns_conn headers]
  set browser [ns_set iget $headers User-Agent]
  set time [clock seconds]
%>
<html>
  <body>
    Time: <%= $time %>
    Browser: <%= $browser %>
  </body>
</html>
```

The template engine replaces the embedded Tcl code and produces proper HTML output.

The CONTENT FORMAT TEMPLATE pattern offers a set of benefits: For simple scenarios, template production is very simple and straightforward. That is, Web page design can be separated from program development, and it is possible for Web designers to create dynamic pages. In general, the approach is more efficient than purely constructive approaches on top of CONTENT CREATORS. In contrast to FRAGMENTS, more high-level dynamic interactions can be supported in the content format. Simple behavioral customizations can be performed by the Web designer.

The CONTENT FORMAT TEMPLATE pattern can also incur the following liabilities: In many approaches, such as JSP and ASP, the promise to be simple and straightforward turns out to be unrealistic in practice, because complex programming language elements have to be understood by the Web designers. Real applications have complex interdependencies. Since templates only act at the local level of a single document, they can hardly cope with these issues. A second liability results from this problem: Recurring elements often have to be recoded for every use in a template; that is, there is only limited reuse of template code. The page design and business logic of the application are often not separated.

CONTENT CREATORS operate in the same context as CONTENT FORMAT TEMPLATE. But they build up the content in a programmatic and constructive approach. In some domains, this can lead to significant liabilities regarding end-user customizability and performance compared to static HTML content.

The CONTENT FORMAT TEMPLATE can internally be realized using CONTENT CREATORS. Other combinations of the patterns are also possible. For instance, templates may be embedded in CONTENT CREATOR'S client code. It is also useful to reference FRAGMENTS or CONTENT CREATORS directly from the embedded template code written in the content format.

A FRAGMENT is another template-based approach. It codes only the fragment ID into the document, but it does not include the dynamic content itself. Thus, dynamic behavioral aspects of content that can be coded into the documents themselves are limited.

There are many CONTENT FORMAT TEMPLATE variants based on popular programming languages that are embedded in HTML code. We can generally distinguish between approaches aiming at the end-user and Web-designer level, and more complex approaches. Another aspect to distinguish the approaches is caching and interpretation. Some approaches always compile pages, some approaches cache pages once they are created, and other approaches always interpret the pages.

Fowler [Fowler2003] documents a variant of this pattern called TEMPLATE VIEW, which renders information into HTML by embedding meta-information as comments in the HTML page.

FRAGMENTS

Instead of providing static Web pages only, today's Web sites offer dynamically generated Web pages enriched with real time information such as stock quotes in a sometimes highly personalized manner. Examples of such Web sites are financial, news, and sports sites. You are developing a Web application serving Web pages containing dynamic content.

The different parts of your Web page can have a different lifetime, be highly personalized, or be redundant. You have to ensure that the content presented is consistent. You have to provide these dynamic Web pages in a highly efficient manner.

Generating Web pages from dynamic content is an expensive task because content has to be fetched from data stores like RDBMS, XMLDBMS, or even from other Web systems by accessing Web services. This leads to increased I/O operations and often network overhead as backend systems are incorporated over the intranet or even the internet.

Furthermore, assembling of the retrieved content to Web pages results in a processing overhead. Content might have to be converted into a GENERIC CONTENT FORMAT and Web pages are regenerated completely, because no means are available to determine which parts of a Web page have changed. Often Web pages as a whole are the finest-grained building blocks of Web systems. Therefore, Web pages cannot be served in an efficient manner if the whole Web page is regenerated.

The consistency of the content displayed on the Web page is another key challenge. Different parts of a Web page should be consistent. Consider a Web page showing stock quotes belonging to the user's portfolio. To get more detailed information on a specific stock, the user can click on a hyperlink that opens a details page. The information on that page cannot be older or inconsistent with what was displayed on the first page. To ensure that Web pages are generated consistently, intelligent means must be available to verify that underlying content has changed. This enforces flexible and intelligent information architectures.

Therefore:

Provide an information architecture that represents Web pages from smaller building blocks called FRAGMENTS. Connect these FRAGMENTS so that updates and changes can be propagated along a FRAGMENTS chain.

FRAGMENTS are pieces of information that have an independent meaning and identity. Single stock quotes, news, or user profiles are examples of FRAGMENTS. These independent parts can be assembled into compound parts such as whole Web pages. FRAGMENTS can thus contain other FRAGMENTS and reference still others. FRAGMENTS can thereby build a dependency chain or object dependency graph. If FRAGMENTS lower in the chain change, the higher FRAGMENTS have to be revalidated and regenerated. Thus, only the parts of a Web page that have actually changed are regenerated, which leads to a decreased processing overhead.

Because FRAGMENTS have an independent meaning in the user's conceptual model, they can build the basic entities for caching strategies. It is important to understand that FRAGMENTS are a concept of the information architecture used and are completely independent of base technologies like J2EE or .NET. Therefore, the same information architecture can be used on different technology platforms [Kriha2001]. A FRAGMENTS-based information architecture fits nicely into the overall software architecture of a Web application system because FRAGMENTS can be represented by conventional means like classes.

The illustration in Figure 11–7 shows a Web page of a financial portal site constructed from smaller building blocks. The portal logo and the navigation menu are user-independent and thus appear on every portal page. The uncustomized

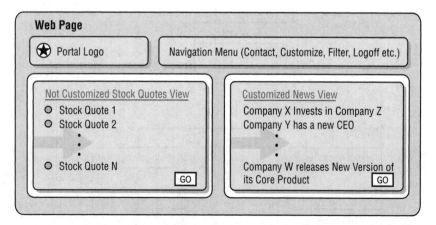

Figure 11–7 *An example Web page containing personalized and non-personalized parts*

stock quotes view is built upon dynamic content but not personalized. Therefore, it can be reused across different portal pages.

In contrast, the customized news view is personalized by the user and is specifically generated for that particular user. However, several users could have the very same configuration, or different news items could appear on different Web pages as well. Thus, there is a reuse potential for the news view and news items. Furthermore, the stock quotes view and the news view are themselves built from smaller building blocks, namely, stock quotes or news items, respectively.

Using the FRAGMENTS concept, the Web page is a compound FRAGMENT containing the portal logo FRAGMENT, the navigation menu FRAGMENT, the stock quotes FRAGMENT, and the news FRAGMENT. The stock quotes and news FRAGMENTS are compound FRAGMENTS as well built from stock quote and news item FRAGMENTS. Like the GENERIC CONTENT FORMAT, a FRAGMENTS architecture can be designed using the COMPOSITE pattern.

Using the COMPOSITE pattern, arbitrary fragment trees can be assembled, as shown in Figure 11–8. In order to tell which fragments make up which other fragments, Fragment Definition Sets (FDS) are used. Fragment Definition Sets are fragments themselves and build an object dependency graph necessary to invalidate fragments and to detect which parts of a fragment have to be regenerated. The Fragment Definition Sets can themselves be modeled using the COMPOSITE pattern (see Figure 11–9).

FRAGMENTS are defined by FRAGMENT definitions. Combining the definition and the instance level of the information architecture leads to a dynamic object model system as described in [Riehle+2001].

Besides using FRAGMENTS to structure Web pages, FRAGMENTS are also ideal candidates to model dependencies between different formats of the same content.

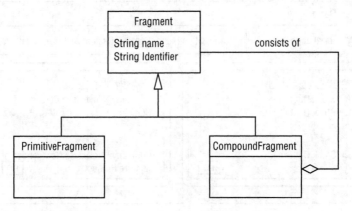

Figure 11–8 *Generic Fragments structure using the Composite pattern*

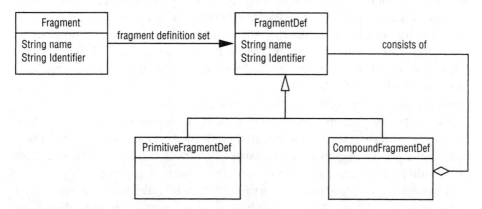

Figure 11–9 *Generic Structure of a Fragment Definition Set*

In Figure 11–10, we can see a typical FRAGMENTS dependency graph of the same content. If any part of the FRAGMENTS dependency graph changes, its successor has to be revalidated and regenerated. The upper part in the dependency graph, the rendered FRAGMENT, is usually part of a Web page dependency graph triggering the revalidation of the affected parts of the Web page after its regeneration. To detect and to propagate fragment changes, special algorithms can be used. For example, a Data Update Propagation (DUP) algorithm can be used to

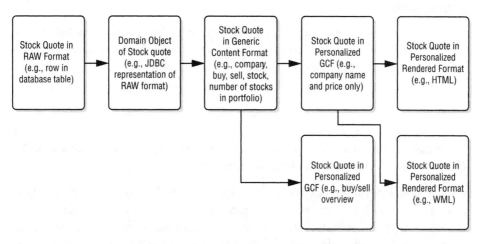

Figure 11–10 *Fragment dependency graph of the same content*

propagate changes along the FRAGMENT dependency graph by assuring consistent updates as described in [Challenger+2000]. Another approach is to include special validator objects containing the logic necessary to determine if FRAGMENTS have become invalid and therefore have to be updated. The validators can either be configured using a rule-based approach or be created programmatically [Kriha2001]. Moreover, caching can be integrated within the FRAGMENTS architecture, as explained in CONTENT CACHE.

The FRAGMENTS pattern offers a set of benefits: Compared to the other content generation patterns, FRAGMENTS potentially offer the highest performance. Fragments offer good integration with a layered CONTENT CACHE. The other content generation patterns can be combined with the FRAGMENT approach.

The FRAGMENTS pattern can also incur the following liabilities: FRAGMENTS only assemble pre-built parts. They are not highly programmable and do not offer behavioral abstractions. However, these problems can be eliminated by combining them with the other content-generation patterns. In pre-built FRAGMENTS, content changes have to be detected and propagated to ensure content consistency.

In their internal structure, FRAGMENTS can be atomic, chained, COMPOSITES, or cascaded COMPOSITES. Fragments can only have an object representation, or they can also cache the GENERIC CONTENT FORMAT representation that corresponds to their internal representation. Then only one of these representations has to be valid, and the other one can be computed lazily.

Content Cache

You are developing a Web application system targeting many users that has to support dynamic content in an efficient way. You are using FRAGMENTS to structure your content. The processing time required to render Web pages should be reduced.

How can you increase the performance of Web page delivery and thereby increase the efficiency of the Web architecture?

Dynamic Web application systems often do not provide Web pages efficiently. A FRAGMENTS architecture can be used to reduce the number of parts of a Web page that have to be regenerated every time a new request enters the system. However, the performance of the overall Web architecture might still be insufficient.

Content changes that affect already created content have to be detected and propagated to avoid content inconsistencies.

Therefore:

Provide a central cache for caching already created dynamic content. Let the PUBLISHER AND GATHERER enter newly created or updated FRAGMENTS in the cache. When the content changes, invalidate the respective content entries in the cache. When a client wants to access some content, let the PUBLISHER AND GATHERER check the cache before dynamically creating the requested content.

The main reason for caching is to increase throughput and thereby increase performance. According to a report by Yahoo [Manber+2000], 80% of all users do not customize their homepage. This means that besides the welcome message, everything appearing on the individual's portal page stays the same. Caching these parts truly increases the performance of the overall Web site tremendously.

However, enabling caching in a consistent way is challenging because accurate cache invalidation algorithms have to be applied. Moreover, client- and server-side caching has to be considered. Whereas server-side caching enables cache invalidation by introducing validator objects containing the knowledge of when a cached piece of content becomes invalid, client-side caching is often quite cumbersome.

First of all, clients, which in most cases are Web browsers, must adhere to a protocol supporting the control of client-side caching from the server side. Although, the common protocol HTTP allows for setting certain caching parameters, most popular Web browsers still do not implement the HTTP specification accurately. This makes caching of dynamic content on the client side unreliable, because it is not clear how the client's browser implements the specification. One can limit access to Web sites to certain, tested browsers only. But the next version or the same version on another platform might still behave differently. Thus, often the only choice is to turn off client-side caching completely, which leads to a decrease of performance.

Server-side caching is an effective means of speeding up overall request satisfaction. To support efficient server-side caching, information architecture must be in place that decomposes the information space along the dimensions of time and personalization and that distinguishes clearly between global pieces, individual selections of global pieces, and truly individual pieces [Kriha2001]. An information architecture based on FRAGMENTS can be used to classify content. Moreover, validator objects can be applied to determine if a piece of information is still valid according to time and personalization constraints. The validator objects can either be configured using a rule-based approach or implemented programmatically. Different validator algorithms can be supplied using the STRATEGY pattern [Gamma+1995].

Assuming that hundreds of requests for the same stock quote are entering the system, the same number of requests to the backend system requesting the same information would be required. Thus, the system performance would be influenced very negatively. Only the first request should trigger the retrieval of the information; all subsequent requests should receive the information from the server-side cache, as long as it is valid. For most types of information, an accuracy of a few seconds is acceptable. Therefore, every request should go through a CONTENT CACHE. The CONTENT CACHE checks to see if the requested piece of information is in the cache and if it is valid. If it is not, the content is loaded from the backend system, stored in the cache, and returned to the client. This applies to whole Web pages as well as to parts of Web pages.

Content can be gathered and published by using the PUBLISHER AND GATHERER pattern. CONTENT CONVERTERS are typically triggered before and/or after the content is placed in the CONTENT CACHE. The PUBLISHER AND GATHERER checks whether the CONTENT CACHE contains a valid entry before it re-creates content dynamically.

The ContentCache itself contains Fragments as well as FragmentDefs and uses associated FragmentValidators to validate Fragments of certain types (see Figure 11–11).

Chains or dependency graphs of FRAGMENTS representing the same content in different formats can be cached in the ContentCache too. Because of the behavior of FragmentChains, the ContentCache is not the only active component within the caching process. FRAGMENTS within a chain automatically notify its successors upon content change, triggering their revalidation and probably

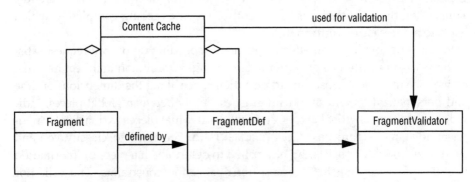

Figure 11–11 *Internal Structure of a Content Cache*

leading to the invalidation of the ContentCache. Thus, FRAGMENTS play an active role in the caching process as well.

The CONTENT CACHE pattern offers a set of benefits: In combination with FRAGMENTS, the patterns allows for highly efficient information architectures. Together with a PUBLISHER AND GATHERER, it integrates well with CONTENT CONVERTERS.

The CONTENT CACHE pattern can also incur the following liabilities: Possible inconsistencies in the CONTENT CACHE have to be resolved. In exceptional cases, change detection and propagation can be more costly than the performance gain of caching. In multithreaded environments, a CONTENT CACHE requires mutex locks, which can result in lock contention. Therefore, it is important to monitor hit rates and contention closely.

There are different variants of CONTENT CACHES. A cache can be supplied as one central instance. As a variant, there can also be multiple caching instances, one for each content element. For instance, in Tcl, Tcl_Objs use this style of caching: Each Tcl_Obj is one cached element plus a CONTENT CONVERTER to/from a generic, string-based representation.

A CONTENT CACHE can support automatic invalidation of all dependent objects, or invalidation has to be handled by hand. Moreover, CONTENT CACHES can also support more advanced forms of content change detection and propagation such as object dependency graphs [Challenger+2000].

If personalized FRAGMENTS are supported, an important variant is a layered CONTENT CACHE. Each caching layer then reflects one personalization layer in the FRAGMENTS.

Implementation Example in Java

In this section, we provide a few Java code examples to illustrate the practical use of the patterns. In the pattern language, the PUBLISHER AND GATHERER pattern is used as the central pattern for architecturally integrating the other patterns of the language. Let us consider PUBLISHER AND GATHERER realized as two separate Java classes with methods for each type of source content. In a simple publisher class, methods for retrieving each individual content type are provided. A document in the GENERIC CONTENT FORMAT (here, XML) can directly be delivered with getXml, if it is found in the cache. Each document has a unique document ID, for instance, denoted by an URL. We would have to trigger building a page from FRAGMENTS here as well if this functionality is supported. Internally, the document FRAGMENTS consist of an object tree corresponding with the GENERIC CONTENT FORMAT's information architecture. XML and HTML text are just views on this generic representation; however, the XML view has a one-to-one correspondence.

Other formats such as HTML are either already converted or stored in the generic cache, or they have to be converted from XML. If a conversion took place, we can put the generated HTML document into the cache.

```
class Publisher {
  CacheHandler xmlCache;
  CacheHandler htmlCache;
  ContentConverter htmlConverter;
  ...
  public XmlDocument getXml (DocumentID docID) {
    return xmlCache.get(docID);
  }
  public HtmlDocument getHtml (DocumentID docID) {
    HtmlDocument htmlDoc = htmlCache.get(docID)
    if (htmlDoc == null) {
      XmlDocument xmlDoc = getXml(docID);
      htmlDoc = htmlConverter.convertFromXml(xmlDoc);
      if (htmlDoc != null)
        htmlCache.enter(docID, htmlDoc);
    }
    return htmlDoc;
  }
  ...
}
```

Similarly, a gatherer can directly store XML input into the document cache (or on any other storage device), and entries for the document in depending caches, such as the HTML cache, are invalidated. If HTML input is received, the XML and HTML cache entries are invalidated, and the new document is converted to XML.

```
class Gatherer {
  CacheHandler xmlCache;
  CacheHandler htmlCache;
  ContentConverter htmlConverter;
  ...
  public void storeXml (DocumentID docID,
                        XmlDocument xmlDoc) {
    xmlCache.store(xmlDoc);
    xmlCache.propagateChangeToDependingCaches(xmlDoc);
  }
```

```
public void storeHtmlAsXml (HtmlDocument htmlDoc) {
  invalidateAllCaches(docID);
  xmlCache.store(docID,
    htmlConverter.convertToXml(htmlDoc));
}
...
}
```

CONTENT CONVERTERS are triggered by the PUBLISHER AND GATHERER. We will now discuss code examples for input processing with the tree-based model on the basis of the Document Object Model (DOM). The CONTENT CONVERTER has to wrap and trigger a DOM CONTENT CREATOR. Before parsing, we have to instantiate a document tree creator object first. Then we have to parse the file as well:

```
DocumentBuilderFactory factory =
  DocumentBuilderFactory.newInstance();
factory.setValidating(false);
DocumentBuilder builder =
  factory.newDocumentBuilder();
...
Document document = builder.parse(file);
```

A tree structure is generated in memory. DOM provides a low-level API to traverse this tree as an intermediate format in memory, for example:

```
NodeList nodes_i =
  document.getDocumentElement().getChildNodes();
for (int i = 0; i < nodes_i.getLength(); i++) {
  Node node_i = nodes_i.item(i);
  if (node_i.getNodeType() == Node.ELEMENT_NODE &&
      ((Element) node_i).getTagName().equals("A")) {
    handleElementA();
  }
  ...
}
```

A CONTENT CONVERTER wraps these low-level details of XML processing and generates the appropriate GENERIC CONTENT FORMAT with its corresponding information architecture. Usually, only the Java FRAGMENT objects are created from the DOM tree and the corresponding XML text and other content formats are created lazily on demand.

Alternatively, we can use event-based XML processing models, such as SAX or Expat, or rule-based processing models, such as XSLT.

CONTENT CREATORS can be used in this architecture to generate XML and HTML text from the FRAGMENTS that are created after input processing. Here, the FRAGMENTS are ordered hierarchically in a COMPOSITE structure. For each element of the content format, the CONTENT CREATOR has methods for starting the element and ending it. For instance, a paragraph in an HTML creator may have children; thus, it has to be started and ended:

```
void startParagraph(String attributes) {
  addStringIncr("<P ");
  addString(parseArguments(attributes));
  addStringIncr(">\n");
}
void endParagraph() {
  addStringDecr("</P>");
}
```

Leafs, such as strings, have only a method for adding the leaf. In startParagraph and endParagraph we have used the methods addStringIncr, addString, and addStringDecr for adding the leafs that mark up the paragraph. Only addString is a method supported by the abstract CONTENT CREATOR. addStringIncr and addStringDecr are methods for increasing and decreasing the indent level of HTML text before adding a string. Thus, they represent a specialty of the HTML format.

An XML CONTENT CREATOR usually has a one-to-one mapping of content FRAGMENTS and CONTENT CREATOR methods, because there is a one-to-one correspondence between those elements in the GENERIC CONTENT FORMAT pattern. A mapping method for each FRAGMENT type defines the correspondence between the semantic content in the FRAGMENTS and basic content layout, such as HTML or WML. Further layout refinements can be added with different means, such as Cascading Style Sheets (CSS) and XSLT processing.

As an alternative, we can enhance given content with CONTENT FORMAT TEMPLATES. A simple example of CONTENT FORMAT TEMPLATE is JSPs that contain Java code to be substituted. The substitution rules can also be applied with XML. The template engine finds special tags containing the Java code and executes this code before delivering the pages. Here, the data for date and time is computed dynamically:

```
<%@page import="java.util.*" %>
<HTML>
...
<BODY>
```

```
<H2>Date and Time</H2>
  Today's date is: <%= new Date() %>
</BODY>
</HTML>
```

Of course, CONTENT FORMAT TEMPLATES are especially valuable if they are combined with the other patterns in the language. For instance, the called methods can refer to FRAGMENTS that are dynamically computed and/or cached. This computation can be done with CONTENT CREATORS.

Known Uses and Related Work

There are different commercial Web service and portal architectures that are based on parts of the pattern language. For instance, BEA WebLogic Integration uses a GENERIC CONTENT FORMAT to receive and send data from and to clients connected to its integration platform. Oracle's PortalToGo uses a SimpleResult data structure to represent content in a device-independent manner. It generates device-specific pages based on the content represented in the GENERIC CONTENT FORMAT. The Java Connector Architecture (JCA) provides ResultSets, MapResultsSets, and other generic formats to represent data coming from different backend systems.

Different Web standards and their implementations are also based on parts of the pattern language: SOAP [Box+2000] is an XML-based remote procedure call (RPC) protocol. SOAP envelopes are a typed GENERIC CONTENT FORMAT. RDF [Lassila+1998] is a graph-based GENERIC CONTENT FORMAT for providing metadata on the Web.

Servers that allow for putting and retrieving data (and programs) are simplistic implementation variants of the PUBLISHER AND GATHERER pattern with one entity; examples are FTP servers and HTTP PUT/POST-enabled HTTP servers.

There are numerous XML-based CONTENT CONVERTERS based on the different processing standards: SAX [Megginson1999] parsers and Expat are the basis for numerous event-based parsing architectures, DOM [W3C2000] is the basis for numerous tree-based parsing architectures, and XSLT [Clark1999] is the basis for numerous rule-based parsing architectures.

xoComm [Neumann+2000] is a extensible Web server architecture that has a worker object for each request and a central server for handling incoming and outgoing HTTP requests. Thus, this Web server architecture is also a PUBLISHER AND GATHERER variant. xoComm provides a CONTENT CACHE structure on the client side. Actiweb [Neumann+2001] is a Web object and mobile code system based on xoComm. It uses the "events" generated by the corresponding worker of the Web server. It translates the URLs in an invoker component. Depending on the URL, normal Web pages are delivered, an agent immigration or RPC invocation is handled, or a Web object is triggered. In this framework, xoRDF [Neumann+2002] is a tree-based CONTENT CONVERTER architecture for RDF data that is extensible with multiple other interpretations using a VISITOR framework. Antti Salonen's Htmllib is a CONTENT CREATOR written in XOTcl for the HTML target format that is integrated in ActiWeb. It builds up a Tcl list dynamically on the creator object and supports the most important parts of HTML's functionality. The conference management system, described in [Zdun2002a], uses these HTML creator objects extensively.

The Credit Control Platform has been developed for a leading Swiss bank. The platform stores credit control information coming from different credit control systems in GENERIC CONTENT FORMAT and uses it to render HTML pages. Credit Control Platform uses efficient, format-specific, code-generated CONTENT CONVERTERS to convert credit reports from different credit control systems into a GENERIC CONTENT FORMAT [Vogel2000]. A modeling tool can be used to describe the schema of the input format. Based on the schema-specific CONTENT, CONVERTERS are created. Credit Control Platform supports different CONTENT FORMAT TEMPLATES. Data Visualizers can be specified on a meta level using a special modeling tool [Bredenfeld+2000]. Concrete CONTENT FORMAT TEMPLATES can be generated for different technologies like JSP, ASP, and XSLT.

The document archiving system in [Goedicke+2002] provides a GENERIC CONTENT FORMAT in the form of a data capsule format for document archiving. The capsules contain the document plus metadata. In future system versions, the capsule format should be XML. The system provides central GATHERER entities for archiving of different content formats and a document retrieval handler. All handlers are daemons that are provided for initial access only. Upon request, a PUBLISHER handler is forked from the central instance and handles the request. The system supports CONTENT CONVERTERS for converting all inputs into an archive capsule format.

In the document management system DocMe, a central gatherd and publishd are provided to realize the pattern PUBLISHER AND GATHERER. Internally, all gathered information is converted. Here, different constructive CONTENT CONVERTERS are provided, for example, from MS Word format and similar formats used by end users as content editors. The system approximates how the documents should look in different formats, such as HTML or TV broadcast data. Using the central PUBLISHER AND GATHERER, the system caches the information, handles multiple document versions in the CONTENT CACHE, change detection and propagation, user and rights management, and document classification issues.

AOL Digital City, based on AOL Server [Davidson2000], has an architecture with a central Pub server and multiple front-end servers as a variant of PUBLISHER AND GATHERER. A switch server multiplexes a client onto one of the front-end servers. AOL Server's SOB (small objects) is an interface for dynamic publishing of editorial content. SOBs can be placed as FRAGMENTS in templates. They are aggressively cached in a CONTENT CACHE, for example, in AOL Movie Guide. AOL Server implements a CONTENT CACHE in a multithreaded environment. Here, the cached data has to be mutex-protected during writing. AOL Digital City and Movie Guide use this functionality for central content caching servers. AOLServer's ADP templates are CONTENT FORMAT TEMPLATES that integrate HTML, Tcl, and the AOL Server interfaces. They are used on numerous high-performance Web sites, including AOL Digital City and Movie Guide.

The Olympic Games 2000 Web Site [Challenger+2000] is built by IBM using a FRAGMENTS-based system for dynamic creation of Web content. It uses a server-side CONTENT CACHE to cache dynamic content [Challenger+2000].

Edge Side Includes are a new evolving FRAGMENT technology used to describe cacheable and non-cacheable Web page components. These components can be aggregated, assembled, and delivered at runtime [ESI2002].

WebShell [Vckovski2001] uses Tcl procedure to implement each part of the construction of a Web page as a CONTENT CREATOR. These are combined in a special method that assembles and delivers the Web page. The code of this procedure already resembles the document to be created, but actually Tcl commands and lists are used.

In the TPMHP project, we are building a Java-based CONTENT CREATOR for the Multimedia Home Platform (MHP), which should support DVB-J, HTML, and MMS pages.

There are several different languages and platforms that support CONTENT FORMAT TEMPLATES natively. ASP and JSP are approaches that use tags to allow embedded code in an HTML page. ASP pages are written in Visual Basic, and JSP pages are written in Java. ASPs offer a CONTENT CACHE for all created pages. As a disadvantage, both approaches require "low-level" programming and are therefore hardly applicable at the end-user level. Scripting approaches for building templates on the Web are often easy to customize. PHP introduces a new language for Web page templates. It is small, lightweight, efficient, and easy to use for non-programmers. However, as a disadvantage, the language is only created for one use: on the Web. The Apache modules mod_perl, mod_tcl, and WebShell [Vckovski2001] allow for combining templates written in Tcl and Perl with the Apache Web server. Zope is a rather complex and powerful system for integrated Web development that resides on the Python language, and also allows for templates.

Some approaches provide combinations of CONTENT FORMAT TEMPLATES and CONTENT CREATORS: WebShell [Vckovski2001], ActiWeb [Neumann+2001], and Brent Welch's TclHttpd can construct pages dynamically, and embedded template elements in the HTML code are used to construct an HTML page.

Conclusion

In this chapter we have presented patterns for dynamic content conversion and generation on the Web. The patterns are used in many different Web architectures, and to a certain extent, different available technological instances can be exchanged. For instance, different models of CONTENT CONVERTERS or different content generation techniques can easily be exchanged. However, the baseline architecture stays the same despite such important technological decisions. Since most basic technologies are based on XML, and since components such as parsers and processors are widely available for many different programming languages, we can assert that the patterns can be used for architectural decisions apart from concrete technological realizations. Therefore, they provide a good communication means with different stakeholders of the system in focus.

In our experience, the patterns yield architectures with a set of benefits and liabilities that vary slightly for the different implementation technologies used, for different combinations of the patterns, for different sequences through the language, and for different variants of the patterns.

The patterns strongly encourage architectures that provide a separation of concerns between content, styles, formats, and channels. That is the reason that different technological choices can relatively easily be exchanged against each other. MESSAGE REDIRECTORS [Goedicke+2001] can be used to implement the indirection to the channels, and add-ons for the channels can be transparently provided, such as logging or authentication.

With a SERVICE ABSTRACTION LAYER [Vogel2001], multiple representation channels may be supported. CONTENT CREATOR and CONTENT FORMAT TEMPLATE can be used to abstract from different content formats. Thus, a common denominator can be implemented with minimal programming effort. Both patterns provide a programmable alternative to using FRAGMENTS alone, and both can be integrated with FRAGMENT approaches.

Generational aspects in the pattern language can be handled at runtime. Therefore, introducing changes into a running program is natively supported by much architecture based on the pattern language. However, since generation is always more performance-intensive than delivering static HTML pages (e.g., stored in files or in a database), performance may be influenced negatively.

Therefore, the balance between CONTENT CREATORS, CONTENT FORMAT TEMPLATES, and static content often has to be considered very carefully. In different applications, performance impacts may significantly vary. Thus, often combinations of the patterns and caching architectures are necessary in order to reach acceptable results. These forces are primarily resolved by the FRAGMENT and CONTENT CACHE patterns.

If CONTENT CREATORS are used exclusively, the user interfaces are reduced to the common denominator defined in the abstract creator. Of course, certain CONTENT CREATORS may also ignore certain formatting instructions, such as a WML CONTENT CREATOR that does not fully support the HTML subset.

On first sight, the complexity of architectures based on the pattern language is higher than simple architectures such as template-based approaches or CGI scripts. However, for larger tasks, the complexity of the simpler models usually grows exponentially, for example, because of cut-and-paste code and missing integration models. Therefore, in our experience, in real-world, large-scale Web applications, the complexity and thus the maintainability and understandability is influenced rather positively by applying the pattern language.

Acknowledgments

We wish to thank our EuroPLoP shepherd Markus Voelter for his valuable comments during the shepherding process. We wish to also thank the participants of the EuroPLoP 2002 Writer's Workshop, who also provided substantial feedback that helped us to improve the chapter.

References

[Alexander+1977] C. Alexander, S. Ishikawa, M. Silverstein, M. Jakobson, I. Fiksdahl-King, and S. Angel. *A Pattern Language—Towns, Buildings, Construction*. Oxford University Press, 1977.

[Box+2000] D. Box, D. Ehnebuske, G. Kakivaya, A. Layman, N. Mendelsohn, H. F. Nielsen, S. Thatte, and D. Winer. Simple Object Access Protocol (SOAP) 1.1, 2000. Available: *http://www.w3.org/TR/SOAP/*.

[Bredenfeld+2000] A. Bredenfeld, E. Ihler, and O. Vogel. "GENVIS, Model Based Generation Of Data Visualizers." In *Proceedings of Technology of Object Oriented Languages and Systems Conference*, France, 2000. Available: *http://www.ovogel.de/publications/GENVIS.pdf*.

[Challenger+2000] J. Challenger, A. Iyengar, K. Witting, C. Ferstat, and P. Reed. "A Publishing System for Efficiently Creating Dynamic Web Content." In *Proceedings of IEEE INFOCOM 2000*, Tel Aviv, Israel, March 2000.

[Clark1999] J. Clark. *XSL Transformations (XSLT)*. 1999. Available: *http://www.w3.org/TR/xslt*.

[Davidson2000] J. Davidson. "Tcl in AOL Digital City the Architecture of a Multithreaded High-Performance Web Site." In *Keynote at Tcl2k: The 7th USENIX Tcl/Tk Conference*, Austin, Texas, February 2000. Available: *http://www.aolserver.com/docs/intro/tcl2k/*.

[ESI2002] ESI. *Edge Side Includes (ESI) Overview*, 2002. Available: *http://www.esi.org*.

[Fowler2003] M. Fowler. *Patterns of Enterprise Application Architecture*. Boston: Addison-Wesley, 2003.

[Gamma+1995] E. Gamma, R. Helm, R. Johnson, and J. Vlissides. *Design Patterns: Elements of Reusable Object-Oriented Software*. Reading, MA: Addison-Wesley, 1995.

[Goedicke+2002] M. Goedicke and U. Zdun. "Piecemeal Legacy Migrating with an Architectural Pattern Language: A Case Study." In *Journal of Software Maintenance and Evolution: Research and Practice*, 14:1–30, 2002.

[Goedicke+2001] M. Goedicke, G. Neumann, and U. Zdun. "Message Redirector." In *Proceedings of EuroPlop 2001*, Irsee, Germany, July 2001.

[Kircher2001] M. Kircher. "Lazy Acquisition." In *Proceedings of EuroPlop 2001*, Irsee, Germany, July 2001.

[Kriha2001] W. Kriha. *Advanced Enterprise Portals*, 2001. Available: *http://www.kriha.org*.

[Manber+2000] U. Manber, A. Patel, and J. Robison. "Experience with Personalization on Yahoo!" In *Communications of ACM*, 43 (8), pp. 107–111, 2000.

[Lassila+1998] O. Lassila and R. R. Swick. *Resource Description Framework (RDF) Model and Syntax Specification*, WD-rdf-syntax-19981008, 1998. Available: *http://www.w3.org/RDF*.

[Megginson1999] D. Megginson. SAX 2.0: *The Simple API for XML*, 1999. Available: *http://www.megginson.com/SAX/index.html*.

[Neumann+2000] G. Neumann and U. Zdun. "High-Level Design and Architecture of an HTTP-Based Infrastructure for Web Applications." *World Wide Web Journal*, 3(1), 2000.

[Neumann+2001] G. Neumann and U. Zdun. "Distributed Web Application Development with Active Web Objects." In *Proceedings of The 2nd International Conference on Internet Computing (IC'2001)*, Las Vegas, Nevada, June 2001.

[Neumann+2002] G. Neumann and U. Zdun. "Pattern-Based Design and Implementation of an XML and RDF Parser and Interpreter: A Case Study." In *Proceedings of the 16th European Conference on Object-Oriented Programming (ECOOP 2002)*, pp. 392–414, Malaga, Spain, June 2002. LNCS 2374, Springer-Verlag.

[Riehle+2001] D. Riehle, M. Tilman, and R. Johnson. "Dynamic Object Model." In *Proceedings of 7th Pattern Languages of Programs Conference (Plop 2000)*, Monticello, Illinois, August 2000.

[Vckovski2001] Andrej Vckovski. "TclWeb." In *Proceedings of 2nd European Tcl User Meeting*, Hamburg, Germany, June 2001.

[Vogel2000] O. Vogel. "Usability of XML, Generation of Efficient XML Content Converters." Speech at XML for Business, Switzerland, Zuerich/Regensdorf, 2000. Available: *http://www.ovogel.de/publications/XML4Business.pdf*.

[Vogel2001] O. Vogel. "Service Abstraction Layer." In *Proceedings of EuroPlop 2001*, Irsee, Germany, July 2001. Available: *http://www.ovogel.de/publications/ServiceAbstraction-Layer.pdf*.

[W3C2000] W3C. *Document Object Model*. 2000. Available: *http://www.w3.org/DOM/*.

[Zdun2002a] U. Zdun. "Dynamically Generating Web Application Fragments from Page Templates." In *Proceedings of Symposium of Applied Computing (SAC 2002)*, Madrid, Spain, 2002.

[Zdun2002b] U. Zdun. "Reenginering to the Web: Towards a Reference Architecture." In *Proceedings of 6th European Conference on Software Maintenance and Reengineering*, Budapest, Hungary, 2002.

[Zdun2003] U. Zdun. "Patterns of Tracing Software Structures and Dependencies." In *Proceedings of 8th European Conference on Pattern Languages of Programs (EuroPlop 2003)*, pp. 581–616, Irsee, Germany, June 2003.

[Zdun2004] U. Zdun. "Some Patterns of Component and Language Integration." In *Proceedings of 9th European Conference on Pattern Languages of Programs (EuroPlop 2004)*, pp. 1–26, Irsee, Germany, July 2004.

PART V

Architecture Patterns

Chapter 12: Patterns for Plug-Ins

The ability to modify and extend software represents one of the characteristics that set software engineering apart from most other engineering disciplines. Plug-ins represent a popular technique for extending applications that allows users to late-bind new functionality. But how do people who build applications that must be extended with plug-ins design their applications? Klaus Marquardt answers this question based on insight from several systems that use plug-ins. The Patterns for Plug-Ins pattern language covers techniques mined from a wide body of software, including operating systems, Web browsers, graphics programs, and development environments.

Chapter 13: The Grid Architectural Pattern: Leveraging Distributed Processing Capabilities

Grid computing represents one of the promising developments of the last few years (and regrettably also one of the terms heavily abused by marketers). By regarding computational resources as the elements of an interconnected grid, it allows their sharing within or between organizations. Raphael Y. de Camargo, Andrei Goldchleger, Márcio Carneiro, and Fabio Kon adopt a pattern-oriented approach to describe the issues that this architecture must deal with as it strives to provide for ubiquity of the power grid. The Grid Architectural Pattern covers the architectural elements of grid middleware as well as guidelines for implementing and deploying them.

Chapter 14: Patterns of Component and Language Integration

Seasoned programmers know to pick the most powerful language or tool for the problems that they solve. Sometimes this means building applications using more than one programming language or multiple kinds of components. This brings to the table the problem of integrating components written in different languages or built with heterogenous component concepts. Uwe Zdun presents a pattern language that focuses on this type of component integration. Targeting application developers working in such a heterogeneous environment, the Patterns of Component and Language Integration distill insight from systems that include Apache Axis and the Simplified Wrapper Interface Generator (SWIG).

Chapter 15: Patterns for Successful Framework Development

Frameworks represent a side effect of many software development projects. However, in many instances framework development doesn't start with several concrete applications. Sometimes the development of new frameworks even lies on the project's critical path. This context represents a radical departure from the advice provided by framework experts. Andreas Rüping presents a set of patterns for mitigating the mismatch between the recommended practice and the reality of many software development projects. These patterns provide guidance to practitioners who are building applications and frameworks at the same time.

CHAPTER 12

Patterns for Plug-ins

Klaus Marquardt

Software is cheap. Ever more functions in technical devices are implemented in software, because software is much more flexible than hardware or mechanics. But this flexibility, adaptability, and extensibility does not come for free. The costs in software development and ownership during a product's lifetime are significant and often underestimated. Measures to minimize them are of great interest in the industry.

Flexibility in software can be achieved by careful design, by configurability, and by using software components. These techniques supplement each other, and a careful design is prerequisite for the latter ones. Both configuration and component installation add flexibility by deferring software changes and decisions from the initial development of an application to late phases, installation, and deployment.

- Carefully designed software separates different aspects explicitly and anticipates certain kinds of changes. These changes then have a limited impact on the software structure and can be implemented easily. Because other changes require rewriting large parts of the software, management of internal dependencies is a key to maintainability. Each change migrates through the complete line from development to the customer.

- Configurable software determines parts of its behavior at runtime, when it reads and interprets its configuration. The initial development and test effort is high, but a larger variety of changes can be treated without changing the delivered software itself.

- Using software components requires dividing the software into parts that can be developed and exchanged independently. The flexibility gained is virtually infinite, because components contain executable code. Preparing for exchangeable components increases the development effort, but the ability to change the software by adding or exchanging distinct parts of it reduces the costs during the product lifetime.

Configurability inevitably adds to the complexity of the software and can make projects suffocate from their own weight. Thus, component-based development has become more popular for large systems. Plug-in components are a special flavor of components that have advantages over standard components. The key difference is the responsibility for integration. Plug-in components integrate themselves into an existing context that is defined by a hosting application and extend that application in ways that are potentially unforeseen by the initial concept.

Plug-ins are not intended to be of general purpose but are made for a particular application and domain. This has two effects. First, the application defines the ways and means of the functionality and its integration. This allows limiting the integration infrastructure to the minimum required, but an apparently seamless semantic integration can be achieved by defining a large number of fine-grained integration points. Second, the initial responsibility for integration is shifted from the application to the components. This defers some of the complexity and effort from the initial application development to the plug-in development and ensures that integration is manageable, even in large development efforts.

The power of the plug-in component approach is amazing. Software systems can be delivered almost "nakedly," and most user value is added by plug-ins that are developed separately. Existing applications can be extended without change to support new file formats, additional procedures and abilities, or further customer devices.

While plug-ins were an established base technique for business applications [Fowler2003] even before their first description as patterns [Marquardt1999], the plug-in idea has become most popular through the Eclipse platform [Eclipse]. The patterns presented here treat the role of software components in the context of a hosting software application, ranging from specification and design to shipment and organizational issues.

The Plug-in Flavor of Components

Components [Völter+2002] based on a standard component infrastructure such as EJB or .NET solve problems similar to those that plug-in components solve. In both cases, the main driver is the need for extensibility, that is, the possibility to "plug" together the application software. However, there are some differences that distinguish plug-ins from other components.

- Plug-ins are extensions for a particular application in a particular domain. Standard components and containers are more generic and meant for multipurpose reuse. This allows the hosting containers to define more generic interfaces and a less tight integration.

- With plug-in architectures, the hosting applications are often useful without any plug-in installed yet. Plug-ins typically extend the functionality by certain aspects, like PDF viewing in Internet browsers. This is different for components. The container, which resembles the hosting application, does not do anything useful without installed components.

- Components present software with completed functionality. They bring everything they need and can be installed and employed by other components. Plug-ins are much more tightly integrated with the hosting application and extend it by aspects that are more specific and less general. Accordingly, the contracts between hosting application and plug-in are more specific than component-ware interfaces—but the latter may become a part of the plug-in contract.

- Component infrastructures (such as EJB, CCM, and .NET) divide the functionality along technical concerns (Container) and application logics (Component). Plug-in architectures separate different areas of the application logic in the first place, and only in the second place do they also separate technology from application—via different areas in the contract.

- Plug-ins are complete extensions that contribute their knowledge across different technical layers. This thematic closure is missing with other components. Plug-in packages can be shipped independently of their hosting application, and they enable a separate licensing model.

A plug-in architecture should be considered when the kind of extensibility is defined by the application domain, independent development is important, and a high amount of specific integration points add value to the user. [Marquardt+2003]

Example

The patterns usage is illustrated by the fictitious Argus example. Argus is the central software of a security company that integrates security systems of single buildings. Within each building, an independent local system observes doors, windows, and parameters such as temperature and humidity to identify (possibly illegal) access, fire, or other problems. The Argus central connects to a number of individual local security systems, retrieves their data, and reports all violations both visibly and audibly, depending on their priority.

The local building security systems come from different vendors and have different sizes and abilities. At the Argus central, each of them is represented by a plug-in component that takes care of the communication to its corresponding local system and for the translation of received data into the model of the Argus central.

Known Uses

The use of plug-ins is common in a large variety of applications. The patterns refer to the following known uses:

- *Eclipse* is an application that hosts plug-ins for development tasks. Some of the more generic plug-ins define interfaces themselves where further, more specialized plug-ins can contribute [Eclipse].

- *Internet Explorer, Firefox, Netscape* and other browsers present Web pages that combine text, pictures, and movies with navigation facilities and elements that initiate an action.

- *Adobe Photoshop* and *Adobe Acrobat* provide their functions via plug-ins that are loaded at startup.

- *Microsoft Word* and *Rational Rose*, like many other applications, provide extensibility through an application-specific interpreted language (BASIC) and customizable GUI elements (menus and tool bars) that call further executables.

- *Windows, Linux, VxWorks*, and virtually every operating system can be adapted to different hardware devices and allow the user to start programs.

- *LSM*, the Laboratory Systems Manager for laboratory automation systems, controls a number of chemical analyzers and integrates them into a laboratory or hospital information system [Roche].

- *Zeus* is an anaesthesia workplace that observes and controls a patient's health. Each Zeus controls a number of replaceable sensors and actors, or packages of them, that change with the shipped configuration, and it integrates them into a combined intelligence and user interface [Dräger].

Roadmap

The patterns for plug-ins deal with the definition of a plug-in and its context, its relation to the application, packaging, and activation. The patterns are of a general technical nature, applicable in a wide range of development environments and methods.

Figure 12–1 shows the patterns and their main relations. PLUG-IN describes how functionality can be added to applications at runtime. Each PLUG-IN lives in a context, the activating application. This FRAMEWORK PROVIDING APPLICATION provides access to services and domain objects. FRAMEWORK PROVIDING APPLICATION and PLUG-IN share a PLUG-IN CONTRACT defined by the application that describes duties that each PLUG-IN has to fulfill, options for specific extensions, and functions and libraries that the application offers to all connected PLUG-INS.

PLUG-INS are accompanied by additional programs and files forming a shippable PLUG-IN PACKAGE. The PLUG-IN BASED PRODUCT is the customer-usable package of a hosting application and a set of PLUG-IN PACKAGES that comprise functionality of value to a customer.

Further patterns clarify the relation between application and plug-in, and among different plug-ins. The PLUG-IN REGISTRATION enables the application to find and invoke its functional extensions. PLUG-IN LIFECYCLE and its management are a fundamental part of the PLUG-IN CONTRACT. A single PLUG-IN may not be

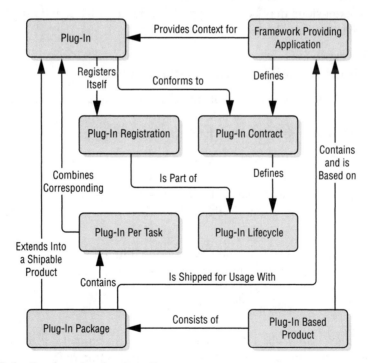

Figure 12–1 *Roadmap for plug-in patterns*

sufficient to fulfill the complete extensibility task. Large functional parts can be separated into multiple cooperating PLUG-INS, with COOPERATING PLUG-INS.

Plug-in

Context

An application that is required to be highly adaptable, or to be extensible to support future functionality or modules.

Problem

How can functionality be added late? How can the functionality be increased after shipping?

Forces

The application is extended by additional functionality,
... but the extensions may be developed by a different team and on a different schedule than the initial application.

Shipping is expensive,
... but early delivery increases market share and profit.

At application shipping time, not all functional components are known or available
... but the kind of additional or exchanged functionality can be well known.

The kind of additional or exchanged functionality can be well known,
... but specifically added functionality cannot be foreseen, and the application must not presume that a particular functional component is available, and which functionality is dynamically added when may only be determined at runtime

The application core is not changed by additional functionality,
... but as technology evolves, the application will be used in unforeseen ways.

Solution

Factor out functionality, and place it in a separate component that is activated at runtime. This component is called a PLUG-IN. The application defines functionality that it does not provide itself, but that must be added by PLUG-INS. The application is shipped with a well-defined interface for PLUG-INS (PLUG-IN CONTRACT). A PLUG-IN consists of executable code that the application loads dynamically at runtime [Fowler2003]. The mechanism used for the late binding is also part of the contract, like a DLL linkage or component-ware infrastructure.

Each PLUG-IN complies with the defined interface in technical and application domain aspects. The application does not depend on a PLUG-IN's internals, and often not on the presence of a particular plug-in kind. PLUG-INS can be used to factor out essential functionality. In this case, the presence of a particular PLUG-IN is required and the application is always shipped with that PLUG-IN.

Terminology

"Plug-in kind"—Different PLUG-INS are of the same kind when they conform to the same predefined interface. The object-oriented analogue would be a super-class.

"Plug-in type"—The plug-in implementation denotes the type. Each type adheres to a different interface and serves a different purpose. The object-oriented analogue would be a (derived) class.

"Plug-in instance"—A currently or potentially invoked plug-in. The object-oriented analogue would be a class instance.

Consequences

☺ Functionality can be developed and added or changed after shipping the application.

☺ The application with factored functionality can be shipped earlier than a similar application with full embedded functionality.

☺ An application with defined plug-ins can be shipped while a fully functional application may never reach a shippable state at all.

☺ The application is not updated when adding functionality, and is not affected by any plug-in.

☺ Delayed developed plug-ins must be shipped separately, but can also be sold separately.

☹ The kind of extensibility must be foreseen, because the interface for plug-ins must be defined in advance.

Implementation

To identify functions that can be placed into a plug-in, look out for open points in the application requirements. Frequently, a specific kind of extensibility is required or implied when the specification contains "etc." phrases. Multiple subclasses of key abstraction are also candidates, if your analysis shows that extending the system would add another subclass.

Plug-ins can be implemented using any component technology that allows for deferred loading, such as DLL or .NET. The application decides about the activation time and conditions (PLUG-IN LIFECYCLE). A plug-in may start and use helper applications when useful.

Separate between physical design (execution) and logical design (basic and added functionality). Physical design is up to the application that decides when which plug-in is activated in which process; for plug-in internals, occasionally a resource budget [Noble+2000] is defined as part of the interface. The application can also define the outline of the logical design, but internals are completely up to the plug-in.

Organizational Issues

Plug-ins can be used to develop customer specific solutions. In this case plug-ins can be organized as separate projects, after the application is available. Products based on plug-ins can then be customized to a specific client's needs. This enables a large-scale reuse of ready-to-use software, i.e., the entire hosting application and all available plug-ins, and minimal development time and effort.

Plug-ins can serve as separate products that either the application vendor or an independent manufacturer can develop and distribute. The first case is common with video games that can be extended by scenarios, and in other narrow domains. The latter is common in technical domains where plug-in vendors intend to advertise their own products and services such as screen savers and Web browser plug-ins.

When applications are shipped together with available plug-ins, plug-ins are developed as subprojects simultaneously with the application project (developing the market-visible product). Especially in nontechnical domains, the application's market success can depend heavily on the existence and number of available plug-ins. In this case, the application project has to take care of plug-in projects as preferred customers.

Known Uses

Adobe Photoshop uses plug-ins extensively to factor out internal as well as extensible functionality. Development of plug-ins is considered part of the application project. Some externally developed plug-ins can be purchased, such as Kai's Power Tools.

Web browsers place viewing functionality into plug-ins, each of which interprets a specific graphics or movie format. Third parties provide additional plug-ins for less common or new formats. Some of the plug-ins for browsers are almost as well known as the browsers themselves.

Eclipse offers to plug in development support tools like compilers, source control management, and groupware solutions. The plug-ins are developed independent of the Eclipse platform and enjoy fairly different reception by different communities.

Device drivers for most operating systems are plug-ins provided by the hardware vendor. Each commercial application (like Microsoft Word) is a plug-in to an operating system.

The Windows OS family has factored out the screen saver functionality, which must be provided by a separate plug-in. Windows is shipped with a variety of different plug-ins; the user can select one of them to be activated.

LSM has separated the analyzer-handling know-how and code into plug-ins. The user selects the kind and amount of analyzers in the laboratory, and a corresponding number of the appropriate plug-ins is activated.

Zeus has separated the sensor- and actor-handling know-how and code into plug-ins. By installing the appropriate plug-in, physically attached sensor packages are activated and can be used.

Example

The Argus central can connect to a variety of different observation systems. The specific, mostly proprietary transmission protocols are factored into plug-ins. This way, the Argus application is prepared to connect to a variety of different systems from different vendors. Each plug-in is activated according to a schedule (when the corresponding local monitor becomes inactive).

Argus defines a superclass LocalSystemPlugin for this plug-in kind from which local systems must derive:

```
class LocalSystemPlugin {
public:
  virtual void initialize( const Services &) = 0;
        // pass reference to services of the host application
  virtual ~LocalSystemPlugin() = 0;
  // ...
};
```

The plug-in representing the local system is placed in a DLL that exports a trader function. This function must have the same name for all plug-in types, and it returns a plug-in instance of the specific type. The passed specification defines the name of the local system and communication settings like the network address.

```
#include "PluginDefinition\LocalSystemPlugin.h"
_declspec(dllexport) LocalSystemPlugin* getLocalSystem( const Spec&);
```

For application implementation convenience, the plug-in class and the DLL loading is encapsulated by a class LocalSystem that forwards all requests to the plug-in and has additional member functions for loading and unloading. The DLL name is passed with the Specification, and GetProcAddress obtains the published trader function.

Related Patterns

FRAMEWORK PROVIDING APPLICATION: The application is implemented as FRAMEWORK PROVIDING APPLICATION to enable a larger amount of reuse and increase the lifetime of PLUG-IN BASED PRODUCTS in the market.

PLUG-IN CONTRACT: The interface that the PLUG-IN must conform to, and the interface the PLUG-IN may use to perform its task, are defined by the application.

PLUG-IN PACKAGE: A single PLUG-IN is often not shippable on its own, but needs other PLUG-INS, or a context of accompanying files. The package may become very large.

COOPERATING PLUG-INS: To keep each plug-in interface and duties compact and concise, an extension that covers multiple functional layers can be split into a number of corresponding plug-ins.

Plug-in Contract

Context

The application and plug-in projects are established, and the core purpose of plug-ins is defined.

Problem

How does the application define and describe the interface for plug-ins?

Forces

The development of application and plug-ins shall be decoupled to proceed faster and keep the system manageable,
... but clients expect similar behavior from different plug-ins, a common look and feel, and seamless integration.

Different plug-ins are developed by different teams or companies,
... but steering different plug-ins in an identical direction is difficult, expensive, and tedious.

A plug-in needs access to key classes and services of the application,
... but the application may need to be portable, and it may be necessary to replace, remove, or activate any plug-in at runtime.

Solution

Publish the interface the plug-in is expected to fulfill, and the interface offered to it. This contract needs to be available in code and documentation. The contract must support late binding and preserve the hosting application from depending on any particular plug-in or its implementation.

The broadness of the published interface and the number of integration points define how tightly the plug-ins can integrate with the application and how specific they are to the application domain. The plug-in uses not only system services, but application services as well. Also the expected plug-in functionality requires a custom interface. Figure 12–2 shows the major components and their dependencies.

Plug-in Definition is the interface the framework requires from the plug-in (Required Interface [Köthe1998]). The plug-in is modeled as one or several abstract classes, together with their respective abstract factories or factory methods.

Plug-in adds specific knowledge to the application. It offers a factory or method that returns classes conforming to the expected interface. The internal implementation is hidden, and the visible class can serve as a Façade [Gamma+1995] to it. The plug-in may use services of the application and must use the domain objects the framework provides.

Framework Interface defines the services and domain objects of the framework. Their implementation is hidden from the plug-in by (abstract) factories [Gamma+ 1995] or product traders [Bäumer+1997].

Implementation provides a process for execution, implements the framework services and domain objects, invokes the Framework Interface component, and activates the plug-in by calling the factory and giving references to the framework objects.

All clients to the plug-in can only access it through the plug-in Definition component and interface, and the plug-in can only access those instances and services published by the Framework Interface.

To identify the interface that is published for the plug-ins, decide whether to mandate a particular container infrastructure (like EJB) or develop and define a minimal infrastructure yourself. Are there foundations that the application is built upon that can seriously be considered stable? These are candidates to become part of the published Framework Interface. Class libraries are a perfect start to check for candidates.

Besides purely technical interfaces, the application defines an expected user-visible functionality that each plug-in has to provide. A common example is a top-level configuration dialog at a predictable location in the applications menu structure. Depending on the application, a large number of additional dialogs and controls may also be expected as essential functionality. Each of these mandated or optional contributions by a plug-in is called an integration point and resembles a hot spot in framework development [Pree2000]. When desired, enforce large parts of the mandatory contract by technical means such as by defining required products from the plug-in (see [Bäumer+1997]).

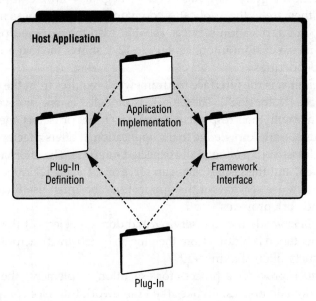

Figure 12–2 *Major packages of a hosting application using plug-ins*

Consequences

☺ A clear dependency structure guides development and organization.

☺ The internals of application and plug-in are invisible from the outside.

☺ A bidirectional separation of implementation and interface enables independent development.

☺ Plug-ins can be added and removed at any time.

☺ Users can treat different plug-ins identically, decreasing their mental integration effort.

☺ A detailed contract enables seamless integration.

☺ Each plug-in has access to uniform and reused application classes and services.

☹ The application is bound to the classes and services it offers; its evolution potential is limited when the interfaces are published.

☹ Only parts of the contract can be enforced technically. To increase their probability for success, applications should have organizational influence on plug-in development.

☹ A plug-in Contract is not sufficient for seamless integration and common "look and feel." Additional style guides are needed.

Implementation

Keep track of the invocation state of the plug-in and make that become part of the PLUG-IN DEFINITION. The application initiates state transitions to control the plug-ins.

A manageable PLUG-IN CONTRACT aiming to reach closure must remain at a generic level and not depend on particular plug-ins. Consequently, the contract should impose restrictions on whether different plug-ins may know about each other. Independent, uncoupled plug-ins allow for parallel development and deployment in PLUG-IN BASED PRODUCTS; see the variants when higher flexibility is needed.

A stable PLUG-IN CONTRACT is critical to a FRAMEWORK PROVIDING APPLICATION's lifetime. This lifetime can be increased by simple interfaces with flexible parameters at the price of potential misunderstandings and creeping compatibility issues.

Variants

Plug-in Subcontract: Not only the hosting application can define a plug-in contract. Plug-ins themselves can also define contracts for further plug-ins at a finer granularity. This can be useful if an aspect of the application domain allows for different levels of abstraction.

Extended Plug-in Contract: A plug-in may not only adhere to a predefined contract, but it may also offer further interfaces for more control opportunities. This can be useful when an integrating PLUG-IN BASED PRODUCT desires more detailed knowledge to establish semantic links between otherwise independent plug-in types.

Multiple Plug-in Contracts: When the application identifies several distinct opportunities for extensibility in different areas, it may define a separate contract for each of these. Each particular contract is defined for a specific plug-in kind. Typically, the technical side and some fundamental domain portions will be identical among different contracts.

Example

Argus offers superclasses and services like error log and alarm handler. It requires that plug-ins implement a subclass of `LocalSystemPlugin` and overload polymorphic functions that the application calls.

Here's the `LocalSystemPlugin` class in more detail. It allows the application to control the way of communication and to initiate functions that are executed asynchronously.

```
class LocalSystemPlugin {
public:
  enum State {
    undefined,   // before initialization
    inactive,    // no connection
    online,      // reports on communication events
    offline      // reports on application requests only
  };
  // ...
  virtual State setState( State) = 0;
  virtual State getState() = 0;
  virtual void initiateStatusReport() = 0; // demand report of system
  virtual void initiateSensorStatus( Sensor &) = 0; // demand sensor rep
  virtual void inhibitLocalMonitor( bool) = 0; // switch local monitor
    on/off
  // ...
};
```

The application must in turn provide references to interfaces that the plug-in can use to fulfill the requested tasks. These references are provided by the `Services` class.

```
class Services {
public:
    ErrorLog& getErrorLog() const;
    AlarmHandler& getAlarmHandler() const;
// ...
};
```

Known Uses

The contract of an operating system for executables includes the load procedure, where the system expects code and data segments, and the API the system offers.

Eclipse defines a common purpose and infrastructure. The Java environment is part of the contract.

LSM and Zeus frameworks both offer access to their generic application objects, to services like an error log, and to a library of customized GUI widgets. In turn, they expect plug-ins to create specific application knowledge using the generic structures and services, and they require usage of the custom widgets by convention (style guide).

Related Patterns

PLUG-IN: PLUG-IN CONTRACT defines the boundaries for the PLUG-IN.

FRAMEWORK PROVIDING APPLICATION: PLUG-IN CONTRACT defines its services and dependencies towards the Plug-In.

PLUG-IN LIFECYCLE is an essential part of the PLUG-IN CONTRACT.

PLUG-IN BASED PRODUCT: The product's integration abilities depend on the contract. More specific integration requires multiple contracts for different plug-in kinds or contract extensions for specific access to individual plug-ins beyond the generic contract.

Framework-Providing Application
Also Known As

Host Application, Plug-in Context

Context

An application has factored out some functionality that is now implemented by plug-ins. Plug-ins implement a specific functionality that requires usage of the application, such as subclasses or specific parameterized instances of common application domain classes.

Problem

How can a plug-in add its unique knowledge to create and use specific application domain data and algorithms?

Forces

The application knows and defines the domain,
... but the plug-in must be as independent as possible from the application.

The application provides services for infrastructure and generic knowledge,
... but the plug-in knows which domain objects it needs to employ, subclass or instance.

Products desire a minimal time to market, especially in families of customized similar products,
... but independent plug-in components would require significant integration.

Solution

The application offers a framework. This is a black box framework offering no insights about the host application but defining opportunities for subclassing and parameterization. Only a part of the application is a framework. Other parts relevant for plug-ins control loading and activating the plug-ins, or offer technical services. Each interface for a plug-in kind corresponds to a set of related "hot spots" [Pree2000], [Roberts+1997]. Beyond the portions related to plug-ins, the application may offer functionality immediately useful to the user.

Consequences

☺ PLUG-IN integration is the purpose and focus of the application.

☺ All PLUG-INS use the same infrastructure and domain abstraction.

☺ PLUG-INS can be reused by other applications and products that offer the same framework. This enables product lines and product families.

☺ Plug-ins do not depend on the application implementation. With a consequently abstracted infrastructure (like the operating system), the application may define the plug-ins to be portable when it provides all services necessary for the plug-ins' execution.

☺ Different plug-ins of the same kind do not know each other. Products integrating them with intelligent combinations need to take special measures.

☹ The development effort of the application increases significantly, depending on the size of the framework part.

Implementation

Check out the standard literature on framework development (such as Johnson [Johnson1999] or Fayad [Fayad+2000]).

Parameterization instead of subclassing is especially useful when plug-in subclasses would have to use internal application services. A common example is persistence, which would require the plug-in to extend or change the database scheme (see plug-in Registration, and [Bäumer+1997], [Szyperski1998], [Szyperski1999]).

Variant

Safe Framework Providing Application: When the application has no control over future plug-ins, but will be held responsible for their failures, it needs to protect itself against ill-behaved plug-ins. This can be done by adding Facades [Gamma+1995] that narrow and control the access from the PLUG-IN to the application. The key advantage of the Safe Framework Providing Application is that the published Framework Interface (of the PLUG-IN CONTRACT) can cope with plug-ins from sources that are not organizationally related and controlled. Disadvantages are increased development effort, performance penalties, and possibly lessened functionality that the plug-in is allowed to provide or use.

Example

Argus delivers a large number of application objects that the plug-ins for specific local observation systems use. Some can be parameterized (like Room, Alarm, Sensor); others are intended for subclassing (such as LocalSystemPlugIn).

The framework defines an `Alarm` class that is constructed via a factory (to hide persistence and other implementation details):

```
class Alarm {
// ...
    bool isVisible() const;
    bool isAudible() const;
    void confirm(); // user has seen and confirmed this alarm
    void remove(); // creator/owner: alarm cause has vanished
};
class AlarmFactory {
// ...
    Alarm& createAlarm( LocalSystemPlugin& owner, int resourceId, int
                        priority);
// ...
};
```

The specific plug-in creates its `Alarm`s during initialization or registration (PLUG-IN REGISTRATION). Status reports and communication messages are converted to `Alarm` function calls.

Known Uses

Most of the known uses are hosting applications. They vary in the amount of domain context they proscribe, and services they offer to their plug-ins.

Operating systems define no application but provide a technical context.

Eclipse provides a plug-in infrastructure, but its concept includes only minimal application beyond the essential plug-in handling [Birsan2005].

Applications like Microsoft Word and Internet browsers define an application domain. Unlike Eclipse, they offer core functionality independent of loaded plug-ins.

LSM implements the "safe" variant: Access to most objects is limited to reading attributes and changing only that subset of them where a connected analyzer is the only legitimated source of information.

Related Patterns

PLUG-IN: Hosted and employed by the FRAMEWORK PROVIDING APPLICATION.

PLUG-IN CONTRACT: Defines the relation between PLUG-IN and FRAMEWORK PROVIDING APPLICATION.

PLUG-IN REGISTRATION is used to make a PLUG-IN known to the FRAMEWORK PROVIDING APPLICATION.

PLUG-IN BASED APPLICATION: The organizational means of the framework related to the plug-in should be separated from the product-related functionality. Products need to care for relations between different plug-ins, e.g. if different plug-ins may interfere, or depend upon each other.

Plug-in Registration

Context

The hosting application has defined Framework Interfaces and Plug-in Definitions (as in Figure 12–2). Plug-ins are available. User or application decides at startup or runtime which plug-in to activate.

Problem

How are the plug-ins to be invoked known to the application?

Forces

Prior to immediate usage, the application does not need to know about available plug-ins,
... but each plug-in needs to announce its presence before it can be used.

User-initiated activation can become repetitive and tedious,
... but automatic installation can take place without active involvement of the application.

The application knows about the trigger points when plug-ins need to be invoked,
... but the plug-in itself knows which specific trigger is meant for itself.

Solution

The application defines a place where available plug-ins register themselves. Each plug-in installs itself there and defines its invocation triggers. When the application receives the trigger, it starts the respective plug-in. The plug-in Registration includes information about where to locate the plug-in and how to invoke it.

The complexity of the registration depends on the complexity of the tasks the hosting application requires prior to invocation. In the ideal cases, it establishes registration conventions that do not demand runtime interaction with the framework or services. However, a container infrastructure or complex services such as persistency mechanisms may require that the application is actively addressed from an installation program.

Consequences

☺ Application startup time does not depend on available plug-ins.

☺ Depending on the trigger mechanism, user interaction is not required with later activation.

☺ Plug-ins can be installed at any time.

☺ Plug-in installation can be automated and initiated remotely.

☹ Depending on the implementation, registration might require a distinct installation program.

☹ A complex registration process may require the application or some services to be active.

☹ Version conflicts may appear that require a resolution policy.

Implementation

The simplest solution allows the application to scan a directory for a specific filename extension. More common are explicit registries where plug-ins define their trigger point, such as a file type they can interpret or a menu entry that invokes them. Both approaches are a passive form of registration where the plug-in does not directly contact the application.

When a plug-in type needs to react on different simultaneous triggers, the registration needs to facilitate that several instances may run in parallel.

Variants

Active Registration: Registration can come in an active flavor. Plug-ins may contact the running application and announce their properties there. Furthermore, the application may then prepare for optimized execution, such as predefining internal structures or creating indexes and queries.

The active registration broadens the PLUG-IN CONTRACT and requires more development effort, but it can lead to a tighter integration of plug-in properties and to much quicker invocation.

Active Registration in combination with the directed dependencies of the contract is the foundation of the Dependency Injection technique [Fowler2004].

The key feature of this technique is that the hosting application defines a PLUG-IN CONTRACT, including abstract services, where the plug-in can make its concrete services known to the application at runtime.

Trigger-Based Registration: Registration can be offered to the user upon receipt of unknown triggers, when the trigger the application receives contains a link to the installation program of the respective plug-in. This technique is especially useful in domains that do not require real-time responses and are prepared for frequent changes and functional extensions.

Example

The Argus central shall include a connection schedule, and know in advance which local systems have to be connected when. This schedule can most easily be built when the plug-ins for the respective local security systems register themselves. Thus, the Active Registration variant is chosen.

Known Uses

Operating systems have defined registration mechanisms for various kinds of plug-ins. Modern systems make efforts to allow device driver registration at runtime, while traditionally adding an essential driver requires a very intrusive active registration with a kernel rebuild. Outside of the world of embedded systems, executables are registered passively by placing them into the directory structure where the user can find and activate them.

Eclipse systems require the plug-in to be present in the runtime system prior to startup.

LSM and Zeus need to change configuration data of the FRAMEWORK PROVIDING APPLICATION and use active registration.

Related Patterns

PLUG-IN CONTRACT: The application must include the installation services in the published interfaces.

PLUG-IN PACKAGE: Active registration requires additional files such as the installation program. These are packaged and shipped together with the plug-in.

PLUG-IN LIFECYCLE: The registration is the first step in the lifecycle of a plug-in type.

Plug-in Lifecycle

Context

A PLUG-IN CONTRACT is defined. The application needs to make use of PLUG-INS.

Problem

How can the application invoke and control plug-ins?

Forces

Plug-ins can be installed, activated, and deactivated during application runtime,
… but both the application and the plug-ins need to take special actions in different employment phases.

Plug-ins do not decide about their invocation,
… but the application invokes, controls, and checks the employed plug-ins.

Solution

The application defines the lifecycle of the plug-in. The lifecycle for a plug-in instance contains at least loading, activation, deactivation, and unloading. For a plug-in type, the lifecycle includes registration. Each lifecycle transition corresponds to member functions within the plug-in Definition to allow the plug-in to react.

The lifecycles for a plug-in instance, and for a plug-in type, must be distinguished, especially when registration is done the active way and may occur during runtime of the application. Both lifecycles may only be merged when just one plug-in instance per kind may be active at a time.

Consequences

☺ The plug-in lifecycle is defined and controllable.

☺ The application can control the plug-in's state, and the plug-in can react to it.

☺ The application can check the states of all registered plug-ins.

Implementation

When the application shall be able to control the lifecycle at runtime, the application checks at startup what plug-ins are registered and offers a choice. The user selects one or more to become active, do its job, and become inactive again. The application invokes the plug-in without knowing more than the registered information that is also displayed to the user. The plug-in decides itself about its normal inactivation.

Without the need for manual user control, time-consuming tasks can be preferred or deferred [Marquardt1998] [Kircher+2004]. To minimize the activation time of plug-ins, adopt the PLUG-IN LIFECYCLE to shift load to the most appropriate situations. This can be the startup time if immediate reaction on a trigger is demanded, or the time of first invocation. The application's loading policy is important here, so that a published "performance style guide" becomes useful [Noble+2000]. The choice of how to use the lifecycle is done by the PLUG-IN BASED APPLICATION.

Dynamic loading and unloading of plug-ins requires special attention from the hosting application:

- The trigger event reaction described by the registration needs to be adapted dynamically.

- All services provided by plug-ins need to be maintained in dynamic registries.

- The services of the hosting application need to scale to a large number of parallel uses.

- The plug-in implementation must be free of resource leakages, or the hosting application needs to provide cleanup routines that allow for multiple restarts.

- There must be no deviation from the mandate that the hosting application does not depend on a plug-in.

Variants

Scheduled Invocation: After the user has selected the desired plug-in, activation is delayed according to a schedule, or until an external event occurs.

Automatic Invocation: The application detects during normal operation (data procession) that it needs to activate a specific plug-in. The appropriate plug-in is determined from registration data.

Event Driven Invocation: Applications receive requests (such as a user interaction or network message), search the registry for a specific plug-in, and start it. The plug-in does its job until the application receives a request to stop it or an error condition occurs.

Example

Argus connects to local systems according to a schedule. The user configures at which time which registered plug-in should become active. For performance issues, an additional communication state is introduced that controls the local system's responsiveness.

```
class LocalSystem {
public:
    enum State {
        unloaded,
        loaded,
        active
    };
    enum CommunicationState {
        undefined,   // before initialization
        inactive,    // no connection
        online,      // reports on communication events
        offline      // reports on application requests only
    };
// ...
    virtual void setState( State) = 0;
    virtual CommunicationState setComState( CommunicationState) = 0;
    virtual CommunicationState getComState() = 0;
// ...
};
```

Known Uses

Eclipse, Adobe Photoshop, Microsoft Word, and LSM activate plug-ins on user demand.

Operating systems activate their drivers at startup or on external events.

Screen savers are invoked according to a timer, that is, they are scheduled.

Browsers automatically activate their plug-ins when the corresponding page content appears.

Zeus activates all plug-ins at application startup to avoid peak loads and minimize response times.

Related Patterns

PLUG-IN CONTRACT: PLUG-IN LIFECYCLE is an essential part of the PLUG-IN CONTRACT.

PLUG-IN REGISTRATION is the first step in the lifecycle of a PLUG-IN type.

PLUG-IN BASED PRODUCT decides about performance optimizations in the lifecycle of the PLUG-IN instances.

Plug-in Package

Context

Defined application functionality is factored into plug-ins, and the Plug-in Contract definitions are available. Shipping a plug-in as a stand-alone extension component requires consideration of non-functional issues like installation and localization.

Problem

How to extend a plug-in to turn it into a shippable component?

Forces

Small and custom interfaces allow for self-consistent plug-ins,
... but custom interfaces require a learning curve of the plug-in developer and are less stable than available standards.

Separation into areas of different concerns dilute the unity of purpose of a plug-in,
... but separate interface parts allow parallel development of different plug-in parts.

Solution

Define and ship the functional extension as a package consisting of many files of many different types. The plug-in interface consists of the custom plug-in definition classes and a number of additional files. The central plug-in is packed together with related executables, plug-ins, resource files, and "little helpers" such as icons, sound files, or shortcuts. The application requests resources and utilities in standard formats.

To determine which files and file kinds to pack, start by identifying the functions throughout the lifecycle that the functional extension is expected to fulfill. Then try to find technical interfaces for these functions. Prefer technical standards of a long (expected) lifetime, and use custom PLUG-IN CONTRACT definitions where necessary.

Typical aspects of lifecycle support include:

- Plug-in (or a number of cooperating plug-ins)
- Installation program

- Help text files (one per language or locale)
- Resource files (one per language or locale)
- "Little helpers": Icons, sounds, movies, and so on

Whenever features are loosely coupled to the application domain and increase user comfort and application accessibility (such as via the "little helpers"), the application should avoid addressing them through customized plug-in Definitions and thus keep the custom interfaces minimal by using a standard format to provide the feature. The PLUG-IN PACKAGE must include the required files.

Consequences

☺ The solution partly relies on existing standards, increasing the interface stability.

☺ The application is open to future use—the number of offered standard interfaces to future extension packages can be enhanced.

☺ Package parts can be developed in parallel, and by a wider range of developers.

☺ An inherent cohesion of related plug-ins is maintained.

☺ Users experience comfort and convenience.

☹ The extension component becomes broad instead of complex, still requiring development effort and logistics.

☹ An additional policy for versioning of the complete shipped package is required.

☹ Parts of the interfaces are not controlled by the application.

Implementation

While developing PLUG-INS, take care to constantly integrate the whole PLUG-IN PACKAGE and keep it up to date. The PLUG-IN PACKAGE is the granule of plug-in releases and shipment.

For the versioning strategy, take care to define a version nomenclature and checking mechanism that ensures interoperation without ending in a nightmare of testing combinations and that ensures backward compatibility.

Example

When observed buildings are connected to the central Argus workstation, it is helpful when each audible and visible violation announcement allows for immediate recognition of the affected building. Thus, a specific sound, delivered in an additional WAV file, and an icon of the particular building, delivered in an additional ICO file, become part of the driver software for each building.

Known Uses

Like most complex applications, Microsoft Word consists of many different files and file kinds: Executables, help files, converters, dictionaries, registry entry file, document templates, and many more. An extension for a specific country also comes as a collection of files, such as help file, menu file, dictionary file, hyphenation rules file, thesaurus file, and grammar file.

A Plug-in Package for Rational Rose could combine a VBA program script and an installation program extending the user-visible menus.

LSM requires one plug-in for communication to the analyzer, one for specific GUI screens, an icon used by the "lab overview" screen, and an installation program that adds the analyzer's properties to the common database.

Plug-in Packages for Zeus consist of several plug-ins, some of them optional, and resource files containing language-specific texts for the specific GUI portions and for the alarms that the connected sensor package may issue.

Related Patterns

PLUG-IN: One or multiple PLUG-INS are the central parts of the package.

COOPERATING PLUG-INS: PLUG-IN PACKAGES are especially useful for packaging related plug-ins together that only in conjunction provide a completed functionality.

PLUG-IN REGISTRATION: The PLUG-IN PACKAGE is the granule of registration at a product. Packages that contain several plug-ins need to register all of these, possibly in different ways.

PLUG-IN BASED PRODUCT: A product comprises a hosting application and a number of PLUG-IN PACKAGES.

Cooperating Plug-ins

Also Known As

One Plug-in per Task

Context

An application has defined a Plug-in Contract. Seamless integration requires specific additions beyond the plug-in's model extension, such as specific view and control, and possibly data exchange.

Problem

How can functional additions span multiple layers?

Forces

The functional plug-in Definition should be concise and complete,
... but specific data requires specific interpretation and specific view.

It is helpful to find everything available in one place,
... but Swiss army knife interfaces are difficult to learn and handle.

Solution

Define a distinct plug-in Definition for each distinct task or domain. Provide an identifier for the plug-ins so that the application can activate all plug-ins that cooperate for a common purpose. Cooperating plug-ins solve the problems that arise when functionality on different technical layers needs to be contributed to pursue a closed functionality.

A typical example for a plug-in for connecting a remote device could include a network communication application level protocol, data storage and triggers, and a graphical display for the remotely connected device. The data model plug-in would contribute specific data and classes added to the overall model. This data is known only to the other cooperating plug-ins, is written by the communication plug-in, and is viewed by the user interface plug-in. The application cares for the data exchange and processing in between and ensures that the corresponding plug-in gets in control on the viewing side. Each extension, a set of cooperating plug-ins, consists of one plug-in type of each predefined plug-in kind.

With regard to the definition of the plug-in Contract for cooperating plug-ins, avoid addressing all extension functionality through one interface. Such a contract interface would look like a Swiss army knife [Webster1995]. Separate the interface into consistent domains. Where behavior-less configuration or assistant "little helpers" are required, refrain from defining another plug-in interface and employ standard file formats as in PLUG-IN PACKAGE instead.

Consequences

☺ Each plug-in Definition is limited to one technical domain and can be functionally closed.

☺ Extension-specific data can be passed through all system layers.

☺ An extra level of packaging must be introduced.

☺ Specific domain object instances must identify to which extension they belong.

☹ When less generic objects and policies are used, integration between different plug-in types of different extensions becomes impossible without a PLUG-IN BASED PRODUCT.

Implementation

The application must define the division into several plug-ins. Each plug-in kind gets its own PLUG-IN CONTRACT. For development and learning efficiency, only the Plug-in Definitions (part of the contract) deviate between the plug-in kinds, whereas the Framework Interface is the same for all of them. Dividing the Framework Interface into different sections, and documenting which section is useful for which plug-in kind, further flattens the learning curve.

On the plug-in side, typically all cooperating plug-ins are developed by one team and share significant amounts of code. This pattern gives each single plug-in a distinct technical domain focus and helps to separate different concerns.

Example

One of the local observation systems cares for the size of the rooms in which the smoke detectors are placed and determines an event priority from this. To support this, the Room class must be subclassed, and this subclass must be fed, read, and displayed by appropriate code knowing of this subclass.

For this kind of extensibility, the Argus system prepares by separating each functional extension into a communication plug-in, an application plug-in, and a GUI plug-in. All these plug-ins work together; the functional extension is opaque to other system components. This way, functional specifics of a plugged-in addition can be handled in all functional layers.

Known Uses

LSM and Zeus define distinct plug-ins for communication and for display purposes that are packaged and versioned together.

Related Patterns

PLUG-IN is the granule of which corresponding plug-ins are composed.

PLUG-IN CONTRACT addresses each kind of the corresponding plug-ins.

FRAMEWORK PROVIDING APPLICATION defines the division into multiple cooperating plug-ins.

PLUG-IN PACKAGE ensures that different parts of the extension are packed and shipped together.

Plug-in Based Product

Context

A Framework Providing Application is defined, and several plug-ins or Plug-in Packages are available.

Problem

How can the pieces be set together to increase end-user satisfaction?

Forces

All functional parts are available,
… but the end user expects a product of a shrink-wrap quality.

The hosting application is unaware of the available plug-ins,
… but the combination of installed plug-ins defines the user value.

The separation into different components is technically helpful,
… but it does not add functional user value.

Solution

Package a product comprising the FRAMEWORK PROVIDING APPLICATION *and several* PLUG-IN PACKAGES. Do not exhibit this technical separation to the end user.

Select those available plug-ins that build a homogenous suite of functionality. Depending on marketing strategy and availability, different products of one family may consist of different sets of plug-ins. Establish a pricing model based on the user perceived value.

Different versions of the product may contain upgrades of the employed plug-ins. Product upgrades might comprise additional plug-ins that provide further functionality.

Consequences

☺ The product portion could be defined without any coding and consist of packaging aspects only.

☺ The responsibility for a product is explicitly defined and not mixed with other duties.

☺ A business model can be defined that makes use of technical infrastructure and existing plug-ins.

☺ The focus on end-user value is addressed.

☺ An upgrade strategy can be defined and controlled.

☹ An organizational entity is defined for something that is potentially obsolete.

Implementation

Some products do not make any sense without at least one active plug-in. In this case, the hosting application should not be shipped without any plug-in and might rely on integration of a particular one. The PLUG-IN LIFECYCLE can be decoupled from the product lifecycle by introducing stubs that adhere to the generic and extended PLUG-IN CONTRACT and that the product may rely on. The hosting application then needs to support dynamic loading and unloading to replace the stub by an actual implementation.

Applications and products can define more than one plug-in interface and expect different kinds of plug-ins simultaneously. When a combinatory intelligence across different plug-ins is required, it can be useful to define the integration responsibility as a distinct plug-in kind as described in Figure 12–3.

Some applications allow only one active plug-in at a time; others support an (almost) arbitrary number of different plug-ins of the same kind in parallel. Some applications even allow multiple plug-in instances of identical type in parallel.

Organizational Issues

A product is naturally closely coupled to the providing framework, because that defines the application domain, the PLUG-IN CONTRACT, and the degree of seamless integration. However, without meaningful plug-ins, no product can come to life. It is reasonable to develop key plug-ins within the same team, or to contract them out but retain control of their development. Alternatively, especially after

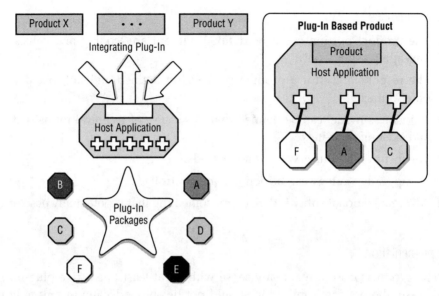

Figure 12–3 *A product consisting of a hosting application using plug-ins. The product integration is defined as a distinct plug-in kind.*

the first market introduction, it is useful to see further PLUG-INS under development as special customers to the FRAMEWORK PROVIDING APPLICATION and to support their success to enable further product sales [Marquardt1999].

Example

Two major vendors of security systems make use of the Argus platform. They closely integrate their own building observation systems, especially the most recent ones. Extended versions of their products offer integration of systems from different vendors, that is, they include further plug-ins.

Known Uses

Eclipse: Many vendors of development tools ship their recent compiler, linker, and so on with the Eclipse platform, and they combine their plug-ins into a product that includes all facets of versioning, service, hot line, licensing, and customer care.

Zeus: Olymp is the hosting application below the Zeus products. Further plug-ins are developed on that platform and added to new versions of the Zeus, offering extended connectivity and features.

Related Patterns

FRAMEWORK PROVIDING APPLICATION defines the domain of all products built on the application and plug-ins.

PLUG-IN PACKAGES are the building and shipping blocks of the products.

Acknowledgments

I would like to thank my current and former colleagues for their assistance in this successful and exciting work. These patterns are another result of our shared experience.

Special thanks to John Vlissides for shepherding this paper before EuroPLoP 1999, and to Dirk Riehle for his feedback during the shepherding period. Further thanks to Neil Harrison for guiding feedback on an earlier version of this paper, and to Markus Völter for his help in telling plug-ins from components. The workshop participants at EuroPLoP 1999 gave valuable and encouraging feedback.

References

[Bäumer+1997] D. Bäumer and D. Riehle. "Product Trader." In R. C. Martin, D. Riehle, and F. Buschmann (eds.), *Pattern Languages of Program Design 3.* Reading, MA: Addison-Wesley, 1998.

[Birsan2005] Dorian Birsan. "On Plug-ins and Extensible Architectures." ACM Queue 3(2), March 2005.

[Dräger] Zeus description. Available: *http://www.draeger.com/MT/Internet/EN/us/ CareAreas/ORAnesthesia/AnesthesiaWorkstations/zeus/pd_zeus.jsp.*

[Eclipse] Eclipse home page. Available: http://eclipse.org.

[Fayad+2000] M. Fayad, D. Schmidt, and R. Johnson (eds.). *Building Application Frameworks: Object Oriented Foundations of Framework Design.* New York: John Wiley & Sons, 2000.

[Fowler2003] M. Fowler. *Patterns of Enterprise Application Architecture.* Boston: Addison-Wesley, 2003.

[Fowler2004] M. Fowler. Inversion of Control. Containers and the Dependency Injection Pattern. Available: *http://www.martinfowler.com/articles/injection.html*.

[Gamma+1995] E. Gamma, R. Helm, R. Johnson, and J. Vlissides. *Design Patterns: Elements of Reusable Object-Oriented Software*. Reading, MA: Addison-Wesley, 1995.

[Johnson1999] Frameworks home page. Available: *http://st-www.cs.uiuc.edu/users/johnson/frameworks.html*.

[Kircher+2004] M. Kircher and P. Jain. *Pattern-Oriented Software Architecture, Volume 3: Patterns for Resource Management*. New York: John Wiley & Sons, 2004.

[Köthe1998] U. Köthe. "Design Patterns for Independent Building Blocks." In J. Coldewey and P. Dyson (eds.), *Proceedings of the Third European Conference on Pattern Languages of Programming and Computing* (EuroPLoP 1998), Universitätsverlag Konstanz, 1999.

[Marquardt1998] Klaus Marquardt. "Patterns for Software Packaging, Installation, and Activation." In Jens Coldewey and Paul Dyson (eds.), *Proceedings of the Third European Conference on Pattern Languages of Programming and Computing* (EuroPLoP 1998), Universitätsverlag Konstanz, 1999.

[Marquardt1999] K. Marquardt. "Patterns for plug-ins." In P. Dyson and M. Devos (eds.), *Proceedings of the Fourth European Conference on Pattern Languages of Programming and Computing* (EuroPLoP 1999), Universitätsverlag Konstanz, 2001.

[Marquardt+2003] K. Marquardt and M. Völter: Plug-Ins—Applikationsspezifische Komponenten. Javaspektrum 2/2003, March 2003. Available: *http://www.sigs.de/publications/js/2003/02/marquardt_JS_02_03.pdf*.

[Noble+2000] J. Noble, C. Weir, and D. Bibby. *Small Memory Software: Patterns for Systems with Limited Memory*. Boston: Addison-Wesley, 2001.

[Pree2000] W. Pree. "Hot-Spot-Driven Framework Development." In M. Fayad, D. Schmidt, and R. Johnson (eds.), *Building Application Frameworks: Object Oriented Foundations of Framework Design*. New York: John Wiley & Sons, 2000.

[Roberts+1997] D. Roberts and R. Johnson. "Patterns for Evolving Frameworks." In R. C. Martin, D. Riehle, and F. Buschmann (eds.), *Pattern Languages of Program Design 3*. Reading, MA: Addison-Wesley, 1997.

[Roche] Laboratory Systems Manager Specification. Available: *http://www.sdm.de/en/unternehmen/referenzen/projekte/roche/*.

[Szyperski1998] C. Szyperski. *Component Software: Beyond Object-Oriented Programming.* Reading, MA: Addison-Wesley, 1998.

[Völter+2002] M. Völter, A. Schmid, and E. Wolff. *Server Component Patterns— Component Infrastructures Illustrated with EJB.* New York: John Wiley & Sons, 2002.

[Webster1995] B. Webster. *Pitfalls of Object-Oriented Programming.* M&T Books, 1995.

CHAPTER 13

The Grid Architectural Pattern: Leveraging Distributed Processing Capabilities

Raphael Y. de Camargo, Andrei Goldchleger,
Márcio Carneiro, and Fabio Kon

Intent

The GRID architectural pattern describes the required software necessary to allow the sharing of distributed and potentially heterogeneous computational resources for execution of applications. The middleware deals with aspects such as resource management, scheduling, and security in an efficient and transparent manner. This pattern addresses both the architecture and implementation of the middleware.

Example

Weather forecasting is a typical computationally intensive problem. Data about the area subject to forecasting is split into smaller pieces or fragments, each one corresponding to a fraction of the total area. Each fragment is then assigned to a computing resource, typically a node on a cluster or a processor in a parallel machine. During the computation, nodes need to exchange data, since their neighbors influence the forecasting in each of the fragments. After several hours of processing, the results of the computation are expected to reflect the weather in the given area for a certain period of time, such as a few days. Figure 13–1 shows the results of a simulation where the total area was divided into 16 fragments.

There are several other applications that can be broken into smaller pieces and require large amounts of computational power, such as financial market simulation, image processing, three-dimensional image generation, bioinformatics, and signal analysis.

To perform large computations such as the ones cited here, one typically uses dedicated infrastructures such as parallel machines or dedicated clusters. Institutions usually have a limited number of these resources, and many users in need of processing power compete for their use. At the same time, it is very likely that in these same institutions there will be hundreds of workstations sitting idle for most of the time. If these workstations could be used for processing during these idle periods, they would greatly increase the processing power available to users.

A *Grid* [Berman+2003] [Foster+2003] is a collection of loosely coupled, geographically distributed supercomputers and clusters of computers. *Grid Computing* denotes the coordinated sharing of these distributed resources that provides ubiquitous access to remote resources and thus increases the amount of available computing power. Grid computing requires sophisticated middleware to coordinate the resource sharing process and deal with resource management, scheduling, and security in an efficient and transparent manner.

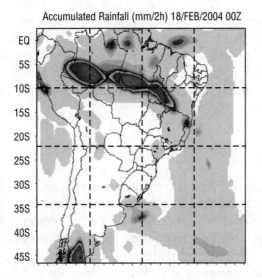

Figure 13–1 *Result from a weather forecasting simulation*

Grid Computing is a vast and active research area that encompasses aspects of distributed computing such as seamless access to distributed data (Data Grids) and collaborative distributed environments (Service Grids). The Grid Architectural Pattern focuses on grids for running computationally intensive applications (Computational Grids) and grids that leverage the idle capacity of commodity workstations (Opportunistic Grids).

Context

Sharing of computational resources in heterogeneous distributed systems to improve the availability of computing resources for the execution of computationally intensive applications.

Problem

Using the idle periods of available computing resources can greatly increase the amount of computing power available to users in an organization. A software middleware infrastructure that allows the use of these shared computing resources must address aspects such as application deployment, distributed scheduling, collection of execution results, fault-tolerance, and security. When developing such an infrastructure, it is necessary to consider the following forces:

- Grids can be composed of thousands of machines. The design and implementation of the Grid should be scalable.
- The Grid will encompass heterogeneous resources having different computing architectures and operating systems. The middleware system must account for this diversity.
- In the normal case, underlying mechanisms of the Grid middleware should be transparent for end users. The system can optionally allow the user to specify some aspects of application execution, such as manually selecting the machines that will execute the application.
- Different administrative domains have different policies for resource sharing and usage. The middleware should be flexible enough to allow these different policies to be enforced.
- To gain widespread acceptance, the middleware must be easy to deploy without requiring extensive reconfiguration on existing systems.

- Security must be provided for both resource owners and users submitting applications to the Grid. Machines sharing their resources need protection against malicious code. Grid users should have some guarantees regarding data confidentiality and integrity.

- A large number of existing parallel applications exist that could benefit from the Grid. The middleware must provide grid-enabled libraries supporting standard parallel programming models that allow for easy porting of applications to the Grid environment.

Solution

Use a middleware infrastructure to manage distributed and potentially heterogeneous resources without changing the underlying operating system. The middleware will allow users to access these resources for the execution of computationally intensive applications.

A user interested in executing applications submits a request via an *access agent*. The applications can be either regular applications consisting of a single process or parallel applications. The *scheduling service* receives the execution request, checks the identity of the user who submitted the application, and uses a *resource management service* to discover which machines (nodes) have available resources to execute the application. These nodes, which must run the *resource provision service*, are called *resource providers*. If there are nodes with free resources, the scheduler sends an execution request to the selected nodes. If there are no free resources in nodes, the request waits in an execution queue. When the execution is finished, the resource providers return the results to the user.

Structure

The structure of the GRID pattern is composed of five major elements. Figure 13–2 shows the interactions between them.

- The *access agent* is the primary access point for users who interact with the Grid. It runs on each node from which users submit application execution requests. Besides the submission of execution requests, it allows the user to specify application requirements, monitor executions, and collect execution results.

- The *resource provision service* runs on each machine that exports its resources to the Grid. It is responsible for servicing execution requests by retrieving application code, starting application execution, reporting errors on application execution, and returning application results. It is also responsible for managing local resource usage and providing information about resource availability.

- The *resource management service* is responsible for maintaining information about the state of shared resources and responding to resource availability queries. It keeps a dynamic list of available resource providers and the state of their resources, such as processor usage and memory availability. This service can also detect resource provider failures and notify the access agent when an execution fails due to a resource failure.

- The *scheduling service* schedules the execution of applications on Grid nodes. It receives application execution requests, obtains available resources with the resource management service, and then determines which application process will execute on each node.

- The *security service* is responsible for three major tasks: (1) protecting shared resources so that a node sharing its resources with the Grid does not suffer the effects of a rogue application, (2) authenticating users so that application ownership can be established in order to enable relations of trust and accountability, and (3) securing Grid communications in order to provide information confidentiality and integrity.

We define a *Grid cluster* as a collection of resource providers managed by a cluster management node. A Grid is composed of several Grid clusters, as shown in Figure 13–3.

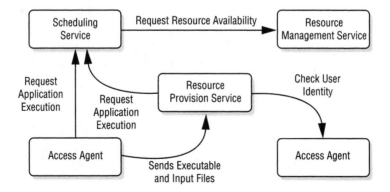

Figure 13–2 *Interactions between Grid module.*

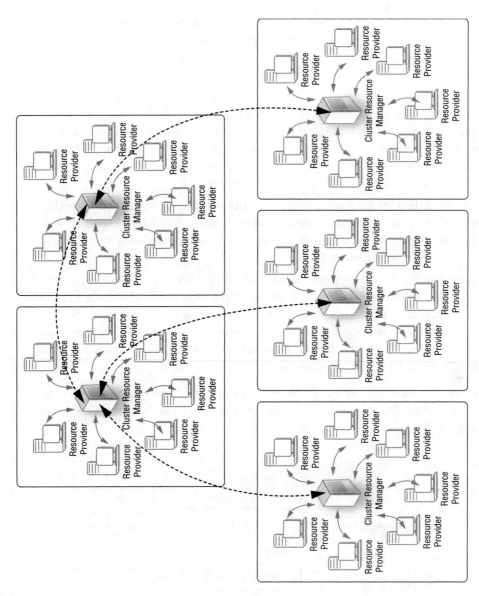

Figure 13–3 *A typical Grid deployment*

Dynamics

Figure 13–4 illustrates the behavior of the Grid components when an access agent requests an application execution (presuming that no errors occur during the execution of the application).

1. The access agent sends an execution request to the scheduling service, possibly with some information about the required resources.

2. The scheduling service queries the resource monitoring service for nodes meeting the request requirements, and the resource monitoring service returns a list containing the location of nodes satisfying the query.

3. The scheduling service determines whether it is possible to execute the application on the available nodes. If the execution is possible, the scheduling service forwards the execution request to the selected resource providers. If the execution is not possible, the scheduling service queues the request for later execution.

4. The resource providers download the application code from the access agent that submitted the execution request.

5. The resource providers use the security service to verify the identity and permissions of the code owner.

6. The resource providers execute the application. When the execution is finished, the results are sent back to the access agent.

Implementation

Implementing the Grid pattern is a complex process. We present here some guidelines for the implementation and deployment of the pattern.

1. A *communication infrastructure* is necessary to allow Grid components to locate each other and exchange information. It should provide a reliable communication mechanism, such as remote procedure calls (RPC) or asynchronous messaging, and work on all platforms where Grid components will be installed.

   It is easier to use an already existing communication infrastructure that satisfies the Grid requirements. To permit the usage of heterogeneous machines, the infrastructure should be language- and platform-independent; for example, one could use either CORBA [OMG2004] or Web Services [W3C2004]. They permit decoupling the component interfaces from their implementations and

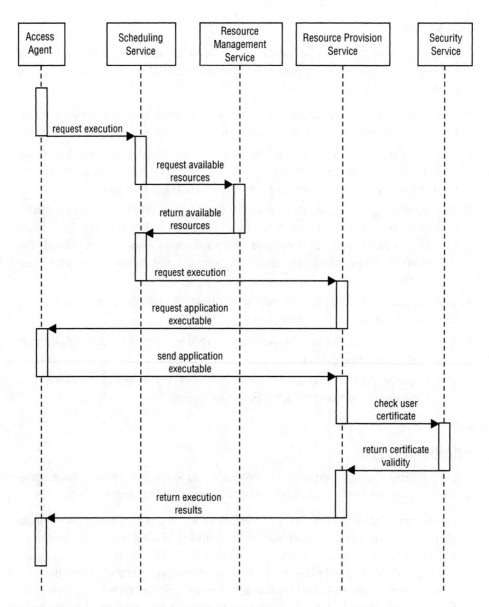

Figure 13–4 *Dynamics of a successful execution request*

allow multiple interchangeable implementations that support different architectures. Both are implementations of the `Broker` [Buschmann+1996] pattern.

Another possibility is to develop a new communication infrastructure from scratch. Here, it is necessary to deal with several aspects of the infrastructure, such as communication reliability, event dispatching, machine heterogeneity, and component interfaces. Several patterns can be used for the construction of this communication infrastructure [Hohpe+2003] [Schmidt+1999].

2. The *access agent* is typically implemented as a proxy that receives user requests and forwards them to other `Grid` components. It must provide a well-defined interface that allows one to make execution requests, specify application requirements and preferences, monitor application execution, and collect executions results. A friendly interface to the access agent should be provided to permit users to interact with the Grid. This user interface can be implemented as a shell-like interface that uses UNIX-like commands, a graphical interface, or a Web portal.

During an execution request, the access agent usually sends the application executable directly to the resource providers. Another approach is to upload the executable to a remote code repository in the network, from which resource providers can fetch the executables. For dealing with the input and output files, a first possibility is to allow the access agent to send the input files with the request and, when the execution finishes, to download the output files directly from the resource providers. Another option is to define a data repository in the Grid and upload the input and output files to this repository. Finally, it is possible to link the Grid applications with a remote I/O library that allows reading and writing files remotely from the machine that initiated the execution request.

When preparing the execution request, the user may want to specify application constraints and preferences. Typical constraints are the architecture for which the executable was compiled and the amount of required RAM to run it. A preference can be, for example, selecting machines that belong to a particular administrative domain. The access agent should provide a constraint language that allows the specification of application constraints and preferences.

3. The *resource provision service* runs permanently on each of the nodes that share its resources with the Grid. This service should have a small memory footprint when deployed on shared machines in order to help ensure that resource owners will not perceive degradations in the quality of service provided by their machines.

When this service receives an application execution request from the scheduling service, it first obtains the application executables and other input files required for its execution. It is then necessary to create an execution environment for the application, for example, by creating a separate file system directory for each execution and launching a new process for execution on that directory. After the execution finishes, its output files must be returned to the user. In the case of abnormal terminations, partial results and error messages should be returned to the access agent to allow the user to analyze the cause of failure.

This service is also responsible for sending periodic *resource usage information* to the resource management service in order to keep it up to date. A shorter update interval leads to higher network traffic, while longer intervals can lead to stale information. One should send updates only when a substantial change occurs. Keep-alive messages can be used to determine if the resource provider is active.

Local scheduling can be performed either by the operating system scheduler or by a custom scheduler. By using a custom scheduler associated with the resource provision service, it is possible to achieve better resource utilization by Grid applications. Support for resource reservation permits better QoS guarantees, but it requires a custom local scheduler for most operating systems, which do not support this feature.

Finally, the resource provision service should provide an interface to allow the resource owner to specify *constraints on resource sharing*. It should provide for specifying restrictions such as which users can access the resources, the period of the day during which the resources can be shared, and the amount of resources to be shared.

4. The *resource management service* needs to provide interfaces for both queries and updates about the availability of resources from resource providers. It maintains a list containing the registered resource providers, their characteristics, and dynamic information about the currently available resources. To match resource requests and offers, it should support a query language that allows the specification of application requirements and preferences.

To keep information up to date, this service receives periodic updates from resource providers with their resource availability state. It is possible to use push, pull, or push/pull approaches [Zdonik+1997] for the periodic update. These updates also allow the monitoring service to detect when resource providers are not reachable, which can happen due to hardware, software, or network failures. When it detects that a node is unreachable, the service should notify the scheduler or access agent about the node failure and the processes that were executing on that node so that these processes can be instantiated on other resource providers.

The storage of dynamic resource availability information can be implemented easily on top of existing services such as the CORBA Trading Service

[OMG2000] or LDAP [Yeong1995]. Another possibility is to implement the service using a database that provides a custom front end for queries and updates.

5. The *scheduling service* is responsible for a particularly complex aspect of Grid computing: deciding where and when each application process will execute. There are many types of applications with different requirements, which makes one-fit-all algorithms inappropriate. Another complication is that the scheduler typically does not have reliable information about the state of all resources of the Grid and does not have full control over these resources. Finally, the heterogeneity of resources makes scheduling an even harder task; machines have different processor speeds, memory and disk sizes, network bandwidths, and so on.

   A possible approach is to assign the responsibility for scheduling the received execution requests to the access agent. It prompts the resource manager for available resources and schedules the requests on these resources. This allows different clients to employ different scheduling strategies, including the definition of user priorities. Another possibility is to implement the scheduling service as a separate component that contains a default scheduler and domain-specific schedulers. Applications can choose one of these schedulers or implement a custom one. The STRATEGY pattern [Gamma+1995] can be used to allow the scheduler to employ these different scheduling strategies.

   The service should signal an error to the user when it cannot find the resources required by the application. The error message may provide some information about available resources so that the user can relax application requirements to meet the current resource availability.

6. The *security service* protects resource providers by limiting system privileges for Grid applications. This can be accomplished by presenting a restricted execution environment for Grid applications, usually called sandbox [Goldberg+1996] [Dodonov+2004]. It can be implemented by intercepting system calls or using a virtual machine, as in a Java environment. Typical restrictions include disallowing the application to fork new processes, access some peripherals such as printers, and obtain unrestricted access to the file system. The authorization mechanism should allow resource owners to specify these security restrictions, which can be different depending on the administrative domain. This can be implemented by using access control lists (ACL), which are composed of lists of actions that are allowed or disallowed for a user or group of users. Since the resource provider protection is enforced by the operating system, a mapping between Grid users and local machine users may be required.

   The user authentication mechanism should provide a single sign-on facility for Grid users. The most common way of authenticating users is by using passwords. After checking the password, the authentication mechanism can generate a certificate that identifies that user. Grid components can verify these certificates with the user public key to confirm the identity of users and their access rights.

Communication security by means of encryption incurs a significant execution overhead, especially for parallel applications that exchange large amounts of data. For applications that do not need information confidentiality, it should be possible to disable this mechanism. Application security requirements could be included in the application preferences defined before application submission.

The implementation of both user authentication and data encryption can be greatly simplified by leveraging existing security libraries. For example, GSS (Generic Security Services) [Linn+2000] is a standard API for managing security; it does not provide the security mechanisms itself but can be used on top of other security methods such as Kerberos [Neuman+1994]. CorbaSEC [OMG2002] is another alternative that can be used if communication is based on CORBA.

7. *Libraries for parallel computation* permit the execution of parallel applications in the Grid. It is desirable to implement Grid-specific libraries for well-known APIs for parallel programming, such as MPI [MPIForum1993], BSP [Valiant1990], and PVM [Sunderam1990], since they permit easier migration of legacy software. It is possible to implement these libraries either from scratch or by modifying existing libraries to use the Grid middleware communication and resource management infrastructures.

8. *Organizing the* Grid *as a cluster federation allows* dealing with thousands of geographically distributed machines spanning different administrative domains. In this scenario, a centralized solution would become a bottleneck since it lacks scalability, contains single points of failures, and concentrates management under a single administration.

Organizing the Grid as a collection of clusters prevents single servers from having complete knowledge of the system, which would hinder scalability, and is usually more tolerant to node and network failures. It is also usually easier for each organization to manage and deploy its own resource management service that applies desired policies to shared resources. The implementation of cluster federation will require the careful design of inter-cluster protocols for disseminating information across Grid clusters and for locating resources and executing applications on remote clusters.

To enable the implementation of the Grid as a cluster federation (as shown in Figure 13–3), it is necessary to modify several of its services. The access agent communicates with the resource management and scheduling services of its own cluster, so no major changes are required in this module. The security service may have to deal with differences in the security infrastructures of different administrative domains, for example, by performing a mapping between these infrastructures. The resource management service should contain a server for each cluster; each cluster server should then maintain full information about machines on that cluster and statistical information about resources on other clusters. Servers should not maintain full information about all the Grid resources, since this would limit the scalability of the system. Finally, the scheduling service will query the resource manager in its cluster for available resources. If resources are not available there, the system should query resource managers in other clusters throughout the Grid.

When combining clusters in different administrative domains, the messages sent by Grid nodes will probably need to cross several firewalls. Most certainly, many of the Grid nodes will not have a real IP address. The communication substratum will have to deal with these limitations, for example, by tunneling RPC messages via HTTP or SSL and by using proxies strategically located in the distributed system.

9. *Opportunistic computing* consists of using the idle periods of shared workstations to run Grid applications. In this case, it is necessary to preserve the quality of service (QoS) of workstation owners, who should not perceive performance degradation. When the owner of an idle workstation decides to use the machine, the resource that is providing service must kill or suspend Grid application processes running on that machine.

Since, in this situation, the rate at which processes are killed is much higher than in the case where resources are dedicated to Grid processes, it is important to be able to restart the execution of these processes from an intermediate state, not from its beginning. In the case of parallel applications, this is particularly important because the failure of any of the application processes can require all the remaining processes to be restarted. *Checkpointing* [Elnozahy+2002] is a mechanism that allows the reinitialization of an application from an intermediate execution state. It consists in periodically saving the application state as a checkpoint, which allows the recovery of application execution from the last saved checkpoint.

Even using checkpointing, part of the computation performed by the application is always lost. In addition, the application files need to be uploaded to another node. This makes the reinitialization process expensive. To reduce the number of these reinitializations, *usage patterns* for the resource providers can be determined by using clustering algorithms [Arabie+1996] on the usage history of the offered resources. The scheduling service can use this data to select machines with a higher probability of remaining free for a longer period.

10. The *deployment of the Grid middleware* requires launching each of its services. The resource provision service must be started on each machine that will export its resources to the Grid. Each organization then defines policies for the shared resources. Access agents are deployed on machines belonging to users who submit applications for execution on the Grid.

When using a distributed resource manager service, a resource manager server is deployed on each administrative domain. These servers are responsible for the resource providers in their domains. Security deployment is dependent on the implementation. When using centralized certificate-based approaches, it is necessary to deploy certificate servers. Figure 13–3 shows a typical Grid deployment.

Known Uses

Condor [Litzkow+1988] [Berman+2003] is a pioneer work in the area of cluster and opportunistic computing. The *Agent* module implements the functionality of the access agent and is also responsible for the scheduling process. The *Matchmaker* is responsible for the resource management service, and the *Resource* module implements the resource provision service. A Condor Grid is composed of several Condor pools, which are a group of machines connected to a single Matchmaker. A number of parallel programming libraries are available to Condor, including PVM, MPI, and one based on the master-worker model. Finally, applications can benefit from a transparent checkpointing mechanism.

Legion [Lewis+1994] [Berman+2003] treats everything in the Grid as an object, including hosts, users, schedulers, applications, and data. It started as an academic project and was later transformed into a commercial product. The services are implemented by Legion core objects. *Host* objects are responsible for the resource provision service and resource protection. *Scheduler* objects implement different scheduling strategies, whereas *Collection* objects maintain lists of Host objects. On Legion, each user receives an identification object used for authentication. The security also includes authorization and data confidentiality. Finally, Legion provides support for the execution of MPI applications.

Globus [Foster+1997] [Berman+2003] is the most widely used Grid middleware infrastructure. It implements most of the services described in this pattern. The *Monitoring and Discovery Service (MDS)* [Czajkowski+2001] and the *Globus Resource Allocation Manager (GRAM)* [Czajkowski+1998] are cooperatively responsible for the resource management and resource provision services. The *Grid Security Infrastructure (GSI)* implements the security service by using GSS over Kerberos. PVM and MPI parallel programming libraries are available for running parallel applications.

InteGrade [Goldchleger+2004] [Camargo+2004] provides most of the services of the Grid pattern. Its resource management and scheduling services are implemented as a single module, the *Global Resource Manager (GRM)*. The resource provision service is called *Local Resource Manager (LRM)*, a very lightweight component that imposes a small overhead on shared resources. The *Application Submission and Control Tool (ASCT)* module performs the access agent role. InteGrade uses CORBA for the communication infrastructure and includes support for portable checkpointing of sequential and BSP applications as well as a security service based on GSS over Kerberos.

OurGrid [Andrade+2003] [Cirne+2005] organizes grids as a peer-to-peer network of resources. Resource sharing is based on the concept of network of favors; that is, priority for the use of resources is determined by the amount of resources one has previously donated to the community. The *MyGrid* module implements the access agent and performs the scheduling of applications submitted from it. The *UserAgent* module is responsible for the resource provision service, whereas *OurGridPeer* modules implement the resource management service functionality in a peer-to-peer fashion. Resources can be a single machine or a cluster of machines. The OurGrid security service implements authentication, communication security, and authorization. The *SWAN (Sandboxing Without A Name)* module is responsible for shared resources security. Finally, OurGrid allows the execution of sequential and bag-of-tasks applications with no communication among computing nodes.

Consequences

The GRID pattern provides the following benefits:

- *Reusability.* Once implemented, the Grid middleware infrastructure works for many applications that share the same services and programming libraries. Since the system is a middleware that provides an abstraction layer for the development of applications, it can be easily installed as an off-the-shelf component on different systems with little or no modification to the underlying system.

- *Encapsulation of heterogeneity.* The Grid middleware hides the specific details of communications, computer architectures, and operating systems. Consequently, application development is much easier, because there is no need to worry about details that vary from one operating system to the other.

- *Easy application deployment.* The Grid middleware manages the details of resource allocation, scheduling, security, and application deployment. This facilitates the execution process, since the user does not have to worry about the details of reserving computing resources and deploying the application on various machines.

- *Efficient resource usage.* Resource idleness may be reduced significantly when using the Grid. This applies both to workstations and to specialized and expensive resources. During normal operation, their owners suffer no degradation in their quality of service. However, when idle, these resources can be shared and utilized by applications running on the Grid. The more efficient use of resources means that less hardware will have to be purchased and maintained, which results in a significant cost reduction.

- *Integration of distributed resources.* The use of the Grid middleware eases the integration of distributed resources, including geographically distant ones. When these resources are spread across administrative domains, different policies for resource sharing such as access restrictions can be implemented for each domain, especially if the Grid middleware is structured as a federation of clusters.

However, the GRID pattern has the following liabilities:

- *High complexity.* The implementation of the Grid pattern involves many challenges that still do not have a dominant solution. Implementing the Grid pattern demands a considerable amount of time and effort from talented people, which can incur a high cost. The investment must be justified by using the Grid for many applications and environments.

- *Necessity to change applications.* To take advantage of the Grid, it may be necessary to change parts of the application. This requires access to the application source code, which is rare on commercial applications. Even when the source code is available, its adaptation to use the Grid can consume a considerable amount of time and money, for example, if the application is written using a parallel programming API not supported by the Grid.

- *Harder to debug and test applications.* Applications submitted for execution on the Grid are harder to test and debug. This happens because the user has no control over where the application processes are executed. In addition, the current availability of tools for testing and debugging applications in a distributed environment is extremely limited.

- *Security exposures.* Executing foreign code on a resource provider machine is a potential security breach. It is possible to minimize the risk by restricting the execution environment, but it is difficult to guarantee full security for the machine.

Related Patterns

The LOOKUP pattern [Kircher+2004] uses a lookup service for finding and accessing computational resources and has a structure similar to the GRID pattern. Its participants correspond to the resource management service, resource provision service, access agent, and resources of the GRID pattern. The main difference is that the LOOKUP has a smaller scope that does not involve issues such as security, sharing policies, and scheduling.

The RESOURCE LIFECYCLE MANAGER pattern [Kircher+2004] separates resource usage from resource management by introducing a Resource Lifecycle Manager. It is similar to the resource provision service in that it is responsible for accepting resource usage requests and managing the resources according to defined policies. However, it does not address the security concerns brought by the Grid environment.

The BROKER pattern [Buschmann+1996] coordinates the communication among interacting distributed components. Like the GRID pattern, its goal is to encapsulate several details regarding the implementation of distributed systems, which simplifies the development of applications. Nevertheless, it does not require many of the features available in the Grid, such as the scheduling and resource monitoring services. Since the BROKER encapsulates details such as the communication with remote entities, it can be used as a substrate for the implementation of the GRID pattern. InteGrade uses CORBA, an implementation of the BROKER pattern, as the basis for its communication.

The MASTER-SLAVE pattern [Buschmann+1996] consists of having a central coordinator that distributes tasks for execution on servants and then collects the results. In contrast to the GRID pattern, the pattern only applies to problems that can be solved by the "divide and conquer" approach. However, this specificity allows for a simpler system that can be easily implemented and optimized. Application developers can use this pattern as a model for parallel applications to execute on the Grid.

Acknowledgments

We would like to thank Eugenio Sper de Almeida for providing the weather forecasting image used in our example, Walfredo Cirne for the help with the OurGrid description, and Francisco Gatto for the paper revision. Special thanks go to Michael Stal, whose innumerable suggestions during the shepherding process of the PLoP 2004 conference were invaluable for improving the quality of this pattern. Finally, this work would not be possible without the financial support from the Brazilian Research Council (CNPq).

References

[Andrade+2003] N. Andrade, W. Cirne, F. Brasileiro, and P. Roisenberg. "Our-Grid: An Approach to Easily Assemble Grids with Equitable Resource Sharing." In D. G. Feitelson, L. Rudolph, and U. Schwiegelshohn (eds.), *Proceedings of the 9th Workshop on Job Scheduling Strategies for Parallel Processing*, Seattle, WA, June 2003. *Lecture Notes on Computer Science*, vol. 2862. New York: Springer-Verlag, 2003.

[Arabie+1996] P. Arabie, L. J. Hubert, and G. D. Soete (eds.), *Clustering and Classification*. Singapore and River Edge, NJ: World Scientific Publishers, 1996.

[Berman+2003] F. Berman, G. Fox, and T. Hey. *Grid Computing: Making the Global Infrastructure a Reality*. Chichester, UK: John Wiley & Sons, 2003.

[Buschmann+1996] F. Buschmann, R. Meunier, H. Rohnert, P. Sommerlad, and M. Stal. *Pattern-Oriented System Architecture: A System of Patterns*. Chichester, UK: John Wiley & Sons, 1996.

[Camargo+2004] R. Y. de Camargo, A. Goldchleger, F. Kon, and A. Goldman. "Checkpointing-based Rollback Recovery for Parallel Applications on the InteGrade Grid Middleware." In B. Schulze, R. Nandkumar, and F. Kon (eds.), *Proceedings of the 2nd Workshop on Middleware for Grid Computing*, pp. 35–40, Toronto, ON, Canada, October 2004. New York: ACM Press, 2004.

[Cirne+2005] W. Cirne, F. Brasileiro, N. Andrade, R. Santos, A. Andrade, R. Novaes, and M. Mowbray. Labs of the World, Unite!!! Technical Report 01/2005, Universidade Federal de Campina Grande. Available: *http://walfredo.dsc.ufcg.edu.br/resume.html#publications*.

[Czajkowski+1998] K. Czajkowski, I. Foster, N. Karonis, C. Kesselman, S. Martin, W. Smith, and S. Tuecke. "A Resource Management Architecture for Metacomputing Systems." *Proceedings of IPPS/SPDP 98 Workshop on Job Scheduling Strategies for Parallel Processing*, Orlando, FL, March 1998. *Lecture Notes in Computer Science*, vol. 1459, pp. 62–82. New York: Springer-Verlag, 1998.

[Czajkowski+2001] K. Czajkowski, S. Fitzgerald, I. Foster, and C. Kesselman. "Grid Information Services for Distributed Resource Sharing." In I. Foster and W. Johnston (eds.), *Proceedings of the 10th IEEE International Symposium on High-Performance Distributed Computing* (HPDC-10), San Francisco, CA, August 2001. IEEE Computer Society Press, 2001.

[Dodonov+2004] E. Dodonov, J. Quaini Sousa, and H. C. Guardia. "GridBox: Securing Hosts from Malicious and Greedy Applications." In B. Schulze, R. Nandkumar, and F. Kon (eds.), *Proceedings of the 2nd Workshop on Middleware for Grid Computing*, pp. 17–22, Toronto, ON, Canada, October 2004. New York: ACM Press, 2004.

[Elnozahy+2002] M. Elnozahy, L. Alvisi, Y.-M. Wang, and D. B. Johnson. "A Survey of Rollback-recovery Protocols in Message-passing Systems." *ACM Computing Surveys*, 34(3):375–408, May 2002.

[Foster+1997] I. Foster and C. Kesselman. "Globus: A Metacomputing Infrastructure Toolkit." *International Journal of Supercomputing Applications*, 2(11):115–128, 1997.

[Foster+2003] I. Foster and C. Kesselman. *The Grid 2: Blueprint for a New Computing Infrastructure*, 2nd ed. San Francisco, CA: Morgan Kaufmann, 2003.

[Gamma+1995] E. Gamma, R. Helm, R. Johnson, and J. Vlissides. *Design Patterns: Elements of Reusable Object-Oriented Software*. Reading, MA: Addison-Wesley, 1995.

[Goldberg+1996] I. Goldberg, D. Wagner, R. Thomas, and E. Brewer. "A Secure Environment for Untrusted Helper Applications." In *Proceedings of the 1996 USENIX Security Symposium*, San Jose, CA, July 1996. USENIX Association, 1996.

[Goldchleger+2004] A. Goldchleger, F. Kon, A. Goldman, M. Finger, and G. C. Bezerra. "InteGrade: Object-Oriented Grid Middleware Leveraging Idle Computing Power of Desktop Machines." *Concurrency and Computation: Practice and Experience*, 16:449–459, March 2004.

[Hohpe+2003] G. Hohpe and B. Woolf. *Enterprise Integration Patterns: Designing, Building, and Deploying Messaging Solutions*. Boston: Addison-Wesley Professional, 2003.

[Kircher+2004] M. Kircher and P. Jain. *Pattern-Oriented Software Architecture, Volume 3: Patterns for Resource Management*. Chichester, UK: John Wiley & Sons, 2004.

[Lewis+1994] M. Lewis and A. Grimshaw. "The Core Legion Object Model." In S. Hariri and G. C. Fox (eds.), *Proceedings of the 5th IEEE International Symposium on High-Performance Distributed Computing* (HPDC-96), Syracuse, NY, August 1996. IEEE Computer Society Press, 1996.

[Linn+2000] J. Linn. Generic Security Service Application Program Interface, Version 2, Update 1, January 2000. Network Working Group RFC 2743. Available: *http://www.ietf.org/rfc/rfc2743.txt*.

[Litzkow+1988] M. Litzkow, M. Livny, and M. Mutka. "Condor—A Hunter of Idle Workstations." In *Proceedings of the 8th International Conference of Distributed Computing Systems* (ICDCS '88), pp. 104–111, San Jose, California, June 1988. IEEE Computer Society Press, 1988.

[MPIForum1993] MPI Forum. "MPI: A Message Passing Interface." In *Proceedings of 1993 Supercomputing Conference*, pp. 878–883, Portland, WA, November 1993. IEEE Computer Society Press, 1993.

[Neuman+1994] B. C. Neuman and T. Tso. "Kerberos: An Authentication Service for Computer Networks." *IEEE Communications*, 32:33–38, September 1994.

[OMG2000] Object Management Group. Trading Object Service Specification, June 2000, version 1.0. OMG document formal/00-06-27. Available: *http://www.omg.org/technology/documents/formal/trading_object_service.htm*.

[OMG2002] Object Management Group. Security Service Specification, March 2002, version 1.8. OMG document formal/02-03-11. Available: *http://www.omg.org/technology/documents/formal/security_service.htm*.

[OMG2004] Object Management Group. CORBA v3.0.3 Specification, March 2004. OMG Document formal/04-03-01. Available: *http://www.omg.org/technology/documents/formal/corba_iiop.htm*.

[Schmidt+1999] D. C. Schmidt and C. Cleeland. "Applying Patterns to Develop Extensible ORB Middleware." *IEEE Communications*, 37(4):54–63, May 1999.

[Sunderam1990] V. S. Sunderam. "PVM: A Framework for Parallel Distributed Computing." Concurrency, Practice, and Experience, 2(4):315–340, 1990.

[Valiant1990] L. G. Valiant. "A Bridging Model for Parallel Computation." *Communications of the ACM*, 33:103–111, 1990.

[W3C2004] W3C Working Group. Web Services Architecture, February 2004. Available: *http://www.w3.org/TR/2004/NOTE-ws-arch-20040211/*.

[Yeong1995] M. Wahl, T. Howes, and S. Kille. Lightweight Directory Access Protocol, version 3. Network Working Group RFC 2251, December 1997. Available: *http://www.ietf.org/rfc/rfc2251.txt*.

[Zdonik+1997] S. Zdonik and M. Franklin. "A Framework for Scalable Dissemination Based Systems." In *Proceedings of the 1997 ACM SIGPLAN Conference on Object-oriented Programming Systems, Languages, and Applications*, pp. 94–105, Atlanta, GA, October 1997. ACM SIGPLAN Notices, 1997.

CHAPTER 14

Patterns of Component
and Language Integration

Uwe Zdun

Integration is an important concern in many software systems. In this chapter, we present a number of patterns that are used to improve the integration of a system with components or code that is written in different languages than the system itself. Component integration is necessary when (foreign) components must be used within a system. The challenge of integrating components into a system lies in the fact that heterogeneous kinds of components exist that may not have distinct interfaces or other component boundaries. The task of the component integration code is to provide suitable, stable invocation interfaces and to compose the components within the system. Sometimes, however, invocation and composition of components is not enough and deeper language integration is required. Examples of what might be needed are automatic type conversions between languages, preserving the destruction order of the other language, automatic forwarding of invocations into the other language, and runtime integration of foreign language components. The patterns presented in this chapter are successful solutions in these areas. Each of these patterns plays an important role in different integration architectures. We will give examples from the areas of distributed systems, reengineering projects, scripting languages, and aspect-oriented programming systems. There are many other fields where the patterns are used as well.

Introduction

Software Integration

Integration of software systems is needed in many situations. Consider two enterprise applications that need to be integrated after acquisition of one company by another, or a reengineering project in which a terminal-based legacy system must be reengineered to the Web and thus integrated with a modern application server. The capability of the system's architecture to integrate foreign components and be integrated with other systems is thus considered an important quality attribute [Bass+1998]. There are many integration concerns to be considered when integrating software architectures. These include the integration of:

- Data, data models, and queries
- Various software components
- Various programming languages
- Distributed systems
- Systems with legacy systems
- Different software paradigms such as the object-oriented and procedural paradigms

In this chapter, we present patterns that describe solutions in the area of software component and language integration. These patterns are not a complete pattern language for the broad field of software architecture integration. Instead, they are examples of patterns that work mainly in the area of component, language, and paradigm integration. There are also many patterns from other pattern collections that interact closely with the patterns presented in this chapter. These are referenced in the pattern texts appearing here.

The patterns presented in this chapter are applied where simple, ad hoc integration solutions fail. Thus, the main audiences of the patterns are experienced software architects and developers.

Pattern Language Outline

In this section, we provide short thumbnails for the patterns and important external patterns, as well as a pattern map as an overview.

The following patterns are presented in this chapter:

- A COMMAND LANGUAGE is a language that is implemented within another language (called "host language"). It uses COMMANDS [Gamma+1995] implemented in that host language as implementations of its language elements. The COMMAND LANGUAGE lets the COMMANDS be assembled in scripts, and it provides an INTERPRETER [Gamma+1995] or another interpretation mechanism such as an on-the-fly compiler for these scripts.

- A COMPONENT WRAPPER is an object implemented as part of a component that represents another component. The wrapped component is imported into the wrapping component, and the COMPONENT WRAPPER handles all details of the import. It utilizes other patterns for the integration such as WRAPPER FACADE [Schmidt+2000] or PROXY [Gamma+1995]. The COMPONENT WRAPPER is an accessible white box representing the component within another component's scope, where adaptations such as interface adaptations or version changes can take place.

- An OBJECT SYSTEM LAYER [Goedicke+2000] implements an object system as a LAYER [Buschmann+1996] in another system. This way, we can extend systems written in non-object-oriented languages with object-oriented concepts, integrate different object concepts, and extend existing object concepts. A part of an OBJECT SYSTEM LAYER is a MESSAGE REDIRECTOR [Goedicke+2001] that forms a FACADE [Gamma+1995] to the object system; all invocations into the OBJECT SYSTEM LAYER from the rest of the system are sent to their MESSAGE REDIRECTOR and dispatched here to the objects in the object system.

- An AUTOMATIC TYPE CONVERTER converts types at runtime from one type to another. There are two main variants of the pattern: one-to-one converters between all type bindings and converters utilizing a canonical format to/from which all supported types can be converted. AUTOMATIC TYPE CONVERTER can, for example, be used in a COMMAND LANGUAGE to convert types to/from the host language, in SPLIT OBJECTS to convert between the split object halves, and in COMPONENT WRAPPERS to convert invocations to the types of the wrapped component and vice versa.

- A SPLIT OBJECT is an object that is split across two languages. The SPLIT OBJECT is treated logically like a single example, but it is implemented by two physical entities, one in each language. That is, both halves can forward invocations to the other half, access the inner state of the other half, and usually—to a certain extent—the user-defined class hierarchies of each half is mimicked by the respective other half.

There are a number of external patterns documented elsewhere that play an important role in the patterns described in this chapter. We want to explain some of them briefly:

- A COMMAND [Gamma+1995] encapsulates an invocation to an object and provides a generic (abstract) invocation interface. COMMANDS alone only allow for adaptation by changing the association link to a COMMAND. In the

COMMAND LANGUAGE pattern, the COMMAND abstraction is extended with a binding of COMMANDS to language elements and an interpretation mechanism for that language.

- The important interpretation step in a COMMAND LANGUAGE can be implemented using another pattern [Gamma+1995], the INTERPRETER pattern. In general, an INTERPRETER defines a representation for a grammar along with an interpretation mechanism to interpret the language.

- The pattern INTERFACE DESCRIPTION [Völter+2004] describes how to specify interfaces of an object so that external clients of the object can reliably access the object. The pattern is originally described in the context of distributed systems: In this context, an INTERFACE DESCRIPTION specifies the interface of a remote object for remote clients but can also be used in other scenarios. Generating type conversion code from an INTERFACE DESCRIPTION is the most important alternative solution to using an AUTOMATIC TYPE CONVERTER. AUTOMATIC TYPE CONVERTERS can also be applied according to an INTERFACE DESCRIPTION.

- A MESSAGE REDIRECTOR [Goedicke+2001] receives symbolic invocations—for example, provided in form of strings—and redirects these invocations to objects implementing the invocation behavior. This way, for example, a dynamic object dispatch mechanism can be implemented. A MESSAGE REDIRECTOR can also be used to integrate some non-object-oriented invocation interface with an object system. The MESSAGE REDIRECTOR pattern is an inherent part of an OBJECT SYSTEM LAYER: It is used to dispatch the invocations of OBJECT SYSTEM LAYER to its objects.

Figure 14–1 shows an overview of the patterns described in this chapter and the relationships explained above. In the pattern map, the most important relationships of the patterns are represented by labeled arrows.

Patterns for Component and Language Integration

In this section, we present the five patterns for component and language integration summarized in Figure 14–1. Note that we first describe the patterns with only simple example scenarios and a few known uses. More detailed known uses and technology projections can be found in the section that follows this one. These known uses and technology projections are used as examples for the patterns; instead of giving an example for each pattern on its own, we can better describe the interactions of the patterns.

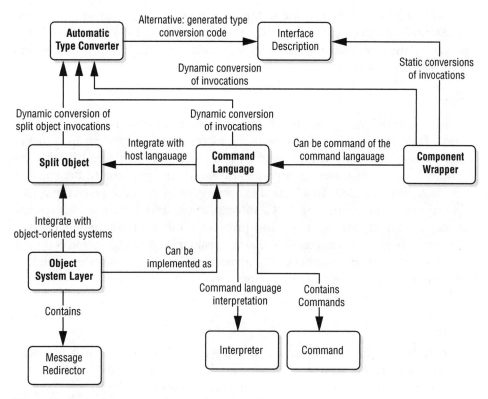

Figure 14–1 *Pattern interactions in the pattern language*

Command Language

Context

Some code needs to be executed by other code and needs to be exchangeable at runtime. In static languages, you cannot simply exchange code. In such situations, COMMANDS provide a standard solution used in object-oriented and procedural systems: They encapsulate the implementation of an invocation and provide a generic, abstract invocation interface.

Problem

Using many COMMANDS without further support can be cumbersome in some cases, where the COMMANDS have to be composed in various different ways. Such situations occur frequently, when using COMMANDS for composing components or configuring a system, because in these situations a large number of different COMMANDS need to be composed. Runtime composition of the COMMANDS is not possible if the composition solution is hard-coded in static, compiled languages such as C, C++, or Java.

Scenario

Consider the following scenario: A system is built from a number of C components. Different customers require different components running in different configurations. The system needs to be composed and configured flexibly according to these customers' requirements. Rapid configuration to the customers' demands is needed. This is hard to achieve, however, because changing the system means programming in C, recompilation, and restart of the system. COMMANDS can be used to avoid this problem up to a certain degree, because they provide a way to encapsulate the composition and configuration code and exchange it at runtime. However, the composition and configuration of components is still hard-coded in the system, and COMMAND-based composition is rather cumbersome.

Forces

Composition in static, compiled languages, such as C, C++, or Java, is inflexible for situations where runtime behavior modification is required, because programming, recompilation, and restart are required for each change.

It is hard to implement simple, domain-specific languages, for example, for rapid configuration of software systems written in those languages, because this requires writing a parser, preprocessor, and interpreter for that language. Even if an existing parser, such as an XML parser, can be reused, the mapping of language elements to implementations still needs to be programmed by hand. For simple configuration options, this is easily done, but for more complex languages that can handle behavior definitions, this can quickly result in a complex task.

The code of multiple, consecutive COMMAND invocations might be hard to read, as seen in the following simple example:

```
if (expressionCommand.execute().toBoolean()) {
  result = command1.execute();
  command2.value = result;
  command2.execute();
}
```

Solution

Express COMMAND composition in a COMMAND LANGUAGE, instead of calling the COMMANDS directly using an API. Each COMMAND is accessed with a unique command name. The host language, in which COMMANDS are implemented, embeds the COMMAND LANGUAGE. In the host language, the COMMAND LANGUAGE'S INTERPRETER or compiler is invoked at runtime to evaluate the COMMANDS expressed in the COMMAND LANGUAGE. Thus COMMANDS can be composed freely using COMMAND LANGUAGE scripts, even at runtime.

Discussion

A part of the COMMAND LANGUAGE is either an INTERPRETER or an on-the-fly compiler. Note that often byte-code compilers are used for COMMAND LANGUAGES. A byte-code compiler can also be part of an INTERPRETER. From a language user's perspective, all these alternatives look the same: The user operates in a language that is interpreted at runtime.

Almost all elements of a COMMAND LANGUAGE are COMMANDS, which means that a COMMAND LANGUAGE'S syntax and grammar rules are usually quite simple. There are some additional syntax elements, such as grouping of instructions in blocks, substitutions, and operators:

- Grouping of instructions in blocks is required to build larger instruction sets, such as method bodies, lists of arguments, and so forth. Brackets are most often used to delimit grouping in blocks.

- Substitutions are required in a COMMAND LANGUAGE to hand over the results of one COMMAND to another. Other substitutions than COMMAND substitution are also possible, such as variable substitution or character substitution.

- Assignment operators are an alternative to COMMAND substitutions for handing over the results of one COMMAND to another. Other operators can also be implemented.

- The end of instructions has to be found during parsing. Usually, line ends or special characters (like ";") are used to mark an instruction end. A grouping can also mark an instruction end.

These COMMAND LANGUAGE elements are usually evaluated by the INTERPRETER before the COMMANDS are evaluated. In general, the INTERPRETER evaluates one instruction after another according to grouping and instruction end rules. Then it performs substitutions, if necessary. Finally, it finds the COMMAND in the instruction and invokes it with the rest of the instruction as arguments.

Note that all further syntactic elements, as well as the semantics of the COM-MAND LANGUAGE, must be well-defined, as in any other programming language. Finding the optimal syntax and semantics for a particular COMMAND LANGUAGE is beyond this pattern description, because these issues depend on the concrete, domain-specific tasks for which the COMMAND LANGUAGE is used. When the COMMAND LANGUAGE pattern is chosen as foundation of an integration architecture, there is one important rule, however: Before building a COMMAND LAN-GUAGE from scratch, one should always consider reusing an existing language that supports COMMAND execution, such as an extensible scripting language or an existing domain-specific language. It is often much easier to adapt an existing language infrastructure to the concrete requirements of a software system than to build a language implementation from scratch.

Consider again the simple example presented earlier. Using a COMMAND LAN-GUAGE, we can provide the dynamic expression by variable substitution (with '$') and pass the result of command1 as an argument to command2 (with '[...]'). These changes shorten the resulting code and make it much more readable:

```
if {$expression} {
   command2 [command1]
}
```

COMMAND LANGUAGE code is typically expressed as strings of the host language in which the COMMAND LANGUAGE is implemented. From within the host language, code can be evaluated in the COMMAND LANGUAGE, and the results of these evaluations can be obtained. A central strength of the COMMAND LANGUAGE is that scripts can be (dynamically) assembled in strings and (also dynamically) evaluated later in time. In other words, we can write dynamically assembled and evaluated programs in host languages that do not support this feature natively. For example, we can put the script just presented into a host language string, change this string at runtime, and evaluate it later in the program.

```
StringBuffer script =
   new StringBuffer("if {$expression} {command2 [command1]}");
...
// later change the script (here: append logging code)
script.append("\nputs \"evaluating expression: \$expression\"");
...
// later evalute the script
interpreter.eval(script.toString());
```

COMMANDS of a COMMAND LANGUAGE are typically implemented in the host language and bound to command names. The command names and implementations are registered in the INTERPRETER of the COMMAND LANGUAGE. When the INTERPRETER evaluates a COMMAND, it looks up the implementation registered for a command name and invokes it.

All language elements of the COMMAND LANGUAGE are usually implemented in the same way as user-defined COMMANDS. For example, control statements such as if or while are implemented as predefined COMMANDS. An if-command can be realized by first evaluating the expression given as first argument. If this expression returns true, the "then" part of the if-statement is evaluated in the INTERPRETER. An example is shown in Figure 14–2.

Interaction between code in the COMMAND LANGUAGE and the host language is sometimes necessary. Defining COMMANDS and using eval, as in the examples just shown, is one simple way of language integration. "Deeper" language integration is supported by the pattern SPLIT OBJECT. For all kinds of interaction, type conversion between the COMMAND LANGUAGE and the host language is necessary. This can be done by letting the user deal with type casting manually, or it can be automated using the pattern AUTOMATIC TYPE CONVERTER.

The PIGGYBACK pattern [Spinellis2001] uses the capabilities of a host language as a hosting base for a new language, such as a domain-specific language (DSL). The COMMAND LANGUAGE pattern follows the PIGGYBACK structure and uses COMMANDS to realize the definition of the new language. The LANGUAGE EXTENSION pattern, also described in [Spinellis2001], is used to add new features to an

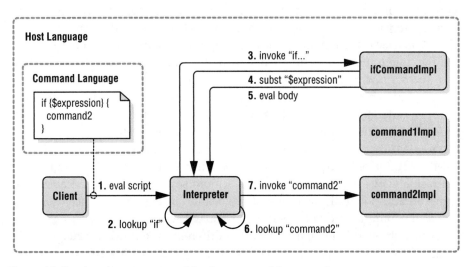

Figure 14–2 *A script gets executed by the command language interpreter*

existing language. It is thus a general alternative to defining a new language following the PIGGYBACK pattern, as described by the COMMAND LANGUAGE pattern.

Scenario Resolved

Consider again the following scenario: When using a COMMAND LANGUAGE to integrate multiple C components, we can flexibly assemble these components and change the COMMAND LANGUAGE scripts even at runtime. Once a C component is integrated in the COMMAND LANGUAGE, it can be used without C programming or recompilation. For example, the three COMMANDS in the example in Figure 14–2 are implemented in the host language and can be freely composed using scripts. These scripts can be provided as stand-alone scripts to the COMMAND LANGUAGE'S INTERPRETER, read from files, for example. Alternatively, they can be evaluated as strings of the host language using the host language API of the COMMAND LANGUAGE.

Consequences

COMMAND LANGUAGE composition is very flexible, because COMMAND LANGUAGE scripts can be evaluated and changed at runtime. COMMAND LANGUAGES are thus well suited for rapid prototyping and for implementing domain-specific languages. Any data can be treated as program code of a COMMAND LANGUAGE.

A COMMAND LANGUAGE is primarily designed for being easily extensible with COMMAND implementations. Thus, it is simple to extend the COMMAND LANGUAGE with new components, typically written in another language. This is usually done by registering COMMANDS with command names in the COMMAND LANGUAGE'S INTERPRETER. In many COMMAND LANGUAGES, solutions exist for automating the integration of components into the COMMAND LANGUAGES as new COMMANDS. How this is realized depends on the language features of the host language in which the COMMAND LANGUAGE is implemented. For example, a wrapper generator can be used, or if it is supported, reflection can be used for performing a runtime lookup of the COMMAND implementation.

COMMAND composition in the host language is very efficient, because COMMAND execution only requires one additional invocation in the host language. In contrast, a COMMAND LANGUAGE means a more severe overhead, because it requires an additional dispatch of each invocation in the COMMAND LANGUAGE as well as the interpretation of COMMAND LANGUAGE scripts.

Because the two languages have quite different tasks, each language can be designed for its particular task: the host language for writing efficient and reliable system components, and the COMMAND LANGUAGE for flexible component composition and other integration tasks.

When using a COMMAND LANGUAGE together with a host language, developers have to learn two languages. This is often not a great problem: Many COMMAND LANGUAGES are easy to learn because they a have a simple syntax, and only a limited number of language elements is required for COMMAND composition and configuration.

Implementing a COMMAND LANGUAGE from scratch might be a substantial effort, depending on the language features required. Thus, reusing an existing language infrastructure (such as an existing scripting language or domain-specific language) should be considered before implementing the language from scratch.

Using a COMMAND LANGUAGE consumes resources. Invocations that are sent through the COMMAND LANGUAGE have a weaker performance than directly invoked COMMANDS. The language implementation requires additional memory, too.

Known Uses

Some known uses of the pattern are as follows:

- Most scripting languages, such as Tcl, Python, and Perl are implemented as COMMAND LANGUAGES. That is, the language elements of the scripting language are implemented in another language; the languages named above are implemented in C. The INTERPRETER of the scripting language maps the command names in the scripts to the respective implementations in C. The scripting languages can thus be extended with new language elements implemented either in C or in the scripting language.

- A domain-specific language is a programming language tailored specifically to an application domain; it is not a general-purpose language. Many interpreted domain-specific languages are implemented as COMMAND LANGUAGES. This is because COMMAND LANGUAGES are easy to implement, easy to extend, or simply because another COMMAND LANGUAGE'S INTERPRETER is used for implementing the domain-specific language.

- The aspect-oriented framework of JAC [Pawlak+2001] implements a COMMAND LANGUAGE for aspect composition and configuration. Operations of an aspect component can thus be provided as command implementations and invoked from the configuration file. Each aspect can define its own "little" configuration language. This aspect can be configured with custom parameters and behavior without the need for programming and recompilation.

Component Wrapper

Context

A system is composed from a number of black-box components. Component configurations and other component variations are handled by parameterization using the components' interfaces.

Problem

You require a flexible composition of the system's components, but this is difficult if component variations can only be introduced using parameterizations or exchange of the component. This is because parameters have to be foreseen by the component developers and thus are not well suited for dealing with unanticipated changes. Exchanging the component often means rewriting the component from scratch. We need to somehow deal with unanticipated changes for a component without sacrificing the black-box property.

Scenario

Consider the following scenario: A company has two related products, one implemented in C and one in C++. Both are monoliths; each consists of a number of hard-wired subsystems. Consider that the systems should be evolved into a product line consisting of a number of products. It should be possible to flexibly assemble products according to customer demands. That is, it should be possible to compose new products from the existing system components. Composition often requires little extensions and changes to the existing components. The product line architecture should provide some concept for integrating components into products and for extending individual components in the context of a product with new state or behavior.

Forces

If the component's source code is available, one way to cope with unanticipated changes is to change the component itself. This is problematic, because the black-box property of the component should not be violated: Black-box reuse eases understandability because the component can be reused without intimate knowledge of the component's internals. The component's internal implementation can even be replaced by another implementation that allows us to get independent from implementation details. These are central reasons for using the component-based approach—and thus should not be sacrificed without need.

Components—especially third-party components—change over time. Even though the black-box abstraction aims at stable interfaces, often the interfaces change. The client's developer should be able to cope with these changes without having to seek access to components through the source code of the client. In many situations, one and the same client version has to deal with several component versions. In those cases, adaptations to interfaces and to relevant internal implementation details have to take place within the same client implementation. With techniques such as preprocessor directives or if/switch control structures, this may result in hard-to-read code.

A client of a black-box component usually should be independent of the internal implementation of the component. But sometimes implementation details of the component implementation, such as access to shared resources, performance issues, and memory consumption, do matter and need to be accessed somehow.

Solution

Let the access point to a component that is integrated into a system be a first-class object of the programming language. Indirection by a COMPONENT WRAPPER object gives the application a central, white-box access point to the component. Here, the component access can be customized without interfering with the client or the component implementation. Because all components are integrated in the same way, a variation point for white-box extension by the component's clients is provided for each black-box component in a system.

Discussion

The COMPONENT WRAPPER provides access to a component using the object abstraction of the component's client. A simple case is when both the component implementation and the component client use the same object abstraction; however, this is not always the case. In fact, a major goal of the COMPONENT WRAPPER pattern is to integrate components that are written in different paradigms and languages by using the same integration style. To reach this goal, the COMPONENT WRAPPER pattern can use some other patterns within its internal implementation (there are many other integration styles, though):

- In the simple case that another object-oriented component is integrated, the COMPONENT WRAPPER can use the PROXY pattern [Gamma+1995]. A PROXY is a placeholder object for another object offering the same interface. Note that a COMPONENT WRAPPER interface can also be different than the component's interface or only provide an excerpt of it, such as an "exported" interface. If two different object-oriented languages with slightly different object and type concepts are integrated, adaptations and type conversions can take place on the COMPONENT WRAPPER.

- When we want to integrate a procedural paradigm component into an object-oriented implementation, we apply the WRAPPER FACADE pattern [Schmidt+ 2000]. It uses one or more objects to represent a procedural component. The wrapper object forwards object-oriented messages to the procedures (or functions).

- If a COMMAND LANGUAGE is also used, the COMPONENT WRAPPERS can be exposed as COMMANDS of the COMMAND LANGUAGE. As a consequence, COMPONENT WRAPPERS can then be flexibly assembled using COMMAND LANGUAGE scripts. That is, two variability mechanisms are combined here: The COMPONENT WRAPPER allows for variation of the individual components and their integration in the system; the COMMAND LANGUAGE scripts allow for flexibly composing multiple COMPONENT WRAPPERS in the system. The COMPONENT WRAPPER is exposing the component's export interface as operations of the COMMAND, one for each exported functionality of the component. The arguments of the COMMAND in the COMMAND LANGUAGE script are used to dispatch the correct COMPONENT WRAPPER operation.

In each of the three variants, the COMPONENT WRAPPER can expose the same interface as the wrapped component (it is then a PROXY) or a different one. When changes to types of the interface are necessary during an invocation by a COMPONENT WRAPPER, the COMPONENT WRAPPER can either contain the conversion code or use an AUTOMATIC TYPE CONVERTER for the conversion.

COMPONENT WRAPPERS are used to provide a uniform way of wrapping blackbox components. The component client does not know about the style of wrapping or other implementation details. Moreover, the indirection to a COMPONENT WRAPPER object provides an accessible white box on the client side. This placeholder provides a central access point to the component. DECORATORS [Gamma+1995], ADAPTERS [Gamma+1995], MESSAGE INTERCEPTORS [Zdun2003b], and other kinds of extensions, variations, or customizations can be optionally added to the COMPONENT WRAPPER. Only changes that necessarily have to interfere with the component's internals cannot be handled this way.

COMPONENT WRAPPERS can easily be generated if the component's interface is electronically documented with an INTERFACE DESCRIPTION [Völter+2004]. The default implementation of such generated COMPONENT WRAPPERS just forwards the invocation to the component, but the client is able to extend the generated code. Using techniques such as subclassing, polymorphism, or MESSAGE INTERCEPTORS [Zdun2003b], we can avoid the problem that regenerated code overwrites client extensions of the COMPONENT WRAPPER.

Using COMPONENT WRAPPERS, we can modularize the "integration of another component" aspect. COMPONENT WRAPPERS are thus well suited to be applied together with an aspect-oriented approach [Kiczales+1997]. That is, an aspect composition framework can be used to weave the aspect represented by the COMPONENT WRAPPER into the system.

Scenario Resolved

Consider again the following scenario: Two monolithic products must be evolved into a product line architecture. This can be done in an incremental fashion using COMPONENT WRAPPERS: They are used to decouple the components of the legacy systems step by step. Figure 14–3 shows that COMPONENT WRAPPERS are implemented as part of the product line and instantiated by a new product. There is one COMPONENT WRAPPER for each of the export interfaces of the products. For the C product, the pattern WRAPPER FACADE is used, and for the C++ product, we use a PROXY. In the example, we can see that one COMPONENT WRAPPER performs an interface adaptation; the PROXY only forwards the invocation. On the COMPONENT WRAPPERS, individual products composed from the existing components can add behavior or state to the components.

Consequences

Customizability of black-box components is enhanced by using COMPONENT WRAPPERS. Different styles of wrapping are conceptually integrated from a component client's perspective. Application developers can flexibly adapt and change

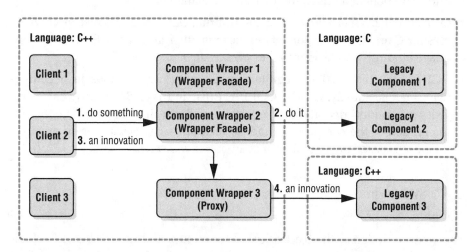

Figure 14–3 *A number of component wrappers are integrated into a C++/C system; some are wrapper facades, and some are proxies.*

component interfaces at a central access point. For example, slight version changes in component versions can be hidden by the COMPONENT WRAPPERS so that clients do not have to contain the adaptation code (such as #IFDEF directives). In other words, COMPONENT WRAPPERS reduce tangled code caused by component integration, composition, and configuration.

Using COMPONENT WRAPPERS, an external component is used as an internal, first-class entity of the object system. That is, once integrated, all external and internal components look the same to component clients. The component use is decoupled from the internal realization. Therefore, the component itself is exchangeable with another implementation.

The indirections to the COMPONENT WRAPPER slightly reduce performance. More classes and flexibility hooks can result in a higher complexity of the application and thus reduce understandability. COMPONENT WRAPPERS introduce additional code. Thus, there is more code to test and understand. Due to the indirection and the additional code, systems using COMPONENT WRAPPERS might be slightly harder to debug.

Known Uses

Some known uses of the pattern are:

- We have used the COMPONENT WRAPPER pattern in a reengineering project for a document archive system implemented in C [Goedicke+2002]. In this project, we use COMPONENT WRAPPERS for migrating the existing C implementation into a component architecture in a stepwise manner.

- SWIG [Swig2003] is a wrapper generator that can generate COMPONENT WRAPPERS for C and C++ components in various other languages. SWIG uses language bindings and header files as INTERFACE DESCRIPTIONS.

- VCF [Oberleitner+2003] integrates components from various Java component models, namely, COM+, CORBA, EJBs, and Java Beans. A FACADE provides a common denominator interface of the technologies to clients. For integration of the component models, the approach uses a plug-in architecture that is based on a number of COMPONENT WRAPPERS.

Object System Layer

Context

You want to design with object-oriented techniques and use the benefits of advanced object-oriented concepts. Parts of a system implementation are realized in a language that does not support object-orientation, such as C, Tcl, or COBOL, or the implementation is realized in an object system that does not support desired object-oriented techniques. For example, C++ and Object COBOL do not implement reflection or interception techniques, or foreign object concepts are used, such as those of a middleware system like CORBA.

Problem

Suppose you are faced with target programming languages that are non-object-oriented, or with legacy systems that cannot quickly be rewritten, or with target object systems that are not powerful enough or not properly integrated with other used object systems. But the target language is chosen for important technical or social reasons, such as integrating with legacy software, reusing knowledge of existing developers, and customer demands, so it cannot be changed. Somehow, the object-oriented and non-object-oriented concepts need to be integrated in one design and implementation model.

Scenario

Consider the following scenario: Legacy applications are often written in procedural languages such as C or COBOL. A complete migration of a system to a new object-oriented language often makes the integration with the existing legacy components difficult and forces a reimplementation of several well-functioning parts. The costs of such an evolution are often too high to permit even considering complete migration to object technology. Most often, the costs are very hard to estimate in advance.

Forces

Situations in which we require some integration with an object system include the following:

- Legacy systems offering no support for object-orientation need to be supported, even though many modern systems are based on object-oriented concepts.

- When two or more different object-oriented languages need to be integrated, we can use COMPONENT WRAPPERS for integration. However, we should avoid implementing this integration for each individual COMPONENT WRAPPER on its own.

- The need for integration of object concepts might also occur in only one object-oriented language when foreign object concepts need to be integrated. For example, the CORBA or COM object systems are not exactly the same as the object systems of object-oriented languages such as C++ or Java in which they are used. This problem arises for all kinds of technologies that introduce object concepts, such as distributed object systems, application servers, transaction monitors, and relational and object-oriented databases.

- Many applications use an object system of a mainstream programming language, such as C++, Java, or Object COBOL. Those object systems only implement standard object-oriented techniques. Thus, extensions of object concepts, such as interception techniques, reflection and introspection, role concepts, or aspect-orientation, are not provided natively.

Manual integration of object systems often means that developers are performing the integration over and over again, which is cumbersome and error-prone. Instead, the integration of object systems should be reusable.

Solution

Build or use an object system as a language extension in the host language and then implement the design on top of this OBJECT SYSTEM LAYER. Provide a well-defined interface to components that are non-object-oriented or implemented in other object systems. Make these components accessible through the OBJECT SYSTEM LAYER, and then the components can be treated as black boxes. The OBJECT SYSTEM LAYER acts as a layer of indirection for applying changes centrally.

Discussion

An OBJECT SYSTEM LAYER requires some dispatch mechanism that translates invocations in the host language into invocations to the objects of the OBJECT SYSTEM LAYER. This can be done using a MESSAGE REDIRECTOR [Goedicke+2001]. It acts as a FACADE [Gamma+1995] to the whole OBJECT SYSTEM LAYER and is not bypassed. For example, the MESSAGE REDIRECTOR invocations might be string-based messages that are translated into the respective invocations.

The OBJECT SYSTEM LAYER can be part of a COMMAND LANGUAGE if the COMMAND LANGUAGE implements an object system. Then the OBJECT SYSTEM LAYER'S MESSAGE REDIRECTOR is part of the COMMAND LANGUAGE'S INTERPRETER. Once a script is parsed, the INTERPRETER uses a MESSAGE REDIRECTOR to indirect the invocation to the implementation of the COMMAND LANGUAGE element. A typical integration of the patterns OBJECT SYSTEM LAYER and COMMAND LANGUAGE uses one object per COMMAND, and the command name is used as an object ID for the OBJECT SYSTEM LAYER object.

The SPLIT OBJECT pattern is used if the OBJECT SYSTEM LAYER needs to be integrated with a host language object system. Using COMPONENT WRAPPERS, foreign paradigm elements such as procedural APIs can be integrated into the OBJECT SYSTEM LAYER'S object system.

Besides the conceptual integration with host language concepts, an OBJECT SYSTEM LAYER also must deal with other potential mismatches of the host language and the OBJECT SYSTEM LAYER'S model. For example, mismatches in the threading models or mismatches in transaction contexts must be resolved.

The OBJECT SYSTEM LAYER can be used to introduce extensions of the object concept of an object-oriented language. Typical examples are the introduction of runtime dynamic object and class concepts such as TYPE OBJECTS [Johnson+1998], ADAPTIVE OBJECT MODEL [Yoder+2002], role concepts, or MESSAGE INTERCEPTORS [Zdun2003b].

Many technologies integrated into a system, such as distributed object systems, application servers, transaction monitors, and databases, implement an OBJECT SYSTEM LAYER. If needed, an OBJECT SYSTEM LAYER can also be introduced as a superset of (a part of) two or more object concepts and used for integrating them. For example, the OBJECT SYSTEM LAYERS of technologies that are implemented in multiple languages, such as distributed object frameworks, are primarily used for integrating the object concepts of these languages.

Scenario Resolved

Consider again the following scenario: Procedural components must be composed using object-oriented concepts. An OBJECT SYSTEM LAYER can be used for this purpose, as depicted in Figure 14–4. The benefit is that we do not have to translate the system into an object-oriented language completely. Instead, existing components can be incrementally evolved; others can stay in the procedural language and be integrated into the OBJECT SYSTEM LAYER using COMPONENT WRAPPERS.

Consequences

When using an OBJECT SYSTEM LAYER, the flexibility of the application can be improved, since the OBJECT SYSTEM LAYER allows us to introduce variation points and to implement high-level language constructs such as interception, reflection, and adaptation techniques.

The complexity of the application can be reduced, because—in scenarios where they are really needed—more high-level concepts, such as roles, interceptors, or aspects, can simplify the program code and eliminate the need for complex workarounds.

The complexity of the application can also increase if the client has to maintain the OBJECT SYSTEM LAYER. Issues such as garbage collection, object destruction,

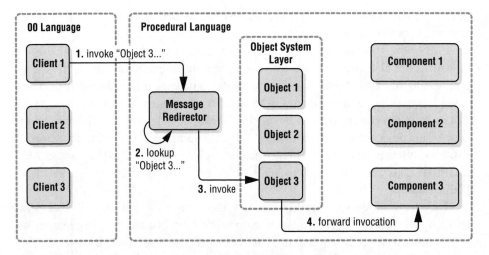

Figure 14–4 *An object system layer is embedded in a procedural language*

relationship dynamics, reflection, and so forth then have to be programmed by hand. But this problem can be avoided by using an existing OBJECT SYSTEM LAYER as a library.

Performance can be decreased due to additional indirections.

The OBJECT SYSTEM LAYER's conventions and interfaces have to be learned by the developers in addition to the system's APIs.

Known Uses

Some known uses of the pattern are the following:

- Object-oriented scripting languages implemented in C, such as Python or XOTcl [Neumann+2000], provide an OBJECT SYSTEM LAYER for C. These languages provide a C API—that means the object models can be accessed and used from C for using object-oriented abstractions in C programs.

- The Redland RDF library [Beckett2004] implements a simple OBJECT SYSTEM LAYER for C to use object-oriented abstractions for RDF nodes, models, streams, and other elements of the library. The library implements classes, object IDs, constructors, and destructors.

- Procedural implementations of object-oriented middleware, such as C or Tcl implementations of CORBA or Web services, provide the object abstractions of the middleware in the procedural language. Thus, in the distributed context, these implementations provide an OBJECT SYSTEM LAYER.

Automatic Type Converter

Context

Languages or systems supporting different types are used in one system.

Problem

When two different types of systems must be integrated, it is necessary to convert corresponding types. An INTERFACE DESCRIPTION can be used to describe the type differences, and the corresponding type conversion code can be generated. Conversion code for each particular invocation can only be generated, however, if the signatures of all operations are known during generation. Sometimes operation signatures are not known before runtime. In many integration situations, it is also necessary for it to be easy to add new type bindings rapidly.

Scenario

Consider the following scenarios:

* In Web services frameworks, remote invocations and other messages are transferred using SOAP [Box+2000] as a XML-based payload format. In SOAP, invocations containing parameter and return types are encoded in string format. To be interpreted by a programming language, the SOAP messages must be converted to native programming language formats. From an INTERFACE DESCRIPTION, we can generate client proxy and server stubs that perform the type conversion. This, however, only works if the types are known before runtime. For dynamic deployment of services, we basically have two choices: We can generate a server stub while the system runs or perform type conversions at runtime.

* A COMMAND LANGUAGE is embedded in a statically typed language. The COMMAND LANGUAGE is given in form of scripts that are interpreted at runtime. That is, all types to be accessed by the COMMAND LANGUAGE need to be dynamically convertible to and from strings. To ease type integration, it should be simple to integrate new types.

Forces

Different languages support different types that cannot be exchanged directly. This problem also arises for other systems supporting types—not only for programming languages. For example, most distributed object frameworks support their own type system for integration across languages or platforms. Systems supporting dynamic types—for example, using the patterns TYPE OBJECT [Johnson+1998] or ADAPTIVE OBJECT MODEL [Yoder+2002]—require some way to cast the dynamic types into other dynamic types or static types of the host language. Some languages and typed systems only support canonical types such as strings. To integrate them with a strongly typed system, we need to convert the types to the canonical format and vice versa.

When an INTERFACE DESCRIPTION of all operation signatures exists, an option is to generate the type conversion code. This option is often chosen, for example, in the proxies and stubs generated by many distributed object frameworks. However, this does not work for more dynamic or complex type conversion situations. For example, generation is not as well suited for dynamic typing or runtime deployment, because here the operation signatures are not known before runtime of the system. Note that runtime generation of conversion code is possible—it is just more complex than writing simple wrappers.

Also, it is necessary in many cases to provide a very simple kind of type conversion, because it should be easily extensible: Only the type binding and the conversion code should be needed to be specified.

Solution

Provide an AUTOMATIC TYPE CONVERTER as a means to convert an instance of a particular type supported by the AUTOMATIC TYPE CONVERTER to a particular target type, and vice versa. The AUTOMATIC TYPE CONVERTER is either extensible with new type bindings for one-to-one transformations, or it converts every type to a canonical format, such as strings, and can convert the canonical format to any supported type. If no user-defined type binding is found, the AUTOMATIC TYPE CONVERTER should execute a default conversion routine.

Discussion

In general, an AUTOMATIC TYPE CONVERTER should be able to deal with all kinds of conversions that occur at runtime, because manual intervention is not possible at runtime and a conversion that fails leads to a runtime error. That is, all kinds of AUTOMATIC TYPE CONVERTERS should always provide a default conversion routine that takes place when no custom type binding is defined. Hooks for type conversion are provided so that users can extend the type converter with additional conversions.

There are two main variants of AUTOMATIC TYPE CONVERTERS:

• There might be a canonical format, such as strings, void* in C/C++, Object in Java, supported by the AUTOMATIC TYPE CONVERTER and a number of other types. The AUTOMATIC TYPE CONVERTER can convert any type to the canonical format and the canonical format to any type. This way, any type can be converted into any other type by a two-step conversion. Note that it is the developer's responsibility to provide sensible canonical representations of the various types that allow for conversion without information loss and that are efficient. Also, it is the developer's burden to request only sensible conversions. For example, converting a whole database into an in-memory string representation is problematic; it might be better to convert a database handle only. The system must be designed in such a way that continuous back-and-forth conversions are avoided where possible.

- An alternative to using a canonical format is to use direct, one-to-one conversion. This is usually faster, because only one conversion is required. The drawback of this variant is that we might have to write more converters: If each type can be mapped to each other type, we have to write $N * (N - 1)$ converters, instead of $2 * N$ converters, needed to support a canonical format. Therefore, one-to-one conversion is often chosen if there is only one target type for each type. A second reason for using one-to-one conversion is that specialties of the individual types must be considered during conversion, for example, because information would get lost during conversion to a canonical format. Finally, a third reason for choosing one-to-one conversion might be the better performance, because conversion to/from the intermediate canonical representation can be avoided.

An AUTOMATIC TYPE CONVERTER can also be used for more than two types. Thus, for example, it can also be used to implement polymorphism for TYPE OBJECTS [Johnson+1998] or other dynamic typing solutions. The AUTOMATIC TYPE CONVERTER can convert an object to all types supported by its classes and delivers the casted type, as requested by the client. This is useful if an AUTOMATIC TYPE CONVERTER is combined with an OBJECT SYSTEM LAYER or SPLIT OBJECTS.

A COMMAND LANGUAGE implemented in a host language usually requires an AUTOMATIC TYPE CONVERTER. In this scenario, the canonical format variant is often supported because the COMMAND LANGUAGE scripts are represented as strings, and these strings can be used as a canonical format. Thus, the AUTOMATIC TYPE CONVERTER is used as a mechanism to exchange data, specify operation parameters, and receive operation results between a COMMAND LANGUAGE and its host language.

An AUTOMATIC TYPE CONVERTER is a flexible alternative to type conversion code generated from an INTERFACE DESCRIPTION. In many cases, generated type conversion code uses the AUTOMATIC TYPE CONVERTER internally. An AUTOMATIC TYPE CONVERTER can also use INTERFACE DESCRIPTIONS as an aid in the type conversion decision.

The pattern CONTENT CONVERTER [Vogel+2002] is a similar pattern describing content integration. It also can be used with a canonical format or using one-to-one integration. If the content of a CONTENT CONVERTER is typed, an AUTOMATIC TYPE CONVERTER can be used as part of a CONTENT CONVERTER used for the type conversion task.

Scenario Resolved

Consider again the following scenarios:

- In a Web services framework, we usually can map every programming language type to one type in the INTERFACE DESCRIPTION. Thus, here we can use a one-to-one converter between INTERFACE DESCRIPTION type, transmitted over the network, and the type of the programming language.

- A COMMAND LANGUAGE needs to be integrated with a statically typed language. The COMMAND LANGUAGE uses scripts consisting of strings. Thus, for each host language type that we want to expose, we need a converter that converts the host language type to strings and from strings. Figure 14–5 sketches a solution using a string representation as a canonical format. Each AUTOMATIC TYPE CONVERTER object internally has two representations: a string representation and an internal representation containing the target type of the statically typed host language. The AUTOMATIC TYPE CONVERTER class provides an operation for converting the internal representation to strings, an

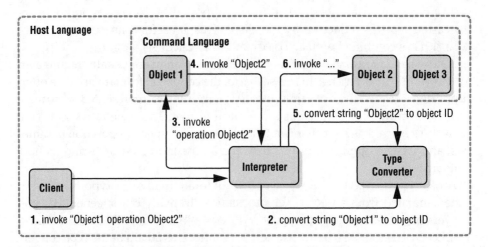

Figure 14–5 *A host language client invokes a command language object and the interpreter performs automatic type conversions*

operation for converting strings to the internal representation, getter/setter operations for both representations, and operations for discarding one of the two representations. At each point in time, at least one of the two representations must be valid.

Consequences

An AUTOMATIC TYPE CONVERTER is in many scenarios slower than a solution generated from an INTERFACE DESCRIPTION because it performs the conversion at runtime, whereas the generated solution only performs a single cast. The benefit of an AUTOMATIC TYPE CONVERTER is that it is more flexible than generated solutions. This way, dynamic typing can be supported. Type mappings can be changed at runtime. Also, the type mappings in an AUTOMATIC TYPE CONVERTER are easy to extend.

Known Uses

Some known uses of the pattern are as follows:

- The scripting language Tcl uses an AUTOMATIC TYPE CONVERTER for converting the string-based scripts to native types in C and vice versa. Strings are used as a canonical format.

- IONA Artix is a Web services framework that supports conversion between different protocols (HTTP, IIOP, WebSphere MQ, Tuxedo, etc.) and payload formats (SOAP, Tuxedo's FML, GIOP, etc.). To increase conversion performance, Artix uses one-to-one converters. An AUTOMATIC TYPE CONVERTER for each converter is needed to recognize the types in one payload format and translate them into the target format.

- Apache Axis is a Web services framework that uses AUTOMATIC TYPE CONVERTERS for one-to-one conversion between programming language types in Java and the payload format SOAP.

Split Object

Context

Two languages need to be used together in one system.

Problem

To integrate two languages, one can write simple wrappers that allow for invocations in the other language. However, pure wrapping poses some problems in more complex language integration situations. A wrapper provides only a "shallow" interface into a system, and it does not reflect further semantics of the two languages. Examples of such semantics are class hierarchies or delegation relationships. Further, a wrapper does not allow one to introspect the system's structure. The logical object identity between wrapper and its wrappees is not explicit. Complex wrappers that are implemented manually are hard to maintain.

Scenario

Consider the following scenario: One language embeds another language, such as a COMMAND LANGUAGE that is embedded in a host language for configuring host language objects. That is, the COMMAND LANGUAGE requires access to its host language, and vice versa. Here "access" means, for example, performing lookups, invocations, creations, and destructions of objects and methods.

Forces

A main driving force for considering deeper language integration than COMPONENT WRAPPERS is that it is cumbersome to write wrappers for each and every element that requires language integration. To a certain degree, wrappers can be generated, but still we would require custom code for each language integration situation. Instead, it should be possible to reuse language integration code. Automation and reuse would also foster maintainability; in general, complex wrapping structures can quickly get quite complex and thus hard to maintain. Scattering wrapping code across the functional code should particularly be avoided.

Simple wrappers are usually realized by a single indirection, and thus they are relatively fast and consume little extra memory. A deeper language integration needs to be compared to simpler wrapper solutions with regard to resource consumption.

Solution

A SPLIT OBJECT is an object that physically exists as an instance in two languages but is logically treated like a single instance. Both SPLIT OBJECT halves can delegate invocations to the other half. The SPLIT OBJECT halves mimic the user-defined class hierarchy of the counterpart, variables are automatically traced or shared, and methods can be wrapped. Depending on the language features of the two languages, these functionalities can either be implemented by extending the language's dispatch process, using reflection, or using program generation.

Discussion

There are different ways for a SPLIT OBJECT half to communicate with its counterpart in the other language:

- A method can be provided, for example, by a superclass of all SPLIT OBJECTS, that allows for sending an invocation to the other half. The invocation parameters are usually provided as arguments using a generic type (such as strings or Object in Java) and converted using an AUTOMATIC TYPE CONVERTER. Depending on the language features, the method implementation on the other split object half can be looked up using reflection, using a dynamic dispatch mechanism, using a registration in a method table (provided by the developer), or using a generated method table.

- A wrapper generator can generate a method on a SPLIT OBJECT half for each exported method of the other SPLIT OBJECT half. This generated method is a simple forwarder to the other split object half. The invocation parameters can be provided using the correct types required by the counterpart, if possible, or an AUTOMATIC TYPE CONVERTER may be needed for conversion. This variant is very efficient because it requires no dynamic lookup.

- If the language's dispatch mechanism can be extended and method dispatch is performed at runtime, we can implement an automatic forwarding mechanism. Whenever a method cannot be found for the SPLIT OBJECT half, the "method not found" error is not raised directly, but it is first tried in order to find the method on the other SPLIT OBJECT half. If this succeeds, the method is invoked there, if not, the error is raised. In this variant, the same means for method lookup as in the first alternative can be used.

- In dynamic languages (e.g., a COMMAND LANGUAGE), wrapper methods can also be generated at runtime. Again, these methods are simple forwarders, as in the second alternative, but the means for method lookup described in the first alternative are used.

Note that clients recognize that the object does not itself implement the method only in the first variant; in the following three variants, the client can use the same invocation style as used for methods implemented in the same language. SPLIT OBJECTS assume a language integration structure following the PIGGYBACK pattern [Spinellis2001]. This pattern generally describes how to use the capabilities of a host language as a hosting base for a new language, such as a domain-specific language (DSL) or a COMMAND LANGUAGE.

In many cases, split object halves will mimic the user-defined class hierarchy of the other half. For example, when you generate forwarder methods to the other split object half, you face the problem of name clashes: Methods on different classes of one object might have the same name. This problem does not arise if every class for which a forwarder method is generated exists within both languages. For this to work, to a certain extent we need to integrate the class concepts of the two languages. For example, if one language supports multiple inheritance, and the other does not, we need to simulate multiple inheritance in the other language. To mimic a class hierarchy in a procedural language or integrate different class concepts in two object-oriented languages, you might consider implementing a simple OBJECT SYSTEM LAYER.

From the COMMAND LANGUAGE, we can automatically forward invocations into the host language. In turn, ordinary host language invocations bypass the SPLIT OBJECT in the COMMAND LANGUAGE. Thus, from within the host language, we have to use the INTERPRETER'S eval method to access a SPLIT OBJECT. To avoid this additional invocation style, the pattern HOOK INJECTOR [Zdun2003b] can be used to replace host language invocations with indirections to SPLIT OBJECTS.

Scenario Resolved

Consider again the following scenario: When integrating a COMMAND LANGUAGE with a host language, we can provide a method for invoking the COMMAND LANGUAGE from the host language. The COMMAND LANGUAGE object in turn provides an automatic forwarding mechanism to invoke the host language half of a SPLIT OBJECT. As an example, Figure 14–6 shows a host language client that needs to invoke a host language object Object1. This object is a SPLIT OBJECT: Instead of invoking this object directly, the counterpart in the COMMAND LANGUAGE is in-

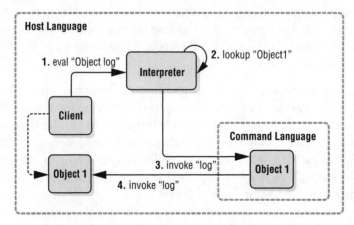

Figure 14–6 *Invoking a split object through the command language*

voked first, which forwards the invocation back into the host language. This way, the COMMAND LANGUAGE can intercept the invocation.

Consequences

SPLIT OBJECTS can be used to deeply integrate two object systems. Concepts realized in one object system can be used from within the other object system. The language integration code in the SPLIT OBJECT implementation can be reused. Thus, language integration is easier to apply and the code is easier to maintain than integration code based on COMPONENT WRAPPERS only. SPLIT OBJECTS can be used as a model to automate wrapper generation for two languages.

Working with two languages might make debugging more difficult, because you have to align the debugging information in the two languages and maybe even integrate debugging tools. On the other hand, SPLIT OBJECTS can even be used to provide debugging information for other languages (see [Zdun2004a] for examples).

SPLIT OBJECTS pose a memory and performance overhead. This overhead can be minimized by not using dynamic lookup and dispatch mechanisms and using generative techniques instead. However, generated code is hard to change at runtime (if this is possible at all); that is, using generative techniques means less flexibility.

Known Uses

Some known uses of the pattern are:

- The network simulator [UCB2000a] and Open Mash [OpenMash2000] are two projects that are implemented in C++ and use OTcl [Wetherall+1995] for configuring and customizing the C++ applications. The integration of the two languages is performed by a SPLIT OBJECT solution called Tclcl [UCB2000b].

- Split objects are also used for dynamically performing maintenance tasks such as component testing, feature tracing, and variation and configuration management [Zdun2004a]. For example, the language Frag [Zdun2003a] is used to configure and compose AspectJ [Kiczales+2001] aspects dynamically to perform these tasks in Java.

- The Redland RDF library [Beckett2004] contains a C-based OBJECT SYSTEM LAYER. The Perl interface to that system uses a hand-built SPLIT OBJECT solution: When a Perl wrapper is created, the respective C-based object is created as well—object IDs are thus mapped one to one. Similarly, the C destructors are automatically invoked in the correct order upon destruction of the Perl wrapper object.

Known Uses and Technology Projections

In this section, we discuss some known uses and examples for the patterns in an integrated manner. We concentrate on a few interesting technology projections from the areas of distributed object frameworks, reengineering, scripting languages, configuration and composition of components, and dynamic aspect configurations. There are many other systems in each of these areas using some of the patterns described in this chapter.

Reengineering a Document Archive System

We have reengineered a documented archive system implemented in C to a component-oriented architecture [Goedicke+2002]. An important concern in this project was incremental evolution of the system. Here, the pattern COMPONENT WRAPPER played a central role. The idea was to start off with simplistic wrappers, in particular WRAPPER FACADES for the original procedural components—these were more or less similar to the original subsystems of the system. The COMPONENT WRAPPERS provided a means of unifying wrapping styles and handling extensions or adaptations. For example, they allowed us to deal with situations in which different component versions had to be supported, interface changes had to be handled, and components with other wrapper styles had to be integrated.

To objectify the system, we applied the pattern OBJECT SYSTEM LAYER. We provided a simple object system with which the components can be treated in an object-oriented manner and easily integrated with the object systems of distributed object systems (in [Goedicke+2002]: CORBA).

New requirements impose changes on the wrappers constantly. Such extensions or adaptations can be transparently handled by MESSAGE INTERCEPTORS [Zdun2003b]. Here, the pattern OBJECT SYSTEM LAYER is beneficial again, because the MESSAGE REDIRECTOR of the OBJECT SYSTEM LAYER can be used to apply the MESSAGE INTERCEPTORS. It can also trigger an AUTOMATIC TYPE CONVERTER where necessary.

Hardware Selection for an MHP Product Line

The TPMHP project [Goedicke+2004] is concerned with developing a product line of software components for the Multimedia Home Platform (MHP) [ETSI2001]. The MHP specification is a generic set of APIs for digital content broadcast applications, interaction via a return channel, and Internet access on an MHP terminal. Typical MHP terminals are, for example, digital set-top boxes, integrated digital TV sets, and multimedia PCs. The MHP standard defines a client-side software layer for MHP terminal implementations, including the platform architecture, an embedded Java virtual machine implementation running DVB-J applications, broadcast channel protocols, interaction channel protocols, content formats, application management, security aspects, a graphics model, and a GUI framework.

Even though there are just a few MHP set-top boxes available right now, a great diversity of products can be foreseen in this field. In addition, there will be a great number of supporting systems, such as input devices. The whole variety of different TV systems and PCs also might be used as an MHP client platform.

Software products that should run on a MHP platform need to consider multiple kinds of variations regarding the hardware environment. As MHP applications are broadcasted, the earliest possible binding time for the variation points is during startup of the application on the client platform.

Let us consider a few typical hardware selection problems. Different input devices offer various input events, and the MHP application needs to dynamically configure itself to these hardware elements. Graphical elements in the MHP API include a few graphic functions of Java as well as the more advanced GUI elements of the HAVI standard [HAVI2001]. It depends on the type of set-top box if HAVI is supported or GUI elements have to be painted using the graphic functions of Java. Different back-channels can be identified at runtime and may in some situations be handled differently.

In pure Java, these issues are typically handled by loose associations with objects. This, however, does not provide a central variation point management architecture that, for example, supports querying various hardware options or reconfiguring them at runtime with a common model.

The solution, proposed in [Goedicke+2004], is to use a COMMAND LANGUAGE to handle the composition and configuration tasks for hardware-related software components. We use scripts like the following example for behavioral compositions and configurations:

```
...
MHPButton create OK -set parent OKBOX
MHPButton create CANCEL -set parent OKBOX
if {$earlyVisible == 1} {
  CANCEL setVisible
  OK setVisible
}
...
```

In the script, two button components are created and composed with another component OKBOX. Then the components are configured conditionally: If the variable `earlyVisible` is true, the configuration option `visible` is set on both components.

Scripts like this example can be rapidly composed and changed, and they can be stored in a central repository. COMPONENT WRAPPERS for the respective GUI components (such as the `MHPButton` in the example) are implemented in Java. Both types, HAVI and Graphics, support a common interface. In the COMPONENT WRAPPERS, the common interface is mapped to the HAVI API or the Java-based Graphics API, respectively:

```
class HAVI_Button implements MHP_Button {
  HtextButton button;
  // use HAVI HtextButton to draw a button
  ...
}
class Graphics_Button implements MHP_Button {
  // use Graphics API to draw a button
  ...
}
```

The COMPONENT WRAPPERS are integrated into the COMMAND LANGUAGE as SPLIT OBJECTS. Each SPLIT OBJECT realizes one COMMAND in the COMMAND LANGUAGE. At application startup, we can select which of the two COMPONENT WRAPPER sets is bound to the COMMANDS. That is, we can use the COMPONENT WRAPPER indirection to select between the HAVI implementation and the Graphics implementation at runtime. The same COMMAND LANGUAGE scripts can be used for both implementations.

The resulting object structure of the example, if HAVI is selected, is shown in Figure 14–7.

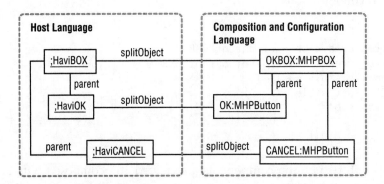

Figure 14–7 *Object structure of the example*

Let's compare the solution briefly to composition and configuration using hard-coded invocations in Java. The solution has many benefits; behavioral composition and configuration is not tangled in the business logic code. Thus, the solution fosters understandability and maintainability. The developer does not have to attend at all to language integration; this is done automatically by using the SPLIT OBJECT solution. The solution is thus easy to use. The composition and configuration behavior can be changed at runtime. Thus, the solution supports unanticipated software evolution. There are a few disadvantages as well; each composition and configuration object consumes memory, and invocations routed through two languages are slower than invocation performed in only one language. This is not a big drawback, because it only applies to composition and configuration code, which is not a large part of the system and does not affect performance-critical parts of the system. A second drawback is that more learning effort is required; developers must learn the Java MHP system plus the configuration options and the COMMAND LANGUAGE syntax. Overall, the benefits outweigh the drawbacks in this example.

TclCL and XOTcl/SWIG

TclCL [UCB2000b] is an integration of OTcl [Wetherall+1995] and C++. It utilizes SPLIT OBJECTS for language integration. TclCL is used as follows:

- Mash [OpenMash2000] is a streaming media toolkit for distributed collaboration applications based on the Internet Mbone tools and protocols.

- The Network Simulator (NS) [UCB2000a] supports network simulation including TCP, routing, multicast, network emulation, and animation.

In both projects, TclCL is applied to utilize the two language concept. The COMMAND LANGUAGE OTcl is used for high-level tasks such as configuration and testing, and C++ is used for the efficient implementation of the core tasks as C++ COMMANDS. The user-defined OTcl classes mimic the C++ class hierarchy. This is mainly done because the C++ variables/methods can be dynamically registered for OTcl in the C++ constructors of the respective classes. The OTcl counterpart remembers the capabilities of the C++ half and thus can forward invocations that are implemented on the C++ half into the other language. OTcl is an OBJECT SYSTEM LAYER that adds dynamic object-oriented language concepts to the static languages C and C++.

XOTcl [Neumann+2000] is the successor of the language OTcl. We have implemented a C++/XOTcl binding using the wrapper generator SWIG [Swig2003]. This project has similar goals and a similar architecture as the TclCl solution just explained. The main difference is that in this solution the variable/method bindings are not registered in the C++ constructors but are generated from an INTERFACE DESCRIPTION (the SWIG header file—which is similar to a C++ header file).

As Tcl extensions, both OTcl and XOTcl use strings in scripts to represent primitive data types. Internally, all primitive data types of XOTcl, such as ints, floats, doubles, booleans, strings, lists, and XOTcl objects, are presented by so-called `Tcl_Objs`. These are AUTOMATIC TYPE CONVERTERS that contain data structures for a string representation and an internal representation for the respective type implemented in C. They also contain conversion routines for each type to strings and for strings to each type—also implemented in C. `Tcl_Objs` use an abstract interface—using C function pointers—so that the Tcl INTERPRETER can automatically convert each type without knowing any more details of the types.

Configuring Aspects using Split Objects

A more sophisticated SPLIT OBJECT solution [Zdun2004a] is implemented in Frag [Zdun2003a]. Frag is a Tcl variant that can be completely embedded in Java. It is implemented on top of Jacl [DeJong+2003], a Tcl INTERPRETER implemented in Java. Frag also exploits SPLIT OBJECTS for language integration, but in contrast to the OTcl and XOTcl solutions just explained, it does not use registration or generative programming for access to the other SPLIT OBJECT half—it uses Java Reflection. Frag can thus be embedded in Java as a COMMAND LANGUAGE and be dynamically connected to Java classes.

Within Frag, a Frag class `JavaClass` is provided. This class is used for wrapping a Java class with a Frag object. When an object is derived from this class or any of its subclasses, a SPLIT OBJECT consisting of a Java half and a Frag half is created.

All SPLIT OBJECTS in Frag inherit from a class `Java`. The method `dispatcher` of the class `Java` is responsible for forwarding all invocations that cannot otherwise be dispatched to the Java half. `dispatcher` is automatically invoked as a default behavior when a method cannot be dispatched in Frag. Both, wrapping a Java class and forwarding invocations, are implemented using Java reflection. Internally, primitive Java types are automatically converted to and from strings. Non-primitive Java types have to be used as SPLIT OBJECTS in order to be accessed from Frag.

Figure 14–8 shows the structure for an example Java class `AJavaClass` that has a SPLIT OBJECT in Frag.

When the goal is to configure a Java application, typically the Frag scripts are used from within Java. However, Java invocations require the developer to

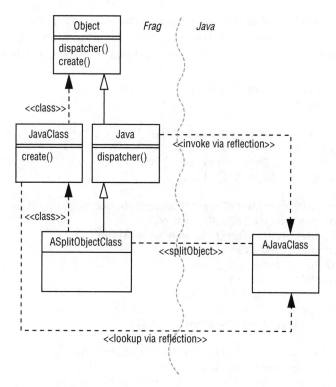

Figure 14–8 *Frag split object structures example*

know which objects are SPLIT OBJECTS. Consider a Java object `circle` that is defined as a SPLIT OBJECT; the following Java invocation is performed:

```
circle.setRadius(2.0);
```

This Java invocation bypasses the COMMAND LANGUAGE Frag. What would be needed instead is an invocation sent through the COMMAND LANGUAGE:

```
frag.eval("circle setRadius 2.0");
```

The pattern HOOK INJECTOR [Zdun2003b] provides a solution. For different languages, different tools exist that can perform static hook injections. For example, for Java we can use AspectJ. The following aspect associates statically with a Frag INTERPRETER. It contains one advice that is invoked before the constructors of user-defined classes. It calls `makeSplitObject` to create a SPLIT OBJECT half in

Frag. All other methods of the user-defined classes are intercepted by an around advice. The method invokeSplitObject sends the invocation to the SPLIT OBJECT half first, and if next is invoked, it is sent to the Java implementation as well.

```
abstract aspect FragSplitObject {
  static Frag frag;
  ...
  protected static void makeSplitObject(
    JoinPoint jp, Object o) {...}
  protected static Object invokeSplitObject(
    JoinPoint jp, Object o) {...}

  abstract pointcut splitObjectClasses(Object obj);
  pointcut theConstructors(Object obj):
    splitObjectClasses(obj) && execution(new(..));
  pointcut theMethods(Object obj):
    splitObjectClasses(obj) &&
    execution(* *(..)) &&
    !execution(String toString());
  before(Object obj): theConstructors(obj) {
    makeSplitObject(thisJoinPoint, obj);
  }
  Object around(Object obj) : theMethods(obj) &&
    !cflow(execution(* invokeSplitObject(..))) {
      return invokeSplitObject(thisJoinPoint, obj);
  }
}
```

Note that this aspect excerpt is simplified. The actual aspect implementation in the Frag distribution is more complex because it treats all Java primitive types by separate pointcuts and advices. (This terminology stems from AspectJ [Kiczales+2001]).

The aspect is defined as an abstract aspect. In concrete aspects, the pointcut splitObjectClasses is refined. Here, the classes can be defined by the user to which the aspect is applied. For example, we can apply the split objects to the classes Circle and Square:

```
public aspect FragSplitObjectCircleSquare
  extends FragSplitObject {
  pointcut splitObjectClasses(Object obj):
    this(obj) &&
    (within(Circle) || within(Square));
  ...
}
```

The default behavior of this aspect is that all invocations are sent through the COMMAND LANGUAGE, but the invocations are not altered. By redefining the classes in the dynamic Frag language, one can dynamically compose the internals of the aspect. Thus, here we have applied the SPLIT OBJECT pattern for integrating AspectJ aspect with the Frag COMMAND LANGUAGE. That is, we can compose and configure aspect implementations dynamically at runtime. The same Frag code used for specifying a Java aspect can also be used to specify an aspect in another language (e.g., Tcl, C, or C++). We only have to use another aspect framework for weaving the aspect.

Semantic Lookup Service

In many distributed systems, servers offer services to clients. Time and again, services get added or removed. Clients need to know which services are currently offered by which server application running at which location. To allow for efficient, inexpensive, and timely publication of services, the LOOKUP pattern is used as a service by most distributed object frameworks (see [Völter+2004]). Typical implementations of lookup services, such as naming or trading services, can be queried using a name (or a set of properties). As a result of the lookup, the ABSOLUTE OBJECT REFERENCE [Völter+2004] of a remote object matching the query is returned, or other location information such as an INTERFACE DESCRIPTION [Völter+2004] like a WSDL-file.

Today, we see many new requirements for lookup services arising that are due to new kinds of applications for these services and new lookup requirements. For example, Web services frameworks and other emerging kinds of middleware, such as P2P systems, GRIDs, or spontaneous networks, require highly dynamic lookup repositories with services that can connect, disconnect, move, and change their properties dynamically. In many existing lookup implementations, however, the properties and relationships of elements in the lookup service are too simple or hard to extend. Also, more advanced lookup functionality might be needed, such as ontology-based queries, behavioral extension, query extension, load-balancing, and fault tolerance. This requires high flexibility with regard to inputs, processing, and outputs of the lookup service.

This section discusses a semantic lookup service [Zdun2004b] that is used to cope with these challenges. The basic idea is to make the lookup service itself an extensible Semantic Web repository and make it programmable at runtime. We offer the Redland RDF store [Beckett2004] remotely, in which we can define resources and resource relationships according to different Semantic Web ontologies, such as RDFS, OWL, Dublin Core, or LOM. In contrast to most existing solutions in the Semantic Web area, we do not use a logic reasoner; we use an OBJECT SYSTEM LAYER as part of a COMMAND LANGUAGE that provides a dynamic, imperative interface to the RDF repository.

As a solution to these problems, we use mobile code that is sent from the client to the server, and an INTERPRETER on the server side for interpreting the lookup queries. In particular, this architecture consists of the following components:

- All metadata about the services is stored in an *RDF store* (the Redland RDF store [Beckett2004]), which stores semantic metadata about Web resources described in some ontology or schema.

- The RDF store is accessed on the server side using a *script interpreter* (the XOTcl [Neumann+2000] INTERPRETER is used here). Queries are executed in a (safe) sub-interpreter that can read the data from the RDF store. Each script interpreter runs in its own thread of control to make the architecture scalable and efficient.

- A *remote query interface* is offered so that remote clients can send scripts to the lookup service. The lookup service evaluates the scripts using its embedded script interpreter.

Figure 14–9 shows how these components are assembled to a remote service architecture and how this architecture is used by services and clients for lookups. Redland is implemented as a set of C libraries. XOTcl is used as an OBJECT SYSTEM LAYER that provides an object-oriented interface to the Redland store. Scripts can use this interface for their queries. The class diagram in Figure 14–10 gives an overview of the object-oriented interface to the Redland RDF store library. Each class depicted in the figure is a COMPONENT WRAPPER that wraps one of the Redland C libraries.

Based on this infrastructure, we can build the lookup and query models. In fact, the basic lookup model is just the object-oriented COMPONENT WRAPPER interface. The basic model can be used for simple RDF graphs with ABSOLUTE OBJECT REFERENCES, properties, and relationships. In the case of ordinary Web services, we simply announce the services with a service name, their WSDL INTERFACE DESCRIPTION, and other information such as the service's URL. More sophisticated descriptions might contain properties provided as domain-specific ontologies. For example, information in the WSDL-file (like operation names and supported protocols) can be reflected in the RDF graph as well—then this information can be included in queries.

The benefit of this architecture is that clients can construct complex queries in an imperative, object-oriented script language. For example, the following sim-

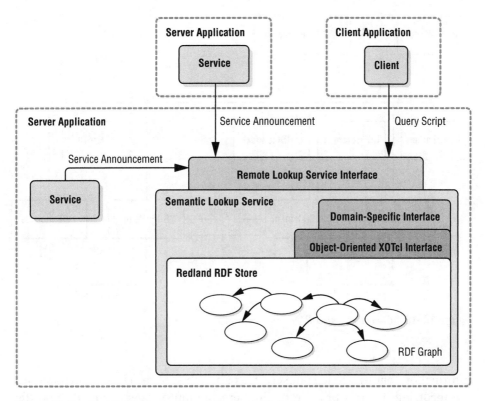

Figure 14–9 *Architecture overview of the semantic lookup service*

ple query produces a list of all the contents of all statements that have a creator (according to the Dublin Core ontology) and the value of the creator is "Jim":

```
set results ""
Statement queryStatement
queryStatement predicate "http://purl.org/dc/elements/1.1/creator"
queryStatement object "Jim"
set stream [m findStatements queryStatement]
while {![$stream end]} {
  lappend results [[$stream current] toString]
  $stream proceed
}
set results
```

It is also easy to extend the server-side INTERPRETER with predefined query methods. Consider the previous example: Here, the client knows what to do with the

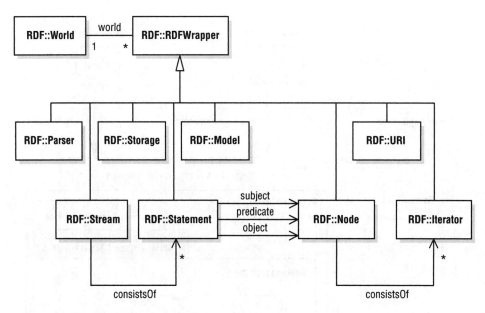

Figure 14–10 *Object-oriented RDF store interface*

information that someone is the creator of a Web service. Thus, if such queries are recurring, we can provide the implementation of query semantics on the server side so that the client does not have to provide the query logic with each request but can reuse the predefined methods instead. Such an interface must then be loaded into the server-side INTERPRETER before the query happens. Of course, this kind of server-side extension is only needed for convenience. Any kind of query can also be defined at the client side and be sent with each query—thus the query model is fully extensible without the need for changes in the server.

Apache Axis

We want to discuss the Web services framework Apache Axis as an example of a distributed object framework. In many other distributed object frameworks, similar concerns occur and similar solutions are applied.

The MARSHALLER [Völter+2004] of the Web services framework needs to convert the types of remote invocations into strings to be transported across the network using the SOAP protocol, and on the server side, it needs to convert the strings into the respective types again. In Axis, the XML Schema Data (XSD) types are used, and WSDL files are used as an INTERFACE DESCRIPTION. Thus Axis only requires one-to-one conversion between programming language types and the string representation of the XSD types. This is done using an AUTOMATIC TYPE CONVERTER. This way, type conversion is flexibly extensible with new type converters.

In Axis, a type converter consists of a factory for a serializer and de-serializer, as well as an implementation of serializer and de-serializer. Besides primitive types that can use a simple converter because type conversion is supported by Java, Axis can convert many more complex types, such as arrays, dates, calendars, DOM documents, object references, vectors, beans, and others. In a class containing the type bindings, these AUTOMATIC TYPE CONVERTERS are mapped to the XSD types. According to the INTERFACE DESCRIPTION, Axis can look up the Java type converter corresponding to an XSD type and perform the conversion automatically.

A Web services framework usually supports the heterogeneity of backends implementing the service. For example, a service might be implemented as a Java class, a procedural library, an EJB component, a COM component, and many others. Axis provides a "provider" abstraction. One provider class for each type of backend service is provided. The provider can be dynamically configured for particular invocations, and the framework can be extended with new providers for new types. This is a variant of the pattern COMPONENT WRAPPER: Each backend component type can be flexibly integrated, and we can manipulate the mapping by either providing new provider types or by configuring the provider objects.

A distributed object framework is an implementation of a canonical object system, often implemented in many languages. Thus, it can be used as an OBJECT SYSTEM LAYER to provide objectified access to non-object-oriented languages as well as unified access to the object systems of the language supported. The object concepts of this OBJECT SYSTEM LAYER are usually described by a language for INTERFACE DESCRIPTIONS, such as WSDL for Web services and IDL for CORBA.

Conclusion

In this chapter, we have presented a number of patterns for software architecture integration from the specific areas of language integration and component integration. The patterns play a central role in a huge number of integration architectures. There are many external patterns and many patterns needed in this broad area in order to provide a full pattern language for this important field.

Acknowledgments

Many thanks go to Charles Weir for his attention as a EuroPLoP 2004 shepherd and his constructive comments. Also, thanks go to the participants of the EuroPLoP 2004 Writers' Workshop who provided valuable feedback.

References

[Bass+1998] L. Bass, P. Clement, and R. Kazman. *Software Architecture in Practice*. Reading. MA: Addison-Wesley, 1998.

[Beckett2004] D. Beckett. Redland RDF Application Framework. 2004. Available: *http://www.redland.opensource.ac.uk/*.

[Box+2000] D. Box, D. Ehnebuske, G. Kakivaya, A. Layman, N. Mendelsohn, H. F. Nielsen, S. Thatte, and D. Winer. Simple Object Access Protocol (SOAP) 1.1. 2000. Available: *http://www.w3.org/TR/SOAP/*.

[Buschmann+1996] F. Buschmann, R. Meunier, H. Rohnert, P. Sommerlad, and M. Stal. *Pattern-Oriented Software Architecture: A System of Patterns*. John Wiley & Sons, 1996.

[DeJong+2003] M. DeJong and S. Redman. Tcl Java Integration. 2003. Available: *http://www.tcl.tk/software/java/*.

[ETSI2001] ETSI. MHP specification 1.0.1. ETSI Standard TS101-812, October 2001.

[Gamma+1995] E. Gamma, R. Helm, R. Johnson, and J. Vlissides. *Design Patterns: Elements of Reusable Object-Oriented Software*. Reading, MA: Addison-Wesley, 1995.

[Goedicke+2000] M. Goedicke, G. Neumann, and U. Zdun. "Object System Layer." In *Proceedings of EuroPlop 2000*. Irsee, Germany, July 2000.

[Goedicke+2001] M. Goedicke, G. Neumann, and U. Zdun. "Message Redirector." In *Proceedings of EuroPlop 2001*. Irsee, Germany, July 2001.

[Goedicke+2002] M. Goedicke and U. Zdun. "Piecemeal Legacy Migrating with an Architectural Pattern Language: A Case Study." *Journal of Software Maintenance and Evolution: Research and Practice*, 14:1–30, 2002.

[Goedicke+2004] M. Goedicke, C. Koellmann, and U. Zdun. "Designing Runtime Variation Points in Product Line Architectures: Three Cases." *Science of Computer Programming*, 53(3):353–380, 2004.

[HAVI2001] HAVI. HAVI specification 1.1., May 2001. Available: *http://www.havi.org*.

[Johnson+1998] R. Johnson and B. Woolf. "Type Object." In R. C. Martin, D. Riehle, and F. Buschmann (eds.), *Pattern Languages of Program Design 3*. Reading, MA: Addison-Wesley, 1998.

[Kiczales+2001] G. Kiczales, E. Hilsdale, J. Hugunin, M. Kersten, J. Palm, and W. G. Griswold. "Getting Started with AspectJ." *Communications of the ACM*, October 2001.

[Kiczales+1997] G. Kiczales, J. Lamping, A. Mendhekar, C. Maeda, C. V. Lopes, J. M. Loingtier, and J. Irwin. "Aspect-Oriented Programming." In *Proceedings of ECOOP'97*. Finland, June 1997. *LCNS 1241*, Springer-Verlag.

[Neumann+2000] G. Neumann and U. Zdun. "XOTcl, an Object-Oriented Scripting Language." In *Proceedings of Tcl2k: The 7th USENIX Tcl/Tk Conference*. Austin, Texas, February 2000.

[Oberleitner+2003] J. Oberleitner, T. Gschwind, and M. Jazayeri. "Vienna Component Framework Enabling Composition across Component Models." In *Proceedings of the International Conference on Software Engineering* (ICSE 2003), Portland, Oregon, May 2003.

[OpenMash2000] Open Mash Consortium. The Open Mash consortium. 2000. Available: *http://www.openmash.org*.

[Pawlak+2001] R. Pawlak, L. Seinturier, L. Duchien, and G. Florin. "JAC: A Flexible Framework for AOP in Java." In *Reflection 2001: Meta-Level Architectures and Separation of Crosscutting Concerns*, Kyoto, Japan, Sept. 2001.

[Schmidt+2000] D. C. Schmidt, M. Stal, H. Rohnert, and F. Buschmann. *Patterns for Concurrent and Distributed Objects: Pattern-Oriented Software Architecture*. John Wiley & Sons, 2000.

[Spinellis2001] D. Spinellis. "Notable Design Patterns for Domain Specific Languages." *Journal of Systems and Software*, 56(1):91–99, February 2001.

[Swig2003] Swig Project. Simplified Wrapper and Interface Generator. 2003. Available: *http://www.swig.org/*.

[UCB2000a] UCB Multicast Network Research Group. Network Simulator - NS (Version 2). 2000. Available: *http://www.isi.edu/nsnam/ns/*.

[UCB2000b] UCB Multicast Network Research Group. Tclcl. 2000. Available: *http://www.isi.edu/nsnam/tclcl/*.

[Völter+2004] M. Völter, M. Kircher, and U. Zdun. *Remoting Patterns—Foundations of Enterprise, Internet, and Realtime Distributed Object Middleware*. Wiley Series in Software Design Patterns. John Wiley & Sons, 2004.

[Vogel+2002] O. Vogel and U. Zdun. "Content conversion and generation on the web: A Pattern Language." In *Proceedings of EuroPlop 2002*, Irsee, Germany, July 2002.

[Wetherall+1995] D. Wetherall and C. J. Lindblad. "Extending Tcl for Dynamic Object-Oriented Programming." In *Proceedings of the Tcl/Tk Workshop '95*, Toronto, July 1995.

[Yoder+2002] J. W. Yoder and R. Johnson. "The Adaptive Object-Model Architectural Style." In *3rd Working IEEE/IFIP Conference on Software Architecture* (WICSA'02), Montreal, Canada, August, 2002.

[Zdun2003a] U. Zdun. Frag. 2003. Available: *http://frag.sourceforge.net/*.

[Zdun2003b] U. Zdun. "Patterns of tracing software structures and Dependencies." In *Proceedings of EuroPlop 2003*, Irsee, Germany, June 2003.

[Zdun2004a] U. Zdun. "Using Split Objects for Maintenance and Reengineering Tasks." In *Proceedings of 8th European Conference on Software Maintenance and Reengineering* (CSMR'04), Tampere, Finland, Mar 2004.

[Zdun2004b] U. Zdun. Semantic Lookup in Service-Oriented Architectures. In *Proceedings of Fourth International Workshop on Web-Oriented Software Technologies*, pp. 101–110, Munich, Germany, July 2004.

CHAPTER 15

Patterns for Successful Framework Development

Andreas Rüping

Introduction

Object-oriented frameworks play an important role in many IT projects these days. Frameworks allow us to reuse not only code, but abstractions and designs as well. Projects typically build a framework with the intention of large-scale reuse.

It's a difficult job, though. There are things that make framework development particularly hard. Reuse may be a promising goal, but finding abstractions is difficult. Frameworks can easily become too generic and, as a consequence, too complex and difficult to understand. Framework development can use up a lot of time and resources before it pays off.

Moreover, the context for framework development can be difficult. Ideally, a framework evolves from long-term experience acquired while building several similar applications [Brugali+1997] [Johnson+1998]. It's fairly common, however, for a software development project to decide to build a framework after identifying a potential for reuse across several applications that are going to be developed, although this means that the framework and the applications will have to be developed more or less simultaneously.

Is this even possible? Is there a chance that a framework developed in such a difficult context can live up to its promise—the reuse of code and design?

This chapter presents a collection of patterns that address these questions. It is targeted at software architects and developers who consider building a framework to meet requirements for reuse. The patterns assume an overall context in which framework and application development take place, at least to some extent, simultaneously. Many of the solutions that the patterns recommend actually apply to framework development in general, but they are particularly useful in this specific context.

The patterns address a framework's architecture, its development process, and questions of team collaboration. I have observed the patterns throughout many projects. The collection isn't necessarily complete, but it does represent a useful set of core strategies.

Project Background

I'd like to explain the patterns by using my experience with two projects that both decided to build a framework in order to facilitate application development. My experience in these projects were both positive and negative, and I'll use the projects as running examples throughout this chapter. Let's therefore first take a look at the two projects.

The Data Access Layer Framework

An insurance company faced the problem of having a large number of legacy systems that didn't work together well. The company felt it was time for a change and decided to build several new applications, including new policy systems for health insurance, life insurance, and property insurance, as well as new customer, payment, commission, and workflow systems. It was a huge endeavor involving several teams, ranging from 8 to 40 people each, working on the various applications more or less simultaneously.

Early on, the project established a team that worked on what was called the "horizontal tasks": the specification, design, and coding of modules that many—and perhaps all—other teams could use. The motivation was to save time and costs, and to ensure a consistent architecture across the new applications.

It soon became clear that providing database access would be among these horizontal tasks. All applications required database access, and in order to hide the objects' physical representations from the applications, all applications were supposed to introduce a data access layer into their architecture.

The team decided to build a framework that would provide the data access layer. The framework had to abstract over the individual applications' data models and therefore allowed application developers to specify a mapping from domain-specific objects onto database tables. The framework also provided a mechanism for object versioning that was quite powerful. Application developers could tailor the framework to the individual needs of their projects by configuring the extent of object versioning that they needed.

The framework offered the advantage that the application programmers didn't have to bother with the details of database access, including the intricate versioning mechanisms.

The Web Portal Framework

The goal of this project was to develop a Web portal for the financial industry. The portal included both Web content and applications, and was used by a bank to sell insurance products. The Web content covered general information about the available products, while the applications provided access to different insurance systems running on various back-end servers that stored and processed contracts and customer information.

Several of these applications had existed for a while when the plans for the portal were made, but a few still had to be developed. The project's main task was to integrate old and new applications into the portal. The team decided to develop a J2EE-based framework that would provide a reusable infrastructure for all applications that had to be integrated into the portal.

The framework extended over the Web server and application server layers. Its task was to take user requests, forward them to the back-end applications, transform the results into HTML and integrate them into a Web presentation. The framework also managed the use cases for the entire portal and performed the necessary session handling.

Application developers essentially had to define the use cases their application required, and to provide a mapping from client requests onto application calls. They could then rely on the mechanisms the framework provided. The definition of the use cases required a bit of programming, but the bulk of integration work was done by the framework and hidden from the application developers.

Roadmap

Figure 15–1 gives an overview of the patterns presented in this chapter and briefly sketches the relationships between them.

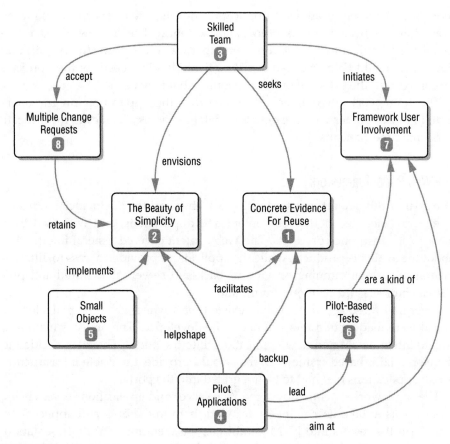

Figure 15–1 *Overview*

1. Concrete Evidence for Reuse

Problem

How can you make sure that in your project building a framework is justified?

Context

You're working on a project that will see the development of several applications. You have identified some functionality that all applications will probably require. The question of whether it would be useful to have a framework that could provide this functionality arises.

Forces

It is of course tempting to design a framework—the framework could provide a set of common abstractions and could serve as a blueprint for functionality that could then be reused many times. Building a framework can be attractive whenever there is some functionality that several applications will require, though in slightly different ways.

But reuse isn't the only aspect that lets a framework appear attractive. If you decide to build a framework, many design decisions will be made only once, leading to a consistent architecture across all applications.

Moreover, not all application developers will have to be concerned with all aspects of the software architecture if some of these aspects can be assigned to the framework. In this case, the framework designers can provide an implementation that all applications can inherit. This is particularly useful when it comes to intricate techniques that not all developers have the skill to use.

On the other hand, there is no way to deny that building a framework takes significantly more time than building a normal application. A rough estimate is that developing a framework takes about three times longer than developing an application, though the exact figure depends upon the framework's size and its degree of abstraction.

In a similar vein, the literature on reuse has a "rule of three," which says that an effort to make software reusable is worth it only when the software is reused at least three times [Jacobsen+1997] [Tracz1995]. A framework needs to be used for three different applications before the break-even point is reached and the investment pays off.

All this suggests that building a framework is justified only if the project can name at least three applications that are going to use it.

A higher number of applications sounds even more promising, but then, there is also a drawback if too many applications are supposed to use the framework: the number of stakeholders can increase to a point where reaching an agreement on the framework's scope and functionality becomes extremely difficult. The larger the number of potential framework users, the more you need to ensure that using the framework isn't just an abstract idea, but a concrete possibility.

The dilemma, however, is that you must make the decision for (or against) a framework at the beginning of the project. The application development teams must know as early as possible whether or not there will be a framework they can use. At the beginning of the project, however, the architecture of the individual applications might still be unclear. Perhaps there is even uncertainty about what applications are going to be developed. In other words, you may have to make a decision for or against a framework without knowing much about the applications that might possibly use it.

Solution

Build a framework only if there is concrete evidence that several applications are going to use it.

The emphasis here is on the word *concrete*. If all you know is that there are several applications that *might* use the framework, all you can conclude is that framework development *might* pay off. Or perhaps it won't.

Therefore, before you decide to build a framework, you must make sure that the preconditions are met:

- Three expected uses is a must. If there are four or five applications that you can expect to use the framework, that's even better, since as a project goes on, things can change, applications may be cancelled, and you may lose a potential user of your framework more quickly than you might think.

- Checking for concrete evidence includes seeking an agreement with all stakeholders of the application programs.

- The teams who build the applications must make a commitment to using the framework. This is not so much a protection against the not-invented-here syndrome, but a cross-check that using the framework is indeed appropriate. Only the application developers can evaluate how much they could benefit from the framework-to-be.

If you choose to build the framework, calculate about three times the budget you would need to build a single application. If you have concrete evidence for reuse, you can explain why the expected benefits will outweigh the costs.

Examples

The Data Access Layer Framework   At first it looked as if six applications were going to use the database access framework. In the end, one of them didn't use it for "political" reasons—a consequence of teams from many companies with conflicting goals working on one large project. With five applications remaining (and more expected), building a framework was still justified.

It took the team about 30 person months to complete the database access layer framework. The team estimated that it would have taken about 12 person months to develop a database access layer for one specific application that is equally powerful with respect to business objects and versioning. (However, exact figures would depend on the size of the application's data model.) Given the fact that building an application using the framework also takes some time, three instances of reuse seemed to be the break-even point in this project.

The Web Portal Framework When the project started, the decision to build a framework was motivated by the perspective that a number of applications were going to be integrated into the Web portal. After all, the portal was supposed to offer a rich functionality to its users. Work on the framework began quickly, and soon the life insurance system and the customer system were integrated into the portal.

After a while, however, it was recognized that not as many applications were going to be integrated into the portal as had originally been planned, and that for some of these applications a less powerful solution was sufficient. The potential for reuse turned out much smaller than the project had assumed. As of now, the framework has only been used twice, and so far, hasn't paid off. The budget calculation says the framework might pay off in the future, but only if at least one more application is going to use it which, at this time, is uncertain.

Discussion

In their patterns for evolving frameworks, Don Roberts and Ralph Johnson suggest that THREE EXAMPLES [Johnson+1998] be developed before building a framework. This recommendation intends to prevent you from not finding the right abstractions or generally heading in the wrong direction with your framework—an easy consequence of a lack of experience.

Yet in many practical scenarios, there are no three examples on which you could possibly rely since the applications will be developed more or less simultaneously to the framework. Is there anything you can do instead to make sure that the framework benefits from experience with application development?

Yes, there is. Because you have concrete evidence for reuse, you must have a good idea of applications that can benefit from the framework, and how. If you choose one or two of those as PILOT APPLICATIONS (4), you can incorporate feedback from application development into the framework development.

Next, a SKILLED TEAM (3) is certainly helpful. Ideally, team members have developed a framework in such a context before. The more the team members are aware of typical pitfalls in framework development, the better.

Finally, a larger framework will have a higher risk of wrong abstractions and hopes for reuse that won't materialize. Aim at THE BEAUTY OF SIMPLICITY (2).

2. The Beauty of Simplicity

Problem

How can you prevent your framework from becoming unmanageable?

Context

You have come to the conclusion that building a framework in your project is justified. Several applications are going to be developed and it's clear that they will benefit from the framework. You are now in discussions with the potential framework users about what functionality the framework should cover.

Forces

Obviously, the application development teams will come up with requirements for the framework. After all, they are supposed to use the framework, so the framework better meet the requirements they have. However, application developers are sometimes inclined to place more and more requirements on the framework; greater functionality offered by the framework means more time and effort the application development teams can save.

Moreover, framework developers sometimes flirt with wanting to build the *perfect* framework. Just one more abstraction here, and another generic parameter there, and the framework can grow incredibly powerful.

All these things easily lead to the framework's architecture becoming rather complex. However, there is much danger in complexity.

First, a complex architecture is difficult to build, maintain, understand, and use. Excessively complex frameworks can therefore create a challenge for designers and users alike, perhaps more of a challenge than they can meet.

Second, complexity, in the context of framework development, often means additional abstractions that are often reflected by generic algorithms and data structures. Genericity, however, is often the enemy of efficiency, and too many abstractions can easily lead you into efficiency problems you cannot resolve.

Third, the more complex the framework is, the longer it takes to build it. If the framework is supposed to "solve all problems on earth," it won't be available anytime soon.

This, however, is unacceptable. You don't have much time to build your framework. The teams that build the applications rely on the framework, and they won't be willing to wait for you. A specification of the framework has to be available when the other teams start designing, and a first version of the framework has to be completed before the other teams start coding. If you don't manage to get the framework ready in time, this will turn out extremely expensive for the entire project.

And no, you cannot rescue the situation by adding more people to the framework team when the deadline is approaching and the schedule is getting tight. We all know that adding people to a late project makes the project later [Brooks1995].

Solution

Design your framework to be small and to focus on a few concrete tasks.

Try to limit the scope of the framework to what is truly necessary:

- Focus on a small number of core concepts. Avoid too much abstraction. A framework that embodies too much abstraction tries to do too much and is likely to end up doing little.

- Perhaps your framework can be a framelet [Pree+1999]. A framelet is a very small framework that defines an abstract architecture that's not for an entire application but for some well-defined part of an application. It follows the "don't call us, we'll call you" principle, but only for that part of the application.

Much in the vein of agile development methods [Ambler2002][Cockburn2002], try "the simplest thing that could possibly work" [Beck2000]. Go with a small solution that works, rather than with a complex solution that promises more than it can deliver.

Examples

The Data Access Layer Framework When assembling the requirements for the database access framework, the team had to work hard to exclude any application logic from the framework. Many applications were going to use the framework's versioning features, but all had different ideas on how to use them. The team had to fight to avoid a versioning system that could be used in many different modes. Had the framework team agreed to include all the features that some of the other teams desired, it would have blown up the framework to incredible proportions.

In order to not overcomplicate the framework, the team also had to restrict the mapping of logical entities onto physical tables. Only simple mappings were possible; advanced techniques such as overflow tables had to be left to the applications. Generating the database access functions would otherwise have become unmanageable.

Nonetheless, the data access layer framework did suffer from too much complexity. The composition of business objects from smaller entities turned out to be extremely complicated. The team managed to implement it properly in the end, but only after much unexpected work. In addition, this complexity made the framework more difficult to use than had been intended. Looking back, the team felt the framework should have done without this mechanism, which required much effort and did little good.

To summarize, the team was successful in keeping the framework simple in many instances but felt they should have made simplicity an even more important issue.

The Web Portal Framework   Providing a portal infrastructure is a concrete task, and certainly one that can be addressed by a framework. Like so many other frameworks, however, this Web portal framework suffered from becoming too powerful and, as a consequence, too complex. For instance, parameters need to be passed between the Web browser and the applications running on the mainframe, and the framework includes a mechanism that manages parameter passing in an entirely generic way. It's powerful, but it's difficult to understand and rather inefficient. A simpler mechanism would have been better.

But there is a success story as well. The framework wasn't only supposed to provide an infrastructure for the Web portal; it was also supposed to provide one for integrating Web services (which don't expect results from the applications to be represented as HTML). The framework team managed to meet these requirements in a simple and elegant way. The framework features a layered architecture: presentation issues are dealt with only in the servlet engine, while use-case management is concentrated on the application server layer. Web services can use the application server layer exactly as the portal does and simply not make use of any HTML generation.

Discussion

Reducing a framework's complexity is a strategy generally approved of in the literature. For instance, Art Jolin recommends that frameworks be simple and modeless [Jolin1999]. And in our particular context—time constraints along with framework and application development happening simultaneously— keeping the framework simple was crucial.

Simplicity also contributes to longevity. For instance, Brian Foote and Joseph Yoder propose THE SELFISH CLASS [Foote+1998]—a class that represents an artifact that reliably solves a useful problem in a direct and comprehensible fashion. In a similar vein, a framework that focuses on a set of core abstractions has a relatively high ability to evolve gracefully and therefore stands the best chance for longevity [Foote+1996].

In order to keep the framework simple as the project goes on, you must be careful with change requests that other teams might have, as they might introduce more, and unwanted, complexity. As a general rule of thumb, only accept MULTIPLE CHANGE REQUESTS (8)—change requests that are made by several, at least two, application development teams.

And of course a Skilled Team (3) is critical to keeping the framework simple. Framework development requires a team that is aware of the problems complexity brings and that is able to see the beauty of simplicity.

3. Skilled Team

Problem

How can you make sure that the framework is designed in a clear and consistent way?

Context

You are going to develop a framework in your project. You now have to assemble a team that can perform the requirements analysis for the framework, define its architecture, and ultimately design and implement it.

Forces

Framework development is hard. But when framework and application development are strongly interwoven, things are even harder.

First, you have only a little time to develop your framework, because the other teams of the project are already counting on it. If your team is either inexperienced with framework development or with the application domain, there is no chance for success. The team would need too much time for familiarization.

Second, the framework team will have to take care of not only framework development and maintenance, but coaching as well. A crucial part of the framework team's job is to explain to the users how to work with the framework properly, which represents quite some time and effort.

Third, several applications are going to use the framework, so it is likely that many different parties would like to put their stake in it. You have to expect many different requirements and requests to influence the framework's design and scope.

And while such influences can give the framework designers valuable input, there is also the danger that the framework evolves into more and more variations. If different parties are free to request functionality as they see fit, the framework is likely not only to become complex, but to also split into inconsistent variations.

Solution

One team of skilled individuals must take care of framework design and development.

A skilled team is important in every development project, but it is crucial to framework development and even more crucial if framework and application development happen simultaneously.

Check the following, carefully and in detail, when assembling the framework team:

- The team members must have the necessary skills to design a framework. Experience with framework design and managing abstraction are required.

- The team members must adopt a strategy to keep the framework reasonably simple and to avoid unnecessary complexity.

- The team must have the experience and the skill to ensure that the framework's scope stays on target.

- The team must have the communication skills that are necessary to collaborate closely with the framework users and to incorporate feedback the users may have into the design.

- At least some team members must be familiar with the application domain.

In order to collaborate smoothly, the team should be large enough to accomplish the task, but no larger. Interestingly, a small team is sometimes more effective than a large team.

Examples

The Data Access Layer Framework Five people were involved in building the data access layer framework, although some only with a small percentage of their time. A stable core team of two people worked on the framework full-time for more than a year. When it came to introducing the framework into the applications, these two people were faced with the problem of doing three things at a time: maintaining the just-released version, preparing a new version, and coaching. Though they eventually managed this, there were some delays.

In retrospect, it became clear that a team of three or four people would have been necessary for timely releases and appropriate user support. A still larger team, however, wouldn't have done any good; the fact that only a handful of people designed the framework added much to its consistency.

The Web Portal Framework The good news here was that framework designers brought the necessary skills; they had developed frameworks before on other projects. The team size was also appropriate; about five people worked on the Web portal framework, which allowed for efficient teamwork.

However, a number of ad hoc corrections were made to the framework by people outside the framework team. This led to some irritation, since at some point responsibility for the framework wasn't clearly defined. After a major re-factoring, the framework's consistency was reestablished, and responsibility for the framework was reassigned to the framework team.

Discussion

If too many people work on the framework, it's hard to develop one consistent architectural vision, which is what your framework needs. A small team can en-vision THE BEAUTY OF SIMPLICITY (2).

Likewise, a small team can take responsibility for how the framework evolves by making sure only MULTIPLE CHANGE REQUESTS (8) are accepted.

In his generative development-process pattern language, Jim Coplien explains that it is important to SIZE THE ORGANIZATION [Coplien1995] and to SIZE THE SCHED-ULE [Coplien1995] when building a software development organization in general. The importance of having the right number of people, as well as the right people from the start, is even more true for building frameworks since the additional level of abstraction makes adding people to the project even more difficult.

4. Pilot Applications

Problem

How can you detail the requirements for your framework?

Context

Work on the framework has begun. You're in the process of defining the frame-work's functionality. At the same time, some application development teams have already kicked off, while others perhaps haven't started yet.

Forces

There is some functionality that several of the applications-to-be will have in common. They will use it in slightly different ways, but they will share a set of common abstractions. However, none of these applications have been built so far.

You're locked in some kind of chicken-and-egg problem: The framework team needs to know quite a bit about the applications to be able to define the framework's functionality, while the application development teams rely on the framework to build the applications. It's hard to come up with the requirements for the framework in such a context.

Still, you have to find the right abstractions for your framework.

What makes things even more difficult is that different application development teams will place many, possibly conflicting, requirements on your framework. You'll have to prioritize those requirements in order to achieve a consistent framework design. If you try to please everybody, the framework will become very complex and might ultimately become a failure.

Solution

Discuss the framework's functionality with several pilot applications that are going to use the framework.

The pilot applications will use the first versions of the framework as soon as they are released. This may well include versions that feature only a partial functionality or that are otherwise still constrained in their usage. In a way, the pilot application developers act as beta testers and provide valuable feedback to the framework team.

In most cases, two pilot applications are appropriate. One pilot application alone might not be representative, and perhaps you cannot say whether a required function is crucial or just nice to have. On the other hand, three or more pilots might simply become difficult to handle. Two pilot applications still seem manageable, and it's unlikely that important requirements go unnoticed.

Keep in mind the following when choosing pilot applications:

- The pilot applications must be fairly typical of others that might use the framework.

- The pilot applications should be significant, so that the framework team keeps in close touch with some of the framework's premier users.

- The pilot applications must be applications that are being built relatively early in the time frame of the overall project.

Collaborating with the teams who work on the pilot applications will increase the knowledge exchange in both directions; you'll get feedback on how good your framework is, and the other teams will learn how to use it. Pilot applications will also force you to adopt a policy of early delivery, which is a well-established strategy for project risk reduction [Cockburn1998].

Unfortunately, pilot users can get the impression that they're doing your work when they use the framework at a very early stage, when its functionality is still incomplete and has a few bugs. Be aware of this, and make clear to the pilot users that in return they have the chance to influence the system they'll have to use.

Examples

The Data Access Layer Framework   Among the new systems, the health insurance system was a very typical one. The framework team had many discussions with the team that built this system. These discussions particularly helped shape the understanding of two-dimensional versioning of application data—versioning that makes a difference between when a change becomes effective and when it becomes known. It's a subtle topic, and it was quite significant for the requirements analysis and for the framework design in the earliest stage of the project. The framework didn't feel on safe ground, though, until they got into detailed discussions with the team who built the new customer system. The new customer system had slightly different requirements on application data versioning. Both systems complemented each other well as far as architectural requirements were concerned.

The Web Portal Framework   The life insurance system and customer system served as pilot applications for the Web portal framework. This was clearly a good choice, since these applications were typical for the portal's usage. For instance, a typical use case is that of a bank assistant who looks up a customer in the customer system and recommends certain life insurance products to back up a bank credit. This typical use case involves exactly the two applications that were chosen as pilot applications. The framework designers received a lot of input from collaborating with the application developers.

Discussion

Collaborating with the pilot users is a kind of FRAMEWORK USER INVOLVEMENT (7), but it's actually more than that. Involving the framework users has the primary goal of achieving a better understanding of the framework among the users once the framework is released, whereas the knowledge exchange with the pilot users is bi-directional.

Prototyping is a strategy generally approved of in the literature on reusable software. Brian Foote and William Opdyke recommend to PROTOTYPE A FIRST-PASS DESIGN [Foote+1995] when the goal is to design software that is usable today and reusable tomorrow, as is certainly the case with frameworks that are developed with large-scale reuse in mind.

The importance of feedback from users is generally acknowledged. In his generative development-process pattern language, Jim Coplien stresses that it is important to ENGAGE CUSTOMERS [Coplien1995], in particular, for quality assurance, mainly during the analysis stage of a project but also during the design and implementation stages. Along similar lines, speaking of customer interaction,

Linda Rising emphasizes that IT'S A RELATIONSHIP NOT A SALE [Rising2000]. Speaking openly with customers—the framework users in this case—will give you valuable feedback about your product.

The pilot applications are not only useful for finding out the requirements for the framework; they also form the precondition for setting up PILOT-BASED TESTS (6).

5. Small Objects

Problem

How can you increase the framework's flexibility while restricting its complexity?

Context

The overall scope and functionality for the framework is clear. You're now in the process of breaking the overall functionality down into smaller pieces, such as individual objects or functions that applications can use.

Forces

Maybe your framework offers an interface to the applications that use it. Maybe it offers abstract classes that the concrete applications have to implement. Either way, it provides a certain amount of functionality to the applications. This functionality is typically expressed by a set of objects or methods—or functions, depending on the underlying technology. This invites the question of how these artifacts should be designed.

There are essentially two opposite approaches you can take. You can choose either a larger number of less powerful objects or a smaller number of more powerful objects.

From the application programmer's viewpoint, both a smaller number of objects and simpler objects are desirable, because both make the framework easier to understand. But because you have to offer a certain amount of functionality, you cannot reduce both the number of objects and the individual objects' complexity. You have to choose one and sacrifice the other.

Which option should be preferred?

You have to keep in mind that different applications will probably use your framework in slightly different ways. Combinatorics tell us that a larger number of less complex objects can be combined in many more different ways than a small number of very powerful objects. This flexibility represents a clear advantage.

In addition, complex objects are generally difficult to understand and difficult to reuse. This is true especially for objects with huge interfaces and methods that require many parameters.

Solution

When breaking down functionality into individual objects, favor a larger number of less powerful objects over a smaller number of more powerful objects.

Applications can then combine several objects to obtain a behavior that is tailored to their specific needs. This policy offers several advantages:

• The objects the framework offers will be better understood.

• Smaller objects have a better chance of meeting the users' needs, since they are less specific to a certain context.

• A larger number of smaller, somewhat atomic, objects allows for more combinations, and hence for an increased configurability of the application.

The price you have to pay for this strategy is that you cannot minimize the number of objects, but as long as the objects are fairly easy to understand, this seems a reasonable price to pay.

Examples

The Data Access Layer Framework   The data access layer framework allows the loading of business objects into its cache where they can be processed. Typically, an application loads a policy object and changes it, thereby also changing the policy's state, which can be active, under revision, or offered to customers.

What happens when a policy object, one that is already in the cache, is requested? Should it be updated? Should the version in the cache be used instead? Different applications had different requirements. Some applications even needed to define a priority among states; for instance, an active object should be replaced by an object under revision but not vice versa. The framework team refused to include such a logic into the framework's function for loading objects. Instead, they implemented two smaller functions: one that tells applications whether a certain object is already available in the cache, and another that loads objects. Applications can combine these functions to implement their specific logic.

Another example: The data access layer keeps track of which objects have been changed. At the end of a session, applications can commit all or some of the changes to the database. The team decided not to implement a complex function that saved all changed objects, but again decided to offer two functions: one that listed all changed objects, and one that saved individual objects to the database. Applications can combine these functions to implement their strategies of which changes should be committed to the database as they see fit.

The Web Portal Framework The Web portal framework allows the applications to define certain use cases that specify the order in which user requests are processed and mapped onto calls of the back-end systems. The framework team decided to let the use cases' objects consist of smaller entities—so-called "user-steps"—that the application developers could aggregate to full-fledged use cases according to their specific needs.

This solution turned out quite successfully. The definition of use cases was easy to understand, and the flexibility of the use case definitions made the concept useful for many applications.

Discussion

A framework should display THE BEAUTY OF SIMPLICITY (2). Less functionality is often better than more functionality. But at some point we know that a certain functionality is not debatable, but strictly necessary. This pattern deals with the question of how this functionality can be implemented in such a way that different applications can use it most easily.

The suggestion to have small objects is similar to Don Roberts' and Ralph Johnson's suggestion to build frameworks from FINE-GRAINED OBJECTS [Johnson+ 1998] and Brian Foote's and Joseph Yoder's recommendation to design objects with a LOW SURFACE-TO-VOLUME RATIO [Foote+1998], that is, objects with small external interfaces.

The benefit of using small objects is also related to the observation that small modules are more likely to be reusable, because smaller modules make fewer assumptions about the architectural structure of the overall system [Garlan+1995]; hence the risk of an architectural mismatch between components is reduced.

6. Pilot-Based Tests
Problem

How can you test the framework sufficiently and reliably?

Context

You are in the process of coding the framework. Tests are necessary to make sure that the framework works correctly and reliably.

Forces

Testing is an important aspect of quality assurance. Testing is particularly important when you build a framework, since bugs would quickly manifest in all applications that use the framework.

However, testing a framework is difficult [Fayad+1999]. A framework alone is just an abstract architecture, not something that can be executed. In order to test the framework, you need a sample application that uses the framework and so acts as a test driver.

Moreover, when you test software, you need test cases with sufficient coverage. Using just one application as a test driver is probably insufficient, because this one application might not use all the features the framework offers.

In addition, it can be difficult to find realistic test scenarios when there are no precursor applications that you could use.

Solution

Set up tests based on the pilot applications.

These tests can take different forms:

- Identify core components from the pilot applications that call the framework, and then use these components as test drivers for the framework.

- Find typical use cases from the pilot applications and maintain them as a test suite.

- Shape these test cases into regression tests that you can run before every release of a new version of your framework.

However, you can't rely on the pilot applications alone. You also have to include some exotic scenarios in your test suite, ones that take your framework to its limits and that can detect more unexpected bugs.

In addition, you need test cases that test the time, performance, and stability of your framework under load.

Examples

The Data Access Layer Framework   The two-dimensional versioning of application data had to be tested with real-world examples. The first time the framework team performed such realistic tests was in a two-week workshop together with the team that developed the health insurance system. In this workshop, the framework team learned some subtle details about two-dimensional versioning that they had not yet implemented. The framework team was therefore able to do some fine-tuning at a relatively early stage. Overall, these tests were very successful, because the few changes that were necessary could quickly be made. These tests would not have been possible without the pilot users—the health insurance application team.

Moreover, the realistic examples that were used in the workshop represented typical use cases for the health insurance system. The framework team used these scenarios as a test suite for a series of future framework versions.

The customer system acted as the second pilot application. The framework team occasionally tested together with the customer system team, since this reduced the necessary testing effort for both teams. Everybody was able to fix problems very quickly, which was equally good for both teams.

The Web Portal Framework   Tests of the Web portal framework were always performed using the pilot applications. It was extremely convenient to have two applications at hand that provided realistic test cases. New versions of the framework were only released after they had been approved by test teams that had checked whether the integration of the life insurance system and the customer system worked smoothly.

In addition to this, performance tests were carried out from time to time to check the portal's time performance.

Discussion

Testing is an activity where the PILOT APPLICATIONS (4) are particularly helpful. Finding real-world test scenarios would otherwise be very difficult.

Joining efforts with the users for testing is a particular kind of FRAMEWORK USER INVOLVEMENT (7) from which both the framework developers and users can benefit. The framework developers receive valuable test scenarios, while the framework users can run tests with the framework developers readily available for immediate bug fixing, if necessary.

7. Framework User Involvement

Problem

How can you make sure that members of the other teams will be able to use your framework when they build their applications?

Context

You have completed a first version of the framework. It's now the application developers' turn to use the framework in their applications.

Forces

Other teams depend on your framework in order to complete their applications—that is, to be successful in what they're doing. They want to know what the framework does and how it works. That's fair enough; you should let them know.

Empirical studies have shown that most people are willing to reuse software if it fits their needs [Frakes+1995]. You can therefore assume that the other teams are generally willing to use the framework as long as you can convince them that the framework offers the necessary functionality and that using the framework is easier than developing the functionality from scratch.

Moreover, frameworks often trade efficiency for flexibility, at least to some degree [Fayad+1999]. When efficiency is critical, applications built with the framework may need some fine-tuning. They may also have to replace certain generic mechanisms with more concrete and more efficient ones. In any case, users might need help using the framework or even customizing it a bit.

Ultimately, it's your goal that the other teams use the framework successfully. If they don't, the failure will be blamed on you, the framework team, rather than on them, the application team.

Solution

Involve the teams that use your framework.

You must show the users how they should use the framework. The users must get an understanding of the framework's feel, so that they understand what they can and what they cannot expect from the framework and how they can integrate it into their applications.

Possible actions include:

- Run common workshops. Explain the steps that users have to take when they build applications with the framework.

- If possible, provide tools that support the framework's instantiation process and demonstrate how to use these tools.

- Provide examples of how an application and your framework collaborate.

- If necessary, show the users how to optimize the applications they are building using the framework.

- Prepare tutorials and documentation and make them available early. Make sure the documentation directly addresses the framework users as its TARGET READERS [Rüping2003] and maintains a FOCUS ON LONG-TERM RELEVANCE

[Rüping2003]—things that application developers will need to know in the long term, when the framework team might not be available anymore on a day-to-day basis.

• Combine written documentation and interactive workshops with the application developers to establish an atmosphere in which team members can share information of different kinds and formats—an atmosphere that can be described as an INFORMATION MARKETPLACE [Rüping2003].

The drawback is that involving the users a lot costs a lot of time and will probably take place while the framework is still developed further. You must make sure that framework development doesn't grind to a halt while you're busy running workshops.

Examples

The Data Access Layer Framework After the release of the first version of the framework, the framework team had a two-week workshop together with the team that developed the health insurance system. The health insurance team wanted to know what they had let themselves in for—how they could use the framework. The framework team showed them and at the same time had the opportunity to fine-tune the two-dimensional versioning of application data, since it was tested with real-life examples for the first time.

At some point, the framework team learned that the commission system had special efficiency requirements. The commission system team had to define a sophisticated mapping of business objects onto database tables—more sophisticated than could be defined in the framework's meta information. Both teams discussed a way to extend the data access layer of the application with a special module that implemented the special mapping.

The framework team provided a usage document that explained the necessary steps that application developers had to take to configure the framework and to use it in their specific context. The document was helpful, especially in combination with workshops like the ones just mentioned, in which the application programmers were shown how to do what was written in the document.

The Web Portal Framework The project managed to integrate the life insurance system and the customer system into the Web portal, despite the portal's relative complexity. Crucial for this success was the fact that the framework team and the application development team had offices next door to one another and that they were able and willing to collaborate closely. Informal communication was no problem, and communication channels were fast. The framework developers were available all the time to answer questions from the application developers. Actually, the framework developers and the application developers felt they were one team, sharing the common goal of bringing the portal to life.

Discussion

Unlike the collaboration with the PILOT APPLICATIONS (4), this pattern doesn't put the emphasis on how the framework team can learn from the framework's users (although it's fine if they do). The focus here is to provide a service to the users and help them.

Involving the users and working jointly on their tasks is generally acknowledged as a successful strategy to use to achieve this goal. In particular, this is true of frameworks, due to the additional level of abstraction and the sometimes non-trivial instantiation process [Eckstein1999].

Moreover, listening to the users, running common workshops, and so forth, helps to BUILD TRUST [Rising2000]. Trust is important because the users will view your framework as a third-party component; they will only be successful building their application if the framework works as it is supposed to.

When you explain how to use the framework, using design patterns is often useful, since they describe typical ways in which application programs can be put together [Johnson1997]. If you consider developing a tool that helps users build applications, keep in mind that a complicated mechanism is probably not justified. However, a simple script, perhaps based on object-oriented scripting languages, might save a lot of work [Ousterhout1999].

8. Multiple Change Requests

Problem

How can you prevent the framework from growing too complex as a consequence of change requests?

Context

Several applications use your framework. Application developers approach you with requests for additional functionality.

Forces

Regardless of how much functionality you have already included in your framework, some people will always ask you to include more. After all, if you add functions to the framework, the members of the other teams won't have to implement these functions themselves.

But if you accept all change requests, the framework might end up over-loaded with functionality. Worse yet, different users might come up with conflicting change requests, and if you accept all of them, you put the framework's consistent architecture at risk.

You absolutely must keep the framework simple. In particular, you should avoid building the framework to run in different modes [Jolin1999]. So what should you do?

If only one application is interested in the additional functionality, that application's team can implement the desired functions on a concrete level at a much lower cost than would result if you implement them on an abstract level.

However, if several applications need additional functionality, it's probably useful to include that functionality—for all the reasons that justify a framework in the first place.

Solution

Accept change requests only if several teams will use the additional functionality. What the word *several* means will depend on the concrete situation. If a framework is used by just three or four applications, the fact that a change request is supported by two of them can be evidence enough to show that the change request is justified. If there are more applications that use the framework, the threshold might be higher. Either way, you must make sure that you add functionality only if it is of general use, not just useful in rare cases.

The following guidelines are helpful for dealing with change requests:

- Be active. Once you have received a change request, it's your job to figure out if it could be useful for more than just one team.

- Help users of the framework to add application-specific functions when their change request is rejected and they need to find an individual solution to solve their problem.

When a change request is accepted, make sure that it doesn't invalidate the framework's design. Apply refactoring techniques if necessary [Fowler1999].

Examples

The Data Access Layer Framework   The data access layer framework normally allows committing changes to the database only at the end of a session. After a while, it turned out that both the workflow system and the printing system required an exception to this rule; certain changes had to be visible on the database immediately. Given the fact that two applications requested the change, the framework team decided to offer an additional function that commits changes to the database immediately as long as these changes are atomic and consistent.

The customer system needed special search functions that allowed searching for a person with an arbitrary combination of name, phone number, address, and other data. The data access layer framework never included such arbitrary queries, since they would have been very complex to implement and they might have easily ruined the system's time performance. Because no other team needed such queries, the framework team decided not to extend the framework but to show the customer system team how to extend their concrete application with the necessary functionality.

At some point, the framework team received several requests from different teams for extending the two-dimensional versioning. It turned out that what those teams needed could already be expressed. The desired extensions would have made things a little more comfortable for the other teams. However, everybody requested different comfort functions that, if implemented together, would have overcomplicated the framework. The framework team thus declined the change requests.

The Web Portal Framework   Of all the change requests concerning the Web portal, the first thing the project had to decide was whether they addressed the framework or any of the applications. The rule of thumb was this: Only if both applications would benefit would the change request be justified. Only a change request made by both applications was thus a candidate that the framework team would consider. This policy avoided having the applications' functionality intrude into the framework.

Discussion

We know that building a framework is justified only when there is CONCRETE EVIDENCE FOR REUSE (1). This pattern is in sync with the principle that functionality should be added to a framework only if at least two applications can use it. It can be acceptable to bend the rule of three a little if a technically plausible change request is made by two applications, but if the requested functionality is useful only for one individual application, it certainly doesn't belong in the framework.

Conclusions

I'd like to conclude this chapter by considering the patterns and the core principles expressed by them from a slightly different perspective.

Over the last couple of years there have been many successful frameworks in the world of open source software. Examples include, but aren't limited to, frameworks that have emerged from the Apache Software Foundation [www.apache.org], such as Struts and Cocoon. Let's take a brief look at the characteristics of these frameworks and see if we can find evidence for why they have been (and still are) so successful.

- The frameworks keep a clear focus on their core tasks. You can say what these framework do in just a few words. Struts is a framework for the implementation of the model view controller pattern. Cocoon is a framework for XML-processing organized in a pipeline style. None of these frameworks tries to solve every problem on earth. Instead, the developers worked hard to retain the frameworks' scope.

- The frameworks address areas with a concrete potential for reuse. Web development is central to today's world of software, and you can find the aspects that the frameworks address in many applications worldwide.

- The frameworks are relatively easy to use. This doesn't mean they're trivial to use, but the frameworks aim to avoid unnecessary complexity and keep an eye on a straightforward usage process.

- There is a strong collaboration between the framework developers and the framework users. These frameworks haven't been developed in an ivory tower. We speak of the open source community—the word *community* alone suggests that there is a massive exchange of information involved. It's this community that gives the framework developers much useful feedback on what they do and what they plan to do.

Keeping a clear focus, aiming for straightforward solutions, avoiding complexity whenever possible—these appear to be key factors in many success stories on frameworks. I think it's important to understand that to achieve these things, a certain frame of mind is required to be shared among the project team members that gives preference to smaller and practical solutions over higher, but unachievable, goals. In addition, a strong collaboration between framework developers and users seems to be an equally important ingredient to successful framework development.

You can find all this advice running like an undercurrent through the patterns presented in this chapter and in the solutions they suggest. In this sense, the patterns should help you with your decision if you're considering building a framework and should provide you with much useful experience in running your framework projects successfully.

Acknowledgments

First, I'd like to thank the people who shared their ideas on framework development with me throughout the last couple of years. Special thanks go to the colleagues of sd&m software design & management AG, Germany, with whom I was happy to collaborate on the two projects described in this chapter.

Sending a paper to a pattern conference always gives you a huge amount of valuable feedback. This chapter has gone through the process twice. Neil Harrison was the shepherd for an earlier version at PLoP 2000, and Dragos Manolescu shepherded the current version for EuroPLoP 2003. Both provided useful comments and suggestions, and they helped me improve the chapter. Thanks also go to the participants of the PLoP 2000 and EuroPLoP 2003 workshops in which this chapter was discussed.

References

[www.apache.org] Apache Software Foundation. *www.apache.org*.

[Ambler2002] S. Ambler. *Agile Modeling: Effective Practices for eXtreme Programming and the Unified Process*. New York: John Wiley & Sons, 2002.

[Beck2000] K. Beck. *Extreme Programming Explained: Embrace Change*. Boston: Addison-Wesley, 2000.

[Brooks1995] F. P. Brooks. *The Mythical Man-Month*. Reading, MA: Addison Wesley, 1995.

[Brugali+1997] D. Brugali, G. Menga, and A. Aarsten. "The Framework Life Span." In *Communications of the ACM*, Vol. 40, No. 10. ACM Press, October 1997.

[Cockburn1998] A. Cockburn. *Surviving Object-Oriented Projects—A Manager's Guide*. Reading, MA: Addison-Wesley, 1998.

[Cockburn2002] A. Cockburn. *Agile Software Development*. Boston: Addison-Wesley, 2002.

[Coplien1995] J. O. Coplien. "A Generative Development-Process Pattern Language." In J. Coplien and D. Schmidt (eds.), *Pattern Languages of Program Design*. Reading, MA: Addison-Wesley, 1995.

[Eckstein1999] J. Eckstein. "Empowering Framework Users." In M. Fayad, R. Johnson, and D. Schmidt (eds.), *Building Application Frameworks—Object-Oriented Foundations of Framework Design*. New York: John Wiley & Sons, 1999.

[Fayad+1999] M. E. Fayad, R. E. Johnson, and D. C. Schmidt. "Application Frameworks." In M. Fayad, R. Johnson, and D. Schmidt (eds.), *Building Application Frameworks—Object-Oriented Foundations of Framework Design*. New York: John Wiley & Sons, 1999.

[Foote+1995] B. Foote and W. F. Opdyke. "Lifecycle and Refactoring Patterns That Support Evolution and Reuse." In J. Coplien and D. Schmidt (eds.), *Pattern Languages of Program Design*. Reading, MA: Addison-Wesley, 1995.

[Foote+1996] B. Foote and J. Yoder. "Evolution, Architecture, and Metamorphosis." In J. Vlissides, J. Coplien, and N. Kerth (eds.), *Pattern Languages of Program Design 2*. Reading, MA: Addison-Wesley, 1996.

[Foote+1998] B. Foote and J. Yoder. "The Selfish Class." In R. Martin, D. Riehle, and F. Buschmann (eds.), *Pattern Languages of Program Design 3*. Reading, MA: Addison-Wesley, 1998.

[Fowler1999] M. Fowler. *Refactoring: Improving the Design of Existing Code*. Addison-Wesley, 1999.

[Frakes+1995] W. B. Frakes and C. J. Fox. "Sixteen Questions About Reuse." In *Communications of the ACM*, Vol. 38, No. 6. ACM Press, June 1995.

[Garlan+1995] D. Garlan, R. Allen, and J. Ockerbloom. "Architectural Mismatch, or Why it's Hard to Build Systems out of Existing Parts." In *Proceedings of the International Conference on Software Engineering, ICSE 17*. ACM Press, 1995.

[Jacobsen+1997] I. Jacobsen, M. Griss, and P. Jonsson. *Software Reuse: Architecture, Process and Organization for Business Success*. ACM Press, 1997.

[Johnson1997] R. E. Johnson. "Frameworks = (Components + Patterns)." In *Communications of the ACM*, Vol. 40, No. 10. ACM Press, October 1997.

[Johnson+1998] R. Johnson and D. Roberts. "Patterns for Evolving Frameworks." In R. Martin, D. Riehle, and F. Buschmann (eds.), *Pattern Languages of Program Design 3*. Reading, MA: Addison-Wesley, 1998.

[Jolin1999] A. Jolin. "Usability and Framework Design." In M. Fayad, R. Johnson, and D. Schmidt (eds.), *Building Application Frameworks—Object-Oriented Foundations of Framework Design*. New York: John Wiley & Sons, 1999.

[Ousterhout1999] J. K. Ousterhout. "Scripting: Higher Level Programming for the 21st Century." In *IEEE Computer*, Vol. 32, No. 3, March 1999.

[Pree+1999] W. Pree and K. Koskimies. "Framelets—Small is Beautiful." In M. Fayad, R. Johnson, and D. Schmidt (eds.), *Building Application Frame-*

works—Object-Oriented Foundations of Framework Design. New York: John Wiley & Sons, 1999.

[Rising2000] L. Rising. "Customer Interaction Patterns." In N. Harrison, B. Foote, and H. Rohnert (eds.), *Pattern Languages of Program Design 4*, Boston: Addison-Wesley, 2000.

[Rüping2003] A. Rüping. *Agile Documentation—A Pattern Guide to Producing Lightweight Documents for Software Projects*. New York: John Wiley & Sons, 2003.

[Tracz1995] W. Tracz. *Confessions of a Used Program Salesman*. Reading, MA: Addison-Wesley, 1995.

PART VI

Meta-Patterns

Chapter 16: Advanced Pattern Writing

Writing good patterns is hard. Besides a solid understanding of the problem domain, it also requires experience with the patterns format—dealing with the problem, forces, solution, and trade-offs in a way that pattern readers have come to expect. Distilling from ten years of writing and reviewing patterns, Neil Harrison's pattern language provides advice for improving pattern writing. The language has a dual audience and is addressed to shepherds (i.e., people who help authors to improve their pattern writings) and authors alike.

Chapter 17: A Language Designer's Pattern Language

In the patterns community, the shift from patterns to pattern languages represents a sign of maturity. But how does one generate a pattern language from a system of forces? Tiffany Winn's pattern language provides an elaborate answer to this question, with parallels to existing theory of system design and evolution in the context of building architecture and biology. This pattern language targets people who explore patterns at a deeper level than the casual patterns user and provides insight about identifying and understanding the nature of relationships between patterns.

Chapter 18: The Language of Shepherding

When casual pattern readers think about the patterns community, they typically see the pattern authors. Unbeknownst to them, many of these patterns (such as the ones from the PLoP conferences) go through several intermediate phases. One of these phases involves a shepherd who works with the author to prepare the patterns for a writer's workshop. Based on his extensive experience, Neil Harrison distilled a pattern language that focuses on analyzing and providing feedback about patterns. This language is addressed to shepherds, pattern authors, and readers—as well as to problem solvers in general.

Chapter 19: Patterns of the Prairie Houses

Most practitioners who adopt patterns recognize their value quickly and start using them regularly for communication as well as for learning about proven solutions. In fact, some of them like patterns so much that they start writing their own. But how does one write patterns in an effective way? Paul Taylor uses the design themes of Frank Lloyd Wright's prairie houses as an exploratory vehicle for showing how people should approach pattern mining and writing. Although not addressing a software problem, this language demonstrates the underlying pedagogical themes to those interested in distilling experience into pattern form.

CHAPTER 16

Advanced Pattern Writing

Patterns for Experienced Pattern Authors

Neil B. Harrison

Introduction

Ten years ago, a group of us met at Allerton Park in Illinois and began a tradition of unique conferences, dedicated to creating a body of software pattern literature. That's a tall order, but we have done well. We have created a significant body of well-written patterns. They may not be literature yet, but they have improved much over the years. In short, we write a lot better than we used to.

It's time to raise the bar again. Some have criticized patterns for being too fluffy—lacking content and substance. I fear that in some cases they may be right. As a result, I wrote the patterns presented in this chapter. I offer them in the hope that they will help authors improve their patterns, particularly with respect to the substance in them.

These patterns are for two closely related audiences: the authors and the shepherds. Why have one set of patterns for two audiences? The obvious reason is that authors and shepherds are often the same people, and much of the advice is the same. But more importantly, an author can gain great insights by understanding what a reader—in this case, the shepherd—is looking for. So I modified the pattern format slightly. Each pattern has two solution summary statements. The main one is for the author, and the second one is especially for the shepherd.

These patterns form a little language. There are several possible paths through the language, but here is probably the most common sequence of the patterns:

"WHAT"-SOLUTIONS: *Write the core idea of the pattern in one or two key sentences that capture what the pattern is all about.*

"HOW"-PROCESS: *Extend the core idea with a detailed explanation of how to implement the solution.*

"WHY"-PROBLEMS: *Make the problem statement explain the main consequence of not having the solution in place.*

DEAD WEASELS: *Replace words that imply meaning but have little substance with a full, specific explanation.*

FORCES HINT AT SOLUTION: *Write forces so that they lead the reader from the problem to the general direction of the solution.*

CONSISTENT "WHO": *Make sure the pattern language focuses on the same audience throughout.*

POINTERS TO DETAIL: *Point to other sources for details that aren't germane to the solution, especially previously published material.*

Figure 16–1 shows a few more paths through the language. As you can see, there are many ways to use these patterns together! Note that lines indicate typical logical flows from one pattern to another. Cycles show the iterative nature of pattern writing.

Existing Work

These are not the first patterns to have been written about pattern writing and shepherding. There are two bodies of patterns that this pattern language builds on. The first is "A Pattern Language for Pattern Writing," by Gerard Meszaros and Jim Doble [Meszaros+2000]. The pattern thumbnails relevant to these patterns are given in this section. Note especially that there are three patterns about naming patterns; there is no additional pattern in the present language about pattern names since these three cover the topic thoroughly.

EVOCATIVE PATTERN NAME: Choose a pattern name that conjures up images that convey the essence of the pattern solution.

NOUN PHRASE NAME: Name the pattern after the result it creates.

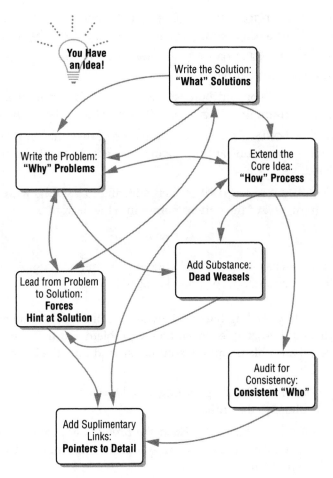

Figure 16–1 *The Advanced Pattern Writing Pattern Language*

MEANINGFUL METAPHOR NAME: Find a meaningful metaphor and name the pattern after it.

SKIPPABLE SECTIONS: Clearly identify the Problem, Context, and Solution parts so that the readers can quickly determine whether this pattern applies to them.

VISIBLE FORCES: Regardless of the style chosen for the pattern description, ensure that the forces are highly visible.

CLEAR TARGET AUDIENCE: Identify a clear target audience and keep this audience in mind while writing the pattern.

TERMINOLOGY TAILORED TO AUDIENCE: Use only those terms with which the typical member of the audience can reasonably be expected to be comfortable.

RELATIONSHIP TO OTHER PATTERNS: Read other pattern languages and describe the relationships to other patterns.

CODE SAMPLES: Provide one or more implementation code examples, written in a prevalent programming language, to illustrate the pattern concepts.

CODE SAMPLES AS BONUS: Ensure that the pattern can stand on its own; make sure it is able to communicate its essential concepts even if the code examples were deleted.

READABLE REFERENCES TO PATTERNS: When referring to patterns within the body of your pattern, weave the pattern names into the narrative.

The following patterns are in "The Language of Shepherding: A Pattern Language for Shepherds and Sheep" [Harrison2006].

BIG PICTURE: Start by reading the problem and solution of the pattern to get the main idea, and then give feedback on the problem and the solution first. By themselves, the problem and the solution should give the big picture of the pattern.

THREE ITERATIONS: Plan the shepherding to take three iterations of comments from the shepherd to the author.

MATCHING PROBLEM AND SOLUTION: Read the problem and solution together to make sure they match. The solution must address the whole problem, but not more than the problem.

FORCES DEFINE PROBLEM: The problem statement should describe the visible manifestation of something wrong. The forces give substance to the problem, and insight into what is behind the symptoms.

"What"-Solutions

…well begun is half done.

You know of a really neat solution. It looks like it would make a good pattern, but it isn't a pattern (yet).

This is where most of us begin with a pattern. We have found a design, an implementation, or some other idea that has worked well for us in solving a problem. A pattern is an attractive way to convey that information to others.

Unfortunately, it's often surprisingly hard to write a pattern, particularly to start writing it. You may have a really good idea, but writing it down is daunting.

One of the problems is that we geeks aren't necessarily good writers. It's hard to describe an idea that works well in software in a natural language.

Another problem is that a pattern needs not only a solution, but also a problem, and lots of other information besides. The breadth of knowledge required to write a complete pattern may intimidate us. But we have to start somewhere.

Therefore:

Write the core idea of the pattern as the first sentence or two of the solution. Try to capture the essence of the solution in these few words.

It is crucial that the essence of the solution be absolutely clear, unambiguous, and understandable.

The solution summary should go right at the beginning of the solution, or somewhere else where it is obvious and can be easily picked out on first reading of the pattern. In the Alexandrian form, the solution summary is set in bold just after the "Therefore." In the GOF form [Gamma+1995], the solution summary finds itself in the "Intent" section at the very beginning of the pattern.

The solution summary may be a statement that describes the structure of the solution. The solution summary in this pattern is such an example. Or the solution summary may be an imperative; an instruction to do something. Other patterns in this language show this style. Pick whichever one works for you. In general, the structural statement is harder to come up with, but produces a stronger solution.

Occasionally, you may get stuck trying to come up with the core idea of the pattern. If so, see the following hints to shepherds.

Shepherds: Find and read just the solution summary. It should give you the general idea of the pattern.

The solution summary is usually the place to start with shepherding. If the author doesn't have this right, then the rest of the pattern doesn't matter.

It is very often helpful to compare the solution summary to the name of the pattern. Names generally evoke the solution. If the name and the solution summary don't seem to match, ask the author about it. Usually, one or the other needs to change.

Ask the author to tell you what the pattern is all about in one or two sentences. Alternatively, ask the author what is the most important point of the pattern.

Occasionally an author will struggle with this. If so, you might try asking the author to explain how the pattern came about. That often uncovers the real point of the pattern.

Note how this follows Alexander's philosophy of a pattern being a "thing, and the process to build that thing." The first few sentences state what the "thing" is. Note that additional explanation may be needed to describe the "thing."

Note that this is half of the BIG PICTURE pattern [Harrison2006]. You will later write the problem so that the author can get the big picture of the pattern quickly. Note that you want to make the solution (as well as the problem) prominent, as described in SKIPPABLE SECTIONS [Meszaros+2000].

As of yet, you haven't described "the process to build that thing." This is a critical element of a pattern; the reader needs information on how to implement the solution. This is where the pattern HOW-PROCESS comes in.

"How"-Process

With the solution summary in hand, you can see the pattern taking shape. But this doesn't mean that the reader can use or even understand the pattern yet. The pattern, particularly the solution, needs additional substance.

The pattern has the core of a solution, and perhaps a brief problem statement, but a person couldn't pick up the pattern and use it yet.

As the author of a pattern, you are already living in the solution space. Things that seem obvious or even trivial to us may be neither trivial nor obvious to the reader. Because the material is new to the reader, the reader often must be led step by step through the solution.

At the same time, though, you must help the new reader get a picture of what the pattern is all about. You can't allow details to obscure the main message of the pattern.

Therefore:

Extend the core of the solution with an explanation of the solution in more detail, giving instruction on what to do, how to do it, and why to do it that

way. Put this information after the solution summary, set off from it, but with information that logically leads from the summary to the explanation.

The second part of the solution describes the "process to build that thing." This is the information the reader needs to implement the solution.

Make sure your solution details include these elements:

- Explain how the solution balances the forces, and tell which forces are not addressed. This may include discussion of tradeoffs; for example, size versus performance. Note that depending on the order that you write the pattern, you may not have written any forces yet. So you may have to defer this part of the solution until after you write forces. In infrequent cases, writing the "how" of the solution actually calls forces to mind, so you may find yourself iterating between forces and solution. See the pattern FORCES HINT AT SOLUTION.

- Explain why this is a good solution—why it works. It is as important to understand why a solution works as to understand how it works. That is what distinguishes patterns from ordinary instruction sheets. Some patterns put this in a section called "Rationale," but I prefer to weave it together with explanation of the resolution of the forces. The two are inextricably intertwined.

- Provide implementation hints for the solution. It is often a very good idea to draw a picture of it. Many patterns have sections called "Implementation." Structure diagrams or message sequence charts may be appropriate. This often includes recommended steps for implementing the solutions. This is usually the largest part of the solution.

- If the implementation has different options, provide hints for choosing which option. For example, the paragraphs following this list describe options about the order of writing the solution, and hints about which option to choose.

- Provide references to other patterns that may be needed.

- Provide pointers to additional details that do not contribute directly to the understanding of the pattern or its core issues (see POINTERS TO DETAIL).

- Discuss alternatives to the pattern and alternative implementations within the pattern as appropriate.

Which do you write first, the summary or the process to create it? While I tend to recommend writing the summary first, and then the process, the real key is your own preferences. Many people in software patterns think intuitively. They think of the big picture first. Process details come later, and come in the context of how they relate to the big picture. In this case, write the solution summary first, and then the process. Be careful not to skimp on the process details.

On the other hand, some people are detail-oriented. They derive the big picture (when forced to) from the details. If you think this way, it is probably much easier to write the implementation process, and then the solution summary. Be careful that your solution summary captures the essence of the solution, and isn't just a process step.

Shepherds: After reading the solution summary, read the entire solution to learn how to achieve the idea given in the summary.

The easiest place to start is to ask the author how to implement the solution. Or you can simply request more detail.

Don't forget to check to see that the summary matches the solution details. This usually isn't a problem, but demands immediate attention if it is.

In some cases, the solution may lack credibility. Refer to DEAD WEASELS for help here.

The result of a carefully crafted solution is that it contains the following parts:

- A sentence that gives the fundamental idea of the solution. This is not the structure to be created but its intention.

- The concrete thing to be built. In Alexander's words, the spatial configuration of the elements and their cooperation.

- The process of how to create the structure.

- An explanation of why this solution resolves the core problem and balances the forces.

- A discussion of what the solution does not cover, such as unresolved forces.

The other result may be that the pattern becomes bloated.

"Why"-Problems

We write patterns because we have a neat solution. But because of that, we naturally have trouble remembering the problems behind the solutions. This is illustrated in the saying, "To someone with a hammer, everything looks like a nail."

Many pattern descriptions are colored by the solutions they suggest, which result in patterns that are tautologies. This is not particularly helpful to the reader, who has a problem, not a solution.

In far too many immature patterns, the problem and solution are basically re-statements of each other. In other words, the pattern really has no problem. It may have something that is labeled as a problem, but when you put it next to the solution, they pretty much match.

A real example, excerpted from the pattern MIND YOUR MANNERS ([Rising 2000–1], used by permission):

Problem: When we interact with customers, we don't always think about etiquette, dress, and behavior.

Solution: MIND YOUR MANNERS. Be polite. Be aware of body language. The way you dress and behave influences the way the customer sees you and our company.

Clearly, this pattern contains very valuable advice. But the problem statement does not give any insight to the real problem; it is actually a reflection of the solution. It says that we don't think about etiquette and appearance, and the solution says to think about them. The general form is as follows:

Problem: You aren't doing X.

Solution: Do X.

Another common form is as follows:

Problem: How do you do X?

Solution: Do X.

Note that some patterns have this form of problem and solution, and are perfectly legitimate, but many such pairs are simply tautologies. Read the pattern carefully to determine whether or not it is a tautology.

The major reason this happens is that once we have a solution that we are excited about, it colors our thinking. It becomes difficult to imagine struggling without the pattern—it is just obvious that everyone should be able to see that this pattern is really great!

So we have to consciously step back and think about what the problem really is and why the solution is important.

Therefore:

The problem statement should reflect reasoning about the main consequence of not having the solution in place.

A good way to start is to ask yourself how the world would be worse if you don't use this pattern. Of course, you make "the world" specific to your pattern: If it is an OO design pattern, ask how your design would look if you didn't use the solution.

In the example just presented, imagine that you go into a sales call and don't pay attention to appearance and mannerisms. What is the consequence? Perhaps it is that the customer gets annoyed or offended by your actions, appearance, or odor. This draws their attention away from the nifty product you are selling, and they don't buy from you. It shouldn't be, but it is. Here is a possible improved problem statement:

> Successful business, be it acquiring a new customer, finalizing a new contract, or getting your ideas accepted in an organization is not just a matter of the quality of the offering. Often, the success or failure of a business is decided within the first 30 seconds, simply based on whether or not the other party likes the way you look.

It is sometimes helpful to ask yourself "why" questions about the solution, specifically why the solution is significant, or why one would want to apply the solution. You may find that you have to ask why several times to get to the heart of the problem.

Shepherds: Read just the problem and solution, and see how similar they are. See whether the problem points directly to the solution. If so, probe with questions to help the author unearth the real problem.

This is similar to MATCHING PROBLEM AND SOLUTION [Harrison2006]. That pattern points out that the problem and solution must be consistent with each other. This pattern explains what to do if the problem and solution are too similar to each other.

The questions are the same as those just presented for the author. The most effective is usually, "How would the world be different if you didn't have this pattern?"

Don't be surprised if the author doesn't understand right away. After all, the author is sitting firmly in the solution space, and everything has the rosy glow of the solution. You may have to ask more than once, and may have to try different approaches, such as the "why" questions. This is yet another reason to plan for THREE ITERATIONS [Harrison2006].

The process of discovering the problem is akin to peeling layers of an onion. It may take several tries to arrive at the real problem, so keep peeling! The result of all this peeling is sometimes astounding: The problem doesn't seem to resemble the solution at all! Yet you can see how they relate, and that's very cool. But now you may need to write material that ties the problem and solution back together.

Dead Weasels

The initial problem and solution are in place. But they are often much easier said than done.

The solution sounds plausible, but it is unclear how to make it work. In fact, you wonder if the author really understands what to do.

These can be the most frustrating of patterns. They sound right. You know you should follow them. But when you go to apply them, you feel that you have been cheated: You can't get from step A to step B. The author just happened to gloss over that with a few slick words. You have just encountered weasel words.

Weasels are traditionally sly, underhanded creatures. Likewise, weasel words are sly. They convey some meaning, but under the façade, there is nothing there.

The following statements were taken from real patterns; see if you can spot the weasel word in each:

- Hire a good consultant.
- Carefully design the system.
- Create a user-friendly interface
- Build strong teamwork

What is a "good consultant?" Under what conditions would you want to *carelessly* design a system? The phrase "user-friendly interface" is better than the previous two, but still doesn't give the reader much help. After all, would you ever recommend creating a *user-hostile* interface? And what does it mean to build strong teamwork? It has even less meaning than building strong teams.

Therefore:

Read through your pattern to find weasel words; words that imply meaning but have no substance. In nearly all cases, replace the weasel word with a phrase or paragraph that is more specific than the word it replaces.

Most weasel words are easy to spot. Look for adjectives or adverbs; they are the most likely candidates for weasel words. Also look for phrases that are platitudes, or always desirable. When you find such words, read the phrase, and ask what point you are trying to make. Then make the necessary corrections. For example:

"Hire a consultant with experience in working with geographically distributed teams. The consultant should have expertise with OO design, although this is of secondary importance."

In some cases, you can drop the adjective or adverb, or the phrase altogether. In extreme cases, the pattern may be too superficial to save. Throw it out.

Note that in a few cases, weasel words may be all right. For example, pattern names that contain weasel words may be acceptable. But in every case, at least consider replacing the weasel word with more substantive wording.

Shepherds: Ask the author what each weasel word or surrounding phrase means. Then have the author replace the word.

For example, you might ask the author, "What do you mean by 'good consultant'?" Or you could ask, "How do you tell a good consultant from a bad one?" Another possible question might be, "What is the difference between carefully designing a system and carelessly designing it?" Or, "Under what conditions would I not want to carefully design my system?"

This causes patterns to grow, often substantially. Sometimes a pattern will get too big, and will become too awkward to use easily. Then you have to balance detail in the pattern with detail outside the pattern. One way to do this is to apply POINTERS TO DETAIL.

Forces Hint at Solution

In the most interesting patterns, the problem and solution are not close in cognition. When we think about the problem, the solution does not come to mind at all. This can make the solution seem particularly elegant, but it can also make it difficult to understand just how the solution solves the problem.

Though the solution matches the problem, you don't see how the two fit together. Even after you read the entire pattern, the solution isn't intuitive.

One problem is that if the solution doesn't feel like it intuitively fits the problem, you won't remember it. You will always have to go back to the reference; it will never become part of you.

We have often said that the emergent patterns are the ones where the problem and solution are separate in time or space, or in different conceptual areas. In other words, the action one takes is not directly connected to the problem. But it causes something to happen (emerge) that solves the problem. But that makes it difficult to understand how a solution solves the problem.

In these cases, the author has had a flash of insight, and the insight is the real heart of the pattern. Now the trick is to convey that insight to the reader. A problem and solution alone is simply not enough; they need to be tied together.

So that means that you need to prepare the reader for the solution. The logical place to do that is in the space between the problem and the solution, where the forces live.

Therefore:

Write the forces so they lead the reader from the problem and point in the general direction of the solution. It is not necessary to be able to derive the solution from the forces. Instead, write the forces to be the foundation of a bridge to the solution.

This sequence of writing seems to work best:

1. Write a sentence or two for the solution first. Try to capture the essence of the solution, but don't go into much detail yet.

2. Write the problem in one or two sentences. If you aren't sure of the problem, write something down as a starting point.

3. Once you have those in place, you can fill in the forces between them. The first paragraph after the problem generally gives more detail about how gnarly the problem is.

4. The paragraph just before the solution sets the stage for the solution.

5. Work both ends toward the middle.

Of course, every pattern is different. If you are like me, you will flit from the forces to add more detail to the solution, and back again. And of course, you will modify the problem and the solution statements as you go along.

Many patterns have bullet lists of forces. Such lists may benefit from a reordering. Begin with the forces that are most "problem-like" and that explain the problem in more detail, or that show the contradictions inherent in the problem.

They may lead naturally to other forces. In any case, order the forces so that the forces most indicative of the solution end up just before you state it.

Shepherds: Ask the author to trace a logical sequence through the forces. Look for places where there are large nonintuitive leaps.

In some patterns, it may be difficult to find the forces, contrary to VISIBLE FORCES [Meszaros+2000]. In that case, you will have to work with the author to make the forces more obvious. This does not necessarily mean that the author has to create a section called "Forces" in the pattern. There are other ways to make the forces clear.

Doesn't this pattern contradict FORCES DEFINE PROBLEM [Harrison2006], one of the beginning shepherding patterns? No, forces do both; they help one understand the problem, but they also give subtle hints in the general direction of the solution. Sometimes the author struggles with the problem; it just won't come. In that case, writing the forces can help illuminate the problem. After you write the problem, you will probably need to order the forces and fill in any missing ones.

There are two things that go on here. The most obvious is that the pattern flows better, particularly between the problem and the solution. The second is that you as the pattern writer begin to think in terms of logical flow from problem to solution, rather than a list of forces to be filled in.

Consistent "Who"

When we write patterns, we often try to make them useful to as many people as possible. We try to address every issue that might come up so that everybody can understand and apply the pattern. But this makes the pattern a jack-of-all-trades—but a master of none.

The pattern is hard to use, because the pattern is unfocused.

This is often because the author doesn't really know whom the pattern is for. So the author tries to make the pattern useful to everyone.

Shepherding and writer's workshops can actually make this problem worse. Writer's workshops tend to cause patterns to become more general and to appeal to a wider circle of people. The author may receive advice that the pattern should address needs of a certain audience in addition to the audiences already in the pattern. But this can dilute the focus of the pattern.

The habits of readers complicate this problem somewhat. A reader new to the pattern wants to find out as soon as possible whether the pattern applies to him or her. A combination of the problem and the audience of the pattern determine this.

One can easily state the intended audience at the beginning of a pattern or pattern language. This is very useful, but has two drawbacks. The first is that it is easy to drift from the intended audience; the flow of writing can easily pull us from our moorings. The second drawback is that you can't depend on the readers to have well-behaved reading habits. Some may skip the introduction and jump in at the first pattern. Others may just read the problems and solutions. There are even some who start at the beginning and read the whole thing sequentially! For each of these groups of readers, you need to catch their interest early in their reading.

A pattern may solve the right problem for the right people, but it does them no good if they don't read it.

Therefore:

Ask yourself who will use this pattern, and make the pattern focus on one audience. Make this clear at different points throughout the pattern. Be consistent.

There are a few key places where it is good to establish who the audience is. The first is the title of the pattern collection. In the ideal cases, the title screens the audience effectively. For example, the title "Smalltalk Scaffolding Patterns" [Doble+2000] keeps the C++ and Java riffraff away. Another is the introduction to the work. Note that the introduction to these patterns talks about the audience. Within a single pattern, one might focus the audience in the context section, in the problem statement, and/or in the solution statement. These are the bold sections, if using the Alexandrian form. The pattern name is usually too short to establish audience focus.

It often isn't necessary to explicitly state who the target audience is. Or in some cases, a single word suffices to establish the audience.

This is similar to CLEAR TARGET AUDIENCE [Meszaros+2000] and TERMINOLOGY TAILORED TO AUDIENCE [Meszaros+2000]. This pattern explains various places to establish the audience, and it stresses the necessity of maintaining consistency throughout the pattern.

Shepherds: As you read the pattern, ask yourself whom the pattern is intended for. Although it may be stated explicitly, watch for cues in the pattern that the audience focus has shifted.

The biggest difference in audience is in experience level, either general or specific to a technology or technique. Watch to see if the pattern begins to assume experience levels that are inconsistent. For example, the pattern may begin to use acronyms or jargon that the stated audience wouldn't know. On the other hand, watch for excessive explanations and definitions of terms the audience should know already.

So why does this pattern have two audiences? Isn't this pattern in direct violation of itself? It isn't, for two reasons. The first reason is that all the patterns consistently address both authors and shepherds. The second reason is that shepherds are a subset of authors; they must know how to write patterns. Advice to the shepherds is good for regular authors to see, and vice versa.

Pointers to Detail

In the patterns world, we exercise an "aggressive disregard for originality." Sometimes we take it too far.

The patterns community has been justly criticized for rehashing previously published material.

Many patterns contain restatements of older material. The material may be previously published, or sometimes unpublished common knowledge. There are often good reasons for writing such material as patterns. In some cases, the previous material was not written well enough to be easily approachable by most readers; in other cases, the material fits into a larger whole such as a pattern language. The language would be incomplete without the duplicate patterns. But in many cases, the material has already been published.

Yet even if there are good reasons for repeating existing material, there are three significant problems with doing so. The first is that it makes finding and referring to patterns more difficult; in effect, it pollutes the namespace. For example, the index of *The Pattern Almanac* [Rising2000–2] devotes more than a page to layers, and includes the following: Layers, Layered Architecture, Layered and Sectioned Architecture, Four-Layer Architecture, Three-Tier Architecture, Two-Tier Architecture, Hierarchy of Control Layers, and more.

The second problem is that duplication simply looks bad to the outside world. It makes the patterns community look unprofessional.

The third reason is that if you put enough material in the pattern to make the pattern really useful by itself, the pattern will be long and probably pretty hard to use. On the other hand, if the pattern is succinct enough to be easy reading, it runs the risk of missing important substance.

Therefore:

Balance needed detail with conceptual flow in the pattern by using pointers to details that aren't germane to the key points of the pattern, particularly previously published patterns.

The challenge is always what to put in the pattern and what to have pointers to. Remember that you want to get the main idea across. So work with flow—the main pattern should establish a conceptual flow. You don't want to break the conceptual flow with momentary dives into unwanted detail or into unwanted tangents. So you dive into enough detail to firmly establish the idea, and then use pointers to more detailed information.

We are not good judges of our own work, because we already have intimate knowledge of the subject. We tend not to notice when our patterns are too superficial, since we know what is behind them. Similarly, we aren't bothered by breaks in the flow because we already know what the flow is. The obvious answer is another pair of eyes.

Make judicious use of examples, including code examples. Examples should be used to help clarify a point, but excessive detail can actually distract from the main point. As a rule, the longer and more detailed the example, the later in the pattern it should be.

An alternate approach with examples is to use formatting to set them off from the main text of the pattern so that the reader can skip them if desired. You can put examples in a sidebar, for example. Code examples are set off naturally by the typical format of the code. In these cases, make sure that the pattern can stand on its own without the example. See CODE SAMPLES [Meszaros+2000] and CODE SAMPLES AS BONUS [Meszaros+2000] for further information.

Of course, not all patterns need the same level of examples. Technical patterns, such as OO design patterns, simply beg for code examples. On the other hand, patterns of process and behavior, such as these, don't lend themselves quite so much to examples. But on the other hand, such patterns lend themselves to simplistic platitudes for solutions. In either case, experience and comparison to other similar patterns will help.

Where do you point? In general, favor pointing to somewhere in the work itself, such as an appendix, over an outside source. That way, the reader doesn't have to get another document or buy another book.

Are hyperlinks a good way to implement pointers to detail? Hyperlinks can be good as long as the primary medium of the pattern is electronic. With hyperlinks, try to get all the hyperlinks at the same level.

Thumbnails—one- or two-sentence summaries of patterns—can often be very useful. The pattern READABLE REFERENCES TO PATTERNS [Meszaros+2000] suggests weaving the name into the text to increase readability.

How do you handle using a previously published pattern? If it is part of a pattern, then start with a thumbnail of the pattern, and then add more detail as necessary. Be sure to clearly explain the RELATIONSHIP TO OTHER PATTERNS [Meszaros+2000]. However, don't rewrite a previously published pattern and slap a new name on it. If you need to write something up, write it up as an example usage of the pattern in your context. Note, for example, CONSISTENT "WHO" in this collection. It is similar to an existing pattern. So it explains how it differs, and what it adds beyond that pattern. This issue might be a point of discussion at the writer's workshop.

Shepherds: Do a "two-pass" read of the pattern. In the first pass, read the problem and solution to get the essence of the pattern. Then read the complete pattern and note where the detail detracts from the basic flow as established by the problem and solution.

Use your personal reaction to the pattern to give you cues about the level of detail. Are there sections of the pattern that you feel like skipping or that put you to sleep? Are there places where you don't have enough information to do what the pattern suggests? These things may indicate excessive or insufficient detail.

Another thing to watch for during the two-pass read is whether the pattern is a duplicate of an existing pattern. The first clue will be in the first pass; it may sound suspiciously like some other pattern. In the second pass, you should be able to pick up the essential differences from the existing pattern. If you don't see them, ask the author how the pattern is different from the existing pattern. (Note, of course, that this requires a familiarity with the pattern literature; check the pattern literature and any domain-specific pattern Web sites.)

❖ ❖ ❖

One of the purposes of patterns is to raise the context of our communication, which allows the communication to flow better. We can discuss that our software design should be based on MVC without delving into the details of the responsibilities of the Model, the View, and the Controller. That same type of flow works within a pattern itself, with the caveat that a pattern is meant to teach, so it may need to explain details more often.

Acknowledgments

Over the years, I have had the privilege of reading hundreds of patterns. All the authors of these patterns have helped me, through their patterns, to learn what makes a good pattern. Those who have allowed me to be their shepherd, as well as those who have shepherded my patterns, deserve special thanks. My shepherd for this work was Frank Buschmann, who gave me outstanding advice on this work. Many thanks! Thanks also go to the participants of my EuroPLoP 2003 writers' workshop, who gave me many helpful suggestions.

These patterns were partly inspired by a set of patterns I presented at MensorePLoP in Okinawa, Japan in 2001. The comments I received from my shepherd Jim Coplien, Linda Rising, Tiffany Winn, and the writers' workshop there provided some insights for this work.

Thanks to Linda Rising for graciously allowing me to use part of the pattern MIND YOUR MANNERS as an example of what not to do!

References

[Doble+2000] J. Doble and K. Auer. "Smalltalk Scaffolding Patterns." In N. Harrison, B. Foote, and H. Rohnert (eds.), *Pattern Languages of Program Design 4*. Reading, MA: Addison-Wesley, 2000.

[Gamma+1995] E. Gamma, R. Helm, R. Johnson, and J. Vlissides, *Design Patterns: Elements of Reusable Object-Oriented Software*. Reading, MA: Addison-Wesley, 1995.

[Harrison2006] N. Harrison. "The Language of Shepherding: A Pattern Language for Shepherds and Sheep." In D. Manolescu, J. Noble, and M. Voelter (eds.), *Pattern Languages of Program Design 5*. Boston: Addison-Wesley, 2006.

[Meszaros+1997] G. Meszaros and J. Doble. "A Pattern Language for Pattern Writing." In R. C. Martin, D. Riehle, and F. Buschmann (eds.), *Pattern Languages of Program Design 3*. Reading, MA: Addison-Wesley, 1997.

[Rising2000–1] L. Rising. "Customer Interaction Patterns." In N. Harrison, B. Foote, and H. Rohnert (eds.), *Pattern Languages of Program Design 4*. Reading, MA: Addison-Wesley, 2000.

[Rising2000–2] L. Rising. *The Pattern Almanac 2000*. Reading, MA: Addison-Wesley, 2000.

CHAPTER 17

A Language Designer's Pattern Language

Tiffany Winn and Paul Calder

This chapter focuses on how to help pattern language writers build better pattern languages. It presents a pattern language called Language Designer's Pattern Language (LDPL) that itself articulates the structure of pattern languages and key processes by which they form and evolve, and thus guides the building of pattern languages. The focus of LDPL is semantic, rather than syntactic; it focuses on how patterns work together to build a system. The theoretical foundation of LDPL is Alexander's [1977; 1979] work on pattern languages and Stewart and Golubitsky's [1992] work on symmetry-breaking as a means of analyzing complex systems.

Introduction

Several key assumptions are behind the development of LDPL. These are outlined in the section A Basis for LDPL. The Key Insights from Design Theorists section outlines key insights from design theorists relevant to the development of LDPL, and the Examples Used in the LDPL section provides introductory background for using LDPL.

A Basis for LDPL

The main assumptions underlying the development of LDPL are as follows:

- It is valid to treat a pattern language as a designed system, and therefore valid to develop a pattern language for building pattern languages, based on theory about system design and evolution.

- A pattern language is both a complex system and a means of analyzing complex systems.

- Evolved systems provide insight useful for building and maintaining designed systems.

A Pattern Language Is a Designed System

In a discussion example related to garden design, Alexander points out that a pattern language is, in fact, a designed system:

> ... the design of the garden lies within the language for the garden. ...
>
> We tend to imagine that the design of a building or a garden takes a long time; and that the preparation for the process of design is short. But in the process where the language plays its proper part, this gets reversed. ...
>
> Essentially, this means that the language which you have prepared must be judged as if it were itself a finished garden (or a finished building). ...
>
> ... if you think of the language merely as a convenient tool, and imagine that the garden of the building you create will become beautiful later, because of the finesse with which you handle it, but that the collection of patterns which lie in the language now are not enough to make it beautiful, then there is something deeply wrong with the language ...
>
> So, the real work of any process of design lies in this task of making up the language, from which you can later generate the one particular design.
>
> You must make the language first, because it is the structure and the content of the language which determine the design.
>
> [Alexander1979]

A consequence of being a designed system is that a pattern language is structural. It is not simply a guide to some kind of process of design. It is a structural entity that articulates design structure as well as design process and is more powerful than an isolated pattern. An individual pattern has structure; it is "both a process and a thing" [Alexander1979]. The structure of a pattern language comes both from the individual patterns and from their interaction. The patterns in a language work together to generate a system. Coplien describes a pattern language as follows:

> [A pattern language is] … a collection of patterns that build on each other to generate a system. A pattern in isolation solves an isolated design problem; a pattern language builds a system. [Coplien 1996]

A Pattern Language Is a Complex System

A complex system is "a system formed out of many components whose behavior is emergent, that is, the behavior of the system cannot be simply inferred from the behavior of its components" [Bar-Yam1997]. Governments, families, and the human body are all examples of complex systems, whereas a pendulum, spinning wheel, and orbiting planet are all simple systems. The amount of information needed to describe a complex system provides a measure of its complexity. Understanding a complex system requires understanding its individual parts, their interdependencies, and how those parts act together to form the behavior of the whole system. Complex systems may have been designed, or have evolved, or have partly evolved and partly been designed. Systems in domains as diverse as nature, software, economics, and ecology can thus be classified as complex systems.

According to Alexander's [1979] work, a pattern language fits the above definition of a complex system, because it is made up of components and its overall behavior is emergent. A pattern language is made up of components called patterns:

> … it is possible to put these patterns together to form coherent languages. …

> The structure of a pattern language is created by the fact that individual patterns are not isolated. …

> Each pattern then, depends both on the smaller patterns it contains, and on the larger patterns within which it is contained.

> [Alexander1979]

Furthermore, the behavior of a pattern language cannot be explained simply by studying individual patterns:

> A collection of these deep patterns, each one a fluid field, capable of being combined, and overlapping in entirely unpredictable ways, ... [is] capable of generating an entirely unpredictable system of new and unforeseen relationships.

> [Alexander1979]

Evolved Systems Provide Insight

Both some evolved and some designed systems can be classified as complex systems, and therefore have underlying, common properties [Bar-Yam1997]. Recognizing those common properties enables insights from evolved systems to be used to understand and build designed systems. Dasgupta [1991] actually argues that it is valid and worthwhile to view design, and in particular design in computer science, as an evolutionary process. While in the Darwinian view, evolution is a process of variation and natural selection (and design is not such a process), key aspects of solution development related to testing and adaptation are the same across domains. In particular, solving complex problems typically requires making choices involving many alternative and mutually interacting factors. Design solutions to complex problems are therefore "satisficed", by which Dasgupta means that they are good solutions, suboptimal but workable, rather than the best solution. As a separate but related issue, sometimes the optimal solution cannot be comprehended, and even if it can, it may not be practical to use it. In addition, many models suggest that computer science design is a process of iterative refinement, as is evolution. Any design solution should therefore be viewed as tentative and likely to evolve further.

From the point of view of this language, evolved systems in nature are particularly relevant for two reasons.

First, systems in nature and the patterns in those systems have been formally characterized in terms of symmetry and symmetry breaking [Stewart+1992]. Such systems provide a useful reference point for the analysis of patterns in other domains in terms of symmetry and symmetry breaking. As symmetry breaking is one explanation of the processes by which systems in nature form and evolve, system designers in other domains may benefit from understanding the role of symmetry and symmetry breaking in nature, and in their systems.

Second, some of the properties inherent to natural systems are significant for software. In particular, systems in nature are inherently stable: "Natural systems must be stable; that is, they must retain their form even if they're disturbed" [Stewart+1992]. System designers who seek to build systems that are stable (behave predictably) and yet able to change (to adapt in a dynamic environment) may be able to build better systems by learning from the patterns and systems of nature.

The symmetry-breaking theory on which LDPL is based has its foundations in mathematics. Complex systems in biology and physics have been formally analyzed in terms of symmetry-breaking theory as defined by the mathematics of group theory [Stewart+1992]. No such formal analysis, however, exists for systems in many other domains, although Coplien and Zhao [2001; 2002] are in the process of establishing a formal basis for symmetry-breaking analysis of software. The development of the LDPL thus rests on an informal analysis of concepts of symmetry and symmetry breaking in systems in several application domains.

Rather than focus directly on system design, LDPL aims to help designers create the conditions necessary for good design to happen. In a sense, then, LDPL is about meta-design, which can be defined as follows:

> [Meta-design is about creating] the enabling conditions for design activities. In other words [it provides] a perspective of design in which the user is a designer.
>
> An important aspect of meta-design is to design not just an artifact, but a life-cycle that anticipates changes that may occur over a long period of time.
>
> [Ostwald2002]

Examples Used in LDPL

LDPL is intended for use in the development of *pattern languages*. Those pattern languages can then in turn be used in the development of *physical systems*, as shown in Figure 17–1. For example, LDPL could be used to help build a pattern language for C++ programs, which could then be used to help develop C++ programs.

The existence of each pattern in LDPL is confirmed by using examples from existing pattern languages for system development—languages at the second level of the diagram shown in Figure 17–1. The examples are drawn from several different languages in several different application domains, substantiating the multidisciplinary nature of LDPL and validating that the symmetry-breaking theory underlying LDPL is, in fact, fundamental. This validation is particularly important in the given context, in which formal analysis of

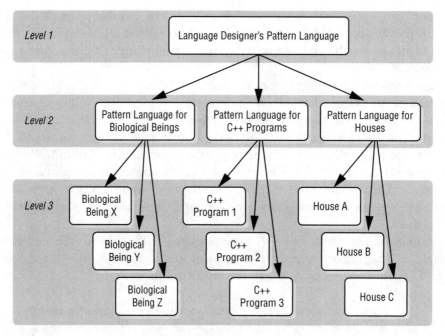

Figure 17-1 *The Language Designer's Pattern Language helps build pattern languages for system design, that in turn help build physical systems.*

symmetry-breaking concepts in many domains has not yet been fully developed. Software is one domain from which pattern language examples are drawn, as it is the domain of interest for this work. Architecture is another, because of architect Christopher Alexander's [1977; 1979] foundational work on pattern languages and their subsequent influence on the development of the software patterns discipline.

Each pattern in LDPL also includes examples drawn from biological systems—entities at the third level of the diagram shown in Figure 17-1. Biological examples are of particular interest because of the existence of formal analysis of biological systems in terms of the symmetry and symmetry-breaking theory [Stewart+1992] on which LDPL is based. Ideally, any biological examples would be drawn from biological pattern languages rather than biological systems, but such languages have not yet been explicitly articulated. The biological examples have therefore been carefully chosen to reflect structures likely to be present in a biological pattern language.

The multidisciplinary examples included with each pattern in LDPL come from a variety of sources. From the domain of software patterns and pattern languages, Coplien's [2000] C++ idioms language, the CHECKS Pattern Language of Information Integrity [Cunningham1995], and the HALF-OBJECT PLUS PROTOCOL (HOPP) pattern [Meszaros1995], are used extensively as examples. Alexander's [1977] architectural patterns provide a rich source of architectural pattern language examples. The biological examples relate to diverse processes and structures, including the processes by which cells develop and regenerate, and the social structures of insect communities.

The C++ Idioms Language [Coplien2000] draws on idioms from earlier work by Coplien [1992] to develop a pattern language that guides the building of an inheritance hierarchy in C++, with particular focus on algebraic types. Key issues in building such a hierarchy include efficient and effective memory management, placement of algebraic operations in the hierarchy, and implementation of operations that depend equally on more than one operand without multiple inheritance.

The CHECKS pattern language [Cunningham1995] guides the development of software that accepts user input. The language shows how to separate good from bad input and how to minimize the amount of bad input recorded. It consists of ten patterns relating to quantifying the domain model, providing feedback about the domain model to the user as transparently as possible, and addressing the long-term integrity of information.

The HOPP pattern [Meszaros1995] describes how to decompose a concept that exists across multiple address spaces. It splits an original, whole object into two half-objects plus a communication protocol between them. For the examples in LDPL, HOPP is discussed in the context of how it interacts with various other patterns to provide language-like examples rather than examples focused on one pattern.

Alexander [1977] developed an architectural pattern language for towns, buildings, and construction. The language provides "a coherent picture of an entire region," from large-scale regional design down to the details of construction of particular buildings. The patterns can be combined in many different ways to generate a variety of structures.

The Pattern Language

LDPL addresses the following key issues:

- Generating patterns from a system of forces
- Identifying and understanding the nature of relationships between patterns

- Adding new patterns to, and removing patterns from, a pattern language
- Maintaining stability in a pattern language over time

These issues are important because they are key issues from the point of view of building pattern languages for complex systems, where those systems need to function effectively, over the long term, in a dynamic environment. They relate both to how patterns work together and to the structural properties of systems generated with pattern languages built from this pattern language.

LDPL identifies ten patterns, as shown in the language structure diagram in Figure 17–2. LOCAL REPAIR is the pattern largest in scale, and it highlights the importance of structural transformations being small-step and local in scope but in accord with global needs. CLUSTER OF FORCES focuses on how to identify and group together related forces, and RESOLUTION OF FORCES focuses on balancing identified groups of forces to create patterns. LOCAL SYMMETRIES shows how to connect patterns in a language and LEVELS OF SCALE ensures that connected patterns are relatively close in scale. CROSS LINKAGES addresses the problem of

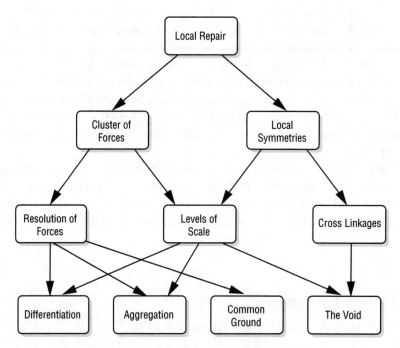

Figure 17–2   *The language structure of the LDPL. The higher a pattern in the diagram, the larger in scale it is. An arrow from pattern A to pattern B indicates that B builds on A.*

the language structure being complex enough to generate complex system structure. DIFFERENTIATION, AGGREGATION, and COMMON GROUND show different ways patterns are added to a language. DIFFERENTIATION shows how to elaborate an existing pattern when finer structure is needed, AGGREGATION shows how to incorporate structure that appears new and different, and COMMON GROUND points out that a new pattern may arise out of existing patterns in different contexts with underlying commonality. THE VOID focuses on removing a pattern or patterns from a language.

In this section, the description of each pattern in the LDPL begins with a patlet that conveys the intent of the pattern, followed by Context, Problem, Forces, Solution, and Rationale sections. Each pattern then has examples from software and architectural pattern languages, and a biological system example.

Local Repair

If you have an isolated or unbalanced force,
then try to fit it in an existing pattern.

Context

You have a pattern language that at one time has balanced its forces, but now you have a force that is isolated or disturbs the balance of the language.

Problem

You need to incorporate the force into the language in a way that minimizes the changes required and that benefits rather than detracts from the whole language.

Forces

The information available about forces will never be complete.

The process of finding a solution that balances the forces will cause other forces to arise; it is not possible to enumerate all the forces before attempting a solution. [Grabow1983]

The world is always changing, so new forces are always coming and going from the design. [Grabow1983]

No force can be considered in isolation. Forces are interrelated, and a given pattern resolves a given set of forces: "*In short, a pattern lives when it allows its own internal forces to resolve themselves. ... The 'bad' patterns are unable to contain the forces which occur in them.*" [Alexander1979]

A collection of patterns works together to resolve a systemwide set of forces:

> *The individual configuration of any one pattern requires other patterns to keep itself alive. ...*
>
> It is true that each [pattern] can be explained, in its own terms, as an isolated thing, which is needed to resolve certain forces. But, also, these few patterns form a whole, they work as a system ....
>
> [The] life of [a] pattern ... [depends on] the self-sustaining harmony, in which each process helps sustain the other processes, and in which the whole system of forces and processes keeps itself going, over and again, without creating extra forces that will tear it down.
>
> [Alexander1979]

There are many ways to cluster a given field of forces. Even if reclustering the forces from scratch produces an entirely different but workable solution, work done on the basis of the previous solution would be wasted.

The need for local repair to a language is driven by the need for repair in systems generated by the language.

Reclustering the forces from scratch could lead to instability in systems generated with the language, because the patterns in the new language have not been validated [Winn+2002] by their repeated occurrence in existing systems.

Focus is by nature local; a designer can only be attentive to one thing in one place at a time. [Raskin2000]

Solution

Identify the pattern that can best accommodate the isolated or unbalanced force (where the force best fits in) and focus on that pattern. Often, the new force is implicit in an existing solution and simply needs to be explicitly stated; the force can then be added to the pattern without disturbing the balance of the forces. When the force is truly new, the old solution can often be adapted to rebalance the forces. Even if it turns out that the new force requires a new solution, the old solution will often serve as a solid basis for the new solution.

Doing local repair on a language might require adding a pattern, removing a pattern, or modifying a pattern. As a result of these changes, the interconnections between patterns may also need to be modified.

Rationale

In *The Nature of Order* [2002a][1996], Alexander describes what he calls "the fundamental process," which he argues is the key process governing the development of self-sustaining systems. The fundamental process drives change through local and small-step modification that has a global focus. Change happens by evaluating the system to see which small-scale, local change would best impact the whole. That local change is made, and its effect on the whole evaluated. If the effect on the whole is negative, the change is wiped out, and the process begins again.

Awareness of the impact of local change on a system as a whole is critical, because in an interconnected system, change to one part of a system inevitably affects other parts of the system. Alexander [1996] argues that the fundamental process helps build stable systems for a number of reasons. Change is based on what has worked in the past rather than what is anticipated to happen in the future. Change is incremental and thus gives an opportunity for feedback; the effects of small changes are available for study before other changes are made, and changes can be altered, if necessary. Further, such incremental change implies a willingness to live with unpredictability—to resist defining a priori the nature of major change and let that change unfold step by step.

In his book *How Buildings Learn* [1997], Stewart Brand argues that slow, small-step growth is what makes a building grow gradually better rather than gradually worse over time. Such growth is not just healthy for individual buildings. Brand argues that much wholesome evolution of cities can be explained by the persistence of site—in other words, by the fact that property lines and thoroughfares in cities do not change even when, for example, hills are leveled and waterfronts filled in. Brand also points out that most building design is vernacular and vernacular design is inherently small-step and localized.

Senge [1990] emphasizes the importance of local but globally aware change in his study of complex systems. He argues that when making changes to a system, global awareness is critical, but it is not the scale on which most changes should be made. Dynamic complexity must be managed locally [Senge 1990], but local management of dynamic complexity must be driven by global as well as local concerns. Senge points out the typical cycle that happens in many complex systems when local repair is driven by local concerns and the needs of the whole are ignored:

> In the short run, individuals gain by acting selfishly. This selfishness leads to success, which reinforces the actions that led to the success. ... But, the sum total of all the individuals acting in their self-interest ...

add up to a "total activity" with a life of its own. Eventually … the unsustainable "gain per individual activity" … begins to decline, and the benefit to each individual begins to reverse. By the time they realize the import of that common error, it's too late to save the whole, and all the individuals fall with it. It's not enough for one individual to see the problem; the problem cannot be solved until most decision makers act together for the good of the whole. [Senge 1990]

Alexander uses a biological analogy to make the same point:

Each part (cell) is free to adapt locally to its own processes, and is helped in this process by the genetic code which guides its growth.

Yet at the same time, this same code contains features which guarantee that the slow adaptation of the individual parts is not merely anarchic, and individual, but that each part simultaneously helps to create those larger parts, systems, and patterns which are needed for the whole.

And, just as the flower needs a genetic code to keep the wholeness of its parts, so do the building and the town.

[Alexander1979]

The structure of a pattern language is such that each pattern is smaller in scale than the patterns above it, and each pattern, by definition, takes into account the structure of the patterns above it. This structure inherently takes into account global context and ensures that implementing change by focusing on one pattern incorporates global awareness:

At any given moment in the unfolding of a sequence of patterns, we have a partly defined whole, which has the structure given to it by the patterns that come earlier in the sequence.

… in every case, there is some sequence of patterns which is most appropriate for that design; and you can get this sequence more or less directly from your knowledge of the size of the morphological effect which each pattern has, compared with all the others.

The sequence of the patterns for a design—as generated by the language—is therefore the key to that design. …

At every level, certain broad patterns get laid down: and the details are squeezed into position to conform to the structure of these broader patterns. Of course, under these circumstances, the details are always slightly different, since they get distorted as they are squeezed into the larger structure already laid down. In a design of this type, one naturally senses that the global patterns are more important than the details, because they dominate the design. Each pattern is given the importance and control over the whole which it deserves in the hierarchy of patterns.

Each pattern encompasses, and contains, the forces which it has to deal with; and there are no other forces in the system. Under these circumstances, each event which happens is resolved. The forces come into play, and resolve themselves, within the patterns as they are.

Each pattern helps to sustain other patterns.

The language will evolve, because it can evolve piecemeal, one pattern at a time.

[Alexander1979]

Example (C++ Idioms Language)

One force missing from the idioms language [Coplien2000] is that in C++ interface can be separated from implementation using pointers, but this is not effective because it makes it impossible to overload built-in operators. This new force clearly fits best with the HANDLE/BODY pattern, whose other forces also relate to separating interface and implementation. The solution structure of the existing HANDLE/BODY pattern already balances the new force—it overcomes the problems of using pointers to separate interface and implementation—so all that is needed is for the force to be explicitly stated; this is the simplest kind of LOCAL REPAIR.

An early version of PROMOTION LADDER [Coplien2003] was based on a class promoting objects of derived class types to its own type. This set the scene for HOMOGENOUS ADDITION to work. At some point, however, the author realized that there was a force that PROMOTION LADDER needed to resolve but did not. Specifically, the original version of PROMOTION LADDER allowed base classes to know about their children. This prevented important forces about encapsulation—for example, that a class should not know about its derived classes—from being resolved. The author recognized that the new force belonged with PROMOTION LADDER and adjusted the solution of PROMOTION LADDER to take account of the newly recognized force. The change was to make derived classes promote themselves to their base class type, rather than the other way around. This change allowed all forces to be resolved, and represents an example of LOCAL REPAIR where existing structure is modified.

The idioms language was originally developed without DETACHED COUNTED BODY, which shows how to keep track of the number of handles to a body without modifying Body code. At some later point, the author realized that some systems generated with the language needed to be able to add to a HANDLE/BODY context the capacity to manage multiple handles for one body, but without access to Body code. This realization represented a new force: that the Body code could not be modified. While this force is most closely related to the forces in the existing COUNTED BODY pattern, it cannot be potentially balanced together with those forces, because one of the forces already implicit in COUNTED BODY and critical to its solution is that the Body code can be modified. The force therefore required a new pattern; COUNTED BODY and DETACHED COUNTED BODY both represent valid solutions to a problem, each appropriate in a different context. This example of LOCAL REPAIR resulted in existing structure being further elaborated and a new pattern being incorporated in the idioms language.

Example (CHECKS Language)

WHOLE VALUE [Cunningham1995] suggests that specialized values meaningful in the application domain should be constructed and used for message arguments and as input/output units. In the context of a document editor, where characters represent fundamental domain values, WHOLE VALUE suggests that characters should be implemented as objects. Implementing characters as objects offers several advantages [Gamma+1995]. It allows the "application's object structure ... [to] mimic the document's physical structure," which allows characters and more complex elements to be "treated uniformly with respect to how they are drawn and formatted."

However, the cost of representing characters as objects can become prohibitive, as "even a moderate-sized document may require hundreds of thousands of character objects." This prohibitive cost represents a new force, which becomes operative at the point at which cost is unmanageable. One way of incorporating the new force is to represent characters as built-in types, rather than objects. Such a solution, though, comes at a high cost because it negates the advantages of representing characters as objects. Moreover, it requires changing the system globally and does not preserve existing symmetry; the draw method for characters is no longer tied to the subclass representing the particular character being drawn, but to some other unrelated subclass in the system.

FLYWEIGHT [Gamma+1995] shows how to retain the benefits of storing simple entities as objects but defray the potentially high storage cost of doing so. FLYWEIGHT shows how to use sharing to support large numbers of simple objects efficiently. In the document editor, one FLYWEIGHT object can be created for each character in a character set and a single instance of that object shared amongst all occurrences of the character in the document. Information that differs between character instances, such as font, size, and position on a page, can be calculated "from text layout algorithms and formatting commands in effect wherever the character appears."

In the context of a pattern language incorporating WHOLE VALUE, and at the point at which the cost of representing particular entities as objects becomes unmanageable, the addition of FLYWEIGHT to the language represents LOCAL REPAIR of the language, in the region of WHOLE VALUE.

Example (Biological System)

When a tree grows, it begins with a trunk and then splits into various branches. The way the branches form is for each split to form smaller and smaller branches. For example, the trunk might split into two branches each about half the size of the original trunk, then each of those halves might split into two pieces, smaller again, and so on. Whenever the leaves on a branch begin to get too heavy, this represents a new force acting on the system. The branch responds by growing a new, smaller sub-branch; the change is local and fits with the global needs of the tree in the sense that the tree doesn't collapse because of the new sub-branch that has grown.

Related Patterns

CLUSTER OF FORCES shows how to identify where a force belongs in the language. LOCAL SYMMETRIES shows how to connect patterns in the language together. LEVELS OF SCALE shows how the language as a whole is organized.

Cluster of Forces

If there are too many forces to think about all at once,
then use domain knowledge and structure to make clusters of forces.

Context

You are developing a pattern language. A pattern language is a field of forces. The forces are numerous, interrelated and often conflicting. You have a force or forces that you need to place into the language.

Problem

You need to partition forces into patterns so that each pattern is as independent as possible, allowing patterns to be applied one at a time, in sequence.

Forces

Where there are many interrelated forces to be considered, their interactions are too complex for the designer to grasp simultaneously. [Alexander1964]

It is important to take account of how responding to one force affects other forces; responding to forces in isolation leads to inequilibrium. [Alexander196]

Forces in a pattern should not cause or reflect needless change. Otherwise, minor disturbances will take hold of the pattern and distort it. [Alexander1964]

For any one force or collection of forces, there are certain other forces that must be considered simultaneously with it in order for the overall system of forces to be balanced. [Alexander1964]

"[There] is a deep and important underlying structural correspondence between the pattern of a problem and the process of designing a physical form which answers that problem." [Alexander1964]

Solution

Group forces together so that they form clusters that maximize the interaction of forces within clusters and minimize it between clusters [Alexander1964].

Each cluster will form the basis for a pattern in the language. To work out which forces interact the most, use domain knowledge. A main consideration in this is to cluster those forces that relate to the same domain structure [Alexander1964].

Rationale

Designers using a pattern language will often not fully understand all of the forces at play. The pattern language should enable the designer using the language to create well-structured entities in the domain of interest without having to fully comprehend the interrelationships of the forces they are dealing with. Maximizing the interaction of forces within patterns and minimizing the interaction between patterns enables designers to apply patterns one at a time, with each pattern independently resolving a different set of forces.

Patterns in a pattern language represent subdivisions of the design problem into smaller problems whose forces are as independent as possible. This facilitates pattern language users addressing potentially large problems with a sequence of small changes, and makes it easier for a pattern language to evolve over time:

> Since the patterns are independent, then you can change one at a time, and they can always get better, because you can always improve each pattern, individually. [Alexander1979]

Each pattern is thus a cluster of the forces in the domain of systems being implemented with the language. Developing a pattern language requires identifying key structures in the domain of implementation and articulating those structures as patterns that build on each other.

Example (Architectural Pattern Language)

FAMILY OF ENTRANCES argues that entrances to a building complex or group of related buildings should be designed to be broadly similar and arranged so that each is visible from all others. If this is not done, then a person arriving at the building is likely to have trouble finding which entrance they need.

The forces addressed by FAMILY OF ENTRANCES are as follows [Alexander+ 1977]:

- Each building in a group of buildings or each section in a building complex needs an entrance.
- Each entrance needs to be distinguishable from others in the group.
- The collection of entrances needs to be recognizable as such.

These forces all relate to being able to easily identify a particular entrance within a collection of entrances. They are thus semantically related and relate to a common structure: the collection of entrances in a group of buildings or building complex.

ENTRANCE TRANSITION addresses the problem of making a person feel comfortable when they enter a building. The forces it addresses are as follows:

- People behave differently in public and private places.
- People need time and space in which to adjust their behavior from public to private and vice versa.
- People want their houses and, to some degree, other buildings, to be private domains.

- People expect the street to be a public domain.
- An entrance marks a transition from public to private space.
- Physical changes help create psychological changes.
- The experience of entering a building affects how you feel inside the building.

These forces all relate to facilitating a shift in behavior from public to private and vice versa. The common structure that they relate to is the particular entrance being built.

Although both FAMILY OF ENTRANCES and ENTRANCE TRANSITION relate to creating entrances for buildings, none of the forces addressed by ENTRANCE TRANSITION pertain to distinguishing an individual entrance within a collection of entrances. Similarly, none of the forces addressed by FAMILY OF ENTRANCES relate to smoothing the transition between the space inside and outside a building. The interaction of forces between the patterns is thus not significant, and these patterns thus cluster forces.

Example (CHECKS Pattern Language)

WHOLE VALUE argues that specialized values that are meaningful in the application domain should be constructed and used for message arguments and as input/output units. For example, a contract duration should be specified in units of weeks or days, rather than as an integer.

The forces addressed by WHOLE VALUE are as follows:

- Literal values offered by the language and standard objects used as values will not correspond to meaningful quantities in a business domain.
- When quantifying a domain model, people want to use the most fundamental units possible.
- Communication between program and users needs common units.

These forces are semantically related because they all relate to the *fundamental units* used in the domain model. The forces also relate to a common structure: the units used to quantify the domain.

EXCEPTIONAL VALUE addresses the problem of categorizing user input values that do not fit into the range of attributes covered by WHOLE VALUE. For example, if "agree" and "strongly agree" are two typical responses to a query, an answer such as "illegible" will not be able to be quantified in the domain model. EXCEPTIONAL VALUE suggests that "one or more distinguished values [be used] to represent exceptional circumstances," rather than extending the range of attributes covered by WHOLE VALUE. EXCEPTIONAL VALUE incorporates into the domain model a place for missing data that may appear at a later stage.

The forces addressed by EXCEPTIONAL VALUE are as follows:

- Anticipating every possible business category in the domain hierarchy can be confusing and difficult.
- There will be a normal range of answers and other answers that are more exceptional.
- There needs to be a place in the class hierarchy for exceptional values.

These forces are semantically related because they all focus on categorizing the range of values in the domain. The forces all pertain to some classification structure for the values.

Although both WHOLE VALUE and EXCEPTIONAL VALUE relate to quantities used by the domain model, none of the forces addressed by EXCEPTIONAL VALUE pertain to identifying what units to use to quantify the domain. Likewise, none of the forces in WHOLE VALUE address how to categorize the range of values in the domain. The interaction of forces between the patterns is therefore not significant. The patterns thus cluster related forces.

Related Patterns

RESOLUTION OF FORCES shows how to create structure that holds a cluster of forces in tension.

Local Symmetries

If you need to understand how patterns are related,
then connect them according to the ways they break symmetry.

Context

You have a collection of patterns, each of which solves a key problem in a domain. At least one of those patterns is not connected to other patterns in the language, or even if all the patterns are connected, you may feel that some connections are missing.

Problem

Patterns by themselves cannot solve complex problems. You need to connect them so that they form a language.

Forces

System structure is defined by symmetry: "One of the great themes of the past century's mathematics is the existence of deep links between geometry and symmetry." [Stewart+1992]

Preserving symmetry preserves stability: "Generally, the lowest energy state of an assembly is a symmetrical one." [Blundell+1996]

Local symmetry, rather than global symmetry, is critical to a system's stability. A system needs more fine structure—more local symmetries—to be stable:

> In general, a large symmetry of the simplified neoclassicist type rarely contributes to the life of a thing, because in any complex whole in the world, there are nearly always complex, asymmetrical forces at work—matters of location, and context, and function— which require that symmetry be broken. [Alexander2002]

> ... saying these patterns are alive is more or less the same as saying they are stable. [Alexander1979]

Each pattern exists in the context of other patterns and smaller-scale patterns complete larger-scale ones. [Alexander+1977]

While the cluster of forces in each pattern is independent, the patterns themselves work together and are interrelated:

> Each pattern encompasses, and contains, the forces which it has to deal with; and there are no other forces in the system. Under these circumstances, each event which happens is resolved. The forces come into play, and resolve themselves, within the patterns as they are.

> *Each* pattern *helps to sustain other patterns.*

> The quality without a name occurs, not when an isolated pattern occurs, but when an entire system of patterns, interdependent, at many levels, is all stable and alive. ...

> So, somehow, this system of patterns, which I have loosely sketched, forms the basis for what is needed ... and these patterns are a system; they are interdependent. It is true that each one can be explained, in its own terms, as an isolated thing, which is needed to resolve certain forces. But, also, these few patterns form a whole, they work as a system.

[Alexander1979]

Solution

Connect the patterns so that smaller-scale patterns break the symmetry of the larger-scale patterns to which they are connected. The scale of a pattern relates to the size of the artifact being shaped by the application of the pattern.

Find a larger-scale pattern that provides a context such that the pattern you are considering elaborates the symmetries provided by that context, thus preserving the overall structure of the larger pattern. Connect the isolated pattern below the larger pattern in the language. If there are several patterns that provide a suitable context for the isolated pattern, then use domain knowledge to choose the right one or to decide whether more than one should be connected.

The new structure added to the language by the previously isolated pattern should create local symmetries; it should replicate and refine symmetry created by the solution structure of the pattern above. Then it will strengthen or refine the existing, overall structure created by the other patterns, making the overall structure more "whole."

Continue connecting patterns until all are connected. Since a pattern language has partial ordering, according to the levels of scale of the patterns, you will eventually converge on the same structure independent of the order in which you connect the patterns.

Rationale

Smaller-scale patterns elaborate larger-scale patterns by a process of differentiation [Alexander1979]. Differentiation is not a process of combining preformed parts to make a whole, but rather one in which the whole gives birth to its parts by splitting, like the development of an embryo [Alexander1979]. Differentiation of structure goes hand in hand with specialization: each pattern creates structure that is "specialized" to balance a given system of forces. Since patterns are transformations that break symmetry [Stewart+1992], smaller-scale patterns will elaborate on the structure of larger-scale patterns by transforming existing, latent symmetries in the larger-scale patterns and expressing those symmetries more locally. The pattern language structure should reflect this relationship.

Czarnecki and Eisenecker [2000] affirm the importance of differentiation to system structure. They note that undifferentiated components are too large to be effective units of reuse, and that classes and objects alone are too small to have system impact. Alexander makes the same point in BUILDING COMPLEX [1977]: "... the more monolithic a building is, and the less differentiated, the more it presents itself as an inhuman, mechanical factory." Alexander argues that it is important that building structures reflect the different social identities of people who use the buildings. In buildings that do so, a person's experience of using the building is more likely to be positive, and their interactions with other people in the building more likely to be regarded as personal, rather than impersonal.

Example (C++ Idioms Language)

HANDLE/BODY splits a design-time class into two implementation classes, one of which is the interface (Handle) and the other the actual implementation (Body).

HANDLE/BODY creates local symmetry by redistributing type symmetry, as shown in Figure 17–3. The original type (before HANDLE/BODY is applied) expresses symmetry over a related set of objects (the objects of that type) in the system. That is, there are elements of the interface and elements of the implementation that are invariant across all the objects of the type. Specifically, the interface member functions, their parameter and return types, their pre- and post-conditions, are all the same. Similarly, the structure of all of the objects is the same.

HANDLE/BODY redistributes this symmetry in two parts: the handle and the body. One part (the Handle) carries the original interface symmetry, and the other

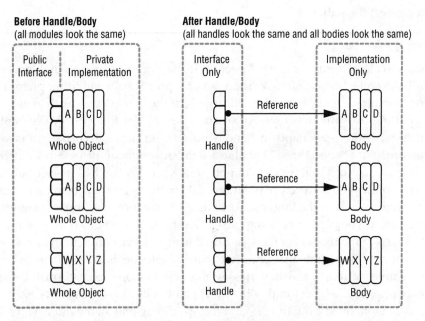

Figure 17–3 *Handle/Body transforms a design-time class into two distinct implementation classes, Handle and Body. In the process, the type symmetry of the original class is redistributed, with the Handle expressing the interface symmetry and the Body the implementation symmetry.*

(the Body) carries the original implementation symmetry. Each of these parts expresses its own local symmetry—all handles of the type look the same, and all bodies of the type look the same. Conceptually, the Handle and Body are each still part of one whole object: the HANDLE/BODY object. Each of these local symmetries derives from the original symmetry; the original symmetry is preserved.

Using HANDLE/BODY creates a situation where more than one Handle can potentially refer to the same Body. For example, the top two handles in Figure 17–3 both refer to identical bodies, which represents a source of inefficiency. COUNTED BODY, illustrated in Figure 17–4, addresses this problem by adding a reference counter to the body objects, thus allowing more efficient memory use while still preserving the independence of the HANDLE/BODY objects.

In the idioms language, COUNTED BODY is connected to HANDLE/BODY, indicating that the language structure of the idioms language reflects the symmetry-breaking relationships between HANDLE/BODY and COUNTED BODY. COUNTED BODY builds on HANDLE/BODY by preserving the existing type symmetry but elaborating on it more locally. The symmetry that COUNTED BODY preserves has

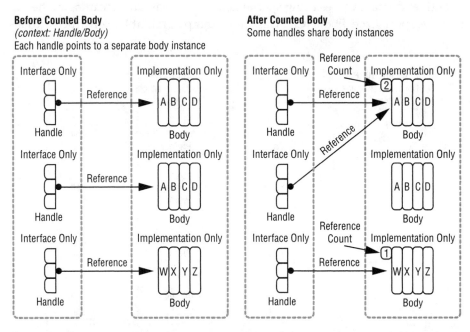

Figure 17–4 *Counted Body transforms Handle/Body by maintaining a reference count and allowing multiple handles to refer to the same body. This preserves the symmetry whereby each client of a Handle/Body object views it (locally) in the same way, regardless of which handle provides access.*

to do with the relationship between HANDLE/BODY and client objects. Each client of a Handle/Body object "sees" the object in the same way, because all of the object functionality is accessed through the one Handle. From the client's (local) point of view, all objects look the same. But from the system (global) point of view, only the handles that share a body are the same; a handle for one body is different from a handle for a different body. Thus COUNTED BODY preserves the symmetry created by HANDLE/BODY (from the client's point of view) while enabling greater efficiency (from the system's point of view).

Example (Half-Object Plus Protocol Pattern)

HALF-OBJECT PLUS PROTOCOL (HOPP) represents a transformation of a system in which a concept that has been implemented in exactly one address space splits across two or more address spaces. The object implementing that concept is transformed such that it comprises two (or more) "half-objects" plus a protocol that manages interaction between the half-objects. The protocol and half-objects together make up the HOPP object, as shown in Figure 17–5.

The HOPP pattern builds on WHOLE VALUE [Cunningham1995], because it quantifies domain values using specialized values that have meaning in the domain. A specialized Phone Call class, for example, might be constructed to al-

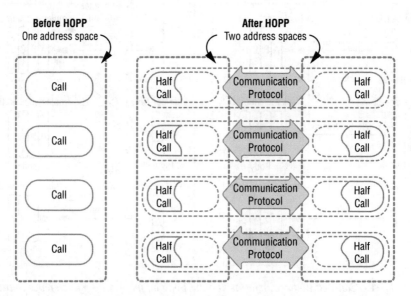

Figure 17–5 *An example of HOPP for Call objects. The key to recognizing the symmetry breaking in HOPP is to recognize that each half-object is created as like the original full object as possible.*

low Phone Call objects to represent phone calls in a telecommunications system. In a system implementing WHOLE VALUE, the relationship between a particular object and each of its client objects is the same: Each of the client objects "sees" the given object in the same way, because all of the object's functionality is in the same place. This sameness of relationship between object and *all* client objects is a symmetry; the invariant is the relationship between object and client, and what changes is the structure of the client itself. This symmetry might be lost when a concept is split across object spaces, but HOPP preserves it, by transforming the object into a HOPP object and redistributing symmetry *inside* what is now a HOPP object to create local symmetries. Each half-object is created as like the original as possible, even if that means duplicating some functionality. Clients can interact with each half-object as if it were the original, whole object.

When forces require a concept to be implemented across multiple address spaces, HOPP thus indicates how to change the system to allow the distribution, yet still preserve the symmetry of the original system as much as possible. HOPP provides an implementation that preserves a conceptual symmetry of relationship between object and client, by creating local symmetries in the system implementation [Coplien1998a; Coplien1998b]. Within the context of a pattern language, HOPP would thus be connected to a pattern like WHOLE VALUE, because it breaks the symmetry of WHOLE VALUE.

Example (Biological System)

In many species, the embryo is initially spherically shaped. As it develops, the embryo changes shape, but not randomly; the embryo of a given species follows a predictable pattern of development. Many major events in embryo development break symmetry, and this symmetry breaking is a key to the predictability of the developmental process [Harris2004].

CLEAVAGE is the name given to the initial period of embryo development and is an example of a pattern in embryo development that breaks symmetry. During cleavage, an embryo repeatedly doubles the number of cells of which it is made up, as shown in the top row of Figure 17–6. Each cell of the embryo repeatedly splits into two copies of itself; this process is called mitosis. Throughout cleavage, there is no growth of the embryo. The embryo splits into ever smaller cells [Kimball2004], creating local symmetries; the structures of the original zygote are replicated on a smaller and smaller scale, and still form part of an identifiable whole.

GASTRULATION, shown in the second row of Figure 17–6, is another example of a pattern in embryo development that breaks symmetry. During gastrulation, cells in the embryo reposition themselves to form the three primary germ

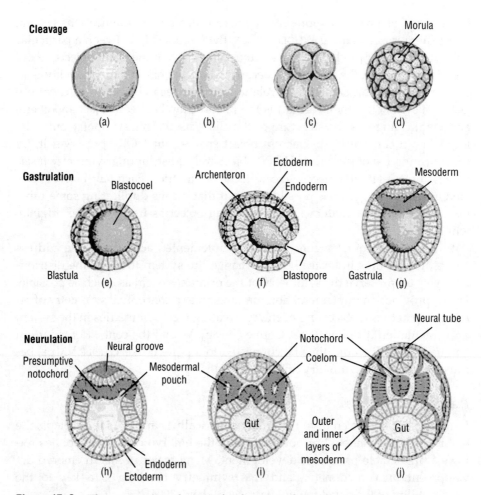

Cleavage

(a)   (b)   (c)   (d) Morula

Gastrulation

Blastocoel   Archenteron   Ectoderm   Endoderm   Mesoderm

Blastula (e)   (f) Blastopore   Gastrula (g)

Neurulation

Neural tube

Presumptive notochord   Neural groove   Mesodermal pouch   Notochord   Coelom

Gut   Outer and inner layers of mesoderm   Gut

(h) Endoderm Ectoderm   (i)   (j)

Figure 17–6 *Three stages in embryonic development: cleavage, gastrulation, and neurulation.*

layers, each of which has a special role in building the complete animal [Kimball2004]. During gastrulation the embryo develops a definite anterior and posterior, and left and right orientation. Gastrulation replaces axial symmetry with bilateral symmetry; the embryo moves from having an infinite number of planes of reflection symmetry to having only one plane of reflection symmetry [Harris2004]. The embryo thus retains some, but not all of its original symmetry, and the full reflectional symmetry is found more locally in smaller areas within the embryo.

Related Patterns

LEVELS OF SCALE shows what to do when the difference in scale between patterns is too great for a connection to be made. CROSS LINKAGES highlights the importance of the overall language structure being more than a simple, tree-like structure.

Resolution of Forces

If you need to balance a cluster of forces,
then build a structure that holds the forces in tension.

Context

You have identified the pattern that a new force belongs with, but that force cannot be resolved within the pattern as it stands.

Problem

You need to resolve the new cluster of forces.

Forces

The forces within a cluster need to hold each other in tension to produce a stable structure. Alexander notes that each pattern is stable, or self-sustaining, to the degree that it is capable of "containing its own forces, and keeping them in balance." [Alexander1979]

Not all forces should pull in the same direction; otherwise there is no tension to be held.

Each cluster of forces relates to a single, common physical form: "The ultimate object of design is form." [Alexander1964]

You will not know that you have resolved forces until you have built a physical form that resolves them.

Balancing forces will cause new forces to arise in the patterns.

Solution

Balance the cluster of forces by building a structure that holds the forces in tension. This structure will become a pattern. Use domain knowledge to determine when forces are balanced. If you cannot balance the clustering using domain insight, then look for a missing force. If a missing force cannot be found, then the clustering is probably wrong; discard the cluster of forces and try again.

Rationale

In a very pragmatic sense, you need to write a solution for your patterns, and this is where you do it.

You will not be able to work out simply by theoretical means whether or not your clusters of forces are the right ones, and whether they will resolve into good patterns. Some clusters of forces cannot be balanced using cursory domain information, and there is no simple rule with which to verify that a pattern does resolve its forces. Alexander [1979] notes that it requires an intangible mix of analytical and practical understanding, and that "we must rely on feelings more than intellect." You will have to create the patterns—create the structures—before you can work out whether they resolve forces:

> We cannot decide whether a misfit has occurred either by looking at the form alone, or by looking at the context alone. Misfit is a condition of the ensemble as a whole, which comes from the unsatisfactory interaction of the form and context. [Alexander1964]

Creating the patterns may also reshape your understanding of the forces:

> A well-designed house not only fits its context well but also illuminates the problem of just what the context is, and thereby clarifies the life which it accommodates. Thus Le Corbusier's invention of new house forms in the 1920's really represented part of the modern attempt to understand the twentieth century's new way of life. ...

> At the time of its invention the geodesic dome could not be calculated on the basis of the structural calculations then in use. Its invention not only solved a specific problem, but drew attention to a different way of thinking about load-bearing structures.

> In all these cases, the invention is based on a hunch which actually makes it easier to understand the problem. Like such a hunch, a constructive diagram will often precede the precise knowledge which could prescribe its shape on rational grounds.

> It is therefore quite reasonable to think of the realization as a way of probing the context's nature, beyond the program but parallel to it. This is borne out, perhaps, by the recent tendency among designers to think of their designs as hypotheses. Each constructive diagram is a tentative assumption about the nature of the context. Like a hypothesis, it relates an unclear set of forces to one another concep-

tually; like a hypothesis, it is usually improved by clarity and economy of notation. Like a hypothesis, it cannot be obtained by deductive methods, but only by abstraction and invention. Like a hypothesis, it is rejected when a discrepancy turns up and shows that it fails to account for some new force in the context.

[Alexander1964]

Example (Architectural Pattern Language)

FAMILY OF ENTRANCES addresses the problem of easy identification of building entrances within a collection of related buildings or building complex. The solution it proposes is twofold. It suggests making each entrance distinguishable by some feature, such as a number, or being on a corner, or having a particular kind of tree or bush near it. It also suggests laying out the collection of entrances so that they "form a family." Laying out the entrances so that they form a family requires the following:

> 1. They [the entrances] form a group, are visible together, and each is visible from all the others.

> 2. They are all broadly similar, for instance all porches, or all gates in a wall, or all marked by a similar kind of doorway.

[Alexander+1977]

This solution balances the forces addressed by FAMILY OF ENTRANCES because it identifies a way of making an entrance both distinguishable from yet similar to other entrances at the same time.

ENTRANCE TRANSITION addresses the problem of how to make people feel comfortable when they enter a building. The solution it proposes is as follows:

> Make a transition space between the street and the front door. Bring the path which connects street and entrance through this transition space, and mark it with a change of light, a change of sound, a change of direction, a change of surface, a change of level, perhaps by gateways which make a change of enclosure, and above all with a change of view. [Alexander+1977]

This solution balances the forces addressed by ENTRANCE TRANSITION. Those forces include that people behave differently in public and private places, and that they want their homes and to some degree other buildings to be relatively private, while expecting the street to be a public place. Recognizing that the experience of entering a building affects how a person feels inside that building, ENTRANCE TRANSITION creates a physical structure that provides time and space in which psychological transitions can happen, and helps trigger those transitions with changes in the physical space, such as a change of light or sound.

Example (CHECKS Pattern Language):

WHOLE VALUE addresses the problem of what kind of units to use in a programming language to model a domain, and offers the following solution:

> [construct] specialized values to quantify [the] domain model and use these values as the arguments of their messages and as the units of input and output. [Cunningham1995]

This solution balances the forces clustered by WHOLE VALUE. The first of those forces notes that values in the programming language lack meaning in the domain. Yet, as the second force notes, people tend to use those values anyway; people tend to want to use the most fundamental units possible, regardless of domain meaning. The third force notes that effective communication between program and users requires common units. WHOLE VALUE balances these forces by providing values in a programming language that represent meaningful quantities in a domain. This both enables effective communication between program and users and allows meaningful domain quantities to be represented, while helping the programmer resist the temptation to use the most fundamental units possible to quantify the domain model.

EXCEPTIONAL VALUE addresses the problem of categorizing the range of input values to a program, providing the following solution:

> Use one or more distinguished values to represent exceptional circumstances. Exceptional values should either accept all messages, answering most of them with another exceptional value, or reject all messages (with doesNotUnderstand), with the possible exception of identifying protocols like isNil or printOn:. [Cunningham1995]

This solution balances the forces clustered by EXCEPTIONAL VALUE. The first of those forces is the difficulty of anticipating every possible business category. Yet, despite this difficulty, there still needs to be a way of storing values that don't fit in an identified and expected category; this is the third force. The second force points out that values can at least be categorized as normal and exceptional. By categorizing values into normal and exceptional, EXCEPTIONAL VALUE provides a way of catering to unexpected values, balancing the forces, without having to anticipate every unexpected value. The independence of forces across WHOLE VALUE and EXCEPTIONAL VALUE means that even though EXCEPTIONAL VALUE builds on WHOLE VALUE, it can be added to the language without affecting WHOLE VALUE.

Related Patterns

DIFFERENTIATION shows how to create new structure by refining existing structure, AGGREGATION shows how to incorporate new structure by molding it to fit the existing structure, even if it is different, and COMMON GROUND shows how to incorporate new structure by drawing out underlying similarities in existing structure.

Levels of Scale

If the difference in scale between patterns is too great,
then add patterns that make the difference smaller.

Context

You have a collection of interconnected patterns of different levels of scale that form a language.

Problem

You cannot connect patterns with the right differences in scale between them. The scale of a pattern relates to the size of the artifact being shaped by the application of the pattern.

Forces

Patterns in a language must be of different levels of scale, even in software [Fincher1999].

The complex systems that pattern languages generate have patterns on many different levels of scale, and the language needs to reflect this: "Multiscale descriptions are needed to understand complex systems." [Bar-Yam2005]

Patterns at different levels of scale are interrelated: "Each pattern then, depends both on the smaller patterns it contains, and on the larger patterns within which it is contained." [Alexander1979]

If connected patterns are too different in scale, then the language will lack coherence:

> ... I must also make sure that the patterns below a given pattern are its principal components.
>
> There must not be too many patterns underneath a given pattern. Consider HALF-HIDDEN GARDEN this time. There is one corner of the garden which will be the SUNNY PLACE; another place will be an OUT-DOOR ROOM perhaps; there is a need for trees, forming a place; there is the character of the garden as a whole; GARDEN GROWING WILD; there is the relation between the garden and the street, in detail; PRIVATE TERRACE ON THE STREET. There is the possibility of the relation between the house and the garden: covered perhaps by GREENHOUSE .... There is the character of flowers in the garden: perhaps RAISED FLOWERS, and the need for vegetables and fruit: VEGETABLE GARDEN and FRUIT TREES ....
>
> But not all of these need to be directly underneath HALF-HIDDEN GARDEN. The reason is that some of them embellish *each other*. For example, GARDEN GROWING WILD, which gives the gardens global character, is itself filled out and completed by RAISED FLOWERS and VEGETABLE GARDEN; and TREE PLACES is itself filled out by FRUIT TREES. These patterns which can be "reached" through another pattern, do not need to appear directly below the pattern HALF-HIDDEN GARDEN.
>
> It is essential to distinguish those patterns which are the principal components of any given pattern, from those which lie still further down.
>
> If I have to make a HALF-HIDDEN GARDEN and I can understand it as a thing which has three or four parts, I can visualize it, and begin to create one, for myself, in my own garden.
>
> But if the HALF-HIDDEN GARDEN has twenty or thirty patterns, all equally its parts, I will not be able to imagine it coherently.
>
> [Alexander1979]

Symmetries in a design must gradually unfold to give it order:

> ... the presence of this "objective beauty" was closely tied to the presence of symmetries and subsymmetries that balance the use of contrasting space, light, and color to form fields of visual centers. Feelings

of beauty and order would increase when these visual centers unfolded recursively at multiple hierarchical levels of granular scale throughout a design (much like fractals). [Appleton2000]

Solution

Make sure the connections between patterns reflect differences in scale of roughly 2:1 to 7:1. If necessary, create patterns whose scale is appropriate to fill the gaps that are too large in scale in the language. Those new patterns will break the symmetry of larger-scale patterns, and will have their symmetry broken by smaller-scale patterns.

Rationale

In *The Nature of Order* [2002], Alexander points out that artifacts that exhibit certain jumps in levels of scale have much more of the essential, structural quality that he calls "life" than artifacts that don't. Specifically, if jumps in scale between patterns are deliberate and evenly spaced and of a magnitude from 10:1 to 2:1, then the patterns of an artifact intensify each other and increase the life of the whole artifact. Salingaros goes further and argues that three architectural laws can be extracted from physics and mathematics by looking at how nature is put together:

> Order on the smallest scale is established by paired contrasting elements, existing in a balanced visual tension.
>
> Large-scale order occurs when every element relates to every other element at a distance in a way that reduces the entropy.
>
> The small scale is connected to the large scale through a linked hierarchy of intermediate scales with scaling factor approximately equal to $e = 2.718$.
>
> [Salingaros1995]

The entropy of a design relates to the innate human ability to perceive connections. Salingaros argues that when all components of a design interact harmoniously, the design will resonate with people's innate perception of connections, and this corresponds to states of least entropy. Salingaros further notes that pattern languages can be represented as multilevel hierarchical systems, and that in such systems:

> Even though disconnected lower-level patterns can work without necessarily forming a higher-level pattern, such a system is not

cohesive, because it exists on only one level. Each level in a complex hierarchical system is supported by the properties of the next-lower level. [Salingaros2000]

Alexander also points out that the measured jumps in scale that he argues are key to good design are intrinsic to biological organisms. Limburg, for example, notes that in ecological systems, connections tend to be strongest across similar scales:

"In general ... there will be tighter coupling among processes and components with similar rates and overlapping spatial scales." [Limburg+2002]

Patterns of the same scale work together, but this relationship is implicit in the language structure and the way the language is supposed to be used (patterns of the same size applied consecutively), rather than being shown in the drawn connections between patterns.

Alexander points out that the presence of a continuous range of structures at different scales is widespread throughout many natural systems. Some of those systems include:

The tree: trunk, limbs, branches, twigs. The cell: cell wall, organelles, nucleus, chromosomes. A river: bends in the river, tributaries, eddies, pools at the edge. A mountain range: highest mountains, individual peaks, surrounding foothills, still smaller sub-hills. Limestone: large particles, smaller particles, smallest particles each in the interstices of larger ones. The sun and solar system: planets and their orbits, satellites and their orbits. A molecule: component complexes, individual atoms and ions, neutrons, protons, electrons. A flower: individual flower heads, center and petals, sepals, stamens, pistils. [Alexander2002]

Example (Architectural Pattern Language)

In Alexander's language for creating a garden, shown in Figure 17–7 (see page 490), if the patterns between HALF-HIDDEN GARDEN and GARDEN SEAT were not part of the language, it would be hard to envision what kind of garden could be created by the two patterns HALF-HIDDEN GARDEN and GARDEN SEAT. It can be argued that GARDEN SEAT breaks the symmetry of HALF-HIDDEN GARDEN, creating local symmetries simply because it adds structure to what is otherwise an almost blank slate; a garden that will be half-hidden but has little other speci-fied structure. In contrast, when you follow the language through from HALF-HIDDEN GARDEN to GARDEN GROWING WILD, then to TREE PLACES, then to FRUIT TREES, and finally to GARDEN SEAT, you have a much better picture in your mind of what kind of garden is being envisaged; the language is much more coherent.

Example (CHECKS Pattern Language)

WHOLE VALUE argues that values corresponding to key values in the application domain should be created in the software domain. VISIBLE IMPLICATION argues that derived or redundant quantities implied by entered values should be com-puted and displayed to the user. Given just these descriptions, it is hard to see exactly how these two patterns could be connected. It can be argued that VISIBLE IMPLICATION breaks the symmetry of WHOLE VALUE by making communication happen from system to user, as well as from user to system, but when ECHO BACK is added to the language, the symmetry-breaking connections become much clearer. ECHO BACK displays back to the user any information (any whole value) written into the domain model. It breaks the symmetry of WHOLE VALUE, creating local symmetries by replicating the communication from user to do-main in the opposite direction every time it occurs. VISIBLE IMPLICATION then breaks the symmetry created by ECHO BACK and WHOLE VALUE. VISIBLE IMPLICA-TION computes values defined as key by WHOLE VALUE and implied by entered information, and echoes them back to the user, so that ECHO BACK now applies to computed values as well as entered values.

Related Patterns

New patterns may be fleshed out with DIFFERENTIATION, COMMON GROUND, or PIECEMEAL GROWTH. The connections to the new patterns will fit the overall scheme of LOCAL SYMMETRIES. If the language becomes too crowded, it will be cleaned out with THE VOID.

Cross Linkages

> *If the pattern language structure cannot express essential complexity,*
> *then look for other linkages that express that complexity.*

Context

You are developing the structural interconnections between patterns in a pat-tern language that generates complex systems.

Problem

You need to make the language rich enough to be able to generate complex systems.

Forces

A simple hierarchical structure will not solve complex problems. [Alexander1988]

System structure needs to be in alignment with fundamental domain structure. [Winograd+1986]

Containment or specialization is not the only kind of structural relationship in many domains.

Every pattern is connected to other patterns: "Each pattern sits at the center of a network of connections which connect it to certain other patterns that help to complete it." [Alexander1979]

Solution

Connect patterns according to how they break symmetry, expecting that some patterns will break the symmetries of more than one larger-scale pattern.

Rationale

The structure of complex systems cannot be articulated in a simple, tree-like hierarchy, because elements of such systems sometimes overlap, rather than being either wholly contained in or disjointed from other system elements. Overlap is, in fact, an essential generator of complex structure. A better representation of a complex system is a semi-lattice, which allows its elements to overlap. The main constraint on a semi-lattice is that "when two overlapping sets belong to the collection [semi-lattice], the set of elements common to both also belongs to the collection" [Alexander1979].

In *A City is Not a Tree* [1988], Alexander argues that the structures of a city are too complex to be captured in a simple, tree-like structure. Further, he argues that cities whose design is based on such a tree structure are unsuccessful and will fail in their ultimate aim to improve the human condition. In contrast, successful cities have a more complex structure of interactions or cross-linkages that can be represented by a semi-lattice.

Many of Alexander's patterns reflect the need for systems generated with those patterns to exhibit cross linkages. One such pattern is SCATTERED WORK [1977], in which Alexander argues that work zones need to be decentralized and woven in with residential zones, because a complete separation does not reflect the integrated nature of people's lives. People need interconnections between the many different aspects of their lives.

Alexander notes that the structure of a pattern language must be complex enough to generate complex systems, and describes the connections between patterns as reflecting more than a simple hierarchy, with patterns building on potentially more than one other pattern:

> Suppose we use a dot to stand for each pattern, and use an arrow to stand for each connection between two patterns. Then [A• →• B] means that the pattern A needs the pattern B as part of it, in order for A to be complete; and that the pattern B needs to be part of the pattern A, in order for B to be complete.
>
> If we make a picture of *all* the patterns which are connected to the pattern A, we see then that A sits at the center of a whole network of patterns, some above it, some below it.
>
> Each pattern sits at the center of a similar network.
>
> And it is the network of these connections between patterns which creates the language.
>
> [Alexander1979]

Example (Architectural Pattern Language)

As shown in Figure 17–7, in the diagram of a language for a HALF-HIDDEN GARDEN, some patterns build on more than one other pattern. For example, TREE PLACES builds on both GARDEN GROWING WILD and COURTYARDS WHICH LIVE because the latter two patterns together define the space of the garden. Trees can be added to the garden to create TREE PLACES that are partly contained in the GARDEN GROWING WILD and partly contained in the COURTYARDS WHICH LIVE areas of the garden.

Example (C++ Idioms Language)

The relationships between patterns in the idioms language are represented in a structural diagram [Coplien2000] that draws an arrow from PATTERN A to PATTERN B where PATTERN B builds directly on PATTERN A. These arrows illustrate the links existing between patterns in the language. The fact that some patterns build on more than one other pattern (that is, have arrows from more than one other pattern to themselves) indicates that the structure of the language cannot be represented as a simple hierarchy.

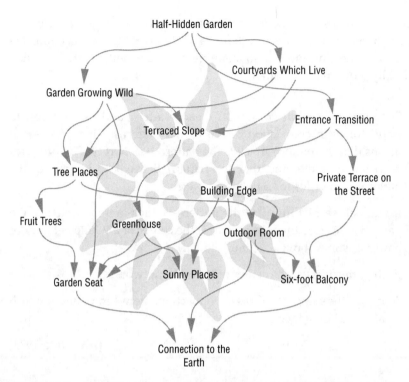

Figure 17–7 *A diagram of the structure of a language for creating a garden. Note that several patterns have more than one arrow coming to them from other (larger-scale) patterns, indicating the complexity of the relationships between patterns.*

One pattern that builds on more than one other pattern is PROMOTE AND ADD. It implements heterogenous addition where the operands are of the same hierarchy. It builds on both PROMOTION LADDER and HOMOGENOUS ADDITION, using PROMOTION LADDER repetitively to promote the object of more specific type to the more general type and HOMOGENOUS ADDITION to then perform the addition. The language structure diagram shows arrows to PROMOTE AND ADD from both PROMOTION LADDER and HOMOGENOUS ADDITION.

Example (CHECKS Pattern Language)

While no language structure diagram is provided for CHECKS [Cunningham 1995], the descriptions of the patterns indicate that interconnections between them are more complex than a simple hierarchy. For example, MEANINGLESS BEHAVIOR builds on both WHOLE VALUE and EXCEPTIONAL VALUE. The latter pattern suggests working with entities in the domain model that have meaning in the domain. It shows how to create space in the domain model for unexpected input values that have no meaning in the domain. MEANINGLESS BEHAVIOR suggests not attempting to attach meaning to errors when that meaning is actually unpredictable from the information at hand. Instead, MEANINGLESS BEHAVIOR suggests expecting input/output widgets to recover from any failure and continue processing. Failure is simply displayed as a blank line. MEANINGLESS BEHAVIOR is most powerful in a context where both WHOLE VALUE and EXCEPTIONAL VALUE are used, because these two patterns constrain the situations that MEANINGLESS VALUE needs to deal with.

Example (Biological System)

Storch and Gaston [2002] note that while "general macroecological patterns are quite simple, the relationships between them are complex and not straightforward." They analyze ecological complexity on different scales of space and time, identifying key macro-ecological patterns and analyzing their interconnections. They note that some patterns must reflect a multidimensional relationship that is not simply hierarchical. For example, one pattern they identify is SPECIES – AREA RELATIONSHIP, which notes that species richness tends to increase with area. They note that this pattern must be connected in some way to all patterns relating to commonness and rarity. Patterns related to commonness and rarity include SPATIAL VARIATION IN ABUNDANCE, which notes that "abundance of a species is highly unequally distributed within its range," and LOCAL-REGIONAL SPECIES RICHNESS RELATIONSHIP, which notes that local and regional species richness tend to correlate.

Related Patterns

LOCAL SYMMETRIES guides the connections between patterns.

Differentiation

If incorporating a new force requires finer-scale structure,
then create a new pattern that breaks the symmetry of an existing pattern.

Context

You have identified the pattern most closely related to a new force that needs to be incorporated in the language, but the new force cannot be successfully incorporated within that pattern.

Problem

In order to incorporate the new force, you need finer-scale structure.

Forces

Maintaining the stability of the existing structure is important, and system structure is defined by symmetry. [Stewart+1992]

The largest-scale patterns in a language are of greatest morphological importance with respect to the artifact being built. Smaller-scale patterns therefore need to conform to the structure of larger-scale patterns. [Alexander1979]

Design can be viewed as "a sequence of acts of complexification" [Alexander 1979]. New structure is always laid down on the basis of existing structure.

The structure of patterns in the language must have reached a certain level of detail in order to be useful, because the language must have enough levels of scale to be compatible with the application domain.

Particular patterns must become specialized for particular tasks. [Alexander+1977]

Solution

Add a new pattern whose structure elaborates that of the identified pattern by breaking symmetry. The new pattern should express latent symmetry in the original pattern more locally.

Rationale

Alexander informally defines "differentiation" as smaller patterns building on larger patterns by a process of elaboration, rather than one of combining preformed parts. It is like the process by which an embryo develops: A whole gives birth to its parts by splitting. It is a process in which existing symmetry is preserved as much as possible. As system structure is defined by symmetry, preserving symmetry preserves structure and thus promotes stability of system structure.

Warren Montgomery noted the importance of preserving symmetry in the context of development of telecommunications software:

> Consider a distributed system in which the HOPP pattern is present. If the system needed to expand from, say, two to three sites, it could do so easily by transforming the existing HOPP structure from two half-calls to three, and so on for further adaptation. The relationship between client and existing "half-objects" does not need to change, and the new client object relationship is the same as that for existing

client/object pairs. It is this preservation of symmetry that enables this kind of incremental growth, by allowing the growth to be based on existing system structure.

Making the model symmetric, if you can, leads to great simplifications. [A system I worked on] started out symmetric, no notion of originating and terminating terminal process, just terminal processes. The call protocols were all symmetric. This made it very easy to take the next step of going to multi-party calls …

[Montgomery1998]

In terms of the language, adding the new pattern differentiates the local structure produced by the language, because it introduces a new pattern that replicates and refines an existing pattern.

Example (C++ Idioms Language)

HANDLE/BODY shows how to split a class into interface (Handle) and implementation (Body) classes in a way that provides effective memory management. The forces it addresses relate to the separation of interface and inheritance in a C++ context. One issue that arises out of using HANDLE/BODY relates to memory usage; it is potentially wasteful not to allow multiple handles to reference the same body. At the point at which memory usage becomes critical, this force needs to be incorporated into the language. It is a force that clearly belongs in a HANDLE/BODY context, but the HANDLE/BODY pattern does not resolve it. The force can be resolved, though, by creating a new, more specialized pattern; COUNTED BODY works within a HANDLE/BODY context to do reference counting. It solves the problem of providing multiple handles for the same body by adding a reference count to the body class and memory management features to the handle class. The addition of COUNTED BODY to the idioms language at the point when reference counting becomes a critical issue represents DIFFERENTIATION.

Example (Biological System)

Mitosis refers to the process of cell division in which chromosomes are equally partitioned and replicated into two identical groups. As most biological organisms develop, cells initially simply divide and replicate, or undergo mitosis. At this stage, all cells are called "stem cells" because they are "undifferentiated" then; all cells appear alike and each cell has the potential to become any more specialized kind of cell. If the only biological patterns in existence were patterns to do with cell division, however, many biological structures would not exist. At some point during the development process, there is a need for cells to specialize for particular tasks in order for the organism's structure to develop beyond that of an indistinctive blob and for the organism's functionality to develop to an appropriate level. At the point at which this need becomes operative, this need represents a new force that can be addressed by a Stem Cell Specialization pattern. Stem cells begin to progressively specialize, with cells initially being able to be distinguished as organ, skin-and-gut, or nerve cells. Each of those groups of cells then further specializes. For example, skin-and-gut cells specialize into cells for the skin or cells for the lining of the gut. The transformation whereby stem cells specialize represents a refinement of existing structure rather than a fundamental modification of existing structure:

> The cells of the body differ in structure and function not because they contain different genes, but because they express different portions of a common genome. [Campbell1996]

If a biological pattern language had been developed without STEM CELL SPECIALIZATION, then the addition of STEM CELL SPECIALIZATION at the point when the need for cells to specialize for particular tasks became an issue would represent DIFFERENTIATION.

Related Patterns

This pattern is closely related to AGGREGATION. Use LOCAL SYMMETRIES to connect patterns in the language. If further specialization is ineffective, then clean out with THE VOID.

Aggregation

If a different kind of structure needs to be added to the language,
then mold it so that it specializes existing larger-scale structure.

Context

You have identified the pattern most closely related to a new force that needs to be incorporated in the language, but the new force cannot be successfully incorporated within that pattern.

Problem

In order to accommodate the new force you need a solution structure that represents an alternative to that provided by the identified pattern.

Forces

A system will need to evolve over time; new structure will need to be added. Systems grow; pattern languages, being a system, also grow. But they must grow in an orderly way if they are to remain stable.

The need for finer structure does not drive all system growth. Sometimes new structure is needed for other reasons, such as to cope with environmental change or increased demands. While such new structure ought to be molded to fit with existing structure, and at some level of scale will represent a specialization of existing structure, in the context in which the change is made, new structure may not always be a specialization of existing structure but rather a new kind of structure.

Change does not happen in isolation; change to one part of a system will affect other parts.

Yet you want to localize the effects of change as much as possible.

Maintaining overall stability may result in a particular solution being suboptimal.

Solution

Use the pattern that you have identified as the basis for developing a new pattern. The two patterns will represent alternative solutions to a particular problem and will build on the same pattern(s). When creating the new pattern, discard forces that contradict the new force that you need to incorporate, and modify the solution structure appropriately.

Rationale

A pattern language is a continually evolving artifact. As it is being developed, new patterns will be added: "We must ... invent new patterns, whenever necessary, to fill out each pattern which is not complete." [Alexander1979]

Not every pattern will be easily identifiable as refining some slightly larger-scale pattern. Some patterns will incorporate new structure into a language:

> ... I argued that an organic whole could only be created by a differentiating process.

> I explained that only a process of differentiation, because it defines the parts within the whole, can generate a natural thing; because only this kind of process can shape parts individually, according to their position in the whole.

We see now that there is a second, complementary process which produces the same results, but works piecemeal, instead.

When a place grows, and things are added to it, gradually, being shaped as they get added, to help form larger patterns, the place also remains whole at every stage—but in this case the geometric volume of the whole keeps changing, because there is an actual concrete aggregation of matter taking place.

[Alexander1979]

The key to effectively incorporating new structure is to remember that every act of growth is an act of repair in a broader context [Alexander1979]. So, for example, adding extensions to a house might add new structure to the house, but it is an act of repair to the larger environment that the house is part of:

… suppose that you have built a small laboratory building.

It has a kitchen, a library, four labs, and a main entrance. You want to add a fifth laboratory to it … .

Don't look for the best place right away. First, look at the existing building, and see what is wrong with it. There is a path where tin cans collect; a tree which is a beautiful tree, but somehow no one uses it; one of the four labs is always empty, there is nothing obviously wrong with it, but somehow no one goes there; the main entrance has no places to sit comfortably; the earth around one corner of the building is being eroded.

Now, look at all these things which are wrong, and build the fifth lab in such a way that it takes care of all these problems, and also does, for itself, what it has to do.

[Alexander1979]

Example (C++ Idioms Language)

At some point in the development of the idioms language, the author realized that some systems generated with the language needed to be able to adapt HANDLE/BODY code to implement reference counting, but without the access to Body code assumed by COUNTED BODY. The new force addressed by DETACHED COUNTED BODY—that the Body code is immutable—cannot be incorporated into the solution structure of COUNTED BODY because it contradicts a force implicit in the solution to COUNTED BODY, the force that the Body code can change. This suggests using AGGREGATION to create a new pattern. COUNTED BODY can be cloned as a starting point for developing DETACHED COUNTED BODY. The force that the Body code can be modified is deleted from the new pattern and the force that the Body code be immutable added. According to this change, DE-TACHED COUNTED BODY ought to sit under HANDLE/BODY in the idioms language. While this is not where the author put DETACHED COUNTED BODY, he agrees that this is a reasonable refactoring [Coplien 2003]. Incorporating DE-TACHED COUNTED BODY into the idioms language is thus an example of the kind of LOCAL REPAIR where a new force cannot be balanced within an existing cluster of balanced forces. It is an example of AGGREGATION.

Example (Biological System)

Social insects such as ants live in colonies where a mature colony has one or multiple queens and a collection of workers [Oster+1978]. When a colony is first started, though, it may consist only of a queen who does all the work herself. It is only as more and more young are reared that the colony develops a structure in which particular ants become specialized for particular tasks. As particular ants become specialized for particular tasks, the structures of a colony change. Instead of EVERYONE DOES EVERYTHING being the most efficient way to operate, EVERYONE SPECIALIZES becomes more efficient. EVERYONE SPECIALIZES is not a specialization of EVERYONE DOES EVERYTHING; it is a different way of working. Incorporating this pattern into a language describing the structure of an ant colony thus represents AGGREGATION.

Related Patterns

This pattern is closely related to DIFFERENTIATION. Use LOCAL SYMMETRIES to connect patterns in the language. If further specialization is ineffective, then clean out with THE VOID.

Common Ground

If several patterns have underlying similarities,
then reformulate the patterns into a more general, slightly larger-scale pattern, able
to be applied in a greater variety of situations.

Context

You have identified the pattern most closely related to a new force that needs to be incorporated in the language, but the new force cannot be successfully incorporated within that pattern.

Problem

The new force relates closely to several patterns.

Forces

Some patterns address similar clusters of forces.

Some patterns have a similar solution structure.

Different patterns "… have underlying similarities, which suggest that they can be reformulated to make them more general, and usable in a greater variety of cases." [Alexander1979]

Solution

Create a new pattern that draws out underlying similarity in the identified pattern and other similar, existing patterns. In particular, find two or more patterns of a similar level of scale that have underlying similarities because they address similar forces and have similar solution structures. The scale of a pattern relates to the size of the artifact being shaped by the application of the pattern. Create a new pattern that is larger in scale than the selected patterns. The new pattern should explicitly cluster the underlying forces that the other patterns have in common and it should build a structure that balances those forces.

Rationale

As Alexander [1979] notes, some patterns identified in different contexts reflect the same structural configuration, yet each pattern is in a slightly different context with slightly different forces and a different finer structure. Drawing out the underlying structural commonality in the patterns into a new pattern may help identify new contexts where that structure may be used. The new pattern may also add a necessary level of scale to an existing language, and identifying the new pattern may lead to additional, more specific, smaller-scale patterns also being identified.

Example (Architectural Pattern Language)

In their work of developing the campus of the University of Oregon, Alexander and colleagues [Alexander1975] noted that a department building that is just a collection of offices does not facilitate the development of community or the exchange of ideas. DEPARTMENT HEARTH addresses this issue. It notes the need, within a departmental building, for a common area, close to well-used paths, where people feel comfortable to sit and have coffee and chat. The pattern FAMILY ROOM CIRCULATION [Alexander1979] addresses a similar issue, but in the context of Peruvian houses. It recognizes the need for a room that allows those living in the house to interact easily with visitors without disrupting the privacy of the rest of the house. TANGENT PATHS again addresses a similar issue, but this time in the context of the development of clinics. It notes the need for paths to pass tangent to social areas in order for those areas to be used.

Alexander notes that underlying each of these patterns is the same bundle of relationships; they each require "a common area at the heart of a social group, placed in such a way that people's natural paths passed tangent to this common area, every time that they moved in and out of the place" [Alexander1979]. Out of these patterns Alexander and colleagues identified the more general and slightly larger-scale pattern COMMON AREA AT THE HEART.

Example (C++ Idioms Language)

Both COUNTED BODY and DETACHED COUNTED BODY are patterns of similar level of scale. They could both be positioned in the idioms language directly underneath HANDLE/BODY, since they can be thought of as representing alternative ways of building on HANDLE/BODY. Both COUNTED BODY and DETACHED COUNTED BODY each cluster forces that primarily have to do with some aspect of reference counting; the forces listed for COUNTED BODY discuss how to best manage multiple handles for one body, and those for DETACHED COUNTED BODY discuss how to do the same without modifying Body code. The link to reference counting is not picked up in the idioms language as it stands. A REFERENCE COUNTER pattern could be added to the idioms language, as shown in Figure 17–8. Together with HANDLE/BODY, such a pattern would provide a helpful basis from which to implement COUNTED BODY or DETACHED COUNTED BODY.

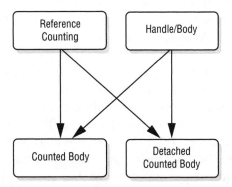

Figure 17–8 *A diagram showing the language structure of part of the Idioms Language if a Reference Counting pattern were to be included in the language.*

Related Patterns

Use LOCAL SYMMETRIES to connect patterns in the language. If further specialization is ineffective, then clean out with THE VOID.

The Void

> *If the overall language structure gets too tangled,*
> *then clean it out to create space for more development.*

Context

The existing language structure has become convoluted and tangled.

Problem

You need to further grow the language without increasing the tangling.

Forces

Adding more local symmetries will make the language more convoluted.

Structure that is all detail diffuses itself, destroying its own structure; "calm is needed to alleviate the buzz" [Alexander2002].

Solution

Excise the tangle by breaking some connections in the language, and possibly removing some patterns, thus creating space for new growth.

Rationale

Alexander [2002] points out the importance of emptiness for good design. He argues that some spaces must be empty in order for the overall structure to be effective. For example, Alexander points out that when using building materials, it is much more common for large amounts of one substance surrounded by small amounts of another to be economical and efficient, rather than equal amounts of two substances. He notes that a concept of The Void is central to many of the architectural patterns he describes, including Bathing Room, which provides a necessary calm space amidst the busy life of a household. POSITIVE OUTDOOR SPACE [Alexander+1977] describes the kind of shapes that buildings should create around them, by their shape. It argues that buildings that create convex spaces around them create a positive space, or "void." Buildings that do not create convex spaces around them do not create any distinctly identifiable spaces around them. When a building creates positive outdoor space, that space works as a void, or space between buildings, that people identify as distinct and feel comfortable in.

Natural processes also work by periodically "cleaning out" when things get too tangled. For example, forest fires regenerate forests. Plants and animals die to give space for new plants and animals to live.

A designed system should therefore be cleaned out when it becomes too tangled.

Example (Architectural Pattern Language)

Alexander points out that the pattern language he wrote with colleagues is continually evolving. As part of that process, some patterns are removed from the language:

> A group of us began to construct such a language eight or nine years ago. To do it, we discovered and wrote down many hundreds of patterns. Then we discarded most of these patterns during the years … [Alexander1979]

For example, when designing new buildings for the University of Oregon, as documented in *The Oregon Experiment* [1975], Alexander discarded many patterns from his original pattern language [1977] and incorporated some new patterns specific to the university context. Discarding many unnecessary patterns allowed designers to focus on those few patterns most important to the design at hand.

Example (CHECKS Pattern Language)

Many patterns exist that potentially build on patterns in the CHECKS language. NULL OBJECT, for example, is a SPECIAL case of EXCEPTIONAL VALUE [Walker2003]. An EXCEPTIONAL VALUE "will either absorb all messages or produce MEANINGLESS BEHAVIOR … A Null Object is one such EXCEPTIONAL VALUE."

Many other patterns are related to NULL OBJECT in various ways. Since every NULL OBJECT has no internal state that could change, and multiple instances would act exactly the same, SINGLETON [Gamma+1995] can be used to implement NULL OBJECT. FLYWEIGHT [Gamma+1993] can be used for more efficient implementation where multiple null objects are implemented as instances of a single NULL OBJECT class. As part of the STRATEGY [Gamma+1993] pattern, NULL OBJECT can be used to represent the strategy of doing nothing. The STATE [Gamma+1993] pattern often includes representation of a state in which the client should do nothing; NULL OBJECT is often used to represent this state. ITERATORS [Gamma+1993] can use NULL OBJECT to represent the special case of not iterating over anything, and ADAPTERS [Gamma+1993] can use NULL OBJECT so that they can pretend to adapt another object and yet not actually be adapting anything.

While all of these patterns could potentially be part of the CHECKS language, the language would then become overly complicated. At least some of the patterns would need to be removed in order to give the language back its focus.

Example (Biological System)

As part of the process of development, stem cells specialize for particular tasks. The first specialization is into organ, skin-and-gut, or nerve cells. Taking cells for organ development as an example, in order for those cells to continue to divide and replicate and form a distinct entity that is an organ, they need to be more separate from the mass of cells that they are originally part of. They cannot develop a distinct identity while remaining fully connected to all the other cells around them. Thus, a sac of fluid (fluid not being made up of cells but simply being a chemical solution) forms around the organ cells, creating a "void" in which the organ can develop.

Related Patterns

Once a language has been cleaned out with THE VOID, it will gradually grow again following a process of LOCAL REPAIR.

Conclusion

This language has sought to better define patterns and pattern language concepts. Two conclusions from this work stand out as particularly significant:

It is valid to develop a pattern language for building pattern languages.

The development of this language was based on the assumption that a pattern language is a complex, designed system and that therefore, as for other such systems, it makes sense to use a pattern language to describe, generate, and analyze pattern languages. The assumption is validated by the wide variety of patterns that LDPL can analyze. Given that success, it is likely that system designers across a wide variety of fields will be able to use pattern languages to describe and analyze their systems, both statically and dynamically, as those systems are transformed over time.

Pattern language designers can benefit by understanding symmetry breaking in natural, physical systems.

The development of this language was based on the assumption that analysis of evolved systems offers useful insights to system designers. In particular, the symmetry-breaking processes taking place in natural, physical systems lead to the formation of patterns in those systems, and so it is worthwhile for pattern language designers to understand those processes. The assumption is validated by the development of LDPL, which defines patterns and the connections between them in terms of the creation of local symmetries. Such a definition requires an acknowledgment of the importance of scale; smaller-scale patterns break the symmetry of larger-scale patterns. It also requires an acknowledgment of the importance of forces. It is forces that dictate the need for structure to change, and that define the parameters for the structure of a pattern; the symmetry breaking must generate structure that holds a set of forces in tension. Even in domains that do not appear to be geometric, such as software, forces still drive the need for change. Given the success of analyzing the idioms and CHECKS languages in terms of symmetry breaking, it is likely that many other software patterns can be understood by noting symmetries that are transformed through the application of a pattern.

References

[Alexander1964] C. Alexander. *Notes on the Synthesis of Form.* Cambridge, MA: Harvard University Press, 1964.

[Alexander1975] C. Alexander. *The Oregon Experiment.* New York: Oxford University Press, 1975.

[Alexander1979] C. Alexander. *The Timeless Way of Building.* New York: Oxford University Press, 1979.

[Alexander+1977] C. Alexander, S. Ishikawa, and M. Silverstein. *A Pattern Language: Towns, Buildings, Construction.* New York: Oxford University Press, 1977.

[Alexander1988] C. Alexander. "A City is not a Tree." In J. Thackera (ed.), *Design After Modernism: Beyond the Object.* London: Thames and Hudson, 1988.

[Alexander2002] C. Alexander. *The Nature of Order (Book One): The Phenomenon of Life.* Berkeley, CA: The Center for Environmental Structure, 2002.

[Alexander2002a] C. Alexander. *The Nature of Order (Book Two): The Process of Creating Life.* Berkeley, CA: The Center for Environmental Structure, 2002.

[Altshuller1984] C. Altshuller. *Creativity as an Exact Science: The Theory of the Solution of Inventive Problems.* New York: Gordon and Breach, 1984.

[Appleton2000] B. Appleton. "Patterns and Software: Essential Concepts and Terminology." Available: *http://www.cmccrossroads.com/bradapp/docs/patterns-intro.html.* Accessed March 17, 2003.

[Bar-Yam1997] Y. Bar-Yam. *Dynamics of Complex Systems.* Reading, MA: Addison-Wesley, 1997.

[Bar-Yam2005] Y. Bar-Yam. "About Complex Systems." Available: *http://www.necsi.org/projects/yaneer/points.html.* Accessed August 4, 2004.

[Blundell+1996] T. L. Blundell and N. Srinivasan. "Symmetry, Stability, and Dynamics of Multidomain and Multicomponent Protein Systems." Proceedings of the National Academy of Sciences, 93:53–63, 14243–14248, 1996.

[Brand1997] S. Brand. *How Buildings Learn: What Happens After They're Built.* London: Phoenix Illustrated, 1997.

[Campbell1996] N. A. Campbell. *Biology.* Menlo Park, CA: Benjamin Cummings, 1996.

[Coplien1992] J. O. Coplien. *Advanced C++ Programming Styles and Idioms.* Reading, MA: Addison-Wesley, 1992.

[Coplien2000] J. O. Coplien. "C++ Idioms Patterns." In N. Harrison, B. Foote, and H. Rohnert (eds.), *Pattern Languages of Program Design 4.* Boston: Addison-Wesley, 2000.

[Coplien1996] J. O. Coplien. *Software Patterns.* New York: SIGS Books, 1996.

[Coplien1998a] J. O. Coplien. "The Column Without a Name: Space, the Final Frontier." *C++ Report,* 10(3):11–17, 1998.

[Coplien1998b] J. O. Coplien. "The Column Without a Name: Worth a Thousand Words." *C++ Report,* 10(5):51–54 and 71, 1998.

[Coplien2000] J. O. Coplien. Multi-Paradigm Design. PhD Thesis, Vrije Universiteit Brussel, Brussels, Belgium, May 2000.

[Coplien2003] J. O. Coplien. Promotion Ladder. Personal communication, October 2003.

[Coplien+2001] J. O. Coplien and L. Zhao. "Symmetry Breaking in Software Patterns." *Lecture Notes in Computer Science,* 2177:37–54, 2001.

[Cunningham1995] W. Cunningham. "The CHECKS Pattern Language of Information Integrity." In J. O. Coplien and D. C. Schmidt (eds.), *Pattern Languages of Program Design.* Reading, MA: Addison-Wesley, 1995.

[Czarnecki+2000] K. Czarnecki and U. W. Eisenecker. *Generative Programming: Methods, Tools, and Applications.* Boston: Addison-Wesley, 2000.

[Dasgupta1991] S. Dasgupta. *Design Theory and Computer Science.* Cambridge, MA: Cambridge University Press, 1991.

[Dooley1997] K. J. Dooley. "A Complex Adaptive Systems Model of Organizational Change." *Nonlinear Dynamics, Psychology, and Life Sciences*, 1(1):69–97, 1997.

[Fincher1999] S. Fincher. "What is a Pattern Language?" Interact'99: Seventh IFIP Conference on Human Computer Interaction, Edinburgh, UK, August/September 1999.

[Gamma+1993] E. Gamma, R. Helm, R. Johnson, and J. Vlissides. "Design Patterns: Abstraction and Reuse of Object-Oriented Design." *Lecture Notes in Computer Science*, 707:406–431, 1993.

[Gamma+1995] E. Gamma, R. Helm, R. Johnson, and J. Vlissides. *Design Patterns: Elements of Reusable Object-Oriented Software.* Reading, MA: Addison-Wesley, 1995.

[Grabow1983] S. Grabow. *Christopher Alexander: The Search for a New Paradigm in Architecture.* Northumberland, England: Stockfield Press, 1983.

[Harris2004] A. Harris. "Mechanical Forces, Geometrical Shapes, and Asymmetry." Available: *http://www.bio.unc.edu/courses/2003spring/biol104/lecture22.html.* Accessed July 30, 2004.

[Kimball2004] J. W. Kimball. "Frog Embryology." Available: *http://users.rcn.com/jkimball.ma.ultranet/BiologyPages/F/FrogEmbryology.html.* Accessed July 30, 2004.

[Limburg+2002] K. E. Limburg, R. V. O'Neill, R. Costanze, and S. Farber. "Complex Systems and Valuation." *Ecological Economics*, 41(3):409–420, 2002.

[Meszaros1995] G. Meszaros. "Half-object+Protocol (HOPP)." In J. O. Coplien and D. C. Schmidt (eds.), *Pattern Languages of Program Design.* Reading, MA: Addison-Wesley, 1995.

[Montgomery1998] W. Montgomery. As quoted in J. O. Coplien. "The Column Without a Name: Worth a Thousand Words." *C++ Report*, 10(5):51–54 and 71, 1998.

[Oster+1978] G. F. Oster and E. O. Wilson. *Caste Ecology in the Social Insects.* New Jersey: Princeton University Press, 1978.

[Ostwald2002] J. Ostwald. "Meta-Design." Available: *http://webguide.cs.colorado.edu:9080/entwine/Concepts.* Accessed January 13, 2004.

[Raskin2000] J. Raskin. *The Humane Interface: New Directions for Designing Interactive Systems*. Boston: Addison-Wesley, 2000.

[Salingaros1995] N. A. Salingaros. "The Laws of Architecture from a Physicist's Perspective." *Physics Essays*, 8(4):638–643, 1995.

[Salingaros2000] N. A. Salingaros. "The Structure of a Pattern Language." *Architectural Research Quarterly*, 4:149–161, 2000.

[Senge1990] P. M. Senge. *The Fifth Discipline: The Art and Practice of the Learning Organization*. New York: Doubleday, 1990.

[Stewart+1992] I. Stewart and M. Golubitsky. *Fearful Symmetry: Is God a Geometer?* Oxford, UK: Blackwell Publishers, 1992.

[Storch+2002] D. Storch and K. J. Gaston. Untangling Ecological Complexity on Different Scales of Space and Time. Technical Report CTS-02-07, Center for Theoretical Study, Charles University, Jilska 1, 110-00 Praha 1, Czech Republic, July 2002.

[Walker2003] J. Walker. "Null Object Design Pattern." Available: *http://www.cs.oberlin.edu/~jwalker/nullObjPattern*. Accessed December 10, 2004.

[Winn+2002] T. Winn and P. Calder. "Is This a Pattern?" *IEEE Software*, 19(1):59–66, 2002.

[Winograd+1986] T. Winograd and F. Flores. *Understanding Computers and Cognition*. Reading, MA: Addison-Wesley, 1986.

[Zhao+2002] J. O. Coplien and L. Zhao. "Symmetry in Class and Type Hierarchy" In *Proceedings of the Fortieth International Conference on Technology of Objects, Languages, and Systems* (TOOLS Pacific 2002), pp. 181–190, Sydney, New South Wales, Australia, January 2002.

CHAPTER 18

The Language of Shepherding

A Pattern Language
for Shepherds and Sheep

Neil B. Harrison

Many of us have submitted patterns to our colleagues for feedback prior to a writers' workshop or other type of review. In fact, at PLoP conferences, all submissions are subjected to shepherding before they are evaluated for acceptance. Unfortunately, the quality of shepherding varies widely. Some people receive extremely helpful comments, but others receive only cursory remarks and a "looks good" endorsement.

Yet shepherding can be a very powerful tool for improving patterns. It can go well beyond hints for grammar and usage to the heart of the work being shepherded. In fact, shepherding can turn a paper about a solution into a pattern. But it requires more than a casual reading by the shepherd: It requires attention and actions such as the ones described in the patterns in this chapter.

These patterns have been gleaned from significant experience with shepherding, both as a shepherd and as a "sheep." This experience is augmented with experience from giving and receiving feedback for non-pattern technical works, from teaching, and from observing. The patterns should help you become a better shepherd, both in a formal pattern-shepherding setting and in other situations.

Imagine that you have agreed to be a shepherd for an upcoming PLoP. You have had some experience with shepherding; at the very least, you have been a sheep yourself. You know what it feels like. In addition, you know about patterns. You have an idea of what makes up a good pattern. Ideally, you have been to writers' workshops, perhaps at a PLoP.

Setting the Stage

You just received mail from the program chair informing you of your shepherding assignment. She notes that you have not quite a month before the final papers are due, so you need to start soon. You immediately take a look at the paper you have been assigned. As you read it, you recognize your responsibility—your help may make the difference between acceptance and rejection. You want to do the best job for the author that you can. Now what?

It is likely that you will run across several of the problems described here. The patterns presented in this chapter will help you to more successfully assist the pattern author in improving his or her work.

A Map of the Patterns

The patterns here can be grouped into two major groups that interact very closely with each other. The first group contains patterns that deal with the shepherding process itself, with the tactics of shepherding. These patterns are:

- THREE ITERATIONS: How to budget your time and effort to make shepherding effective.

- THE SHEPHERD KNOWS THE SHEEP: How to establish a productive relationship with the author.

- HALF A LOAF: How to make sure that shepherding continues to move forward.

- BIG PICTURE: How to grasp the gist of the pattern immediately.

- AUTHOR AS OWNER: How to keep from writing the pattern for the author.

- FORCES DEFINE PROBLEM: How to understand the problem at a deeper level.

The shepherding process is essentially a reviewing process, as is the writers' workshop. Therefore, it should come as no surprise that these patterns are closely tied to "A Pattern Language for Writers' Workshops" [Coplien2000].

Since shepherding is all about improving the pattern itself, the second group of patterns deals with aspects of the pattern itself. These are areas that the shepherd should look closely at, because they tend to be troublesome. Therefore, there is often great potential for improvement in these areas. Interestingly, it isn't easy to separate these two groups of patterns. In fact, the first pattern in the second group also appears in the preceding list! In other words, if you apply BIG PICTURE with the intent of helping yourself shepherd, you are automatically helping improve the pattern itself. Conversely, if you apply it with the goal of helping improve the pattern, you are making life easier for yourself as a shepherd. This is true to a lesser extent with many of the patterns in this language. The patterns in the second group are:

- BIG PICTURE: How to make the essence of a pattern immediately clear to the reader.
- MATCHING PROBLEM AND SOLUTION: How to ensure that the pattern really is pattern-ish.
- CONVINCING SOLUTION: How to make the pattern believable.
- FORCES DEFINE PROBLEM: How to strengthen the problem.
- BALANCED CONTEXT: How to help get the pattern at the right scope.
- WAR STORIES: How to help the pattern flow.
- FORM FOLLOWS FUNCTION: How to put a new form into a pattern.
- SMALL PATTERNS: How to keep patterns easily digestible

These patterns look more at content than do the first group. They relate to patterns in "A Pattern Language for Pattern Writing" [Meszaros+1997]. These will be referred to as "Pattern Writing Patterns."

During the course of shepherding, one tends to use more of the tactical patterns initially, but then tends to mix the patterns of the two groups. Figure 18–1 shows all the patterns, illustrating the rough order in which they might be applied. An arrow from one pattern to another indicates that the first pattern helps set the stage for use of the second.

Three Iterations

When you receive a pattern to shepherd, you have an unknown amount of work ahead of you. Pattern languages have different levels of maturity, quality, and size. The amount and type of work varies widely, and it's pretty hard to predict what the pattern might be like before you see it. You may have a better idea of what to expect from the pattern if you know the author. However, different works from the same author will require different amounts of shepherding, sometimes widely different amounts.

All too often, the author receives poor feedback from the shepherd: It comes late, it is incomplete, and superficial. The author has no chance to bounce corrections off the shepherd, or even to find out what the shepherd really meant.

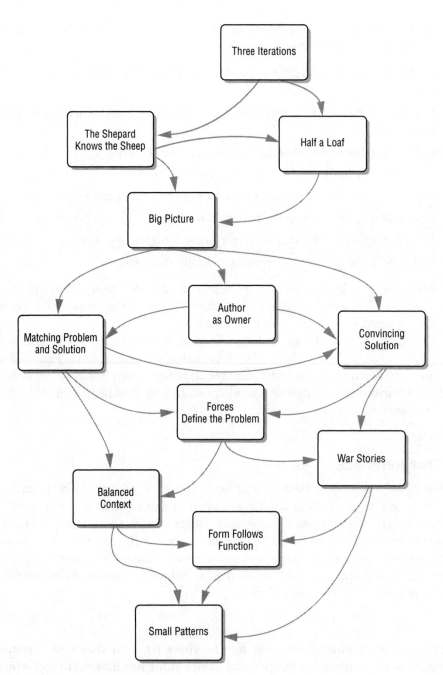

Figure 18–1 *The Shepherding Pattern Language*

Actually, most patterns need a fair amount of work when they come in for shepherding. One reason for this is that the shepherd may well be the first real "outsider" to examine the work closely. It takes someone who is removed from the pattern to really see the strengths and weaknesses of the pattern.

Most shepherds begin with the best intentions. But shepherding is a volunteer activity, and your real job gets in the way. The time slips by, and soon all you can do is to skim the patterns and dash off a hurried set of comments to the author. You feel vaguely guilty but console yourself that the patterns did indeed look pretty good. At least they did during your quick pass through them …

Therefore:

Plan the shepherding effort to take three iterations of comments from the shepherd to the author. In order to make three iterations possible in the time generally allotted to shepherding, it is almost always necessary to start immediately. Both the shepherd and the author must be prepared to respond quickly—the shepherd must send suggestions to the author, and the author must prepare revisions of the work.

Three iterations helps you budget your time so that you have enough time to give meaningful comments to the author. In addition, it helps you avoid the tendency to dump all your comments on the author three days before the deadline. The author gets manageable chunks of information and can respond to them better. HALF A LOAF expands on this point.

If you are a natural procrastinator, it may be especially difficult to do this. In order to help you motivate yourself, immediately tell the author when to expect each batch of comments. External commitment is a wonderful goad.

Some works may need only two iterations, while others might require more than three sets of comments. If the work is in good shape after one or two iterations, you can rejoice in the gift of unexpected time. However, it is the rare paper that cannot benefit from three sets of comments. It is much more common that a paper needs more than three iterations. If you can fit an additional iteration into the schedule, feel free to do so. But after three iterations, the work tends to become stale to the shepherd as well as to the author; you have moved "too close to the coalface,"[1] and you find yourself repeating the same suggestions to the author. After three iterations, the effectiveness of one shepherd tends to decrease. Regardless of the state of the work, three seems to be the best number of iterations.

---

1. Thanks to Alan O'Callaghan for this British metaphor.

A typical consequence of having three iterations is that shepherding takes more effort, but the quality of the shepherding will be much higher. As a shepherd, you must plan for this. Recognize that the time you spend will be well worth it to the author.

THREE ITERATIONS sets the stage for the shepherding session, but it cannot succeed by itself. In order to effectively budget one's time, one must also budget the information flow; HALF A LOAF makes this happen. In addition, THREE ITERATIONS assumes an implicit contract of cooperation between the shepherd and the sheep. Use THE SHEPHERD KNOWS THE SHEEP to make this happen.

Thanks to Jim Coplien and Dirk Riehle.

The Shepherd Knows the Sheep

Now that you have the pattern in hand and are ready to begin shepherding, what is the first thing you do? You have planned out your schedule to accommodate THREE ITERATIONS. However, you realize that there is no way to ensure that sheep will pay attention to your comments.

Because the shepherd is essentially a critic, there is a natural barrier between the shepherd and the sheep—the sheep feels vulnerable and defensive. This attitude can hinder effective communication and can even foster a tendency for the sheep to ignore comments from the shepherd.

On the one hand, you might feel inclined to give lots of comments to the author in order to be the most help. But it is discouraging if the author ignores most of your comments. So you might be tempted to gloss over the difficult items and give only cosmetic suggestions, since they are non-threatening.

Most shepherding is done via e-mail. While e-mail is nearly ideal for shepherding, it is detached and somewhat anonymous. That makes it easy to ignore.

Since most shepherds are also authors, one can follow the Golden Rule—I should respond quickly and positively to my shepherd, and perhaps my author will be responsive to me. But positive example only goes so far; there are no guarantees. We are dealing with other people, and we have no real power over them.

Therefore:

Start immediately to build a relationship with the author, and maintain it throughout the shepherding. Contact the author right away, even before reading the patterns, and tell the author about yourself. Tell him or her what to expect from you (such as three iterations) and establish what you expect in return. Above all, follow through on your commitments.

It is important to make the shepherding personal. Authors need to feel like they know you and can trust you. It helps if they know that you have been a sheep yourself. You are, in essence, establishing a SAFE SETTING[2] for the author.

Early contact is important. The author will have been informed of your stewardship, and he or she will be expecting to hear from you. Establishing contact immediately shows that you care, and the author will thus be more willing to listen to your comments. This embodies the old adage, "They don't care how much you know until they know how much you care."

You can maintain the personal relationship over time through the manner in which you give feedback. Don't forget to give positive reinforcement as well as suggestions for improvement. Try to give POSITIVE FEEDBACK FIRST,[3] and to finish up each group of suggestions with POSITIVE CLOSURE.[4]

An important aspect of a relationship is that both parties understand what the other expects. Establish ground rules that encompass what you will do and what you expect the author to do. Include, for example, dates of trips or events that could prevent you from responding quickly.

If you begin shepherding by establishing a relationship, both shepherd and author will be edified by the process. You will build relationships that last beyond the shepherding period, because you will have built a COMMUNITY OF TRUST.[5] On

---

2. Writers' Workshop Pattern SAFE SETTING: How to make feedback more open and effective by raising the comfort level, particularly for the author.

3. Writers' Workshop Pattern POSITIVE FEEDBACK FIRST: How to give the gathering a supportive tone, and to start with feedback that will put the author in a receptive mood.

4. Writers' Workshop Pattern POSITIVE CLOSURE: How to leave the author with a positive feeling at the end of the feedback.

5. Writers' Workshop Pattern COMMUNITY OF TRUST: How to help authors feel that the experience will help them, rather than tear them down.

several occasions, people I have met first through shepherding have become close personal friends, as well as professional colleagues.

Half a Loaf

Shepherding is now under way. By using THREE ITERATIONS, you have established an approximate schedule, and you and the author understand what each expects of the other (THE SHEPHERD KNOWS THE SHEEP). Now the author is ready to receive your first batch of comments.

With zeal to help the author, the shepherd often sends every possible correction to the author all at once. This overwhelms the author and disrupts the schedule.

It's natural to want to send a comprehensive list of comments to the author all at once. But you can't possibly comment on every little thing and still maintain three iterations; there just isn't time. Even if you were able to do so, the author couldn't respond in time. After all, the job of revision is even bigger than the job of criticism.

Not all corrections are created equal. Some are absolutely critical; others are trivial. But if the author receives all the comments at once, it is difficult to know which are the important ones. The author may spend excessive time making minor changes and not have time for the big ones. This is a natural tendency: It's easy to correct grammar and spelling, and we tend to like to do the easy things first.

Therefore:

Send the author small bites of comments. Start with the biggest issues, and work to the most trivial. If you run out of time but haven't assembled all the comments you wish to make, send what you have. The author can start on whatever comments you send. Half a loaf is better than none.

Comments, unlike software, don't need to be complete before they are released. In fact, they don't even need to be debugged. The author will be able to make sense of them. If the author can't, you can expect some e-mail asking for clarification.

The schedule is more important than the completeness of the comments. For one thing, if you miss the time, you put an iteration of comments in jeopardy, and they can't be made up. For another thing, the author can begin with what you send. If necessary, you can always complete your comments a few days after you send the first part.

Now you are off and running. Well, maybe. There is still this gnawing question: If you are supposed to begin with the most important issues, how do you know what they are? Where do you start? The answer is found in BIG PICTURE.

Thanks to David DeLano, Jutta Eckstein, and Dirk Riehle.

Big Picture

Now that you are ready to give a small dose of feedback (see HALF A LOAF), the task before you is to understand the pattern and find the most important issues to highlight first. But this is easier said than done.

It's often hard to know where to start shepherding. You need to understand the pattern in order to make effective suggestions, but draft patterns are often pretty arcane. Patterns that are small and concise at this stage of maturity often lack substance. On the other hand, large patterns often have extraneous details that obscure the main ideas.

Upon first reading, one can find many areas for improvement in a draft pattern. But time is limited. So it's critical to call out the most important issues first and get them straight. Furthermore, some of the minor issues may change, or even take care of themselves as you tackle the big issues. But it isn't always clear what the most important issues are.

It's not uncommon for a draft pattern to be pretty muddy—it's hard to figure out what the pattern is all about. There may be a great pattern struggling to get out, but it takes work to unearth it. To put it bluntly, a lot of engineers are poor writers.

Of course, the shepherd's initial experience with a pattern will likely mirror the experience of the general populace. First impressions tend to stick. So the way a pattern is presented can make all the difference.

Therefore:

Start by reading the problem and solution of the pattern to get the main idea and by giving feedback at first just on them. The problem and solution together should give the big picture of the pattern.

You start here for three reasons. First, it gives you an idea of the pattern very quickly and helps frame your subsequent study of the pattern. Second, it helps you see how (or if) the author understands the pattern. Third, the essence of a pattern should be easy to pick out of the pattern itself. The reader must be able to find what the pattern is about relatively easily. By the way, it's best to give your first impression feedback very soon after you read the big picture, similar to READING JUST BEFORE REVIEWING.[6]

A good place for this information is at the beginning of the problem and solution sections. Look at the first two sentences in each section. You should be able to understand the basic idea of the pattern upon first reading. This is evocative of SINGLE-PASS READABLE PATTERN.[7] If you can't understand the basic idea on first reading, you can ask the author to explain what the pattern is all about as succinctly as possible and ask the author to incorporate that into the pattern. You might have the author use a 'patlet' form and work from the patlet for a while.

Note that some patterns (like the ones in this chapter) don't have sections explicitly called "Problem" and "Solution." Nevertheless, they should be easy to find (see FINDABLE SECTIONS.[8]) In these patterns, for example, problems and solutions are in bold. Note that the problem and solution are the key elements of MANDATORY ELEMENTS PRESENT.[9]

Shepherding tends to be more effective when you start with the BIG PICTURE. It helps get the shepherd and the author on the same page. It can avoid costly (in time) misunderstandings, and it helps place the focus on the most important issues first. (See MATCHING PROBLEM AND SOLUTION.)

An interesting parallel pattern for reviewing papers is EVALUATE PAPERS FAST,[10] by Jens Parlsberg.

---

6. Writers' Workshop Pattern READING JUST BEFORE REVIEWING: How a reviewer should avoid over-preparing or under-preparing for the workshop.
7. Pattern Writing Pattern SINGLE-PASS READABLE PATTERN: How to make it easy for the reader to understand the gist of the pattern on first reading.
8. Pattern Writing Pattern FINDABLE SECTIONS: How to make key information easy to find.
9. Pattern Writing Pattern MANDATORY ELEMENTS PRESENT: How to make sure all the necessary information is present in a pattern.
10. EVALUATE PAPERS FAST: How to quickly get an idea of the merits of a paper to be reviewed for a conference or a journal [Parlsberg1999].

Author as Owner

You have read through the pattern, and have probably used BIG PICTURE to help you identify the highest priority issues of the pattern. You know that you want to send a limited amount of comments (see HALF A LOAF); at this point, the style of the comments is important.

Developing a strong relationship with the author can cause the author to lean on you too much. In particular, the author may use your suggestions verbatim.

It is somewhat flattering to have the author use your words exactly, but it has negative consequences. First, you aren't the expert, so your comments may not be completely accurate. After all, the author should be the expert, not the shepherd.

A second problem is that it makes you, in a small way, a part owner of the work. This is usually inappropriate, and it's a burden that most shepherds don't want.

Perhaps the biggest problem is that the author doesn't learn by simply copying your suggestions. Grappling with technical issues as well as stylistic pattern problems is one of the best ways to grow; the author shouldn't be deprived of this opportunity.

However, time pressure encourages the author to simply incorporate the comments into the pattern without giving them much thought.

Therefore:

Establish the author as the clear owner of the work by not spoon-feeding answers to the author. Instead, ask questions in order to nudge the author in the right direction. Phrase much of your feedback as thought-provoking questions.

It's often hard to turn your criticisms into questions that will help the author come up with the answers. Think about "what," "how," and "why" questions, such as, "What problem are you solving?" or "How does the solution solve the problem?" or "Why is this force important?" You might even use other journalistic "w" questions, such as, "When does this solution not work?"

Questions force the author to think about the problem and to come up with the right words (and concepts) rather than taking your words without much thought. The author will therefore learn about the topic and patterns in general. Meanwhile, you become an invisible hand behind the work without becoming overly involved in it.

Note that this approach takes more work on your part than does writing suggestions to the author. As a shepherd, you need to think carefully about what questions to ask the author, because your questions will also be creating more work for the author. But this extra time and effort pays off for both of you in a more consistent, higher quality pattern.

A side effect of questions is that your comments are not direct attacks on the work, and thus are less likely to offend the author.

Matching Problem and Solution

Once you are on your way with the BIG PICTURE, you need to know what to do with it. Most patterns that are being shepherded need some work to make the BIG PICTURE hold together.

Often, an immature pattern doesn't hang together well. It may feel like a solution looking for a problem, or maybe the purpose of the pattern isn't clear.

Patterns are not written front to back. Authors bounce around in the patterns as they write them. So the BIG PICTURE of the pattern—the problem and solution—are often written at different times. But the reader reads the pattern from front to back. This often leads to a BIG PICTURE that is distorted or fuzzy.

We tend to focus on solutions; indeed patterns are about solutions. This focus leads to strong solutions with problem statements that are little more than afterthoughts. But we need strong problem statements to know when we might need a pattern.

Some patterns are pretty complex, so they are naturally hard to understand. They require a great deal of detail, yet this detail can obscure the meaning of the pattern. This is exacerbated by the fact that the author, who is an expert on the topic, tends to focus on the details; the gist of the pattern is now so obvious (to the author) that it gets little attention. Yet it may not be obvious to the reader.

Therefore:

Read the problem and solution together to make sure they match. The solution must address the whole problem, but not more than the problem. Identify which of the two sections is weak with respect to the other, and ask

the author to focus on that section first. In general, work on the solution first, then the problem.

This is all about balance. The problem and solution must fit together in order for the pattern to feel whole. One aspect of this is the breadth of the pattern. The problem and solution must cover the same ground. A broad problem requires a general solution, and a narrow problem is covered by a specific solution. Another issue is depth. The solution and problem should match here as well. If a solution addresses one issue in depth, and that issue is germane to the solution, it must be reflected in the problem, or perhaps in the context.

You may still be on the first pass over the pattern at this point, so it still may be helpful to read just the problem and solution, and skip the other sections. This will help give you a sense of the pattern's balance. However, you will need to begin to bring in the surrounding information of forces, context, and implementation to fill in some holes.

Because we write patterns based on our experience with the solutions, we tend to write the solution of a pattern first. At least, that's what we have in mind first; the solution motivates us to write the pattern. So the solution is usually more mature than the problem. This is why we start with the solution.

Using MATCHING PROBLEM AND SOLUTION helps you see what part of a pattern might need work. It also helps the author understand the interaction of problems and solutions. But beyond identification of issues in the problem and the solution, you need to recommend specific action for the author to take. See CONVINCING SOLUTION and FORCES DEFINE PROBLEM.

Convincing Solution (The "Aha" Effect)

By now, the pattern is taking shape. It has a solid BIG PICTURE. The problem and the solution are beginning to work together (MATCHING PROBLEM AND SOLUTION). As the shepherd, you may have helped the author apply BIG PICTURE and MATCHING PROBLEM AND SOLUTION, but in many cases, the pattern already has these characteristics when it comes to you. On the surface, the pattern looks good.

But something about the pattern just doesn't feel right. In particular, you are skeptical of the solution; you aren't convinced that it works. Perhaps the problem is that the pattern does not show evidence that the pattern has been successfully used. Or maybe the pattern exhibits the "World Peace" syndrome; the solution is easy to say, but hard to do. Once in a while, the solution actually seems wrong.

Sometimes the solution is really weak; it just doesn't do anything for you.

Patterns should capture proven knowledge. But sometimes authors write up a single-instance solution as a pattern. In rare cases, they write up a proposed solution; one that hasn't even worked once (these tend to look like "World Peace"). (Catching unproven solutions during shepherding will help save the author embarrassment later; unfortunately, writers' workshops do not always catch them.)

The author is often so close to the pattern that some important aspects of the solution seem obvious or even trivial. So they aren't mentioned. But that can cause the credibility of the pattern to suffer. Not mentioning things can make the pattern look like a "World Peace" solution, because information that would help us understand the pattern is missing. So we wonder whether the author has really successfully used the pattern.

Some people write a form of patterns they call "anti-patterns," which describe a common problem, and then advise against the destructive behavior. Such works miss the point of patterns, which is to convey insight about what works. They are not very helpful, since most of us already know dozens of ways to fail.

Therefore:

Look for a solution in the pattern that is strong, even compelling. Ideally, the solution should have the "Aha" effect. If it doesn't, ask direct, pointed questions so that the author can revise the solution. For example, tell the author that you are not convinced that the solution works; please convince me. Ask how to implement it, or ask where the author has seen the pattern in practice.

Watch for tip-offs such as the word "should" or little evidence of known uses. Above all, trust your own instincts. If something sounds too good to be true, it probably is not true.

Solutions that are extremely broad tend to lack credibility. Help the author make the solution narrower and deeper by asking for specific examples of usage. You can also present counterexamples and narrow the solution space by exclusion.

Expressing doubt about the validity of a solution is a direct challenge to the author. There is danger of damaging relationships here; that's why it's important to have established a relationship with the author (see THE SHEPHERD KNOWS THE SHEEP.) However, you must not back away. Being openly skeptical now can save the author no end of trouble later.

After (and only after) the solution is in reasonably good shape, you can move on to the problem with FORCES DEFINE PROBLEM.

Forces Define Problem

Generally, after you have worked with the author on a CONVINCING SOLUTION, the solution of the pattern is in good shape. But that was the easy part. Because patterns come from proven solutions, the solution is the strongest part of an emerging pattern. But what is the nature of the problem that it solves?

Many patterns have poor problem statements. Sometimes they are too vague. More often, though, they point directly to the solution and only the solution. In some cases, you can't even find a statement of a problem.

The problem is the key to the pattern; if the solution is the heart of the pattern, the problem is its soul. A carefully crafted problem statement can be a boon to a person who is looking for a solution to that problem. However, many authors don't understand this, and instead focus exclusively on the solution.

Problem statements are hard. We tend to be solution-oriented; once we've solved a problem we think only of the solution. Thus, we usually begin by writing the solution, and then we write the problem as an afterthought. This leads to problem statements that presuppose the solution. In extreme cases, the problem statement is nothing but a restatement of the solution.

Because the problem comes first, authors occasionally write the problem before they write the solution. But this is also problematic. The temptation is to write a problem down even before the solution is well understood. Unless the author has thought through the solution in detail, such problem statements tend to be vague and overly broad.

Problems are complex. They have various aspects that may suggest different approaches to solutions, not all of which may work. Furthermore, the external manifestation of a problem is often not the problem itself; measles is a bodily illness that presents itself as small red dots on the skin.

Therefore:

The problem statement should describe the visible manifestation of something wrong. The forces then give substance to the problem and insight into what is behind the symptoms. The author should alternate between the forces and the problem statement to improve them both.

Note that the problem statement in FORCES DEFINE PROBLEM points out that problem statements tend to be weak (which is visible), and the next paragraphs (forces) point out the reasons behind it. Note also that in this particular form, the forces are not explicitly labeled. As a shepherd, you may have to hunt for the forces in the pattern.

If the author has a good start on the problem, but the forces are weak, ask what makes the problem difficult. Also ask what is the real problem that lurks behind the symptoms described in the problem. Make sure, though, that the problem statement focuses on the external symptoms, for this is what the reader will encounter and be able to relate to.

If there are forces, but a problem is not articulated, ask the author to summarize the forces in a single statement that describes the problem, and then go from there. If the pattern is weak in both forces and problem, start by asking something like, "So what problem are you trying to solve?" or "What is wrong with the world that this pattern solves?"

If you can't find the forces at all, it's time to apply VISIBLE FORCES.[11]

Be particularly wary of problem statements that are questions, because they are easy to abuse, such as a problem that reads something like, "How do you do X?" Such a problem statement very often presupposes the solution. Read the forces to see whether there is a real problem lurking in them.

You may find that you spend the bulk of the shepherding effort working on the problem. This is appropriate. Once the problem and solution are in good shape, the pattern emerges. I have seen many alleged patterns where there was indeed a pattern struggling to get out. The pattern became apparent as the problem crystallized.

---

11. Pattern Writing Pattern VISIBLE FORCES: How to make sure the reader understands the choice of solution.

Balanced Context

As the pattern takes shape through Matching Problem and Solution, Convincing Solution, and Forces Define Problem, it becomes more clear where the author's pattern can and cannot be used. The problem is well understood. The solution is now better defined, which puts natural limits on the pattern's applicability. But all too often, we don't think about the effects of the solution; we just assume that it solves the problem, and that's that. But such an assumption is in reality naïve. Any action, including applying a perfectly good solution, has consequences. A pattern owes it to its users to explain the consequences.

The pattern suffers from the "And They Lived Happily Ever After" syndrome: If you apply this pattern, all will be right with the world. Or it may have the "Good For What Ails You" syndrome: You can use this pattern for whatever problem you happen to have at the moment. Or it has both.

These two syndromes are really the same problem: The context of the pattern is not well described. On the one hand, the context for applying the pattern may be inadequate or too broad. On the other hand, the consequences, or the context that results from applying the pattern, is ignored. Both contexts are easy to forget, particularly for the author, who is so close to the pattern.

In many cases, the pattern tries to be all things to all people. The author has received comments from others about how the pattern might be applied in this or that situation, and the author tries to expand the pattern to cover the new areas. So the pattern grows, and tends to lose focus.

If it is easy to lose focus about where a pattern might be applied, it's even easier to lose focus about what the application of the pattern does to the world. One major reason for this is that the consequences of a pattern are often added last, almost as an afterthought. Consequences can get neglected in the heat of battle.

Therefore:

Look at the context before and after the solution to see how the world changes as a result of applying the pattern. Compare the beginning and the resulting contexts to each other. Also compare the beginning context to the problem, and then compare the resulting context to the solution.

The beginning context lays the groundwork, setting the stage for what will come, namely, the problem. The resulting context should explain how the world has changed through the application of the solution. The resulting context should also show how the forces have been balanced.

Compare the beginning and the resulting contexts. The overly rosy resulting context statements are usually pretty short on specifics, and so they do not show how the context has changed or how the forces are balanced. So use them to guide you as you ask the author how each force has been addressed. Ask for specifics and examples. WAR STORIES may help.

Context is difficult to get one's arms around, so it is often impossible or impractical to state the context with a great deal of rigor. So don't be too hard on the pattern writer. But do watch for obvious traps. An overly broad beginning context or a very optimistic resulting context must be tightened.

Patterns that have matching beginning and ending contexts tend to be crisp. It can also help keep the patterns focused on what is important and make them more useable out of the box. The user will know better what to expect and won't be built up and then disillusioned by grandiose expectations.

War Stories

The pattern should be improving nicely by now. The problem and solution should be clear, and one should be able to understand where to apply the pattern. But it's not. It's still difficult to understand the pattern. Furthermore, and maybe because of that, the pattern is boring.

The pattern is unclear, or sterile, and no matter what you suggest, it's not getting any better.

The pattern writer is often faced with requests to add this or that to the pattern to make it more broadly applicable, easier to use, and so forth. But if the author adds everything in, the result is huge, unwieldy, and obtuse. In addition, as patterns grow, they tend to become more abstract and less approachable. Yet the information requested is important.

The author is very close to the pattern and has experienced it firsthand. So the pattern is perfectly clear to the author. But it isn't to many readers. Among other things, the author has unwritten knowledge that seems obvious, but is not obvious, to the outside world. Sometimes there is so much missing that the shepherd knows that the pattern isn't clear but can't even figure out what to ask to gain the necessary clarification.

Therefore:

Ask the author to relate real-life experiences ("war stories") to clarify the pattern.

War Stories can be extremely powerful instruments to show what a pattern is all about and how one can use it.

One way to use a War Story is to make it a RUNNING EXAMPLE.[12]

An important aspect of a War Story is that it be appropriate for the intended audience. See CLEAR TARGET AUDIENCE[13] for help.

One way to draw out relevant stories from the author is to ask how the pattern came about. I was mentoring two people at a EuroPLoP, and the pattern was just hard to grasp. We struggled together for a while, and then I asked them to tell me how they came across the pattern. They immediately lit up and talked animatedly about their use of the pattern. All of a sudden, their pattern made sense, so I then told them to write down what they had told me. The improvement to the pattern was dramatic.

War stories can really make a pattern come alive. They help illustrate principles and reinforce the credibility of the pattern, and they make it more interesting as well. The price for this is that the pattern gets longer. Two or more stories, particularly running examples, in the same pattern can feel overdone.

Note that some cultures tend to discourage the sharing of personal experiences. Where this is the case, this pattern may be inappropriate.

Form Follows Function

(Or: Functional Form, Fitting Form)

Applying patterns such as FORCES DEFINE PROBLEM and BALANCED CONTEXT often causes large chunks to be added to a pattern. Sometimes they don't fit well with what is already there. In addition, sometimes the material in the various sections of the pattern seems somewhat contrived. This may be apparent early on,

---

12. Pattern Writing Pattern RUNNING EXAMPLE: How to make it easier for the reader to put the pattern into practice by using a single example through several patterns.

13. Pattern Writing Pattern CLEAR TARGET AUDIENCE: How to make sure the pattern reaches the intended audience by clearly identifying a primary target audience.

but in some cases might not become glaringly obvious until after one has wrestled with MATCHING PROBLEM AND SOLUTION, forces, and context.

Sometimes the pattern and the form the author picked just don't go together.

Some authors have limited exposure to patterns and therefore may know only one or two pattern forms. For example, many people's first experience with patterns is the GoF book (*Design Patterns: Elements of Objected-Oriented Software Design*), which uses a different pattern form than many patterns in the PLoPD (*Pattern Languages of Program Design*) series. You stick with what you know.

However, some patterns just work better in one form than another. The author may have a much easier time with a different form. I remember once writing a group of patterns in a particular form. I struggled with them until I started over using a different form. Then the patterns almost wrote themselves.

But a form change can be major. The author may be (understandably) reluctant to make such a big change, especially when there is little time in which to rework the patterns. It's hard to change one's methodology in the middle of a process.

Therefore:

Find a form that fits the pattern and slide the new form into the pattern, one part at a time.

If you ask the author to provide some information, use that as an opportunity to suggest putting that information into a section with an appropriate name. For example, if the target pattern form has a separate problem statement, you might draw out the problem as described earlier, and suggest that it be set off with a "Problem" heading. Conversely, you can eliminate sections by suggestions to remove them or to combine them with other sections.

The goal, of course, is to make the form serve the pattern, rather than the other way around. As you gradually introduce the desired form, the author should see how the new form is useful.

Of course, like all the other patterns, FORM FOLLOWS FUNCTION will not force the author to write a certain way. It's still up to the author. At the very least, though, the author will be exposed to new pattern forms.

Note that this pattern works very closely with SMALL PATTERNS, which follows.

Small Patterns

(Or: Small is Beautiful)

Most of the previous patterns focus on enhancing and clarifying the substance of a pattern. This means adding material to the pattern. Sometimes that material can be substantial.

Revising a pattern, especially with input from others (such as shepherds), naturally causes it to grow into a behemoth.

It is vital that a pattern have enough information to be usable. However, if the pattern is too big, the readers get lost.

As the author adds to the pattern, the new information may well overlap with the old parts of the pattern. But that may not be initially obvious. On top of that, the author is understandably not eager to rip anything out. After all, he wrote everything for a reason.

One might consider trying to keep the pattern small by ongoing pruning efforts. But it often isn't clear what information is needed in a pattern until it has been worked quite a bit. But by then, the author may be reluctant to change the pattern any more at all, particularly if it involves removing material.

Therefore:

Allow the pattern to grow at first, and then cut the pattern down. Identify extraneous chunks of the pattern and remove them.

Although one can usually tighten the prose of a pattern, redaction yields only minor reductions. You need to find whole parts of the pattern that are unnecessary and take them out. For each candidate section, ask what it adds to the pattern and whether it is covered elsewhere. Doing that will help make it clear to the author which parts of the pattern should be removed. This activity is often done together with FORM FOLLOWS FUNCTION.

Using hypertext allows inclusion of detail that can be hidden on first reading and brought forth if desired.

If the pattern is very large, it may actually be several patterns. You might suggest that the author consider whether the pattern should be broken into multiple smaller patterns. A sign of this being the case is when a pattern contains multiple solutions; a single pattern should contain one problem, one context, and one solution.

❖ ❖ ❖

The resulting pattern is smaller and cleaner than before, but it is almost always larger than it was at the beginning of shepherding. That's usually all right; if it isn't, you can make multiple passes on the pattern. Cutting can be a difficult process, but it is still easier with prose than it is with source code.

Epilogue

On the surface, the patterns presented here are all about how to help someone improve their patterns. Yes, that is what they are all about. But they are deeper than that. For the most part, these patterns are all about the things that make patterns good. For example, WAR STORIES is all about making the pattern more concrete and approachable. MATCHING PROBLEM AND SOLUTION helps the shepherd, and therefore the author, focus on the essence of the pattern—the solution and what problem it solves. Many of the patterns seek to improve the quality of the problem statement. If the solution is the heart of a pattern, the problem is its soul. In my experience, the problem statements are typically weak, so using the patterns presented in this chapter can directly influence the quality of the pattern.

But one can go still deeper. These patterns can help us solve problems more effectively; they can guide us in how we approach a problem; they can help us think. For example, BIG PICTURE and MATCHING PROBLEM AND SOLUTION can help us get started right. I have been in several meetings where my friend and colleague Jim Coplien has asked, "Wait a minute! What problem are you solving?" This question helps us focus on what we are really trying to accomplish and steers us away from ineffective actions. In a like manner, all these patterns can help us, not only in shepherding, but in general problem solving and in relationships with others.

Acknowledgments

Sometimes I think acknowledgments should go up front, so that you, dear reader, know who contributed to the material even as you read it. There have been many people who have helped. Thanks go to Jim Coplien, who provided thought-provoking comments on an early version of the paper. Special thanks to Ward Cunningham, who took on the daunting task of shepherding a paper on shepherding. He also recommended that I ask the shepherd pool for comments, which resulted in suggestions from the following shepherds: Brad Appleton, Mark Bradac, Ward Cunningham (again), Dennis DeBruler, David DeLano, Jutta Eckstein, Robert Hanmer, William Opdyke, Dirk Riehle, Antonio

Rito Silva, and Andreas Rüping. They have certainly enriched this language. Thanks also to my PLoP99 writers' workshop group for their insightful comments. They were Brad Appleton, Ali Arsanjani, Ralph Cabrera, Ralph Johnson, John Liebenau, Cameron Smith, Carol Stimmel, and Terunobu Fujino.

References

[Coplien2000] J. Coplien. "A Pattern Language for Writers' Workshops." In N. Harrison, B. Foote, and H. Rohnert (eds.), *Pattern Languages of Program Design 4*. Boston: Addison-Wesley, 2000.

[Meszaros+1997] G. Meszaros and J. Doble. "A Pattern Language for Pattern Writing." In R. C. Martin, D. Riehle, and F. Buschmann (eds.), *Pattern Languages of Program Design 3*. Reading, MA: Addison-Wesley, 1997.

[Parlsberg1999] J. Parlsberg. Evaluate Papers Fast. Available: *http://c2.com/cgi/ wiki?EvaluatePapersFast*.

CHAPTER 19

Patterns of the Prairie Houses

Paul R. Taylor

On the Prairie

This chapter attempts distillation of the essential design themes of Frank Lloyd Wright's Prairie Houses in pattern form. The result is a pattern language fragment that documents the key features of Wright's architectural style and an interpretation of Wright's design justifications and motivations. The exercise serves to illustrate the use of patterns and pattern languages in post hoc design documentation and design rationale recovery.

> "We of the Middle West are living on the prairie. The prairie has a beauty of its own and we should recognize and accentuate this natural beauty, its quiet level. Hence, gently sloping roofs, low proportions, quiet sky lines, suppressed heavy-set chimneys." —Frank Lloyd Wright (1908)

Frank Lloyd Wright, arguably America's most celebrated architect, designed houses for the Midwest prairie. By 1901, Wright had fleshed out his ideal house on paper, and "A Home in a Prairie Town" appeared that year in the February edition of *Ladies' Home Journal*. Its shady roofs, bands of windows, outstretching and suspended terraces, free-flowing interiors, and ground-hugging form finally put Wright on the architectural map. His inspiration was the Midwestern prairie, with its "quiet level" and far horizon signifying a new sense of freedom. For the next decade, this horizontal line became for Wright "the line of domesticity," the template for several hundred designs, of which about 120 were built.

He furnished his Prairie Houses with art-glass windows of intricate geometric designs and a superb sense of scale, prominent hearths, and custom designed and built furniture in the colors of nature, binding each house to its natural context and initiating a reversal of attitude to the environment [Maddex2000].

These houses are famous not just because they became synonymous with Wright's signature design style, but because they announced a new period in which domestic design turned from its introverted obsession and refocused outward, to embrace environment, even to invite it to enter a kind of dialogue. In Australia, a similar design movement found expression a decade later in the wave of bungalow designs from California that swept through the new automobile-accessible suburbs. These houses of the 1920s and 1930s lowered their European predecessor's lofty ceilings; sported larger, airier rooms and windows; and bore heavy, overhanging gables to protect the inhabitants from the harsh antipodean sun. The bungalow houses dissolved formal rooms into free-flowing living spaces and embraced the car by giving it pride of place next to the house itself, while sprawling across and down their blocks in homage to the idealized ranch that every family apparently aspired to. In twentieth-century architecture, Wright's Prairie Houses set the foundation for the golden era of the nuclear family, which was the sociological fabric of the emerging American middle classes. Rarely has a type of domestic house design had such sociological and cultural impact.

Wright's houses clearly had (and still have) an almost mystical appeal. Hildebrand's book, "The Wright Space—Pattern and Meaning in Frank Lloyd Wright's Houses" [Hildebrand1991], describes a search for the reasons for the overwhelming appreciation of Wright's houses, particularly by lay people, despite many inhabitants' descriptions of functional problems inherent in the buildings. Hildebrand summarizes the generally ecstatic responses of past and present owners of Wright's houses, and their overwhelmingly positive responses to the experience of working with the architect. Evidence of this can be found in the rate of return business—some clients returned for more than one subsequent engagement. Robert Twombly, described by Hildebrand as a "careful and balanced biographer," notes that "as questionnaires and interviews establish again and again, his clients love their homes, indeed, are more than ordinarily enthusiastic, and leave, if they have to, with considerable reluctance" [Twombly1979]. Hildebrand notes that the public is equally enthusiastic and appreciative of the designs.

Hildebrand's attempts to analyze this appeal led him to describe a "pattern" and raise interesting themes of aesthetics and beauty in design. Wright himself tried to explain the appeal of his work through references to a belief in the organic, a sympathy with nature, the art and craft of the machine, the countenance of principle, and a sense of shelter. Art historians have proposed analogies to natural forms or to contemporary, primordial, or exotic architectural examples; they have analyzed abstract compositional processes and devices; they have offered explanations about the liberation of space and have discussed the metaphor of expansive democratic life. While much of this work helps us to understand what differentiates Wright's designs, it does not explain the basic appeal, particularly to lay observers of Wright's houses.

Prospect and Refuge

The identification of the essence of this appeal is informed by Hildebrand's interest in the work of English geographer Jay Appleton, the author of a theory of "prospect and refuge" [Appleton1975]. Appleton argues that there is a deeply seated, genetically driven human predilection for conditions of prospect and refuge within landscape settings. By "prospect" Appleton means a place from which one can see over a considerable distance, and by "refuge" he means a place where one can hide—as a pair, they reinforce each other by creating the ability to see without being seen, a combination that once had survival value. Appleton claims that this habitat-selecting is enacted just for the inherent pleasure it yields, without conscious recognition of the inherent species survival conditions. Hildebrand claims that in the years since the theory's appearance, it has received "a fair amount of empirical substantiation," and while not wishing to claim it as immutable truth, Hildebrand believes it has progressed somewhat beyond the stage of speculation.

Prospect and refuge have poignant meanings on the prairie in the summer heat of the Midwest or on Australia's coastal fringe, and Wright's designs provide both. To the extent that Wright's implementation of "prospect and refuge" is structural and can be abstracted from the plans of his Prairie Houses, a pattern exists. Other common characteristics of the designs yield naturally to pattern form, and if we consider Wright's Prairie Houses a design genre, a pattern language seems a natural way of explicating the content of the designer's mind.

Hildebrand's Essential Characteristics

In fact, Hildebrand has explicated the content of the designer's mind, although not in Alexanderian pattern form. Hildebrand classifies the recurring elements of all of Wright's Prairie Houses as follows:

- The major spaces are elevated well above the terrain they overlook.
- The fireplace is withdrawn to the center of the house and to the internal edge of the room it serves.

- The withdrawal of the fireplace is emphasized by a low ceiling edge and flanking built-in seating and cabinetwork.

- The ceiling forward of the fireplace sweeps upward into the roof, echoing its form.

- The distant edges of the ceiling then return to a low elevation like that near the fireplace.

- There are anterior views to contiguous spaces seen beyond architectural screening devices.

- Glass and glazed doors are located on walls distant from the fire.

- A generous elevated terrace lies beyond.

- The exterior consists of deep, overhanging eaves; an evident central chimney; broad horizontal groupings of window bands; conspicuous balconies or terraces.

- The connection from exterior to interior is by means of a long and circuitous path.

Interestingly, Hildebrand selects the word "pattern" for this statement of abstracted form, or canonical state—"this repetitive configuration of domestic architectural elements" [Hildebrand1991]. According to Hildebrand, the pattern occurs in its entirety for the first time in the Heurtley house, which is comprised of these thirteen characteristics, and that for the next fifty years of Wright's professional life, all of his houses (with the exception of the Ocatillo camp and Taliesin West) will have at least ten of these characteristics, and many will have all thirteen. Thus, this "pattern" underlies all of Wright's Prairie houses, Taliesin, the Californian houses of the 1920s, Fallingwater, and the Usonians.

Nowhere in his voluminous writings did Wright explicitly describe this pattern, which Hildebrand does not find surprising, because "such things develop as often by intuition as by conscious thought." There is nothing to suggest that Wright ever generalized his style, although he often referred to his work as "the destruction of the box," by which he meant the opening up of views between rooms and to the outdoors by means of broad horizontal expanses of windows.

An Alexanderian Rendition

Alexander regards all of the great architects of history, and indeed all of us mortals as well, as having internalized "pattern languages" of our own, from which we arrange our personal spaces and form our own designs. "When a person is faced with an act of design," writes Alexander, "what he does is governed entirely by the pattern language which he has in his mind at the moment":

> Palladio used a pattern language to make his designs. And Frank Lloyd Wright too used a pattern language to make his designs. Palladio happened to record his patterns in books, with the idea that other people could use them too. Wright tried to keep his patterns secret, like a master chef who keeps his recipes secret. But this difference is inessential. What matters is that both of them, and all the other great architects who have ever lived, have had their own pattern languages, the condensation of their own experience, in the form of private rules of thumb, which they could use whenever they began to make a building [Alexander1979].

Thus, if the master architects of yesteryear did not explicate their recipes, perhaps today's distant disciples could show their appreciation by doing it for them. But the would-be masters must be clear on their motivations. Why pursue the essence of Frank Lloyd Wright's Prairie House style in Alexander's [1977] pattern form? After all, it is not as if anyone will attempt to reproduce these houses now.

While the resultant extracted patterns from any such effort would provide little more than an exercise for the writer, the experience of effectively reverse-engineering them could draw out valuable insights for the reader into how pattern languages should be approached. The world does not need Prairie House patterns, but the (software and systems development) world does need mechanisms to extract the essence of proven or outstanding designs and ways of supporting learning from exemplary designs. Mining patterns from architectural masterpieces has potential to satisfy both needs, and the Prairie Houses, as instances of a master designer's oeuvre, offer the advantage of a closely studied collection of works that embody a set of unified, internalized principles that have time-proven appeal and endurance. It is difficult to think of another collection of designed artifacts that offers similar consistency and faithfulness to its designer's objectives and vision.

Although Hildebrand listed thirteen common characteristics of these houses and their occurrences, he did not consciously mine Wright's design intentions or motivations. It is impossible to write patterns without doing so. The patterns in this paper represent the author's attempt to answer the question "Why did he choose this design from all other possibilities?" In adopting the pattern form, you must read Wright's intentions, and go further by knitting them together through a web of pattern relationships. This is a challenging task, despite the obvious clarity and purity of Wright's designs. To successfully write Wright's patterns is to attempt to think like the architect—just for a moment.

Author's Note

During the shepherding process, the comment was made that Alexander would not approve of the concept of this paper. The reasons for and counterfoils against this statement would constitute a workshop in their own right—but if we look closely, we find that Alexander does have something to say about Wright's style. In a passage expounding the innocent nature of the "quality without a name," he writes:

> This innocence will only come about when people honestly forget themselves.
>
> It goes without saying that the vast steel and glass concrete structures of our famous architects do not have this quality.
>
> It goes without saying that the mass-produced development houses, built by big developers, do not have this quality.
>
> But it is true that even the more "natural" architects, like Frank Lloyd Wright and Alvar Aalto, also do not reach this quality.
>
> These places are not innocent, and cannot reach the quality without a name, because they are made with an outward glance. The people who make them make them the way they do because they are trying to convey something, some image, to the world outside. Even when they are made to seem natural, even their naturalness is calculated; it is in the end a pose. [Alexander1979]

It seems that it might be impossible for a working architect in the commercial world to achieve Alexander's quality without a name in its purest form. If Wright's Prairie style is indeed "a pose," I am prepared to turn a blind eye to any hint of self-conscious arrogance in the designer's stance because the designs themselves and the ideas they present are so compelling. They work as art should work, igniting flashes of inspiration and bringing insight to otherwise uninspiring places. The historically maligned Midwest prairie has become a beautiful place in our collective consciousness because an artisan chose to render it differently.

Alexander's alleged disapproval of his pattern form being used to document the design style of America's most prominent architectural hero might turn out to be a brief bitter moment in the sweet pattern renaissance that the software community has brought about. For now, there is much to be learned from an experiment such as this one.

Form Follows Predominant Feature

"Architecture is the scientific art of making structure express ideas."
—Frank Lloyd Wright (1932)

"I loved the prairie by instinct as a great simplicity, the trees and flowers, the sky itself, thrilling by contrast." —Frank Lloyd Wright (1931)

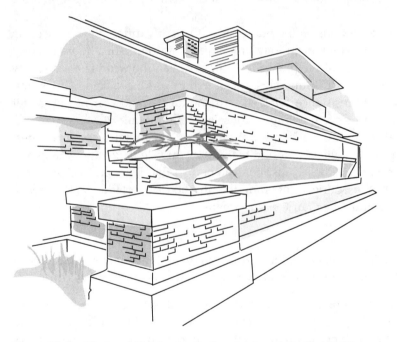

Figure 19–1 *Horizontality dominates the prairie and the Prairie House*

. . . good design forms a response to the features of its surroundings, and domestic architecture can either isolate us from, or integrate us with, our surroundings. The prairie's dominant features of flatness, the horizon, prospect, and the sky overhead dictate a new architectural style that must be articulated. Just how that articulation is voiced is the designer's challenge.

What should the relationship between the Prairie House form and the prairie be? What forms will open the house up to the prairie, embrace and integrate with it, be instantaneously recognizable, and yet still provide everything that a house must provide for shelter and domestic well-being?

Traditional house designs balance horizontal spread with vertical height in an aspect ratio that has become somewhat predictable across many cultures and times. These designs, born in cities, were motivated in part by the need to minimize the footprint of the house, for heating, cooling, and security reasons. The prairie knows no such space limitations. More importantly, a multi-story villa cannot freely associate with any natural features of the prairie, and it is doubtful whether any existing domestic house design can achieve such integration more convincingly.

The weather conditions on the prairie are sufficiently different from those on the East Coast to warrant an entirely different configuration of a house's aspect ratio. At certain times of the prairie inhabitant's year, the wind is a seemingly constant companion. On some days, it can make working outside almost impossible. Low wind resistance, wind screens and breaks, and year-round shelter must be made intrinsic to the Prairie House's configuration.

The Prairie House needs a single, unifying idea, one that drives every aspect of the design, and results in a design that fits the prairie landscape snugly and naturally. The Prairie House must be designed so that it echoes the predominant features of the prairie, celebrating the uniqueness, isolation, and forces of nature that constitute the prairie environment.

Therefore:

Emphasize the horizontal over the vertical, so that all the main externally visible lines of the house integrate with the prairie's flatness and endless horizon.

All good design embodies a central idea—a "seed" or "generator," that manifests in the building on every scale, from the conceptual to the structural and down to the minutiae of the finest detail. For a house on a prairie, the primary generator should be the prairie's fundamental characteristic—the horizontality of the plane (Figure 19–1).

But it would be a mistake to simply take the elements of a "conventional" urban house and stretch them sideways in a single-level, horizontal, pancake fashion, because when you change a structural assumption of a design as fundamental as its aspect ratio, you must rethink every part of the design. Most existing elements (such as windows, doors, chimneys, verandas, and rooflines) are designed for conventional placements on equally conventional house designs, and so the act of reorienting the house to integrate with the prairie renders the existing language of domestic design irrelevant.

Fortunately, there are some straightforward ways of emphasizing the horizontal. Keep the center of gravity low in order to anchor the house firmly to the ground. Mimic the sharp horizon of the plains with long, projecting cantilevered rooflines and terraces that appear to stretch the house into its environment without visible reference to the ground for support. Trim the Prairie House along horizontal lines, allowing these lines to run parallel with the horizon unimpeded around the full perimeter of the house.

A horizontal emphasis will visibly and structurally tie the house to the prairie. A house design that is based on horizontality will achieve a strong sense of PROSPECT AND REFUGE. Many of the house's features can be designed in accord with this primary concept. A CHIMNEY AS ANCHOR will provide an axis of symmetry, and a CANTILEVERED TERRACE will extend the house's horizontality out into space, parallel to and above the prairie plane. BANDS OF WINDOWS can double as an externally visible horizontal trim, and CIRCUITOUS APPROACH will emphasize the house's strong integration with its context to approaching visitors.

Prospect and Refuge

Figure 19–2 *View of the woods and prairie from Fallingwater living room*

. . . house designs throughout history reveal the ways that their designers and occupiers chose to balance refuge (the degree of enclosure) with prospect (the occupant's ability to see out to the horizon). The privacy of the prairie affords an opportunity to reassess this balance, to allow new freedoms to open up and even merge internal and external spaces.

In designing the living spaces in a house on the prairie, how do you provide a sense of connection with the wide, flat, surrounding open landscape, while at the same time providing equally important senses of privacy, shelter, and refuge from the harsh realities of the external environment?

Traditional European and early American colonial houses used design elements such as multiple stories, small windows, and single front and rear external doors to effectively exclude the extremes of weather, unwanted visitors, disease, and other threats from outside. These designs assumed that the primary purpose of a house was refuge. In increasing the thickness of the street-facing wall, reducing the door and window sizes, and elevating the floor well above street level, such houses deliberately isolated occupants from perceived dangers outside. But in the 1920s in the American Midwest, most of these dangers had ceased to be real.

As a domestic environment, the prairie offers an unprecedented sense of space. The individual lots, with space for automobile access and storage on one side and generous gardens on the other, large front gardens and even larger rear gardens, and expansive grassy areas between fence and road, offer unparalleled privacy and uninterrupted views from internal living spaces. By opening up sight lines from the internal living spaces to the outside, emphasizing the prairie's expansive field, we emphasize the inhabitant's sense of prospect—of being able to see without being seen.

But the prairie is no year-round Garden of Eden. It can be a harsh environment, and a house must fundamentally provide shelter. In winter, the northern prairie is blanketed in snow, so an overly open design with too much glass will be impossible to heat, and midwinter sun hitting fresh powder snow should not be allowed to blind the inhabitants.

People also want and need privacy from the eyes of passersby in both private and shared rooms. But it can be difficult to provide such privacy in a house designed with wide or unchangeable openings between internal and external spaces. There are two conflicting forces in the design of the spaces of a house on the prairie—we want to open up the house to the prairie outside, but we do not want to compromise the inhabitant's sense of shelter.

Therefore:

Elevate the house's major living spaces well above the terrain they overlook.

Use just enough elevation so that the house is visually distinct from the plain, but not so much as to create a second story underneath. The actual height needs to be determined at each site, but it should be determined experimentally, by standing on successive steps of a ladder, or at different heights on a movable platform until the best sense of prospect is attained.

Surround the elevated external living surfaces with wide, solid fences and railings to secure the inhabitants, but keep them low enough so that they do not impede the view of the prairie from inside (Figure 19–2).

Exaggerate the projection of the house's eaves horizontally so that they become a sun and weather visor while trimming but not obscuring the view from inside.

Raising the level of the living spaces will distinguish between the house and the prairie and will enhance the sense of prospect without turning the Prairie House into a multi-story building. Enclosing terraces with solid but low walls provides a similar limited screening effect. Other design elements can be used to further enhance the occupant's sense of prospect, such as providing alternate PROSPECTIVE VIEWS. The occupant's sense of refuge is served by using the CHIMNEY AS ANCHOR and by creating a FIREPLACE AS REFUGE. A CIRCUITOUS APPROACH serves to enhance the approaching visitor's appreciation of both prospect and refuge.

Chimney as Anchor

The Midwestern prairie is subject to freezing temperatures in winter, and a generous and functional fireplace is a mandatory inclusion in any house in the region. A fireplace implies a hearth, an informal social space, and a chimney. An important concern for the designer of a house on the prairie is the position and relationship of this assembly with the other main elements of the house so as to make them usable and functional.

Figure 19–3 *Substantial central chimney (Fallingwater)*

Where should you place the fireplace and chimney so as to integrate them with the social flows of the household?

Fireplaces are a natural point of refuge in any house, but not all houses are designed to enhance this sense of refuge. If you place the fireplace on an outer wall, people are forced to adhere to that wall, like insects clinging to a lighted window at night. The off-center fireplace breaks their sense of connection with the rest of the house, which may remain cold and seemingly unwelcome.

The Prairie House with its large living spaces that open onto expansive terraces through horizontal bands of windows suffers noticeably from this problem. In the winter evenings, the house must beckon its inhabitants inward from the cold of the prairie toward a solid, stable, unchanging core.

Therefore:

Make the fireplace and chimney large and solid. Place them in the center of the house and to the internal edge of the room they serve. Ensure that they form the pivot upon which all of the main structural features of the house's plan revolve.

A large and solid chimney offers a solidity that seemingly anchors the house to the ground, thereby enhancing the sense of permanence (Figure 19–3). Placing the fireplace in the center of the house plan allows its heat to radiate outward into all adjacent rooms, which typically serve a range of functions. The hearth is also withdrawn into the center of the house, to its core, and away from external windows and terraces. With a central hearth, the occupants will feel a sense of retreat from the other more open spaces of the house to an internal space that provides seemingly constant warmth and refuge.

A central hearth additionally provides a pleasing symmetry to the house's plan, allowing the wings and terraces of the house to radiate out horizontally in all directions. A symmetrical, strongly anchored house plan provides a comforting orientation for their inhabitants.

CHIMNEY AS ANCHOR works hand in hand with FIREPLACE AS REFUGE so that the solid, central fireplace affords opportunities for refuge on all sides. With the CHIMNEY AS ANCHOR, a CANTILEVERED TERRACE can extend out from the central anchor in any direction.

Cantilevered Terrace

Figure 19–4 *Cantilevered terrace (Fallingwater)*

If a house is to integrate with its natural context, then its designer must find ways of connecting its occupants with nature in a way that allows free movement between "inside" and "outside." To achieve this, the conventional notions of doors, windows, and walls may need to be rethought. At all times, people must be able to move freely between a natural and a domestic space.

How do you connect domestic living spaces with nature outside? How do you blur the distinction between inside and outside spaces?

As we have seen in earlier patterns, traditional urban house designs reinforce the distinction between inside and outside for reasons that are not important on the prairie. There, we must look for ways of melding the two experiences of space.

We can bring light and a sense of outside into the inside by using large, open, unimpeded windows. However, experiencing nature from behind glass is only half the experience—it is reminiscent of being stopped by a shop window from touching, smelling, and feeling fresh fruit. Oversized sets of windows make heating in winter problematic and reduce privacy.

Many houses in the United Kingdom and Europe include small glass-roofed sunrooms on their south wall to catch sun in the winter. But a glass-roofed structure would quickly turn into an uninhabitable sauna on the prairie in summertime, where a solid roof is required all year round.

Neither of these potential solutions addresses the problem of nature being "out there," at a "safe" distance from the house, because in all cases, the house boundary sets the limit of proximity. An alternate solution must be found—one that brings nature in close, that protects from weather extremities, and that allows free flow between internal and external living spaces.

Therefore:

Thrust the terrace out from the house's main structure and into the air beyond. Do not use vertical supports of any kind—instead, use cantilevered steel girders hidden within the floor of the terrace for structural support.

By extending horizontal roofed terraces out from the house, a living space is created that appears to "hover" above the prairie, pushing the inhabitant out into the environment while still providing sufficient sense of refuge. If the terrace extends far enough, the house's living spaces can literally come close to touching the surrounding trees. The omission of vertical supports emphasizes this projection both visually and experientially. The terrace may be designed to provide external space or internal space behind walls and windows, or both (Figure 19–4).

A CANTILEVERED TERRACE implements the horizontality demanded when FORM FOLLOWS PREDOMINANT FEATURE on a prairie and strongly contributes to the inhabitant's experience of Prospect and Refuge. A Cantilevered Terrace should ideally extend out from the centrally located Chimney as Anchor so that one end of the terrace is firmly anchored while the other end flies cantilevered out into the air. A Cantilevered Terrace is an ideal setting for Bands of Windows.

Bands of Windows

Windows say a lot about the designer's intentions, the builder's skill, and the client's means. They are critically important in setting the mood and tone of the rooms inside because they control the available light that falls upon the faces and features of the inhabitants. Windows have probably more semiotic significance than just about any other house feature—if the designer exhibits sufficient taste and skill, and the client exhibits sufficient means, the windows can become the most architecturally decorative and thematically integrated feature of a house.

How do you insert windows into a Prairie House wall so that the horizontality is not lost?

Windows are conventionally tall and narrow, and are set in walls in symmetric pairs. This historical window treatment is out of place in the Prairie House with its sweeping horizontal lines.

It might be possible to design and fabricate a long horizontal window set, but such an arrangement would present design and manufacturing problems, and it divorces the window from the human scale. Ideally, we wish to keep the conventional window design and aspect ratio with its human scale, its standard sashes, and hardware.

Therefore:

Replace the solid wall punctuated with the occasional window at symmetrical centers with a low wall and a horizontal band of a large number of identical windows with conventional aspect ratios. Leave as little space between the windows as possible so that they merge into a continuous band of light. If possible, sweep the band of windows right around three sides of the room.

This array of conventional vertical windows of standard scale and ratios solves window scaling problems, serves to flood the living space with light, and provides visual lines of sight from inside to nature outside. An array of windows provides a natural gallery for exhibiting repeating patterns of design motifs in art-glass.

Alexander has much to say about the way light from multiple sources enhances people's experience of habitation (LIGHT ON TWO SIDES OF EVERY ROOM). BANDS OF WINDOWS implements the horizontality demanded when FORM FOLLOWS PRE-DOMINANT FEATURE on the prairie. BANDS OF WINDOWS allow the transparent flows of vision and light that the inhabitant's experience of PROSPECT AND REF-UGE requires and belongs naturally on a CANTILEVERED TERRACE.

Fireplace as Refuge

Using CHIMNEY AS ANCHOR provides a point of symmetry for the house plan and a point of reference for the inhabitants. It also ensures a sense of solidity, as if the house were anchored to a central monolith. But the internal design of the fireplace and hearth needs further consideration before it becomes the social center of the house.

How do you design the space around the fireplace so that people are encour-aged to relax, to feel a sense of refuge, as they assemble in small informal groups during a winter's day, or sit comfortably at the end of an evening?

In the winter months, people will spend a great deal of their time gathered around the fireplace. Its immediate surroundings must facilitate this. Some rooms have large open spaces around the fireplace, so that the inhabitants are free to place furniture, rugs, bookshelves, and low tables to suit themselves. But this means that people facing the fire sit in the midst of a large space, with their back to the open room behind them. It is difficult to feel a sense of refuge when the other inhabitants of the house are freely moving behind you. It is also com-mon for the ceiling of the room to continue its height into the wall on which the fireplace is set. This cavernous space over the heads of the inhabitants also lim-its the sense of refuge.

In these settings, people often drag their chairs over against one of the two walls in order to reduce movement behind them, and they may artificially crowd their space with low tables or lamps that create a superficial "nook."

Therefore:

Emphasize the fireplace's withdrawal and create a sense of refuge with a low ceiling edge, and add adjacent built-in seating and cabinetwork. Make the ceiling forward of the fireplace sweep upward into the roof, echoing its form. To ensure symmetry, make the distant edges of the ceiling then return to a low elevation like that near the fire.

Making the fireplace with these characteristics helps to draw the social flows inward, toward the center of the house, and this is the easiest place in which to arrange things so as to create a sense of refuge. A central fireplace is never too far from any wing of the house and can be designed to be accessible from all sides.

To achieve a balance between the refuge of the fireplace and the prospect of an elevated living floor of a Prairie House, always ensure that prospective views are not more than a few steps away from the fireplace.

FIREPLACE AS REFUGE is the primary mechanism by which the Prairie House can provide the refuge part of its PROSPECT AND REFUGE. A FIREPLACE AS REFUGE, with its graduated ceilings and its alcove or inglenook features, is perfectly paired with having the CHIMNEY AS ANCHOR, because both draw the chimney and fireplace to the center of the Prairie House. If a CANTILEVERED TERRACE extends the living space out from the chimney and fireplace, then the room offers both fireplace refuge at one end and openness to nature at the other.

Prospective Views

> "Human use and comfort should have intimate possession of every interior… should be felt in every exterior." — Frank Lloyd Wright (1932)

The degree to which the Prairie House is elevated to provide a sense of PROSPECT AND REFUGE, and the distance that its CANTILEVERED TERRACE extends the living space out into nature, and the number and size of the horizontal BANDS OF WINDOWS that flood the living spaces with light needs to be chosen with care. Opening up the Prairie House integrates it and its inhabitants' lives with the natural context, but the house must always retain a sense of refuge and a character of its own.

How do you find a balance between opening up the design of the house to the prairie outside and providing a permanent or occasional sense of privacy? How do you stop the prairie's overpowering nature from dominating every aspect of the inhabitants' lives?

It is tempting when designing for the prairie, with its non-negotiable expansiveness, to think of using floor-to-ceiling glass walls and doors to flood the house with light. However, nature and the elements must be moderated so that the house's year-round sense of refuge will be not be compromised. In Prospect and Refuge, we noticed that a balance between the dominance of the prairie could be achieved by finding the right elevation. But beyond this, seasonal weather variations on the prairie are considerable, and the need for privacy or shelter will change with the seasons.

Therefore:

Arrange the house's position on the site, and its windows and living spaces, so that there are forward views to contiguous spaces beyond architectural screening devices.

These may be fixed or movable screens. They may be naturally occurring obstacles such as trees or a more distant grove of trees, or they may be designed and placed outside the house deliberately.

By alternating between views of the horizon and views into screened-off spaces or "garden rooms," the inhabitant is afforded a chance to discover prospective views and to choose, explicitly or tacitly, between different prospective views. As a result of this choice, inhabitants personalize their experience of living on the prairie, and the Prairie House unfolds and reveals itself over time and as the seasons change.

Prospective Views helps the house to reveal the right balance of Prospect and Refuge.

Concealed Verticals

Figure 19–5 *Concealed vertical entrance, Thomas House*

Given that the predominant sense of the prairie is flat, the Prairie House must do as little as possible to disturb this sense of horizon. Its horizontal lines should not be broken by features or fixtures, especially by those that are essentially vertical in their shape or design.

How can the unavoidable verticality of some mandatory features, such as the entrance door, be concealed and yet remain discernible to the approaching visitor?

Every house needs an entrance, but the basic shape of the conventional entrance is one of vertical height. Features around the conventional entrance door, such as leadlight windows and "fan-lights" (the small windows over the top of the door), emphasize this verticality. And yet we must preserve the horizontality of the Prairie House at all cost.

One potential solution is to place the vertical entrance door on a large wall, or façade, so that the scale of the façade overwhelms the verticality of the door, making it appear as less of an interruption in the horizontality of the house. However, large facades break from the nature of the prairie too strongly and must therefore be used with caution.

It is, of course, also impossible to make all features and house design elements horizontal—people and furniture must have easy and unimpeded access through doors that must extend up vertically.

Therefore:

Conceal the vertical dimensions of the entrance door behind a screen, and create a path that leads the approaching visitor past the screen to the door.

Use horizontally integrated features of the façade to mask verticality, such as that of the door. For example, visitors must pass through an archway that creates a cave-like pathway that is separate from the outside of the house. Thus, visitors can find the door, but to do so they must pass beyond the house's façade or integrated wall and into a welcoming realm in which verticality is acceptable.

Alexander's pattern ENTRANCE TRANSITION resolves the problem of transition from street to house. It may be similar to CONCEALED VERTICALS in its implementation, but its purpose differs. CONCEALED VERTICALS is intended only to preserve the Prairie House's uninterrupted horizontal lines—if concealment creates an ENTRANCE TRANSITION, it should be considered a desirable side effect of this pattern.

Circuitous Approach

The use of CONCEALED VERTICALS means that the house's main entrance door will be partially or entirely concealed. On the prairie, a well-marked entrance pathway is essential, because neither the prairie nor the shape of the house will emphasize the approach.

If the entrance door is concealed, how can it be discernible to the approaching visitor?

Traditional vertical doors in city villas are frequently teamed with formal, linear paths that extend from the door straight to the gate. On the prairie, the house is surrounded by lawn, woodlands, and low garden beds. There is no obvious self-suggesting approach, and the formality of linear paths does not belong there.

We also do not want the main entrance to face onto the prairie directly, because this would eliminate the inhabitants' privacy and risk exposure to the extremes of prairie weather. The inhabitants' perception of the house as shelter and protector will be enhanced by requiring them to make a conscious transition as they approach from the edge of the prairie and as they leave the protection of the house.

Therefore:

Make the connection from exterior to interior by means of a long and circuitous pathway. Signify the beginning of the path with pillars, a garden transition, or some other means. If possible, lead the path past views of the site and the house that emphasize the transition from outside to inside.

A CIRCUITOUS APPROACH will guide the approaching visitor through the open prairie spaces to the entrance door. On the way, the path can be placed to afford views of the house and its situation. In doing so, it can add a sense of drama and occasion to the approach, serving to celebrate the house and its integration with its natural surroundings. The CIRCUITOUS APPROACH can also serve to emphasize the entrance transition.

Alexander's pattern ENTRANCE TRANSITION resolves the problem of transition from street to house, but it does not address how the visitor should approach the entrance from afar. CIRCUITOUS APPROACH, by comparison, guides the visitor over the expansive open spaces in front of the house.

Assessment and Conclusion

With the performance complete, and the resultant patterns aired, what can we take away of lasting value from this exercise? Can we conclude that the major value to be had from this kind of endeavor is that which is derived from writing or performing a toccata—a challenging exercise of perception and performance for the pattern author? As such, it brings useful personal insights and builds authoring expertise, but there are other lessons.

The task of tracing patterns from indirect observation of a designer's work is made difficult for a number of reasons, some of which may have become obvious to the reader as the extracted patterns were read. While the structural solution of each of these patterns can be justified in its own right, what cannot be justified is the exact reasoning behind the pattern—we simply cannot second-guess the designer with any degree of confidence. When Wright employed CIRCUITOUS AP-PROACH on the Thomas, Heurtley or Robie Houses, exactly why did he do so in each case? Was it, as the author's pattern suggests, to screen the main entrance from prairie extremes? Was he primarily motivated by his penchant for preserving the horizontality of the house from vertical interruption? Or perhaps his well-known predilection to posture repeatedly got the better of him, and these circuitous approaches are actually intended to parade the visitor past the best perspectives on Wright's masterpieces every time they enter the building. We simply cannot know.

Other questions plagued the author—the selection of which patterns should be documented and which should not, the precedence of patterns, and of course, the thorny issue of the relationship between the patterns and the degree to which they form a language. These patterns do not knit into a comprehensive language. Thus, they illustrate only some of the power of pattern theory. If time and means permitted, more patterns could surely be identified; the author could spend time visiting Wright's structures and reading architectural analyses of his work. More investment in the project would also increase the confidence level for each pattern and the relationships between the patterns. These are resource limitations and do not reflect negatively on the core concept of mining design knowledge from a master designer's collection of works.

There is little doubt that recurring strong design themes can be adequately documented in individual patterns, and the patterns presented in this chapter demonstrate this. They are reasonable, feasible, and believable. But the value of the exercise as an attempt to capture the essence of the designer's capability is limited. These patterns are illustrative, but they are not as strongly generative as they could be. Making them into a generative pattern language would require such a degree of interpretation and projection on the part of the author that their link with the original designer would become tenuous. We cannot get inside Wright's head, as much as we would like to. And in making the effort to find the measure of his genius, we fall short. We are left with impressions and shadows rather then the form itself.

Alexander's primary motivation in writing and promoting patterns followed from his negative experience of the built world in the modernist era. Alexander (along with other theorists) concluded that modern design regarded humans as little more than an appliqué on an egoistic, heroic rationalist master plan. In proposing and popularizing patterns, he became the great anti-modernist, intent on restoring basic habitability on the scarred face of the built world and driven by the desire to see design subservient to human scale and need. This historical perspective reminds us that all good patterns exist primarily for moral purposes—to improve the well-being of ordinary people as they inhabit their predominantly man-made places and spaces. This is the ultimate test of a pattern or a pattern language—does it improve the well-being of people? Does it improve people's experience of living and being? Is its moral fiber fully intact? The reader has two conclusions to draw. Was Frank Lloyd Wright pursuing the agenda we just stated? And if he was (as I believe he was), do the patterns of the Prairie Houses express these aims? If they do, then the author has performed a workmanlike job in "reading" and translating to pattern form.

Our inability to know for certain what was actually going through Wright's mind, of course, does nothing to diminish the skill or creativity of the master designer whose work survives and is valued more and more each year. A simple visit to these houses will no doubt serve to inspire more attempts to understand Wright in the future. The present exercise is subject to a critical view—the author's desire to reduce Wright's uniquely brilliant designs to a set of templates reflects most strongly on the author's desire to reduce the gap between the master and the apprentice, between Wright as visionary synthesizer and ourselves as routine assemblers and bricklayers. It serves our egos well to reduce genius to a flattened, universal set of rules. We continue to pursue the myth of the one universal methodology because we find it personally or professionally difficult to accept inferiority or diversity. In the end, we benefit as professional designers by confronting our ordinariness and celebrating the luminosity of exceptional designers.

Acknowledgments

The author would like to thank Richard Gabriel for his thoughtful shepherding of the original submission to KoalaPLoP 2002, James Coplien for his analysis of the author's intentions and for his encouragement, Brian Foote for his incisive commentary on the author's use of language, James Noble for his support with KoalaPLoP, and the remaining workshop members for stretching their minds across such an atypical patterns paper.

References

[Alexander1979] C. Alexander. *The Timeless Way of Building*. Oxford, UK: Oxford University Press, 1979.

[Appleton1975] J. Appleton. *The Experience of Landscape*. London, UK: John Wiley & Sons, 1975.

[Hildebrand1991] G. Hildebrand. *The Wright Space—Pattern and Meaning in Frank Lloyd Wright's Houses*. Seattle: University of Washington Press, 1991.

[Maddex2000] D. Maddex. *50 Favourite Houses by Frank Lloyd Wright*. London, UK: Thames and Hudson, 2000.

[Twombly1979]. R. Twombly. *Frank Lloyd Wright: His Life and Architecture*. New York: John Wiley & Sons, 1979.

About the Authors

Rossana Maria de Castro Andrade received her bachelor's degree in computer science from the State University of Ceará in 1989 and her master's degree from Federal University of Paraíba (now Federal University of Campina Grande) in 1992. She received her Ph.D. from the School of Information Technology and Engineering (SITE) of the University of Ottawa, Ottawa, Canada, in 2001. Her thesis on capture, reuse, and validation of patterns for mobile systems was written under the supervision of Luigi Logrippo. She is now an adjunct professor at Federal University of Ceará, Brazil, in the Computer Science Department. Andrade does research in the areas of computer networks and software engineering. Specifically, she is looking at the application of formal and semiformal techniques to specify mobile systems, capture, reuse, and validation of software patterns, and alternative solutions to increase security in wireless mobile systems.

Paul Calder is an associate professor in the School of Informatics and Engineering at Flinders University. His research interests include object-oriented software design, component-based software reuse, graphical interfaces, and data visualization. He is a member of the IEEE Computer Society, ACM SIGCHI, and ACM SIGPLAN. He earned his Ph.D. in electrical engineering from Stanford University, where he was one of the developers of the InterViews user interface toolkit. Contact him at the School of Informatics and Engineering, Flinders University, GPO Box 2100, Adelaide, SA 5001, Australia; Paul.Calder@flinders.edu.au; *www.infoeng.flinders.edu.au/people/pages/calder_paul*.

Raphael Y. de Camargo is a doctoral candidate in the Department of Computer Science at the University of São Paulo. He received a bachelor's degree in molecular sciences and a master's degree in physics from the University of São Paulo, where he did research in the area of computational neuroscience. His current research interests include grid computing, fault-tolerance, and distributed object systems. He has published in conferences including the 11th Conference on Pattern Languages of Programs (PLoP2004) and the ACM/IFIP/USENIX International Workshop on Middleware for Grid Computing.

Márcio Carneiro works as an expert in informatics at the Brazilian Federal Police. He received a bachelor's degree in computer science from the University of São Paulo and published in the 11th Conference on Pattern Languages of Programs (PLoP2004).

Pascal Costanza is a research assistant at the Vrije Universiteit Brussel, Belgium, where he currently explores possibilities for making object-oriented programs better adaptable to the dynamic context of their use. He has served as a program committee member and shepherd for numerous conferences, including EuroPLoP, Viking PLoP, International Lisp Conference, NetObjectDays, and the Object-Oriented Programming Languages and Systems track at the ACM Symposium on Applied Computing.

Pasi Eronen is a research scientist at Nokia Research Center in Helsinki, Finland. His research interests include network security and cryptographic protocols.

Andrei Goldchleger is a systems developer and architect currently working at The Brazilian Mercantile & Futures Exchange (BM&F). In 2001, he received a bachelor's degree in computer science from the University of São Paulo, with honors, and received a master's degree in 2004. He has published in conferences and journals including The Brazilian Symposium on Computer Networks (SBRC), the ACM/IFIP/USENIX International Workshop on Middleware for Grid Computing, and *Concurrency and Computation: Practice and Experience*. His research interests include grid computing, object-oriented programming, and middleware for distributed systems.

Manfred Gruber received his doctor's degree in physics at the Vienna University of Technology in 1989. He has thirteen years of experience in software engineering and IT project management through his participation as developer and project manager in large international IT projects carried out by Alcatel, Phillips, and Frequentis/Eurocontrol. At Alcatel he designed and implemented dependable systems in the railway and telecommunications area. Since 2003, he has worked with ARCS, where he now coordinates the integrated project DECOS within the EU Frame Programme 6, which addresses the development of integrated architecture and high-level services for dependable real-time systems, based on the time-triggered model.

Arno Haase is an independent software architect based in Bonn, Germany. He specializes in model-driven development and agile methods. He has worked on large, distributed business systems in various sectors, including telecommunications, public administration, banking, and the chemical industry. He is the author of numerous patterns and magazine articles and is a regular speaker at international software conferences.

Robert S. Hanmer is a consulting member of the technical staff at Lucent Technologies. He has consulted on architecture, performance, reliability, and patterns and now consults on third-party and open source software technologies. Hanmer is a past program chair or co-chair for a number of Pattern Languages of Programming conferences, including PLoP and SugarLoaf PLoP. He is active in TelePLoP, an informal collection of pattern advocates and authors interested in the patterns of telecommunications. He is also active in the Hillside Group. He has published patterns and articles on patterns in earlier PLoPD volumes, some of which have been re-published. In 2002 he participated in a three-person art exhibition presenting the aesthetics of software to a non-technical audience. He received bachelor's and master's degrees in computer science from Northwestern University.

Neil B. Harrison is an assistant professor of computer science at Utah Valley State College in Orem, Utah. Until recently, he was a distinguished member of technical staff at Avaya Labs, where he developed communications software. He has been involved in software development and research for more than twenty years, both as a developer and team leader. He has studied software development organizations for more than ten years, and is a coauthor of *Organizational Patterns of Agile Software Development*. He is acknowledged as the world's leading expert on pattern shepherding, and the PLoP shepherding award is named after him.

Wolfgang Herzner received his doctorate in computer science at the Vienna University of Technology in 1984. He has supported the establishment of the Dependable Embedded Systems (DES) group within ARCS as principal scientist since 2002. Herzner's interests include safe software engineering and related disciplines such as (design) patterns, object-orientation, UML, model-based software development, or aspect-orientation, as well as fault-tolerance and real-time aspects, not necessarily restricted to embedded systems. He is member of ACM, IEEE Computer Society, the Austrian Computer Society (OCG), and a reviewer for *IEEE Software* and *Computer*.

Ralph Johnson is one of the object-oriented community's best known and most effective evangelists. During the 1980s as an early voice in the software engineering wilderness, he was instrumental in launching a Smalltalk revival in the academic community. His early missives on object-oriented reuse and framework design are still read today. In 1994, he coauthored *Design Patterns: Elements of Reusable Object-Oriented Software*. Ralph received his Ph.D. in computer science from Cornell University in 1985. He lives in Champaign, Illinois, with his wife Faith, his children Joy, Grace, and Caleb, and their dog, Shirley. He works at the University of Illinois at Urbana-Champaign.

Allan Kelly has more than ten years professional programming experience with a wide range of organizations. He is an active member of the Hillside Europe patterns community and a regular contributor to ACCU magazines and conferences. He holds a B.Sc from the University of Leicester and an M.B.A. from Nottingham University Business School.

Fabio Kon is an associate professor in the Department of Computer Science at the University of São Paulo. In 2000, Fabio received a Ph.D. in computer science from the University of Illinois at Urbana-Champaign. His research interests include distributed object systems, reflective middleware, dynamic (re)configuration and adaptation, mobile agents, computer music, multimedia, grid computing, and agile methods. He is a member of ACM and the Hillside Group, and he has been in the program committee of international conferences and workshops such as Middleware, DOA, OOPSLA, RM, and MGC.

Teemu Koponen received a master's degree in computer science from Helsinki University of Technology, Finland, where he is currently working toward a Ph.D. He also works as a consultant for software technology and engineering in the telecommunications industry. His principal research interests focus on software architecture, wide-area networking, network security, and mobility.

Wilfried Kubinger received his Diplom-Ingenieur in 1995 and a doctorate in 1999, both in electrical engineering, from Vienna University of Technology, Austria. He worked at the Institute for Flexible Automation from 1996 to 2000 and at Siemens Austria from 2000 to 2003. Since 2003, he has been with the Dependable Embedded Systems Group at Seibersdorf research. His current research interests include embedded real-time systems, computer vision, and embedded vision applications in general.

John Liebenau is a software architect and project manager with more than ten years of experience in the financial trading domain. His work has focused on object-oriented frameworks, design patterns, evolutionary architecture, adaptive systems, and agile methodologies in the development of equity trading and reporting systems. John has a bachelor's degree in computer science from California State University, Long Beach, and a master's degree in computer science from Loyola Marymount University.

Luigi Logrippo received a "laurea" in law from the University of Rome in 1961, and in the same year he wrote his first computer program. Until 1967 he worked with Olivetti, Olivetti-Bull, General Electric, and Siemens as a programmer and systems analyst. From 1967 to 1969 he was a research associate at the Institute for Computer Studies, University of Manitoba, where he obtained a master's degree in computer science in 1969. He then obtained a Ph.D. in computer science at the University of Waterloo in 1974. From 1973 to 2002 he was with the University of Ottawa, first in the Department of Computer Science and then in the School of Information Technology and Engineering (SITE). He was chair of the Computer Science Department from 1991 to 1997 and administrative director of SITE from 1997–1998. Since 2002, he has been a professor at Université du Québec en Outaouais, Département d'informatique et ingénierie. He is a member of the ACM and of IFIP WG 6.1. He participates in ITU-T WG 11 and 17.

Dragos Manolescu, lead editor for this volume, is a software architect with ThoughtWorks, Inc., where he works on architecture evaluation and enterprise integration projects. Dragos has been involved with the patterns community since 1996. He chaired the PLoP 1999 conference, contributed to the PLoPD4 volume, and coauthored *Integration Patterns* (Microsoft Press, 2004). He frequently speaks at conferences and to corporate audiences. He can be reached via micro-workflow.com.

Klaus Marquardt works in object-oriented projects in different roles, including engineer, team leader, architect, coach, and consultant. He is currently a technical manager and system architect for Dräger Medical in Lübeck, Germany. His experiences cover information systems and life-supporting systems, distributed development, introduction of new ideas, processes, and technology into organizations, and a broad range of technologies from distributed systems to hard real-time control. His main interests are people: linking different worlds and views, patterns, and processes with their interdependencies to people and technology. He has contributed to conferences, including OOPSLA, JAOO, OOP, EuroPLoP, VikingPLoP, ACCU, and OT/SPA. In 2004, he was program chair of EuroPLoP. His Web site is *www.kmarquardt.de*.

James Noble, co-editor of this volume, is professor of computer science and software engineering at Victoria University of Wellington, New Zealand. His research centers around software design. This includes the design of the user interface (the parts of software that users have to deal with every day) and the programmer interface (the internal structures and organizations of software that programmers see only when they are designing, building, or modifying software). His research in both of these areas is colored by his long-standing interest in object-oriented approaches to design.

Carlos O'Ryan received his Ph.D. in information and computer science from the University of California, Irvine in 2002, where his research focused on patterns and optimizations for real-time publish/subscribe middleware. He is currently the chief technology officer for Automated Trading Desk in Charleston, North Carolina.

Juha Pärssinen works as a senior research scientist at VTT Technical Research Centre of Finland. He received his M.Sc in 1998 and Lic.Sc. in 2003 from Helsinki University of Technology, Department of Computer Science and Engineering. His current research interests include patterns, object oriented- and conceptual modeling, and network protocol modeling, design, and implementation aspects. He was the chair of VikingPLoP2005.

Irfan Pyarali received his Ph.D. in computer science from Washington University in 2001, where his research focused on optimization techniques for distributed real-time and embedded systems and middleware. He is currently developing financial trading systems on Wall Street.

Dirk Riehle is a software entrepreneur and researcher. He is currently the chief scientist and a co-founder of Bayave Software, a Berlin, Germany-based software company that provides on-demand business solutions to small businesses. Dirk has worked in Germany, in Switzerland, and in Boston and the Silicon Valley in the United States. He was the leader of the team that designed and implemented the first UML virtual machine, and he still runs the JValue open source project. Dirk holds a Ph.D. in computer science from ETH Zürich and an M.B.A. from Stanford University. His Web site is *http://www.riehle.org*, and he welcomes feedback at dirk@riehle.org.

Andreas Rüping is an independent software architect in Hamburg, Germany. Before going independent, he worked at Forschungszentrum Informatik (FZI) for six years and sd&m software design & management AG for seven years. He has worked on framework development and reuse throughout several research and development projects. His current focus is on the architecture and design of Web-based systems and content management. Andreas is also interested in all aspects of knowledge management and documentation and is the author of *Agile Documentation—A Pattern Guide to Producing Lightweight Documents for Software Projects* (John Wiley & Sons, 2003). He graduated from the University of Dortmund and holds a Ph.D. in computer science from the University of Karlsruhe. Andreas is a long-term member of the pattern community, was program chair for EuroPLoP 2001, and is currently president of Hillside Europe e.V. He can be reached at *www.rueping.info.*

Douglas C. Schmidt is a full professor in the Electrical Engineering and Computer Science Department, the associate chair of Computer Science and Engineering, and a senior researcher at the Institute for Software Integrated Systems (ISIS) at Vanderbilt University. For over a decade, his research has focused on patterns, optimization techniques, and empirical analyses of object-oriented and component-based frameworks as well as model-driven development tools that facilitate the development of distributed real-time and embedded (DRE) middleware and applications on parallel platforms running over high-speed networks and embedded system interconnects.

Dietmar Schütz is Principal Software Architect for Siemens AG in the Corporate Technology Department for Software Architecture. He has published several patterns in software design and engineering. He is especially active and recognized in the European pattern community, acting as shepherd, PC member, and as conference chair for the EuroPLoP conferences in 2003 and 2004.

Michel Tilman graduated *summa cum laude* in mathematics at the Brussels Free University in 1981. In 1985 he joined the new Programming Technology Lab, where he participated in research on reflective object-oriented programming languages for concurrent systems. In 1989 he joined SoftCore as Research Manager where he investigated the design of object-oriented application-server frameworks for workflow applications. From 1994 to 2002 he worked at Unisys, where he designed the Argo framework, which features an adaptive model-driven application development approach for database, document management, workflow, and Web applications. For the next eighteen months he designed software for the public and commercial broadcasting industry at MediaGeniX. In 2002 he joined Real Software where he designed a scalable, highly configurable rule engine based on an adaptive model-driven architecture for Belgian Social Security. His interests include reflective architectures for real-life frameworks, aspect-oriented programming, adaptive model-driven architectures, and "smart" development tools.

Paul R. Taylor is a business and systems consultant, project and solution architect, software designer, and part-time writer with twenty years of experience in a wide range of industry and business contexts. His software engineering and consulting career has taken him from message-oriented real-time systems, via object-oriented systems, to agent-oriented systems. His ongoing interest in the philosophical and pragmatic issues that arise when people design systems and software transcends these specific technologies.

Markus Voelter, co-editor of this volume, works as an independent consultant and coach for software technology and engineering. He focuses on software architecture, middleware, and model-driven software development. Markus is the coauthor of several books on middleware patterns and model-driven software development and is a regular speaker at conferences worldwide. Markus can be reached via *www.voelter.de.*

Oliver Vogel is an IT architect with IBM Business Consulting Services. He has worked on various international projects where he was responsible for the design and realization of complex software architectures. Currently he is responsible for introducing and controlling a model-driven software development process on a very large project. He is also a lecturer at the University of Applied Sciences Furtwangen and the author of articles and of a book about software architecture. His IT interests include software architecture, software design, and patterns, as well as model-driven software development.

Tiffany Winn is a Ph.D. student in computer science at Flinders University, where she received her BSc (Hons.) in computer science. She is a part of the Knowledge Discovery and Intelligent Systems group. Her research interests are in patterns and pattern languages, software design, and complex systems and how they evolve over time. Contact her at the School of Informatics and Engineering, Flinders University, GPO Box 2100, Adelaide, SA 5001, Australia; Tiffany.Winn@flinders.edu.au; *www.infoeng.flinders.edu.au/people/pages/winn_tiffany.*

Uwe Zdun is currently an assistant professor in the Department of Information Systems at the Vienna University of Economics and Business Administration. He received his doctoral degree from the University of Essen in 2002. His research interests include software patterns, software architecture, scripting, object-orientation, AOP, and Web engineering. Uwe has published in many journals, and is coauthor of the book *Remoting Patterns—Foundations of Enterprise, Internet, and Realtime Distributed Object Middleware* (John Wiley & Sons). Uwe is (co)author of open-source software systems, such as Extended Object Tcl (XOTcl), ActiWeb, Leela, Frag, and many others, and acts as a reviewer for journals and conferences. He has co-organized workshops at conferences such as EuroPLoP, CHI, and OOPSLA and served as conference chair for EuroPLoP 2005.

Index

a-periodic messages, 98
a-periodic tasks, 121
Aalto, Alvar, 536
Abnormal network conditions, 167
ABSOLUTE OBJECT REFERENCE pattern, 393
AC (Authentication Center), 226
Access agents, 340, 343–345
Account class, 4–6, 17–19
AccountType class, 4–6, 17, 19–20
Acrobat plug-ins, 304
Action class, 55
Activation time of plug-ins, 323
Active Directory, 200
Active Object Model. *See* DYNAMIC OBJECT MODEL pattern
Active Registration, 320
Actiweb system, 291–292
ADAPTERS pattern
    COMPONENT WRAPPER, 370
    VOID, 502
ADAPTIVE OBJECT MODEL pattern, 375
Adjectives, 444
ADP templates, 278
Advanced pattern writing
    acknowledgments, 451
    CONSISTENT "WHO", 446–448

DEAD WEASELS, 443–444
existing work, 434–436
FORCES HINT AT SOLUTION, 444–446
"HOW"-PROCESS, 438–440
introduction, 433–434
POINTERS TO DETAIL, 448–451
references, 451–452
"WHY"-PROBLEMS, 440–443
Adverbs, 444
Agent module, 350
AGGREGATION pattern, 461, 494–497
    DYNAMIC OBJECT MODEL, 12–13
    RESOLUTION OF FORCES, 483
Aha effect, 519–521
Air interface, 217
Airplane Information Management System (AIMS), 122
Alarm class, 318
Alexander, Christopher
    biological analogy by, 464
    on city structure, 488
    on complex systems, 455–456, 489
    on context, 498
    on designed systems, 454–455
    on differentiation, 473, 492
    on emptiness, 500
    on entrances, 481

Alexander, Christopher, *continued*
  on evolution, 501
  on forces, 461–462, 468–469, 472,
      480–483, 488, 498
  on fundamental process, 463
  on HALF-HIDDEN GARDEN, 484
  and LDPL, 453, 458
  motivation of, 552
  on paths, 499
  on pattern growth, 495–496
  *Pattern Language, A—Towns, Build-
      ings, Construction*, 259
  on pattern sequences, 464–465
  on scale, 485–486
Alexandrian pattern form, 437–438
  Prairie Houses, 534–537
  Web content conversion and gener-
      ation, 259
ALIGN DIRECTORIES WITH ORGANIZA-
    TION pattern, 199–200
  CONSULT DIRECTORY, 196
  OVERLAY NETWORK, 193
  SERVER DOES HEAVY WORK, 205
Ambiguous comparands, 180
Analog mobile wireless systems, 227
Analysis Patterns (Fowler), 22
Analyzers, 309
Anchor entities
  in mobile wireless systems, 220,
      242–244
  summary, 255
"And They Lived Happily Ever After"
    syndrome, 523
Andrade, Rossana Maria de Castro
  biographical information, 555
  MoRaR, 213
Anti-patterns, 520
  Blob, 53, 58–59
  Poltergeist, 47
AOL Server, 293

Apache Axis framework, 381, 396–397
Appleton, Jay
  on prospect and refuge, 533
  on symmetries, 484–485
Application/Communication Buffer
    pattern. *See* TEMPORAL APPLICA-
    TION DECOUPLING pattern
Application servers, 32
Application Submission and Control
    Tool (ASCT) module, 351
Application tasks, 116–117
Applications
  configurable. *See* Plug-ins
  deployment of, 351–352
  development of, 102
Apptimizer system, 60
Architectural concepts for MoRaR,
    215–218
Architectural pattern languages,
    299–300, 458
  CLUSTER OF FORCES, 469
  COMMON GROUND, 498
  CROSS LINKAGES, 489
  HALF-SYNC/HALF-ASYNC, 120
  LEVELS OF SCALE, 486–487
  RESOLUTION OF FORCES, 481–482
  VOID, 501
Arguments Object pattern, 62
ARINC 659 standard
  BIUs in, 115
  in hard real-time systems, 122
  in SYNC FRAME, 111
  in TEMPORAL APPLICATION DECOU-
      PLING, 119
Artix framework, 381
ASCT (Application Submission and
    Control Tool) module, 351
ASK LOCAL NETWORK pattern, 191–192
  CONSULT DIRECTORY, 196
  LISTEN TO ADVERTISEMENTS, 194

PLACE DIRECTORIES DYNAMICALLY, 201

SEPARATE IDENTITY FROM LOCATION, 202

SERVICES REGISTER IN DIRECTORY, 197
in SLP, 206

USE ADVERTISER, 195

ASP pages, 293

Aspect configuration, 390–393

Aspect ratio in Prairie Houses, 538

Asynchronous-Change Commands pattern, 84–85

Attribute reuse, 178

Audiences, 447

Authentication
in mobile wireless systems, 215, 220, 225–227, 229–232
summary, 254

Authentication Centers (ACs), 215, 226

Authenticator pattern, 232

Author as Owner pattern, 508, 517–518

AUTOMATIC CONTROLS pattern
in Equitable Resource Allocation, 146
in Real Time and Resource Overload language, 132, 148

Automatic Invocation application, 323

AUTOMATIC OUT-OF-CHAIN ROUTING pattern
in Equitable Resource Allocation, 147
in Real Time and Resource Overload language, 132, 148

AUTOMATIC TYPE CONVERTER pattern, 359–360, 377–381
COMMAND LANGUAGE, 365
COMPONENT WRAPPER, 370
CONTENT CONVERTER, 273
SPLIT OBJECT, 383, 386, 390, 397

Automation, DYNAMIC OBJECT MODEL for, 10

Availability in distributed systems, 157

Available bandwidth for a-periodic transmissions, 98

Axis framework, 381, 396–397

BACKEND pattern, 30, 35

BALANCED CONTEXT pattern, 509, 523–525

BANDS OF WINDOWS pattern, 539, 545–547

Bandwidth utilization
in hard real-time systems, 96
in PRESCHEDULED PERIODIC TRANS-MISSION, 98, 101
in SYNC FRAME, 110

Banking systems. *See* DYNAMIC OBJECT MODEL pattern

Bar-Yam, Y., 483

Base station controllers (BSCs), 216–218

Base station transceivers (BSTs), 217–218

Base stations, 217

Bathing Room pattern, 500

BEA WebLogic Integration, 291

BEAUTY OF SIMPLICITY pattern, 407–411, 413, 418

Behavioral patterns in MoRaR, 218–221

BIG PICTURE pattern, 436, 438, 508–509, 515–516

Biological systems
AGGREGATION, 497
CROSS LINKAGES, 491
DIFFERENTIATION, 493–494
in LDPL, 458, 464, 467
LOCAL SYMMETRIES, 477–478
VOID, 502

Bit masks, 141–142
BIUs (Bus Interface Units), 115, 119
Blob antipattern, 53, 58–59
Bottlenecks, 58
Boundary conditions, 177
Brake control systems. *See* Hard real-time systems
Brand, Stewart, 463
BROKER pattern, 345, 353
Browsers
  FRAMEWORK PROVIDING APPLICATION, 318
  PLUG-IN, 309
BSCs (base station controllers), 216–218
BSP API, 348
BSTs (base station transceivers), 217–218
BUILD TRUST pattern, 423
Bus cycles, 102
BUS GUARDIAN pattern
  consequences, 114
  context, 111
  examples, 112, 114
  in hard real-time systems, 92, 97
  implementation, 113–114
  known uses, 115
  problem, 111
  related patterns, 115
  solution, 112
  in SYNC FRAME, 109
Bus Interface Units (BIUs), 115, 119
Business logic, 25–26, 32
Business rules engine, 21
Buy class, 47
Byzantine situations, 109, 111

C language
  AUTOMATIC TYPE CONVERTER, 381
  dispatching in, 79
  OBJECT SYSTEM LAYER, 376

C++ language
  dispatching in, 79
  encapsulation in, 50, 60–61
  OBJECT SYSTEM LAYER, 374
  and OTcl, 389–390
  sameness in, 177, 183
  wrappers in, 371–373
C++ Idioms Language, 459
  AGGREGATION, 496
  COMMON GROUND, 499
  CROSS LINKAGES, 489–490
  DIFFERENTIATION, 493
  LOCAL SYMMETRIES, 474
  operator overloading in, 465
Calder, Paul
  biographical information, 555
  LDPL, 453
Camargo, Raphael Y. de
  biographical information, 555–556
  GRID, 337
CANTILEVERED TERRACE pattern, 543–545
  BANDS OF WINDOWS, 546
  FIREPLACE AS REFUGE, 547
  for horizontal spread, 539
Car brake control systems. *See* Hard real-time systems
Carneiro, Marcio
  biographical information, 556
  GRID, 337
CAVE (Cellular Authentication and Voice Encryption), 232
Cells in mobile wireless systems, 215
Central Bus Guardian, 113–114
CHAIN OF RESPONSIBILITY pattern
  CONTENT CONVERTER, 271–272
  DYNAMIC OBJECT MODEL, 13
  ENCAPSULATED CONTEXT, 61
Change requests in framework development, 423–425

Channel-specific formats, 264
CheckingAccount class, 17
Checkpointing, 349
CHECKS pattern language, 459, 466–467
    CLUSTER OF FORCES, 470
    CROSS LINKAGES, 490–491
    LEVELS OF SCALE, 487
    RESOLUTION OF FORCES, 482
    VOID, 501
CHI (controller host interfaces), 119
CHIMNEY AS ANCHOR pattern, 539, 541–543
    CANTILEVERED TERRACE, 545
    FIREPLACE AS REFUGE, 547
Ciphering
    in mobile wireless systems, 215, 220, 223, 226–229
    summary, 253
CIRCUITOUS APPROACH pattern, 539, 541, 550–551
City is Not a Tree, A (Alexander), 488
Classes, comparable, 176–177
CLEAR TARGET AUDIENCE pattern, 435, 447, 525
CLEAVAGE pattern, 477–478
Client class, 9
CLIENT-DISPATCHER-SERVER pattern, 203
CLIENT KNOWS BEST pattern, 203–204
Clients
    DECENTRALIZED LOCKING, 157–158
    in Service Discovery, 189
Cliques in SYNC FRAME, 109
Clock synchronization, 103–105
Clone comparisons, 175–176
CLUSTER OF FORCES pattern, 460, 467–471
CNI (communication network interface), 119
Cocoon framework, 426
CODE SAMPLES pattern, 436, 449

CODE SAMPLES AS BONUS pattern, 436, 449
Collaborations, 7–8, 30–31
Collection Framework, 177
Collections
    COMPARAND, 183–184
    GRID, 350
Collisions on Ethernet, 94–95
COM (Component Object Model), 182
COMMAND pattern, 359–360
    ENCAPSULATED CONTEXT, 47, 61
    substitutions in, 363
COMMAND LANGUAGE pattern, 358–360
    AUTOMATIC TYPE CONVERTER, 377, 379–380
    COMPONENT WRAPPER, 370
    consequences, 366–367
    context, 361
    discussion, 363–366
    forces, 362
    known uses, 367
    OBJECT SYSTEM LAYER, 374
    problem, 361–362
    scenarios, 362, 366
    solution, 363
    SPLIT OBJECT, 382, 384–385, 387–389, 391, 393–394
COMMANDS pattern, 358–360
    COMMAND LANGUAGE, 365
    COMPONENT WRAPPER, 370
Comments in shepherding, 514
COMMON AREA AT THE HEART pattern, 499
COMMON GROUND pattern, 497–500
    in LDPL, 461
    LEVELS OF SCALE, 487
    RESOLUTION OF FORCES, 483
Communication
    in DISASTER NOTIFICATION, 135
    in GRID, 343, 348

Communication handlers, 116–117
Communication network interface (CNI), 119
COMMUNITY OF TRUST pattern, 513
COMPARAND pattern
acknowledgments, 187
conclusion, 186–187
consequences, 183–184
context, 170
example, 169–170
implementation, 174–183
known uses, 184–186
overview, 169
problem, 171–173
references, 187–188
related patterns, 186
solution, 173–174
ComparandFactory class, 176
Comparisons
operations, 178–179
semantics, 174
Complex systems, pattern languages as, 455–456
Complexity
in BUS GUARDIAN, 114
COMPARAND, 183
DYNAMIC OBJECT MODEL, 6–7
in framework development, 408, 416
GRID, 352
in SYNC FRAME, 110
Component and language integration, 357
acknowledgments, 398
AUTOMATIC TYPE CONVERTER, 377–381
COMMAND LANGUAGE, 361–367
COMPONENT WRAPPER, 368–372
conclusion, 397
introduction, 358–360

OBJECT SYSTEM LAYER, 372–376
patterns, 360–361
references, 398–400
SPLIT OBJECT. See SPLIT OBJECT pattern
Component class, 7, 9
Component Object Model (COM), 182
COMPONENT WRAPPER pattern, 368–372
implementation, 359
OBJECT SYSTEM LAYER, 373
SPLIT OBJECT, 394, 397
COMPONENT WRAPPERS pattern
AUTOMATIC TYPE CONVERTER, 359
OBJECT SYSTEM LAYER, 374
SPLIT OBJECT, 382, 386, 388
Components
in hard real-time systems, 120
vs. plug-ins, 302–303
ComponentType class, 7, 9, 14
Composability, 101
COMPOSITE pattern
DYNAMIC OBJECT MODEL, 22
FRAGMENTS, 281, 284
GENERIC CONTENT FORMAT, 265, 267
Compound comparands, 180–182
CompoundContent class, 266
Computations, grid, 338–339
Computed comparands, 182
CONCEALED VERTICALS pattern, 549–550
CONCRETE EVIDENCE FOR REUSE pattern, 404–407, 425
CONCRETEFINDER pattern, 30
CONCRETEMANAGER pattern, 30, 34
Concurrency in reference counting, 79
Condor Grids, 350
Configurable software. See Plug-ins
"Connecting Business Object to Relational Databases" (Yoder), 40

Connection interface, 30
CONSISTENT "WHO" pattern, 434,
    446–448
Constraints
    DYNAMIC OBJECT MODEL, 13
    GRID, 346
    in PRESCHEDULED PERIODIC TRANS-
        MISSION, 97
    in TEMPORAL APPLICATION DECOU-
        PLING, 119
CONSULT DIRECTORY pattern,
    195–196
    CONSULT DIRECTORY, 196
    LISTEN TO ADVERTISEMENTS, 194
    SEPARATE IDENTITY FROM LOCATION,
        202
    in SLP, 206
    USE ADVERTISER, 195
Consumer/user behavior in OVER-
    LOAD EMPIRES, 134
CONTENT CACHE pattern, 257, 264
    CONTENT CONVERTER, 272
    FRAGMENTS, 283
    overview, 262
    PUBLISHER AND GATHERER, 268
    Web content conversion and gener-
        ation, 284–287
CONTENT CONVERTER pattern, 257
    AUTOMATIC TYPE CONVERTER, 380
    CONTENT CREATOR, 275
    GENERIC CONTENT FORMAT, 266
    overview, 261
    Web content conversion and gener-
        ation, 270–274, 289
CONTENT CREATOR pattern, 257, 260
    CONTENT CONVERTER, 273
    CONTENT FORMAT TEMPLATE, 279
    overview, 261
    Web content conversion and gener-
        ation, 274–277, 290

CONTENT FORMAT TEMPLATE pattern,
    257, 260
    overview, 262
    Web content conversion and gener-
        ation, 277–279
Context, encapsulated. *See* ENCAPSU-
    LATED CONTEXT pattern
Context Beans, 61
Context class, 51–59
Controller host interfaces (CHI), 119
Conversions
    AUTOMATIC TYPE CONVERTER. *See*
        AUTOMATIC TYPE CONVERTER
        pattern
    content. *See* CONTENT CONVERTER
        pattern
    Web. *See* Web content conversion
        and generation
CONVINCING SOLUTION pattern, 509,
    519–521
COOPERATING PLUG-INS pattern, 306,
    310, 327–330
Coordinated comparands, 182–183
Copies
    COMPARAND, 172
    ENCAPSULATED CONTEXT, 50–51, 57,
        61
Coplien, Jim
    C++ Idioms Language, 459, 465
    ENGAGE CUSTOMERS, 415
    "Pattern Language for Writers'
        Workshops", 508
    on pattern languages, 455
    SIZE THE ORGANIZATION, 413
    on symmetry breaking, 457
    THREE ITERATIONS, 512
COPY-ON-DEMAND pattern, 82–84
COPY-THEN-DISPATCH pattern, 81–82
CORBA Object Adapter component,
    71–73

CORBA Object Factories component, 39
CORBA Relationship Service, 185
CorbaSEC security, 348
CosObjectIdentity module, 185
Costanza, Pascal
  biographical information, 556
  COMPARAND, 169
Costs in BUS GUARDIAN, 114
COUNTED BODY pattern, 466
  AGGREGATION, 496–497
  COMMON GROUND, 499
  DIFFERENTIATION, 493
  LOCAL SYMMETRIES, 475–476
Counting references in dispatch, 78–80
Coupling encapsulated context, 50, 57
COURTYARDS WHICH LIVE pattern, 489
CPU utilization, 119, 133
Credibility, 520
Credit Control Platform, 292
CROSS LINKAGES pattern, 460, 487–491
CRUD pattern, 40
Cunningham, W., 482
Czarnecki, K., 473

D-AMPS (Digital Advanced Mobile Phone System), 213
DA (Directory Agent), 196
Dasgupta, S., 456
Data access layer framework
  background, 402–403
  evidence for reuse, 406
  framework user involvement, 422
  multiple change requests, 424–425
  pilot applications, 415
  pilot-based tests, 419–420
  simplicity, 409–410
  skilled teams, 412
  small objects, 417–418

Data conversion
  AUTOMATIC TYPE CONVERTER. See AU-TOMATIC TYPE CONVERTER pattern
  content. See CONTENT CONVERTER pattern
  Web. See Web content conversion and generation
Data copying, 50–51, 57, 61
Data Router system, 60
Data Update Propagation (DUP) algorithms, 282
Data Visualizers, 292
Databases
  in mobile wireless systems, 215, 220, 223, 225–226, 235–237
  in paging, 233–234
  summary, 253–254
DEAD WEASELS pattern, 434, 443–444
Debugging
  COMPARAND for, 170
  GRID for, 352
DECENTRALIZED LOCKING pattern
  acknowledgments, 167–168
  consequences, 166–167
  context, 156
  dynamics, 159–161
  example, 155–156, 164
  implementation, 161–164
  introduction, 155
  known uses, 165–166
  problem, 156–157
  references, 168
  related patterns, 167
  solution, 157
  structure, 157–158
  variants, 165
Decentralized start-up, 110
DECORATOR pattern
  COMPARAND, 171, 175
  COMPONENT WRAPPER, 370

Deferred plug-in loading, 308
DeLano, David, 515
DEPARTMENT HEARTH pattern, 498
Dependency Injection technique, 320
Dependent Demand pattern, 22
Deployment structure in DECENTRAL-
    IZED LOCKING, 157
*Design Patterns: Elements of Object-
    Oriented Software Design*, 526
Designed systems, pattern languages
    as, 454–455
Destruction in encapsulation, 50
DETACHED COUNTED BODY pattern, 466
    AGGREGATION, 496–497
    COMMON GROUND, 499
Device drivers, 309
DIFFERENTIATION pattern, 491–494
    LEVELS OF SCALE, 487
    purpose, 461
    RESOLUTION OF FORCES, 483
Digital Advanced Mobile Phone Sys-
    tem (D-AMPS), 213
Directory Agent (DA), 196
DIRECTORY FINDS SERVICES pattern,
    197–199
DISASTER NOTIFICATION pattern
    in Equitable Resource Allocation,
        147
    in Real Time and Resource Over-
        load language, 134–136
Discovering services. *See* Service
    discovery
Dispatching components, 69
    conclusion, 85–86
    introduction, 69–70
    multiple objects, 80–85
    overview, 70–73
    references, 86–88
    single objects, 74–80
    SPLIT OBJECT, 383

Distributed environments, 179–180
Distributed Locking. *See* DECENTRAL-
    IZED LOCKING pattern
Distributed object computing (DOC)
    middleware, 69–70
Distributed processing capabilities.
    See GRID pattern
Distributed resources, 352
Distributed systems, 153–154, 173
Disturbances in PRESCHEDULED
    PERIODIC TRANSMISSION, 102
DNS
    ALIGN DIRECTORIES WITH ORGANIZA-
        TION, 200
    SEPARATE IDENTITY FROM LOCATION,
        202
    SERVICES REGISTER IN DIRECTORY, 198
Doble, Jim, "Pattern Language for Pat-
    tern Writing", 434
DOC (distributed object computing)
    middleware, 69–70
DocMe system, 292
Document archiving systems
    SPLIT OBJECT, 386
    Web content conversion and gener-
        ation, 292
DOM (Document Object Model), 289,
    291
Domain names, 202
DOMAIN OBJECT MANAGER pattern, 25
    acknowledgments, 41
    applicability, 28–29
    collaborations, 30–31
    consequences, 32
    implementation, 32–35
    intent, 25
    known uses, 39
    motivation, 25–28
    participants, 29–30
    references, 42–43

DOMAIN OBJECT MANAGER pattern, *continued*
 related patterns, 40
 sample code, 35–38
 structure, 29
Domain-specific languages, 7, 367
Domain-specific patterns, 211–212
DOMAINOBJECT pattern, 30, 32–33
Dominant siblings, 59–60
DUP (Data Update Propagation) algorithms, 282
Dynamic behavior, 11–12
Dynamic consumer subscriptions, 73
Dynamic languages, wrappers for, 383
Dynamic loading of plug-ins, 323
DYNAMIC OBJECT MODEL pattern, 3
 acknowledgments, 22
 dynamic behavior, 11–12
 end-user configuration, 11
 extensions, 12–13
 flexibility, 10
 implementation, 13–15
 known uses, 20–21
 motivation, 3–6
 portability, 12
 problem, 6–7
 programming environment, 11
 references, 22–24
 related patterns, 22
 runtime typing, 12
 sample code, 15–20
 simplicity, 9–10
 solution structure, 7–9
DYNAMIC OVERLOAD CONTROL pattern
 DISASTER NOTIFICATION, 136
 in Real Time and Resource Overload language, 132, 148

ECHO BACK pattern, 487
Eckstein, Jutta, 515

Eclipse application plug-ins, 304, 309
 PLUG-IN BASED PRODUCT, 332
 PLUG-IN CONTRACT, 315
 PLUG-IN LIFE CYCLE, 324
 PLUG-IN REGISTRATION, 321
Edge Side Includes, 293
Editing databases, 21
Eisenecker, U. W., 473
Electro Mechanical Brake (EMB) systems. *See* Hard real-time systems
Elevation in Prairie Houses, 541
Embedded systems, 90
Emergency braking, 92
Emptiness, 500
ENABLING THE SYSTEM TO SHARE LOAD pattern, 133
ENCAPSULATED CONTEXT pattern
 acknowledgments, 63–64
 audience, 45
 consequences, 56–60
 examples, 45–48, 63
 forces, 49–51
 implementation, 52–54
 known uses, 60–61
 problem, 49
 references, 64–65
 related patterns, 61–63
 resolution, 54–55
 solution, 51–52
 summary, 63
 variations, 55–56
Encapsulation of heterogeneity, 351
Encryption, 223, 226–229
End-user configuration in DYNAMIC OBJECT MODEL, 11
ENGAGE CUSTOMERS pattern, 415
Enterprise Java Beans
 COMPARAND, 185
 DOMAIN OBJECT MANAGER, 39
 ENCAPSULATED CONTEXT, 61

Entities in mobile wireless systems, 220

ENTRANCE TRANSITION pattern
  CIRCUITOUS APPROACH, 551
  CONCEALED VERTICALS, 550
  forces for, 469–470, 481–482

Equation constraints, 119

Equitable manner, 132

Equitable Resource Allocation
  OVERLOAD EMPIRES, 133
  in Real Time and Resource Over-
    load language, 146–147

Eronen, Pasi
  biographical information, 556
  Service Discovery, 189

Erroneous node detection, 101

Errors
  in hard real-time systems, 120
  in Real Time and Resource Over-
    load language, 130
  SOS, 112

Ethernet-like communications, 94–95

EVALUATE PAPERS FAST pattern, 516

Event and Notification Services, 72

Event channel dispatching components, 72

Event-driven communication, 94–95

Event Driven Invocation, 323

EVERYONE DOES EVERYTHING pattern,
  497

EVERYONE SPECIALIZES pattern, 497

Evidence for reuse, 404–407, 425

EVOCATIVE PATTERN NAME pattern, 434

Evolution of systems, 6–7

Evolved systems, pattern languages
  as, 456–457

EXCEPTIONAL VALUE pattern, 470–471
  CROSS LINKAGES, 491
  RESOLUTION OF FORCES, 482–483
  VOID, 501

Expat standard, 291

Extended Plug-in Contract pattern,
  314

External comparisons, 178–179

FACADE pattern
  COMPONENT WRAPPER, 372
  FRAMEWORK PROVIDING APPLICA-
    TION, 317
  OBJECT SYSTEM LAYER, 359, 374

Fail silent systems, 120

Failures in hard real-time systems, 120

Fallback operations, 166

FAMILY OF ENTRANCES pattern,
  469–470, 481

FAMILY ROOM CIRCULATION pattern,
  498

Fault containment units (FCUs), 121

Fault hypotheses, 121

Fault-tolerance
  in Real Time and Resource Over-
    load language, 131
  in safety-critical systems, 92
  in SYNC FRAME, 110
  in TIME-TRIGGERED CLOCK SYNCHRO-
    NIZATION, 105

Fault-tolerant units (FTUs), 121

Faults in hard real-time systems, 120

FCUs (fault containment units), 121

FDSs (Fragment Definition Sets),
  281–282

Feedback from shepherds, 509

FINAL HANDLING pattern
  in Equitable Resource Allocation,
    147
  in Real Time and Resource Over-
    load language, 131–132, 148

Financial industry. *See* Web portal
  framework

FINDABLE SECTIONS pattern, 516

FINE-GRAINED OBJECTS pattern, 418FINDER pattern, 30, 33–35
FINISH WORK IN PROGRESS pattern, 129
  OVERLOAD EMPIRES, 134
  Real Time and Resource Overload language, 131, 148
  REASSESS OVERLOAD DECISION, 136
Firefox plug-ins, 304
FIREPLACE AS REFUGE pattern, 541, 543, 546–547
Fitting Form pattern, 525–526
Flexibility
  COMPARAND, 183
  DYNAMIC OBJECT MODEL, 10
  in PRESCHEDULED PERIODIC TRANS-MISSION, 102
FlexRay architecture
  in hard real-time systems, 122–123
  in PRESCHEDULED PERIODIC TRANS-MISSION, 102–103
FLYWEIGHT pattern, 467, 501
FOCUS ON LONG-TERM RELEVANCE pattern, 421–422
Foote, Brian
  LOW SURFACE-TO-VOLUME RATIO, 418
  PROTOTYPE A FIRSTPASS DESIGN, 415
  SELFISH CLASS, 410
FORCES DEFINE PROBLEM pattern, 436
  FORCES HINT AT SOLUTION pattern, 446
  FORM FOLLOWS FUNCTION, 525
  in shepherding, 508–509, 521–522
FORCES HINT AT SOLUTION pattern, 434, 444–446
FORM FOLLOWS FUNCTION pattern, 509, 525–527
FORM FOLLOWS PREDOMINANT FEATURE pattern, 537–539
  BANDS OF WINDOWS, 546
  CANTILEVERED TERRACE, 544

Forwarding functions, 56
Fowler, Martin
  Analysis Patterns, 22
  on knowledge level, 5
  TEMPLATE VIEW, 279
Frag language, 385, 390–393
Fragment Definition Sets (FDSs), 281–282
FRAGMENTS pattern, 257, 260
  CONTENT CACHE, 264, 285–287
  CONTENT CONVERTER, 272–273
  CONTENT FORMAT TEMPLATE, 277–279
  GENERIC CONTENT FORMAT, 267
  overview, 262
  PUBLISHER AND GATHERER, 268
  Web content conversion and generation, 279–284, 287, 290–291
Framegrabbers, 89
Framework development
  acknowledgments, 427
  conclusions, 425–426
  evidence for reuse, 404–407
  framework user involvement, 420–423
  introduction, 401–402
  multiple change requests, 423–425
  pilot applications, 413–416
  pilot-based tests, 418–420
  references, 427–429
  roadmap, 403–404
  simplicity, 407–411
  skilled teams, 411–413
  small objects, 416–418
Framework Interface, 311
FRAMEWORK PROVIDING APPLICATION pattern, 305, 310, 315–319
  COOPERATING PLUG-INS, 330
  PLUG-IN BASED PRODUCT, 333
  PLUG-IN CONTRACT, 313
  PLUG-IN REGISTRATION, 321

FRAMEWORK USER INVOLVEMENT pattern, 415, 420–423
FRESH WORK BEFORE STALE pattern
  in Equitable Resource Allocation, 146
  OVERLOAD EMPIRES, 133, 134
  in Queue for Resources, 143–144
  in Real Time and Resource Overload language, 131, 149
Front distance credibility, 99
FRUIT TREES pattern, 484, 487
FTUs (fault-tolerant units), 121
Functional Form pattern, 525–526
Functors, 55
Fundamental process, 463
Fundamental units, 470

Garbage collection, 79
GARDEN GROWING WILD pattern, 484, 487, 489
GARDEN SEAT pattern, 486, 487
Gaston, K. J., 491
GASTRULATION pattern, 477–478
Gatherer class, 288–289
General Packet Radio Services (GPRS), 213
GENERIC CONTENT FORMAT pattern, 257, 260
  FRAGMENTS, 281, 284
  overview, 261
  PUBLISHER AND GATHERER, 267–268
  Web content conversion and generation, 264–267, 287, 289
Generic representation of Web content, 265
Generic Security Services (GSS), 348
Ginko client, 186
Global Resource Manager (GRM), 351
Global System for Mobile communications 900 (GSM-900), 213
Global variables in encapsulation, 50

GLOBUS grids, 350
Globus Resource Allocation Manager (GRAM), 350
GoF book, 526
GOF pattern form, 437
Goldchleger, Andrei
  biographical information, 556
  GRID, 337
Golubitsky, M., 453
"Good For What Ails You" syndrome, 523
GPRS (General Packet Radio Services), 213
Grabow, S., 461
GRAM (Globus Resource Allocation Manager), 350
Green, R., "Hide Forbidden Globals", 59
GREENHOUSE pattern, 484
Grid clusters, 341–342, 348–349
Grid Computing, 338–339
GRID pattern
  acknowledgments, 353
  consequences, 351–352
  context, 339
  dynamics, 343–344
  example, 337–339
  implementation, 343, 345–350
  intent, 337
  known uses, 350–351
  problem, 339–340
  references, 354–356
  related patterns, 353
  solution, 340
  structure, 340–342
Grid Security Infrastructure (GSI), 350
GRM (Global Resource Manager), 351
Gruber, Manfred
  biographical information, 556
  hard real-time systems, 89

GSI (Grid Security Infrastructure), 350
GSM-900 (Global System for Mobile communications 900), 213
GSS (Generic Security Services), 348
GUIDs, 182

Haase, Arno
  biographical information, 557
  COMPARAND, 169
HALF A LOAF pattern, 508, 511–512, 514–515
HALF-HIDDEN GARDEN pattern, 484, 486–487, 489
HALF-OBJECT PLUS PROTOCOL (HOPP), 459, 476–477
HALF-SYNC/HALF-ASYNC pattern, 120
HANDLE/BODY pattern, 465–466
  AGGREGATION, 496–497
  COMMON GROUND, 499
  DIFFERENTIATION, 493
  LOCAL SYMMETRIES, 474–476
Handoff procedures in mobile wireless systems, 217–221, 240–242
  anchor entities in, 242–244
  failure action for, 246–247
  intersystem, 244–246
  summary, 254–255
Hanmer, Robert S.
  biographical information, 557
  Real Time and Resource Overload language, 127
Hard real-time systems
  brake-by-wire example, 90–92
  BUS GUARDIAN, 111–115
  introduction, 89–90
  known uses, 122–123
  patterns-outline, 92–93
  PRESCHEDULED PERIODIC TRANSMISSION pattern. *See* Prescheduled Periodic Transmission pattern
  references, 124–125

SYNC FRAME, 106–111
TEMPORAL APPLICATION DECOUPLING, 115–120
terminology, 120–122
TIME-TRIGGERED CLOCK SYNCHRONIZATION, 103–106
Hardware selection for MHP product lines, 386–389
Harrison, Neil B.
  advanced pattern writing, 433
  biographical information, 557
  "Language of Shepherding", 436
  shepherding, 507
HashMap class, 4
Hashtables, 14, 20
Haugen, Robert, 22
Herzner, Wolfgang
  biographical information, 557
  hard real-time systems, 89
Hidden Globals, 59
"Hide Forbidden Globals" (Green), 59
Hierarchical directories, 200
Hildebrand, G.
  essential characteristics, 533–534
  Prairie Houses, 535–536
  The Wright Space, 532
HIP host identities, 202
HLRs (home location registers)
  databases for, 236
  in mobile wireless systems, 215
Home databases in mobile wireless systems, 220, 225–226, 235–237
  in paging, 233–234
  summary, 254
"Home in a Prairie Town, A", 531
Home interface, 39
Home location areas, 215
Home location registers (HLRs)
  databases for, 236
  in mobile wireless systems, 215

HOMOGENOUS ADDITION pattern, 465, 490
HOOK INJECTOR pattern, 384, 391
Horizontal splits, 53
Horizontal spread in Prairie Houses, 538–539
Horizontal tasks, 402–403
Host Application, 315–319
Host objects, 350
Hot spots plug-ins, 316
How Buildings Learn (Brand), 463
"HOW"-PROCESS pattern, 434, 438–440
HTML, 258
    CONTENT CREATOR, 274–277
    Web content conversion and generation, 288–290
Htmllib, 292
Hyperlinks, 450

I-frames, 111
ICMPv6 Router Advertisements, 194
IDENTIFICATION patterns, 203
Idioms languages, 459, 465
    AGGREGATION, 496
    COMMON GROUND, 499
    CROSS LINKAGES, 489–490
    DIFFERENTIATION, 493
    LOCAL SYMMETRIES, 474
    operator overloading in, 465
IDL interface, 39
IEEE 802.11 wireless LAN Beacon messages, 194
IMT-200 (International Mobile Telecommunications 2000) Systems, 214
IN THE REGION OF WHOLE VALUE pattern, 467
Indirection, 32
Information Integrity, 459
INFORMATION MARKETPLACE pattern, 422

Information secrecy, 229, 232
Inheritance, 12
Initial Resync, 111
Input processing in CONTENT CONVERTER, 271
Insertion collaborations, 30
Instance class, 9
Instances, plug-in, 307
Instantiation in encapsulation, 50, 58
Insurance, 21, 402–403, 407, 415, 419–422
InteGrade services, 351
Integration, component and language. *See* Component and language integration
Integrity Controller, 138
Intended audiences, 447
Interbase station transceiver handoff, 217
INTERFACE DESCRIPTION pattern, 360
    AUTOMATIC TYPE CONVERTER, 377, 378–381
    COMPONENT WRAPPER, 370
    SPLIT OBJECT, 393–394, 397
Internal comparisons, 178–179
International Mobile Telecommunications 2000 (IMT-200) Systems, 214
Internet browsers
    FRAMEWORK PROVIDING APPLICATION, 318
    PLUG-IN, 309
Internet Explorer plug-ins, 304
INTERPRETER pattern, 359–360
    COMMAND LANGUAGE, 363, 365–367
    DYNAMIC OBJECT MODEL, 13
    ENCAPSULATED CONTEXT, 61
    OBJECT SYSTEM LAYER, 374
    SPLIT OBJECT, 384, 390, 391, 394–396
Intersystem handoffs, 218, 220–221, 244–246, 255
Intrasystem handoffs, 218

Introduce Parameter Object pattern, 62
ITERATORS pattern, 501
IT'S A RELATIONSHIP NOT A SALE pattern, 416
JAC framework, 367
Java and Java-like languages
   comparisons in, 177
   DYNAMIC OBJECT MODEL, 7
   OBJECT SYSTEM LAYER, 374
Java Connector Architecture (JCA), 291
Java Debug Interface (JDI), 169, 184
Java Debug Wire Protocol (JDWP), 169
Java Platform Debugger Architecture
   (JPDA), 169
Java RMI (JRMI), 184
Java Virtual Machine (JVM), 169–170
Java Virtual Machine Debug Interface
   (JVMDI), 169
JCA (Java Connector Architecture),
   291
JDI (Java Debug Interface), 169, 184
JDWP (Java Debug Wire Protocol), 169
Jiffy server, 60
Jini services
   CONSULT DIRECTORY, 196
   SEPARATE IDENTITY FROM LOCATION,
      202
   SERVICES REGISTER IN DIRECTORY,
      197–198
Jitter in hard real-time systems, 121
Johnson, Ralph
   biographical information, 558
   DYNAMIC OBJECT MODEL, 3
   FINE-GRAINED OBJECTS, 418
   THREE EXAMPLES, 407
Join protocols, 197–198
Jolin, Art, 410
JPDA (Java Platform Debugger Architecture), 169
JRMI (Java RMI), 184

JVM (Java Virtual Machine), 169–170
JVMDI (Java Virtual Machine Debug
   Interface), 169

Kelly, Allan
   biographical information, 558
   ENCAPSULATED CONTEXT, 45
Kerberos security, 348
Keys
   DYNAMIC OBJECT MODEL, 14
   JavaBeans, 185
Kinds, plug-in, 307
Knowledge level, 5, 22
Kon, Fabio
   biographical information, 558
   GRID, 337
Koponen, Teemu
   biographical information, 558
   Service Discovery, 189
Kubinger, Wilfried
   biographical information, 558
   hard real-time systems, 89

Laboratory Systems Manager (LSM),
   304, 309
   COOPERATING PLUG-INS, 329
   FRAMEWORK PROVIDING APPLICA-
      TION, 318
   PLUG-IN CONTRACT, 315
   PLUG-IN LIFECYCLE, 324
   PLUG-IN PACKAGE, 327
   PLUG-IN REGISTRATION, 321
Language Designer's Pattern Language (LDPL), 453
   AGGREGATION, 494–497
   basis for, 454–457
   CLUSTER OF FORCES, 467–471
   COMMON GROUND, 497–500
   conclusion, 502–503
   CROSS LINKAGES, 487–491

DIFFERENTIATION, 491–494
  examples, 457–459
  introduction, 453
  LEVELS OF SCALE, 483–487
  LOCAL REPAIR, 461–467
  LOCAL SYMMETRIES, 471–479
  pattern language, 459–461
  references, 502–506
  RESOLUTION OF FORCES, 479–483
  VOID, 500–502
LANGUAGE EXTENSION pattern, 365
"Language of Shepherding, The: A
  Pattern Language for Shepherds
  and Sheep" (Harrison), 436
LANs (Local Area Networks), 214
LAYER pattern, 359
Layers, 448–449
LDAP directory, 200
LDPL. *See* Language Designer's Pat-
  tern Language (LDPL)
LEASING pattern
  DECENTRALIZED LOCKING, 165
  SERVICES REGISTER IN DIRECTORY, 197
Leaves, HTML, 290
Legion grids, 350
LEVELS OF SCALE pattern, 460, 483–487
  LOCAL REPAIR, 467
  LOCAL SYMMETRIES, 479
Libraries
  GRID, 348
  OBJECT SYSTEM LAYER, 376
  SPLIT OBJECT, 385, 393–394, 396
Liebenau, John
  biographical information, 558–559
  DOMAIN OBJECT MANAGER, 25
LIGHT ON TWO SIDES OF EVERY ROOM
  pattern, 546
Limburg, K. E., 486
Linux plug-ins, 304
Liskov Substitution Principle (LSP), 49

LISTEN TO ADVERTISEMENTS pattern,
  193–194
  CONSULT DIRECTORY, 196
  PLACE DIRECTORIES DYNAMICALLY, 201
  SERVICES REGISTER IN DIRECTORY, 197
  in SLP, 206
  USE ADVERTISER, 195
Little helpers, 328
Local Area Networks (LANs), 214
Local Lock Acquisition scenario,
  159–160
LOCAL-REGIONAL SPECIES RICHNESS RE-
  LATIONSHIP pattern, 491
LOCAL REPAIR pattern, 460
  AGGREGATION, 497
  context, 461
  examples, 465–467
  forces, 461–462
  problem, 461
  rationale, 463–465
  solution, 462
  VOID, 502
LOCAL REPAIR OF THE LANGUAGE pat-
  tern, 467
Local Resource Manager (LRM), 351
Local scheduling, 346
LOCAL SYMMETRIES pattern, 460
  AGGREGATION, 497
  COMMON GROUND, 500
  context, 471
  CROSS LINKAGES, 491
  DIFFERENTIATION, 494
  examples, 474–478
  forces, 472
  LEVELS OF SCALE, 487
  LOCAL REPAIR, 467
  problem, 471
  rationale, 473–474
  related patterns, 479
  solution, 473

LocalSystem class, 324

LocalSystemPlugin class, 309–310, 314–315

Locations in mobile wireless systems, 215, 220, 237–239, 254

Lock-Permit. *See* DECENTRALIZED LOCKING pattern

Lock Relay variant, 165

Lock Release scenario, 159–160

Locking Overhead force, 157

LockManager service, 158, 162–165

LockManager Proxy service, 158–161, 165

Locks
  decentralized. *See* DECENTRALIZED LOCKING pattern
  in dispatching components, 75–78

Logical design of plug-ins, 308

Logically deleted objects in reference counting, 80

LogManager class, 48

Logrippo, Luigi
  biographical information, 559
  MoRaR, 213

Long Resync frames, 111

LOOKUP pattern
  GRID, 353
  SPLIT OBJECT, 393

Lookup services, 196

LOW SURFACE-TO-VOLUME RATIO, 418

LRM (Local Resource Manager), 351

LSM. *See* Laboratory Systems Manager (LSM)

LSP (Liskov Substitution Principle), 49

MAHO (mobile station-assisted hand-offs), 241

Maintenance work, 139

MANAGER pattern, 29

MANDATORY ELEMENTS PRESENT pattern, 516

Manolescu, Dragos, 559

Maps
  framework development, 409
  patterns, 508–510
  Real Time and Resource Overload language, 129–130
  UCMs, 218

MarketContext class, 54, 56, 59–60

MarketDataStore class, 48

MarketMessageCommand class, 47–48, 54–55, 59

Marquardt, Klaus
  biographical information, 559
  plug-ins, 301

MARSHALLER pattern, 396

Mash toolkit, 389

MASK PRIORITIES TO SHED WORK pattern
  in Real Time and Resource Overload language, 141–142
  in Working Hard, Don't Fix it, 140

MASTER-SLAVE pattern, 353

MATCHING PROBLEM AND SOLUTION pattern, 436
  FORM FOLLOWS FUNCTION, 526
  problem and solution in, 442, 518–519
  in shepherding, 509

Matchmaker module, 350

MDS (Monitoring and Discovery Service), 350

MEANINGFUL METAPHOR NAME pattern, 435

MEANINGLESS BEHAVIOR pattern
  CROSS LINKAGES, 490, 491
  VOID, 501

MEDL (Message Description List), 102

Memory
  for COMPARAND, 184
  for OVERLOAD EMPIRES, 133
  in TEMPORAL APPLICATION DECOU-
    PLING, 119
MESSAGE INTERCEPTORS pattern
  COMPONENT WRAPPER, 370
  CONTENT CONVERTER, 273
  OBJECT SYSTEM LAYER, 375
  SPLIT OBJECT, 386
Message RAM, 119
MESSAGE REDIRECTOR pattern, 360
  OBJECT SYSTEM LAYER, 359, 374
  PUBLISHER AND GATHERER, 268–270
  SPLIT OBJECT, 386
Message slots, 98
Meszaros, Gerard, "Pattern Language
  for Pattern Writing, A", 434, 509
Meta-patterns, 431–432
Metadata in SPLIT OBJECT, 394
Methods for States pattern, 61
MHP (Multimedia Home Platform),
  276
  products, 386–389
  Web content conversion and gener-
    ation, 293
Middleware, 350
MIND YOUR MANNERS pattern, 441
Minimum front distance, 99
Mobile station-assisted handoffs
  (MAHO), 241
Mobile stations, 215–218
Mobile switching centers (MSCs),
  215–218
Mobility and radio resource manage-
  ment. *See* MoRaR pattern
  language
Mobility management functions,
  221–222
Module Interface, 119

Monitor locks, 75–76
Monitor Object pattern
  in dispatching components, 75
  ENCAPSULATED CONTEXT, 62
Monitoring and Discovery Service
  (MDS), 350
Montgomery, Warren, 492–493
MoRaR pattern language
  acknowledgments, 250
  anchor entities, 242–244
  architectural concepts, 215–218
  authentication, 215, 220, 225–227,
    229–232
  ciphering, 226–229
  handoff decisions, 240–242
  handoff failure actions, 246–247
  home and visitor databases,
    235–237
  intersystem handoffs, 244–246
  introduction, 213–214
  location registration, 237–239
  mobility management functions,
    221–222
  paging, 233–235
  pattern language, 218–221
  radio resource management, 239
  references, 250–253
  releasing resources, 247–248
  security database, 225–226
  summary, 253–255
  temporary identification, 222–224
Motivation, 3
MPI API, 348, 350
MSCs (mobile switching centers),
  215–218
Multimedia Home Platform (MHP),
  276
  products, 386–389
  Web content conversion and gener-
    ation, 293

MULTIPLE CHANGE REQUESTS pattern, 410, 413, 423–425
Multiple objects, dispatching to, 80–85
Multiple Plug-in Contracts pattern, 314
Multiple read permits, 167
Multithreading
    in CORBA Object Adapter, 72–73
    ENCAPSULATED CONTEXT, 58
Mutexes
    ENCAPSULATED CONTEXT, 58
    in serialized dispatching, 76

Naming patterns, 434–436
Natural systems, 456–457
Nature of Order (Alexander), 463, 485
NetBIOS networks, 201
Netscape plug-ins, 304
Network management systems, 155–156
Network Simulator (NS), 385, 389
NEURULATION pattern, 478
Noble, James
    Arguments Object, 62
    biographical information, 560
    OBJECT SYSTEM, 22
Nodes in hard real-time systems, 121
Non-existent objects in CORBA, 72
NOUN PHRASE NAME pattern, 434
NP-complete problems, 121
NP-hard problems, 121
NS (Network Simulator), 385, 389
NULL OBJECT pattern, 501–502

Object activation/deactivation use cases, 72
Object Adapter, CORBA, 71–73
Object COBOL, 373–374
Object Factories, 39
Object ids (OIDs), 32–33
Object Request Broker (ORB), 69

OBJECT SYSTEM pattern. *See* DYNAMIC OBJECT MODEL pattern
OBJECT SYSTEM LAYER pattern, 359–360
    consequences, 375–376
    context, 372–373
    discussion, 374–375
    forces, 373–374
    known uses, 376
    OBJECT SYSTEM LAYER, 374
    problem, 373
    scenario, 373, 375
    solution, 374
    SPLIT OBJECT, 384, 386, 394, 397
Objectivity database system, 165–166
OBSERVER pattern
    CONSULT DIRECTORY, 196
    in dispatching components, 73
    DYNAMIC OBJECT MODEL, 13
    ENCAPSULATED CONTEXT, 61–62
OID pattern, 186
OIDs (object ids), 32–33
OKBOX pattern, 387
Olympic Games 2000 Web Site, 293
One Plug-in per Task pattern, 327
Opdyke, William, 415
Open Mash project, 385
Operational level, 5
Opportunistic computing, 349
Oracle system, 166
ORB (Object Request Broker), 69
Order class, 26, 36–37
Order pattern, 30
Order-processing framework, 26
OrderFinder interface, 26–28, 30, 37
OrderManager interface, 26–29, 35–36
Orders class, 26
Oregon Experiment, The, 501
O'Ryan, Carlos, 69
Ostwald, J., 457
OTcl, 385, 389

OURGRID pattern, 351
OurGridPeer modules, 351
Out-of-sync transmissions, 114
OUTDOOR ROOM pattern, 484
Output processing in CONTENT CON-
    VERTER, 271
Overhead
    in dispatching components, 73
    in Prescheduled Periodic Transmis-
        sion, 102
OVERLAY NETWORK pattern, 192–193
OVERLOAD ELASTICS pattern
    OVERLOAD EMPIRES, 134
    in Real Time and Resource Over-
        load language, 131, 144–145
OVERLOAD EMPIRES pattern
    OVERLOAD ELASTICS, 144
    in Queue for Resources, 143
    in Real Time and Resource Over-
        load language, 131–134
    refinement of, 129
OVERLOAD OUT-OF-CONTROL pattern,
    132
Owner class, 8–9

Paging
    in mobile wireless systems, 215, 220,
        225, 233–235
    summary, 254
Palladio, Andrea, 535
Parallel computation, 348
Parameter Block pattern, 62–63
Parameter Database pattern, 239
Parameter lists in encapsulation, 50
Parameterizing Finders, 33
Parlsberg, Jens, 516
Parsing Web content, 291
Parssinen, Juha
    biographical information, 560
    Service Discovery, 189

Partially removed objects in reference
    counting, 80
Pattern Almanac, The (Rising), 448
*Pattern Language, A—Towns, Buildings,
    Construction* (Alexander), 259
"Pattern Language for Pattern Writ-
    ing, A" (Meszaros and Doble),
    434, 509
"Pattern Language for Writers' Work-
    shops" (Coplien), 508
Pattern Language of Feature Interac-
    tion pattern, 239
Pattern Languages of Program Design,
    526
Pattern Writing Patterns, 509
Patterns
    advanced. *See* Advanced pattern
        writing
    maps of, 508–510
PCS-1900 (Personal Communication
    System 1900), 213
Peer-to-peer file sharing networks, 193
PEOPLE KNOW BEST pattern, 204
Performance in locking, 166
Periodic tasks, 121
Peripheral equipment for OVERLOAD
    EMPIRES, 133
Perl language, 367
Permit Revoke scenario, 160–161
Permits
    in locking, 157
    multiple read, 167
PersistenceManager interface, 39
Persistent states, 28–29, 32–33
Personal Communication System 1900
    (PCS-1900), 213
Phone Call class, 476–477
Photoshop program, 304, 308–309, 324
PHP language, 293
Physical design for plug-ins, 308

Physical systems, 457

PIECEMEAL GROWTH pattern, 487

PIGGYBACK pattern, 365–366

PILOT APPLICATIONS pattern, 407, 413–416, 420, 423

PILOT-BASED TESTS pattern, 416, 418–420

Pipes, 98

PLACE DIRECTORIES DYNAMICALLY pattern, 200–201

  CONSULT DIRECTORY, 196

  OVERLAY NETWORK, 193

Platitudes, 444

PLMN (Public Land Mobile Network), 215

PLUG-IN pattern, 306–310

PLUG-IN BASED APPLICATION pattern, 323

PLUG-IN BASED PRODUCT pattern, 310, 314, 330–333

PLUG-IN CONTEXT pattern, 315–319

PLUG-IN CONTRACT pattern, 305, 310–315

Plug-in Definition interface, 311

PLUG-IN LIFECYCLE pattern, 305, 322–324

PLUG-IN PACKAGE pattern, 305, 310, 325–327

PLUG-IN REGISTRATION pattern, 305, 319–321

PLUG-IN SUBCONTRACT pattern, 314

Plug-ins, 305–310

  acknowledgments, 333

  vs. components, 302–303

  COOPERATING PLUG-INS, 327–330

  example, 303–304

  FRAMEWORK PROVIDING APPLICATION, 315–319

  known uses, 304

  PLUG-IN, 306–310

  PLUG-IN BASED PRODUCT, 330–333

  PLUG-IN CONTRACT, 310–315

  PLUG-IN LIFECYCLE, 322–324

  PLUG-IN PACKAGE, 325–327

  PLUG-IN REGISTRATION, 319–321

  references, 333–335

  roadmap, 304–306

POINTERS TO DETAIL pattern, 434, 444, 448–451

Poltergeist antipattern, 47

Pools in Equitable Resource Allocation, 147

Portability in DYNAMIC OBJECT MODEL, 12

PortalToGo architecture, 291

POSITIVE CLOSURE pattern, 513

POSITIVE FEEDBACK FIRST pattern, 513

POSITIVE OUTDOOR SPACE pattern, 500

Power consumption in Prescheduled Periodic Transmission, 102

Power Tools, 309

Prairie Houses, 531–533

  acknowledgments, 553

  Alexandrian rendition, 534–537

  assessment and conclusion, 551–553

  BANDS OF WINDOWS, 545–546

  CANTILEVERED TERRACE, 543–545

  CHIMNEY AS ANCHOR, 541–543

  CIRCUITOUS APPROACH, 550–551

  CONCEALED VERTICALS, 549–550

  FIREPLACE AS REFUGE, 546–547

  FORM FOLLOWS PREDOMINANT FEATURE, 537–539

  PROSPECT AND REFUGE, 533–534, 539–541

  PROSPECTIVE VIEWS, 547–548

  references, 553–554

PrepStmtOrderFinder interface, 30

PRESCHEDULED PERIODIC TRANSMISSION pattern, 93

  consequences, 101

  context, 93

  example, 93–94, 99–100

implementation, 97–99
known uses, 102–103
problem, 94–96
related patterns, 103
solution, 96–97
Primary keys, 185
PrimitiveContent class, 266
Printers, 206–207
PRIVATE TERRACE ON THE STREET pattern, 484
Processing pipes, 98
Processor CPU time, 133
PROFILE-BASED SERVICE BROWSING pattern, 204
Programming environment, 11
PROMOTE AND ADD pattern, 490
PROMOTION LADDER pattern, 465–466, 490
Property class, 4–7, 9
PROPERTY LIST pattern, 4–5, 8–9, 17–19, 22
PropertyType class, 5–7, 9, 14, 19–20
PROSPECT AND REFUGE pattern, 539–541
    BANDS OF WINDOWS, 546
    CANTILEVERED TERRACE, 545
    FIREPLACE AS REFUGE, 547
    PROSPECTIVE VIEWS, 547–548
PROSPECTIVE VIEWS pattern, 541, 547–548
PROTOTYPE A FIRSTPASS DESIGN pattern, 415
Prototype design patterns, 40
Proven knowledge, 520
PROXY pattern, 359
    COMPONENT WRAPPER, 369–371
    DECENTRALIZED LOCKING, 163–164
Public Land Mobile Network (PLMN), 215
Public switched telephone networks (PSTNs), 128

PUBLISHER AND GATHERER pattern, 257, 260, 264
    CONTENT CACHE, 285–287
    CONTENT CONVERTER, 272
    overview, 261
    Web content conversion and generation, 267–270, 287
PUBLISHER-SUBSCRIBER pattern, 196
PVM API, 348, 350
Pyarali, Irfan, 69
Python language
    COMMAND LANGUAGE, 367
    OBJECT SYSTEM LAYER, 376

Quality of Service standards, 130
Query mechanisms
    CLIENT KNOWS BEST, 204
    DOMAIN OBJECT MANAGER, 30, 32
Queue for Resources
    OVERLOAD EMPIRES, 133
    in Real Time and Resource Overload language, 131, 143–144

Race conditions, 119
Radio resource management, 217, 239
RAISED FLOWERS pattern, 484
Random values in authentication, 230–231
Rational Rose application, 304, 327
RdbOrderManager class, 26–28, 30, 36
RDF library
    OBJECT SYSTEM LAYER, 376
    SPLIT OBJECT, 385, 393–394, 396
Reactive computing systems, 127
Read permits in locking, 167
READABLE REFERENCES TO PATTERNS pattern, 436, 450
Readers/writer locks, dispatching with, 77–78

READING JUST BEFORE REVIEWING pattern, 516

Real Time and Resource Overload language
acknowledgments, 150–151
DISASTER NOTIFICATION, 134–136
Equitable Resource Allocation, 146–147
introduction, 127–129
language context, 130–132
language maps, 129–130
MASK PRIORITIES TO SHED WORK, 141–142
OVERLOAD ELASTICS, 144–145
OVERLOAD EMPIRES, 132–134
previously published patterns, 148–150
Queue for Resources, 143–144
REASSESS OVERLOAD DECISION, 136–138
references, 151–152
Working Hard, Don't Fix it, 138–140

Real-time systems. *See* Hard real-time systems

Reasoning in encapsulation, 57

REASSESS OVERLOAD DECISION pattern
OVERLOAD ELASTICS, 145
in Real Time and Resource Overload language, 136–138
in Working Hard, Don't Fix it, 140

Recursive access in multithreading, 73

Recursive applications, 13

Recursive mutexes, 76

Redland RDF library
OBJECT SYSTEM LAYER, 376
SPLIT OBJECT, 385, 393–394, 396

Redundancy in safety-critical systems, 90

REFERENCE COUNTER pattern, 499

Reference counting in dispatch, 78–80

Reference semantics in comparisons, 171–172

Refresh rate in scheduling, 97–98

Regenerative switching delays, 135

Registering in mobile systems, 215

Relationship Service Specification, 185

RELATIONSHIP TO OTHER PATTERNS pattern, 436, 450

Relationship type objects, 13

Relationships in shepherding, 517

Release Strategy variant, 165

Releasing resources
in mobile wireless systems, 220–221, 247–248
summary, 255

Remote interface, 39

Remote Method Invocation (RMI), 184–185

remote objects, 183

Remote procedure call (RPC) protocol, 291

Remote Proxy, 163

Remote query interface, 394

Removal collaborations, 30

Rendezvous protocol, 192

Repository pattern. *See* DOMAIN OBJECT MANAGER pattern

RESOLUTION OF FORCES pattern, 460, 471, 479–483

RESOURCE LIFECYCLE MANAGER pattern, 353

Resource management services, 340–341, 346

Resource module, 350

Resource providers, 340

Resource provision services, 340–341, 343–346

Resource usage information, 346, 352

Response times in locking, 157
Reuse
  COMPARAND attributes, 178
  in framework development,
    404–407, 425
  GRID, 351
Revocation requests, 160–163
Riehle, Dirk
  biographical information, 560
  DYNAMIC OBJECT MODEL, 3
  HALF A LOAF, 515
  THREE ITERATIONS, 512
Rising, Linda
  IT'S A RELATIONSHIP NOT A SALE, 416
  The Pattern Almanac, 448
RMI (Remote Method Invocation),
    184–185
Roaming, 215
Roberts, Don
  FINE-GRAINED OBJECTS, 418
  THREE EXAMPLES, 407
Round robin scheduling, 145
RPC (remote procedure call) protocol,
    291
Rule of three, 405–406
RUNNING EXAMPLE pattern, 525
Runtime Domain Model. *See* DY-
    NAMIC OBJECT MODEL pattern
Runtime typing, 12
Rüping, Andreas
  biographical information, 560
  framework development, 401

Safe Framework Providing Applica-
    tion, 317
SAFE SETTING pattern, 513
SAFEbus standard
  BIUs in, 115
  in hard real-time systems, 122

  in SYNC FRAME, 111
  in TEMPORAL APPLICATION DECOU-
    PLING, 119
Safety-critical systems, 90, 92
Salingaros, N. A., 485–486
Sameness of objects, 172
Sandboxes in GRID, 347
Sandboxing Without A Name (SWAN)
    module, 351
SavingsAccount class, 15–16
SavingsAccountType class, 6,
    16–17
SAX standard, 291
Scalable processor-independent de-
    sign for electromagnetic resilience
    (SPIDER), 123
Scarce resources, 146
SCATTERED WORK pattern, 488
Scheduled Invocation plug-ins, 323
Scheduler objects, 350
Scheduling
  round robin, 145
  services, 340–341, 343, 346–347
  tasks, 119
Schmidt, Douglas C.
  biographical information, 561
  dispatching components, 69
Schütz, Dietmar
  biographical information, 561
  DECENTRALIZED LOCKING, 155
Screen savers, 324
Screening devices, 548
Script interpreters, 394
Search engines
  CONSULT DIRECTORY, 196
  SERVER DOES HEAVY WORK, 205
Secrecy, 229, 232
Secure-channel communication pat-
    tern, 232

Security databases
  in mobile wireless systems, 220, 225–226
  summary, 253
Security in GRID, 340–341, 347–348, 352
SELECTIVE DYNAMIC OVERLOAD CONTROL pattern
  in DISASTER NOTIFICATION, 136
  in Equitable Resource Allocation, 147
  in Real Time and Resource Overload language, 132, 149
SELECTIVE TRUNK RESERVATION pattern
  in Equitable Resource Allocation, 147
  in Real Time and Resource Overload language, 132, 149
Self-stabilization in SYNC FRAME, 110
SELFISH CLASS pattern, 410
Sell class, 47
Semantic lookup service, 393–396
Semi-lattice systems, 488
Sender authentication pattern, 232
Senge, P. M., 463–464
SEPARATE IDENTITY FROM LOCATION pattern, 201–203
  DIRECTORY FINDS SERVICES, 199
  in SLP, 206
Serialized dispatching, 74–76
Serializer design pattern, 40
Servants in CORBA, 71
SERVER DOES HEAVY WORK pattern, 204–205
Server Lock Acquisition scenario, 159–160
Server-side caching, 285
SERVICE ABSTRACTION LAYER pattern, 260, 269–270
Service centers in locking, 166

Service discovery, 189–190
  acknowledgments, 206
  ALIGN DIRECTORIES WITH ORGANIZATION, 199–200
  ASK LOCAL NETWORK, 191–192
  CLIENT KNOWS BEST, 203–204
  combining patterns, 205–207
  CONSULT DIRECTORY, 195–196
  DIRECTORY FINDS SERVICES, 198–199
  LISTEN TO ADVERTISEMENTS, 193–194
  OVERLAY NETWORK, 192–193
  PLACE DIRECTORIES DYNAMICALLY, 200–201
  references, 206–209
  SEPARATE IDENTITY FROM LOCATION, 201–203
  SERVER DOES HEAVY WORK, 204–205
  SERVICES REGISTER IN DIRECTORY, 196–198
  USE ADVERTISER, 194–195
Service Location Protocol (SLP), 190
  ASK LOCAL NETWORK, 192
  LISTEN TO ADVERTISEMENTS, 194
  in service discovery, 205–207
  SERVICES REGISTER IN DIRECTORY, 197
  USE ADVERTISER, 195
Service registration messages, 197
SERVICES REGISTER IN DIRECTORY pattern, 196–198
  CONSULT DIRECTORY, 196
  DIRECTORY FINDS SERVICES, 199
  SEPARATE IDENTITY FROM LOCATION, 202
  in SLP, 206
Session Beans, 61
Set-top boxes, 386–389
Severity of overloads, 145
SHARE THE LOAD pattern, 131, 149

SHED LOAD pattern
 OVERLOAD EMPIRES, 133
 in Real Time and Resource Over-
  load language, 131, 149
 REASSESS OVERLOAD DECISION,
  136–137
 in Working Hard, Don't Fix it, 139
SHEPHERD KNOWS THE SHEEP pattern,
 508, 512–514
 Shepherding, 507
 acknowledgments, 528–529
 Author as Owner, 517–518
 BALANCED CONTEXT, 523–524
 BIG PICTURE, 515–516
 CONVINCING SOLUTION, 519–521
 epilogue, 528
 FORCES DEFINE PROBLEM, 521–522
 FORM FOLLOWS FUNCTION, 525–526
 HALF A LOAF, 514–515
 map of patterns, 508–510
 references, 529
 SHEPHERD KNOWS THE SHEEP, 512–514
 SMALL PATTERNS, 527–528
 THREE ITERATIONS, 509–512
 WAR STORIES, 524–525
"Should" in patterns, 520
SICO First and Always
 in Real Time and Resource Over-
  load language, 131–132
 REASSESS OVERLOAD DECISION, 138
Simplicity
 DYNAMIC OBJECT MODEL, 9–10
 framework development, 407–411
SimulatorContext class, 60
Single objects, dispatching to, 74–80
SINGLE-PASS READABLE PATTERN pat-
 tern, 516
SINGLETON pattern
 ENCAPSULATED CONTEXT, 61
 VOID, 501

SIP URIs, 202
SIZE THE ORGANIZATION pattern, 413
SIZE THE SCHEDULE pattern, 413
SKILLED TEAM pattern, 407, 411–413
SKIPPABLE SECTIONS pattern, 435, 438
Slightly out of specification (SOS) er-
 rors, 112
SLP (Service Location Protocol), 190
 ASK LOCAL NETWORK, 192
 LISTEN TO ADVERTISEMENTS, 194
 in service discovery, 205–207
 SERVICES REGISTER IN DIRECTORY, 197
 USE ADVERTISER, 195
Small objects in framework develop-
 ment, 416–418
SMALL PATTERNS pattern, 509, 527–528
Smalltalk language
 class modification in, 7
 flexibility of, 10
SOAP standard
 AUTOMATIC TYPE CONVERTER, 377
 Web content conversion and gener-
  ation, 291
SOB interface, 293
Soft real-time systems, 89
Software
 configurable. See Plug-ins
 integration, 358
SOS (slightly out of specification) er-
 rors, 112
SPATIAL VARIATION IN ABUNDANCE pat-
 tern, 491
SPECIAL pattern, 501
SPECIES—AREA RELATIONSHIP pattern,
 491
Specification-based queries, 34–35
Speed in SYNC FRAME, 110
SPIDER (scalable processor-indepen-
 dent design for electromagnetic
 resilience), 123

SPLIT OBJECT pattern, 359, 382–383
  Apache Axis, 396–397
  Aspect configuration, 390–393
  AUTOMATIC TYPE CONVERTER, 379
  COMMAND LANGUAGE, 365
  context, 381
  discussion, 383–384
  document archive systems, 386
  forces, 382
  OBJECT SYSTEM LAYER, 374
  problem, 381–382
  scenario, 382, 384–385
  semantic lookup service, 393–396
  set-top boxes, 386–389
  solution, 382
  TclCL and XOTcl/SWIG, 389–390
Sporadic messages, 98
Sporadic tasks, 121
Start-up in SYNC FRAME, 110
State design pattern, 40
STATE pattern
  DECENTRALIZED LOCKING, 165
  VOID, 501
Statement interface, 30
STEM CELL SPECIALIZATION pattern, 494
Stewart, I., 453
Stock quotes, 280–281, 286
Storch, D., 491
StoredProcOrderFinder class, 30, 37–38
STRATEGIES pattern, 275
Strategized Locking pattern, 74
STRATEGY pattern
  CONTENT CACHE, 286
  in dispatching components, 74
  DYNAMIC OBJECT MODEL, 13
  GRID, 347
  VOID, 501
STRING A WIRE pattern
  in DISASTER NOTIFICATION, 136
  in Real Time and Resource Over-
    load language, 150

Structural patterns in MoRaR, 218–221
Struts framework, 426
Substitutability in encapsulation, 49,
  56
Substitution rules in XML, 290
SUNNY PLACE pattern, 484
SWAN (Sandboxing Without A Name)
  module, 351
SWIG wrapper generator
  COMPONENT WRAPPER, 372
  SPLIT OBJECT, 389
Switching delays, 135
Symmetry breaking, 456–458
SYNC FRAME pattern
  consequences, 110
  context, 106
  example, 106–107, 109–110
  in hard real-time systems, 92
  implementation, 108–109
  known uses, 111
  problem, 106
  related patterns, 111
  solution, 107–108
Synchronization
  in multithreading, 58
  time-triggered, 101, 103–105
System costs in BUS GUARDIAN, 114
System Integrity Control (SICO First
  and Always)
  in Real Time and Resource Over-
    load language, 131–132
  REASSESS OVERLOAD DECISION, 138

T-fault-tolerant midpoint, 105
TANGENT PATHS pattern, 499
TARGET READERS pattern, 421
Tasks
  application, 116–117
  in hard real-time systems, 121
  in TEMPORAL APPLICATION DECOU-
    PLING, 119

Tautologies, 440
Taylor, Paul R.
  biographical information, 561
  Prairie Houses, 531
Tcl language
  AUTOMATIC TYPE CONVERTER, 381
  COMMAND LANGUAGE, 367
Tclcl language, 385, 389
TclHttpd, 294
TDMA (Time Division Multiple Access)
  in hard real-time systems, 122
  in MoRaR, 222
  in Prescheduled Periodic Transmission. *See* PRESCHEDULED PERIODIC TRANSMISSION pattern
Telecommunications Input Output Language, 136
TEMPLATE METHODS pattern, 272
TEMPLATE VIEW pattern, 279
TEMPLATES pattern, 273
TEMPORAL APPLICATION DECOUPLING pattern
  acknowledgements, 120
  consequences, 119
  context, 115
  example, 116
  in hard real-time systems, 93
  implementation, 118–119
  known uses, 119
  problem, 115–116
  related patterns, 120
  solution, 116–118
Temporal splits, 53
Temporary identification
  in mobile wireless systems, 220, 222–224
  summary, 253
Temporary Mobile Subscriber Identity (TMSI), 224
TERMINOLOGY TAILORED TO AUDIENCE pattern, 436, 447

Testing
  ENCAPSULATED CONTEXT, 58
  GRID, 352
This pointers, 55
Thread-Specific Storage pattern, 82
THREE EXAMPLES pattern, 407
THREE ITERATIONS pattern, 436, 442, 508–512
Thumbnails, 450
Tilman, Michel
  biographical information, 561
  DYNAMIC OBJECT MODEL, 3
TIME DIVISION MULTIPLE ACCESS (TDMA)
  in hard real-time systems, 122
  in MoRaR, 222
  in Prescheduled Periodic Transmission. *See* PRESCHEDULED PERIODIC TRANSMISSION pattern
TIME-TRIGGERED CLOCK SYNCHRONIZATION pattern, 103–106
  in hard real-time systems, 92
  vs. PRESCHEDULED PERIODIC TRANSMISSION, 101–102
Time-triggered communication on CAN (TTCAN) protocol
  in hard real-time systems, 123
  in PRESCHEDULED PERIODIC TRANSMISSION, 102–103
  in TEMPORAL APPLICATION DECOUPLING, 119
Time-Triggered Communication pattern. *See* PRESCHEDULED PERIODIC TRANSMISSION pattern
Time-Triggered Protocol (TTP)
  in hard real-time systems, 122
  in Prescheduled Periodic Transmission, 102
Titles of pattern collections, 447
TMSI (Temporary Mobile Subscriber Identity), 224

Token Ring networks, 96
TPMHP project, 293
TradingContext class, 60
TradingDayChange class, 47
Transient states, 28
Transmissions. *See* PRESCHEDULED PERI-
   ODIC TRANSMISSION pattern
TREE PLACES pattern, 484, 487, 489
Trigger-based registration, 321
Trigger events
   for location registration, 239
   for plug-ins, 323
Trigger memory, 119
Triple-T system. *See* Hard real-time
   systems
TTCAN (time-triggered communica-
   tion on CAN) protocol
   in hard real-time systems, 123
   in PRESCHEDULED PERIODIC TRANS-
      MISSION, 102–103
   in TEMPORAL APPLICATION DECOU-
      PLING, 119
TTP (Time-Triggered Protocol)
   in hard real-time systems, 122
   in PRESCHEDULED PERIODIC TRANS-
      MISSION, 102
Two-pass reads, 450
Twombly, Robert, 532
Type-checking property access, 14
TYPE OBJECTS pattern
   AUTOMATIC TYPE CONVERTER, 379
   DYNAMIC OBJECT MODEL, 4, 8–9, 22
   OBJECT SYSTEM LAYER, 375
Types, plug-in, 307

UCMs (Use Case Maps), 218
UDDI protocol
   SERVER DOES HEAVY WORK, 205
   SERVICES REGISTER IN DIRECTORY,
      198

UML
   collaboration, 7–8
   virtual machines, 21
Uncluttered code, 58
Universal Mobile Telecommunica-
   tions System (UMTS), 213
Update collaborations, 30
UPnP protocol
   ASK LOCAL NETWORK, 192
   CLIENT KNOWS BEST, 204
   LISTEN TO ADVERTISEMENTS, 194
   SEPARATE IDENTITY FROM LOCATION,
      202
URLs in service discovery, 202
Usage patterns in GRID, 349
USE ADVERTISER pattern, 194–195
Use Case Maps (UCMs), 218
UserAgent module, 351
Users in framework user involvement,
   421

Validating DomainObjects, 33
Validity time spans
   in hard real-time systems, 122
   in Prescheduled Periodic Transmis-
      sion, 97
Value class, 9
VALUE HOLDER pattern, 4, 9
Value semantics, 171
Variable dispatching times, 73
VCF, 372
VEGETABLE GARDEN pattern, 484
Vertical height in Prairie Houses,
   538
Vertical splits, 53
VISIBLE FORCES pattern, 435, 446,
   522
VISIBLE IMPLICATION pattern, 487
Visited areas in mobile systems,
   215

Visitor databases
  in mobile wireless systems, 215, 220, 223, 225–226, 235–237
  in paging, 233–234
  summary, 254
Visitor design pattern, 40
Visitor location registers (VLRs), 236
Visual Basic pattern, 11
Voelter, Markus, 562
Vogel, Oliver
  biographical information, 562
  Web content conversion and generation, 257
VOID pattern, 461, 500–502
  AGGREGATION, 497
  DIFFERENTIATION, 494
  LEVELS OF SCALE, 487
VxWorks plug-ins, 304

Waiting period in SYNC FRAME, 109
WANs (Wide-Area Networks), 214
WAR STORIES pattern, 509, 524–525
WCET (Worst Case Execution Time)
  in EMB systems, 99
  in hard real-time systems, 122
Weasels, 434, 443–444
Weather forecasting, 337–339
Web-based applications, 258–259
Web browsers
  FRAMEWORK PROVIDING APPLICATION, 318
  PLUG-IN, 309
Web content conversion and generation, 257
  acknowledgments, 295
  conclusion, 294–295
  CONTENT CACHE, 284–287
  CONTENT CONVERTER, 270–274
  CONTENT CREATOR, 274–277
  CONTENT FORMAT TEMPLATE, 277–279

  form, 259–260
  FRAGMENTS, 279–284
  GENERIC CONTENT FORMAT, 264–267
  implementation example, 287–291
  intended audience, 259
  introduction, 257–259
  known uses and related work, 291–294
  overview, 260–264
  PUBLISHER AND GATHERER, 267–270
  references, 295–297
Web portal framework
  background, 403
  evidence for reuse, 407
  framework user involvement, 422–423
  multiple change requests, 425
  pilot applications, 415
  pilot-based tests, 420
  simplicity, 410
  skilled teams, 412–413
  small objects, 418
Web search engines
  CONSULT DIRECTORY, 196
  SERVER DOES HEAVY WORK, 205
WebLogic application servers, 39
WebShell, 293
WebSphere, 39
Welch-Lynch algorithm, 105
"WHAT"—SOLUTIONS pattern, 434
WHOLE VALUE pattern, 466–467
  CLUSTER OF FORCES, 470–471
  CROSS LINKAGES, 491
  HOPP, 476–477
  LEVELS OF SCALE, 487
  RESOLUTION OF FORCES, 482–483
"WHY"—PROBLEMS pattern, 434, 440–443
Wide Area Networks (WANs), 214
Wild clock readings, 104

WIN (Wireless Intelligent Network), 214

Windows (operating system) plug-ins, 304, 309

Windows (Prairie Houses), 545–546

Winn, Tiffany
   biographical information, 562
   LDPL, 453

Wireless Intelligent Network (WIN), 214

Wireless mobile Asynchronous Transfer Mode (WmATM) systems, 214, 241

Wireless systems. *See* MoRaR pattern language

Witthawaskul, W., 21

Word application, 304
   FRAMEWORK PROVIDING APPLICATION, 318
   PLUG-IN LIFECYCLE, 324
   PLUG-IN PACKAGE, 327

WORK SHED AT PERIPHERY pattern, 150

Worker objects, 55–56

Working Hard, Don't Fix it strategy, 138–140

Workloads in real time systems, 128

Workshops
   disadvantages of, 446–447
   framework user involvement, 421

World Peace syndrome, 519–520

Worst Case Execution Time (WCET)
   in EMB systems, 99
   in hard real-time systems, 122

WRAPPER FACADE pattern, 359, 370–371

Wrappers in SPLIT OBJECT, 382–383, 386, 394

Wright, Frank Lloyd. *See* Prairie Houses

Wright Space, The—Pattern and meaning in Frank Lloyd Wright's Houses (Hildebrand), 532

Writer locks, dispatching with, 77–78

WSDL files, 394, 397

X-frames, 111

XML
   CONTENT CREATOR, 274–277
   Web content conversion and generation, 288–290

XML Database Server, 60–61

XML Schema Data (XSD), 396–397

xoComm architecture, 291–292

xoRDF architecture, 292

XOTcl language, 376, 389

XSD (XML Schema Data), 396–397

XSLT standard, 291

Yoder, Joseph
   "Connecting Business Object to Relational Databases", 40
   LOW SURFACE-TO-VOLUME RATIO, 418
   SELFISH CLASS, 410

Zdun, Uwe
   biographical information, 562
   component and language integration, 357
   Web content conversion and generation, 257

Zeus, 304
   COOPERATING PLUG-INS, 329
   PLUG-IN, 309
   PLUG-IN BASED PRODUCT, 333
   PLUG-IN CONTRACT, 315
   PLUG-IN LIFECYCLE, 324
   PLUG-IN PACKAGE, 327
   PLUG-IN REGISTRATION, 321

Zhao, L., 457

Zope system, 293

Addison-Wesley Professional
Is the Ultimate Resource for Patterns!

In 1994, Addison-Wesley published *Design Patterns,* the first and definitive book on patterns for software development. Addison-Wesley continues to publish the thought leaders in the patterns community and remains the most comprehensive and authoritative resource on software patterns for developers of all levels and experience.

0-201-63361-2

0-321-12697-1

CHECK OUT THESE ESSENTIAL TITLES ON SOFTWARE PATTERNS

0-321-12742-0

0-321-33302-0

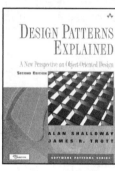

0-321-24714-0

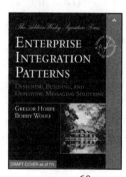

0-321-20068-3

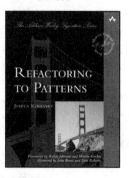

0-321-21335-1

0-321-32194-4